Funk & Wagnalls Hammond WORLD ATLAS

INCLUDING
UNITED STATES AND CANADA
RECREATION AND ROAD ATLAS

Funk & Wagnalls, Inc.

Publishers since 1876

CONTENTS

WORLD STATISTICAL TABLES

Elements of the Solar System

	Mean Distance from Sun: in Miles	in Kilometers	Period of Revolution around Sun	Period of Rotation on Axis	Equatorial Diameter: in Miles	in Kilometers	Surface Gravity (Earth = 1)	Mass (Earth = 1)	Mean Density (Water = 1)	Number of Satellites
MERCURY	35,990,000	57,900,000	87.97 days	59 days	3,032	4,880	0.38	0.055	5.5	0
VENUS	67,240,000	108,200,000	224.70 days	243 days†	7,523	12,106	0.90	0.815	5.25	0
EARTH	93,000,000	149,700,000	365.26 days	23h 56m	7,926	12,755	1.00	1.00	5.5	1
MARS	141,730,000	228,100,000	687.00 days	24h 37m	4,220	6,790	0.38	0.107	4.0	2
JUPITER	483,880,000	778,700,000	11.86 years	9h 50m	88,750	142,800	2.87	317.9	1.3	16
SATURN	887,130,000	1,427,700,000	29.46 years	10h 14m	74,580	120,020	1.32	95.2	0.7	17
URANUS	1,783,700,000	2,870,500,000	84.01 years	10h 49m†	31,600	50,900	0.93	14.6.	1.3	5
NEPTUNE	2,795,500,000	4,498,800,000	164.79 years	15h 48m	30,200	48,600	1.23	17.2	1.8	3
PLUTO	3,667,900,000	5,902,800,000	247.70 years	6.39 days (?)	1,500	2,400	0.03 (?)	0.01(?)	0.7(?)	1

†Retrograde motion

Facts About the Sun

Equatorial diameter	865,000 miles	1,392,000 kilometers
Period of rotation on axis	25-35 days*	
Orbit of galaxy	every 225 million years	
Surface gravity (Earth = 1)	27.8	
Mass (Earth = 1)	333,000	
Density (Water = 1)	1.4	
Mean distance from Earth	93,000,000 miles	149,700,000 kilometers

*Rotation of 25 days at Equator, decreasing to about 35 days at the poles.

Facts About the Moon

Equatorial diameter	2,160 miles	3,476 kilometers
Period of rotation on axis	27 days, 7 hours, 43 minutes	
Period of revolution around Earth (sidereal month)	27 days, 7 hours, 43 minutes	
Phase period between new moons (synodic month)	29 days, 12 hours, 44 minutes	
Surface gravity (Earth = 1)	0.16	
Mass (Earth = 1)	0.0123	
Density (Water = 1)	3.34	
Maximum distance from Earth	252,710 miles	406,690 kilometers
Minimum distance from Earth	221,460 miles	356,400 kilometers
Mean distance from Earth	238,860 miles	384,400 kilometers

Dimensions of the Earth

	Area in Sq. Miles	Sq. Kilometers
Superficial area	197,751,000	512,175,090
Land surface	57,970,000	150,142,300
Water surface	139,781,000	362,032,790

	Miles	Kilometers
Equatorial circumference	24,902	40,075
Polar circumference	24,860	40,007
Equatorial diameter	7,926.68	12,756.4
Polar diameter	7,899.99	12,713.4
Equatorial radius	3,963.34	6,378.2
Polar radius	3,949.99	6,356.7

Volume of the Earth	2.6×10^{11} cubic miles	10.84×10^{11} cubic kilometers
Mass or weight	6.6×10^{21} short tons	6.0×10^{21} metric tons
Maximum distance from Sun	94,600,000 miles	152,000,000 kilometers
Minimum distance from Sun	91,300,000 miles	147,000,000 kilometers

The Continents

	Area in: Sq. Miles	Sq. Km.	Percent of World's Land
Asia	17,128,500	44,362,815	29.5
Africa	11,707,000	30,321,130	20.2
North America	9,363,000	24,250,170	16.2
South America	6,875,000	17,806,250	11.8
Antarctica	5,500,000	14,245,000	9.5
Europe	4,057,000	10,507,630	7.0
Australia	2,966,136	7,682,300	5.1

Oceans and Major Seas

	Area in: Sq. Miles	Sq. Km.	Greatest Depth in: Feet	Meters
Pacific Ocean	64,186,000	166,241,700	36,198	11,033
Atlantic Ocean	31,862,000	82,522,600	28,374	8,648
Indian Ocean	28,350,000	73,426,500	25,344	7,725
Arctic Ocean	5,427,000	14,056,000	17,880	5,450
Caribbean Sea	970,000	2,512,300	24,720	7,535
Mediterranean Sea	969,000	2,509,700	16,896	5,150
Bering Sea	875,000	2,266,250	15,800	4,800
Gulf of Mexico	600,000	1,554,000	12,300	3,750
Sea of Okhotsk	590,000	1,528,100	11,070	3,370
East China Sea	482,000	1,248,400	9,500	2,900
Sea of Japan	389,000	1,007,500	12,280	3,740
Hudson Bay	317,500	822,300	846	258
North Sea	222,000	575,000	2,200	670
Black Sea	185,000	479,150	7,365	2,245
Red Sea	169,000	437,700	7,200	2,195
Baltic Sea	163,000	422,170	1,506	459

Major Ship Canals

	Length in: Miles	Kms.	Minimum Feet	Depth in: Meters
Volga-Baltic, U.S.S.R.	225	362	—	—
Baltic-White Sea, U.S.S.R.	140	225	16	5
Suez, Egypt	100.76	162	42	13
Albert, Belgium	80	129	16.5	5
Moscow-Volga, U.S.S.R.	80	129	18	6
Volga-Don, U.S.S.R.	62	100	—	—
Göta, Sweden	54	87	10	3
Kiel (Nord-Ostsee), W. Ger.	53.2	86	38	12
Panama Canal, Panama	50.72	82	41.6	13
Houston Ship, U.S.A.	50	81	36	11

Largest Islands

	Area in: Sq. Mi.	Sq. Km.		Area in: Sq. Mi.	Sq. Km.		Area in: Sq. Mi.	Sq. Km.
Greenland	840,000	2,175,600	South I., New Zealand	58,393	151,238	Hokkaido, Japan	28,983	75,066
New Guinea	305,000	789,950	Java, Indonesia	48,842	126,501	Banks, Canada	27,038	70,028
Borneo	290,000	751,100	North I., New Zealand	44,187	114,444	Ceylon, Sri Lanka	25,332	65,610
Madagascar	226,400	586,376	Newfoundland, Canada	42,031	108,860	Tasmania, Australia	24,600	63,710
Baffin, Canada	195,928	507,454	Cuba	40,533	104,981	Svalbard, Norway	23,957	62,049
Sumatra, Indonesia	164,000	424,760	Luzon, Philippines	40,420	104,688	Devon, Canada	21,331	55,247
Honshu, Japan	88,000	227,920	Iceland	39,768	103,000	Novaya Zemlya (north isl.), U.S.S.R.	18,600	48,200
Great Britain	84,400	218,896	Mindanao, Philippines	36,537	94,631	Marajó, Brazil	17,991	46,597
Victoria, Canada	83,896	217,290	Ireland	31,743	82,214	Tierra del Fuego, Chile & Argentina	17,900	46,360
Ellesmere, Canada	75,767	196,236	Sakhalin, U.S.S.R.	29,500	76,405	Alexander, Antarctica	16,700	43,250
Celebes, Indonesia	72,986	189,034	Hispaniola, Haiti & Dom. Rep.	29,399	76,143			

Principal Mountains

	Feet	Meters		Feet	Meters		Feet	Meters
Everest, Nepal-China	29,028	8,848	Pissis, Argentina	22,241	6,779	Kazbek, U.S.S.R.	16,512	5,033
Godwin Austen (K2), Pakistan-China	28,250	8,611	Mercedario, Argentina	22,211	6,770	Puncak Jaya, Indonesia	16,503	5,030
Kanchenjunga, Nepal-India	28,208	8,598	Huascarán, Peru	22,205	6,768	Tyree, Antarctica	16,289	4,965
Lhotse, Nepal-China	27,923	8,511	Llullaillaco, Chile-Argentina	22,057	6,723	Blanc, France	15,771	4,807
Makalu, Nepal-China	27,824	8,481	Nevada Ancohuma, Bolivia	21,489	6,550	Klyuchevskaya Sopka, U.S.S.R.	15,584	4,750
Dhaulagiri, Nepal	26,810	8,172	Illampu, Bolivia	21,276	6,485	Fairweather (Br. Col., Canada)	15,300	4,663
Nanga Parbat, Pakistan	26,660	8,126	Chimborazo, Ecuador	20,561	6,267	Dufourspitze (Mte. Rosa), Italy-		
Annapurna, Nepal	26,504	8,078	McKinley, Alaska	20,320	6,194	Switzerland	15,203	4,634
Gasherbrum, Pakistan-China	26,740	8,068	Logan, Canada (Yukon)	19,524	5,951	Ras Dashan, Ethiopia	15,157	4,620
Nanda Devi, India	25,645	7,817	Cotopaxi, Ecuador	19,347	5,897	Matterhorn, Switzerland	14,691	4,478
Rakaposhi, Pakistan	25,550	7,788	Kilimanjaro, Tanzania	19,340	5,895	Whitney, California, U.S.A.	14,494	4,418
Kamet, India	25,447	7,756	El Misti, Peru	19,101	5,822	Elbert, Colorado, U.S.A.	14,433	4,399
Gurla Mandhada, China	25,355	7,728	Pico Cristóbal Colón, Colombia	19,029	5,800	Rainier, Washington, U.S.A.	14,410	4,392
Kongur Shan, China	25,325	7,719	Huila, Colombia	18,865	5,750	Shasta, California, U.S.A.	14,162	4,350
Tirich Mir, Pakistan	25,230	7,690	Citlaltépetl (Orizaba), Mexico	18,855	5,747	Pikes Peak, Colorado, U.S.A.	14,110	4,301
Gongga Shan, China	24,790	7,556	El'brus, U.S.S.R.	18,510	5,642	Finsteraarhorn, Switzerland	14,022	4,274
Muztagata, China	24,757	7,546	Damavand, Iran	18,376	5,601	Mauna Kea, Hawaii, U.S.A.	13,796	4,205
Communism Peak, U.S.S.R.	24,599	7,498	St. Elias, Alaska-Canada			Mauna Loa, Hawaii, U.S.A.	13,677	4,169
Pobeda Peak, U.S.S.R.	24,406	7,439	(Yukon)	18,008	5,489	Jungfrau, Switzerland	13,642	4,158
Chomo Lhari, Bhutan-China	23,997	7,314	Vilcanota, Peru	17,999	5,486	Cameroon, Cameroon	13,350	4,069
Muztag, China	23,891	7,282	Popocatépetl, Mexico	17,887	5,452	Grossglockner, Austria	12,457	3,797
Cerro Aconcagua, Argentina	22,831	6,959	Dykhtau, U.S.S.R.	17,070	5,203	Fuji, Japan	12,389	3,776
Ojos del Salado, Chile-Argentina	22,572	6,880	Kenya, Kenya	17,058	5,199	Cook, New Zealand	12,349	3,764
Bonete, Chile-Argentina	22,541	6,870	Ararat, Turkey	16,946	5,165	Etna, Italy	11,053	3,369
Tupungato, Chile-Argentina	22,310	6,800	Vinson Massif, Antarctica	16,864	5,140	Kosciusko, Australia	7,310	2,228
			Margherita (Ruwenzori), Africa	16,795	5,119	Mitchell, North Carolina, U.S.A.	6,684	2,037

Longest Rivers

	Length in: Miles	Kms.		Length in: Miles	Kms.		Length in: Miles	Kms.
Nile, Africa	4,145	6,671	São Francisco, Brazil	1,811	2,914	Ohio-Allegheny, U.S.A.	1,306	2,102
Amazon, S. Amer.	3,915	6,300	Indus, Asia	1,800	2,897	Kama, U.S.S.R.	1,262	2,031
Chang Jiang (Yangtze), China	3,900	6,276	Danube, Europe	1,775	2,857	Red, U.S.A.	1,222	1,966
Mississippi-Missouri-Red Rock, U.S.A.	3,741	6,019	Salween, Asia	1,770	2,849	Don, U.S.S.R.	1,222	1,967
Ob'-Irtysh-Black Irtysh, U.S.S.R.	3,362	5,411	Brahmaputra, Asia	1,700	2,736	Columbia, U.S.A.-Canada	1,214	1,953
Yenisey-Angara, U.S.S.R.	3,100	4,989	Euphrates, Asia	1,700	2,736	Saskatchewan, Canada	1,205	1,939
Huang He (Yellow), China	2,877	4,630	Tocantins, Brazil	1,677	2,699	Peace-Finlay, Canada	1,195	1,923
Amur-Shilka-Onon, Asia	2,744	4,416	Xi (Si), China	1,650	2,655	Tigris, Asia	1,181	1,901
Lena, U.S.S.R.	2,734	4,400	Amudar'ya, Asia	1,616	2,601	Darling, Australia	1,160	1,867
Congo (Zaire), Africa	2,718	4,374	Nelson-Saskatchewan, Canada	1,600	2,575	Angara, U.S.S.R.	1,135	1,827
Mackenzie-Peace-Finlay, Canada	2,635	4,241	Orinoco, S. Amer.	1,600	2,575	Sungari, Asia	1,130	1,819
Mekong, Asia	2,610	4,200	Zambezi, Africa	1,600	2,575	Pechora, U.S.S.R.	1,124	1,809
Missouri-Red Rock, U.S.A.	2,564	4,125	Paraguay, S. Amer.	1,584	2,549	Snake, U.S.A.	1,000	1,609
Niger, Africa	2,548	4,101	Kolyma, U.S.S.R.	1,562	2,514	Churchill, Canada	1,000	1,609
Paraná-La Plata, S. Amer.	2,450	3,943	Ganges, Asia	1,550	2,494	Pilcomayo, S. Amer.	1,000	1,609
Mississippi, U.S.A.	2,348	3,778	Ural, U.S.S.R.	1,509	2,428	Magdalena, Colombia	1,000	1,609
Murray-Darling, Australia	2,310	3,718	Japurá, S. Amer.	1,500	2,414	Uruguay, S. Amer.	994	1,600
Volga, U.S.S.R.	2,194	3,531	Arkansas, U.S.A.	1,450	2,334	Platte-N. Platte, U.S.A.	990	1,593
Madeira, S. Amer.	2,013	3,240	Colorado, U.S.A.-Mexico	1,450	2,334	Ohio, U.S.A.	981	1,578
Purus, S. Amer.	1,995	3,211	Negro, S. Amer.	1,400	2,253	Pecos, U.S.A.	926	1,490
Yukon, Alaska-Canada	1,979	3,185	Dnieper, U.S.S.R.	1,368	2,202	Oka, U.S.S.R.	918	1,477
St. Lawrence, Canada-U.S.A.	1,900	3,058	Orange, Africa	1,350	2,173	Canadian, U.S.A.	906	1,458
Rio Grande, Mexico-U.S.A.	1,885	3,034	Irrawaddy, Burma	1,325	2,132	Colorado, Texas, U.S.A.	894	1,439
Syrdar'ya-Naryn, U.S.S.R.	1,859	2,992	Brazos, U.S.A.	1,309	2,107	Dniester, U.S.S.R.	876	1,410

Principal Natural Lakes

	Area in: Sq. Miles	Sq. Km.	Max. Depth in: Feet	Meters		Area in: Sq. Miles	Sq. Km.	Max. Depth in: Feet	Meters
Caspian Sea, U.S.S.R.-Iran	143,243	370,999	3,264	995	Lake Eyre, Australia	3,500-0	9,000-0	—	—
Lake Superior, U.S.A.-Canada	31,820	82,414	1,329	405	Lake Titicaca, Peru-Bolivia	3,200	8,288	1,000	305
Lake Victoria, Africa	26,724	69,215	270	82	Lake Nicaragua, Nicaragua	3,100	8,029	230	70
Aral Sea, U.S.S.R.	25,676	66,501	256	78	Lake Athabasca, Canada	3,064	7,936	400	122
Lake Huron, U.S.A.-Canada	23,010	59,596	748	228	Reindeer Lake, Canada	2,568	6,651	—	—
Lake Michigan, U.S.A.	22,400	58,016	923	281	Lake Turkana (Rudolf), Africa	2,463	6,379	240	73
Lake Tanganyika, Africa	12,650	32,764	4,700	1,433	Issyk-Kul', U.S.S.R.	2,425	6,281	2,303	702
Lake Baykal, U.S.S.R.	12,162	31,500	5,316	1,620	Lake Torrens, Australia	2,230	5,776	—	—
Great Bear Lake, Canada	12,096	31,328	1,356	413	Vänern, Sweden	2,156	5,584	328	100
Lake Nyasa (Malawi), Africa	11,555	29,928	2,320	707	Nettilling Lake, Canada	2,140	5,543	—	—
Great Slave Lake, Canada	11,031	28,570	2,015	614	Lake Winnipegosis, Canada	2,075	5,374	38	12
Lake Erie, U.S.A.-Canada	9,940	25,745	210	64	Lake Mobutu Sese Seko (Albert), Africa	2,075	5,374	160	49
Lake Winnipeg, Canada	9,417	24,390	60	18	Kariba Lake, Zambia-Zimbabwe	2,050	5,310	295	90
Lake Ontario, U.S.A.-Canada	7,540	19,529	775	244	Lake Nipigon, Canada	1,872	4,848	540	165
Lake Ladoga, U.S.S.R.	7,104	18,399	738	225	Lake Mweru, Zaire-Zambia	1,800	4,662	60	18
Lake Balkhash, U.S.S.R.	7,027	18,200	87	27	Lake Manitoba, Canada	1,799	4,659	12	4
Lake Maracaibo, Venezuela	5,120	13,261	100	31	Lake Taymyr, U.S.S.R.	1,737	4,499	85	26
Lake Chad, Africa	4,000-10,000	10,360-25,900	25	8	Lake Khanka, China-U.S.S.R.	1,700	4,403	33	10
Lake Onega, U.S.S.R.	3,710	9,609	377	115	Lake Kioga, Uganda	1,700	4,403	25	8

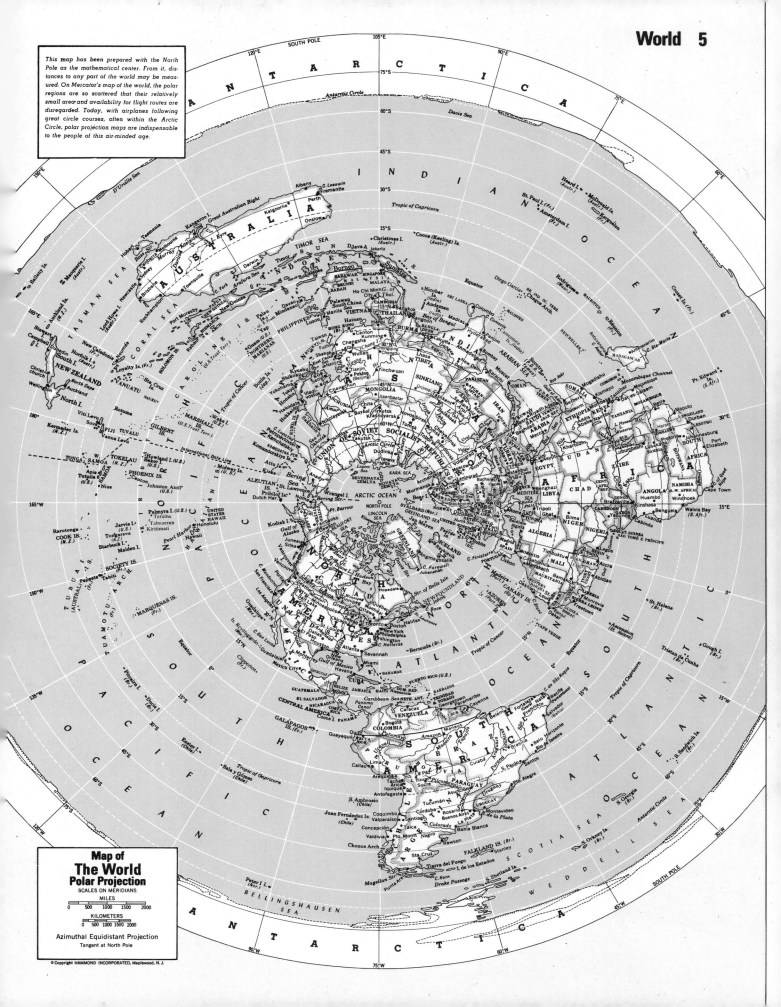

This map has been prepared with the North Pole as the mathematical center. From it, distances to any part of the world may be measured. On Mercator's map of the world, the polar regions are so scattered that their relatively small area and availability for flight routes are disregarded. Today, with airplanes following great circle courses, often within the Arctic Circle, polar projection maps are indispensable to the people of this air-minded age.

Map of
The World
Polar Projection
SCALES ON MERIDIANS

MILES
0   500   1000   1500   2000

KILOMETERS
0   500   1000   1500   2000

Azimuthal Equidistant Projection
Tangent at North Pole

© Copyright HAMMOND INCORPORATED, Maplewood, N.J.

Europe

POLYCONIC PROJECTION

SCALE OF MILES
0 100 200 300 400

KILOMETERS
0 100 200 300 400

Capitals of Countries .... ⊛
Other Capitals .... ⊛
International Boundaries .... —·—·—
Internal Boundaries .... —··—··—
Canals ....

AREA 4,057,000 sq. mi.
(10,507,630 sq. km.)
POPULATION 676,000,000
LARGEST CITY Paris
HIGHEST POINT El'brus 18,510 ft.
(5,642 m.)
LOWEST POINT Caspian Sea -92 ft.
(-28 m.)

Population Distribution

DENSITY PER	
SQ. KILOMETER	SQ. MILE
Over 100	Over 260
50-100	130-260
10-50	25-130
1-10	3-25
Under 1	Under 3

• Cities with over 2,000,000 inhabitants (including suburbs)

○ Cities with over 1,000,000 inhabitants (including suburbs)

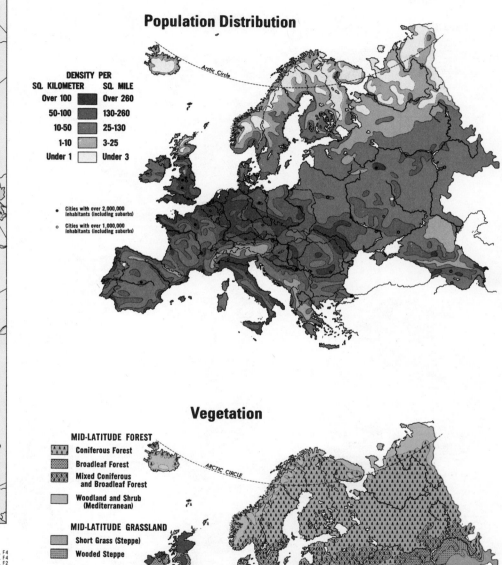

Vegetation

MID-LATITUDE FOREST
- Coniferous Forest
- Broadleaf Forest
- Mixed Coniferous and Broadleaf Forest
- Woodland and Shrub (Mediterranean)

MID-LATITUDE GRASSLAND
- Short Grass (Steppe)
- Wooded Steppe

HEATH AND MOOR

DESERT AND DESERT SHRUB

TUNDRA AND ALPINE

PERMANENT ICE COVER

© Copyright HAMMOND INCORPORATED, Maplewood, N.J.

UNITED KINGDOM

AREA 94,399 sq. mi. (244,493 sq. km.)
POPULATION 55,672,000
CAPITAL London
LARGEST CITY London
HIGHEST POINT Ben Nevis 4,406 ft. (1,343 m.)
MONETARY UNIT pound sterling
MAJOR LANGUAGES English, Gaelic, Welsh
MAJOR RELIGIONS Protestantism, Roman Catholicism

IRELAND

AREA 27,136 sq. mi. (70,282 sq. km.)
POPULATION 3,440,427
CAPITAL Dublin
LARGEST CITY Dublin
HIGHEST POINT Carrantuohill 3,415 ft. (1,041 m.)
MONETARY UNIT Irish pound
MAJOR LANGUAGES English, Gaelic (Irish)
MAJOR RELIGION Roman Catholicism

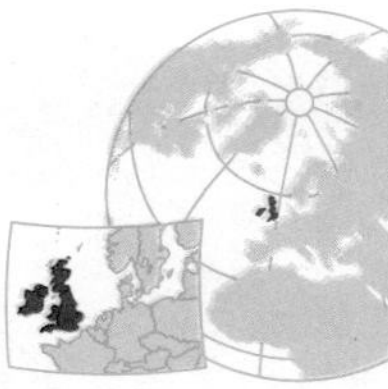

UNITED KINGDOM

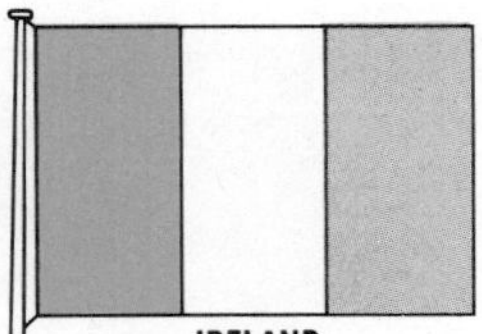

IRELAND

ENGLAND

COUNTIES

n, 920,200 . . . E 6
dfordshire, 491,700 . . . G 5
kshire, 659,000 . . . F 6
ckinghamshire, 512,000 . . . G 6
mbridgeshire, 563,000 . . . G 5
eshire, 916,400 . . . E 4
eveland, 567,900 . . . F 3
rnwall, 405,200 . . . C 7
mbria, 473,600 . . . D 3
rbyshire, 887,600 . . . F 5
von, 942,100 . . . D 7
rset, 575,800 . . . E 7
rham, 610,400 . . . F 3
st Sussex, 655,600 . . . H 7
sex, 1,426,200 . . . H 6
oucestershire, 491,500 . . . E 6
eater London, 7,028,200 . . . H 8
eater Manchester, 2,684,100 . . . H 2
mpshire, 1,456,100 . . . F 6
ereford and Worcester, 594,200 . . E 5
ertfordshire, 937,300 . . . G 6
umberside, 848,600 . . . G 4
le of Wight, 111,300 . . . F 7
les of Scilly, 1,900 . . . A 7
ent, 1,448,100 . . . H 6
ancashire, 1,375,500 . . . E 4
eicestershire, 837,900 . . . F 5
incolnshire, 524,500 . . . G 4
ondon, Greater, 7,028,200 . . . H 8
anchester, Greater, 2,684,100 . . . H 2
erseyside, 1,578,000 . . . G 2
orfolk, 662,500 . . . H 5
orthamptonshire, 505,900 . . . G 5
orthumberland, 287,300 . . . E 2
orth Yorkshire, 653,000 . . . F 3
ottinghamshire, 977,500 . . . F 4
Oxfordshire 541,800 . . . F6
Shropshire (Salop) 359,000 . . . E5
Somerset 404,400 . . . E6
South Yorkshire 1,318,300 . . . F4
Staffordshire 997,600 . . . E5
Suffolk 577,600 . . . H5
Surrey 1,002,900 . . . G6
Sussex, East 655,600 . . . H7
Sussex, West 623,400 . . . G7
Tyne and Wear 1,182,900 . . . H3
Warwickshire 471,000 . . . F5
West Midlands 2,743,300 . . . F5
West Sussex 623,400 . . . G7
West Yorkshire 2,072,500 . . . J1
Wiltshire 512,800 . . . E6
Yorkshire, North 653,000 . . . F3
Yorkshire, South 1,318,300 . . . F4
Yorkshire, West 2,072,500 . . . J1

CITIES and TOWNS

Abingdon, 20,130 . . . F 6
Accrington, 36,470 . . . H 1
Adwick le Street, 17,650 . . . K 2
Aldeburgh, 2,750 . . . J 5
Aldershot, 33,750 . . . G 8
Aldridge Brownhills, 89,370 . . . E 5
Alfreton, 21,560 . . . F 4
Alnwick, 7,300 . . . F 2
Altrincham, 40,800 . . . H 2
Amersham, ⊙17,254 . . . G 7
Andover, 27,620 . . . F 6
Appleby, 2,240 . . . E 3
Arnold, 35,090 . . . F 4
Arundel, 2,390 . . . G 7
Ashford, 36,380 . . . H 6
Ashington, 24,720 . . . F 2
Ashton-under-Lyne, 48,500 . . . H 2
Axminster, ⊙4,515 . . . D 7
Aycliffe, ⊙20,203 . . . F 3
Aylesbury, 41,420 . . . G 7
Bacup, 14,990 . . . H 1
Bakewell, 4,100 . . . J 2
Banbury, 31,060 . . . F 5
Banstead, 44,100 . . . H 8
Barking, 153,800 . . . H 8
Barnet, 305,200 . . . H 7
Barnsley, 74,730 . . . J 2
Barnstaple, 17,820 . . . D 6
Barrow-in-Furness, 73,400 . . . D 3
Barton-upon-Humber, 7,750 . . . G 4
Basildon, 135,720 . . . J 8
Basingstoke, 60,910 . . . F 6
Bath, 83,100 . . . E 6
Batley, 41,630 . . . J 1
Battle, ⊙4,987 . . . H 7
Bebington, 62,500 . . . G 2
Bedford, 74,390 . . . G 5
Bedlington, 27,200 . . . F 2
Bedworth, 41,600 . . . F 5
Beeston and Stapleford, 65,360 . . . F 5
Benfleet, 49,180 . . . J 8
Bentley with Arksey, 22,320 . . . F 4
Berkhamsted, 15,920 . . . G 7
Beverley, 16,920 . . . G 4
Bexhill, 34,680 . . . H 7
Bexley, 213,500 . . . H 8
Biddulph, 18,720 . . . H 2
Birkenhead, 135,750 . . . G 2
Birmingham, 1,058,800 . . . F 5
Bishop Auckland, 32,940 . . . E 3
Bishop's Stortford, 21,720 . . . H 6
Blackburn, 101,670 . . . H 1
Blackpool, 149,000 . . . G 1
Blaydon, 31,940 . . . H 3
Blyth, 35,390 . . . F 2
Bodmin, 10,430 . . . C 7
Bognor Regis, 34,620 . . . G 7
Boldon, 24,430 . . . J 3
Bolton, 154,480 . . . H 2
Bootle 71,160 . . . G2
Boston 26,700 . . . G5
Bournemouth 144,100 . . . F7
Bracknell† 34,067 . . . G8
Bradford 458,900 . . . J1
Braintree and Bocking 26,300 . . . H6
Brent 256,500 . . . H8
Brentwood 58,690 . . . J8
Bridgwater 26,700 . . . E6
Bridlington 26,920 . . . G3
Bridport 6,660 . . . E7
Brigg 4,870 . . . G4
Brighouse 35,320 . . . J1
Brightlingsea 7,170 . . . J6
Brighton 156,500 . . . G7
Bristol 416,300 . . . E6
Broadstairs and Saint Peter's 21,670 . . . J6
Bromley 299,100 . . . H8
Bromsgrove 41,430 . . . E5
Buckfastleigh 2,870 . . . C7
Buckingham 5,290 . . . G6
Bude-Stratton 5,750 . . . C7
Bungay 4,120 . . . J5
Burgess Hill 20,030 . . . G7
Burnham-on-Crouch 4,920 . . . H6
Burnley 74,300 . . . H1
Burntwood† 23,088 . . . F5
Burton upon Trent 49,480 . . . F5
Bury 69,550 . . . H2
Bury Saint Edmunds 26,800 . . . H5
Bushey 24,500 . . . H7
Buxton 20,050 . . . J2
Caister-on-Sea† 6,287 . . . J5
Camborne-Redruth 43,970 . . . B7
Cambridge 106,400 . . . G5
Camden 185,800 . . . H8
Cannock 56,440 . . . E5
Canterbury 115,600 . . . H6
Canvey Island 29,550 . . . J8
Carlisle, 99,600 . . . D 3
Carlton, 46,690 . . . F 5
Caterham and Warlingham, 35,840 . H 8
Chatham, 59,550 . . . J 8
Cheadle and Gatley, 62,460 . . . H 2
Chelmsford, 58,320 . . . J 7
Cheltenham, 75,910 . . . E 6
Chertsey, 45,070 . . . G 8
Chesham, 20,830 . . . G 7
Cheshunt, 45,750 . . . H 7
Chester, 117,200 . . . G 2
Chesterfield, 69,480 . . . J 2
Chester-le-Street, 20,720 . . . J 3
Chichester, 20,940 . . . G 7
Chigwell, 54,220 . . . H 8
Chippenham, 18,550 . . . E 6
Chorley, 31,800 . . . G 2
Christchurch, 31,610 . . . F 7
Cirencester, 14,500 . . . E 6
Clacton, 39,380 . . . J 6
Clay Cross, 9,630 . . . J 2
Cleator Moor, ⊙7,686 . . . D 3
Cleethorpes, 37,200 . . . H 4
Clevedon, 15,140 . . . D 6
Clun, ⊙1,261 . . . D 6
Coalville, 28,740 . . . F 5
Cockermouth, 6,480 . . . D 3
Colchester, 79,600 . . . H 6
Colne, 19,030 . . . H 1
Colne Valley, 21,190 . . . J 2
Congleton, 21,500 . . . H 2
Consett, 35,080 . . . H 3
Corby, 48,850 . . . G 5
Coventry, 336,800 . . . F 5
Cowes, 19,190 . . . F 7
Crawley, 72,600 . . . G 6
Crewe and Nantwich, 98,100 . . . E 4
Cromer, 5,720 . . . J 5
Crook and Willington, 21,120 . . . E 3
Crosby, 56,750 . . . G 2
Croydon, 330,600 . . . H 8
Cuckfield, 26,500 . . . G 6
Darlington, 85,120 . . . F 3
Dartford, 44,130 . . . J 8
Darton, 15,710 . . . J 2
Darwen, 29,290 . . . H 1
Deal, 26,840 . . . J 6
Dearne, 24,780 . . . K 2
Denton, 38,110 . . . H 2
Derby, 213,700 . . . F 5
Dewsbury, 50,560 . . . J 1
Didcot, ⊙14,277 . . . F 6
Doncaster, 81,530 . . . F 4
Dorking, 22,410 . . . G 8
Dover, 34,160 . . . J 6
Downham Market, 4,120 . . . H 5
Droitwich, 13,950 . . . E 5
Dronfield, 20,000 . . . J 2
Dudley, 187,110 . . . E 5
Dunstable, 32,090 . . . G 6
Durham, 88,800 . . . J 3
Ealing, 293,800 . . . H 8
Eastbourne, 73,200 . . . H 7
East Grinstead, 19,420 . . . G 6
Eastleigh, 46,340 . . . F 7
East Retford, 18,260 . . . G 4
Egham, 30,320 . . . G 8
Egremont, ⊙7,253 . . . D 3
Eling, ⊙20,006 . . . F 7
Ellesmere, ⊙2,630 . . . E 5
Ellesmere Port, 63,870 . . . G 2
Enfield, 260,900 . . . H 7
Epsom and Ewell, 70,700 . . . G 8
Esher, 63,970 . . . H 8
Eston, ⊙46,219 . . . F 3
Eton, 4,950 . . . G 8
Evesham, 14,090 . . . F 5
Exeter, 93,300 . . . D 7
Exminster, ⊙3,181 . . . D 7
Exmouth, 26,840 . . . D 7
Falmouth, 17,530 . . . B 7
Fareham, 86,300 . . . F 7
Farnborough, 43,520 . . . G 8
Farnham, 33,140 . . . G 8
Farnworth, 26,110 . . . H 2
Faversham, 15,010 . . . H 6
Felixstowe, 19,460 . . . J 6
Felling, 38,990 . . . J 3
Filey, 5,660 . . . G 3
Fleet, 22,930 . . . G 8
Fleetwood, 30,070 . . . D 4
Folkestone, 45,610 . . . J 6
Formby, 24,850 . . . G 2
Framlingham, ⊙2,258 . . . J 5
Frimley and Camberley, 47,390 . . . G 8
Fulwood, 22,910 . . . G 1
Gainsborough, 17,440 . . . G 4
Gateshead, 91,230 . . . J 3
Gillingham, Dorset, ⊙4,050 . . . E 6
Gillingham, Kent, 93,900 . . . J 8
Glastonbury, 6,580 . . . E 6
Glossop, 24,820 . . . J 2
Gloucester, 91,600 . . . E 6
Godalming, 18,840 . . . G 8
Golborne, 28,720 . . . G 2
Goole, 17,920 . . . G 4
Gosport, 82,300 . . . F 7
Grange, 3,520 . . . E 3
Grantham 27,830 . . . G5
Gravesend 53,500 . . . J8
Great Grimsby 93,800 . . . G4
Great Torrington 3,430 . . . C7
Great Yarmouth 49,410 . . . J5
Greenwich 207,200 . . . H8
Guildford 58,470 . . . G8
Guisborough 14,860 . . . F3
Hackney 192,500 . . . H8
Hale 17,080 . . . H2
Halesowen 54,120 . . . E5
Halifax 88,580 . . . J1
Haltemprice 54,850 . . . G4
Haltwhistle† 3,511 . . . E2
Hammersmith 170,000 . . . H8
Haringey 228,200 . . . H8
Harlow 79,160 . . . H7
Harrogate 64,620 . . . F4
Harrow 200,200 . . . B5
Hartlepool 97,100 . . . F3
Harwich 15,280 . . . J6
Haslingden 15,140 . . . H1
Hastings 74,600 . . . H7
Hatfield† 25,359 . . . H7
Havant and Waterloo 112,430 . . . G7
Haverhill 14,550 . . . H5
Havering 239,200 . . . J8
Hayle† 5,378 . . . B7
Hazel Grove and Bramhall 40,400 . . . H2
Heanor 24,590 . . . F4
Hebburn 23,150 . . . J3
Hedon 3,010 . . . G4
Hemel Hempstead 71,150 . . . G7
Hereford 47,800 . . . E5
Hertford 20,760 . . . H7
Hetton 16,810 . . . J3
Hexham 9,820 . . . E3
Heywood 31,720 . . . H2
High Wycombe 61,190 . . . G8
Hillingdon 230,800 . . . G8
Hinckley 49,310 . . . F5
Hinderwell† 2,551 . . . G3
Hitchin 29,190 . . . G6
Hoddesdon 27,510 . . . H7
Holmfirth 19,790 . . . J2
Horley† 18,593 . . . H8
Hornsea 7,280 . . . G4
Horsham 26,770 . . . G6
Horwich 16,670 . . . G2
Houghton-le-Spring 33,150 . . . J3
Hounslow, 199,100 . . . G 8
Hove, 72,000 . . . G 7
Hoylake, 32,000 . . . G 2
Hoyland Nether, 15,500 . . . J 2
Hucknall, 27,110 . . . F 4
Huddersfield, 130,060 . . . J 2
Hugh Town, ⊙1,958 . . . A 8
Hull, 276,600 . . . G 4
Hunstanton, 4,140 . . . H 5
Huntingdon and Godmanchester, 17,200 . . . G 5
Huyton-with-Roby, 65,950 . . . G 2
Hyde, 37,040 . . . H 2
Ilfracombe, 9,350 . . . C 6
Ilkeston, 33,690 . . . F 5
Immingham, ⊙10,259 . . . G 4
Ipswich, 121,500 . . . J 5
Islington, 171,600 . . . H 8
Jarrow, 28,510 . . . J 3
Kendal, 22,440 . . . E 3
Kenilworth, 19,730 . . . F 5
Kensington and Chelsea, 161,400 . . G 8
Keswick, 4,790 . . . D 3
Kettering, 44,480 . . . G 5
Keynsham, 18,970 . . . E 6
Kidderminster, 49,960 . . . E 5
Kidsgrove, 22,690 . . . E 4
King's Lynn, 29,990 . . . H 5
Kingston upon Thames, 135,600 . . H 8
Kingswood, 30,450 . . . E 6
Kirkburton, 20,320 . . . J 2
Kirkby, 59,100 . . . G 2
Kirkby Lonsdale, ⊙1,506 . . . E 3
Kirkby Stephen, ⊙1,539 . . . E 3
Knutsford, 14,840 . . . H 2
Lambeth, 290,300 . . . H 8
Lancaster, 126,300 . . . E 3
Leatherhead, 40,830 . . . G 8
Leeds, 744,500 . . . J 1
Leek, 19,460 . . . H 2
Leicester, 289,400 . . . F 5
Leigh, 46,390 . . . H 2
Leighton-Linslade, 22,590 . . . F 7
Letchworth, 31,520 . . . G 6
Lewes, 14,170 . . . H 7
Lewisham, 237,300 . . . H 8
Leyland, 23,690 . . . G 1
Lichfield, 23,690 . . . F 5
Lincoln, 73,700 . . . G 4
Liskeard, 5,360 . . . C 7
Litherland, 23,530 . . . G 2
Littlehampton, 20,320 . . . G 7

(continued on following page)

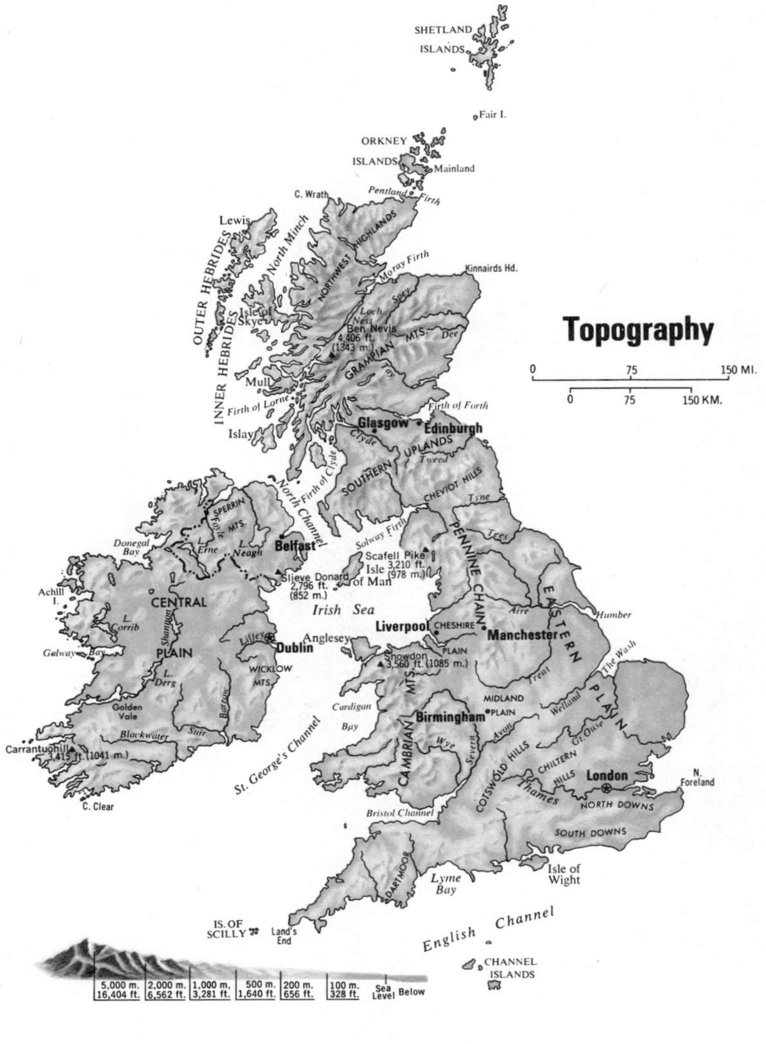
Topography
0 75 150 MI.
0 75 150 KM.
SHETLAND ISLANDS
Fair I.
ORKNEY ISLANDS
Mainland
C. Wrath
Pentland Firth
Lewis
OUTER HEBRIDES
INNER HEBRIDES
North Minch
NORTHWEST HIGHLANDS
Moray Firth
Kinnairds Hd.
Isle of Skye
Loch Ness
Ben Nevis 4,406 ft. (1,343 m.)
GRAMPIAN MTS.
Dee
Mull
Firth of Lorne
Islay
Firth of Forth
Glasgow
Edinburgh
Clyde
SOUTHERN UPLANDS
Tweed
CHEVIOT HILLS
Firth of Clyde
North Channel
Tyne
Tees
Solway Firth
Scafell Pike 3,210 ft. (978 m.)
Isle of Man
PENNINE CHAIN
Belfast
L. Neagh
SPERRIN MTS.
L. Erne
Donegal Bay
Slieve Donard 2,796 ft. (852 m.)
Irish Sea
Achill I.
CENTRAL PLAIN
L. Corrib
Shannon
Galway Bay
Dublin
Liffey
Anglesey
WICKLOW MTS.
L. Derg
Liverpool
CHESHIRE PLAIN
Manchester
Aire
Humber
EASTERN PLAIN
The Wash
Snowdon 3,560 ft. (1085 m.)
Trent
MIDLAND PLAIN
Birmingham
Cardigan Bay
CAMBRIAN MTS.
Golden Vale
Blackwater
Suir
Barrow
Carrantuohill 3,415 ft. (1041 m.)
St. George's Channel
C. Clear
Severn
Wye
Avon
COTSWOLD HILLS
CHILTERN HILLS
Welland
Gt. Ouse
London
Thames
N. Foreland
NORTH DOWNS
SOUTH DOWNS
Bristol Channel
DARTMOOR
Lyme Bay
Isle of Wight
IS. OF SCILLY
Land's End
English Channel
CHANNEL ISLANDS
5,000 m. 16,404 ft.
2,000 m. 6,562 ft.
1,000 m. 3,281 ft.
500 m. 1,640 ft.
200 m. 656 ft.
100 m. 328 ft.
Sea Level
Below

ENGLAND

AREA 50,516 sq. mi. (130,836 sq. km.)
POPULATION 46,220,955
CAPITAL London
LARGEST CITY London
HIGHEST POINT Scafell Pike 3,210 ft. (978 m.)

WALES

AREA 8,017 sq. mi. (20,764 sq. km.)
POPULATION 2,790,462
CAPITAL Cardiff
LARGEST CITY Cardiff
HIGHEST POINT Snowdon 3,560 ft. (1,085 m.)

SCOTLAND

AREA 30,414 sq. mi. (78,772 sq. km.)
POPULATION 5,117,146
CAPITAL Edinburgh
LARGEST CITY Glasgow
HIGHEST POINT Ben Nevis 4,406 ft. (1,343 m.)

NORTHERN IRELAND

AREA 5,452 sq. mi. (14,121 sq. km.)
POPULATION 1,543,000
CAPITAL Belfast
LARGEST CITY Belfast
HIGHEST POINT Slieve Donard 2,796 ft. (852 m.)

10 United Kingdom and Ireland
(continued)

Liverpool, 539,700 G 2
Loftus, 7,850 G 3
London (cap.), 7,028,200 H 8
London, ★12,332,900 H 8
Long Eaton, 33,560 F 5
Longbenton, 50,120 J 3
Looe, 4,060 C 7
Loughborough, 49,010 F 5
Lowestoft, 53,260 J 5
Ludlow, ⊙7,466 E 5
Luton, 164,500 G 6
Lydd, 4,670 H 7
Lyme Regis, 3,460 E 7
Lymington, 36,780 F 7
Lynton, 1,770 D 6
Lytham Saint Anne's, 42,120 G 1
Mablethorpe and Sutton, 6,750 H 4
Macclesfield, 45,420 H 2
Maidenhead, 48,210 G 8
Maidstone, 72,110 J 8
Maldon, 14,350 H 6
Malmesbury, 2,550 E 6
Malton, 4,010 G 3
Malvern, 30,420 E 5
Manchester, 490,000 H 2
Mangotsfield, 23,000 E 6
Mansfield, 58,450 K 2
Mansfield Woodhouse, 25,400 F 4
March, 14,560 H 5
Margate, 50,290 J 6
Market Harborough, 15,230 G 5
Marlborough, 6,370 F 6
Matlock, 20,300 J 2
Melton Mowbray, 20,680 G 5
Merton, 169,400 H 8
Middlesbrough, 153,900 F 3
Middleton, 53,340 H 2
Middlewich, 7,600 H 2
Mildenhall, ⊙9,269 H 5
Millom, ⊙7,101 D 3
Milton Keynes, 89,900 F 5
Minehead, 8,230 D 6
Moretonhampstead, ⊙1,440 C 7
Morpeth, 14,450 F 2
Mundesley, ⊙1,536 J 5
Nelson, 31,220 H 1
Neston, 18,210 G 2
Newark, 24,760 G 4
Newbury, 24,850 F 6
Newcastle upon Tyne, 295,800 H 3
Newcastle-under-Lyme, 75,940 E 4
Newham, 228,900 H 8
Newhaven, 9,970 H 7
Newport, 22,430 F 7
New Romney, 3,830 J 7
Newton Abbot, 19,940 D 7
Newton-le-Willows, 21,780 H 2
New Windsor, 29,660 G 8
Northallerton F 3
Northam, 8,310 C 6
Northampton, 128,290 F 5
Northfleet, 27,150 J 8
North Sunderland, ⊙1,725 F 2
Northwich, 17,710 H 2
Norton, 5,580 G 3
Norton-Radstock, 15,900 E 6
Norwich, 119,200 J 5
Nottingham, 280,300 F 5
Nuneaton, 69,210 F 5
Oadby, 20,700 F 5
Oakham, 7,280 G 5
Okehampton, 4,000 D 7
Oldham, 103,690 H 2
Ormskirk, 28,860 G 2
Oswaldtwistle, 14,270 H 1
Oxford, 117,400 F 6
Padstow, ⊙2,802 B 7
Penryn, 5,660 B 7
Penzance, 19,360 B 7
Peterborough, 118,900 G 5
Peterlee, ⊙21,846 J 3
Plymouth, 259,100 C 7
Polperro, ⊙1,491 C 7
Poole, 110,600 E 7
Porlock, ⊙1,290 D 6
Portishead, 9,680 E 6
Portland, 14,860 E 7
Portslade-by-Sea, 18,040 G 7
Portsmouth, 198,500 F 7
Potters Bar, 24,670 H 7
Poulton-le-Fylde, 16,340 G 1
Preston, 94,760 G 1
Prestwich, 32,850 H 2
Queenborough, 31,550 H 6
Radcliffe, 29,630 H 2
Ramsbottom, 16,710 H 2
Ramsgate, 40,090 J 6
Rawtenstall, 20,950 H 1
Rayleigh, 26,740 J 8
Reading, 131,200 G 8
Redbridge, 231,600 H 8
Redcar, ⊙46,325 F 3
Redditch, 44,750 E 5
Reigate, 55,600 H 8
Richmond upon Thames, 166,800 H 8
Rickmansworth, 29,030 G 8
Ripley, 18,060 F 4
Rochdale, 93,780 H 2
Rochester, 56,030 J 8
Rothbury, ⊙1,818 E 2
Rotherham, 84,770 K 2
Royal Leamington Spa, 44,950 F 5
Royal Tunbridge Wells, 44,800 H 6
Rugby, 60,380 F 5
Rugeley, 24,440 E 5
Runcorn, 42,730 G 2
Rushden, 21,840 G 5
Ryde, 23,170 F 7
Rye, 4,530 H 7
Ryton, 15,170 H 3
Saddleworth, 21,340 J 2
Saint Agnes, ⊙4,747 B 7
Saint Albans, 123,800 H 7
Saint Austell-with-Fowey, 32,710 C 7
Saint Columb Major, ⊙3,953 B 7
Saint Helens, 104,890 G 2
Saint Ives, Cornwall, 9,760 B 7
Saint Neots, 17,940 G 5
Salcombe, 2,370 D 7
Sale, 59,060 H 2
Salford, 261,100 H 2
Salisbury, 35,460 F 6
Saltburn and Marske-by-the-Sea, 21,170 G 3
Sandbach, 14,280 H 2
Sandown-Shanklin, 14,800 F 7
Sandwich, 4,420 J 6
Saxmundham, 1,820 J 5
Scarborough, 43,300 G 3
Scunthorpe, 68,100 G 4
Seaford, 18,020 H 7
Seaham, 22,470 J 3
Seascale, ⊙2,106 D 3
Seaton, 4,500 D 7
Seaton Valley, 35,880 J 3
Sedbergh, ⊙2,741 E 3
Selsey, ⊙6,491 G 7
Sevenoaks, 18,160 J 8
Shaftesbury, 4,180 E 7
Sheffield, 558,000 J 2
Sherborne, 9,230 E 7
Sheringham, 4,940 J 5
Shildon, 15,360 F 3
Shoreham-by-Sea, 19,620 G 7
Shrewsbury, 56,120 E 5
Silloth, ⊙2,662 D 3
Sittingbourne and Milton, 32,830 H 6
Skelmersdale, 35,850 G 2
Skelton and Brotton, 15,930 G 3
Sleaford, 8,050 G 5
Slough, 89,060 G 8
Solihull, 108,230 F 5
Southampton, 213,700 F 7
Southend-on-Sea, 159,300 H 6
Southport, 86,030 G 1
South Shields, 96,900 J 3
Southwark, 224,900 H 8
Southwold, 1,960 J 5
Sowerby Bridge, 15,700 H 1
Spalding, 17,040 G 5
Spenborough, 41,460 J 1
Spennymoor, 19,050 F 3
Stafford, 54,860 E 5
Staines, 56,380 G 8
Stamford, 14,980 G 5
Stanley, 42,280 H 3
Staveley, 17,620 K 2
Stevenage, 72,600 G 6
Stockport, 138,350 H 2
Stockton-on-Tees, 165,400 F 3
Stoke-on-Trent, 256,200 E 4
Stourbridge, 56,530 E 5
Stourport-on-Severn, 19,430 E 5
Stowmarket, 9,020 J 5
Stratford-upon-Avon, 20,080 F 5
Stretford, 52,450 H 2
Stroud, 19,600 E 6
Sudbury, 8,860 H 5
Sunbury-on-Thames, 40,070 G 8
Sunderland, 214,820 J 3
Sutton, 166,700 H 8
Sutton Bridge, ⊙3,113 H 5
Sutton in Ashfield, 40,330 K 2
Swadlincote, 21,060 F 5
Swanage, 8,000 E 7
Swindon, 90,680 F 6
Tamworth, 46,960 F 5
Taunton, 37,570 D 6
Tavistock, ⊙7,620 C 7
Telford, ⊙79,451 E 5
Tenbury, ⊙2,151 E 5
Tewkesbury, 9,210 E 6
Thetford, 15,690 H 5
Thirsk, ⊙2,884 F 3
Thornaby-on-Tees, ⊙42,385 F 3
Thorne, ⊙16,694 F 4
Thornton Cleveleys, 27,090 G 1
Thurrock, 127,700 J 8
Tiverton, 16,190 D 7
Todmorden, 14,540 H 1
Tonbridge, 31,410 H 8
Torbay, 109,900 D 7
Torpoint, 6,840 C 7
Tower Hamlets, 146,100 H 8
Tow Law, 2,460 H 4
Trowbridge, 20,120 E 6
Truro, 15,690 B 7
Turton, 22,800 H 2
Tynemouth, 67,090 J 3
Upton upon Severn, ⊙2,048 E 5
Urmston, 44,130 H 2
Uttoxeter, 9,100 E 5
Ventnor, 6,980 F 7
Wainfleet All Saints, ⊙1,116 H 4
Wakefield, 306,500 J 2
Wallasey, 94,520 G 2
Wallsend, 45,490 J 3
Walsall, 182,430 E 5
Waltham Forest, 223,700 H 8
Waltham Holy Cross, 14,810 H 7
Walton and Weybridge, 51,270 G 8
Walton-le-Dale, 27,660 G 1
Wandsworth, 284,600 H 8
Wantage, 8,490 F 6
Ware, 14,900 H 7
Wareham, 4,630 E 7
Warley, 161,260 E 5
Warminster, 14,440 E 6
Warrington, 65,320 G 2
Warwick, 17,870 F 5
Washington, 27,720 J 3
Watchet, 2,980 D 6
Watford, 77,000 H 7
Wellingborough, 39,570 G 5
Wells, 8,960 E 6
Wells-next-the-Sea, 2,450 H 5
Welwyn, 39,900 H 7
Wem, ⊙3,411 E 5
West Bridgford, 28,340 F 5
West Bromwich, 162,740 F 5
West Mersea, 4,730 H 6
Westminster, 216,100 H 8
Weston-super-Mare, 51,960 D 6
Weymouth and Melcombe Regis, 41,080 E 7
Whickham, 29,710 J 3
Whitchurch, ⊙7,142 E 5
Whitehaven, 26,260 D 3
Whitley Bay, 37,010 J 3
Widnes, 58,330 G 2
Wigan, 80,920 G 2
Wigston, 31,650 F 5
Wilmslow, 31,250 H 2
Wilton, 4,090 F 6
Winchester, 88,900 F 6
Windermere, 7,860 E 3
Winsford, 26,920 G 2
Wirral, 27,510 G 2
Wisbech, 16,990 H 5
Witham, 19,730 H 6
Withernsea, 6,300 H 4
Wivenhoe, 5,630 J 6
Woking, 79,300 G 8
Wokingham, 22,390 G 8
Wolverhampton, 266,400 E 5
Wombwell, 17,850 K 2
Woodhall Spa, 2,420 G 4
Woodley and Sandford, ⊙24,581 G 8
Woodstock, 2,070 F 6
Wooler, ⊙1,833 F 2
Worcester, 73,900 E 5
Workington, 28,260 D 3
Worksop, 36,590 F 4
Worsbrough, 15,180 J 2
Worsley, 49,530 H 2
Worthing, 89,100 G 7
Wymondham, 9,390 J 5
Yateley, ⊙16,505 G 8
Yeovil, 26,180 E 7
York, 101,900 F 4

OTHER FEATURES

Aire (riv.) F 4
Atlantic Ocean A 7
Avon (riv.) F 5
Avon (riv.) F 7
Axe Edge (mt.) H 2
Barnstaple (bay) C 6
Beachy (head) H 7
Bigbury (bay) C 7
Blackwater (riv.) H 6
Bristol (chan.) C 6
Brown Willy (mt.) C 7
Cheviot (hills) E 2
Cheviot, The (mt.) E 2
Chiltern (hills) G 6
Cleveland (hills) F 3
Colne (riv.) G 8
Cornwall (cape) B 7
Cotswold (hills) E 6
Cross Fell (mt.) E 3
Cumbrian (mts.) D 3
Dart (riv.) D 7
Dartmoor National Park C 7
Dee (riv.) D 4
Derwent (riv.) G 3
Derwent (riv.) H 3
Don (riv.) F 4
Dorset Heights (hills) E 7
Dove (riv.) J 2
Dover (str.) J 7
Dungeness (prom.) J 7
Dunkery (hill) D 6
Eddystone (rocks) C 7
Eden (riv.) E 3
English (chan.) D 8
Esk (riv.) D 2
Exe (riv.) D 7
Exmoor National Park D 6
Fens, The (reg.) G 5
Flamborough (head) G 3
Formby (head) G 2
Foulness Island (pen.) J 6
Gibraltar (pt.) H 4
Great Ouse (riv.) H 5
Hartland (pt.) C 6
High Willhays (mt.) C 7
Hodder (riv.) H 1
Holderness (pen.), 43,900 G 4
Holy (isl.), 189 F 2
Humber (riv.) G 4
Irish (sea) B 4
Kennet (riv.) F 6
Lake District National Park D 3
Land's End (prom.) B 7
Lea (riv.) G 6
Lincoln Wolds (hills) G 4
Lindisfarne (Holy) (isl.), 189 F 2
Liverpool (bay) D 4
Lizard, The (pen.), 7,371 B 8
Lundy (isl.), 49 C 6
Lune (riv.) E 3
Lyme (bay) D 7
Manacle (pt.) C 7
Medway (riv.) H 6
Mendip (hills) E 6
Mersea (isl.), 4,423 J 6
Mersey (riv.) G 2
Morecambe (bay) D 3
Mounts (bay) B 7
Naze, The (prom.) J 6
Nene (riv.) H 5
New (for.) F 6
North (sea) J 4
North Downs (hills) G 6
North Foreland (prom.) J 6
Northumberland National Park E 2
North York Moors National Park G 3
Orford Ness (prom.) J 5
Ouse (riv.) G 4
Ouse (riv.) G 6
Parrett (riv.) E 6
Peak District National Park F 4
Peak, The (mt.) J 2
Peel Fell (mt.) E 2
Pennine Chain (range) E 3
Plymouth (sound) C 7
Portland, Bill of (pt.) E 7
Prawle (pt.) D 7
Purbeck, Isle of (pen.), 39,500 F 7
Ribble (riv.) E 4
Saint Alban's (head) F 7
Saint Bees (head) D 3
Saint Martin's (isl.), 106 A 8
Saint Mary's (isl.), 1,958 A 8
Scafell Pike (mt.) D 3
Scilly (isls.), 1,900 A 7
Selsey Bill (prom.) G 7
Severn (riv.) E 6
Sheppey (isl.), 31,550 J 6
Sherwood (for.) F 4
Skiddaw (mt.) D 3
Solent (chan.) F 7
Solway (firth) D 3
South Downs (hills) G 7
Spithead (chan.) F 7
Spurn (head) H 4
Stonehenge (ruins) F 6
Stour (riv.) E 7
Stour (riv.) H 6
Stour (riv.) J 6
Swale (riv.) F 3
Tamar (riv.) C 7
Taw (riv.) D 7
Tees (riv.) F 3
Test (riv.) F 6
Thames (riv.) H 6
Tintagel (head) C 7
Torridge (riv.) C 7
Trent (riv.) G 4
Tresco (isl.), 246 A 8
Tweed (riv.) E 2
Tyne (riv.) F 3
Ure (riv.) F 3
Ver (riv.) H 7
Walney, Isle of (isl.), 11,241 D 3
Wash, The (bay) H 5
Weald, The (reg.) H 6
Wear (riv.) F 3
Weaver (riv.) G 2
Welland (riv.) G 5
Wey (riv.) G 6
Wharfe (riv.) E 3
Wirral (pen.), 432,900 G 2
Witham (riv.) G 4
Wolds, The (hills) G 4
Wye (riv.) D 5
Wyre (riv.) G 1
Yare (riv.) J 5
Yorkshire Dales National Park E 3

CHANNEL ISLANDS

CITIES and TOWNS

Saint Anne E 8
Saint Helier (cap.), Jersey, ⊙28,135 E 8
Saint Peter Port (cap.), Guernsey, ⊙16,303 E 8
Saint Sampson's, ⊙6,534 E 8

OTHER FEATURES

Alderney (isl.), 1,686 E 8
Guernsey (isl.), 51,351 E 8
Herm (isl.), 96 E 8
Jersey (isl.), 72,629 E 8
Sark (isl.), 590 E 8

ISLE of MAN

CITIES and TOWNS

Castletown, 2,820 C 3
Douglas (cap.), 20,389 C 3
Laxey, 1,170 C 3
Michael, 408 C 3
Onchan, 4,807 C 3
Peel, 3,081 C 3
Port Erin, 1,714 C 3
Port Saint Mary, 1,508 C 3
Ramsey, 5,048 C 3

OTHER FEATURES

Ayre (pt.) C 3
Calf of Man (isl.) C 3
Langness (prom.) C 3
Snaefell (mt.) C 3
Spanish (head) C 3

WALES

COUNTIES

Clwyd, 376,000 D 4
Dyfed, 323,100 C 6
Gwent, 439,600 D 6
Gwynedd, 225,100 C 4
Mid Glamorgan, 540,400 D 6
Powys, 101,500 D 5
South Glamorgan, 389,200 A 7
West Glamorgan, 371,900 D 6

CITIES and TOWNS

Aberaeron, 1,340 C 5
Abercarn, 18,370 B 6
Aberdare, 38,030 A 6
Abertillery, 20,550 B 6
Amlwch, 3,630 C 4
Bala, 1,650 D 5
Bangor, 16,030 C 4
Barmouth, 2,070 C 5
Barry, 42,780 B 7
Beaumaris, 2,090 C 4
Bedwellty, 25,460 B 6
Bethesda, 4,180 D 4
Betws-y-Coed, 720 D 4
Brecknock (Brecon), 6,460 D 6
Brecon, 6,460 D 6
Bridgend, 14,690 A 7
Brynmawr, 5,970 B 6
Builth Wells, 1,480 D 5
Burry Port, 5,990 C 6
Caernarfon, 8,840 C 4
Caerphilly, 42,190 B 6
Cardiff, 281,500 B 7
Cardigan, 3,830 C 5
Chepstow, 8,260 E 6
Chirk, ⊙3,564 D 5
Colwyn Bay, 25,370 D 4
Criccieth, 1,590 C 5
Cwmamman, 3,950 D 6
Cwmbran, 32,980 B 6
Denbigh, 8,420 D 4
Dolgellau, 2,430 D 5
Ebbw Vale, 25,670 B 6
Ffestiniog, 5,510 D 5
Fishguard and Goodwick, 5,020 B 5
Flint, 15,070 G 2
Gelligaer, 33,820 A 6
Harlech, ⊙332 C 5
Haverfordwest, 8,930 B 6
Hawarden, ⊙20,389 G 2
Hay, 1,200 D 5
Holywell, 8,570 G 2
Kidwelly, 3,090 C 6
Knighton, 2,190 D 5
Llandeilo, 1,780 C 6
Llandovery, 2,040 D 5
Llandrindod Wells, 3,460 D 5
Llandudno, 17,700 D 4
Llanelli, 25,870 C 6
Llanfairfechan, 3,800 D 4
Llangefni, 4,070 C 4
Llangollen, 3,050 D 5
Llanguicke, ⊙15,029 D 6
Llanidloes, 2,390 D 5
Llantrisant, ⊙27,490 A 7
Llanwrtyd Wells, 460 D 5
Llwchwr, 27,530 D 6
Machynlleth, 1,830 D 5
Maesteg, 21,100 D 6
Menai Bridge, 2,730 C 4
Merthyr Tydfil, 61,500 A 6
Milford Haven, 13,960 B 6
Mold, 8,700 G 2
Montgomery, 1,000 D 5
Mountain Ash, 27,710 A 6
Mynyddislwyn, 15,590 B 6
Narberth, 970 C 6
Neath, 27,280 D 6
Nefyn, ⊙2,086 C 5
Newcastle Emlyn, 690 C 5
Newport, Dyfed, ⊙1,062 C 5
Newport, Gwent, 110,090 B 6
New Quay, 760 C 5
Newtown, 6,400 D 5
Neyland, 2,690 B 6
Ogmore and Garw, 19,680 A 6
Pembroke, 14,570 C 6
Penarth, 24,180 B 7
Penmaenmawr, 4,050 C 4
Pontypool, 36,710 B 6
Pontypridd, 34,180 A 6
Porthcawl, 14,980 D 6
Porthmadog, 3,900 C 5
Port Talbot, 58,200 D 6
Prestatyn, 15,480 D 4
Presteigne, 1,330 D 5
Pwllheli, 4,020 C 5
Rhondda, 85,400 A 6
Rhyl, 22,150 D 4
Risca, 15,780 B 6
Ruthin, 4,780 D 4
Saint David's, ⊙1,638 B 6
Swansea, 190,800 C 6
Tenby, 4,930 C 6
Tredegar, 17,450 B 6
Tywyn, 3,850 C 5
Welshpool, 7,370 D 5
Wrexham, 39,530 E 4

OTHER FEATURES

Anglesey (isl.), 64,500 C 4
Aran Fawddwy (mt.) C 5
Bardsey (isl.), 9 C 5
Berwyn (mts.) D 5
Black (mts.) D 6
Braich-y-Pwll (prom.) C 5
Brecon Beacons (mt.) D 6
Brecon Beacons National Park D 6
Caldy (isl.), 70 C 6
Cambrian (mts.) D 5
Cardigan (bay) C 5
Carmarthen (bay) C 6
Cemmaes (head) C 5
Dee (riv.) D 4
Dovey (riv.) D 5
Ely (riv.) B 7
Gower (pen.), 17,220 C 6
Great Ormes (head) C 4
Holy (isl.), 13,715 C 4
Lleyn (pen.), 25,800 C 5
Menai (str.) C 4
Milford Haven (inlet) B 6
Pembrokeshire Coast National Park C 6
Plynlimon (mt.) D 5
Preseli (mts.) C 6
Radnor (for.) D 5
Rhymney (riv.) B 6
Saint Brides (bay) B 6
Saint David's (head) B 6
Saint George's (chan.) B 5
Saint Gowans (head) C 6
Severn (riv.) E 5
Snowdon (mt.) D 4
Snowdonia National Park D 4
Taff (riv.) B 7
Teifi (riv.) C 5
Towy (riv.) D 6
Tremadoc (bay) C 5
Usk (riv.) B 6
Wye (riv.) D 5
Ynys Môn (Anglesey) (isl.), 64,500 C 4

★Population of met. area.
⊙Population of parish.

SCOTLAND
(map on page 13)

REGIONS

Borders, 99,409 E 5
Central, 269,281 D 4
Dumfries and Galloway, 143,667 E 5
Fife, 336,339 E 4
Grampian, 448,772 F 3
Highland, 182,044 D 3
Lothian, 754,008 E 5
Orkney (islands area), 17,675 E 1
Shetland (islands area), 18,494 F 2
Strathclyde, 2,504,909 C 4
Tayside, 401,987 E 4
Western Isles (islands area) 29,615 A 3

CITIES and TOWNS

Aberchirder, 877 F 3
Aberdeen, 210,362 F 3
Aberdour, 1,576 D 1
Aberfeldy, 1,552 E 4
Aberfoyle, 793 D 4
Aberlady, 737 F 4
Aberlour, 842 E 3
Abernethy, 776 E 4
Aboyne, 1,040 F 3
Acharacle, ⊙764 C 4
Achiltibuie, ⊙1,564 C 3
Achnasheen, ⊙1,078 C 3
Ae, 239 E 5
Airdrie, 38,491 C 2
Alexandria, 9,758 A 1
Alford, 764 F 3
Alloa, 13,558 C 1
Alness, 2,560 D 3
Altnaharra, ⊙1,227 D 2
Alva, 4,593 C 1
Alyth, 1,738 E 4
Ancrum, 266 F 5
Annan, 6,250 E 6
Annat, ⊙550 C 3
Annbank Station, 2,530 D 5
Applecross, ⊙550 C 3
Arbroath, 22,706 F 4
Ardavasar, ⊙449 B 3
Ardersier, 942 E 3
Ardgay, 193 D 3
Ardrishaig, 946 C 4
Ardrossan, 11,072 D 5
Armadale, 7,200 C 2
Arrochar, 543 D 4
Ascog, 230 A 2
Auchenblae, 339 F 4
Auchencairn, 215 E 6
Auchinleck, 4,883 D 5
Auchterarder, 1,738 E 4
Auchtermuchty, 1,426 E 4
Auldearn, 405 E 3
Aviemore, 1,224 E 3
Avoch, 776 D 3
Ayr, 47,990 D 5
Ayton, 410 F 5
Bailivanish, 347 A 3
Baillieston, 7,671 B 2
Balallan, 283 B 2
Balerno, 3,576 D 2
Balfron, 1,149 B 1
Ballantrae, 262 C 5
Ballater, 981 F 3
Ballingry, 4,332 D 1
Ballinluig, 188 E 4
Balloch, Highland, 572 D 3
Balloch, Strathclyde, 1,484 B 1
Baltasound, 246 G 2
Banchory, 2,435 F 3
Banff, 3,832 F 3
Bankfoot, 868 E 4
Bankhead, 1,492 F 3
Bannockburn, 5,889 C 1
Barrhead, 18,736 B 2
Barrhill, 236 D 5
Barvas, 279 B 2
Bathgate, 14,038 C 2
Bayble, 543 B 2
Bearsden, 25,128 B 2
Beattock, 309 E 5
Beauly, 1,141 D 3
Beith, 5,859 D 5
Bellsbank, 3,066 D 5
Bellshill, 18,166 C 2
Berriedale, ⊙1,927 E 2
Bieldside, 1,137 F 3
Biggar, 1,718 E 5
Birnam, 659 E 4
Bishopbriggs, 21,570 B 2
Bishopton, 2,931 B 2
Blackburn, 7,636 C 2
Blackford, 529 E 4
Blair Atholl, 437 E 4
Blairgowrie and Rattray, 5,681 E 4
Blanefield, 835 B 1
Blantyre, 13,992 B 2
Blyth Bridge, ⊙441 E 5
Bo'ness, 12,959 C 1
Boat of Garten, 406 E 3
Boddam, 1,429 G 3
Bonar Bridge, 519 D 3
Bonhill, 4,385 B 1
Bonnybridge, 5,701 C 1
Bonnyrigg and Lasswade, 7,429 D 2
Bowmore, 947 B 5
Braemar, 394 E 3
Breasclete, 234 B 2
Brechin, 6,759 F 4
Bridge of Allan, 4,638 C 1
Bridge of Don, 4,086 F 3
Bridge of Weir, 4,724 A 2
Brightons, 3,106 C 1
Broadford, 310 B 3
Brodick, 630 C 5
Brora, 1,436 E 2
Broxburn, 7,776 D 1
Buchlyvie, 412 B 1
Buckhaven and Methil, 17,930 F 4
Buckie, 8,145 E 3
Bucksburn, 6,567 F 3
Bunessan, ⊙585 B 4
Burghead, 1,321 E 3
Burnmouth, 300 F 5
Burntisland, 5,626 D 1
Cairndow, ⊙874 D 4
Cairnryan, 199 D 6
Callander, 1,805 D 4
Cambuslang, 14,607 B 2
Campbeltown, 6,428 C 5
Cannich, 203 D 3
Canonbie, 234 F 5
Caol, 3,719 C 4
Carbost, ⊙772 B 3
Cardenden, 6,802 D 1
Carloway, 178 B 2
Carluke, 8,864 E 5
Carnoustie, 6,838 F 4
Carnwath, 1,246 E 5
Carradale, 262 C 5
Carrbridge, 416 E 3
Carron, 2,626 C 1
Carsphairn, 186 D 5
Castlebay, 284 A 4
Castle Douglas, 3,384 E 6
Castle Kennedy, 307 D 6
Castletown, 902 E 2
Catrine, 2,681 D 5
Cawdor, 111 E 3
Chirnside, 888 F 5
Chryston, 8,322 C 2
Clackmannan, 3,248 C 1
Clarkston, 8,404 B 2
Closeburn, 225 E 5
Clovulin, ⊙315 C 4
Clydebank, 47,538 B 2
Coalburn, 1,460 E 5
Coatbridge, 50,806 C 2
Cockburnspath, 233 F 5
Cockenzie and Port Seton, 3,539 D 1
Coldingham, 423 F 5
Coldstream, 1,393 F 5
Coll, 305 B 2
Colmonell, 218 D 5
Comrie, 1,119 E 4
Connel, 300 C 4
Cononbridge, 914 D 3
Corpach, 1,296 C 4
Coupar Angus, 2,010 E 4
Cove and Kilcreggan, 1,402 A 1
Cove Bay, 765 F 3
Cowdenbeath, 10,215 D 1
Cowie, 2,751 C 1
Craigellachie, 382 E 3
Craignure, ⊙544 C 4
Crail, 1,033 F 4
Crawford, 384 E 5
Creetown, 769 D 6
Crieff, 5,718 E 4
Crimond, 313 G 3
Crinan, ⊙462 C 4
Cromarty, 492 E 3
Crosshill, 535 D 5
Crossmichael, 317 D 6
Cruden Bay, 528 G 3
Cullen, 1,199 F 3
Culross, 504 C 1
Cults, 3,336 F 3
Cumbernauld, 41,200 C 1
Cumnock and Holmhead, 6,298 D 5
Cupar, 6,607 E 4
Currie, 6,764 D 2
Dailly, 1,258 D 5
Dalbeattie, 3,659 E 6
Daliburgh, 261 A 3
Dalkeith, 9,713 D 2
Dalmally, 283 D 4
Dalmellington, 1,949 D 5
Dalry, 5,833 D 5
Dalrymple, 1,336 D 5
Darvel, 3,177 D 5
Daviot, ⊙513 D 3
Denholm, 581 F 5
Denny and Dunipace, 10,424 C 1
Dervaig, ⊙1,081 B 4
Dingwall, 4,275 D 3
Dollar, 2,573 E 4
Dornoch, 880 D 3
Douglas, 1,843 E 5
Doune, 859 D 4
Drongan, 3,609 D 5
Drumbeg, ⊙833 C 2
Drummore, 336 D 6
Drumnadrochit, 359 D 3
Drymen, 659 B 1
Dufftown, 1,481 E 3
Dumbarton, 25,469 B 1
Dumfries, 29,259 E 5
Dunbar, 4,609 F 4
Dunbeath, 161 E 2
Dunbeg, 939 C 4
Dunblane, 5,222 E 4
Dundee, 194,732 F 4
Dundonald, 2,256 D 5
Dunfermline, 52,098 D 1
Dunkeld, 273 E 4
Dunning, 564 E 4
Dunoon, 8,759 A 2
Dunragit, 323 D 6
Duns, 1,812 F 5
Duntochter, 3,532 B 2
Dunure, 452 D 5
Dunvegan, 301 B 3
Dyce, 2,733 F 3
Eaglesfield, 581 E 5
Eaglesham, 2,788 D 5
Earlston, 1,415 F 5
East Calder, 2,690 D 2
East Kilbride, 71,200 B 2
East Linton, 882 F 5
Eastriggs, 1,455 E 5
Ecclefechan, 844 E 5
Edinburgh (cap.), 470,085 D 1
Edzell, 658 F 4
Elderslie, 5,204 B 2
Elgin, 17,042 E 3
Elie and Earlsferry, 807 F 4
Ellon, 2,855 F 3
Embo, 260 E 3
Errol, 762 E 4
Evanton, 562 D 3
Eyemouth, 2,704 F 5
Fairlie, 1,029 D 5
Falkirk, 36,901 C 1
Falkland, 998 E 4
Fallin, 3,159 C 1
Fauldhouse, 5,247 C 2
Ferness, ⊙287 E 3
Ferryden, 740 F 4
Findhorn, 664 E 3
Findochty, 1,229 E 3
Fintry, 296 B 1
Fochabers, 1,238 E 3
Forfar, 11,179 F 4
Forres, 5,317 E 3
Fort Augustus, 670 D 3
Forth, 2,929 C 2
Fortrose, 1,150 D 3
Fort William, 4,370 C 4
Foyers, 276 D 3
Fraserburgh, 10,930 G 3
Friockheim, 807 F 4
Furnace, 220 C 4
Fyvie, 405 F 3
Gairloch, 125 C 3
Galashiels, 12,808 F 5
Galston, 4,256 D 5
Gardenstown, 892 F 3
Garelochhead, 1,552 A 1
Gargunnock, 457 B 1
Garlieston, 385 D 6
Garmouth, 352 E 3
Garrabost, 307 B 2
Gartmore, 253 B 1
Gatehouse-of-Fleet, 835 D 6
Giffnock, 10,987 B 2
Gifford, 575 F 5
Girvan, 7,597 D 5
Glamis, 190 F 4
Glasgow, 880,617 B 2
Glasgow, ★1,674,789 B 2
Glenbarr, ⊙691 C 5
Glencaple, 275 E 5
Glencoe, 195 C 4
Glenelg, ⊙1,468 C 3
Glenluce, 725 D 6
Glenrothes, 31,400 E 4
Golspie, 1,374 E 3
Gordon, 320 F 5
Gorebridge, 3,426 D 2
Gourock, 11,192 A 1
Grangemouth, 24,430 C 1
Grantown-on-Spey, 1,578 E 3
Greenlaw, 574 F 5
Greenock, 67,275 A 2
Gretna, 1,907 E 5
Gullane, 1,701 F 4
Haddington, 6,767 F 5
Halkirk, 679 E 2
Hamilton, 45,495 C 2
Hamnavoe, 307 G 2
Harthill, 4,712 C 2
Hatton, 315 G 3
Hawick, 16,484 F 5
Heathhall, 1,365 E 5
Helensburgh, 13,327 A 1
Helmsdale, 727 E 2
Hill of Fearn, 233 D 3
Hillside, 692 F 4
Hillswick, ⊙696 G 2
Hopeman, 1,248 E 3
Huntly, 4,078 F 3
Hurlford, 4,294 D 5
Inchnadamph, ⊙833 D 2
Innellan, 922 A 2
Innerleithen, 2,293 E 5
Insch, 881 F 3
Inveraray, 473 C 4
Inverbervie, 853 F 4
Invercassley, ⊙1,067 D 3
Invergordon, 2,385 D 3
Invergowrie, 1,389 E 4
Inverie, ⊙1,468 C 3
Inverkeithing, 6,102 D 1
Inverness, 35,801 D 3
Inverurie, 5,534 F 3
Irvine, 48,500 D 5
Isle of Whithorn, 222 D 6
Jedburgh, 3,953 F 5
John O'Groats, 195 E 2
Johnshaven, 544 F 4
Johnstone, 23,251 B 2
Kames, 230 C 5
Keiss, 344 E 2
Keith, 4,192 F 3
Kelso, 4,934 F 5
Kelty, 6,573 D 1
Kemnay, 1,042 F 3
Kenmore, 211 E 4
Kilbarchan, 2,669 A 2
Kilbirnie, 8,259 A 2
Kilchoan, ⊙764 B 4
Kildonan, ⊙1,105 E 2
Killearn, 1,086 B 1
Killin, 600 D 4
Kilmacolm, 3,348 A 2
Kilmarnock, 50,175 D 5
Kilmaurs, 2,518 D 5
Kilninver, ⊙247 C 4
Kilrenny and Anstruther, 2,951 F 4
Kilsyth, 10,210 B 1
Kilwinning, 8,460 D 5
Kinbrace, ⊙1,105 E 2
Kincardine, 3,278 C 1
Kinghorn, 2,163 D 1
Kingussie, 1,036 D 3
Kinlochewe, ⊙1,794 C 3
Kinlochleven, 1,243 D 4
Kinloch Rannoch, 241 D 4
Kinloss, 2,378 E 3
Kinross, 2,829 E 4
Kintore, 970 F 3
Kippen, 529 B 1
Kirkcaldy, 50,207 D 1
Kirkcolm, 346 C 6
Kirkconnel, 3,318 E 5
Kirkcowan, 354 D 6
Kirkcudbright, 2,690 E 6
Kirkhill, 210 D 3
Kirkintilloch, 26,664 B 2
Kirkmuirhill, 2,575 E 5
Kirkton of Glenisla, ⊙331 E 4
Kirkwall, 4,777 E 2
Kirriemuir, 4,295 E 4
Kyleakin, 268 C 3
Kyle of Lochalsh, 687 C 3
Kylestrome, ⊙745 D 2
Ladybank, 1,216 E 4
Laggan, 393 D 3
Lairg, 572 D 2
Lamlash, 613 C 5
Lanark, 8,842 E 5
Langholm, 2,509 E 5
Larbert, 4,922 C 1
Largs, 9,461 A 2
Larkhall, 15,926 E 5
Lauder, 639 F 5
Laurencekirk, 1,416 F 4

(continued)

England and Wales

CONIC PROJECTION

MILES

KILOMETERS

Capitals of Countries..............⊛
Administrative Centers...........●
Other Capitals......................●
Canals

International Boundaries..........
County Boundaries...............
Other Boundaries................

The administrative centers
for MID GLAMORGAN,
NORTHUMBERLAND and SURREY
are Cardiff, Newcastle upon
Tyne and Kingston upon Thames,
respectively.

© Copyright HAMMOND INCORPORATED, Maplewood, N.J.

United Kingdom and Ireland

(continued)

Lennoxtown, 3,070 .... B 1
Lerwick, 6,195 .... G 2
Leslie, 3,303 .... E 4
Lesmahagow, 3,906 .... E 5
Leswalt, 237 .... C 6
Letham, 804 .... F 4
Leuchars, 2,482 .... F 4
Leurbost, 461 .... B 2
Leven, 9,507 .... F 4
Leverburgh, 223 .... B 3
Lhanbryde, 1,184 .... E 3
Lilliesleaf, 212 .... F 5
Limekilns, 812 .... D 1
Linlithgow, 6,098 .... C 1
Linwood, 10,510 .... B 2
Lionel, 187 .... B 2
Livingston, 21,900 .... C 2
Loanhead, 5,971 .... D 2
Lochailort, ⊙673 .... C 4
Lochaline, 213 .... C 4
Lochans, 355 .... D 6
Locharbriggs, 2,561 .... E 5
Lochawe, 200 .... C 4
Lochboisdale, 382 .... A 3
Lochcarron, 204 .... C 3
Lochgelly, 7,754 .... D 1
Lochgilphead, 1,217 .... C 4
Lochgoilhead, 216 .... D 4
Lochinver, 283 .... C 2
Lochmaben, 1,304 .... E 5
Lochmaddy, 307 .... A 3
Lochore, 2,994 .... D 1
Lochwinnoch, 2,064 .... A 2
Lockerbie, 3,135 .... E 5
Lossiemouth and Branderburgh, 5,817 .... E 3
Lumsden, 248 .... F 3
Luncarty, 584 .... E 4
Lybster, 554 .... E 2
Lyness, ⊙454 .... E 2
Macduff, 3,682 .... F 3
Machrihanish, 212 .... C 5
Maidens, 536 .... D 5
Mallaig, 903 .... C 4
Markinch, 2,366 .... E 4
Mauchline, 3,612 .... D 5
Maud, 634 .... F 3
Maybole, 4,703 .... D 5
Mayfield, 8,232 .... D 2
Meigle, 357 .... E 4
Melrose, 2,197 .... F 5
Melvaig, ⊙1,794 .... C 3
Methlick, 315 .... F 3
Methven, 806 .... E 4
Mid Yell, 220 .... G 2
Millport, 1,161 .... A 2
Milnathort, 1,099 .... E 4
Milngavie, 10,846 .... B 1
Minnigaff, 658 .... D 6
Mintlaw, 657 .... F 3
Moffat, 2,041 .... E 5
Moniaive, 342 .... E 5
Monifieth, 7,100 .... F 4
Montrose, 4,704 .... F 4
Morar, 184 .... C 4
Motherwell and Wishaw, 72,991 .... C 2
Muirkirk, 2,607 .... E 5
Muir of Ord, 1,339 .... D 3
Musselburgh, 17,045 .... D 2
Muthill, 672 .... E 4
Nairn, 5,821 .... E 3
Neilston, 4,358 .... B 2
Nethy Bridge, 431 .... E 3
New Abbey, 339 .... E 6
Newarthill, 7,003 .... C 2
Newburgh, Fife, 2,124 .... E 4
Newburgh, Grampian, 447 .... G 3
Newcastleton, 903 .... F 5
New Cumnock, 5,077 .... D 5
New Deer, 601 .... F 3
New Galloway, 337 .... D 5
Newmains, 6,847 .... C 2
Newmarket, 613 .... B 2
Newmill, 449 .... E 3
Newmilns and Greenholm, 3,509 .... D 5
New Pitsligo, 1,125 .... F 3
Newport-on-Tay, 3,762 .... F 4
New Scone, 3,830 .... E 4
Newtongrange, 4,555 .... D 2
Newton Mearns, 6,901 .... B 2
Newtonmore, 894 .... D 3
Newton Stewart, 1,983 .... D 6
Newtown Saint Boswells, 1,101 .... F 5
Newtyle, 664 .... E 4
North Berwick, 4,317 .... F 4
North Tolsta, 527 .... B 2
Oakley, 3,499 .... C 1
Oban, 6,515 .... C 4
Old Kilpatrick, 3,256 .... B 2
Oldmeldrum, 1,103 .... F 3
Oykel Bridge, ⊙742 .... D 3
Paisley, 94,833 .... B 2
Palnackie, 225 .... E 6
Patna, 2,867 .... D 5
Peebles, 6,049 .... E 5
Penicuik, 10,476 .... D 2
Penpont, 364 .... E 5
Perth, 43,098 .... E 4
Peterculter, 3,226 .... F 3
Peterhead, 14,846 .... G 3
Pierowall, ⊙735 .... E 1
Pitlochry, 2,468 .... E 4
Pitmedden, 313 .... F 3
Pittenweem, 1,548 .... F 4
Plockton, 288 .... C 3
Poolewe, ⊙1,794 .... C 3
Port Appin, ⊙2,172 .... C 4
Port Askaig, ⊙1,795 .... B 5
Port Bannatyne, 730 .... A 2
Port Charlotte, 240 .... B 5
Port Ellen, 932 .... B 5
Port Glasgow, 22,189 .... A 2
Portgordon, 814 .... F 3
Portknockie, 1,217 .... F 3
Portmahomack, 226 .... E 3
Portpatrick, 643 .... C 6
Portree, 1,374 .... B 3
Portsoy, 1,717 .... F 3
Port William, 517 .... D 6
Prestonpans, 3,272 .... D 1
Prestwick, 13,218 .... D 5
Queensferry, 5,339 .... D 1
Reay, 283 .... E 2
Renfrew, 18,880 .... B 2
Renton, 3,443 .... A 1
Rhu, 1,540 .... A 1
Rhynie, 333 .... F 3
Rigside, 1,195 .... E 5
Rosehearty, 1,220 .... F 3
Rosneath, 946 .... A 1
Rothes, 1,240 .... E 3
Rothesay, 6,285 .... A 2
Rutherglen, 24,091 .... B 2
Saint Abbs, 203 .... F 5
Saint Andrews, 12,837 .... F 4
Saint Combs, 738 .... G 3
Saint Cyrus, 340 .... F 4
Saint Margaret's Hope, 210 .... F 2
Saint Monance, 1,205 .... F 4
Saline, 831 .... C 1
Saltcoats, 14,861 .... D 5
Sandbank, 850 .... A 1
Sandhead, 248 .... D 6
Sandwick, 603 .... B 2
Sanquhar, 2,030 .... D 5
Sauchie, 6,082 .... C 1
Scalasaig, ⊙137 .... B 4
Scalloway, 896 .... G 2
Scarinish, ⊙875 .... B 4
Scourie, ⊙745 .... C 2
Scrabster, 273 .... E 2
Selkirk, 5,635 .... F 5
Shader, 258 .... B 2
Shawbost, 458 .... B 2
Shieldaig, ⊙550 .... C 3
Shotts, 9,512 .... C 2
Skateraw, 674 .... F 3
Skelmorlie, 1,535 .... A 2
Skipness, ⊙765 .... C 5
Slamannan, 1,584 .... C 2
Spean Bridge, 235 .... D 4
Springholm, 340 .... E 5
Stanley, 1,385 .... E 4
Stenhousemuir, 8,203 .... C 1
Stevenston, 11,786 .... D 5
Stewarton, 5,165 .... D 5
Stirling, 29,799 .... C 1
Stonehaven, 4,837 .... F 4
Stonehouse, 7,900 .... D 5
Stornoway, 5,371 .... B 2
Stow, 485 .... F 5
Strachan, ⊙390 .... F 3
Strachur Bay, ⊙678 .... C 4
Stranraer, 10,174 .... C 6
Strathaven, 5,464 .... D 5
Strathpeffer, 874 .... D 3
Strichen, 962 .... F 3
Stromeferry, ⊙1,724 .... C 3
Stromness, 1,680 .... E 2
Strontian, ⊙764 .... C 4
Struan, ⊙772 .... B 3
Swinton, 235 .... F 5
Tain, 2,057 .... D 3
Tarbert, Strathclyde, 1,391 .... C 5
Tarbert, W. Isles, 479 .... B 3
Tarbolton, 2,224 .... D 5
Tarland, 452 .... F 3
Tayport, 2,848 .... F 4
Thornhill, Central, 443 .... D 4
Thornhill, Dumf. & Gall., 1,510 .... E 5
Thurso, 9,113 .... E 2
Tillicoultry, 4,320 .... C 1
Tobermory, 652 .... B 4
Tolob, ⊙2,033 .... G 2
Tomatin, 214 .... D 3
Tomintoul, 306 .... E 3
Torphins, 499 .... F 3
Tradespark, 425 .... E 3
Tranent, 7,212 .... F 5
Troon, 11,656 .... D 5
Tullibody, 6,082 .... C 1
Turriff, 3,051 .... F 3
Tweedsmuir, ⊙105 .... E 5
Twynholm, 274 .... D 6
Tyndrum, ⊙1,153 .... D 4
Uddingston, 5,278 .... B 2
Uig, Highland, 103 .... B 3
Uig, W. Isles, ⊙1,948 .... A 2
Ullapool, 807 .... C 3
Uphall, 3,035 .... C 1
Viewpark, 9,812 .... C 2
Walkerburn, 842 .... F 5
Watten, 347 .... E 2
Wemyss Bay, 323 .... A 2
West Barns, 659 .... F 5
West Calder, 2,005 .... C 2
West Kilbride, 3,883 .... D 5
West Linton, 705 .... D 2
Whitburn, 11,647 .... C 2
Whitehills, 875 .... F 3
Whithorn, 990 .... D 6
Whiting Bay, 352 .... C 5
Wick, 7,804 .... E 2
Wigtown, 1,118 .... D 6
Winchburgh, 2,409 .... D 1
Yetholm, 435 .... F 5

OTHER FEATURES

A'Chralaig (mt.) .... C 3
Ailsa Craig (isl.), 3 .... C 5
Almond (riv.) .... E 4
Annan (riv.) .... E 5
Appin (dist.), 2,006 .... C 4
Ardgour (dist.), 315 .... C 4
Ardle (riv.) .... E 4
Ardnamurchan (pen.), 764 .... B 4
Argyll (dist.), 4,940 .... C 4
Arkaig, Loch (lake) .... C 4
Arran (isl.), 3,564 .... C 5
Askival (mt.) .... B 4
Assynt (dist.), 833 .... C 2
Athol (dist.), 1,082 .... D 4
Atlantic Ocean .... B 2
Avon (riv.) .... C 1
Avon (riv.) .... E 3
Awe, Loch (lake) .... C 4
Ayr (riv.) .... D 5
Ayr, Heads of (cape) .... D 5
Badenoch (dist.), 2,717 .... D 4
Baleshare (isl.), 64 .... A 3
Balmoral Castle .... E 3
Barra (sound) .... A 3
Barra (isl.), 1,005 .... A 4
Barra (head) .... A 4
Barra Isles (isls.), 1,092 .... A 4
Battock (mt.) .... F 4
Beauly (riv.) .... D 3
Beinn Dearg (mt.) .... D 3
Beinn a Ghlo (mt.) .... E 4
Bell Rock (isl.), 3 .... F 4
Ben Alder (mt.) .... D 4
Ben Avon (mt.) .... E 3
Benbecula (isl.), 1,355 .... A 3
Ben Cruachan (mt.) .... C 4
Ben Lawers (mt.) .... D 4
Ben Lui (mt.) .... D 4
Ben Macdhui (mt.) .... E 3
Ben Mhor (mt.) .... A 3
Ben More (mt.) .... B 4
Ben More (mt.) .... D 4
Ben More Assynt (mt.) .... D 2
Ben Nevis (mt.) .... D 4
Bernera (isl.), 276 .... B 2
Berneray (isl.), 131 .... A 3
Berneray (isl.), 6 .... A 4
Bidean nam Bian (mt.) .... D 4
Black Isle (pen.), 7,209 .... D 3
Blackwater (res.) .... D 4
Boisdale, Loch (inlet) .... A 3
Bracadale, Loch (inlet) .... B 3
Braemar (dist.), 7,624 .... E 3
Breadalbane (dist.), 3,649 .... D 4
Bressay (isl.), 248 .... G 2
Broad (bay) .... B 2
Broad Law (mt.) .... E 5
Broom, Loch (inlet) .... C 3
Brough Ness (prom.) .... F 2
Buchan (dist.), 40,089 .... F 3
Buddon Ness (prom.) .... F 4
Burray (isl.), 209 .... F 2
Burrow (head) .... D 6
Bute (isl.), 8,423 .... C 5
Bute (sound) .... C 5
Butt of Lewis (prom.) .... B 2
Cairn Gorm (mt.) .... E 3
Cairngorm (mts.) .... E 3
Cairn Toul (mt.) .... E 3
Caledonian (canal) .... D 3
Canna (isl.), 22 .... B 3
Carn Ban (mt.) .... D 3
Carn Eige (mt.) .... C 3
Carrick (dist.), 21,425 .... D 5
Carron (riv.) .... C 1
Carron (riv.) .... C 3
Cheviot (hills) .... F 5
Cheviot, The (mt.) .... F 5
Clisham (mt.) .... B 3
Clyde (riv.) .... D 5
Clyde (firth) .... D 5
Coll (isl.), 144 .... B 4
Colonsay (isl.), 137 .... B 4
Copinsay (isl.), 3 .... F 2
Cowal (dist.), 15,548 .... C 4
Creag Meagaidh (mt.) .... D 4
Cromarty (firth) .... D 3
Cuillin (hills) .... B 3
Cuillin (sound) .... B 3
Dee (riv.) .... D 5
Dee (riv.) .... F 3
Dennis (head) .... F 1
Deveron (riv.) .... F 3
Don (riv.) .... F 3
Doon (riv.) .... D 5
Dornoch (firth) .... E 3
Duirinish (dist.), 1,085 .... B 3
Duncansby (head) .... F 2
Dunnet (head) .... E 2
Earn (riv.) .... E 4
Earn, Loch (lake) .... D 4
Eday (isl.), 179 .... F 1
Eddrachillis (bay) .... C 2
Eden (riv.) .... F 4
Egilsay (isl.), 39 .... F 1
Eigg (isl.), 69 .... B 4
Eil, Loch (lake) .... C 4
Eishort, Loch (inlet) .... B 3
Enard (bay) .... C 2
Eriboll, Loch (inlet) .... D 2
Ericht, Loch (lake) .... D 4
Eriskay (isl.), 219 .... A 3
Erisort, Loch (inlet) .... B 2
Esk (riv.) .... F 5
Etive, Loch (inlet) .... C 4
Ewe, Loch (inlet) .... C 3
Eye (pen.), 850 .... B 2
Fair Isle (isl.), 65 .... F 3
Fetlar (isl.), 88 .... G 2
Fife Ness (prom.) .... F 4
Findhorn (riv.) .... E 3
Flannan (isls.), 3 .... A 2
Formartine (dist.), 10,768 .... F 3
Forth (riv.) .... B 1
Forth (firth) .... F 4
Forth and Clyde (canal) .... B 2
Foula (isl.), 33 .... F 2
Fyne, Loch (inlet) .... C 5
Galloway (dist.), 54,972 .... D 5
Galloway, Mull of (prom.) .... D 6
Gare Loch (inlet) .... A 1
Garioch (dist.), 6,863 .... F 3
Garry, Loch (lake) .... D 3
Gigha (isl.), 174 .... C 5
Girdle Ness (prom.) .... G 3
Glass (riv.) .... D 3
Glen More (dist.), 55,035 .... D 3
Goat Fell (mt.) .... C 5
Gometra (isl.), 10 .... B 4
Grampian (mts.) .... D 4
Great Cumbrae (isl.), 1,296 .... A 2
Gruinard (bay) .... C 3
Hallandale (riv.) .... E 2
Harris (sound) .... A 3
Harris (dist.), 2,175 .... B 3
Hebrides (sea) .... B 3
Hebrides, Inner (isls.), 14,881 .... B 4
Hebrides, Outer (isls.), 29,615 .... A 3
Helmsdale (riv.) .... E 2
Herma Ness (prom.) .... G 2
Holy (isl.), 10 .... C 5
Holy Loch (inlet) .... A 1
Hoy (isl.), 419 .... E 2
Inchcape (Bell Rock) (isl.), 3 .... F 4
Inchkeith (isl.), 3 .... D 1
Indaal, Loch (inlet) .... B 5
Inner (sound) .... C 3
Inner Hebrides (isls.), 14,881 .... B 4
Iona (isl.), 145 .... B 4
Isla (riv.) .... E 4
Islay (isl.), 3,816 .... B 5
Jura (isl.), 210 .... C 5
Jura (sound) .... C 5
Katrine, Loch (lake) .... D 4
Kerrera (isl.), 27 .... C 4
Kilbrannan (sound) .... C 5
Kinnairds (head) .... G 3
Kintyre (pen.), 10,077 .... C 5
Kintyre, Mull of (prom.) .... C 5
Knapdale (dist.), 4,082 .... C 5
Kyle of Tongue (inlet) .... D 2
Laggan (bay) .... B 5
Lammermuir (hills) .... F 5
Lennox (hills) .... B 1
Leven (lake) .... E 4
Leven, Loch (inlet) .... D 4
Lewis (dist.), 20,047 .... B 2
Liddel Water (riv.) .... F 5
Linnhe, Loch (inlet) .... C 4
Lismore (isl.), 166 .... C 4
Little Minch (sound) .... B 3
Lochaber (dist.), 13,813 .... D 4
Lochnagar (mt.) .... E 4
Lochy, Loch (lake) .... D 3
Lomond, Loch (lake) .... D 4
Long, Loch (inlet) .... D 4
Lorne (dist.), 12,162 .... C 4
Lorne (firth) .... C 4
Loyal, Loch (lake) .... D 2
Luce (bay) .... D 6
Luing (isl.), 151 .... C 4
Lyon (riv.) .... D 4
Machers, The (pen.), 6,192 .... D 6
Mainland (isl.), 12,747 .... E 1
Mainland (isl.), 12,944 .... G 2
Mar (dist.), 23,931 .... F 3
Maree, Loch (lake) .... C 3
May, Isle of (isl.), 10 .... F 4
Merrick (mt.) .... D 5
Minginish (dist.), 772 .... B 3
Moidart (dist.), 155 .... C 4
Monach (sound) .... A 3
Monadhliath (mts.) .... D 3
Moorfoot (hills) .... E 5
Moray (firth) .... E 3
Moriston (riv.) .... D 3
Morven (dist.), 398 .... C 4
Morven (mt.) .... E 2
Muck (isl.), 24 .... B 4
Muckle Flugga (isl.), 3 .... G 2
Mull (isl.), 2,024 .... C 4
Mull (head) .... F 1
Mull (sound) .... C 4
Nairn (riv.) .... D 3
na Keal, Loch (inlet) .... B 4
Naver (riv.) .... D 2
Ness, Loch (lake) .... D 3
Nevis, Loch (inlet) .... C 3
Nith (riv.) .... E 5
North (chan.) .... C 5
North (sound) .... F 1
North (sound) .... G 4
North Esk (riv.) .... F 4
North Minch (sound) .... B 3
North Ronaldsay (isl.), 134 .... F 1
North Uist (isl.), 1,469 .... A 3
Oa, Mull of (prom.) .... B 5
Ochil (hills) .... E 4
Oich (riv.) .... D 3
Orchy (riv.) .... D 4
Orkney (isls.), 17,675 .... F 1
Oronsay (isl.), 2 .... B 4
Outer Hebrides (isls.), 29,615 .... A 3
Oykel (riv.) .... D 3
Pabbay (isl.), 4 .... A 3
Papa Stour (isl.), 24 .... F 2
Papa Westray (isl.), 106 .... F 1
Paps of Jura (mt.) .... C 5
Park (dist.), 210 .... B 2
Peel Fell (mt.) .... F 5
Pentland (hills) .... D 2
Pentland (firth) .... E 2
Pladda (isl.), 2 .... C 5
Quoich, Loch (lake) .... C 3
Raasay (isl.), 163 .... C 3
Rannoch (dist.), 1,177 .... D 4
Rannoch, Loch (lake) .... D 4
Rhinns, The (pen.), 8,295 .... C 6
Roag, Loch (inlet) ....
Rona (isl.), 3 ....
Ross of Mull (pen.), 585 ....
Rousay (isl.), 181 ....
Rudha Hunish (cape) ....
Rudh Re (cape) ....
Rum (isl.), 40 ....
Ryan, Loch (inlet) ....
Saint Kilda (isl.), 65 ....
Saint Magnus (bay) ....
Sanda (isl.), 9 ....
Sanday (isl.), 11 ....
Sanday (isl.), 592 ....
Scalpay (isl.), 483 ....
Scalpay (isl.), 5 ....
Scapa Flow (chan.) ....
Scarp (isl.), 12 ....
Scridain, Loch (inlet) ....
Scurdie Ness (prom.) ....
Seaforth, Loch (inlet) ....
Seil (isl.), 326 ....
Sgurr a Choire Ghlais (mt.) ....
Sgurr Alasdair (mt.) ....
Sgurr Mor (mt.) ....
Sgurr na Lapaich (mt.) ....
Shapinsay (isl.), 346 ....
Shetland (isls.), 18,494 ....
Shiant (sound) ....
Shiel, Loch (lake) ....
Shin (falls) ....
Shin, Loch (lake) ....
Shona (isl.), 17 ....
Sidlaw (hills) ....
Sinclair's (bay) ....
Skye, Isle of (isl.), 7,183 ....
Sleat (pt.) ....
Sleat (dist.), 449 ....
Small Isles (isls.), 171 ....
Snizort, Loch (inlet) ....
Soay (isl.), 5 ....
Solway (firth) ....
South Esk (riv.) ....
South Ronaldsay (isl.), 776 ....
South Uist (isl.), 2,281 ....
Spean (riv.) ....
Spey (riv.) ....
Start (pt.) ....
Stinchar (riv.) ....
Strathbogie (dist.), 7,959 ....
Strathmore (valley) ....
Strathspey (dist.), 6,668 ....
Strathy (pt.) ....
Stroma (isl.), 8 ....
Stronsay (isl.), 436 ....
Sumburgh (head) ....
Sunart, Loch (inlet) ....
Swona (isl.), 3 ....
Taransay (isl.), 5 .... A
Tarbat Ness (prom.) ....
Tarbert, East Loch (inlet) .... B
Tarbert, Loch (inlet) .... B
Tarbert, West Loch (inlet) .... A
Tay (riv.) .... E
Tay (firth) .... F
Tay, Loch (lake) .... D
Teith (riv.) .... D
Teviot (riv.) .... F
Thurso (riv.) .... E
Tiree (isl.), 875 .... B
Tolsta (head) .... B
Tor Ness (prom.) .... E
Torridon, Loch (inlet) C
Trossachs, The (valley) .... D
Trotternish (dist.), 1,948 .... B
Tweed (riv.) .... F
Tyne (riv.) .... F
Ulva (isl.), 23 .... B
Unst (isl.), 1,124 .... G
Vaternish (dist.), 162 .... B
Vatersay (isl.), 77 .... A
West Burra (isl.), 501 .... G
Westray (firth) .... E
Westray (isl.), 735 .... E
Whalsay (isl.), 870 .... G
White Coomb (mt.) .... E
Wigtown (bay) .... D
Wrath (cape) C
Wyre (isl.), 36 .... F
Yarrow (riv.) .... E
Yell (isl.), 1,143 .... G
Ythan (riv.) .... F

★Population of met. area
⊙Population of parish.

Agriculture, Industry and Resources

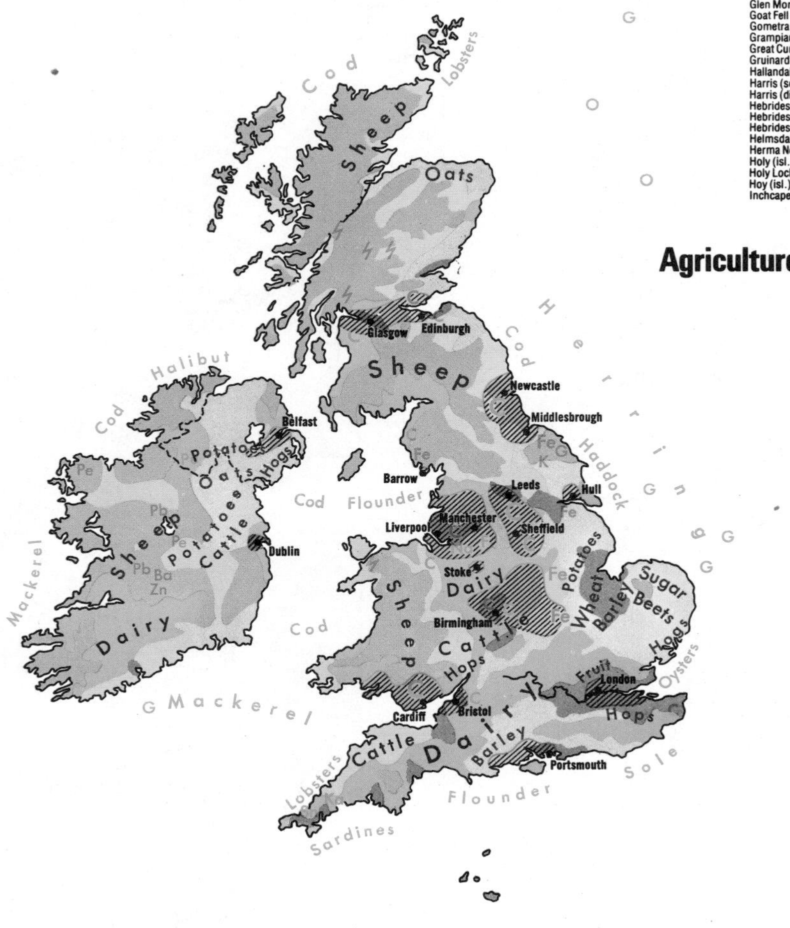

DOMINANT LAND USE

Cereals (chiefly oats, barley)
Truck Farming, Horticulture
Dairy, Mixed Farming
Livestock, Mixed Farming
Pasture Livestock

MAJOR MINERAL OCCURRENCES

Ba Barite
C Coal
F Fluorspar
Fe Iron Ore
G Natural Gas
K Potash
Ka Kaolin (china clay)
Na Salt
O Petroleum
Pb Lead
Pe Peat
Sn Tin
Zn Zinc

Water Power
Major Industrial Areas

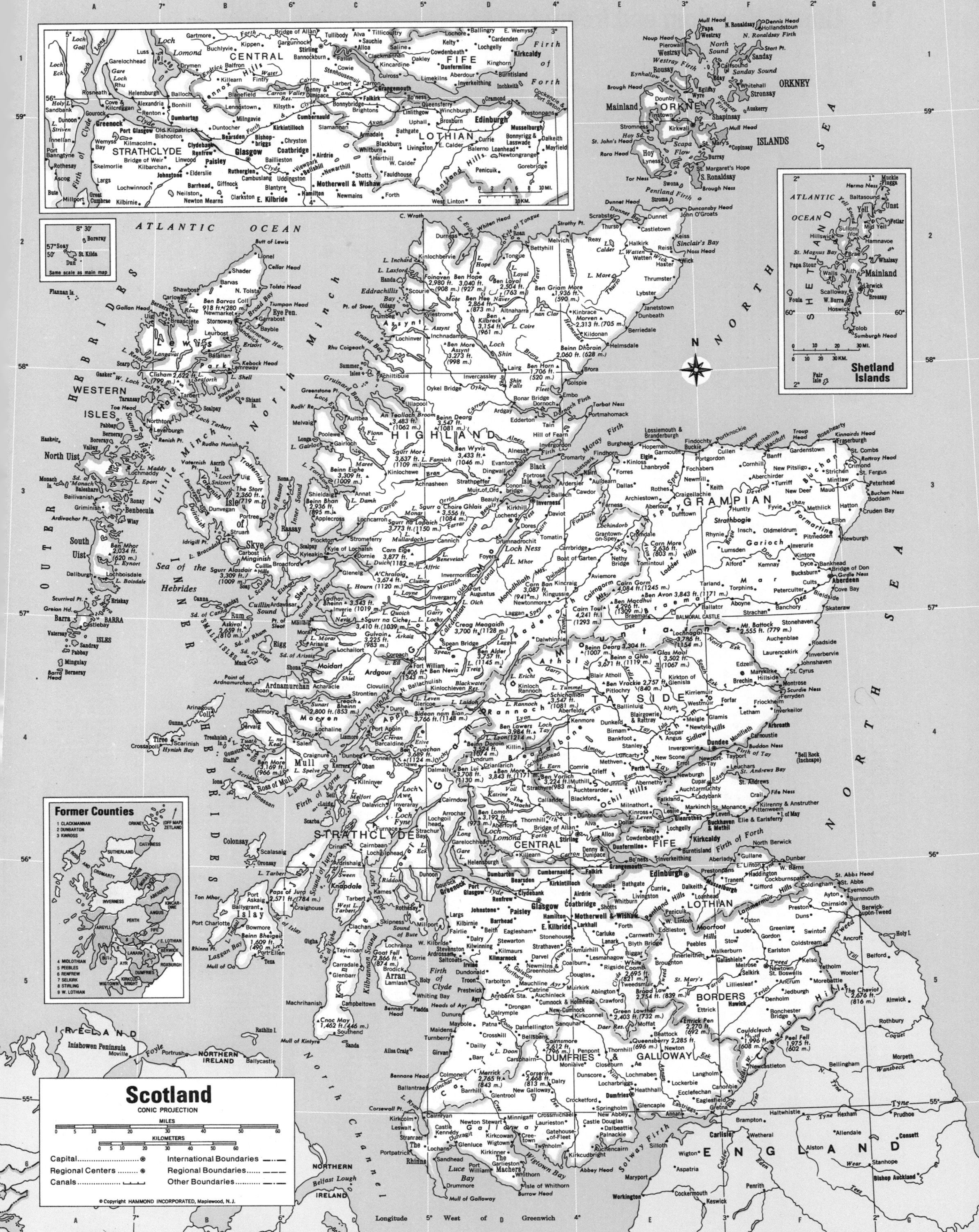

Scotland

CONIC PROJECTION

MILES
0 10 20 30 40 50 60

KILOMETERS
0 10 20 30 40 50 60

Capital	⊛
Regional Centers	⊛
Canals	
International Boundaries	
Regional Boundaries	
Other Boundaries	

© Copyright HAMMOND INCORPORATED, Maplewood, N.J.

Former Counties

1 CLACKMANNAN
2 DUNBARTON
3 KINROSS
4 MIDLOTHIAN
5 PEEBLES
6 RENFREW
7 SELKIRK
8 STIRLING
9 W. LOTHIAN

ORKNEY (OFF MAP)
ZETLAND

CAITHNESS
SUTHERLAND
ROSS AND CROMARTY
INVERNESS
NAIRN
MORAY
BANFF
ABERDEEN
KINCARDINE
ANGUS
PERTH
FIFE
ARGYLL
LANARK
AYR
BUTE
WIGTOWN
KIRKCUDBRIGHT
DUMFRIES
ROXBURGH
BERWICK
E. LOTHIAN

Shetland Islands

ATLANTIC OCEAN

0 10 20 30 MI.
0 10 20 30 KM.

Muckle Flugga
Herma Ness
Baltasound
Unst
Yell
Fetlar
Hillswick
Mid Yell
Hamnavoe
St. Magnus Bay
Sullom
Papa Stour
Whalsay
Walls
Mainland
Lerwick
Foula
W. Burra
Bressay
Hoswick
Tolob
Sumburgh Head
Fair Isle

Orkney Islands

Mull Head
N. Ronaldsay
Dennis Head
Papa Westray
Holland's Head
Westray
N. Ronaldsay Firth
Noup Head
North Sound
Sanday
Sanday Sound
Eynhallow
Roussay
Stronsay
Brough Head
Dounby
Whitehall
Stromness
Finstown
Kirkwall
St. Mary's
Scapa Flow
Hoy Sd.
Lyness
Burray
St. Margaret's Hope
S. Ronaldsay
Brough Ness

ATLANTIC OCEAN

NORTH SEA

WESTERN ISLES (OUTER HEBRIDES)

Butt of Lewis
Lewis
Stornoway
Harris
North Uist
Benbecula
South Uist
Barra

HIGHLAND

GRAMPIAN

TAYSIDE

STRATHCLYDE

CENTRAL

FIFE

LOTHIAN

BORDERS

DUMFRIES & GALLOWAY

Ben Nevis 4,406 ft. (1343 m.)

ENGLAND

NORTHERN IRELAND

IRELAND

Longitude 5° West of 0 Greenwich

(continued)

IRELAND

Carlow 34,237 ..... H6
Cavan 52,618 ..... G4
Clare 75,008 ..... D6
Cork 352,883 ..... D7
Donegal 108,344 ..... K2
Dublin 852,219 ..... J5
Galway 149,223 ..... D5
Kerry 112,772 ..... B7
Kildare 71,977 ..... H5
Kilkenny 61,473 ..... G6
Laois 45,259 ..... G6
Leitrim 28,360 ..... E3
Leix (Laois) 45,259 ..... G6
Limerick 140,459 ..... D7
Longford 28,250 ..... F4
Louth 74,951 ..... J4
Mayo 109,525 ..... C4
Meath 71,729 ..... H4
Monaghan 46,242 ..... H3
Offaly 51,829 ..... F5
Roscommon 53,519 ..... E4
Sligo 50,275 ..... D3
Tipperary 123,565 ..... F6
Waterford 77,315 ..... F7
Westmeath 53,570 ..... G5
Wexford 86,351 ..... H7
Wicklow 66,295 ..... J5

CITIES and TOWNS

Abbeydorney, 188 ..... B 7
Abbeyfeale, 1,337 ..... C 7
Abbeylara, ‡290 ..... F 4
Abbeyleix, 1,033 ..... G 6
Achill Sound, ‡1,163 ..... B 4
Aclare, ‡336 ..... D 3
Adare, 545 ..... D 6
Aghada-Farsid-Rostellan, 461 ..... E 8
Aghadoe, ‡497 ..... B 7
Aghagower, ‡693 ..... C 4
Ahascragh, 221 ..... E 5
Annagry, 201 ..... E 1
Annascaul, 236 ..... B 7
An Uaimh, 4,605 ..... H 4
An Uaimh, *6,665 ..... H 4
Ardagh, Limerick, 213 ..... C 7
Ardagh, Longford, ‡974 ..... F 4
Ardara, 683 ..... E 2
Ardee, *3,183 ..... H 4
Ardee, 3,096 ..... H 4
Ardfert, 286 ..... B 7
Ardfinnan, 510 ..... F 7
Ardmore, 233 ..... F 8
Ardrahan, ‡239 ..... D 5
Arklow, 6,948 ..... J 6
Arthurstown, 1,188 ..... H 7
Arva, 370 ..... F 4
Ashford, 341 ..... J 5
Askeaton, 844 ..... D 6
Athboy, 705 ..... H 4
Athea, 328 ..... C 7
Athenry, 1,240 ..... D 5
Athleague, ‡955 ..... E 4
Athlone, 9,825 ..... F 5
Athlone, *11,611 ..... F 5
Athy, 4,270 ..... H 6
Athy, *4,654 ..... H 6
Aughrim, 451 ..... J 6
Avoca, ‡620 ..... J 6
Bagenalstown (Muinebeag), 2,321 ..... H 6
Baile Átha Cliath (Dublin) (cap.), 567,866 ..... K 5
Bailieborough, 1,293 ..... G 4
Balbriggan, 3,741 ..... J 4
Balla, 293 ..... C 4
Ballaghaderreen, 1,121 ..... E 4
Ballina, Mayo, 6,063 ..... C 3
Ballina, *6,369 ..... C 3
Ballina, Tipperary, 336 ..... E 6
Ballinagh, 459 ..... G 4
Ballinakill, 300 ..... G 6
Ballineen ..... D 8
Ballinamore, 808 ..... F 3
Ballinasloe, 5,969 ..... E 5
Ballincollig-Carrigrohane, 2,110 ..... D 8
Ballindine, 232 ..... C 4
Ballingarry, Limerick, 422 ..... D 7
Ballingarry, Tipperary, ‡574 ..... F 6
Ballinlough, 242 ..... D 4
Ballinrobe, 1,272 ..... C 4
Ballintober, ‡867 ..... E 4
Ballintra, 197 ..... E 2
Ballisodare, 486 ..... E 3
Ballivor, 287 ..... H 4
Ballybay, 754 ..... G 3
Ballybay, *1,159 ..... G 3
Ballybofey-Stranorlar, 2,214 ..... F 2
Ballybunion, 1,287 ..... B 7
Ballycanew, ‡460 ..... J 6
Ballycarney, ‡294 ..... J 6
Ballycastle, ‡724 ..... C 3
Ballyconnell, 421 ..... F 3
Ballycotton, 389 ..... F 8
Ballydehob, 253 ..... C 8
Ballyduff, 406 ..... B 7
Ballygar, 359 ..... E 4
Ballygeary, 725 ..... J 7
Ballyhaise, 274 ..... G 3
Ballyhaunis, 1,093 ..... D 4
Ballyheigue, 450 ..... B 7
Ballyjamesduff, 673 ..... G 4
Ballylanders, 266 ..... E 7
Ballylongford, 504 ..... B 6
Ballymahon, 707 ..... F 4
Ballymakeery, 272 ..... C 8
Ballymore, ‡447 ..... F 5
Ballymore Eustace, 433 ..... J 5
Ballymote, 952 ..... D 3
Ballyporeen, ‡810 ..... E 7
Ballyragget, 519 ..... G 6
Ballyroan, ‡478 ..... G 6
Ballyshannon, 2,325 ..... E 3
Ballytore, ‡580 ..... H 5
Baltimore, 200 ..... C 9
Baltinglass, 909 ..... H 6
Baltray, 236 ..... J 4
Banagher, 1,052 ..... F 5
Bandon, 2,257 ..... D 8
Bandon, *4,071 ..... D 8
Bannow, ‡798 ..... H 7
Bansha, 184 ..... E 7
Bantry, 2,579 ..... C 8
Barna, ‡1,734 ..... C 5
Belmullet, 744 ..... B 3
Belturbet, 1,092 ..... G 3
Bennettsbridge, 367 ..... G 6
Birr, 3,319 ..... F 5
Birr, *3,881 ..... F 5
Blanchardstown, 3,279 ..... H 5
Blarney, 1,128 ..... D 8
Blessington, 637 ..... J 5
Boherbue, 372 ..... C 7
Borris, 430 ..... H 6
Borris-in-Ossory, 276 ..... F 6
Borrisokane, 769 ..... E 6
Borrisoleigh, 471 ..... E 6
Boyle, 1,727 ..... E 4
Boyle, *1,939 ..... E 4
Bray, 14,467 ..... K 5
Bray, *15,841 ..... K 5
Brí Chualann (Bray), 14,467 ..... K 5
Broadford, 226 ..... C 7
Brosna, 250 ..... C 7
Bruff, 547 ..... D 7
Bruree, 243 ..... D 7
Bunbeg-Derrybeg, 878 ..... E 1
Bunclody-Carrickduff, 929 ..... H 6
Buncrana, 2,955 ..... G 1
Buncrana, *3,334 ..... G 1
Bundoran, 1,337 ..... E 3
Burtonport, ‡1,288 ..... E 2
Buttevant, 1,045 ..... D 7
Cahir, 1,747 ..... F 7
Cahirciveen, 1,547 ..... A 8
Callan, 1,283 ..... G 7
Camolin, 306 ..... J 6
Campile, 231 ..... H 7
Cappamore, 567 ..... E 6
Cappawhite, 305 ..... E 6
Cappoquin, 872 ..... F 7
Carbury, ‡894 ..... H 5
Carlingford, 559 ..... J 3
Carlow, 9,588 ..... H 6
Carlow, *10,399 ..... H 6
Carndonagh, 1,146 ..... G 1
Carnew, 570 ..... H 6
Carrickmacross, 2,100 ..... H 4
Carrickmacross, *2,475 ..... H 4
Carrick-on-Shannon, 1,854 ..... F 4
Carrick-on-Suir, 5,006 ..... F 7
Carrigaholt, ‡493 ..... B 6
Carrigaline, 951 ..... E 8
Carrigallen, 230 ..... F 4
Carrigart, ‡753 ..... F 1
Carrigtwohill, 622 ..... E 8
Carrowkeel, ‡326 ..... G 1
Cashel, 2,692 ..... F 7
Castlebar, 5,979 ..... C 4
Castlebar, *6,476 ..... C 4
Castlebellingham, 407 ..... J 4
Castleblayney, 2,118 ..... H 3
Castleblayney, *2,395 ..... H 3
Castlecomer-Donaguile, 1,244 ..... G 6
Castledermot, 583 ..... H 6
Castlefin, 610 ..... F 2
Castlegregory, 216 ..... A 7
Castleisland, 1,929 ..... B 7
Castlemartyr, 491 ..... E 8
Castlepollard, 693 ..... G 4
Castlerea, 1,752 ..... D 4
Castletown, ‡504 ..... F 6
Castletownbere, 812 ..... B 8
Castletownroche, 399 ..... D 7
Castletownshend, 170 ..... C 9
Causeway, 215 ..... B 7
Cavan, 3,273 ..... G 3
Cavan, *4,312 ..... G 3
Ceanannus Mór, 2,391 ..... G 4
Ceanannus Mór, *2,653 ..... G 4
Celbridge, 1,568 ..... H 5
Charlestown-Bellahy, 677 ..... D 4
Charleville (Rathluirc), 2,232 ..... D 7
Clara, 2,156 ..... F 5
Claregalway, ‡594 ..... D 5
Claremorris, 1,718 ..... C 4
Clashmore, ‡379 ..... F 8
Clifden, 790 ..... B 5
Cloghan, 404 ..... F 5
Clogh-Chatsworth, 324 ..... G 6
Clogheen, 530 ..... F 7
Clogherhead, 649 ..... J 4
Clonakilty, 2,430 ..... D 8
Clonaslee, 285 ..... F 5
Clondalkin, 7,009 ..... J 5
Clonegal, 202 ..... H 6
Clones, 2,164 ..... G 3
Clonfert, ‡430 ..... E 5
Clonmany, ‡936 ..... G 1
Clonmel, 11,622 ..... F 7
Clonmel, *12,291 ..... F 7
Clonmellon, 328 ..... H 4
Clonroche, 222 ..... H 7
Clontuskert, 351 ..... E 4
Cloone, ‡460 ..... F 4
Cloughjordan, 480 ..... E 6
Cloyne, 654 ..... E 8
Coachford, 290 ..... D 8
Cóbh, 6,076 ..... E 8
Cóbh, *7,141 ..... E 8
Coill Dubh, 920 ..... H 5
Collon, 262 ..... J 4
Collooney, 546 ..... E 3
Cong, 233 ..... C 4
Convoy, 654 ..... F 2
Coolaney, ‡352 ..... D 3
Coolgreany, ‡603 ..... J 6
Cootehill, 1,415 ..... G 3
Cootehill, *1,542 ..... G 3
Cork, 128,645 ..... E 8
Cork, *134,430 ..... E 8
Corofin, 342 ..... C 6
Courtmacsherry, 210 ..... D 8
Courtown Harbour, 291 ..... J 6
Creeslough, 269 ..... F 1
Crookhaven, ‡400 ..... B 9
Croom, 756 ..... D 6
Crosshaven, 1,222 ..... E 8
Crossmolina, 1,077 ..... C 3
Crusheen, ‡405 ..... D 6
Culdaff, ‡621 ..... G 1
Daingean, 492 ..... G 5
Delvin, 223 ..... G 4
Dingle, 1,401 ..... A 7
Doaghbeg, ‡701 ..... F 1
Donabate, 426 ..... J 5
Donegal, 1,725 ..... F 2
Doneraile, 799 ..... D 7
Dooagh-Keel, 649 ..... A 4
Doon, 387 ..... E 6
Douglas, ‡4,448 ..... D 8
Drimoleague, 415 ..... C 8
Drishane, ‡1,548 ..... C 7
Drogheda, 19,762 ..... J 4
Drogheda, *20,095 ..... J 4
Droichead Nua, 5,053 ..... H 5
Droichead Nua, *6,444 ..... H 5
Dromahair, 177 ..... E 3
Drumcar, ‡1,215 ..... J 4
Drumconrath, ‡1,044 ..... H 4
Drumkeerin, ‡467 ..... E 3
Drumlish, 205 ..... F 4
Drumshanbo, 576 ..... E 3
Dublin (cap.), 567,866 ..... K 5
Dublin, *679,748 ..... K 5
Duleek, 658 ..... J 4
Duncannon, 228 ..... H 7
Dundalk, 21,672 ..... H 3
Dundalk, *23,816 ..... H 3
Dunfanaghy, 303 ..... F 1
Dungarvan, 5,583 ..... F 7
Dungloe, 940 ..... E 2
Dunkineely, 288 ..... E 2
Dún Laoghaire, 53,171 ..... K 5
Dún Laoghaire, *98,379 ..... K 5
Dunlavin, 423 ..... H 5
Dunleer 855 ..... J4
Dunmanway 1,392 ..... C8
Dunmore 522 ..... D4
Dunmore East 656 ..... G7
Dunshaughlin⊙ 283 ..... H5
Durrow, Laois 596 ..... G6
Durrow, Offaly⊙ 441 ..... F5
Easky 184 ..... D3
Edenderry 2,953 ..... G5
Edenderry* 3,116 ..... G5
Elphin 489 ..... E4
Emyvale 281 ..... G3
Ennis 5,972 ..... D6
Ennis* 10,840 ..... D6
Enniscorthy 5,704 ..... J7
Enniscorthy* 6,642 ..... J7
Enniskerry 772 ..... J5
Ennistymon 1,013 ..... C6
Eyrecourt 314 ..... E5
Fahan⊙ 1,023 ..... G1
Falcarragh 506 ..... E1
Feakle⊙ 398 ..... D6
Fenit 360 ..... B7
Ferbane 1,064 ..... F5
Fermoy 3,237 ..... E7
Fermoy* 4,033 ..... E7
Ferns 712 ..... J6
Fethard, Tipperary 1,064 ..... F7
Fethard, Wexford⊙ 637 ..... H7
Foxford 868 ..... C4
Foynes 624 ..... C6
Frankford (Kilcormac) 1,089 ..... F5
Frenchpark⊙ 693 ..... E4
Freshford 585 ..... G6
Galbally 258 ..... E7
Galway 27,726 ..... C5
Galway* 29,375 ..... C5
Geashill⊙ 751 ..... G5
Glandore⊙ 695 ..... C8
Glanmire-Riverstown 1,113 ..... E8
Glanworth 335 ..... E7
Glenamaddy 315 ..... D4
Glenbeigh 266 ..... B7
Glencolumbkille⊙ 787 ..... D2
Glengarriff 244 ..... C8
Glenties 734 ..... E2
Glenville⊙ 264 ..... D7
Glin 623 ..... C6
Golden⊙ 640 ..... F7
Gorey 2,946 ..... J6
Gorey* 3,024 ..... J6
Gormanston⊙ 1,384 ..... J4
Gort 975 ..... D5
Gowran 402 ..... G6
Graiguenamanagh-Tinnahinch 1,303 ..... H6
Granard 1,054 ..... F4
Greencastle 322 ..... H1
Greenore 882 ..... J4
Greystones-Delgany 4,517 ..... K5
Gurteen 165 ..... D3
Hacketstown 574 ..... H6
Headford 673 ..... C5
Holycross⊙ 902 ..... F6
Hospital 525 ..... E7
Inchigeelagh⊙ 516 ..... C8
Inishannon 190 ..... D8
Inistioge 179 ..... G7
Inniscrone 582 ..... C3
Johnstown 303 ..... G6
Kanturk 2,063. ..... D7
Keel-Dooagh 649 ..... A4
Kells⊙ 423 ..... G6
Kells (Ceanannus Mór) 2,391 ..... G4
Kenmare 903 ..... B8
Kilbaha⊙ 471 ..... B6
Kilbeggan 635 ..... G5
Kilcar 273 ..... D2
Kilcock 827 ..... H5
Kilconnell⊙ 629 ..... E5
Kilcoole 679 ..... K5
Kilcormac 1,089 ..... F5
Kilcullen 880 ..... H5
Kildare 3,137 ..... H5
Kildysart 239 ..... C6
Kilfenora⊙ 441 ..... C6
Kilfinane 561 ..... D7
Kilgarvan 228 ..... B8
Kilkee 1,287 ..... B6
Kilkelly 225 ..... D4
Kilkenny 9,838 ..... G6
Kilkenny* 13,306 ..... G6
Killala 368 ..... C3
Killaloe 871 ..... D6
Killarney 7,184 ..... C7
Killarney* 7,541 ..... C7
Killavullen 221 ..... D7
Killenaule 592 ..... F6
Killeshandra 432 ..... F3
Killimor 221 ..... E5
Killinaboy⊙ 297 ..... C6
Killorglin 1,150 ..... B7
Killucan-Rathwire 290 ..... G4
Killybegs 1,094 ..... E2
Kilmacrennan 274 ..... F1
Kilmacthomas 396 ..... G7
Kilmallock 1,170 ..... D7
Kilmeadan⊙ 262 ..... G7
Kilmihill 284 ..... C6
Kilmoganny 181 ..... G7
Kilmore Quay 273 ..... H7
Kilmurry⊙ 387 ..... C6
Kilnaleck 273 ..... G4
Kilronan 243 ..... B5
Kilrush 2,671 ..... C6
Kilsheelan⊙ 665 ..... F7
Kiltimagh 978 ..... C4
Kilworth 360 ..... E7
Kingscourt 1,016 ..... H4
Kingstown (Dún Laoghaire) 53,171 ..... K5
Kinlough 160 ..... E3
Kinnegad 362 ..... G5
Kinnitty⊙ 420 ..... F5
Kinsale 1,622 ..... D8
Kinsale* 1,989 ..... D8
Kinvara 293 ..... D5
Knightstown 236 ..... A8
Knock⊙ 1,202 ..... D4
Knocklong 248 ..... D7
Knocknagashel 168 ..... C7
Labasheeda⊙ 468 ..... C6
Laghy⊙ 625 ..... E2
Lahinch 455 ..... C6
Lanesborough-Ballyleague 906 ..... E4
Laracor⊙ 404 ..... H4
Laytown-Bettystown-Mornington 1,882 ..... J4
Leenane⊙ 271 ..... B4
Leighlinbridge 379 ..... H6
Leitrim⊙ 544 ..... F3
Leixlip 2,402 ..... H5
Letterkenny 4,930 ..... F2
Letterkenny* 5,207 ..... F2
Lifford 1,121 ..... F2
Limerick 57,161 ..... D6
Limerick* 63,002 ..... D6
Liscarroll 231 ..... D7
Lisdoonvarna 459 ..... C5
Lismore 884 ..... F7
Lismore⊙ 1,041 ..... F7
Listowel 3,021 ..... C7
Littleton 322 ..... F6
Longford 3,876 ..... F4
Longford* 4,791 ..... F4
Lorrha⊙ 685 ..... E5
Loughrea 3,075 ..... E5
Louisburgh 310 ..... B4
Louth 208 ..... J4
Lucan-Doddsborough 4,245 ..... J5
Luimneach (Limerick) 57,161 ..... D6
Lusk 553 ..... J4
Macroom 2,256 ..... C8
Malahide 3,834 ..... J5
Malin⊙ 552 ..... G1
Mallow 5,901 ..... D7
Mallow* 6,506 ..... D7
Manorhamilton 858 ..... E3
Manulla⊙ 660 ..... C4
Maryborough (Portlaoise) 3,902 ..... G5
Maynooth 1,296 ..... H5
Meathas Truim 546 ..... G4
Midleton 3,075 ..... E8
Midleton* 4,666 ..... E8
Milford 763 ..... F1
Millstreet 1,319 ..... D7
Milltown 260 ..... A7
Miltown-Malbay 677 ..... C6
Minard⊙ 397 ..... A7
Mitchelstown 2,783 ..... E7
Moate 1,378 ..... F5
Mohill 868 ..... F4
Monaghan 5,256 ..... G3
Monasterevan 1,619 ..... H5
Moneygall 282 ..... F6
Monivea⊙ 405 ..... D5
Mooncoin 413 ..... G7
Mount Bellew 275 ..... D5
Mountcharles 445 ..... E2
Mountmellick 2,595 ..... G5
Mountmellick* 2,864 ..... G5
Mountrath 1,098 ..... F5
Moville 1,089 ..... G1
Moycullen⊙ 498 ..... C5
Moynalty⊙ 583 ..... H4
Muff 240 ..... G1
Muinebeag 2,321 ..... H6
Mullagh 293 ..... H4
Mullaghmore⊙ 629 ..... D3
Mullinahone 262 ..... F7
Mullinavat 343 ..... G7
Mullingar 6,790 ..... G4
Mullingar* 9,245 ..... G4
Naas 5,078 ..... H5
Navan (An Uaimh) 4,605 ..... H4
Nenagh 5,085 ..... E6
Nenagh* 5,174 ..... E6
Newbliss⊙ 547 ..... G3
Newbridge (Droichead Nua) 5,053 ..... H5
Newcastle 2,549 ..... D7
Newcastle* 2,680 ..... D7
Newmarket 886 ..... C7
Newmarket-on-Fergus 1,052 ..... D6
New Pallas⊙ 1,271 ..... E6
Newport, Mayo 420 ..... C4
Newport, Tipperary 582 ..... E6
New Ross 4,775 ..... H7
New Ross* 5,153 ..... H7
Newtown Forbes⊙ 495 ..... F4
Newtownmountkennedy 882 ..... J5
Newtownsandes 268 ..... C6
O'Briensbridge-Montpelier 237 ..... D6
Oldcastle 759 ..... G4
Old Leighlin⊙ 309 ..... G6
Oola 348 ..... E6
Oranmore 440 ..... D5
Oughterard 628 ..... C5
Passage East 408 ..... G7
Passage West 2,709 ..... E8
Patrickswell 415 ..... D6
Pettigo 332 ..... F2
Piltown 456 ..... G7
Portarlington 3,117 ..... G5
Portlaoise 3,902 ..... G5
Portlaoise* 6,470 ..... G5
Portlaw 1,166 ..... G7
Portmarnock 1,726 ..... J5
Portumna 913 ..... E5
Queenstown (Cóbh) 6,076 ..... E8
Rahan⊙ 531 ..... F5
Ramelton 807 ..... F1
Raphoe 945 ..... F2
Rathangan 868 ..... G5
Rathcoole 1,740 ..... J5
Rathcormac 191 ..... E7
Rathdowney 892 ..... F6
Rathdrum 1,141 ..... J6
Rathgormuck⊙ 231 ..... F7
Rathkeale 1,543 ..... D7
Rathluirc 2,232 ..... D7
Rathmore 437 ..... J5
Rathmullen 486 ..... F1
Rathnew-Merrymeeting 954 ..... J6
Rathowen⊙ 294 ..... F4
Rathvilly 230 ..... H6
Ratoath 300 ..... J5
Riverstown 236 ..... E3
Rockcorry 233 ..... H3
Rosapenna⊙ 822 ..... F1
Roscommon 1,556 ..... E4
Roscommon* 2,821 ..... E4
Roscrea 3,855 ..... F6
Rosscarbery 309 ..... C8
Rosses Point 464 ..... D3
Rosslare 588 ..... J7
Rosslare Harbour (Ballygeary) 725 ..... J7
Roundstone 204 ..... A5
Roundwood 260 ..... J5
Rush 2,633 ..... J4
Saint Johnston 463 ..... F2
Scarriff 619 ..... E6
Schull 457 ..... B8
Scotstown 264 ..... H3
Shanagolden 231 ..... C6
Shannon Airport 3,657 ..... D6
Shannon Bridge 188 ..... F5
Shercock 313 ..... G4
Shillelagh 246 ..... J6
Shinrone 365 ..... F5
Shrule 288 ..... C4
Sixmilebridge 567 ..... D6
Skerries 3,044 ..... J4
Skibbereen 2,104 ..... C8
Slane 483 ..... H4
Sligo 14,080 ..... E3
Sligo* 14,456 ..... E3
Sneem 285 ..... B8
Spiddal⊙ 819 ..... C5
Stepaside 748 ..... J5
Stradbally, Laois 891 ..... G5
Stradbally, Waterford 158 ..... F7
Strokestown 563 ..... E4
Swanlinbar 257 ..... F3
Swinford 1,105 ..... C4
Swords 4,133 ..... J5
Taghmon 369 ..... H7
Tallaght 6,174 ..... J5
Tallow, 883 ..... F 7
Tarbert, 485 ..... C 6
Teltown, ‡739 ..... H 4
Templemore, 2,174 ..... F 6
Templetuohy, 197 ..... F 6
Termonfeckin, 328 ..... J 4
Thomastown, 1,270 ..... G 7
Thurles, 6,840 ..... F 6
Thurles, *7,087 ..... F 6
Timoleague, 257 ..... D 8
Tinahely, 450 ..... H 6
Tipperary, 4,631 ..... E 7
Tipperary, *4,717 ..... E 7
Toomevara, 272 ..... E 6
Tralee, 12,287 ..... B 7
Tralee, *13,263 ..... B 7
Tramore, 3,792 ..... G 7
Trim, 1,700 ..... H 4
Trim, *2,255 ..... H 4
Tuam, 3,808 ..... D 4
Tuam, *4,952 ..... D 4
Tubbercurry, 959 ..... D 3
Tulla, 415 ..... D 6
Tullamore, 6,809 ..... G 5
Tullamore, *7,474 ..... G 5
Tullaroan, ‡301 ..... G 6
Tullow, 1,838 ..... H 6
Tullow, *1,945 ..... H 6
Tynagh, ‡452 ..... E 5
Tyrrellspass, 289 ..... G 5
Urlingford, 652 ..... F 6
Virginia, 583 ..... G 4
Waterford, 31,968 ..... G 7
Waterford, *33,676 ..... G 7
Waterville, 547 ..... A 8
Westport, 3,023 ..... C 4
Wexford, 11,849 ..... H 7
Wexford, *13,293 ..... H 7
Whitegate, 370 ..... E 8
Wicklow, 3,786 ..... K 6
Wicklow, *3,915 ..... K 6
Woodenbridge, ‡620 ..... J 6
Woodford, 198 ..... E 5
Youghal, 5,445 ..... F 8
Youghal, *5,626 ..... F 8

OTHER FEATURES

Achill (isl.), 3,129 ..... A 4
Allen (lake) ..... E 3
Allen, Bog of (marsh) ..... H 5
Aran (isl.), 773 ..... D 2
Aran (isls.), 1,499 ..... B 5
Arklow (bank) ..... K 6
Arrow (lake) ..... E 3
Awbeg (riv.) ..... D 7
Ballinskelligs (bay) ..... A 8
Ballycotton (bay) ..... F 8
Ballyheige (bay) ..... B 7
Ballyhoura (hills) ..... E 7
Ballyteige (bay) ..... H 7
Bandon (riv.) ..... D 8
Bann (riv.) ..... J 6
Bantry (bay) ..... B 8
Barrow (riv.) ..... H 7
Baurtregaum (mt.) ..... A 7
Bear (isl.), 288 ..... B 8
Blacksod (bay) ..... A 3
Blackstairs (mt.) ..... H 6
Blackwater (riv.) ..... D 7
Blackwater (riv.) ..... H 4
Blasket (isls.) ..... A 7
Bloody Foreland (prom.) ..... E 1
Blue Stack (mts.) ..... E 2
Boderg (lake) ..... E 4
Boggeragh (mts.) ..... D 7
Boyne (riv.) ..... J 4
Brandon (head) ..... A 7
Bride (riv.) ..... E 7
Broad Haven (harb.) ..... B 3
Brosna (riv.) ..... F 5
Bull, The (isl.), 5 ..... A 8
Caha (mts.) ..... B 8
Carlingford (inlet) ..... J 3
Carnsore (pt.) ..... J 7
Carrantuohill (mt.) ..... B 7
Clare (riv.) ..... D 5
Clare (isls.), 168 ..... A 4
Clear (cape) ..... B 9
Clear (isl.), 192 ..... C 9
Clew (bay) ..... B 4
Comeragh (mts.) ..... F 7
Conn (lake) ..... C 3
Connacht (prov.), 390,902 ..... C 4
Connemara (dist.), 7,599 ..... B 5
Cork (harb.) ..... E 8
Corrib (lake) ..... C 5
Courtmacsherry (bay) ..... D 8
Curragh, The ..... H 5
Dee (riv.) ..... H 4
Deel (riv.) ..... D 7
Deele (riv.) ..... F 2
Derg (lake) ..... E 6
Derravaragh (lake) ..... G 4
Derryveagh (mts.) ..... E 2
Dingle (bay) ..... A 7
Donegal (bay) ..... D 3
Drum (hills) ..... F 7
Dublin (bay) ..... J 5
Dundalk (bay) ..... J 4
Dunmanus (bay) ..... B 8
Dursey (isl.), 38 ..... A 8
Ennell (lake) ..... G 5
Erne (riv.) ..... E 3
Errigal (mt.) ..... E 1
Erris (head) ..... A 3
Fanad (head) ..... F 1
Fastnet Rock (isl.), 3 ..... B 9
Feale (riv.) ..... C 7
Fergus (riv.) ..... D 6
Finn (riv.) ..... F 2
Finn (riv.) ..... G 3
Flesk (riv.) ..... C 7
Foyle (inlet) ..... G 1
Foyle (riv.) ..... G 2
Galley (head) ..... D 9
Galtee (mts.) ..... E 7
Galtymore (mt.) ..... E 7
Galway (bay) ..... C 5
Gara (lake) ..... D 4
Garadice (lake) ..... F 3
Gill (lake) ..... E 3
Glyde (riv.) ..... H 4
Golden Vale (plain) ..... E 7
Gorumna (isl.), 1,108 ..... B 5
Gowna (lake) ..... G 4
Grand (canal) ..... G 5
Greenore (pt.) ..... J 7
Gweebarra (bay) ..... D 2
Hags (head) ..... B 6
Helvick (head) ..... G 7
Hook (head) ..... H 7
Horn (head) ..... E 1
Iar Connacht (dist.), 10,774 ..... C 5
Inishbofin (isl.), 236 ..... A 4
Inishbofin (isl.), 103 ..... E 1
Inisheer (isl.), 313 ..... B 5
Inishmaan (isl.), 319 ..... C 5
Inishmore (isl.), 864 ..... B 5
Inishowen (head) ..... H 1
Inishowen (pen.), 24,109 ..... G 1
Inishtrahull (isl.), 3 ..... G 1
Inishturk (isls.), 83 ..... A 4
Inny (riv.) ..... A 8
Inny (riv.) ..... F 4
Inver (bay) ..... E 2
Ireland's Eye (isl.) ..... K 5
Irish (sea) ..... K 4
Joyce's Country (dist.), 2,021 ..... B 4
Kenmare (riv.) ..... A 8
Kerry (head) ..... A 7
Key (lake) ..... E 3
Kilkieran (bay) ..... B 5
Killala (bay) ..... C 3
Killary (harb.) ..... A 4
Kinsale (harb.) ..... E 8
Kippure (mt.) ..... J 5
Knockboy (mt.) ..... B 8
Knockmealdown (mts.) ..... F 7
Lady's Island Lake (inlet) ..... J 7
Lambay (isl.), 24 ..... K 4
Laune (riv.) ..... B 7
Leane (lake) ..... B 7
Leane (lake) ..... G 4
Lee (riv.) ..... D 8
Leinster (mt.) ..... H 6
Leinster (prov.), 1,498,140 ..... G 5
Lettermullan (isl.), 221 ..... B 5
Liffey (riv.) ..... H 5
Liscannor (bay) ..... B 6
Long Island (bay) ..... B 9
Loop (head) ..... A 6
Lugnaquillia (mt.) ..... J 5
Macgillicuddy's Reeks (mts.) ..... B 7
Macnean (lake) ..... F 3
Maigue (riv.) ..... D 6
Maine (riv.) ..... C 7
Malin (head) ..... F 1
Mask (lake) ..... C 4
Maumturk (mts.) ..... B 5
Melvin (lake) ..... E 3
Mizen (head) ..... B 9
Moher (cliffs) ..... B 6
Monavullagh (mts.) ..... F 7
Moy (riv.) ..... C 3
Mulkear (riv.) ..... E 6
Mullaghareirk (mts.) ..... C 7
Mulroy (bay) ..... F 1
Munster (prov.), 882,002 ..... D 7
Mweelrea (mt.) ..... B 4
Mweenish (isl.), 198 ..... B 5
Nagles (mts.) ..... E 7
Nenagh (riv.) ..... E 6
Nephin (mt.) ..... C 3
Nore (riv.) ..... G 7
North (sound) ..... B 5
Omey (isl.), 34 ..... A 5
Oughter (lake) ..... G 3
Ovoca (riv.) ..... J 6
Owenmore (riv.) ..... D 3
Owey (isl.), 51 ..... D 1
Paps, The (mt.) ..... C 7
Partry (mts.) ..... C 4
Pollaphuca (res.) ..... J 5
Punchestown ..... H 5
Rathlin O'Birne (isl.), 3 ..... C 2
Ree (lake) ..... F 5
Roaringwater (bay) ..... B 9
Rosses (bay) ..... D 1
Rosskeeragh (pt.) ..... D 3
Royal (canal) ..... G 4
Saint Finan's (bay) ..... A 8
Saint George's (chan.) ..... K 7
Saint John's (pt.) ..... D 2
Saltee (isls.) ..... H 7
Seven (heads) ..... D 8
Seven Hogs, The (isls.) ..... A 7
Shannon (riv.) ..... E 6
Sheeffry (hills) ..... B 4
Sheelin (lake) ..... G 4
Sheep Haven (harb.) ..... F 1
Sheeps (head) ..... B 8
Sherkin (isl.), 82 ..... C 9
Silvermine (mts.) ..... E 6
Slaney (riv.) ..... H 7
Slieve Aughty (mts.) ..... D 5
Slieve Bloom (mts.) ..... F 5
Slieve Gamph (mts.) ..... D 3
Slievenaman (mt.) ..... F 7
Sligo (bay) ..... D 3
Slyne (head) ..... A 5
South (sound) ..... C 5
Stacks (mts.) ..... B 7
Suck (riv.) ..... E 5
Suir (riv.) ..... G 7
Swilly (inlet) ..... F 1
Tara (hill) ..... H 4
Tory (isl.), 273 ..... E 1
Tory (sound) ..... E 1
Tralee (bay) ..... B 7
Trawbreaga (bay) ..... F 1
Ulster (part) (prov.), 207,204 ..... G 2
Valencia (Valentia) (isl.), 770 ..... A 8
Valentia (isl.), 770 ..... A 8
Waterford (harb.) ..... G 7
Wexford (bay) ..... J 7
Wicklow (head) ..... K 6
Wicklow (mts.) ..... J 6
Youghal (bay) ..... F 8

NORTHERN IRELAND

DISTRICTS

Antrim, 37,600 ..... J 2
Ards, 52,100 ..... K 2
Armagh, 47,500 ..... H 3
Ballymena, 52,200 ..... J 2
Ballymoney, 22,700 ..... J 1
Bainbridge, 28,800 ..... J 3
Belfast, 368,200 ..... J 2
Carrickfergus, 27,500 ..... K 2
Castlereagh, 63,600 ..... K 2
Coleraine, 44,900 ..... H 1
Cookstown, 27,500 ..... H 2
Craigavon, 71,200 ..... J 3
Down, 48,800 ..... K 3
Dungannon, 43,000 ..... H 3
Fermanagh, 50,900 ..... F 3
Larne, 29,000 ..... K 2
Limavady, 25,000 ..... H 1
Lisburn, 80,800 ..... J 2
Londonderry, 86,600 ..... G 2
Magherafelt, 32,200 ..... H 2
Mourne (Newry and Mourne), 75,300 ..... J 3
Moyle, 13,400 ..... J 1
Newtownabbey, 71,500 ..... J 2
North Down, 59,600 ..... K 2
Omagh, 41,800 ..... G 2
Strabane, 35,500 ..... G 2

CITIES and TOWNS

Ahoghill, ‡1,929 ..... J 2
Annalong, 1,001 ..... K 3
Antrim, 8,351 ..... J 2
Ardglass, 1,052 ..... K 3
Armagh, 13,606 ..... H 3
Armoy, ‡1,051 ..... J 1
Augher, ‡1,986 .....
Aughnacloy, ‡1,885 .....
Ballycastle, 2,899 .....
Ballyclare, 5,155 .....
Ballygawley, ‡2,165 .....
Ballykelly, 1,116 .....
Ballymena, 23,386 .....
Ballymoney, 5,697 .....
Ballynahinch, 3,485 .....
Banbridge, 7,968 .....
Bangor, 35,260 .....
Belfast (cap.), 353,700 .....
Belfast, *551,940 .....
Bellaghy, ‡2,265 .....
Belleek, ‡2,487 .....
Beragh, ‡2,137 .....
Bessbrook, 2,619 .....
Brookeborough, ‡2,534 .....
Broughshane, 1,288 .....
Bushmills, 1,288 .....
Caledon, ‡1,828 .....
Carnlough, 1,416 .....
Carrickfergus, 16,603 .....
Carrowdore, 2,548 .....
Castledawson, 1,162 .....
Castlederg, 1,766 .....
Castlewellan, 1,488 .....
Claudy, ‡2,507 .....
Clogher, ‡1,888 .....
Coalisland, 3,614 .....
Coleraine, 16,354 .....
Comber, 5,575 .....
Cookstown, 6,965 .....
Craigavon, 12,740 .....
Crossgar, 1,098 .....
Crossmaglen, 1,085 .....
Crumlin, 1,450 .....
Cullybackey, 1,649 .....
Derrygonnelly, ‡2,539 .....
Dervock, ‡1,191 .....
Donaghadee, 4,008 .....
Downpatrick, 7,918 .....
Draperstown, ‡2,247 .....
Dromore, Bainbridge, 2,848 .....
Dromore, Omagh, ‡2,224 .....
Drumquin, ‡1,982 .....
Dundrum, ‡2,245 .....
Dungannon, 8,190 .....
Dungiven, 1,536 .....
Dunnamanagh, ‡2,242 .....
Ederny and Kesh, ‡2,497 .....
Enniskillen, 9,679 .....
Feeny, ‡1,459 ..... H
Fintona, 1,190 ..... G
Fivemiletown, ‡1,649 ..... G
Garvagh, ‡2,363 ..... H
Gilford, 1,592 ..... J
Glenarm, ‡1,728 ..... J
Glenavy, ‡2,360 ..... J
Glynn, ‡1,872 ..... K
Gortin, ‡2,033 ..... G
Greyabbey, ‡2,646 ..... K
Hillsborough, 1,021 ..... J
Holywood, 9,892 ..... K
Irvinestown, 1,457 ..... F
Keady, 2,145 ..... H
Kells, ‡2,560 ..... J
Kesh, ‡2,497 ..... F
Kilkeel, 4,090 ..... K
Killough, ‡3,295 ..... K
Killyleagh, 2,359 ..... K
Kilrea, 1,196 ..... H
Kircubbin, 1,075 ..... K
Larne, 18,482 ..... K
Limavady, 6,004 ..... H
Lisburn, 31,836 ..... J
Lisnaskea, 1,443 ..... G
Londonderry, 51,200 ..... G
Loughbrickland, ‡2,056 ..... J
Maghera, 2,085 ..... H
Magherafelt, 4,704 ..... H
Markethill, ‡2,352 ..... H 3
Millisle, 1,172 ..... K 2
Moneymore, 1,178 ..... H 2
Moy, ‡2,349 ..... H 3
Moygashel, 1,086 ..... H 3
Newcastle, 4,647 ..... J 3
Newry, 20,279 ..... J 3
Newtownabbey, 58,114 ..... K 2
Newtownards, 15,484 ..... K 2
Newtownbutler, ‡2,663 ..... G 3
Newtownhamilton, ‡1,936 ..... H 3
Newtownstewart, 1,433 ..... G 2
Omagh, 14,594 ..... G 2
Pomeroy, ‡1,786 ..... H 2
Portaferry, 1,730 ..... K 3
Portavogie, 1,310 ..... K 3
Portglenone, ‡2,061 ..... H 2
Portrush, 5,376 ..... H 1
Portstewart, 5,085 ..... H 1
Randalstown, 2,799 ..... J 2
Rathfriland, 1,886 ..... J 3
Rostrevor, 1,617 ..... J 3
Saintfield, ‡2,198 ..... K 3
Sion Mills, 1,588 ..... G 2
Sixmilecross, ‡1,980 ..... G 2
Stewartstown, ‡1,759 ..... H 2
Strabane, 9,413 ..... G 2
Strangford, ‡1,987 ..... K 3
Tandragee, 1,725 ..... J 3
Tempo, ‡2,282 ..... G 3
Trillick, ‡2,167 ..... G 3
Warrenpoint, 4,291 ..... J 3
Whitehead, 2,642 ..... K 2

OTHER FEATURES

Bann (riv.) ..... H 2
Belfast (inlet) ..... K 2
Blackwater (riv.) ..... H 3
Bush (riv.) ..... H 1
Derg (riv.) ..... F 2
Divis (mt.) ..... J 2
Dundrum (bay) ..... K 3
Erne (lake) ..... F 3
Foyle (inlet) ..... G 1
Foyle (riv.) ..... G 2
Giant's Causeway ..... H 1
Lagan (riv.) ..... K 2
Larne (inlet) ..... K 2
Magee, Island (pen.), 1,581 ..... K 2
Magilligan (pt.) ..... H 1
Main (riv.) ..... J 2
Mourne (mts.) ..... J 3
Mourne (riv.) ..... G 2
Neagh (lake) ..... J 2
North (chan.) ..... K 1
Rathlin (isl.), 109 ..... J 1
Red (bay) ..... K 1
Roe (riv.) ..... H 1
Saint John's (pt.) ..... K 3
Slieve Donard (mt.) ..... K 3
Sperrin (mts.) ..... G 2
Strangford (inlet) ..... K 3
Torr (head) ..... K 1
Ulster (part) (prov.), 1,537,200 ..... G 2
Upper Lough Erne (lake) ..... F 3

*City and suburbs.
‡Population of district.

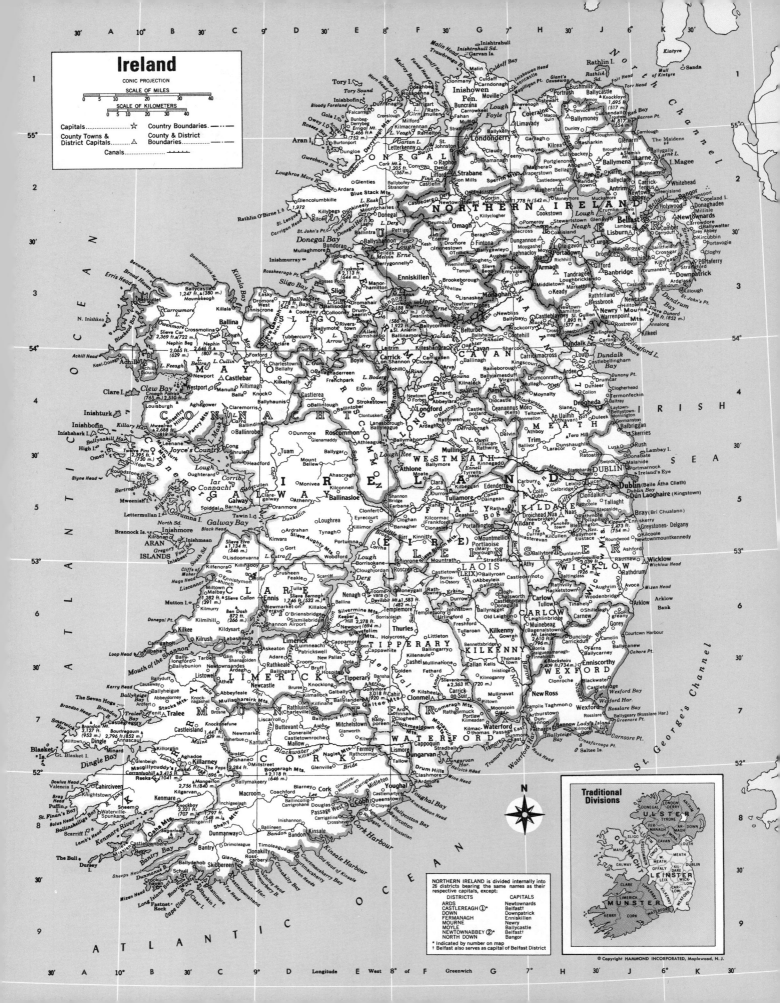

Norway, Sweden, Finland and Denmark

CONIC PROJECTION

SCALE OF MILES
0   50   100   150

SCALE OF KILOMETERS
0   50   100   150   200

Capitals of Countries .... ☆
Administrative Centers .... △
International Boundaries ....
Internal Boundaries ....
Canals ....

SUBDIVISIONS
Indicated by Numbers
Counties in NORWAY
1 Akershus   G 6
2 Vestfold   G 7
3 Østfold   G 7
4 Oslo   G 7

Oslo is the administrative
center for Akershus and
Oslo County.

Counties in SWEDEN
5 Göteborg och
   Bohus   G 7
6 Västmanland   K 7
7 Södermanland   K 7
8 Östergötland   J 7
9 Malmöhus   H 9
10 Kristianstad   J 8

AREA 125,053 sq. mi. (323,887 sq. km.)
POPULATION 4,092,000
CAPITAL Oslo
LARGEST CITY Oslo
HIGHEST POINT Glittertinden 8,110 ft. (2,472 m.)
MONETARY UNIT krone
MAJOR LANGUAGE Norwegian
MAJOR RELIGION Protestantism

AREA 173,665 sq. mi. (449,792 sq. km.)
POPULATION 8,320,000
CAPITAL Stockholm
LARGEST CITY Stockholm
HIGHEST POINT Kebnekaise 6,946 ft. (2,117 m.)
MONETARY UNIT krona
MAJOR LANGUAGE Swedish
MAJOR RELIGION Protestantism

AREA 130,128 sq. mi. (337,032 sq. km.)
POPULATION 4,788,000
CAPITAL Helsinki
LARGEST CITY Helsinki
HIGHEST POINT Haltiatunturi 4,343 ft. (1,324 m.)
MONETARY UNIT markka
MAJOR LANGUAGES Finnish, Swedish
MAJOR RELIGION Protestantism

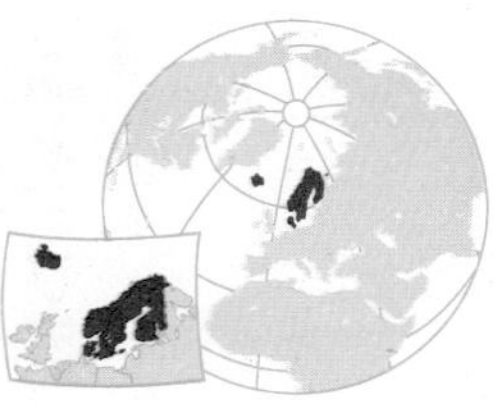

NORWAY

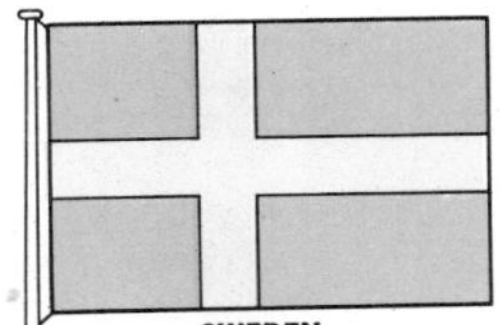
SWEDEN

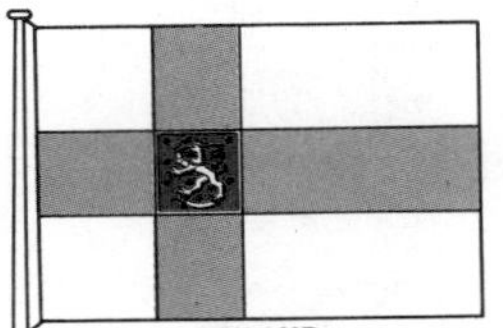
FINLAND

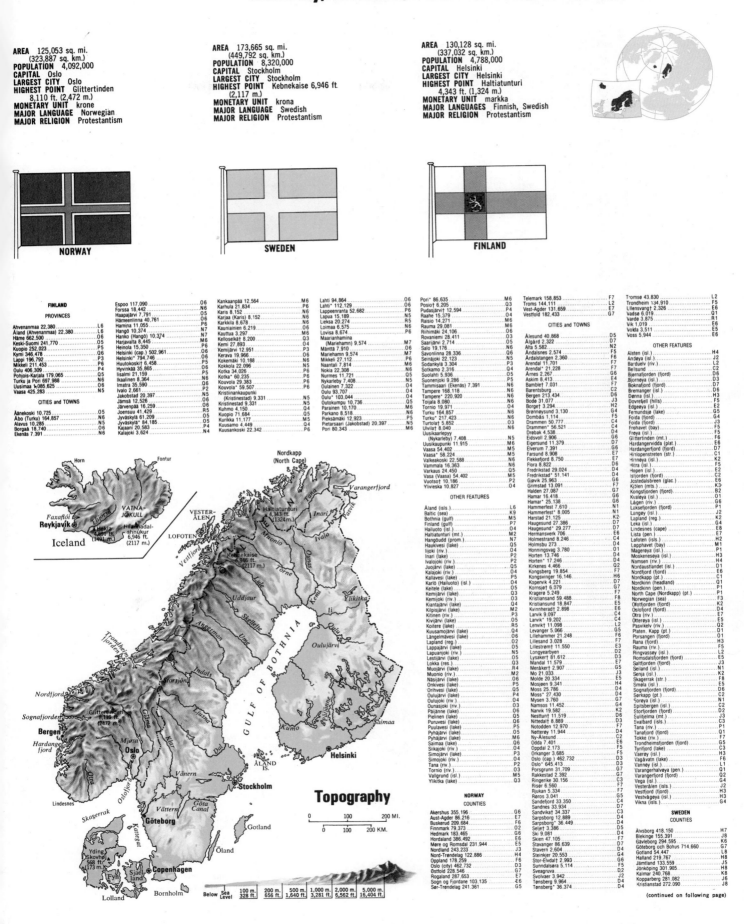

FINLAND

PROVINCES

Ahvenanmaa 22,380 ... L6
Åland (Ahvenanmaa) 22,380 ... L6
Häme 662,500 ... O6
Keski-Suomi 241,770 ... O5
Kuopio 252,023 ... P5
Kymi 346,478 ... Q6
Lappi 196,792 ... P3
Mikkeli 211,453 ... P6
Oulu 406,309 ... P4
Pohjois-Karjala 179,065 ... Q5
Turku ja Pori 697,988 ... N6
Uusimaa 1,085,625 ... O6
Vaasa 425,283 ... N5

CITIES and TOWNS

Äänekoski 10,725 ... O5
Åbo (Turku) 164,857 ... N6
Alavus 10,285 ... N5
Borgaå 18,740 ... O6
Ekenäs 7,391 ... N6
Espoo 117,090 ... O6
Forssa 18,442 ... N6
Haapajärvi 7,791 ... O5
Hämeenlinna 40,761 ... O6
Hamina 11,055 ... P6
Hangö 10,374 ... N7
Hanko (Hangö) 10,374 ... N7
Harjavalta 8,445 ... M6
Heinola 15,350 ... P6
Helsinki (cap.) 502,961 ... O6
Helsinki* 794,746 ... O6
Huutokoski† 6,458 ... P5
Hyvinkää 35,865 ... O6
Iisalmi 21,159 ... P5
Ikaalinen 8,364 ... N6
Imatra 35,590 ... Q6
Ivalo 2,661 ... P2
Jakobstad 20,397 ... N5
Jämsä 12,526 ... O6
Järvenpää 16,259 ... O6
Joensuu 41,429 ... R5
Jyväskylä 61,209 ... O5
Jyväskylä* 84,185 ... O5
Kajaani 20,583 ... P4
Kalajoki 3,624 ... N4
Kankaanpää 12,564 ... M6
Karhula 21,834 ... P6
Karis 8,152 ... N6
Karjaa (Karis) 8,152 ... N6
Karkkila 8,678 ... N6
Kauniainien 6,219 ... O6
Kauttua 3,297 ... M6
Kelloselkä† 8,200 ... Q3
Kemi 27,893 ... O4
Kemijärvi 12,951 ... P3
Kerava 19,966 ... O6
Kokemäki 10,188 ... N6
Kokkola 22,096 ... N5
Kotka 34,026 ... P6
Kotka* 60,235 ... P6
Kouvola 29,383 ... P6
Kouvola* 59,507 ... P6
Kristiinankaupunki (Kristinestad) 9,331 ... N5
Kristinestad 9,331 ... N5
Kuhmo 4,150 ... Q4
Kuopio 71,684 ... Q5
Kurikka 11,177 ... M5
Kuusamo 4,449 ... Q4
Kuusankoski 22,342 ... P6
Lahti 94,864 ... O6
Lahti* 112,129 ... O6
Lappeenranta 52,682 ... P6
Lapua 15,189 ... N5
Lieksa 20,274 ... R5
Loimaa 6,575 ... N6
Lovisa 8,674 ... P6
Maarianhamina (Mariehamn) 9,574 ... M7
Mänttä 7,910 ... O6
Mariehamn 9,574 ... M7
Mikkeli 27,112 ... P6
Naantali 7,814 ... M6
Nokia 22,308 ... N6
Nurmes 11,721 ... Q5
Nykarleby 7,408 ... N5
Oulainen 7,322 ... O4
Oulu 93,707 ... O4
Oulu* 103,044 ... O4
Outokumpu 10,736 ... Q5
Parainen 10,170 ... M6
Parkano 8,518 ... N6
Pieksämäki 12,923 ... P5
Pietarsaari (Jakobstad) 20,397 ... N5
Pori 80,343 ... M6
Pori* 86,635 ... M6
Posio† 6,205 ... Q3
Pudasjärvi† 12,594 ... P4
Raahe 15,379 ... O4
Raisio 14,271 ... M6
Rauma 29,081 ... M6
Riihimäki 24,106 ... O6
Rovaniemi 28,411 ... O3
Saarijärvi 2,714 ... O5
Salo 19,176 ... N6
Savonlinna 28,336 ... Q6
Seinäjoki 22,123 ... N5
Sodankylä 3,304 ... P3
Sotkamo 2,316 ... Q4
Suolahti 5,936 ... O5
Suonenjoki 9,286 ... P5
Tammisaari (Ekenäs) 7,391 ... N6
Tampere 168,118 ... N6
Tampere* 220,920 ... N6
Toijala 8,080 ... N6
Tornio 19,971 ... O4
Turku 164,857 ... N6
Turku* 217,423 ... N6
Turtola† 5,852 ... O3
Ulvila† 8,040 ... N6
Uusikaarlepyy (Nykarleby) 7,408 ... N5
Uusikaupunki 11,915 ... M6
Vaasa 54,402 ... M5
Vaasa* 58,224 ... M5
Valkeakoski 22,588 ... N6
Vammala 16,363 ... N6
Varkaus 24,450 ... Q5
Vasa (Vaasa) 54,402 ... M5
Vuotso† 10,186 ... P2
Ylivieska 10,827 ... O4

OTHER FEATURES

Åland (isls.) ... L6
Baltic (sea) ... K9
Bothnia (gulf) ... M5
Finland (gulf) ... P7
Hailuoto (isl.) ... O4
Haltiatunturi (mt.) ... M2
Hangöudd (prom.) ... N7
Haukivesi (lake) ... Q5
Iijoki (riv.) ... O4
Inari (lake) ... P2
Ivalojoki (riv.) ... P2
Juojärvi (lake) ... Q5
Kalajoki (riv.) ... O4
Kallavesi (lake) ... P5
Karlö (Hailuoto) (isl.) ... O4
Keitele (lake) ... O5
Kemijärvi (lake) ... Q3
Kemijoki (riv.) ... O3
Kiantajärvi (lake) ... Q4
Kilpisjärvi (lake) ... M2
Kitinen (riv.) ... P3
Kivijärvi (lake) ... O5
Koitere (lake) ... R5
Kuusamojärvi (lake) ... Q4
Längelmävesi (lake) ... O6
Lapland (reg.) ... O2
Lappajärvi (lake) ... O5
Lapuanjoki (riv.) ... N5
Lestijärvi (lake) ... O5
Lokka (res.) ... Q3
Muojärvi (lake) ... R4
Muonio (riv.) ... M2
Näsijärvi (lake) ... O6
Onkivesi (lake) ... P5
Orihvesi (lake) ... Q5
Oulujärvi (lake) ... P4
Oulujoki (riv.) ... O4
Ounasjoki (riv.) ... O3
Päijänne (lake) ... O6
Pielinen (lake) ... Q5
Puruvesi (lake) ... Q6
Puulavesi (lake) ... P5
Pyhäjärvi (lake) ... O5
Pyhäjärvi (lake) ... M6
Saimaa (lake) ... Q6
Siikajoki (riv.) ... O4
Simojärvi (lake) ... P3
Simojoki (riv.) ... O4
Tana (riv.) ... P2
Tornio (riv.) ... O3
Vallgrund (isl.) ... M5
Ylikitka (lake) ... Q3

NORWAY

COUNTIES

Akershus 355,196 ... G6
Aust-Agder 86,216 ... E7
Buskerud 209,684 ... F6
Finnmark 79,373 ... O2
Hedmark 183,465 ... G6
Hordaland 386,492 ... E6
Møre og Romsdal 231,944 ... E5
Nordland 243,233 ... J3
Nord-Trøndelag 122,886 ... H4
Oppland 178,259 ... F6
Oslo (city) 462,732 ... D3
Østfold 228,546 ... G7
Rogaland 287,653 ... E7
Sogn og Fjordane 103,135 ... E6
Sør-Trøndelag 241,361 ... G5
Telemark 158,853 ... F7
Troms 144,111 ... L2
Vest-Agder 131,659 ... E7
Vestfold 182,433 ... G7

CITIES and TOWNS

Ålesund 40,868 ... D5
Ålgård 2,322 ... D7
Alta 5,582 ... N2
Åndalsnes 2,574 ... F5
Årdalstangen 2,360 ... F6
Arendal 11,701 ... F7
Arendal* 21,228 ... F7
Årnes 2,267 ... G6
Askim 8,413 ... E4
Bamble† 7,031 ... F7
Barentsburg ... C2
Bergen 213,434 ... D6
Bodø 31,077 ... J3
Borge† 3,294 ... H2
Brønnøysund 3,130 ... G4
Dombås 1,114 ... F5
Drammen 50,777 ... C4
Drammen* 56,521 ... C4
Drøbak 4,538 ... D4
Eidsvoll 2,906 ... G6
Eigersund 11,379 ... D7
Elverum 7,391 ... G6
Farsund 8,908 ... E7
Flekkefjord 8,750 ... E7
Flora 8,822 ... D6
Fredrikstad 29,024 ... D4
Fredrikstad* 51,141 ... D4
Gjøvik 25,963 ... G6
Grimstad 13,091 ... F7
Halden 27,087 ... G7
Hamar 16,418 ... G6
Hamar* 25,138 ... G6
Hammerfest 7,610 ... N1
Hammerfest* 8,005 ... N1
Harstad 21,125 ... K2
Haugesund 27,386 ... D7
Haugesund* 29,277 ... D7
Hermansverk 706 ... E6
Holmestrand 8,246 ... C4
Holmsbu 273 ... D4
Honningsvag 3,780 ... O1
Horten 13,746 ... D4
Horten* 17,246 ... D4
Kirkenes 4,466 ... Q2
Kongsberg 19,854 ... F7
Kongsvinger 16,146 ... H6
Kopervik 4,221 ... D7
Kornsjø† 6,079 ... G7
Kragerø 5,249 ... F7
Kristiansand 59,488 ... F8
Kristiansund 18,847 ... E5
Kvinnherad† 2,898 ... E6
Larvik 9,097 ... C4
Larvik* 19,202 ... C4
Lenvik† 11,098 ... L2
Levanger 5,066 ... G5
Lillehammer 21,248 ... F6
Lillesand 3,028 ... F7
Lillestrøm† 11,550 ... E3
Longyearbyen ... D2
Lysaker† 81,612 ... D3
Mandal 11,579 ... E7
Meråker† 2,907 ... G5
Mo 21,033 ... J3
Molde 20,334 ... E5
Mosjøen 9,341 ... H4
Moss 25,786 ... D4
Moss* 27,430 ... D4
Mysen 3,760 ... G7
Namsos 11,452 ... G4
Narvik 19,582 ... K2
Nesttun† 11,519 ... D6
Nittedal† 8,889 ... D3
Notodden 12,970 ... F7
Nøtterøy 11,944 ... D4
Ny-Ålesund ... C2
Odda 7,401 ... E6
Oppdal 2,173 ... F5
Orkanger 3,685 ... F5
Oslo (cap.) 462,732 ... D3
Oslo* 645,413 ... D3
Porsgrunn 31,709 ... G7
Rakkestad 2,392 ... G7
Ringerike 30,156 ... C3
Risør 6,560 ... F7
Rjukan 5,334 ... F7
Røros 3,041 ... G5
Sandefjord 33,350 ... C4
Sandnes 33,934 ... D7
Sandvika† 34,337 ... C3
Sarpsborg 12,889 ... D4
Sarpsborg* 36,449 ... D4
Selje† 3,386 ... D5
Ski 9,081 ... D4
Skien 47,105 ... F7
Stavanger 86,639 ... D7
Stavern 2,604 ... D4
Steinkjer 20,553 ... G4
Stor-Elvdal† 2,993 ... G6
Sunndalsøra 5,114 ... F5
Sveagruva ... D2
Svolvaer 3,942 ... J2
Tønsberg 9,964 ... D4
Tønsberg* 36,374 ... D4
Tromsø 43,830 ... L2
Trondheim 134,910 ... F5
Ullensvang† 2,326 ... E6
Vadsø 6,019 ... Q1
Vardø 3,875 ... R1
Vik 1,019 ... E6
Volda 3,511 ... E5
Voss 5,944 ... E6

OTHER FEATURES

Alsten (isl.) ... H4
Andøya (isl.) ... J2
Barduelv (riv.) ... L2
Bellsund ... C2
Bjørnafjorden (fjord) ... D6
Bjornøya (isl.) ... D3
Boknafjord (fjord) ... D7
Bremanger (isl.) ... D6
Dønna (isl.) ... H3
Dovrefjell (hills) ... F5
Edgeøya (isl.) ... E2
Femundsjø (lake) ... G5
Folda (fjord) ... G4
Folda (fjord) ... J3
Frohavet (bay) ... F5
Frøya (isl.) ... F5
Glittertinden (mt.) ... F6
Hardangervidda (plat.) ... E6
Hardangerfjord (fjord) ... D7
Hinlopenstreten (str.) ... C1
Hinnøya (isl.) ... K2
Hitra (isl.) ... F5
Hopen (isl.) ... E2
Isfjorden (fjord) ... C2
Jostedalsbreen (glac.) ... E6
Kjölen (mts.) ... K3
Kongsfjorden (fjord) ... B2
Kvaløya (isl.) ... O1
Lågen (riv.) ... G6
Laksefjorden (fjord) ... P1
Langøy (isl.) ... J2
Lapland (reg.) ... K2
Leka (isl.) ... G4
Lindesnes (cape) ... E8
Lista (pen.) ... E7
Lofoten (isls.) ... H2
Løpphavet (bay) ... M1
Magerøya (isl.) ... P1
Moskenesøya (isl.) ... H3
Namsen (riv.) ... H4
Nordaustlandet (isl.) ... D1
Nordfjord (fjord) ... E6
Nordkapp (pt.) ... C1
Nordkinn (headland) ... Q1
Nordkinn (pen.) ... P1
North Cape (Nordkapp) (pt.) ... P1
Norwegian (sea) ... F3
Ofotfjorden (fjord) ... K2
Oslofjord (fjord) ... D4
Otra (riv.) ... E7
Otterøya (isl.) ... E5
Pasvikelv (riv.) ... Q2
Platen, Kapp (pt.) ... D1
Porsangen (fjord) ... O1
Rana (fjord) ... H3
Rauma (riv.) ... F5
Ringvassøy (isl.) ... L2
Romsdalsfjorden (fjord) ... E5
Saltfjorden (fjord) ... J3
Seiland (isl.) ... N1
Senja (isl.) ... K2
Skagerrak (str.) ... F8
Smøla (isl.) ... E5
Sognafjorden (fjord) ... D6
Sørkapp (pt.) ... C2
Sorøya (isl.) ... N1
Spitsbergen (isl.) ... C2
Storfjorden (fjord) ... D2
Sulitjelma (mt.) ... J3
Svalbard (isls.) ... C3
Tana (riv.) ... P1
Tanafjord (fjord) ... Q1
Tokke (riv.) ... F7
Trondheimsfjorden (fjord) ... G5
Tyrifjord (lake) ... C3
Vaerøy (isl.) ... H3
Vagåvatn (lake) ... F6
Vannøy (isl.) ... L1
Varangerhalvøya (pen.) ... Q1
Varangerfjord (fjord) ... Q2
Vega (isl.) ... G4
Vesterålen (isls.) ... J2
Vestfjord (fjord) ... H3
Vestvågøya (isl.) ... H3
Vikna (isls.) ... G4

SWEDEN

COUNTIES

Älvsborg 418,150 ... H7
Blekinge 155,391 ... J8
Gävleborg 294,595 ... K6
Göteborg och Bohus 714,660 ... G7
Gotland 54,447 ... L8
Halland 219,767 ... H8
Jämtland 133,559 ... J5
Jönköping 301,905 ... H8
Kalmar 240,768 ... K8
Kopparberg 281,082 ... J6
Kristianstad 272,090 ... J8

(continued on following page)

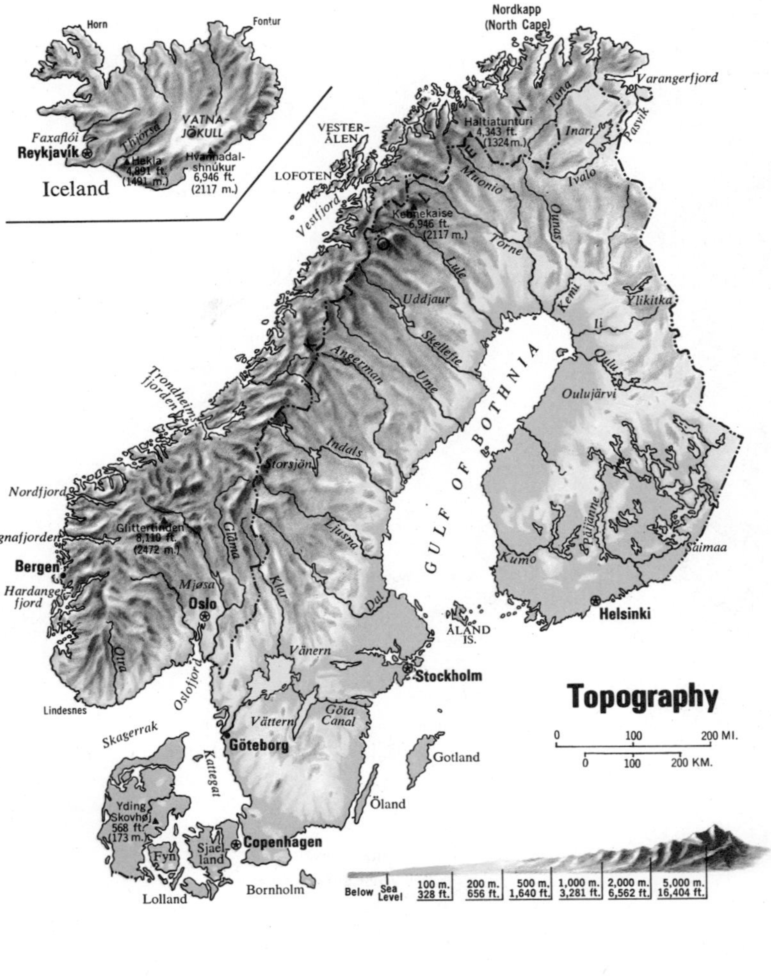

Topography
Horn
Fontur
VATNA-JÖKULL
Faxaflói
Reykjavík
Hekla 4,891 ft. (1491 m.)
Hvannadalshnúkur 6,946 ft. (2117 m.)
Iceland
Nordkapp (North Cape)
Varangerfjord
VESTERÅLEN
LOFOTEN
Vestfjord
Haltiatunturi 4,343 ft. (1324 m.)
Kebnekaise 6,946 ft. (2117 m.)
Inari
Ivalo
Muonio
Torne
Lule
Ylikitka
Uddjaur
Skellefte
Kemi
Oulu
Oulujärvi
GULF OF BOTHNIA
Ångerman
Ume
Indals
Storsjön
Ljusna
Trondheimsfjorden
Nordfjord
Sognafjorden
Glittertinden 8,110 ft. (2472 m.)
Glåma
Klar
Mjøsa
Bergen
Hardangerfjord
Oslo
Otra
Oslofjord
Päijänne
Saimaa
Kumo
Dal
Helsinki
ÅLAND IS.
Vänern
Stockholm
Lindesnes
Skagerrak
Vättern
Göta Canal
Göteborg
Kattegat
Gotland
Öland
Yding Skovhøj 568 ft. (173 m.)
Fyn
Sjælland
Copenhagen
Lolland
Bornholm
0 100 200 MI.
0 100 200 KM.
Below Sea Level
100 m. 328 ft.
200 m. 656 ft.
500 m. 1,640 ft.
1,000 m. 3,281 ft.
2,000 m. 6,562 ft.
5,000 m. 16,404 ft.

Kronoberg 169,454 ... J8
Malmöhus 740,137 ... H9
Norrbotten 264,215 ... L3
Örebro 273,994 ... J7
Östergötland 387,104 ... J7
Skaraborg 263,382 ... H7
Södermanland 252,030 ... K7
Stockholm 1,493,052 ... L7
Uppsala 229,879 ... K7
Värmland 284,442 ... H7
Västerbotten 236,367 ... K4
Västernorrland 268,202 ... K5
Västmanland 259,872 ... K7

CITIES and TOWNS

Åhus 6,125 ... J9
Alingsås 18,892 ... H7
Älmhult 7,390 ... H8
Alvesta 7,261 ... J8
Älvsbyn 4,707 ... M4
Åmål 9,556 ... H7
Ånge 3,760 ... J5
Ängelholm 16,016 ... H8
Arboga 11,819 ... J7
Arbrå 2,734 ... K6
Årjäng† 2,596 ... H7
Arvidsjaur 4,194 ... L4
Arvika 13,934 ... H7
Åseda 2,465 ... J8
Askim 17,609 ... G8
Åtvidaberg 8,436 ... K7
Avesta 19,095 ... J6
Bålsta 8,243 ... G1
Båstad 2,452 ... H8
Bengtsfors 3,535 ... H7
Boden 19,590 ... M4
Bollnäs 13,305 ... K6
Bollstabruk 3,548 ... L5
Borås 67,537 ... H8
Borås* 187,710 ... H8
Borgholm 2,789 ... K8
Borlänge 40,158 ... J6
Brunflo 3,460 ... J5
Dalby† 4,013 ... H6
Danderyd† 36,596 ... H1
Dannemora 291 ... K6
Edsbyn 4,388 ... J6
Eksjö 9,686 ... J8
Emmaboda 5,652 ... J8
Enköping 18,541 ... G1
Eskilstuna 66,409 ... K7
Eslöv 13,629 ... H9
Fagersta† 14,778 ... J6
Falkenberg 14,148 ... H8
Falköping 15,126 ... H7
Falun 30,073 ... J6
Färjestaden 2,995 ... K8
Filipstad 7,835 ... H7
Finspång 16,346 ... J7
Flen 6,770 ... K7
Forshaga 6,000 ... H7
Frösö 10,274 ... J5
Frövi 2,583 ... J7
Gällivare 8,669 ... M3
Gamleby 3,666 ... J8
Gävle 67,454 ... K6
Gimo 3,154 ... K6
Gislaved 8,564 ... H8
Gnesta 3,835 ... G2
Göteborg 444,540 ... G8
Göteborg* 690,767 ... G8
Hagfors 8,060 ... H6
Hällefors 7,862 ... J7
Hallsberg 6,799 ... J7
Hallstahammar 13,583 ... K7
Hallstavik 5,162 ... L6
Halmstad 49,558 ... H8
Haparanda 5,031 ... N4
Härnösand 18,971 ... L5
Hässleholm 16,813 ... H8
Hedemora 7,039 ... K6
Helsingborg 80,986 ... H8
Helsingborg* 215,894 ... H8
Hjo 4,615 ... J7
Hofors 11,459 ... K6
Höganäs 10,866 ... H8
Holmsund 5,467 ... M5
Hörnefors 2,441 ... L5
Huddinge 48,339 ... H1
Hudiksvall 15,004 ... K6
Hultsfred 5,763 ... K8
Husum 2,517 ... L5
Hyltebruk 3,469 ... H8
Iggesund 4,448 ... K6
Järna 6,237 ... G2
Jokkmokk 3,186 ... L3
Jönköping 78,650 ... H8
Jönköping* 131,499 ... H8
Kalix 7,668 ... N4
Kalmar 32,049 ... K8
Karlshamn 17,447 ... J8
Karlskoga† 35,425 ... J7
Karlskrona 33,414 ... J8
Karlstad 51,243 ... H7
Katrineholm 22,884 ... K7
Kinna 13,676 ... H8
Kiruna 25,410 ... L3
Kisa 4,323 ... J7
Köping 20,059 ... J7
Kopparberg 3,942 ... J7
Kramfors 7,719 ... L5
Kristianstad 30,780 ... J9
Kristinehamn 21,146 ... H7
Kumla 11,451 ... J7
Kungälv† 12,764 ... G8
Kungsbacka† 11,986 ... G8
Kvissleby 3,413 ... K5
Laholm 3,898 ... H8
Landskrona 29,486 ... H9
Långshyttan 2,744 ... K6
Laxå 5,166 ... J7
Leksand 4,410 ... J6
Lessebo 2,991 ... J8
Lidingö 30,098 ... H1
Lidköping 21,001 ... H7
Lindesberg 8,247 ... J7
Linköping 80,274 ... K7
Linköping* 132,839 ... K7
Ljungby 12,969 ... J8
Ljusdal 7,075 ... J6
Ljusne 3,578 ... K6
Ludvika 18,217 ... J6
Luleå 42,139 ... N4
Lund 55,047 ... H9
Lycksele 8,586 ... L4
Lysekil 7,815 ... G7
Malmberget 10,239 ... M3
Malmö 241,191 ... H9
Malmö* 453,339 ... H9
Malung 6,211 ... H6
Mariefred 2,553 ... F1
Mariestad 16,454 ... H7
Markaryd 4,266 ... H8
Märsta 17,066 ... K7
Marstrand 1,168 ... G8
Mellerud 3,579 ... H7
Mjölby 12,488 ... J7
Mölndal† 47,248 ... H8
Mönsterås 5,005 ... K8
Mora 8,772 ... J6
Motala 29,454 ... J7
Nacka 19,708 ... H1
Nässjö 18,634 ... J8
Nora 5,515 ... J7
Norberg 5,438 ... K6
Norrköping 85,244 ... K7
Norrköping* 163,206 ... K7
Norrtälje 12,784 ... L7
Nybro 13,010 ... J8
Nyköping 30,352 ... K7
Nynäshamn 11,070 ... L7
Ockelbo 2,810 ... K6
Olofström 10,096 ... J8
Örebro 117,877 ... J7
Örebro* 171,440 ... J7
Örnsköldsvik 29,514 ... L5
Orrefors 919 ... J8
Orsa 5,099 ... J6
Oskarshamn 19,021 ... K8
Östersund 40,056 ... J5
Östhammar 1,783 ... L6
Oxelösund 13,862 ... K7
Piteå 16,169 ... M4
Rättvik 4,087 ... J6
Rimbo 3,404 ... L7
Ronneby 12,086 ... J8
Säffle 11,428 ... H7
Sala 11,216 ... K7
Saltsjöbaden 8,113 ... J1
Sandviken 27,994 ... K6
Säter 4,297 ... J6
Sävsjö 4,913 ... J8
Sigtuna 4,780 ... H1
Simrishamn 5,834 ... J9
Skanör med Falsterbo 4,909 ... H9
Skara 10,138 ... H7
Skellefteå 29,353 ... M4
Skövde 29,945 ... H7
Skutskär 7,174 ... K6
Smedjebacken 8,418 ... J6
Söderhamn 14,673 ... K6
Söderköping 5,310 ... K7
Södertälje 58,408 ... G1
Sollefteå 8,923 ... K5
Sollentuna† 40,905 ... H1
Solna† 53,992 ... H1
Sölvesborg 7,292 ... J9
Stenungsund 8,361 ... G7
Stockholm (cap.) 665,550 ... G1
Stockholm* 1,357,183 ... G1
Storuman 2,587 ... K4
Storvik 2,748 ... K6
Strängnäs 10,255 ... F1
Strömstad 4,735 ... G7
Strömsund 4,119 ... K5
Sundbyberg† 27,058 ... G1
Sundsvall 52,268 ... K5
Sunne 4,273 ... H7
Surahammar 6,509 ... J7
Sveg 2,608 ... J5
Svenljunga 3,189 ... H8
Täby† 41,265 ... H1
Tibro 8,476 ... J7
Tidaholm 8,039 ... J7
Tierp 5,005 ... K6
Timrå 11,416 ... K5
Tomelilla 5,371 ... J9
Torsby 3,632 ... H6
Torshälla 8,231 ... K7
Tranås 14,854 ... J7
Trelleborg 22,559 ... H9
Trollhättan 42,499 ... H7
Trosa 3,128 ... K7
Uddevalla 32,700 ... G7
Ulricehamn 7,827 ... H8
Umeå 49,715 ... M5
Uppsala 101,850 ... K7
Uppsala* 157,202 ... L7
Vadstena 5,294 ... J7
Vaggeryd 3,974 ... J8
Valdemarsvik 3,558 ... K7
Vallentuna 10,477 ... H1
Vänersborg 20,510 ... G7
Vännäs 3,876 ... L5
Vansbro 2,708 ... H6
Vara 3,049 ... H7
Varberg 19,467 ... G8
Värnamo 15,726 ... J8
Västerås 98,858 ... K7
Västerås* 147,508 ... K7
Västerhaninge 14,125 ... H1
Västervik 21,239 ... K8
Vaxholm† 3,744 ... J1
Växjö 40,328 ... J8
Vetlanda 12,358 ... J8
Vilhelmina 4,060 ... K4
Vimmerby 7,405 ... J8
Virserum 2,495 ... J8
Visby 19,886 ... L8
Ystad 14,286 ... H9

OTHER FEATURES

Ångermanälven (riv.) ... K5
Åsnen (lake) ... J8
Baltic (sea) ... K9
Bolmen (lake) ... H8
Bothnia (gulf) ... N4
Dalälven (riv.) ... K6
Fårö (isl.) ... L8
Göta (canal) ... J7
Göta (riv.) ... H7
Gotland (isl.) ... L8
Gräsö (isl.) ... L6
Hanöbukten (bay) ... J9
Hjälmaren (lake) ... J7
Hoburgen (cliff) ... L8
Hornslandet (pen.) ... K6
Indalsälven (riv.) ... H5
Kalixälv (riv.) ... N3
Kalmarsund (sound) ... K8
Kattegat (str.) ... G8
Kebnekaise (mt.) ... L3
Kölen (mts.) ... K3
Klarälv (riv.) ... H6
Lapland (reg.) ... M2
Ljusnan (riv.) ... H5
Luleälv (riv.) ... M4
Mälaren (lake) ... G1
Muonioälv (riv.) ... M2
Öland (isl.) ... K8
Öresund (sound) ... H9
Ornö (isl.) ... J2
Österdalälven (riv.) ... H6
Piteälv (riv.) ... M4
Siljan (lake) ... J6
Skagerrak (str.) ... F8
Sommen (lake) ... J8
Stora Lulevatten (lake) ... L3
Storsjön (lake) ... J5
Sulitelma (mt.) ... K3
Torneälv (riv.) ... M3
Uddjaur (lake) ... L4
Umeälv (riv.) ... L4
Vänern (lake) ... H7
Västerdalälven (riv.) ... H6
Vättern (lake) ... J7

*City and suburbs.
†Population of commune.
†Population of parish.

DENMARK

COUNTIES

Århus 534,333 ... D5
Bornholm 47,241 ... F9
Copenhagen (commune) 622,612 ... F6
Faerøe Islands 41,969 ... B2
Frederiksberg (commune) 101,874 ... F6
Frederiksborg 260,825 ... E5
Fyn 433,765 ... D7
København (Copenhagen) (commune) 622,612 ... F6
Københaven 616,571 ... F6
Nordjylland 457,165 ... D4
Ribe 198,153 ... B7
Ringkøbing 242,006 ... B5
Roskilde 154,314 ... E6
Sønderjylland 238,502 ... C7
Storstrøm 252,780 ... E7
Vejle 306,809 ... C6
Vestsjaelland 259,484 ... E6
Viborg 221,002 ... C4

CITIES and TOWNS

Åbenrå 15,196 ... C7
Åbybro 2,897 ... C3
Åkirkeby 2,001 ... F9
Ålborg 154,582 ... D4
Ålestrup 1,926 ... C4
Århus 245,941 ... D5
Års 4,266 ... C4
Årup 1,675 ... D7
AErøskøbing 1,223 ... D8
Agerbaek 935 ... B6
Allingaåbro 1,385 ... D5
Allinge-Sandvig 1,991 ... F8
Ansager 1,157 ... B6
Arden 1,303 ... C4
Asaå 1,344 ... D3
Askov 904 ... C7
Asnaes 1,413 ... E6
Assens, Århus 1,341 ... D4
Assens, Fyn 5,139 ... D7
Augustenborg 2,628 ... D8
Auning 1,516 ... D5
Avlum 1,729 ... B5
Baelum 1,169 ... D4
Bagenkop 776 ... D8
Ballerup 50,673 ... F6
Bandholm 693 ... E8
Bedsted 965 ... B4
Birkerød 13,663 ... F6
Bjerringbro 4,761 ... C5
Bogense 2,861 ... D6
Bolderslev 774 ... C8
Børkop 1,410 ... C6
Borup 1,591 ... E7
Braedstrup 2,163 ... C6
Bramming 3,678 ... B7
Brande 4,784 ... B6
Bredebro 1,173 ... B7
Broager 2,143 ... C8
Brønderslev 10,247 ... C3
Brørup 2,584 ... C7
Brovst 4,200 ... C3
Bryrup 579 ... C5
Christiansfeld 1,994 ... C7
Copenhagen (cap.) 603,368 ... F6
Copenhagen* 1,327,940 ... F6
Dronninglund 4,661 ... D3
Dybvad 805 ... D3
Ebeltoft 3,017 ... D5
Egernsund 1,323 ... C8
Egtved 1,311 ... C6
Ejby 1,372 ... C7
Esbjerg 68,097 ... B7
Faåborg 6,495 ... D7
Fakse 2,720 ... F7
Fakse Ladeplads 1,799 ... F7
Farsø 2,821 ... C4
Farum 9,936 ... F6
Fjerritslev 2,134 ... C3
Fredensborg 4,709 ... F6
Fredericia 36,157 ... C6
Frederiksberg 101,874 ... F6
Frederikshavn 24,846 ... D3
Frederikssund 11,272 ... E6
Frederiksvaerk 8,903 ... E6
Fuglebjerg 1,094 ... E7
Gedser 1,200 ... F8
Gedsted 1,006 ... C4
Gelsted 1,307 ... C7
Gentofte 77,744 ... F6
Gilleleje 2,943 ... F5
Give 2,366 ... C6
Glamsbjerg 2,226 ... D7
Glostrup 28,326 ... F6
Glumsø 1,027 ... E7
Glyngøre 1,071 ... C4
Gørding 1,261 ... B7
Gørlev 1,542 ... E7
Graested 1,654 ... F5
Gram 2,061 ... C7
Graåsten 2,947 ... C8
Grenaå 12,569 ... D5
Grindsted 7,558 ... B6
Haårby 1,506 ... D7
Haderslev 20,042
Hadsten 3,914
Hadsund 3,652
Hals 1,654
Hammel 3,247
Hammerum 3,227
Hanstholm 1,716
Harboør 1,359
Haårlev 1,228
Hasle 18
Haslev 6,925
Havdrup 1,833
Hedensted 2,659
Hellebaek 2,911
Helsinge 3,613
Helsingør 42,425
Herning 32,973
Hillerød 23,963
Hinnerup 2,061
Hirtshals 6,861
Hjallerup 1,573
Hjerm 647
Hjørring 19,692
Hobro 8,737
Højer 1,416
Højslev 1,641
Holbaek 19,485
Holeby 1,434
Holstebro 25,006
Holsted 1,390
Høng 2,488
Hornslet 2,561
Horsens 44,120
Hørsholm 19,346
Hørve 1,139
Hov 635
Humlum 546
Hundested 5,443
Hurup 2,287
Hvidbjerg 994
Hvide Sande 2,129
Ikast 9,222
Jelling 1,540
Jerslev 798
Juelsminde 1,991
Jyderup 2,901
Kalundborg 12,248
Karise 1,184
Karup 1,694 ... C5
Kastrup† 17,391 ... F6
Kerteminde 5,007 ... D7
Kibaek 1,279 ... B5
Kjellerup 3,245 ... C5
Klitmøller 542 ... B3
København (Copenhagen) (cap.) 603,368 ... F6
Køge 18,608 ... F7
Kolding 41,602 ... C7
Kolind 1,036 ... D5
Korsør 15,502 ... E7
Kvaerndrup 891 ... D7
Langaå 2,320 ... C5
Lem 1,026 ... B5
Lemvig 6,448 ... B4
Løgstør 3,633 ... C4
Løgumkloster 2,091 ... B7
Lohals 580 ... D7
Løjt Kirkeby 1,203 ... C7
Løkken 1,345 ... C3
Løsning 1,967 ... C6
Lundby 747 ... E7
Lunderskov 1,494 ... C7
Lyngby 61,516 ... F6
Malling 1,584 ... D5
Mariager 1,692 ... D4
Maribo 5,287 ... E8
Marstal 4,124 ... D8
Middelfart 13,315 ... C7

Agriculture, Industry and Resources

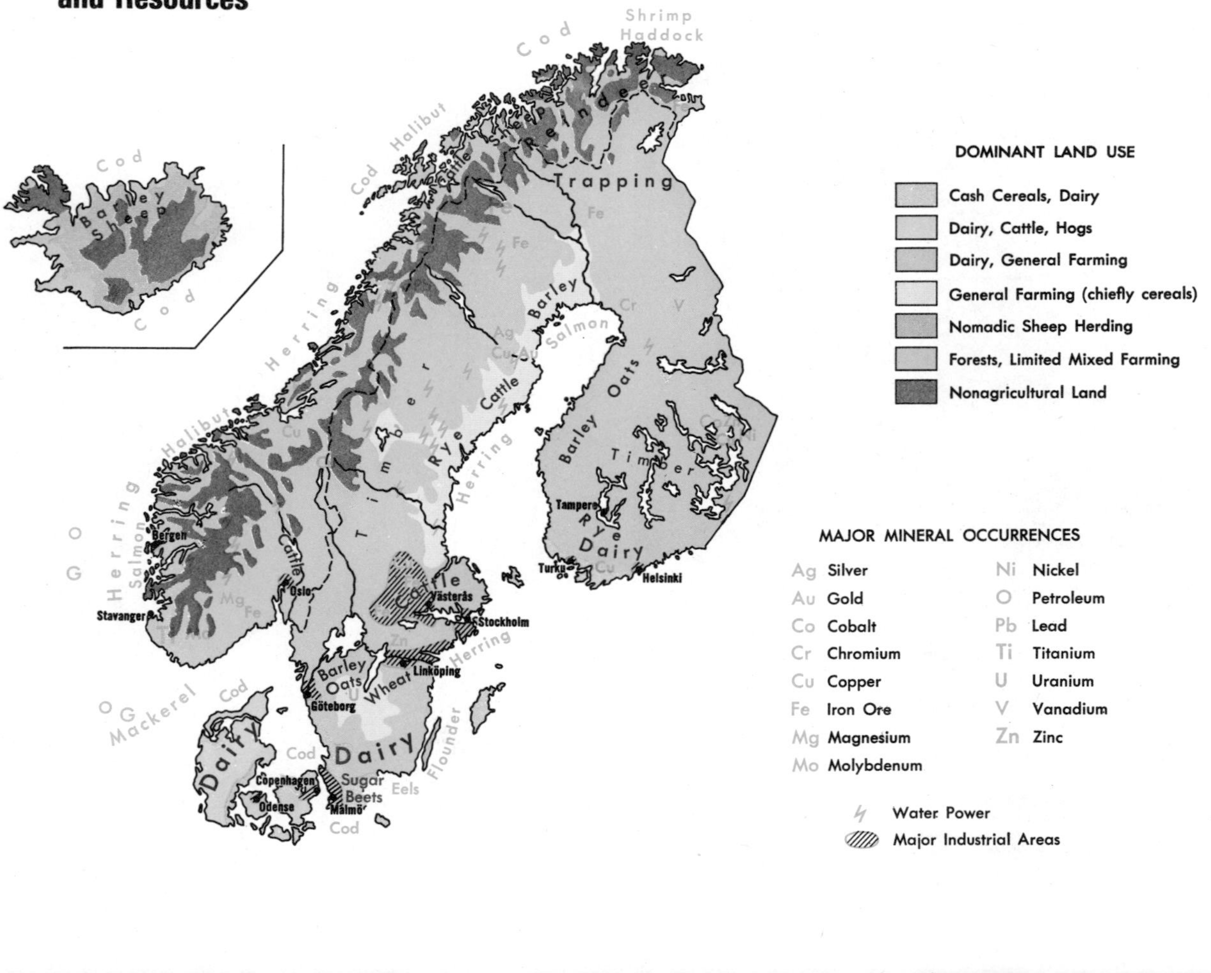

Shrimp
Haddock
Cod
Halibut
Trapping
Reindeer
Barley
Sheep
Herring
Salmon
Cattle
Timber
Rye
Oats
Dairy
Wheat
Sugar Beets
Eels
Flounder
Mackerel
Tampere
Turku
Helsinki
Bergen
Oslo
Stavanger
Västerås
Stockholm
Linköping
Göteborg
Copenhagen
Odense
Malmö
DOMINANT LAND USE
Cash Cereals, Dairy
Dairy, Cattle, Hogs
Dairy, General Farming
General Farming (chiefly cereals)
Nomadic Sheep Herding
Forests, Limited Mixed Farming
Nonagricultural Land
MAJOR MINERAL OCCURRENCES
Ag Silver
Au Gold
Co Cobalt
Cr Chromium
Cu Copper
Fe Iron Ore
Mg Magnesium
Mo Molybdenum
Ni Nickel
O Petroleum
Pb Lead
Ti Titanium
U Uranium
V Vanadium
Zn Zinc
Water Power
Major Industrial Areas

DENMARK

AREA 16,629 sq. mi. (43,069 sq. km.)
POPULATION 5,124,000
CAPITAL Copenhagen
LARGEST CITY Copenhagen
HIGHEST POINT Yding Skovhøj
  568 ft. (173 m.)
MONETARY UNIT krone
MAJOR LANGUAGE Danish
MAJOR RELIGION Protestantism

ICELAND

AREA 39,768 sq. mi. (103,000 sq. km.)
POPULATION 228,785
CAPITAL Reykjavík
LARGEST CITY Reykjavík
HIGHEST POINT Hvannadalshnúkur
  6,952 ft. (2,119 m.)
MONETARY UNIT króna
MAJOR LANGUAGE Icelandic
MAJOR RELIGION Protestantism

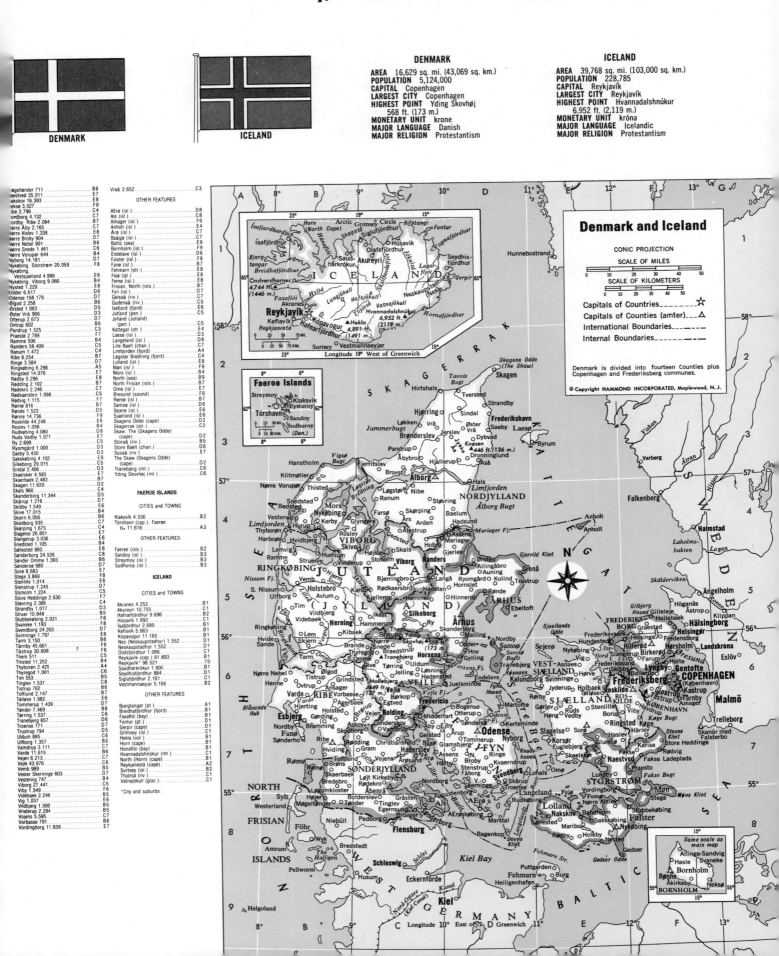

Ægeltender 711 .... B8
Æstved 35,011 .... E7
Ækskov 16,393 .... F9
ekse 3,527 .... F9
ibe 2,796 .... C4
ordborg 4,132 .... C7
ordby, Ribe 2,084 .... B7
ierre Åby 2,165 .... C7
ierre Alslev 1,338 .... E8
ierre Nebel 901 .... B6
ierre Snede 1,461 .... C4
ierre Voruper 644 .... B4
Nyborg 14,181 .... D7
Nykøbing, Storstrøm 20,059 ..... F8
Nykøbing,
  Vestsjælland 4,996 .... E6
Nykøbing, Viborg 9,066 .... B4
Nysted 1,229 .... E8
Odder 6,617 .... D6
Odense 168,178 .... D7
Ølgod 2,258 .... B5
Ørsted 1,093 .... D6
Øster Vrå 676 .... D3
Otterup 2,673 .... D7
Ovtrup 602 .... B6
Pandrup 1,525 .... C3
Praestø 2,789 .... F7
Ramme 506 .... B4
Randers 58,409 .... C4
Ranum 1,472 .... C4
Ribe 8,254 .... B7
Ringe 3,584 .... D7
Ringkøbing 6,298 .... A5
Ringsted 14,076 .... E7
Rødby 5,296 .... E8
Rødding 2,102 .... C7
Rødekro 2,246 .... C7
Rødkaersbro 1,098 .... C4
Rødvig 1,115 .... F7
Rømø 816 .... B7
Rønde 1,523 .... D5
Rønne 14,736 .... F9
Roskilde 44,248 .... E6
Roslev 1,058 .... B4
Rudkøbing 4,080 .... D8
Ruds Vedby 1,071 .... E7
Ry 2,699 .... C5
Ryomgård 1,000 .... D5
Saeby 5,430 .... D3
Sakskøbing 4,102 .... E8
Silkeborg 29,015 .... C5
Sindal 2,406 .... D3
Skaelskør 4,585 .... E7
Skærbaek 2,483 .... B7
Skagen 11,620 .... D2
Skals 960 .... D5
Skanderborg 11,344 .... C5
Skårup 1,216 .... D7
Skibby 1,549 .... E6
Skive 17,015 .... B4
Skjern 6,056 .... B6
Skorborg 935 .... C4
Skørping 1,675 .... C4
Slagelse 26,851 .... E7
Slangerup 3,036 .... E6
Snedsted 1,105 .... B4
Svinninge 1,797 .... E6
Tarm 3,150 .... B6
Tårnby 45,661 .... F6
Tåstrup 30,608 .... F6
Them 511 .... C5
Thisted 11,252 .... B4
Thyborøn 2,425 .... A4
Thyregod 1,001 .... B5
Tim 553 .... B5
Tinglev 1,531 .... C7
Tistrup 762 .... B6
Toftlund 2,147 .... C7
Tølløse 1,982 .... E7
Tommerup 1,439 .... D7
Tønder 7,469 .... B8
Tørring 1,537 .... C6
Tranebjerg 657 .... D6
Troense 771 .... D7
Trustrup 794 .... D5
Uldum 885 .... C6
Ulfborg 1,357 .... B5
Vamdrup 3,111 .... C7
Varde 11,615 .... B6
Vejen 6,213 .... C7
Vejle 43,976 .... B5
Vemb 989 .... B5
Vester Skerninge 603 ..... D7
Vestervig 747 .... B4
Viborg 27,441 .... C4
Viby 1,549 .... F6
Videbaek 2,248 .... B5
Vig 1,037 .... E6
Vildbjerg 1,500 .... B5
Vinderup 2,284 .... B5
Vojens 5,595 .... C7
Vorbasse 791 .... B6
Vordingborg 11,639 .... E7

Vraå 2.652 .... C3

OTHER FEATURES

Ærø (isl.) D8
Als (isl.) F6
Amager (isl.) F6
Anholt (isl.) E4
Åro (isl.) C7
Bågø (isl.) E9
Baltic (sea) F9
Bornholm (isl.) F9
Endelave (isl.) D6
Falster (isl.) E8
Fanø (isl.) B7
Fehmarn (isl.) E8
Fejø (isl.) E8
Femø (isl.) E8
Frisian, North (isls.) B7
Fyn (isl.) D7
Gelså (riv.) C7
Gudenaå (riv.) C5
Isefjord (fjord) E6
Jutland (pen.) C5
Jylland (Jutland)
  (pen.) C5
Kattegat (str.) E4
Læsø (isl.) D3
Langeland (isl.) D8
Lille Baelt (chan.) C7
Limfjorden (fjord) A4
Løgstør Bredning (fjord) C4
Lolland (isl.) E8
Møn (isl.) F8
Mors (isl.) B4
North (sea) B9
North Frisian (isls.) B7
Omø (isl.) E7
Øresund (sound) F6
Rømø (isl.) B7
Samsø (isl.) D6
Sejerø (isl.) E6
Sjaelland (isl.) E6
Skagens Odde (cape) D2
Skagerrak (str.) C2
Skaw, The (Skagens Odde)
  (cape) D2
Storaå (riv.) B5
Store Baelt (chan.) D6
Susaå (riv.) E7
The Skaw (Skagens Odde)
  (cape) D2
Tranebjerg (isl.) C6
Yding Skovhøj (mt.) C6

FAEROE ISLANDS

CITIES and TOWNS

Klaksvík 4,536 .... B2
Tórshavn (cap.) Faeroe
  Is. 11,618 .... A3

OTHER FEATURES

Faeroe (isls.) B2
Sandoy (isl.) B3
Streymoy (isl.) B3
Suduroy (isl.) B3

ICELAND

CITIES and TOWNS

Akranes 4,253 .... B1
Akureyri 10,755 .... C1
Hafnarfjordhur 9,696 .... B2
Húsavík 1,993 .... C1
Ísafjördhur 2,680 .... B1
Keflavík 5,663 .... B1
Kopavogur 11,165 .... B1
Nes (Neskaupstadhur) 1,552 .... D1
Neskaupstadhur 1,552 .... D1
Olafsfjördhur 1,086 .... C1
Reykjavík (cap.) 81,693 .... B1
Reykjavík* 96,521 70
Saudhárkrókur 1,600 .... B1
Seydhisfjördhur 884 .... C1
Siglufjördhur 2,161 .... C1
Vestmannaeyjar 5,186 .... B2

OTHER FEATURES

Bjargtangar (pt.) A1
Breidhafjördhur (fjord) B1
Faxaflói (bay) B1
Fontur (pt.) D1
Gerpir (cape) D1
Grímsey (isl.) C1
Hekla (vol.) B1
Horn (cape) B1
Húnaflói (bay) B1
Hvannadalshnúkur (mt.) C1
North (Horn) (cape) B1
Reykjanestá (cape) A2
Surtsey (isl.) B2
Thjorsá (riv.) C1
Vatnajökull (glac.) C1

*City and suburbs.

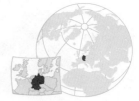

AREA 95,985 sq. mi. (248,601 sq. km.)
POPULATION 61,658,000
CAPITAL Bonn
LARGEST CITY Berlin (West)
HIGHEST POINT Zugspitze 9,718 ft. (2,962 m.)
MONETARY UNIT Deutsche mark
MAJOR LANGUAGE German
MAJOR RELIGIONS Protestantism, Roman Catholicism

AREA 41,768 sq. mi. (108,179 sq. km.)
POPULATION 16,737,000
CAPITAL Berlin (East)
LARGEST CITY Berlin (East)
HIGHEST POINT Fichtelberg 3,983 ft. (1,214 m.)
MONETARY UNIT East German mark
MAJOR LANGUAGE German
MAJOR RELIGIONS Protestantism, Roman Catholicism

WEST GERMANY

EAST GERMANY

Topography

```
0        50       100 MI.
0     50      100 KM.
```

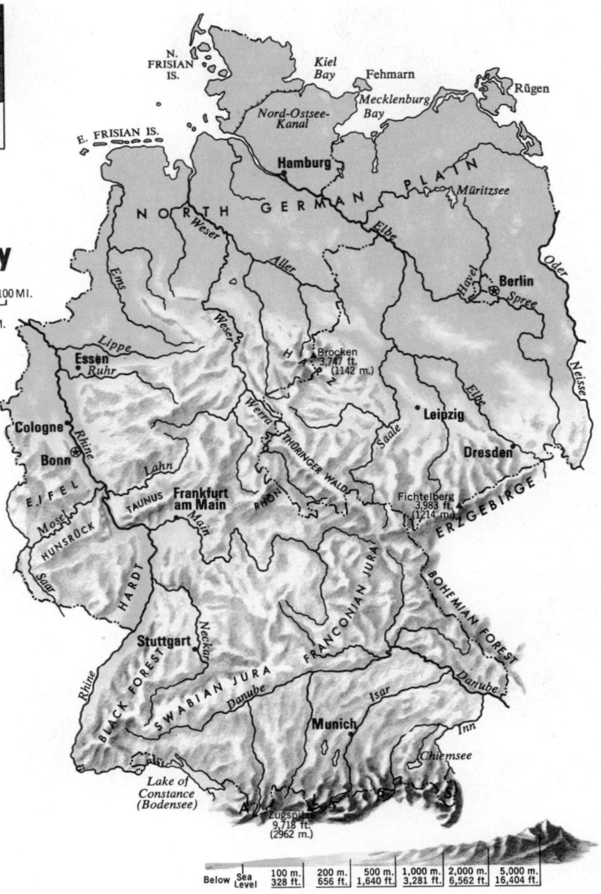

Below Sea Level	100 m. 328 ft.	200 m. 656 ft.	500 m. 1,640 ft.	1,000 m. 3,281 ft.	2,000 m. 6,562 ft.	5,000 m. 16,404 ft.

EAST GERMANY

DISTRICTS

Berlin 1,094,147 .... F4
Cottbus 872,242 .... F3
Dresden 1,845,459 .... E3
Erfurt 1,247,213 .... D3
Frankfurt 688,637 .... D3
Gera 738,847 .... D3
Halle 1,890,187 .... D3
Karl-Marx-Stadt 1,994,115 .... E3
Leipzig 1,457,817 .... E3
Magdeburg 1,297,881 .... D2
Neubrandenburg 628,686 .... E2
Potsdam 1,124,892 .... E2
Rostock 867,806 .... E1
Schwerin 592,334 .... D2
Suhl 550,497 .... D3

CITIES and TOWNS

Aken 11,742 .... D3
Altenburg 51,193 .... E3
Angermünde 11,786 .... E2
Anklam 19,099 .... E2
Annaberg-Buchholz 26,561 .... E3
Apolda 28,649 .... D3
Arnstadt 29,462 .... D3
Aschersleben 36,674 .... D3
Aue 32,622 .... E3
Auerbach 18,168 .... E3
Bad Doberan 12,541 .... D1
Bad Dürrenberg 15,192 .... E3
Bad Langensalza 166,282 .... D3
Bad Salzungen 17,277 .... C3
Barth 12,069 .... E1
Bautzen 45,851 .... F3
Bergen 13,244 .... E1
Berlin, East (cap.) 1,094,147 .... F4
Bernau bei Berlin 15,749 .... E2
Bernburg 44,428 .... D3
Bischofswerda 11,540 .... F3
Bitterfeld 27,062 .... E3
Blankenburg am Harz 18,784 .... D3
Boizenburg an der Elbe 12,428 .... D2
Borna 21,807 .... E3
Brandenburg 94,071 .... E2
Burg bei Magdeburg 29,027 .... D2
Calbe 15,976 .... D3
Chemnitz
 (Karl-Marx-Stadt) 303,811 .... E3
Coswig, Dresden 22,149 .... E3
Coswig, Halle 12,473 .... E3
Cottbus 94,293 .... F3
Crimmitschau 28,845 .... E3
Delitzsch 24,076 .... E3
Demmin 17,270 .... E2
Dessau 100,820 .... E3
Döbeln 27,624 .... E3
Dresden 507,692 .... E3
Ebersbach 12,694 .... F3
Eberswalde-Finow 47,141 .... E2
Eilenburg 22,245 .... E3
Eisenach 49,954 .... D3
Eisenberg 13,450 .... D3
Eisenhüttenstadt 46,455 .... F2
Eisleben 29,297 .... D3
Erfurt 202,979 .... D3
Falkensee 25,295 .... E2
Falkenstein 14,367 .... E3
Finsterwalde 22,466 .... F3
Forst 28,084 .... F3
Frankfurt an der Oder 70,817 .... F2
Freiberg 50,815 .... E3
Freital 46,061 .... E3
Friedland 15,960 .... E2
Fürstenwalde 31,065 .... F2
Gardelegen 12,987 .... D2
Genthin 13,916 .... E2
Gera 113,106 .... E3
Glauchau 30,927 .... E3
Görlitz 84,658 .... F3
Gotha 59,243 .... D3
Greifswald 53,940 .... E1
Greiz 37,612 .... E3
Grevesmühlen 12,005 .... D2
Grimma 17,100 .... E3
Grimmen 14,571 .... E1
Grossenhain 18,712 .... E3
Grossräschen 12,889 .... E3
Guben
 (Wilhelm-Pieck-Stadt) 32,731 .... F3
Güstrow 36,824 .... E2
Halberstadt 46,669 .... D3
Haldensleben 19,194 .... D2
Halle 241,425 .... D3
Halle-Neustadt 67,956 .... D3
Havelberg D2
Heidenau 21,315 .... E3
Heiligenstadt 13,930 .... D3
Hennigsdorf bei Berlin 24,853 .... E3
Hettstedt 20,291 .... D3
Hildburghausen 11,372 .... D3
Hoyerswerda 64,904 .... F3
Ilmenau 22,273 .... D3
Jena 99,431 .... D3
Johanngeorgenstadt 10,328 .... E3
Jüterbog 13,614 .... E3
Kamenz 18,221 .... F3
Karl-Marx-Stadt 303,811 .... E3
Kleinmachnow 14,059 .... E2
Klingenthal 13,614 .... E3
Königs Wusterhausen 11,825 .... E2
Köpenick 130,987 .... F4
Köthen 35,451 .... E3
Kühlungsborn D1
Lauchhammer 26,939 .... E3
Leipzig 570,972 .... E3
Lichtenberg 192,063 .... F4
Limbach-Oberfrohna 25,706 .... E3
Löbau 18,077 .... F3
Lübben 14,224 .... E3
Lübbenau 22,350 .... F3
Luckenwalde 28,544 .... E2
Ludwigslust 13,280 .... D2
Magdeburg 276,089 .... D2
Markkleeberg 22,380 .... E3
Meerane 25,037 .... E3
Meiningen 26,134 .... D3
Meissen 43,561 .... E3
Merseburg 54,269 .... D3
Meuselwitz 13,585 .... E3
Mittweida 19,259 .... E3
Mühlhausen
 (Thomas-Müntzer-Stadt) 44,106 .... D3
Nauen 11,940 .... E2
Naumburg 36,358 .... D3
Neubrandenburg 59,971 .... E2
Neuenhagen bei Berlin 12,603 .... F4
Neuruppin 24,888 .... E2
Neustrelitz 27,074 .... E2
Nordhausen 44,442 .... D3
Oelsnitz 15,084 .... E3
Oelsnitz im Erzgebirge 16,063 .... E3
Olbernhau 13,479 .... E3
Oranienburg 24,452 .... E2
Oschatz 18,974 .... E3
Oschersleben 17,377 .... D2
Pankow 136,527 .... F3
Parchim 22,927 .... D2
Pasewalk 15,099 .... F1
Peenemünde E1
Perleberg 15,029 .... E2
Pirna 49,771 .... E3
Plauen 80,353 .... E3
Pössneck 18,648 .... D3
Potsdam 117,236 .... E2
Prenzlau 22,738 .... E2
Pritzwalk 11,887 .... E2
Quedlinburg 29,796 .... D3
Radeberg 18,528 .... E3
Radebeul 38,383 .... E3
Rathenow 32,011 .... E2
Reichenbach 27,440 .... E3
Ribnitz-Damgarten 17 254 .... E1
Riesa 49,989 .... E3
Rosslau 16,520 .... E3
Rostock 210,167 .... E1
Rudolstadt 31,698 .... D3
Saalfeld 33,648 .... D3
Salzwedel 21,741 .... D2
Sangerhausen 32,721 .... D3
Sassnitz 13,857 .... E1
Schkeuditz 15,585 .... E3
Schmalkalden 15,017 .... D3
Schmölln 13,406 .... E3
Schneeberg 20,376 .... E3
Schönebeck 45,197 .... D2
Schwedt 45,729 .... F2
Schwerin 104,984 .... D2
Sebnitz 13,470 .... F3
Senftenberg 29,953 .... F3
Sömmerda 20,712 .... D3
Sondershausen 23,383 .... D3
Sonneberg 29,193 .... D3
Spremberg 22,862 .... F3
Stassfurt 26,225 .... D3
Stendal 39,647 .... D2
Stralsund 72,167 .... E1
Strausberg 21,334 .... F2
Suhl 36,642 .... D3
Tangermünde 12,898 .... D2
Teltow 16,171 .... E4
Templin 11,718 .... E2
Thale 17,248 .... D3
Thomas-Müntzer-Stadt 44,106 .... D3
Torgau 21,613 .... E3
Torgelow 14,320 .... F2
Treptow 127,448 .... F4
Ueckermünde 11,423 .... F2
Waldheim 11,925 .... E3
Walterschausen 13,893 .... D3
Waren 22,921 .... E2
Weida 11,816 .... E3
Weimar 63,144 .... D3
Weissenfels 43,191 .... D3
Weisswasser 28,451 .... F3
Weisswasser 25,910 .... F3
Werdau 22,249 .... E3
Wernigerode 34,658 .... D3
Wilhelm-Pieck-Stadt 32,731 .... F3
Wismar 56,765 .... D2
Wittenberg 51,364 .... E3
Wittenberge 32,907 .... D2
Wolgast 16,384 .... E1
Wurzen 20,501 .... E3
Zehdenick 12,651 .... E2
Zeitz 44,582 .... E3
Zella-Mehlis 16,301 .... D3
Zerbst 17,960 .... E3
Zeulenroda 13,452 .... D3
Zittau 42,296 .... F3
Zwickau 123,069 .... E3

OTHER FEATURES

Altmark (reg.) D2
Arkona (cape) E1
Baltic (sea) E1
Black Elster (riv.) E3
Brandenburg (reg.) E2
Elbe (riv.) D2
Elde (riv.) D2
Elster, Black (riv.) E3
Elster, White (riv.) E3
Erzgebirge (mts.) E3
Fichtelberg (mt.) E3
Harz (mts.) D3
Havel (riv.) F3
Lusatia (reg.) F3
Mecklenburg (bay) D1
Mecklenburg (reg.) E2
Mulde (riv.) E3
Müritzsee E2
Neisse (riv.) F3
Oder (riv.) F2
Peene (riv.) E2
Pomerania (reg.) E2
Pomerania (bay) F1
Rhön (mts.) D3
Rügen (isl.) E1
Saale (riv.) D3
Saxony (reg.) E3
Spree (riv.) F3
Spreewald (for.) F3
Thüringer Wald (for.) D3
Thuringia (reg.) D3
Ücker (riv.) F2
Unstrut (riv.) D3
Usedom (isl.) F1
Warnow (riv.) D1
Werra (riv.) D3
White, Elster (riv.) E3

WEST GERMANY

STATES

Baden-Württemberg 9,152,700 .... C4
Bavaria 10,810,400 .... D4
Berlin (West) (free
 city) 1,984,800 .... E4
Bremen 716,800 .... C2
Hamburg 1,717,400 .... C2
Hesse 5,549,800 .... C3
Lower Saxony 7,238,500 .... C2
North
 Rhine-Westphalia 17,129,600 .... B3
Rhineland-Palatinate 3,665,800 .... B4
Saarland 1,096,300 .... B4
Schleswig-Holstein 2,582,400 .... C1

CITIES and TOWNS

Aachen 242,453 .... B3
Aalen 64,735 .... D4
Ahaus 27,126 .... B2
Ahlen 54,214 .... B3
Ahrensburg 24,964 .... C2
Alfeld 24,273 .... C2
Alsdorf 47,473 .... B3
Alsfeld 18,091 .... C3
Altena 26,753 .... B3
Altona C2
Alzey 15,190 .... C4
Amberg 44,934 .... D4
Andernach 27,132 .... B3
Ansbach 39,117 .... D4
Arnsberg 80,287 .... C3
Arolsen 15,619 .... C3
Augsburg 249,943 .... D4
Aurich 34,194 .... B2
Backnang 29,614 .... C4
Bad Berleburg 20,415 .... C3
Bad Driburg 17,478 .... C3
Bad Dürkheim 15,133 .... C4
Bad Ems 10,487 .... B3
Baden-Baden 49,718 .... C4
Bad Gandersheim 11,614 .... D3
Bad Harzburg 25,786 .... D3
Bad Hersfeld 29,248 .... C3
Bad Homburg vor der
 Höhe 51,196 .... C3
Bad Honnef 20,903 .... B3
Bad Kissingen 22,279 .... C3
Bad Kreuznach 42,588 .... B4
Bad Lauterberg im Harz 14,715 .... D3
Bad Mergentheim 19,895 .... C4
Bad Münstereifel 14,340 .... B3
Bad Nauheim 25,916 .... C3
Bad Neuenahr-Ahrweiler 26,371 .... B3
Bad Oldesloe 19,640 .... D2
Bad Pyrmont 21,896 .... C3
Bad Reichenhall 13,048 .... E5
Bad Salzuflen 50,924 .... C2
Bad Segeberg 13,320 .... C2
Bad Tölz 12,458 .... D5
Bad Vilbel 25,012 .... C3
Bad Waldsee 14,296 .... C5
Bad Wildungen 15,418 .... C3
Bad Wimpfen 5,536 .... C4
Baiersbronn 14,845 .... C4
Bamberg 70,310 .... D4
Bamberg 74,236 .... D4
Barsinghausen 32,873 .... C2
Bassum 14,740 .... C2
Bayreuth 67,035 .... D4
Bayrischzell 1,586 .... E5
Bebra 15,740 .... C3
Bendorf 15,943 .... B3
Bensheim 32,653 .... C4

Bentheim 13,681 .... B2
Berchtesgaden 8,558 .... E5
Bergisch Gladbach 99,517 .... B3
Berleburg (Bad
 Berleburg) 20,415 .... C3
Berlin (West) 1,984,837 .... E4
Biberach an der Riss 28,891 .... C4
Bielefeld 316,058 .... C2
Bietigheim-Bissingen 34,042 .... C4
Bingen 24,541 .... B4
Birkenfeld 5,883 .... B4
Blaubeuren 11,652 .... C4
Böblingen 40,547 .... C4
Bocholt 65,460 .... B3
Bochum 414,842 .... B3
Bonn (cap.) 283,711 .... B3
Boppard 16,888 .... B3
Borghorst 17,238 .... B2
Borken 30,212 .... B3
Bornheim 32,447 .... B3
Brake 18,089 .... C2
Bottrop 101,495 .... B3
Bramsche 24,119 .... B2
Braunschweig
 (Brunswick) 268,519 .... D2
Breisach am Rhein 9,230 .... B4
Bremen 572,969 .... C2
Bremerhaven 143,836 .... C2
Bremervörde 17,565 .... C2
Bretten 22,140 .... C4
Brilon 24,595 .... C3
Bruchsal 38,929 .... C4
Brühl 44,305 .... B3
Brunsbüttel 11,451 .... C2
Brunswick 268,519 .... D2
Buchholz in der
 Nordheide 26,713 .... C2
Bückeburg 21,393 .... C2
Büdingen 16,845 .... C3
Bühl 21,596 .... C4
Bünde 40,021 .... C2
Büren 17,352 .... C3
Burg auf Fehmarn 5,874 .... D1
Burghausen 16,892 .... E4
Burgsteinfurt 31,367 .... B2
Butzbach 20,932 .... C3
Buxtehude 30,249 .... C2
Castrop-Rauxel 82,373 .... B3
Celle 74,347 .... D2
Cham 12,423 .... D4
Charlottenburg 201,732 .... E4
Clausthal-Zellerfeld 16,690 .... D3
Cloppenburg 19,757 .... B2
Coburg 46,242 .... D3
Coesfeld 30,617 .... B3
Cologne 1,013,771 .... B3
Crailsheim 24,506 .... C4
Cuxhaven 60,353 .... C2
Dachau 33,207 .... D4
Darlem E4
Darmstadt 137,018 .... C4
Deggendorf 25,188 .... E4
Delmenhorst 71,488 .... C2
Detmold 65,609 .... C3
Diepholz 14,201 .... C2
Dillenburg 14,068 .... C3
Dillingen 21,369 .... B4
Dillingen an der Donau 11,601 .... D4
Dingolfing 13,325 .... D4
Dinkelsbühl 10,034 .... D4
Donaueschingen 17,578 .... C5
Donauwörth 17,077 .... D4
Dorsten 65,718 .... B3
Dortmund 630,609 .... B3
Duderstadt 23,255 .... D3
Dudweiler 27,877 .... B4
Duisburg 591,635 .... B3
Dülmen 37,013 .... B3
Düren 29,310 .... B3
Düsseldorf 664,336 .... B3
Eberbach 15,834 .... C4
Ebingen 22,594 .... C4
Eckernförde 22,938 .... C1
Ehingen 21,600 .... C4
Eichstätt 13,080 .... D4
Einbeck 29,821 .... C3
Eiserfeld 22,346 .... C3

Ellwangen 21,994 .... D4
Eppingen 54,365 .... C4
Emden 53,509 .... B2
Emmendingen 24,722 .... B4
Emmerich 29,413 .... B3
Emsdetten 30,195 .... B2
Erlangen 100,671 .... D4
Eschwege 24,882 .... C3
Eschweiler 53,603 .... B3
Espelkamp 22,670 .... C2
Essen 677,568 .... B3
Esslingen am Neckar 95,298 .... C4
Ettlingen 35,159 .... C4
Euskirchen 43,558 .... B3
Eutin 17,701 .... D1
Fellbach 42,501 .... C4
Flensburg 93,213 .... C1
Forchheim 23,430 .... D4
Frankenberg-Eder 15,337 .... C3
Frankenthal 43,684 .... C4
Frankfurt am Main 636,157 .... C3
Frechen 41,453 .... B3
Freiburg im Breisgau 175,371 .... B5
Freising 31,524 .... D4
Freudenstadt 19,454 .... C4
Friedberg 21,918 .... C3
Friedrichshafen 51,544 .... C5
Fulda 58,979 .... C3
Fürstenfeldbruck 27,194 .... D4
Fürth 101,639 .... D4
Füssen 10,506 .... D5
Gaggenau 28,846 .... C4
Garbsen 56,837 .... C2
Garmisch-Partenkirchen 26,831 .... D5
Gatow E4
Geesthacht 24,745 .... D2
Geislingen an der
 Steige 28,693 .... C4
Geldern 24,082 .... B3
Gelnhausen 17,889 .... C3
Gelsenkirchen 322,584 .... B3
Georgsmarienhütte 30,259 .... B2
Geretsried 17,330 .... D5
Germersheim 12,041 .... C4
Gerolstein 6,857 .... B3
Gevelsberg 36,685 .... B3
Gifhorn 23,980 .... D2
Glückstadt 12,159 .... C2
Goch 28,213 .... B3

Göppingen 15,980 .... D4
Göppingen 54,365 .... C4
Goslar 53,957 .... D3
Göttingen 123,797 .... C3
Greven 27,479 .... B2
Grevenbroich 56,392 .... B3
Gronau 40,527 .... B2
Grünberg 18,548 .... C3
Gummersbach 49,316 .... B3
Günzburg 13,528 .... D4
Gunzenhausen 13,565 .... D4
Gütersloh 77,128 .... C3
Haan 29,224 .... B3
Haar 18,824 .... D4
Hagen 229,224 .... B3
Haltern 29,750 .... B3
Hamburg 1,717,383 .... C2
Hameln 61,066 .... C2
Hamm 172,210 .... B3
Hammelburg 12,350 .... C3
Hanau 88,548 .... C3
Hannover 552,955 .... C2
Harburg-Wilhelmsburg C2
Hassloch 17,752 .... C4
Haunstetten 21,810 .... D4
Hechingen 15,926 .... C4
Heide 21,918 .... C1
Heidelberg 129,368 .... C4
Heidenheim an der Brenz 49,943 .... D4
Heilbronn 113,177 .... C4
Helmstedt 28,095 .... D2
Hemer 32,639 .... B3
Herford 64,385 .... C2
Herne 190,561 .... B3
Hildesheim 106,890 .... C2
Hof 54,351 .... D3
Hofgeismar 13,380 .... C3
Holzminden 23,650 .... C3
Homburg 41,861 .... B4
Horn-Bad Meinberg 16,927 .... C3
Höxter 33,759 .... C3
Hückelhoven 34,865 .... B3
Hünfeld 13,873 .... C3
Hürth 51,692 .... B3
Husum 24,882 .... C1
Hüttental 39,561 .... C3
Idar-Oberstein 37,179 .... B4
Immenstadt im Allgäu 13,720 .... C5

Ingolstadt 88,500 .... D4
Iserlohn 96,174 .... B3
Isny im Allgäu 12,367 .... D5
Itzehoe 35,077 .... C2
Jever 12,096 .... B2
Jülich 31,564 .... B3
Kaiserslautern 100,886 .... B4
Karlsruhe 280,448 .... C4
Kassel 205,534 .... C3
Kaufbeuren 42,324 .... D5
Kehl 29,861 .... B4
Kelheim 11,996 .... D4
Kempten 56,944 .... D5
Kevelaer 20,971 .... B3
Kiel 262,164 .... C1
Kirchheim unter Teck 31,666 .... C4
Kitzingen 19,116 .... D4
Kleve 44,043 .... B3
Koblenz 118,394 .... B3
Köln (Cologne) 1,013,771 .... B3
Königswinter 34,586 .... B3
Konstanz 70,152 .... C5
Korbach 22,998 .... C3
Kornwestheim 27,771 .... C4
Krefeld 228,463 .... B3
Kreuztal 30,473 .... C3
Kronach 11,538 .... D3
Kulmbach 25,711 .... D3
Lage 31,724 .... C3
Lahnstein 19,725 .... B3
Lahr 35,570 .... B4
Landau in der Pfalz 37,661 .... C4
Landsberg am Lech 15,862 .... D4
Landshut 55,858 .... D4
Landstuhl 9,227 .... B4
Langen 31,724 .... C4
Langenhagen 47,092 .... C2
Lauenburg an der Elbe 11,077 .... D2
Lauf an der Pegnitz 19,443 .... D4
Lauingen 8,778 .... D4
Lauterbach 15,007 .... C3
Leer 32,785 .... B2
Lehrte 38,272 .... C2
Lemgo 39,660 .... C2
Lengerich 21,600 .... B2
Leutkirchen 165,947 .... D5
Lichtenfels 13,573 .... D3
Limburg an der Lahn 28,606 .... C3
Lindau 23,930 .... C5

(continued on following page)

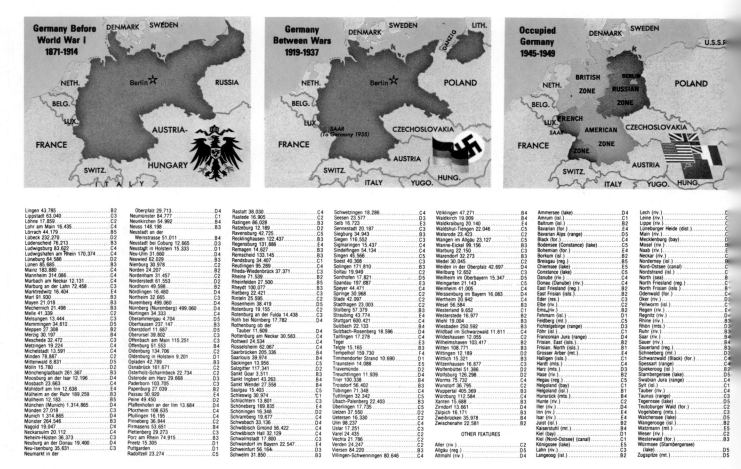

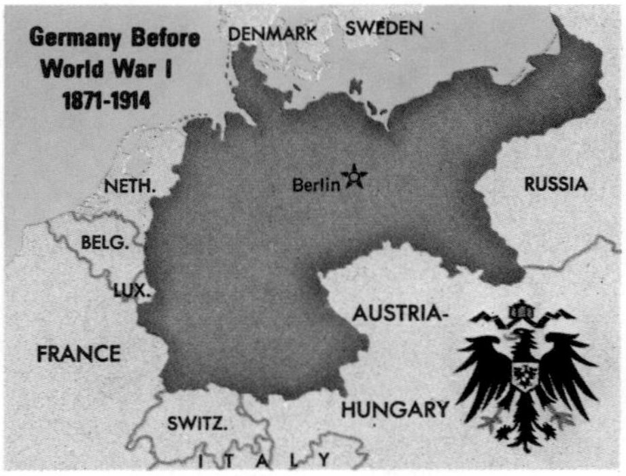
Germany Before World War I 1871-1914
DENMARK
SWEDEN
NETH.
Berlin
RUSSIA
BELG.
LUX.
AUSTRIA-
HUNGARY
FRANCE
SWITZ.
ITALY

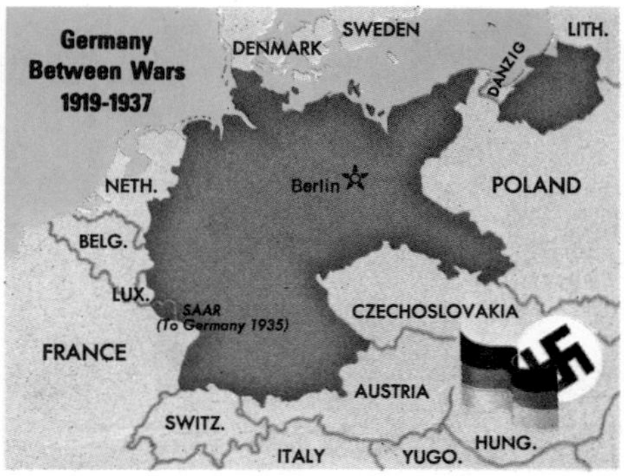
Germany Between Wars 1919-1937
DENMARK
SWEDEN
LITH.
DANZIG
NETH.
Berlin
POLAND
BELG.
LUX.
SAAR
(To Germany 1935)
CZECHOSLOVAKIA
FRANCE
AUSTRIA
SWITZ.
ITALY
YUGO.
HUNG.

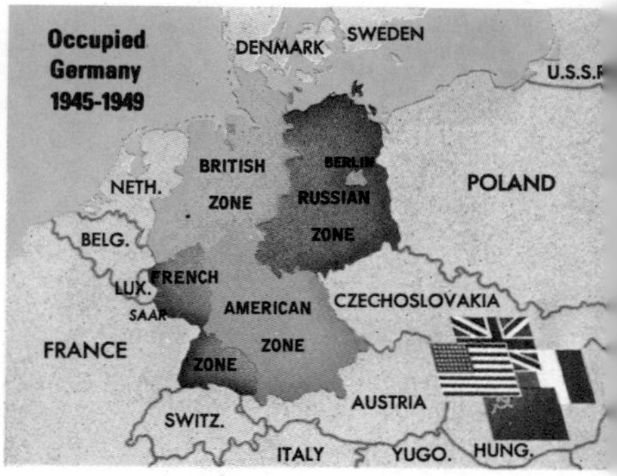
Occupied Germany 1945-1949
DENMARK
SWEDEN
BRITISH ZONE
BERLIN
RUSSIAN ZONE
POLAND
NETH.
BELG.
LUX.
FRENCH ZONE
SAAR
AMERICAN ZONE
CZECHOSLOVAKIA
FRANCE
AUSTRIA
SWITZ.
ITALY
YUGO.
HUNG.

Lingen 43,785 B2
Lippstadt 63,040 C3
Löhne 17,859 C2
Lohr am Main 16,435 C4
Lörrach 44,179 B5
Lübeck 232,270 D2
Lüdenscheid 76,213 B3
Ludwigsburg 83,622 C4
Ludwigshafen am Rhein 170,374 C4
Lüneburg 64,586 D2
Lünen 85,685 B3
Mainz 183,880 C4
Mannheim 314,086 C4
Marbach am Neckar 12,131 C4
Marburg an der Lahn 72,458 C3
Marktredwitz 16,404 E4
Marl 91,930 B3
Mayen 21,018 B3
Mechernich 21,498 B3
Melle 41,339 C2
Melsungen 13,444 C3
Memmingen 34,612 D5
Meppen 27,308 B2
Merzig 30,197 B4
Meschede 32,472 C3
Metzingen 19,224 C4
Michelstadt 13,591 C4
Minden 78,887 C2
Mittenwald 8,831 D5
Mölln 15,780 D2
Mönchengladbach 261,367 B3
Moosburg an der Isar 12,196 D4
Mosbach 23,663 C4
Mühldorf am Inn 12,638 E4
Mülheim an der Ruhr 189,259 B3
Müllheim 12,183 B5
München (Munich) 1,314,865 D4
Münden 27,018 C3
Munich 1,314,865 D4
Münster 264,546 B3
Nagold 19,047 C4
Neckarsulm 20,112 C4
Neheim-Hüsten 36,373 C3
Neuburg an der Donau 19,400 D4
Neu-Isenburg 35,631 C3
Neumarkt in der
Oberpfalz 29,713 D4
Neumünster 84,777 C1
Neunkirchen 54,992 B4
Neuss 148,198 B3
Neustadt an der
Weinstrasse 51,011 B4
Neustadt bei Coburg 12,665 D3
Neustadt in Holstein 15,333 D1
Neu-Ulm 31,660 D4
Neuwied 62,029 B3
Nienburg 30,978 C2
Norden 24,207 B2
Nordenham 31,457 C2
Norderstedt 61,553 D2
Nordhorn 49,598 B2
Nördlingen 16,480 D4
Northeim 32,665 C3
Nuremberg 499,060 D4
Nürnberg (Nuremberg) 499,060 D4
Nürtingen 34,333 C4
Oberammergau 4,704 D5
Oberhausen 237,147 B3
Oberstdorf 11,687 D5
Oberursel 39,802 C3
Offenbach am Main 115,251 C3
Offenburg 51,553 B4
Oldenburg 134,706 C2
Oldenburg in Holstein 9,201 D1
Opladen 42,789 B3
Osnabrück 161,671 C2
Osterholz-Scharmbeck 22,734 C2
Osterode am Harz 29,668 D3
Paderborn 103,705 C3
Papenburg 27,039 B2
Passau 50,920 E4
Peine 49,450 D2
Pfaffenhofen an der Ilm 13,684 D4
Pforzheim 108,635 C4
Pfullingen 16,195 C4
Pinneberg 36,844 C2
Pirmasens 53,651 B4
Plettenberg 29,273 C3
Porz am Rhein 74,915 B3
Preetz 15,305 D1
Puttgarden D1
Radolfzell 23,274 C5
Rastatt 38,030 C4
Rastede 16,905 C2
Ratingen 86,028 B3
Ratzeburg 12,189 D2
Ravensburg 42,725 C5
Recklinghausen 122,437 B3
Regensburg 131,886 E4
Remagen 14,627 B3
Remscheid 133,145 B3
Rendsburg 34,407 C1
Reutlingen 95,289 C4
Rheda-Wiedenbrück 37,371 C3
Rheine 71,539 B2
Rheinfelden 27,500 B5
Rheydt 100,077 B3
Rietberg 22,421 C3
Rinteln 25,595 C2
Rosenheim 38,419 D5
Rotenburg 19,155 C2
Rotenburg an der Fulda 14,438 C3
Roth bei Nürnberg 17,782 D4
Rothenburg ob der
Tauber 11,609 D4
Rottenburg am Neckar 30,583 C4
Rottweil 24,534 C4
Rüsselsheim 62,067 C4
Saarbrücken 205,336 B4
Saarlouis 39,974 B4
Säckingen 13,956 C5
Salzgitter 117,341 D2
Sankt Goar 3,511 B3
Sankt Ingbert 43,263 B4
Sankt Wendel 27,558 B4
Saulgau 15,403 C5
Schleswig 30,974 C1
Schlüchtern 13,801 C3
Schöneberg 169,835 E4
Schöningen 16,348 D2
Schramberg 19,677 C4
Schwabach 33,136 D4
Schwäbisch Gmünd 56,422 C4
Schwäbisch Hall 32,129 C4
Schwalmstadt 17,800 C3
Schwandorf im Bayern 22,547 E4
Schweinfurt 56,164 D3
Schwelm 31,850 B3
Schwetzingen 18,286 C4
Seesen 23,577 D3
Selb 16,723 E3
Sennestadt 20,187 C3
Siegburg 34,943 B3
Siegen 116,552 C3
Sigmaringen 15,437 C4
Sindelfingen 54,134 C4
Singen 45,566 C5
Soest 40,308 C3
Solingen 171,810 B3
Soltau 19,949 C2
Sonthofen 17,821 D5
Spandau 197,687 E3
Speyer 44,471 C4
Springe 30,968 C2
Stade 42,097 C2
Stadthagen 23,003 C2
Stolberg 57,379 B3
Straubing 43,774 E4
Stuttgart 600,421 C4
Sulzbach 22,133 B4
Sulzbach-Rosenberg 18,596 D4
Tailfingen 17,278 C4
Tegel E3
Telgte 15,165 B3
Tempelhof 159,730 F4
Timmendorfer Strand 10,690 D1
Traunstein 14,088 E5
Travemünde D2
Treuchtlingen 11,939 D4
Trier 100,338 B4
Troisdorf 56,402 B3
Tübingen 71,348 C4
Tuttlingen 32,342 C5
Übach-Palenberg 22,403 B3
Überlingen 17,735 C5
Uelzen 37,550 D2
Uetersen 16,330 C2
Ulm 98,237 C4
Uslar 17,251 C3
Varel 24,435 C2
Vechta 21,786 C2
Verden 24,247 C2
Viersen 84,220 B3
Villingen-Schwenningen 80,646 C4
Völklingen 47,271 B4
Waldkirch 19,009 B4
Waldkraiburg 20,140 E4
Waldshut-Tiengen 22,046 C5
Walsrode 23,423 C2
Wangen im Allgäu 23,127 C5
Wanne-Eickel 99,156 B3
Warburg 22,150 C3
Warendorf 32,273 B3
Wedel 30,045 C2
Weiden in der Oberpfalz 42,697 D4
Weilburg 12,652 C3
Weilheim im Oberbayern 15,347 D5
Weingarten 21,143 C5
Weinheim 41,005 C4
Weissenburg im Bayern 16,083 D4
Wertheim 20,942 C4
Wesel 56,584 B3
Westerland 9,652 C1
Westerstede 16,977 B2
Wiehl 19,004 B3
Wiesbaden 250,592 B3
Wildbad im Schwarzwald 11,611 C4
Wildeshausen 12,055 C2
Wilhelmshaven 103,417 B2
Witten 108,771 B3
Wittingen 12,189 D2
Wittlich 15,321 B3
Witzenhausen 16,877 C3
Wolfenbüttel 51,386 D2
Wolfsburg 126,298 D2
Worms 75,732 C4
Wunstorf 36,795 C2
Wuppertal 405,369 B3
Würzburg 112,584 C4
Xanten 15,688 B3
Zirndorf 13,661 D4
Zülpich 16,171 B3
Zweibrücken 35,978 B4
Zwischenahn 22,581 B2

OTHER FEATURES

Aller (riv.) C2
Allgäu (reg.) D5
Altmühl (riv.) D4
Ammersee (lake) D4
Amrum (isl.) C1
Baltrum (isl.) B2
Bavarian (for.) E4
Bavarian Alps (range) D5
Black (for.) C4
Bodensee (Constance) (lake) C5
Bohemian (for.) E4
Borkum (isl.) B2
Breisgau (reg.) B5
Chiemsee (lake) E5
Constance (lake) C5
Danube (riv.) C4
Donau (Danube) (riv.) C4
East Friesland (reg.) B2
East Frisian (isls.) B2
Eder (res.) C3
Elbe (riv.) C2
Ems (riv.) B2
Fehmarn (isl.) D1
Feldberg (mt.) C5
Fichtelgebirge (range) D3
Föhr (isl.) C1
Franconian Jura (range) D4
Frisian, East (isls.) B2
Frisian, North (isls.) B1
Grosser Arber (mt.) E4
Halligen (isls.) C1
Hardt (mts.) C4
Harz (mts.) D3
Hase (riv.) B2
Hegau (reg.) C5
Helgoland (bay) C1
Helgoland (isl.) B1
Hunsrück (mts.) B4
Hunte (riv.) C2
Iller (riv.) D4
Inn (riv.) E4
Isar (riv.) E4
Juist (isl.) B2
Kaiserstuhl (mt.) B4
Kiel (bay) D1
Kiel (Nord-Ostsee) (canal) C1
Königssee (lake) E5
Lahn (riv.) C3
Langeoog (isl.) B2
Lech (riv.) D
Leine (riv.) C
Lippe (riv.) C
Lüneburger Heide (dist.) C
Main (riv.) C
Mecklenburg (bay) D
Mosel (riv.) B
Naab (riv.) E
Neckar (riv.) C
Norderney (isl.) B
Nord-Ostsee (canal) C
Nordstrand (isl.) C
North (sea) B
North Friesland (reg.) C
North Frisian (isls.) B
Odenwald (for.) C
Oker (riv.) D
Pellworm (isl.) C
Regen (riv.) E
Regnitz (riv.) D
Rhine (riv.) B3
Rhön (mts.) D3
Ruhr (riv.) B3
Saar (riv.) B4
Sauer (riv.) B4
Sauerland (reg.) B3
Schneeberg (mt.) D3
Schwarzwald (Black) (for.) C4
Spessart (range) C4
Spiekeroog (isl.) B2
Starnbergersee (lake) D5
Swabian Jura (range) C4
Sylt (isl.) C1
Tauber (riv.) C4
Taunus (range) C3
Tegernsee (lake) D5
Teutoburger Wald (for.) C2
Vogelsberg (mts.) C3
Walchensee (lake) D5
Wangerooge (isl.) B2
Watzmann (mt.) E5
Weser (riv.) C2
Westerwald (for.) B3
Würmsee (Starnbergersee)
(lake) D5
Zugspitze (mt.) D5

Agriculture, Industry and Resources

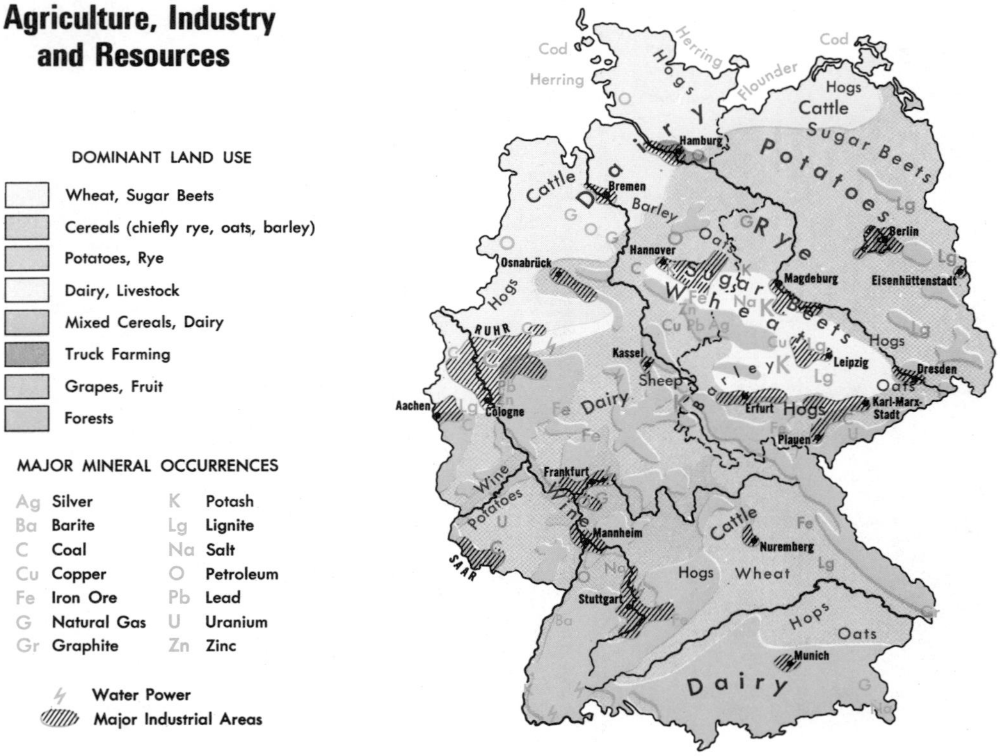
DOMINANT LAND USE
Wheat, Sugar Beets
Cereals (chiefly rye, oats, barley)
Potatoes, Rye
Dairy, Livestock
Mixed Cereals, Dairy
Truck Farming
Grapes, Fruit
Forests
MAJOR MINERAL OCCURRENCES
Ag Silver
Ba Barite
C Coal
Cu Copper
Fe Iron Ore
G Natural Gas
Gr Graphite
K Potash
Lg Lignite
Na Salt
O Petroleum
Pb Lead
U Uranium
Zn Zinc
Water Power
Major Industrial Areas
Cod
Herring
Flounder
Hogs
Cattle
Sugar Beets
Potatoes
Dairy
Hamburg
Bremen
Barley
Berlin
Rye
Oats
Hannover
Osnabrück
Magdeburg
Eisenhüttenstadt
Wheat
RUHR
Kassel
Leipzig
Dresden
Sheep
Erfurt
Karl-Marx-Stadt
Aachen
Cologne
Plauen
Frankfurt
Wine
Mannheim
Nuremberg
SAAR
Stuttgart
Hops
Munich

AREA 15,892 sq. mi. (41,160 sq. km.)
POPULATION 14,227,000
CAPITALS The Hague, Amsterdam
LARGEST CITY Amsterdam
HIGHEST POINT Vaalserberg 1,056 ft. (322 m.)
MONETARY UNIT guilder (florin)
MAJOR LANGUAGE Dutch
MAJOR RELIGIONS Protestantism, Roman Catholicism

AREA 11,781 sq. mi. (30,513 sq. km.)
POPULATION 9,855,110
CAPITAL Brussels
LARGEST CITY Brussels (greater)
HIGHEST POINT Botrange 2,277 ft. (694 m.)
MONETARY UNIT Belgian franc
MAJOR LANGUAGES French (Walloon), Flemish
MAJOR RELIGION Roman Catholicism

AREA 999 sq. mi. (2,587 sq. km.)
POPULATION 364,000
CAPITAL Luxembourg
LARGEST CITY Luxembourg
HIGHEST POINT Ardennes Plateau 1,825 ft. (556 m.)
MONETARY UNIT Luxembourg franc
MAJOR LANGUAGES Luxembourgeois (Letzeburgisch), French, German
MAJOR RELIGION Roman Catholicism

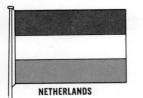

NETHERLANDS

BELGIUM

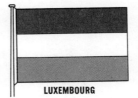

LUXEMBOURG

BELGIUM

PROVINCES

Antwerp 1,533,249	F6
Brabant 2,176,373	F7
East Flanders 1,310,117	D7
Hainaut 1,317,453	D8
Liège 1,008,905	H7
Limburg 652,547	G7
Luxembourg 217,310	G9
Namur 380,561	F8
West Flanders 1,054,429	B7

CITIES and TOWNS†

Aalst 46,659	D7
Aalter 9,173	C6
Aarlen (Arlon) 13,745	H9
Aarschot 12,474	F7
Aat (Ath) 11,842	D7
Aiken 8,677	D7
Alost (Aalst) 46,659	D7
Amay 7,617	G8
Andenne 8,091	G8
Anderlecht 103,796	B9

Anderlues 12,176	E8
Ans 9,173	H7
Antoing 3,426	C7
Antwerp 224,543	E6
Antwerp* 928,000	E6
Antwerpen (Antwerp) 224,543	E6
Ardooie 7,081	C7
Arendonk 9,919	H9
Arlon 13,745	H6
As 5,496	E7
Asse 6,583	E7
Ath 11,842	D7
Attert	H9
Aubange 3,761	H9
Audenarde (Oudenaarde) 26,615	D7
Auderghem 34,546	C9
Auvelais 8,287	F8
Aywaille 3,850	H8
Baerle-Hertog	F6
Balen 15,110	G6
Basse-Sambre	F8
Bastenaken (Bastogne) 6,816	H9
Bastogne 6,816	H9
Beernem	C6
Beloeil	D7
Berchem 50,241	F6

Berchem-Sainte-Agathe 19,087	B9
Bergen (Mons) 59,362	E8
Beringen	H8
Bertogne	G6
Bertrix 4,562	G9
Beveren 15,913	E6
Bilzen 7,178	G7
Binche 10,098	E8
Blankenberge 13,969	C6
Bocholt 6,497	H6
Boom 16,584	E6
Borgerhout 49,002	B7
Borgloon 3,412	G7
Borgworm (Waremme) 10,956	G7
Bourg-Léopold (Leopoldsburg) 9,593	G6
Boussu 11,474	D8
Braine-l'Alleud 18,531	E7
Braine-le-Comte 11,957	D7
Brecht	F6
Bredene 9,244	B6
Bree 10,389	H6
Bruges 117,220	C6
Brugge (Bruges) 117,220	C6
Brussels (cap.)* 1,054,970	C9
Bruxelles (Brussels)	

(cap.)* 1,054,970	C9
Cerfontaine	E8
Charleroi 23,689	E8
Charleroi* 458,000	E8
Chastre	F7
Châtelet 14,752	E8
Chièvres 3,283	D7
Chimay 3,288	E9
Chiny	G9
Ciney 7,536	G8
Comblain-au-Pont 3,582	G8
Comines 8,192	B7
Courcelles 17,015	E8
Courtrai (Kortrijk) 44,961	C7
Couvin 4,234	F8
Damme	C6
De Haan	C6
Deinze 16,711	C7
Denderleeuw 9,925	D7
Dendermonde 22,119	E6
De Panne 6,985	B6
Dessel 7,505	G6
Destelbergen	D6
Deurne 80,766	F6
Diest 10,799	F7
Diksmuide 6,669	B6

Dilbeek 15,108	B9
Dilsen	H6
Dinant 9,747	G8
Dison 8,466	H7
Dixmude (Diksmuide) 6,669	B6
Doische	F8
Doornik (Tournai) 32,794	C7
Dour 10,059	D8
Drogenbos 4,840	B10
Duffel 13,802	F6
Durbuy	H8
Ecaussinnes 6,630	E7
Edingen (Enghien) 4,115	D7
Eeklo 19,144	D6
Eghezée	F7
Eigenbrakel (Braine-l'Alleud) 18,531	E7
Ekeren 27,648	E6
Ellezelles 3,556	D7
Enghien 4,115	D7
Erezée	H7
Erquelinnes 4,471	E8
Esneux 6,183	H7
Essen 10,795	F6
Estampuis	C7
Etterbeek 51,030	B9

Eupen 14,879	J7
Evere 26,957	C9
Evergem 12,886	D6
Farciennes	E8
Fernelmont	F7
Ferrières	H8
Flemalle 8,135	H7
Fleurus 8,523	E8
Florennes 4,107	F8
Forest 55,135	B9
Fosses-La-Ville 3,972	F8
Frameries 11,224	D8
Froidchapelle	E8
Furnes (Veurne) 9,496	B6
Ganshoren 21,147	B9
Geel 29,346	F6
Geldenaken (Jodoigne) 4,132	F7
Gembloux-sur-Orneau 11,249	F7
Genk 57,913	H7
Gent (Ghent) 148,860	D6
Geraardsbergen 17,533	D7
Gerpinnes	F8
Ghent 148,860	D6
Ghent* 477,000	D6
Gistel	B6
Gooik	C7
Gouvy	H8
Grammont (Geraardsbergen) 17,533	D7
Grez-Doiceau	F7
Grimbergen	E7
Haacht 4,436	F7
Habay	H9
Hal (Halle) 20,017	E7
Halen 5,322	G7
Halle 20,017	E7
Hamme 17,559	E6
Hamoir	G8
Hamont-Achel 6,893	H6
Hannut (Hannut) 7,232	G7
Hannut 7,232	G7
Harelbeke 18,498	C7
Hasselt 39,663	G7
Hastière	F8
Heist-Knokke 27,582	C6
Heist-op-den-Berg 13,472	F6
Hensies	D8
Herentals 18,639	F6
Herne	E7
Herselt 7,412	F7
Herstal 29,600	H7
Herve 4,118	H7
Heuvelland	B7
Hoboken 33,693	E6
Hoei (Huy) 12,736	G7
Hoeselt 6,884	G7
Honnelles	D8
Hoogstraten 4,381	F6
Hotton	G8
Huy 12,736	G7
Ichtegem	B6
Ieper 20,825	B7
Ingelmunster 10,245	C7
Ittre	E7
Ixelles 86,450	C9
Izegem 22,928	C7
Jabbeke	C6
Jemappes 18,632	D8
Jette 40,013	B9
Jodoigne 4,132	F7
Kalmthout 12,724	F6
Kapellen 13,352	E6
Kasterlee	F6
Kinrooi	H6
Knokke-Heist 27,582	C6
Koekelare 7,807	B6
Koekelberg 17,570	B9
Koksijde	B6
Kontich 14,432	C6
Kortemark 5,904	C6
Kortrijk 44,961	C7
Kraainem 11,390	C9
La Louvière 23,310	E8
La Louvière* 113,259	E8
Lanaken 8,659	H7
Landen 5,740	G7
Langemark-Poelkapelle 5,457	B7
Lasne	F7
Lede 10,316	D7
Léglise	H9
Leopoldsburg 9,593	G6
Le Roeulx	E8
Lessen (Lessines) 8,906	D7
Lessines 8,906	D7
Leuven 30,623	F7
Leuze-en-Hainaut 7,185	C7
Libin	G9
Libramont-Chevigny 2,975	G9
Lichtervelde 7,459	C6
Liedekerke 10,482	D7
Liège 145,573	H7
Liège* 622,000	H7
Lier 28,416	F6
Lierre (Lier) 28,416	F6
Limburg 3,762	J7
Limburg (Limbourg) 3,762	J7
Linkebeek 4,265	C10

Linter	G7
Lochristi	D6
Lokeren 26,740	D6
Lommel 21,984	G6
Lontzen	H9
Looz (Borgloon) 3,412	G7
Lo-Reninge	B7
Louvain (Leuven) 30,623	F7
Luik (Liège) 145,573	H7
Lummen	G7
Maaseik 8,622	H6
Maasmechelen	H7
Machelen 7,057	C9
Maldegem 14,474	C6
Malines (Mechelen) 65,466	F6
Malmédy 6,464	J8
Manage	E7
Manhay	H8
Marche-en-Famenne 4,567	G8
Marchin 4,206	G8
Mechelen 65,466	F6
Meerhout 8,567	G6
Meise	D6
Menen 22,037	C7
Menin (Menen) 22,037	C7
Merchtem 8,998	E7
Merelbeke 13,837	D6
Merksem 39,768	E6
Merksplas 5,065	F6
Messancy 3,150	H9
Mettet 3,372	F8
Meulebeke 10,458	C7
Middelkerke	B6
Mol 28,823	G6
Molenbeek-Saint-Jean 68,411	B9
Momignies	E9
Mons 59,362	E8
Montigny-le-Tilleul	E8
Moorslede	B7
Mortsel 28,012	E6
Mouscron 37,311	C7
Namen (Namur) 32,269	F8
Namur 32,269	F8
Nassogne	G8
Nazareth	D7
Neerpelt 8,771	G6
Neufchâteau 2,670	G9
Nevele	C6
Nieuport (Nieuwpoort) 8,273	B6
Nieuwpoort 8,273	B6
Nijvel (Nivelles) 16,126	E7
Ninove 12,428	E7
Nivelles 16,126	E7
Ohey	G8
Onhaye	F8
Oostende (Ostend) 71,227	B6
Oostkamp 8,999	C6
Opwijk 9,699	E7
Ostend 71,227	B6
Oudenaarde 26,615	D7
Oudenburg	B6
Oud-Turnhout 9,245	F6
Oupeye	H7
Overijse 16,181	F7
Overpelt 10,470	G6
Paliseul	G9
Peer 7,201	G6
Péruwelz 7,878	D8
Philippeville 2,076	F8
Plombières	J8
†ont-à-Celles	E8
Poperinge 12,671	B7
Profondeville	F8
Putte 6,953	F6
Quaregnon 17,688	D8
Quévy	D8
Quiévrain 5,510	D8
Raeren 3,655	J8
Ravels	G6
Rebecq 3,744	E7
Renaix (Ronse) 25,056	D7
Rendeux	G8
Retie 6,619	G6
Rochefort 4,357	G8
Roeselare 40,428	C7
Ronse 25,056	D7
Roulers (Roeselare) 40,428	C7
Rouvroy	G9
Ruislede	C6
Sainte-Ode	H8
Saint-Georges-sur-Meuse 6,003	G7
Saint-Gilles 55,055	B9
Saint-Hubert 3,001	G8
Saint-Josse-ten-Noode 23,633	C9
Saint-Nicolas	E6
Saint-Trond (Sint-Truiden) 21,473	G7
Saint-Vith (Sankt Vith) 3,001	J8
Sankt Vith 3,001	J8
Schaerbeek 118,950	B9
Schoten 29,914	F6
Seraing 40,545	G7
's-Gravenbrakel (Braine-le-Comte) 11,957	D7
Sint-Laureins	D6
Sint-Niklaas 49,214	E6

(continued on following page)

Agriculture, Industry and Resources

DOMINANT LAND USE

- Dairy, Truck Farming
- Cash Crops, Livestock
- Mixed Cereals, Dairy
- Specialized Horticulture
- Grapes, Wine
- Forests
- Sand Dunes

MAJOR MINERAL OCCURRENCES

- C Coal
- Fe Iron Ore
- G Natural Gas
- Na Salt
- O Petroleum

///// Major Industrial Areas

(continued)

Sint-Pieters-Leeuw 16,856 .... B9
Sint-Truiden 21,473 .... G7
Soignies 12,006 .... D7
Somme-Leuze G8
Spa 9,504 .... H8
Sprimont H8
Staden 5,499 .... B7
Stavelot 4,723 .... H8
Steenokkerzeel 4,037 .... C9
Stekene E6
Stoumont H8
Tamise (Temse) 14,950 .... E6
Tellin G8
Temse 14,950 .... E6
Tenneville H8
Termonde (Dendermonde) 22,119 .... E6
Tessenderlo 11,778 .... G6
Theux 5,316 .... H8
Thuin 5,777 .... E8
Tielt 14,077 .... C7
Tielt-Winge 3,743 .... F7
Tienen 24,134 .... F7
Tintigny G9
Tirlemont (Tienen) 24,134 .... F7
Tongeren 20,136 .... G7
Tongres (Tongeren) 20,136 .... G7
Torhout 15,156 .... C6
Tournai 32,794 .... C7
Trois-Ponts H8
Tubeke (Tubize) 11,507 .... E7
Tubize 11,507 .... E7
Turnhout 38,007 .... F6
Uccle 78,909 .... B9
Ukkel (Uccle) 78,909 .... B9
Vaux-sur-Sûre H9
Verviers 33,587 .... H7
Veurne 9,496 .... B6
Vielsalm 3,587 .... H8
Vilvoorde 34,633 .... F7
Vilvorde (Vilvoorde) 34,633 .... F7
Viroinval F8
Virton 3,558 .... H9
Visé 6,880 .... H7
Vleteren B7
Vorst (Forest) 55,135 .... B9
Vresse-sur-Semois F9
Waarschoot 7,905 .... D6
Wachtebeke D6
Waregem 17,725 .... C7
Waremme 10,956 .... G7
Waterloo 17,764 .... E7
Watermaal-Bosvoorde
(Watermael-Boitsfort C9
Watermael-Boitsfort 25,123 .... C9
Waver (Wavre) 11,767 .... F7
Wavre 11,767 .... F7
Wellin G8
Wemmel 12,631 .... B9
Wervik 12,672 .... B7
Westerlo 14,173 .... F6
Westmalle F6
Wetteren 20,816 .... D7
Wezembeek-Oppem 10,899 .... D9
Wezet (Visé) 6,880 .... H7
Willebroek 15,726 .... E6
Wilrijk 43,485 .... E6
Wingene 7,140 .... C6
Woluwe-Saint-Lambert 47,360 .... C9
Woluwe-Saint-Pierre 40,884 .... C9
Ypres (Ieper) 20,825 .... B7
Zaventem 10,625 .... C9
Zedelgem C6
Zeebrugge C6
Zele 18,585 .... E6
Zelzate 12,785 .... D6
Zemst E7
Zinnik (Soignies) 12,006 .... D7
Zonhoven 13,484 .... G6
Zottegem 21,461 .... D7
Zuienkerke C6

OTHER FEATURES

Albert, (canal) F6
Ardennes, (for.) F9
Botrange, (mt.) J8
Dender, (riv.) D7
Deûle, (riv.) B7
Dyle, (riv.) F7
Hohe Venn, (plat.) H8
Lesse, (riv.) F8
Lys, (riv.) B7
Mark, (riv.) F6
Meuse, (riv.) F8
Nethe, (riv.) F6
North, (sea) D4
Ourthe, (riv.) G8
Rupel, (riv.) F7
Sambre, (riv.) D8
Schelde (Scheldt), (riv.) C7
Scheldt, (riv.) C7
Schnee Eifel, (plat.) J8
Semois, (riv.) G9
Senne, (riv.) E7
Vaalserberg, (mt.) J7
Vesdre, (riv.) H7
Weisserstein, (mt.) J8
Yser, (riv.) B7
Zitterwald, (plat.) J8

LUXEMBOURG

CITIES and TOWNS

Clervaux 916 .... J8
Diekirch† 5,059 .... J9
Differdange 9,287 .... H9
Dudelange† 14,615 .... J10
Echternach† 3,792 .... J9
Esch-sur-Alzette† 27,574 .... J9
Ettelbruck† 5,990 .... J9
Grevenmacher† 2,918 .... J9
Luxembourg (cap.) 78,272 .... J9
Mamer 3,123 .... H9
Mersch 1,869 .... J9
Pétange 6,234 .... H9
Remich† 12,138 .... J9
Viandent† 1,520 .... J9
Wiltz 1,601 .... H9

OTHER FEATURES

Alzette, (riv.) J9
Clerf, (riv.) J8
Eisling, (mts.) H9
Mosel, (riv.) J9
Our, (riv.) J9
Sauer, (riv.) J9

NETHERLANDS

PROVINCES

Drenthe 405,924 .... K3
Dronten 15,343 .... H4
Friesland 560,614 .... H2
Gelderland 1,639,997 .... H4
Groningen 540,062 .... K2
Lelystad H4
Limburg 1,051,620 .... H6
North Brabant 1,967,261 .... F5
North Holland 2,295,875 .... F3
Overijssel 985,569 .... J4
South Holland 3,048,648 .... E5
Utrecht 867,909 .... G4
Zeeland 332,286 .... D6
Zuidelijke
IJsselmeerpolders 14,231 .... H4

CITIES and TOWNS†

Aalsmeer 20,779 .... F4
Aalten 17,486 .... K5
Aardenburg 3,869 .... C6
Akkrum 5,044 .... H2
Alkmaar 65,199 .... F3
Almelo 62,634 .... K4
Alphen aan de Rijn 46,065 .... F4
Amersfoort 87,784 .... G4
Amstelveen 71,803 .... B5
Amsterdam (cap.) 751,156 .... B4
Amsterdam* 987,205 .... B4
Andijk 5,301 .... G3
Apeldoorn 134,055 .... H4
Apeldoorn* 237,231 .... H4
Appingedam 13,295 .... K2
Arnhem 126,051 .... H4
Arnhem* 281,126 .... H4
Assen 43,783 .... K3
Asten 12,295 .... H6
Axel 12,072 .... D6
Baarle-Nassau 5,583 .... F6
Baarn 25,045 .... G4
Barneveld 34,189 .... H4
Bath E6
Beilen 12,948 .... K3
Bemmel 14,218 .... H5
Bergeijk 9,009 .... G6
Bergen 14,306 .... F3
Bergen op Zoom 40,770 .... E5
Bergum 28,047 .... H2
Berkel 9,367 .... F5
Berkhout 5,167 .... F3
Beverwijk 37,551 .... F4
Blerick J6
Bloemendaal 17,940 .... E4
Blokzijl H3
Bodegraven 15,848 .... F4
Bolsward 9,934 .... H2
Borculo 9,859 .... J4
Borger 12,017 .... K3
Borne 18,216 .... K4
Boskoop 12,985 .... F4
Boxmeer 12,662 .... H5
Boxtel 22,465 .... G5
Breda 118,086 .... F5
Breda* 151,182 .... F5
Breezand F3
Breskens C6
Brielle 10,620 .... E5
Brouwershaven 3,263 .... D5
Brummen 20,460 .... J4
Brunssum 26,116 .... J7
Buiksloot C4
Bussum 37,848 .... G4
Capelle 35,696 .... F5
Coevorden 13,089 .... K3
Colijnsplaat D5
Culemborg 17,682 .... G5
Cuyk 15,366 .... H5
Dalen 5,084 .... K3
De Bilt 32,588 .... G4
Dedemsvaart 12,975 .... J3
De Koog F2
Delft 86,103 .... E4
Delfzijl 23,316 .... K2
Den Burg 12,132 .... F2
Denekamp 11,533 .... L4
Den Helder 60,421 .... F3
Deurne 26,539 .... H6
Deventer 65,557 .... J4
Didam 14,263 .... J5
De Wijk 4,631 .... J3
Diemen 13,704 .... C5
Dieren J4
Diever 3,162 .... J3
Dinxperlo 7,296 .... K5
Dirksland 6,495 .... E5
Doesburg 9,759 .... J4
Doetinchem 34,915 .... J5
Dokkum 11,203 .... H2
Domburg 3,874 .... C5
Dongen 19,219 .... F5
Doorn 11,966 .... G4
Dordrecht 101,840 .... F5
Dordrecht* 186,793 .... F5
Drachten 45,390 .... J2
Driebergen 17,022 .... G4
Dronten 16,544 .... H3
Druten 11,113 .... H5
Echt 17,035 .... H6
Edam-Volendam 21,507 .... G4
Ede 79,897 .... H4
Egmond aan Zee 5,734 .... E3
Eindhoven 192,562 .... G6
Eindhoven* 358,234 .... G6
Elburg 18,082 .... H4
Elst 16,686 .... H5
Emmeloord 34,467 .... H3
Emmen 86,700 .... K3
Enkhuizen 13,430 .... G3
Enschede 141,597 .... K4
Enschede* 239,015 .... K4
Epe 32,267 .... H4
Erica K3
Ermelo 23,835 .... H4
Etten-Leur 26,167 .... F5
Europoort E5
Flushing 43,806 .... C6
Franeker 11,415 .... H2
Geertruidenberg 6,185 .... F5
Geldermalsen 8,952 .... G5
Geldrop 25,879 .... H6
Geleen 35,910 .... H7
Gemert 15,267 .... H5
Gendringen 19,086 .... J5
Genemuiden 6,058 .... H3
Gennep 14,773 .... H5
Giessendam-Hardinxveld 15,523 .... F5
Giethoorn J3
Gilze 19,603 .... F5
Goes 28,505 .... D6
Goirle 13,447 .... G5
Goor 11,435 .... K4
Gorinchem 28,337 .... G5
Gorredijk J2
Gouda 56,403 .... F4
Graauw E6
Gramsbergen 5,866 .... K3
Grave 9,492 .... H5
Groenlo 8,693 .... K4
Groesbeek 18,094 .... H5
Groningen 163,357 .... K2
Groningen* 201,662 .... K2
Grouw 8,567 .... H2
Haamstede 4,575 .... D5
Haarlem 164,672 .... F4
Haarlem* 232,048 .... F4
Haarlemmermeer
(Hoofddorp) 72,046 .... F4
Hague, The (cap.) 479,369 .... E4
Hague, The* 682,452 .... E4
Halfweg 4,456 .... B4
Hallum H2
Hardenberg 28,489 .... J3
Harderwijk 28,508 .... H4
Hardinxveld-Giessendam 15,523 .... G5
Harlingen 14,533 .... G2
Hasselt 5,817 .... J3
Hattem 11,074 .... H4
Heemskert 31,728 .... F3
Heemstede 27,376 .... F4
Heer H7
Heerde 16,833 .... H4
Heerenveen 34,948 .... H3
Heerhugowaard 26,019 .... F3
Heerlen 71,500 .... J7
Heesch 8,659 .... G5
Heiloo 20,524 .... F3
Hellendoorn 32,068 .... J4
Hellevoetsluis 14,186 .... E5
Helmond 59,249 .... H6
Hengelo, Gelderland 8,015 .... J4
Hengelo, Overijssel 72,281 .... K4
Heusden 5,542 .... G5
Hillegom 17,489 .... E4
Hilvarenbeek 8,408 .... G6
Hilversum 94,041 .... G4
Hilversum* 110,498 .... G4
Hippolytushoef 7,847 .... G3
Hoek D6
Hoek van Holland (Hook of
Holland) D4
Hoensbroek 22,441 .... H7
Holijsloot C4
Hollum H2
Holwerd H2
Hoofddorp
(Haarlemmermeer) 72,046 .... F4
Hoogeveen 42,673 .... J3
Hoogezand-Sappemeer 33,860 .... K2
Hoogkarspel 5,112 .... G3
Hook of Holland D4
Hoorn 24,609 .... G3
Horst 16,242 .... H6
Huissen 11,049 .... H5
Huizen 25,603 .... G4
Hulst 17,283 .... E6
IJmuiden 6,633 .... E4
IJsselstein 15,450 .... F4
Ilpendam 3,310 .... C4
Joure 14,329 .... H3
Kampen 29,488 .... H3
Katwijk aan Zee 37,437 .... E4
Kerkdriel 7,584 .... G5
Kerkrade 46,609 .... J7
Kesteren 8,257 .... G5
Klazienaveen 9,520 .... L3
Kollum 11,887 .... J2
Krimpen aan den IJssel 26,396 .... F5
Landsmeer 8,082 .... C4
Laren 13,615 .... G4
Leek 15,713 .... J2
Leerdam 15,030 .... F5
Leeuwarden 85,074 .... H2
Leiden 99,891 .... E4
Leiden* 167,554 .... E4
Lelystad H3
Lemmer 10,013 .... H3
Lisse 19,182 .... F4
Lith 5,088 .... G5
Lochem 17,274 .... J4
Lonneker K4
Loon op Zand 18,000 .... G5
Losser 20,688 .... L4
Maarssen 18,346 .... F4
Maasbree 9,462 .... H6
Maassluis 28,170 .... E5
Maastricht 111,044 .... H7
Maastricht* 145,862 .... H7
Margraten 3,318 .... H7
Medemblik 6,432 .... G3
Meerssen 8,414 .... H7
Meppel 21,057 .... J3
Middelburg 36,372 .... C6
Middelharnis 14,245 .... E5
Middenmeer F3
Millingen aan den Rijn 5,035 .... J5
Moerdijk F5
Monnickendam 8,127 .... C4
Montfoort 3,442 .... G4
Muiden 6,567 .... G4
Muntendam 4,147 .... K2
Naaldwijk 24,117 .... E4
Naarden 17,319 .... G4
Nagele H3
Neede 10,842 .... K4
Nes 3,012 .... H2
Nieuwegein 22,648 .... G4
Nieuwe-Pekela 5,086 .... L2
Nieuwkoop 8,923 .... F4
Nieuw-Schoonebeek 7,556 .... L3
Nijkerk 21,615 .... H4
Nijmegen 148,493 .... H5
Nijmegen* 213,981 .... H5
Noordwijk 22,386 .... E4
Norg 6,041 .... J2
Numansdorp 7,072 .... E5
Nunspeet 21,340 .... H4
Odoorn 11,973 .... K3
Oisterwijk 16,263 .... G5
Oldenzaal 26,624 .... K4
Olst 8,480 .... J4
Ommen 16,136 .... J3
Onstwedde K2
Oostburg 18,461 .... C6
Oosterhout 40,077 .... F5
Ooosterwolde 5,845 .... J2
Oostmahorn J2
Oostzaan 6,336 .... C4
Ootmarsum 3,901 .... K4
Oss 45,643 .... H5
Otterlo H4
Oud-Beijerland 14,251 .... E5
Ouddorp 9,091 .... D5
Oudenbosch 11,061 .... E5
Oude-Pekela 8,067 .... K2
Oudewater 6,870 .... F4
Purmerend 32,614 .... F4
Putten 18,243 .... H4
Raalte 23,598 .... J4
Renkum 34,547 .... H5
Reusel 6,901 .... G6
Rheden 49,755 .... J4
Rhenen 16,893 .... H5
Ridderkerk 45,069 .... F5
Rijnsburg 10,698 .... F4
Rijssen 20,008 .... J4
Rijswijk 54,123 .... E4
Roden 16,437 .... J2
Roermond 36,695 .... J6
Roosendaal 51,685 .... F5
Rotterdam 614,767 .... E5
Rotterdam* 1,016,505 .... E5
Rutten H3
Ruurlo 7,557 .... J4
Sappemeer-Hoogezand 33,860 .... K2
Schagen 13,929 .... F3
Scheveningen E4
Schiedam 78,068 .... E5
Schijndel 18,658 .... G5
Schiphol B5
Schoonhoven 10,753 .... F5
's Gravendeel 7,242 .... E5
's Gravenhage (The Hague)
(cap.) 479,369 .... E4
's Gravenhage* 682,452 .... E4
's Gravenzande 15,833 .... E4
's Heerenberg 18,326 .... J5
's Hertogenbosch 86,184 .... G5
Simpelveld 6,783 .... H7
Sint Annaland E5
Sint Jacobiparochie H2
Sittard 34,278 .... H6
Sliedrecht 21,839 .... F5
Slochteren 13,447 .... K2
Sloten, North Holland B5
Sloterdijk B4
Sluis 3,140 .... C6
Smilde 8,247 .... K3
Sneek 28,123 .... H2
Soest 40,165 .... G4
Soesterberg G4
Stadskanaal 13,946 .... L3
Staphorst 11,608 .... J3
Steenbergen 12,930 .... E5
Steenwijk 20,721 .... J3
Stiens 7,711 .... H2
Swifterbant H3
Tegelen 18,386 .... J6
Ter Apel L3
Termunten 4,803 .... K2
Terneuzen 33,731 .... D6
Tholen 17,213 .... E5
Tiel 24,974 .... G5
Tilburg 151,513 .... G5
Tilburg* 212,510 .... G5
Twello 22,542 .... J4
Uden 28,946 .... H5
Uithoorn 22,812 .... F4
Uithuizen 5,194 .... K2
Ulrum 3,665 .... J2
Urk 9,397 .... H3
Utrecht 250,887 .... G4
Utrecht* 464,357 .... G4
Vaals 11,057 .... H7
Vaassen 7,225 .... H4
Valkenswaard 27,121 .... H6
Veendam 26,168 .... K2
Veenendaal 35,845 .... G4
Veenhuizen J2
Veere 4,252 .... D5
Veghel 22,308 .... H5
Veldhoven 30,030 .... G6
Velp J5
Velsen 64,035 .... F4
Venlo 61,659 .... J6
Venraij 31,526 .... H6
Vianen 12,821 .... G5
Vlaardingen 78,311 .... E5
Vlagtwedde 16,719 .... L3
Vlijmen 13,515 .... G5
Vlissingen (Flushing) 43,806 .... C6
Volendam-Edam 21,507 .... G4
Voorburg 45,209 .... E4
Voorst 22,542 .... J4
Vorden 7,276 .... J4
Vriezenveen 16,025 .... K4
Vught 23,261 .... G5
Waalre 13,219 .... G6
Waalwijk 25,977 .... F5
Wageningen 28,659 .... H5
Wamel 8,979 .... H5
Warmenhuizen 3,818 .... F3
Weert 36,850 .... H6
Weesp 17,037 .... C5
West-Terschelling 4,542 .... G2
Wierden 20,618 .... K4
Wijhe 6,888 .... J4
Wijk bij Duurstede 7,927 .... G5
Wijk en Aalburg 9,266 .... F5
Winschoten 19,760 .... L2
Winsum 5,007 .... K2
Winterswijk 27,413 .... K5
Woensdrecht 9,101 .... E6
Woerden 22,064 .... F4
Wolvega 22,812 .... J3
Workum 4,135 .... G3
Zaandam (Zaanstad) 124,795 .... B4
Zaandam (Zaanstad)* 137,371 .... B4
Zaltbommel 8,010 .... G5
Zandvoort 16,289 .... E4
Zeist 58,630 .... G4
Zevenaar 26,560 .... J5
Zevenbergen 13,307 .... E5
Zierikzee 8,816 .... D5
Zundert 12,444 .... F6
Zutphen 29,188 .... J4
Zwartsluis 4,391 .... H3
Zwijndrecht 38,271 .... E5
Zwolle 77,826 .... J3

OTHER FEATURES

Alkmaardermeer (lake) F3
Ameland (isl.) H2
Bergumermeer (lake) J2
Beulaker Wijde (lake) H3
Borndiep (chan.) H2
De Fluessen (lake) G3
De Honte (bay) D6
De Peel (reg.) H6
De Twente (reg.) K4
De Zaan (riv.) B4
Dollard (bay) L2
Dommel (riv.) H6
Duiveland (isl.) D5
Eastern Scheldt (est.) D5
Eems (riv.) K2
Eijerlandsche Gat (str.) F2
Flevoland Polders 35,618 .... G4
Friesche Gat (chan.) J2
Frisian, West (isls.) G2
Galgenberg (hill) H4
Goeree (isl.) D5
Grevelingen (str.) E5
Griend (isl.) G2
Groninger Wad (sound) J2
Groote IJ Polder B4
Haarlemmermeer Polder 72,046 .... B5
Haringvliet (str.) E5
Het IJ (est.) C4
Hoek van Holland (cape) D5
Hondsrug (hills) K3
Houtrak Polder A4
Hunse (riv.) K3
IJmeer (bay) C4
IJssel (riv.) J4
IJsselmeer (lake) G3
Lauwers (chan.) J1
Lauwers Zee (bay) J2
Lek (riv.) F5
Lemelerberg (hill) J4
Lower Rhine (riv.) H5
Maas (riv.) G5
Mark (riv.) F6
Marken (isl.) G4
Markerwaard Polder G3
Marsdiep (chan.) F3
North (sea) E3
North Beveland (isl.) D5
North East Polder 34,467 .... H3
North Holland (canal) C4
North Sea (canal) F4
Old Rhine (riv.) E4
Oostzaan Polder 6,336 .... B4
Orange (canal) K3
Overflakkee (isl.) E5
Pinke Gat (chan.) H2
Regge (riv.) K4
Rhine (riv.) J5
Roer (riv.) J6
Rottumeplaat (isl.) J1
Rottumeroog (isl.) J1
Schiermonnikoog (isl.) J1
Schouwen (isl.) D5
Slotermeer (lake) H3
Sneekermeer (lake) H2
South Beveland (isl.) D6
Terschelling (isl.) G2
Texel (isl.) F2
Tjeukemeer (lake) H3
Tjonger (riv.) J3
Vaalserberg (mt.) J7
Vecht (riv.) F4
Vechte (riv.) J3
Veersche Meer (lake) D5
Veluwe (reg.) H4
Vlieland (isl.) F2
Vliestroom (str.) G2
Voorne (isl.) D5
Waal (riv.) G5
Waddenzee (sound) G2
Walcheren (isl.) C5
Wester Eems (chan.) K1
Western Scheldt (De Honte)
(bay) D6
West Frisian (isls.) F2
Westgat (chan.) F3
Wieringermeer Polder 11,870 .... G3
Wilhelmina (canal) G6
Willems (canal) G5

*City and suburbs.
†Population of cities in Belgium & Netherlands are communes

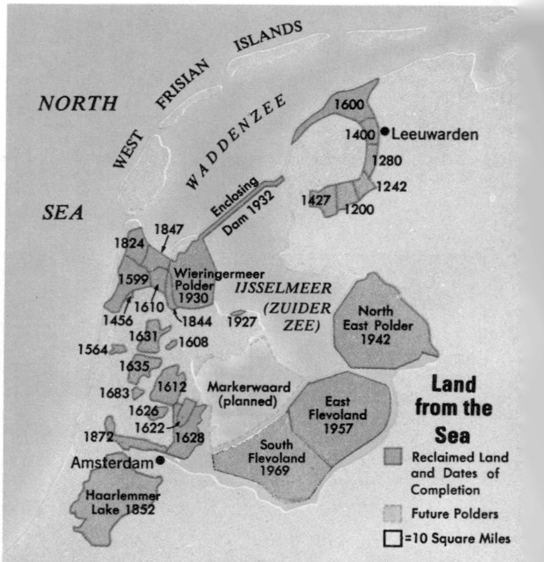
NORTH
SEA
WEST FRISIAN ISLANDS
WADDENZEE
Enclosing Dam 1932
1600
1400
Leeuwarden
1280
1242
1427
1200
1847
1824
Wieringermeer Polder 1930
1599
1610
1844
1927
IJSSELMEER (ZUIDER ZEE)
North East Polder 1942
1456
1631
1608
1564
1635
1683
1612
Markerwaard (planned)
1626
1622
East Flevoland 1957
1872
1628
Amsterdam
South Flevoland 1969
Haarlemmer Lake 1852
Land from the Sea
Reclaimed Land and Dates of Completion
Future Polders
=10 Square Miles
For centuries the Dutch have been renowned for the drainage of marshes and the construction of polders, i.e., arable land reclaimed from the sea. Future projects will convert much of the present IJsselmeer to agricultural land.

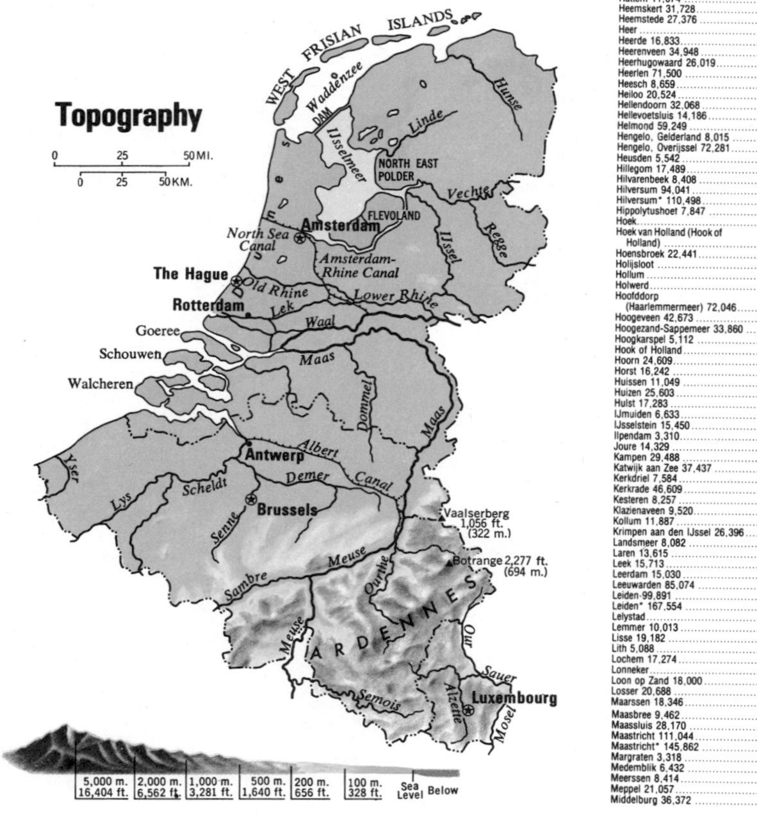
Topography
0 25 50 MI.
0 25 50 KM.
WEST FRISIAN ISLANDS
Waddenzee
DAM
IJsselmeer
NORTH EAST POLDER
Linde
Hunse
Vecht
FLEVOLAND
Regge
IJssel
North Sea Canal
Amsterdam
Amsterdam-Rhine Canal
The Hague
Old Rhine
Lower Rhine
Rotterdam
Lek
Waal
Goeree
Schouwen
Maas
Walcheren
Dommel
Maas
Albert
Yser
Antwerp
Lys
Scheldt
Demer
Canal
Brussels
Senne
Vaalserberg 1,056 ft. (322 m.)
Meuse
Botrange 2,277 ft. (694 m.)
Sambre
Ourthe
ARDENNES
Meuse
Our
Sauer
Semois
Alzette
Luxembourg
Mosel
5,000 m. 16,404 ft.
2,000 m. 6,562 ft.
1,000 m. 3,281 ft.
500 m. 1,640 ft.
200 m. 656 ft.
100 m. 328 ft.
Sea Level
Below

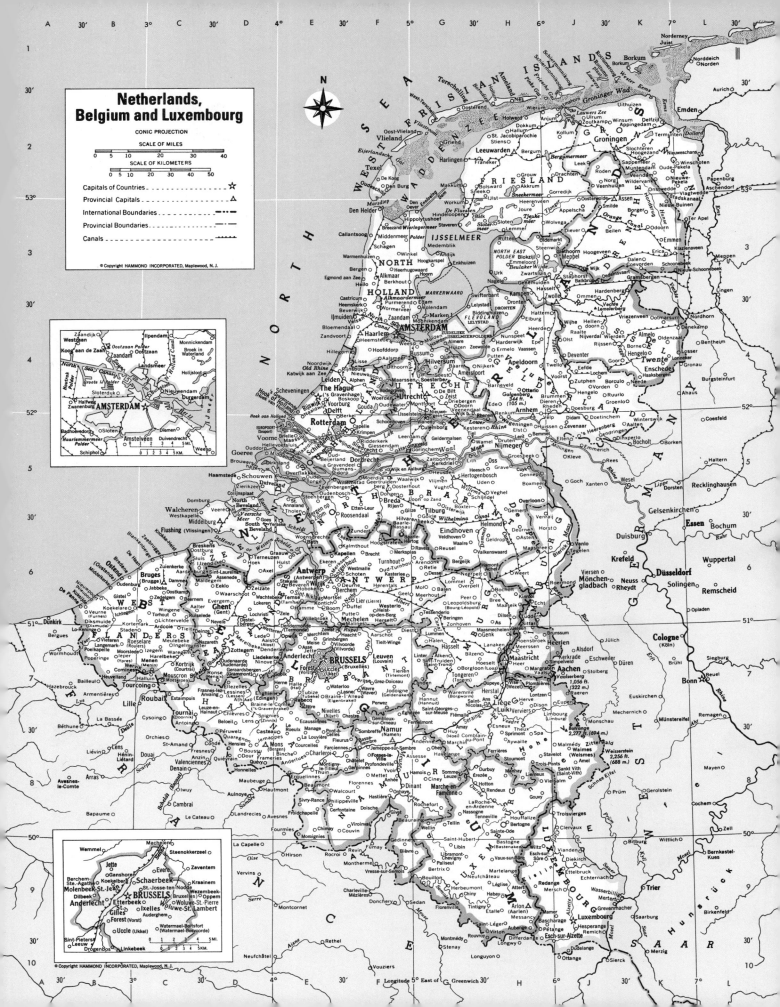

Netherlands, Belgium and Luxembourg

CONIC PROJECTION

SCALE OF MILES

0 5 10 20 30 40

SCALE OF KILOMETERS

0 5 10 20 30 40 50

Capitals of Countries .... ☆
Provincial Capitals .... △
International Boundaries .... — ·· —
Provincial Boundaries .... — · —
Canals .... = = =

® Copyright HAMMOND INCORPORATED, Maplewood, N.J.

DEPARTMENTS

…376,477 F4
…e 533,862 E3
…r 378,406 E4
…s-de-Haute-Provence 112,178 G5
…s-Maritimes 816,681 G6
…che 257,065 F5
…ennes 309,306 F3
…ge 137,857 D6
…e 284,823 E3
…e 272,366 E6
…yron 278,306 E5
…-Rhin 882,121 G3
…ort (terr.) 128,125 G4
…ches-du-Rhône 1,632,974 F6
…ados 560,967 C3
…tal 166,549 E5
…rente 337,064 D5
…rente-Maritime 497,859 C5
…r 316,350 E4
…rèze 240,363 D5
…se du Sud 128,634 B6
…e-d'Or 456,070 F4
…es-du-Nord 525,556 B3
…use 146,214 D4
…x-Sèvres 335,829 C4
…dogne 373,179 D5
…bs 471,082 G4
…me 361,847 F5
…sonne 923,063 E3
…re 422,952 D3
…re-et-Loir 335,151 D3
…istère 804,088 A3
…rd 494,575 F6
…rs 175,366 D6
…onde 1,061,480 C5
…ute-Corse 161,208 B6
…ute-Garonne 777,431 D6
…ute-Loire 205,491 E5
…ute-Marne 212,304 F3
…utes-Alpes 97,358 G5
…ute-Saône 222,254 G4
…ute-Savoie 447,795 G5
…utes-Pyrénées 227,222 D6
…ute-Vienne 352,149 D5
…ut-Rhin 635,209 G4
…uts-de-Seine 1,438,930 A2
…rault 648,202 E6
…e-et-Vilaine 702,199 C3
…dre 248,523 D4
…dre-et-Loire 478,601 D4
…ère 860,339 F5
…ra 238,856 F4
…ndes 288,323 C5
…ire 742,396 F5
…oire-Atlantique 934,499 C4
…oiret 490,189 E4
…oir-et-Cher 283,686 D4
…ot 150,778 D5
…ot-et-Garonne 292,616 D5
…ozère 74,825 E5
…aine-et-Loire 629,849 C4
…anche 451,662 C3
…arne 530,399 F3
…ayenne 261,789 C3
…eurthe-et-Moselle 722,588 G3
…euse 203,904 F3
…orbihan 563,588 B4
…oselle 1,006,373 G3
…ièvre 245,212 E4
…ord 2,510,738 E2
…ise 606,320 E3
…rne 293,523 C3
…aris (city) 2,299,830 B2
…as-de-Calais 1,403,035 E2
Puy-de-Dôme 580,033 E5
Pyrénées-Atlantiques 534,748 C6
Pyrénées-Orientales 299,506 E6
Rhône 1,429,647 F5
Saône-et-Loire 569,810 F4
Sarthe 490,385 D3
Savoie 305,118 G5
Seine-et-Marne 755,762 E3
Seine-Saint-Denis 1,322,127 C1
Somme 538,462 E3
Tarn 338,024 E6
Tarn-et-Garonne 183,314 D5
Val-de-Marne 1,215,713 C1
Val-d'Oise 840,885 E3
Var 626,093 G6
Vaucluse 390,446 F6
Vendée 450,641 C4
Vienne 357,366 D4
Vosges 397,957 G3
Yonne 299,851 E4
Yvelines 1,082,255 D3

CITIES and TOWNS

Abbeville 25,252 D2
Agde 9,856 E6
Agen 33,763 D5
Aix-en-Provence 91,665 F6
Aix-les-Bains 21,884 G5
Ajaccio 47,065 B7
Albert 11,746 E2
Albertville 16,630 G5
Albi 43,942 E6
Alençon 32,917 D3
Alès 33,315 E5
Ambérieu-en-Bugey 9,294 F5
Amboise 10,498 D4
Amiens 129,453 D3
Ancenis 6,689 C4
Angers 136,603 C4
Angoulême 46,293 D5
Annecy 53,058 G5
Annonay 19,234 F5
Antibes 44,226 G6
Antony 57,450 B2
Apt 9,735 F6
Arcachon 13,856 C5
Argentan 16,063 D3
Argenteuil 101,542 A1
Arles 37,337 F6
Armentières 23,850 E2
Arras 45,804 E2
Asnières-sur-Seine 75,328 A1
Aubagne 26,145 F6
Aubenas 11,967 F5
Aubervilliers 72,859 B1
Auch 18,767 D6
Audincourt 18,570 G4
Aulnay-sous-Bois 77,982 B1
Auray 10,006 B4
Aurignac 744 D6
Aurillac 29,458 E5
Autun 19,441 F4
Auxerre 36,039 E4
Auxonne 6,414 F4
Avallon 8,518 E4
Avignon 73,482 F6
Avion 22,860 E2
Avranches 10,128 C3
Ax-les-Thermes 1,456 D6
Bagnères-de-Bigorre 9,080 D6
Bagnolet 35,858 B2
Bagnols-sur-Cèze 13,111 F5
Barbizon 1,189 E3
Barcelonnette 2,523 G5
Barfleur 701 C3
Bar-le-Duc 19,188 F3
Bar-sur-Aube 7,227 F3
Bastia 45,387 B6
Bayeux 13,381 C3
Bayonne 41,281 C6
Beaucaire 10,189 F6
Beaune 16,386 F4
Beauvais 53,493 E3
Belfort 54,469 G4
Belley 6,612 F5
Berck 14,104 D2
Bergerac 25,488 D5
Bernay 9,928 D3
Besançon 119,803 G4
Béthune 26,208 E2
Béziers 79,213 E6
Biarritz 27,453 C6
Blois 49,134 D4
Bobigny 43,041 B1
Bogny-sur-Meuse 6,845 F3
Bolbec 12,347 D3
Bondy 48,285 B1
Bonneville 6,717 G4
Bordeaux 220,830 C5
Boulogne-Billancourt 103,527 A2
Boulogne-sur-Mer 48,309 D2
Bourg-en-Bresse 40,052 F4
Bourges 75,200 E4
Bourgoin-Jallieu 18,504 F5
Bressuire 9,778 C4
Brest 163,940 A3
Briançon 8,523 G5

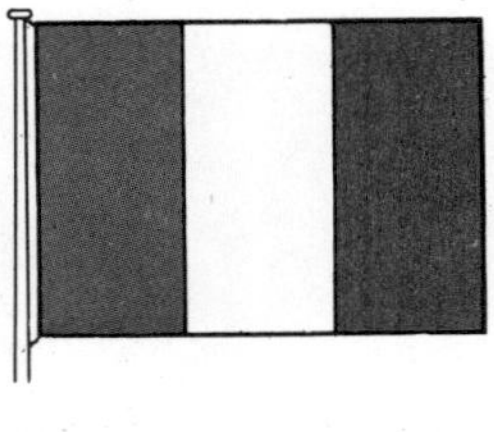

Brignoles 8,784 G6
Brioude 7,756 E5
Brive-la-Gaillarde 49,276 D5
Bruay-en-Artois 25,544 E2
Caen 116,987 C3
Cahors 19,288 D5
Calais 73,009 D2
Caluire-et-Cuire 43,024 F5
Cambrai 38,706 E2
Cannes 70,226 G6
Carcassonne 38,887 D6
Carmaux 11,970 E5
Carpentras 20,169 F5
Castelnaudary 8,947 E6
Castelsarrasin 6,562 D6
Castres 41,037 E6
Cavaillon 17,383 F6
Châlons-sur-Marne 50,870 F3
Chalon-sur-Saône 55,495 F4
Chambéry 52,286 F5
Chambord 166 D4
Chamonix-Mont-Blanc 6,246 G5
Champigny-sur-Marne 80,189 C2
Chantilly 10,517 E3
Charenton-le-Pont 20,383 B2
Charleville-Mézières 59,513 F3
Chartres 38,574 D3
Châteaubriant 12,417 C4
Château-du-Loir 5,598 D4
Châteaudun 14,634 D3
Château-Gontier 8,301 C4
Châteauroux 53,166 D4
Château-Thierry 13,379 E3
Châtellerault 33,811 D4
Châtillon 26,562 B2
Châtillon-sur-Seine 7,367 F4
Chatou 26,415 A1
Chaumont 26,568 F3
Chauny 14,324 E3
Chelles 24,192 C1
Cherbourg 31,333 C3
Chinon 5,378 D4
Choisy-le-Roi 38,629 B2
Cholet 49,887 C4
Clamart 52,881 A2
Clermont 7,834 E3
Clermont-Ferrand 153,379 E5
Clichy 47,731 B1
Cluny 4,335 F4
Cluses 12,713 G4
Cognac 21,567 C5
Colmar 58,585 G3
Colombes 83,241 A1
Commentry 8,074 E4
Commercy 6,918 F3
Compiègne 37,009 E3
Concarneau 15,096 A4
Cosne-Cours-sur-Loire 9,768 E4
Coudekerque-Branche 24,702 E2
Coulommiers 11,363 E3
Courbevoie 54,391 A1
Coutances 8,286 C3
Creil 31,893 E3
Crépy-en-Valois 10,661 E3
Créteil 58,665 B2
Cusset 13,672 E4
Dax 18,019 C6
Deauville 5,655 C3
Decazeville 9,318 E5
Decize 6,853 E4
Denain 26,096 E2
Dieppe 25,607 D3

AREA 210,038 sq. mi. (543,998 sq. km.)
POPULATION 53,788,000
CAPITAL Paris
LARGEST CITY Paris
HIGHEST POINT Mont Blanc 15,771 ft. (4,807 m.)
MONETARY UNIT franc
MAJOR LANGUAGE French
MAJOR RELIGION Roman Catholicism

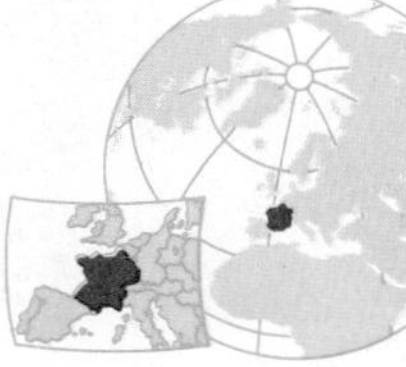

Topography

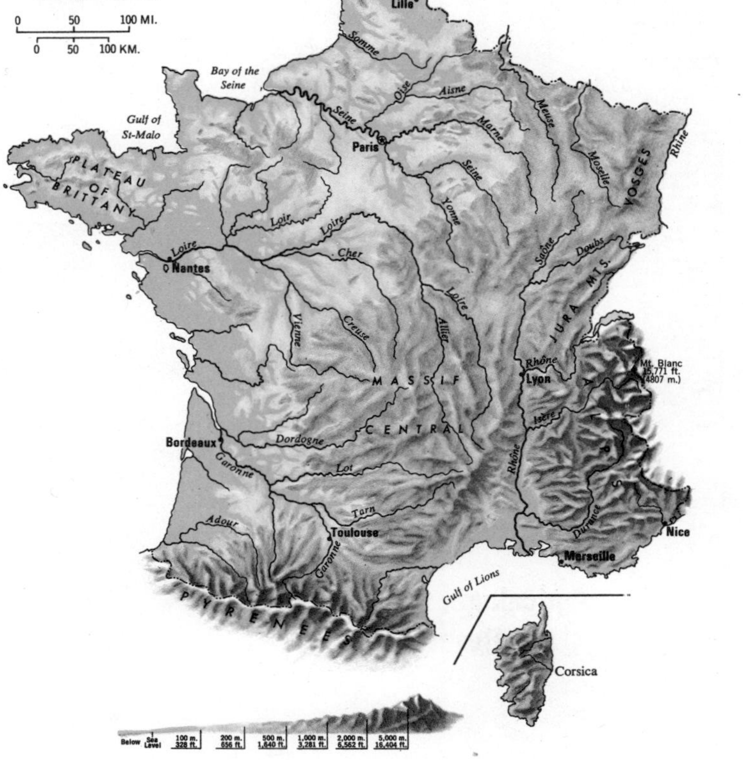
0 50 100 MI.
0 50 100 KM.
Lille
Somme
Bay of the Seine
Oise
Aisne
Meuse
Seine
Marne
Moselle
Rhine
VOSGES
Gulf of St-Malo
Paris
PLATEAU OF BRITTANY
Loire
Yonne
Saône
Doubs
Nantes
Cher
JURA MTS.
Vienne
Creuse
Allier
Rhône
Lyon
Mt. Blanc 15,771 ft. (4,807 m.)
MASSIF CENTRAL
Isère
Bordeaux
Dordogne
Garonne
Lot
Tarn
Adour
Toulouse
Durance
Nice
Marseille
PYRENEES
Gulf of Lions
Corsica
Below Sea Level
100 m. 328 ft.
200 m. 656 ft.
500 m. 1,640 ft.
1,000 m. 3,281 ft.
2,000 m. 6,562 ft.
5,000 m. 16,404 ft.

Historic Provinces

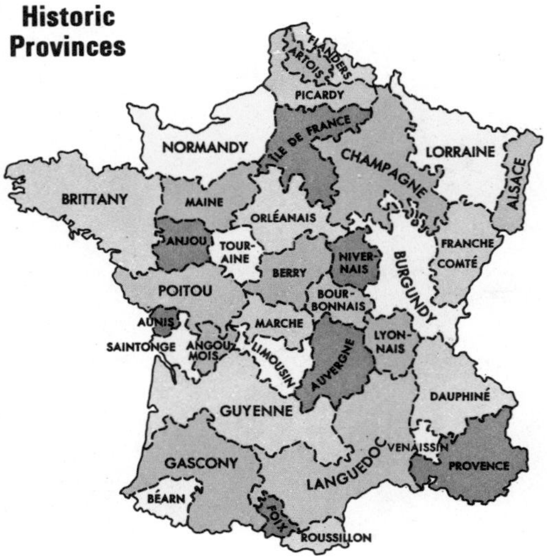
FLANDERS
ARTOIS
PICARDY
NORMANDY
ÎLE DE FRANCE
CHAMPAGNE
LORRAINE
ALSACE
BRITTANY
MAINE
ORLÉANAIS
ANJOU
TOUR-AINE
BERRY
NIVER-NAIS
BURGUNDY
FRANCHE COMTÉ
POITOU
BOUR-BONNAIS
AUNIS
SAINTONGE
ANGOU-MOIS
MARCHE
LIMOUSIN
AUVERGNE
LYON-NAIS
DAUPHINÉ
GUYENNE
GASCONY
LANGUEDOC
VENAISSIN
PROVENCE
BÉARN
FOIX
ROUSSILLON

A resident of the city of Caen thinks of himself as a Norman rather than as a citizen of the modern department of Calvados. In spite of the passing of nearly two centuries, the historic provinces which existed before 1790 command the local patriotism of most Frenchmen.

Digne 13,140 G5
Digoin 10,449 F4
Dijon 149,899 F4
Dinan 13,303 B3
Dinard 9,211 B3
Dôle 28,109 F4
Domrémy-la-Pucelle 190 F3
Douai 43,954 E2
Douarnenez 17,851 A3
Doullens 6,806 E2
Draguignan 19,653 G6
Drancy 64,258 B1
Dreux 31,503 D3
Dunkirk (Dunkerque) 78,171 E2
Elbeuf 18,642 D3
Épernay 29,286 E3
Épinal 39,000 G3
Épinay-sur-Seine 46,458 B1
Erstein 6,494 G3
Étampes 18,810 E3
Étaples 10,423 D2
Eu 8,349 D3
Évreux 46,181 D3
Évry 15,300 E3
Falaise 8,133 C3
Fécamp 20,835 D3
Figeac 8,675 D5
Firminy 23,776 F5
Flers 18,590 C3
Foix 9,569 D6
Fontainebleau 16,436 E3
Fontenay-le-Comte 12,301 C4
Fontenay-sous-Bois 46,200 C2
Forbach 24,812 G3
Fougères 26,260 C3
Fourmies 15,318 F2
Fréjus 27,805 G6
Gagny 36,714 C1
Gaillac 7,653 D6
Gap 24,962 G5
Gardanne 8,175 F6
Gennevillers 50,154 B1
Gentilly 16,843 B2
Gex 3,959 G4
Gien 13,817 E4
Gif 10,866 E3
Gisors 7,591 D3
Givet 7,787 F2
Givors 19,356 F5
Granville 12,869 C3
Grasse 24,260 G6
Graulhet 11,099 E6
Gray 8,718 F4
Grenoble 165,431 F5
Guebwiller 10,477 G4
Guéret 14,418 D4
Guingamp 9,269 B3
Guise 6,642 E3
Haguenau 23,023 G3
Harfleur 9,857 D3
Hautmont 19,130 F2
Hayange 8,479 F3
Hazebrouck 18,867 E2
Hendaye 9,404 C6
Hénin-Beaumont 26,296 E2
Hennebont 8,978 B4
Héricourt 8,481 G4
Hirson 11,909 F3
Honfleur 8,995 D3
Hyères 29,366 G6
Issoire 13,560 E5
Issoudun 15,065 D4
Issy-les-Moulineaux 47,355 A2
Istres 10,127 F6
Ivry-sur-Seine 62,804 B2
Joigny 10,825 E3
La Baule-Escoublac 13,854 B4
La Ciotat 29,290 F6
La Courneuve 37,917 B1
La Flèche 12,743 C4
La Grand-Combe 9,406 E5
L'Aigle 9,198 D3
Landerneau 13,983 B3
Langres 10,745 F4
Lannion 13,692 B3
Laon 27,420 E3
La Pallice C4
La Rochelle 72,936 C4
La Roche-sur-Yon 40,789 C4
La Seyne-sur-Mer 50,059 F6
Laval 50,734 C3
Lavelanet 9,278 E6
Le Blanc 7,431 D4
Le Blanc-Mesnil 49,062 B1
Le-Bourget 10,520 B1
Le Cateau 8,680 E2
Le Chesnay 24,590 A2
Le Creusot 31,643 F4
Le Havre 216,917 C3
Le Mans 150,289 C3
Lens 39,973 E2
Le Puy 24,793 F5
Les Andelys 7,524 D3
Les Sables-d'Olonne 17,157 B4
Le Teil 7,993 F5
Le Tréport 6,463 D2
Levallois-Perret 52,460 A1
Lézignan-Corbières 6,929 E6
Libourne 21,265 C5
Liévin 33,040 E2
Lille 171,010 E2
Limoges 136,059 D5
Limoux 9,595 E6
Lisieux 24,972 D3
Livry-Gargan 32,879 C1
Lodève 7,131 E6
Longwy 20,107 F3
Lons-le-Saunier 20,897 F4
Lorient 68,655 B4
Loudéac 7,173 B3
Loudun 7,060 D4
Lourdes 17,685 C6
Louviers 17,919 D3
Luçon 8,834 C4
Lunel 12,392 E6
Lunéville 22,438 G3
Lure 8,538 G4
Luxeuil-les-Bains 10,061 G4
Lyon 454,265 F5
Mâcon 39,130 F4
Maisons-Alfort 53,963 B2
Maisons-Laffitte 23,465 A1
Malakoff 34,100 A2
Manosque 17,256 G6
Mantes-la-Jolie 42,403 D3
Marmande 13,223 C5
Marseille 901,421 F6
Martigues 26,850 F6
Maubeuge 34,152 F2
Mayenne 11,278 C3
Mazamet 13,148 E6
Meaux 41,831 E3
Mehun-sur-Yèvre 6,533 E4
Melun 36,913 E3
Mende 10,040 E5
Menton 24,736 G6
Metz 110,939 G3
Meudon 31,294 A2
Millau 20,401 E5
Mimizan 6,826 C5
Mirecourt 7,160 G3
Moissac 7,403 D5
Montargis 18,021 E3
Montauban 35,344 D5
Montbard 7,477 F4
Montbéliard 29,968 G4
Montbrison 9,945 E5
Montceau-les-Mines 28,093 F4
Mont-de-Marsan 24,812 C6
Mont-Dore 2,074 E5
Montélimar 25,422 F5
Montfort 2,701 C3
Montigny-les-Metz 24,208 G3
Montluçon 56,337 E4
Montmédy 1,859 F3
Montpellier 178,136 E6
Montreuil, Seine-Saint-Denis 96,441 B2
Montrouge 40,189 B2
Mont-Saint-Michel 88 C3
Morlaix 15,919 B3
Morteau 6,515 G4
Moulins 25,856 E4
Moyeuvre-Grande 12,448 G3
Mulhouse 116,494 G4
Muret 13,041 D6
Nancy 106,906 G3
Nanterre 94,441 A1
Nantes 252,537 C4
Narbonne 36,525 E6
Nemours 11,159 E3
Neufchâteau 8,582 F3
Neuilly-sur-Seine 65,941 A1
Nevers 45,122 E4
Nice 331,002 G6
Nîmes 123,914 F6
Niort 59,297 C4
Nogent-le-Rotrou 12,284 D3
Noisy-le-Sec 37,674 B1
Noyon 13,784 E3
Oloron-Sainte-Marie 11,616 C6
Orange 19,847 F5
Orléans 88,503 D3
Orly 26,090 B2
Orthez 9,639 C6
Oullins 27,731 F5
Oyonnax 22,548 F4
Pamiers 12,906 D6
Pantin 42,651 B1
Paray-le-Monial 11,523 F4
Paris (cap.) 2,291,554 B2
Parthenay 12,549 C4
Pau 81,560 C6
Périgueux 34,779 D5
Péronne 8,358 E3
Perpignan 101,198 E6
Pessac 50,333 C5
Pézenas 6,768 E6
Pithiviers 9,976 E3
Poitiers 78,739 D4
Pont-à-Mousson 14,461 G3
Pontarlier 17,778 G4
Pontivy 9,478 B3
Pont-l'Abbe 6,618 A4
Pontoise 26,702 E3
Port-de-Bouc 20,448 F6
Port-Saint-Louis-du-Rhône 9,649 F6
Port-Vendres 5,448 E6
Privas 9,385 F5
Provins 12,281 E3
Puteau 35,366 A2
Quimper 50,856 A4
Quimperlé 9,783 B4
Rambouillet 18,446 D3
Redon 9,528 C4
Reims 177,320 E3
Remiremont 10,250 G3
Rennes 194,094 C3

(continued on following page)

MONACO
AREA 368 acres (149 hectares)
POPULATION 25,029

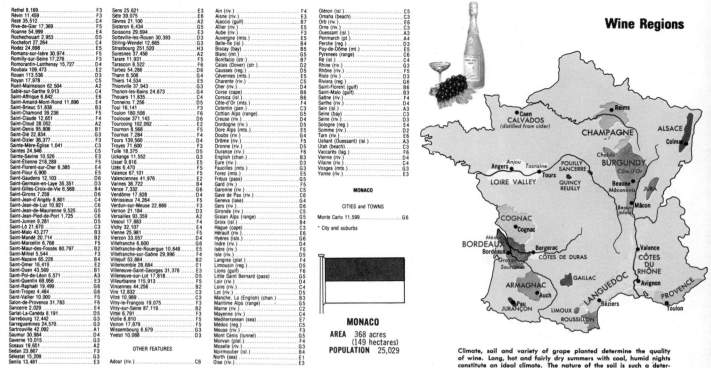

Wine Regions

Climate, soil and variety of grape planted determine the quality of wine. Long, hot and fairly dry summers with cool, humid nights constitute an ideal climate. The nature of the soil is such a determining influence that identical grapes planted in Bordeaux, Burgundy and Champagne, will yield wines of widely different types.

Agriculture, Industry and Resources

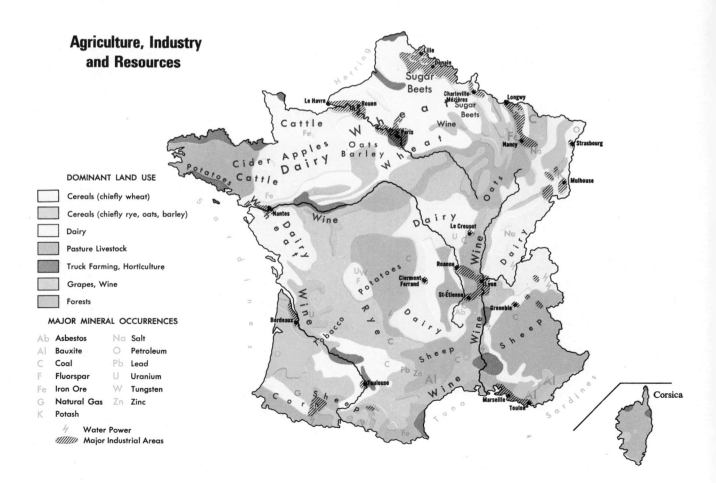

DOMINANT LAND USE
- Cereals (chiefly wheat)
- Cereals (chiefly rye, oats, barley)
- Dairy
- Pasture Livestock
- Truck Farming, Horticulture
- Grapes, Wine
- Forests

MAJOR MINERAL OCCURRENCES

Ab	Asbestos	Na	Salt
Al	Bauxite	O	Petroleum
C	Coal	Pb	Lead
F	Fluorspar	U	Uranium
Fe	Iron Ore	W	Tungsten
G	Natural Gas	Zn	Zinc
K	Potash		

⚡ Water Power
▨ Major Industrial Areas

ANDORRA

SPAIN

PORTUGAL

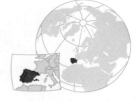

SPAIN
AREA 194,881 sq. mi. (504,742 sq. km.)
POPULATION 37,430,000
CAPITAL Madrid
LARGEST CITY Madrid
HIGHEST POINT Pico de Teide 12,172 ft. (3,710 m.) (Canary Is.); Mulhacén 11,411 ft. (3,478 m.) (mainland)
MONETARY UNIT peseta
MAJOR LANGUAGES Spanish, Catalan, Basque, Galician, Valencian
MAJOR RELIGION Roman Catholicism

ANDORRA
AREA 188 sq. mi. (487 sq. km.)
POPULATION 31,000
CAPITAL Andorra la Vella
MONETARY UNITS French franc, Spanish peseta
MAJOR LANGUAGE Catalan
MAJOR RELIGION Roman Catholicism

PORTUGAL
AREA 35,549 sq. mi. (92,072 sq. km.)
POPULATION 9,933,000
CAPITAL Lisbon
LARGEST CITY Lisbon
HIGHEST POINT Malhão da Estrela 6,532 ft. (1,991 m.)
MONETARY UNIT escudo
MAJOR LANGUAGE Portuguese
MAJOR RELIGION Roman Catholicism

GIBRALTAR
AREA 2.28 sq. mi. (5.91 sq. km.)
POPULATION 29,760
CAPITAL Gibraltar
MONETARY UNIT pound sterling
MAJOR LANGUAGES English, Spanish
MAJOR RELIGION Roman Catholicism

Agriculture, Industry and Resources

DOMINANT LAND USE

- Cereals (chiefly wheat)
- Livestock (chiefly sheep, goats)
- Mixed Cereals, Livestock
- Olives, Fruit
- Grapes, Fruit, Nuts, Mixed Cereals
- Forests
- Nonagricultural Land

MAJOR MINERAL OCCURRENCES

Ag	Silver	Na	Salt
C	Coal	O	Petroleum
Cu	Copper	Pb	Lead
Fe	Iron Ore	Py	Pyrites
G	Natural Gas	Sb	Antimony
Hg	Mercury	Sn	Tin
K	Potash	U	Uranium
Lg	Lignite	W	Tungsten
Mg	Magnesium	Zn	Zinc

⚡ Water Power

▨ Major Industrial Areas

(continued on following page)

Topography

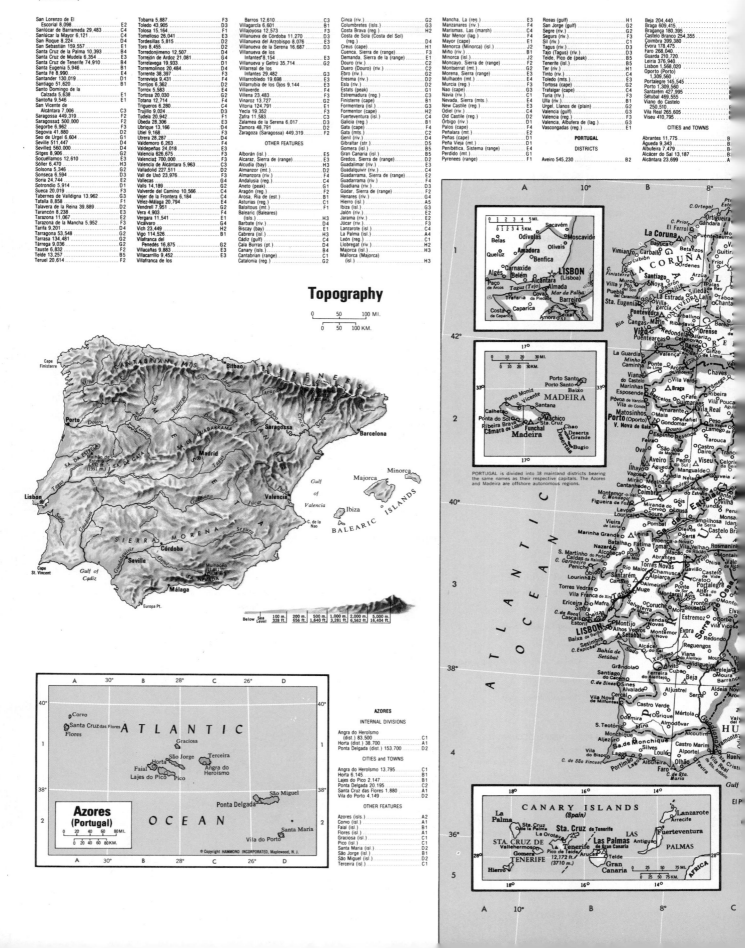

PORTUGAL is divided into 18 mainland districts bearing the same names as their respective capitals. The Azores and Madeira are offshore autonomous regions.

0 50 100 MI.
0 50 100 KM.

| Below Sea Level | 100 m. 328 ft. | 200 m. 656 ft. | 500 m. 1,640 ft. | 1,000 m. 3,281 ft. | 2,000 m. 6,562 ft. | 5,000 m. 16,404 ft. |

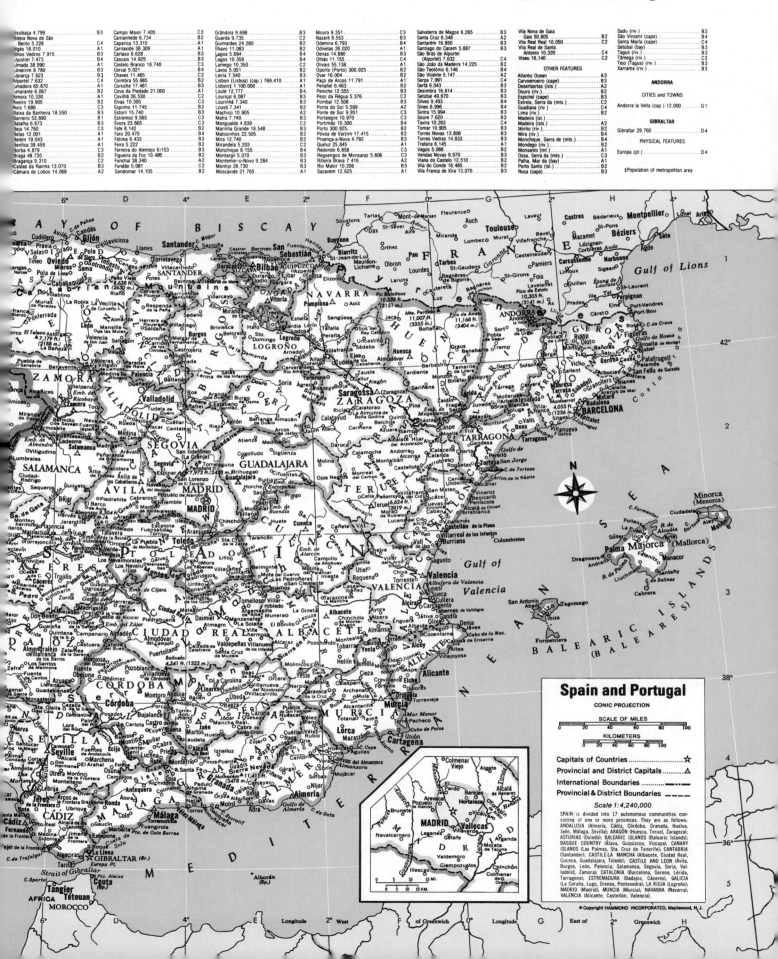

Spain and Portugal
CONIC PROJECTION
SCALE OF MILES
KILOMETERS

Capitals of Countries .... ☆
Provincial and District Capitals .... △
International Boundaries ---·---·---
Provincial & District Boundaries ------

Scale 1:4,240,000

SPAIN is divided into 17 autonomous communities consisting of one or more provinces. They are as follows: ANDALUSIA (Almería, Cádiz, Córdoba, Granada, Huelva, Jaén, Málaga, Sevilla); ARAGÓN (Huesca, Teruel, Zaragoza); ASTURIAS (Oviedo); BALEARIC ISLANDS (Balearic Islands); BASQUE COUNTRY (Álava, Guipúzcoa, Vizcaya); CANARY ISLANDS (Las Palmas, Sta. Cruz de Tenerife); CANTABRIA (Santander); CASTILE-LA MANCHA (Albacete, Ciudad Real, Cuenca, Guadalajara, Toledo); CASTILE AND LEON (Ávila, Burgos, León, Palencia, Salamanca, Segovia, Soria, Valladolid, Zamora); CATALONIA (Barcelona, Gerona, Lérida, Tarragona); ESTREMADURA (Badajoz, Cáceres); GALICIA (La Coruña, Lugo, Orense, Pontevedra); LA RIOJA (Logroño); MADRID (Madrid); MURCIA (Murcia); NAVARRA (Navarra); VALENCIA (Alicante, Castellón, Valencia).

Italy

CONIC PROJECTION

SCALE OF MILES

SCALE OF KILOMETERS

Capitals of Countries .... ☆
Regional Capitals .... ⊞
Provincial Capitals .... △
International Boundaries ━ ━ ━
Regional Boundaries ─ ─ ─

The regions are subdivided into provinces bearing
the same names as their respective capitals, except:

PROVINCE	CAPITAL
MASSA-CARRARA	Massa
PESARO-URBINO	Pesaro

Vatican City

SCALE

St. Peter's

Rome and Environs

© Copyright HAMMOND INCORPORATED, Maplewood, N.J.

Longitude 12° East of Greenwich 14° 16° 18°

VATICAN CITY

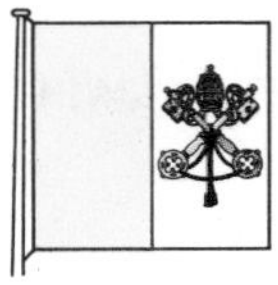

AREA 108.7 acres (44 hectares)
POPULATION 728

SAN MARINO

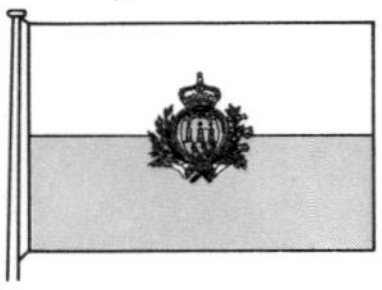

AREA 23.4 sq. mi. (60.6 sq. km.)
POPULATION 19,149

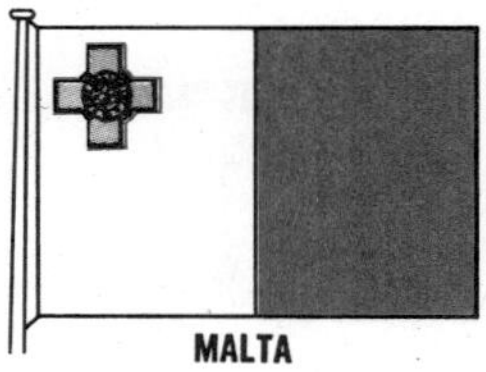

MALTA

AREA 122 sq. mi. (316 sq. km.)
POPULATION 343,970
CAPITAL Valletta
LARGEST CITY Sliema
HIGHEST POINT 787 ft. (240 m.)
MONETARY UNIT Maltese pound
MAJOR LANGUAGES Maltese, English
MAJOR RELIGION Roman Catholicism

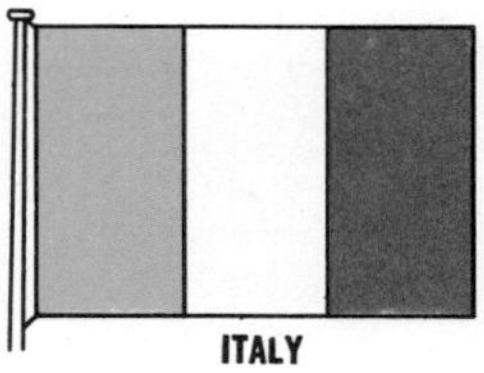

ITALY

AREA 116,303 sq. mi. (301,225 sq. km.)
POPULATION 57,140,000
CAPITAL Rome
LARGEST CITY Rome
HIGHEST POINT Dufourspitze (Mte. Rosa) 15,203 ft. (4,634 m.)
MONETARY UNIT lira
MAJOR LANGUAGE Italian
MAJOR RELIGION Roman Catholicism

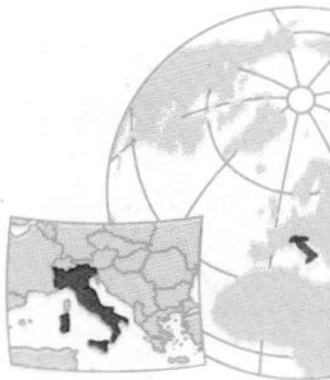

ITALY

REGIONS

zzi 1,166,664 D3
a 109,150 A2
a (Puglia) 3,582,787 F4
icata 603,064 F4
bria 1,988,051 F5
pania 5,059,348 E4
a-Romagna 3,846,755 C2
-Venezia Giulia 1,213,532 D1
m (Lazio) 4,689,482 D3
ria 1,853,578 B2
bardy 8,543,657 B2
che 1,359,907 D3
se 319,807 E4
mont 4,432,313 A2
inia 1,473,800 B4
y 4,680,715 D6
tino-Alto Adige 841,886 C1
cany 3,473,097 C3
bria 775,783 D3
eto 2,109,502 D3

PROVINCES

gento 454,045 D6
sandria 483,183 B2
ona 416,611 D3
a 109,150 A2
zo 306,340 C3
oli Piceno 340,758 D3
218,547 B2
lino 427,509 E4
1,351,288 F4
uno 221,155 D1
evento 286,499 E4
gamo 829,019 B2
ogna 918,844 C2
zano-Bozen 414,041 C1
scia 957,686 C2
Brindisi 366,027 G4
Cagliari 802,888 B5
Caltanissetta 282,069 D6
Campobasso 227,641 E4
Caserta 677,959 E4
Catania 938,273 E6
Catanzaro 718,069 F5
Chieti 351,567 E3
Como 720,463 B2
Cosenza 691,659 F5
Cremona 334,281 B2
Cuneo 540,504 A2
Enna 202,131 E6
Ferrara 383,639 C2
Florence 1,146,367 C3
Foggia 657,292 E4
Forlì 565,470 D2
Frosinone 422,630 D4
Genoa 1,087,973 B2
Gorizia 142,412 D2
Grosseto 216,315 C3
Imperia 225,127 B3
Isernia 92,166 E4
L'Aquila 293,066 D3
La Spezia 244,435 B2
Latina 376,238 D4
Lecce 696,503 G4
Leghorn 335,265 C3
Lucca 380,356 C3
Macerata 286,155 D3
Mantua 376,892 C2
Massa-Carrara 200,955 C2
Matera 194,629 F4
Messina 654,703 E5
Milan 3,903,685 B2
Modena 553,852 C2
Naples 2,709,929 E4
Novara 496,811 B2
Nuoro 273,021 B4
Padua 762,998 C2
Palermo 1,124,015 D5
Parma 395,497 C2
Pavia 526,389 B2
Perugia 552,936 D3
Pesaro e Urbino 316,383 D3
Pescara 264,981 E3
Piacenza 284,881 B2
Pisa 375,933 C3
Pistoia 254,335 C2
Pordenone 253,906 D2
Potenza 408,435 E4
Ragusa 255,047 E6
Ravenna 351,876 D2
Reggio di Calabria 578,323 E5
Reggio nell'Emilia 392,696 C2
Rieti 143,162 D3
Rome 3,490,377 F6
Rovigo 251,908 C2
Salerno 957,452 E4
Sassari 397,891 B4
Savona 296,043 B2
Siena 257,221 C3
Sondrio 169,149 B1
Syracuse 365,039 E6
Taranto 511,677 F4
Teramo 257,080 D3
Terni 222,847 D3
Trapani 405,393 D5
Trento 427,845 C1
Treviso 668,620 D2
Trieste 300,304 E2
Turin 2,287,016 A2
Udine 516,910 D1
Varese 725,823 B2
Venice 807,251 D2
Vercelli 406,252 B2
Verona 733,595 C2
Vicenza 677,884 C2
Viterbo 257,075 C3

CITIES and TOWNS

Acireale 34,081 E6
Acqui Terme 20,099 B2
Acri 8,150 F5
Adrano 31,988 E6
Adria 11,951 D2
Agira 11,262 E6
Agnone 3,965 E4
Agrigento 40,513 D6
Agropoli 9,413 E4
Alassio 13,512 A2
Alatri 5,710 D4
Alba 23,522 B2
Albano Laziale 15,561 F7
Albenga 13,397 B3
Albino 8,837 B2
Alcamo 41,448 D6
Alessandria 78,644 B2
Alghero 28,454 B4
Altamura 44,879 F4
Amalfi 4,205 E4
Amantea 6,132 E5
Amelia 4,331 D3
Ancona 88,427 D3
Andria 76,405 F4
Anguillara Sabazia 3,241 F6
Anzio 14,966 D4
Aosta 35,053 A2
Aprilia 18,412 D4
Aragona 11,213 D6
Arezzo 56,693 C3
Argenta 6,682 D2
Ariano Irpino 9,796 E4
Ariccia 7,287 F7
Artena 5,034 F7
Ascoli Piceno 43,041 D3
Assisi 4,630 D3
Asti 62,277 B2
Atessa 3,079 E3
Atri 4,686 D3
Augusta 32,501 E6
Avellino 44,750 E4
Aversa 46,536 E4
Avezzano 26,456 D3
Avigliano 5,400 E4
Avola 29,089 E6
Bagheria 32,465 D5
Barcellona Pozzo di Gotto 25,280 E5
Bari 339,110 F4
Barletta 75,116 F4
Bassano del Grappa 33,002 C2
Bellagio 3,258 B2
Belluno 22,180 D1
Benevento 48,523 E4
Bergamo 127,553 B2
Biancavilla 18,743 E6
Biella 46,453 B2
Bisceglie 45,014 F4
Bitonto 39,714 F4
Bitti 4,606 B4
Bologna 493,282 C2
Bolzano (Bolzen) 102,806 C1
Bondeno 7,451 C2
Bonorva 5,232 B4
Bordighera 8,994 A3
Borgo 4,013 C1
Borgomanero 16,655 B2
Bôrgo San Lorenzo 7,699 C2
Bosa 8,045 B4
Boves 3,896 A2
Bra 18,399 A2
Bracciano 7,681 C3
Brescia 189,092 C2
Bressanone 12,261 C1
Brindisi 76,612 G4
Bronte 17,823 E6
Brunico 5,175 D1
Budrio 5,635 C2
Busto Arsizio 72,400 B2
Cagli 4,356 D3
Cagliari 211,015 B5
Caltagirone 34,444 E6
Caltanissetta 52,838 D6
Camaiore 8,578 C3
Camerino 4,644 D3
Campobasso 35,551 E4
Campo Tures 1,325 C1
Canicattì 28,761 E6
Canosa di Puglia 30,263 E4
Cantù 28,617 B2
Capua 13,938 E4
Caravaggio 11,298 B2
Carbonia 23,031 B5
Carini 14,255 D5
Carloforte 6,671 B5
Carmagnola 16,469 A2
Carpi 41,789 C2
Carrara 56,236 C2
Casale Monferrato 35,156 B2
Casalmaggiore 6,374 C2
Cascina-Navacchio 28,263 C3
Caserta 51,621 E4
Cassano allo Ionio 9,661 F5
Cassino 14,747 D4
Castelfranco Veneto 16,042 D2
Castel Gandolfo 2,965 F7
Castellammare del Golfo 13,144 D5
Castellammare di Stabia 64,341 E4
Castel San Pietro Terme 6,985 C2
Castelvetrano 29,167 D6
Castiglion Fiorentino 3,797 C3
Castrovillari 15,207 F5
Catania 403,390 E6
Catanzaro 52,054 F5
Caulonia 3,402 F5
Cava de'Tirreni 33,868 E4
Cavarzere 7,917 D2
Cecina 19,415 C3
Cefalù 11,043 E5
Ceglie Messapico 17,512 F4
Celano 9,531 D3
Cerignola 44,648 E4
Cernobbio 8,026 B2
Cerveteri 5,239 E6
Cesano 2,883 F6
Cesena 49,915 D2
Cesenatico 12,805 D2
Chiari 12,017 C2
Chiavari 29,950 B2
Chieri 27,548 A2
Chieti 31,895 E3
Chioggia 24,044 D2
Chivasso 21,369 A2
Ciampino 36,728 F7
Cittadella 9,321 C2
Città di Castello 18,880 C3
Cittanova 11,045 F5
Cividale del Friuli 8,345 D1
Civitavecchia 41,305 C3
Clusone-Fiorine 6,428 C2
Codroipo 6,117 D2
Colle di Val d'Elsa 8,657 C3
Comacchio 10,437 D2
Comiso 24,508 E6
Como 73,257 B2
Conegliano 28,635 D2
Conversano 16,805 F4
Corato 38,163 F4
Cori 6,829 F7
Corigliano Calabro 14,518 F5
Corleone 11,057 D6
Correggio 11,415 C2
Cortina d'Ampezzo 7,285 D1
Cortona 3,482 C3
Cosenza 94,565 F5
Courmayeur 1,401 A2
Crema 26,061 B2
Cremona 75,988 B2
Crotone 44,081 F5
Cuneo 41,633 A2
Cuorgnè 6,752 A2
Desenzano del Garda 14,624 C2
Diano Marina 6,001 B3
Domodossola 18,562 A1
Dorgali 6,714 B4
Eboli 19,787 E4
Edolo 3,707 C1
Empoli 30,526 C3
Enna 27,351 E6
Este 12,992 C2
Fabriano 18,355 D3
Faenza 36,241 D2
Fano 31,238 D3
Fasano 21,247 F4
Favara 27,940 D6
Feltre 11,806 C1
Fermo 17,521 D3
Ferrandina 8,372 F4
Ferrara 97,507 C2
Fidenza 18,064 B2
Fiesole 3,772 C3
Finale Emilia 7,474 C2
Finale Ligure 11,461 B2
Firenze (Florence) 441,654 C3
Fiumicino 13,180 F7
Florence 441,654 C3
Floridia 16,562 E6
Foggia 136,436 E4
Foligno 26,887 D3
Fondi 16,472 D4
Forlì 83,303 D2
Formia 18,978 D4
Fossano 15,857 A2
Fossombrone 5,882 D3
Francavilla Fontana 30,347 F4
Frascati 14,217 F7
Frosinone 34,066 D4
Gaeta 21,973 D4
Galatina 22,137 G4
Galatone 13,880 F4
Gallarate 43,773 B2
Gallipoli 16,878 F4
Garessio 3,359 A2
Gela 66,845 E6
Gemona 6,863 D1
Genoa 787,011 B2
Genova (Genoa) 787,011 B2
Genzano di Roma 14,147 F7
Giarre 18,233 E6
Gioia del Colle 23,299 F4
Gioiosa Ionica 3,811 F5
Giovinazzo 17,768 F4
Giulianova 17,926 E3
Gorizia 35,912 D2
Gravina in Puglia 32,006 F4
Grosseto 48,309 C3
Grottaferrata 10,639 F7
Grottaglie 23,556 F4
Guardiagrele 4,122 E3
Guastalla 7,639 C2
Gubbio 12,371 D3
Guidonia 8,413 F6
Iglesias 24,472 B5
Imola 42,111 C2
Imperia 37,585 B3
Isernia 12,290 E4
Ivrea 26,530 B2
Jesi 33,011 D3
Ladispoli 6,625 E6
Lagonegro 5,613 E4
La Maddalena 10,405 B4
Lanciano 19,652 E3
Lanusei 5,508 B5
Lanuvio 2,970 F7
L'Aquila 36,233 D3
Larino 5,166 E4
La Spezia 121,254 B2
Latina 53,003 D4
Lauria 4,927 E4
Lavello 11,486 E4
Lecce 80,114 G4
Lecco 53,165 B2
Leghorn 170,369 C3
Legnago 15,534 C2
Lendinara 7,079 C2
Lentini 31,429 E6
Leonforte 16,317 E6
Lerici 5,407 B2
Licata 40,997 D6
Lido di Ostia 61,492 F7
Lido di Venezia 18,794 D2
Lipari 3,886 E5
Livigno 2,135 C1
Livorno (Leghorn) 170,369 C3
Lodi 42,489 B2
Lonigo 6,368 C2
Lucca 54,280 C3
Lucera 29,355 E4
Lugo 19,497 D2
Macerata 33,470 D3
Macomer 9,433 B4
Maglie 13,326 G4
Manduria 25,194 F4
Manfredonia 44,463 F4
Mantua 59,529 C2
Marino 12,135 F7
Marsala 34,150 D6
Marsciano 5,372 D3
Martina Franca 31,811 F4
Massa 56,591 C2
Massafra 22,610 F4
Massa Marittima 6,438 C3
Matera 43,026 F4
Mazara del Vallo 37,441 D6
Mazzarino 14,981 E6
Melfi 13,355 E4
Menfi 12,386 D6
Merano 30,951 C1
Mesagne 26,955 G4
Messina 203,937 E5
Mestre 184,818 D2
Milan 1,724,557 B2
Milazzo 18,576 E5
Minturno 2,428 D4
Mirandola 11,551 C2
Mira Taglio 10,194 D2
Mistretta 6,631 E6
Modena 149,029 C2
Modica 31,074 E6
Mola di Bari 23,778 F4
Molfetta 63,250 F4
Moncalieri 49,953 A2
Mondovì Breo 12,524 A2
Monfalcone 29,589 D2
Monopoli 29,776 F4
Monreale 19,348 D5
Monselice 9,047 C2
Montalto Uffugo 3,173 E5
Montebelluna 9,573 D2
Montefiascone 6,885 D3
Montepulciano 4,069 C3
Monterotondo 15,869 F6
Monte Sant'Angelo 17,756 F4
Montevarchi 16,849 C3
Monza 110,735 B2
Mortara 13,929 B2
Naples 1,214,775 E4
Nardò 24,142 F4
Narni 6,213 D3
Naro 13,171 D6
Nettuno 20,927 D4
Nicastro 27,206 F5
Nicosia 13,982 E6
Niscemi 23,925 E6
Nizza Monferrato 7,532 B2
Nocera Inferiore 44,415 E4
Noto 21,606 E6
Novara 92,634 B2
Novi Ligure 29,944 B2
Nuoro 30,551 B4
Olbia 20,998 B4
Oliena 7,030 B4
Orbetello 6,884 C3
Oristano 20,966 B5
Ortona 11,966 E3
Orvieto 8,813 D3
Osimo 12,034 D3
Ostia Antica 2,583 F7
Ostuni 27,241 F4
Otranto 3,707 G4
Ozieri 9,149 B4
Pachino 20,427 E6
Padua 210,950 C2
Palazzolo Acreide 8,981 E6
Palermo 556,374 D5
Palestrina 9,239 F7
Palma di Montechiaro 22,381 D6
Palmi 14,405 E5
Palombara Sabina 5,292 F6
Pantelleria 3,116 C6
Paola 11,330 E5
Parma 151,967 C2
Partanna 10,303 D6
Partinico 25,447 D6
Paterno 41,504 E6
Patti 7,500 E5
Pavia 80,639 B2
Pavullo nel Frignano 5,026 C2
Penne 5,889 D3
Pergine Valsugana 6,248 C1
Pergola 3,866 D3
Perugia 65,975 D3
Pesaro 72,104 D3
Pescara 125,391 E3
Pescia 9,918 C3
Piacenza 100,001 B2
Piazza Armerina 21,754 E6
Pietrasanta 6,620 B3
Pinerolo 33,935 A2
Piombino 35,641 C3
Piove di Sacco 7,035 C2
Pisa 91,156 C3
Pisticci 11,239 F4
Pistoia 55,403 C2
Poggibonsi 21,271 C3
Pomezia 11,915 F7
Pont Canavese 4,075 A2
Pontecorvo 5,986 D4
Pontinia 3,166 D4
Pontremoli 5,222 B2
Popoli 5,372 E3
Pordenone 43,230 D2
Portocivitanova 25,773 D3
Porto Empedocle 15,986 D6
Portoferraio 7,579 C3
Portofino 720 B2
Portogruaro 12,258 D2
Portomaggiore 6,343 C2
Porto Recanati 5,389 D3
Porto Torres 15,422 B4
Potenza 46,869 E4
Pozzallo 12,199 E6
Pozzuoli 53,546 D4
Prato 108,385 C3
Prima Porta 11,393 F6
Priverno 9,950 D4
Putignano 19,290 F4
Quartu Sant'Elena 29,715 B5
Ragusa 55,751 E6
Rapallo 22,272 B2
Ravenna 75,153 D2
Recanati 10,176 D3
Reggio di Calabria 110,291 E5
Reggio nell'Emilia 102,337 C2
Rho 39,206 B2
Riesi 15,855 E6
Rieti 26,775 D3
Rimini 101,579 D2
Rionero in Vulture 11,230 E4
Riva del Garda 8,513 C2
Roccastrada 2,629 C3
Rome (cap.) 2,535,018 F6
Ronciglione 5,900 C3
Rossano 12,119 F5
Rovereto 26,827 C2
Rovigo 31,124 C2
Ruvo di Puglia 23,133 F4

(continued on following page)

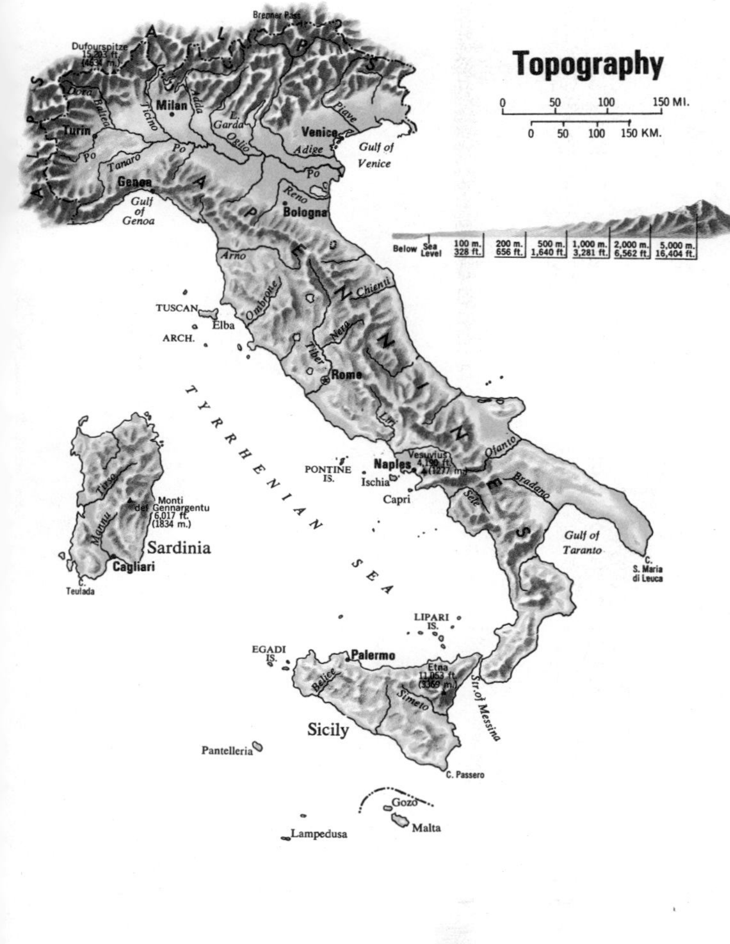

Topography
0 50 100 150 MI.
0 50 100 150 KM.
Below Sea Level
100 m. 328 ft.
200 m. 656 ft.
500 m. 1,640 ft.
1,000 m. 3,281 ft.
2,000 m. 6,562 ft.
5,000 m. 16,404 ft.
Brenner Pass
Dufourspitze 15,203 ft. (4634 m.)
Milan
Turin
Venice
Gulf of Venice
Genoa
Gulf of Genoa
Bologna
Po
Tanaro
Adige
Piave
Reno
Arno
Tiber
TUSCAN ARCH.
Elba
Rome
TYRRHENIAN SEA
PONTINE IS.
Ischia
Naples
Vesuvius
Capri
Gulf of Taranto
C. S. Maria di Leuca
Monti del Gennargentu 6,017 ft. (1834 m.)
Sardinia
Cagliari
C. Teulada
LIPARI IS.
EGADI IS.
Palermo
Etna 11,053 ft. (3369 m.)
Str. of Messina
Sicily
Pantelleria
C. Passero
Gozo
Malta
Lampedusa

34 Italy
(continued)

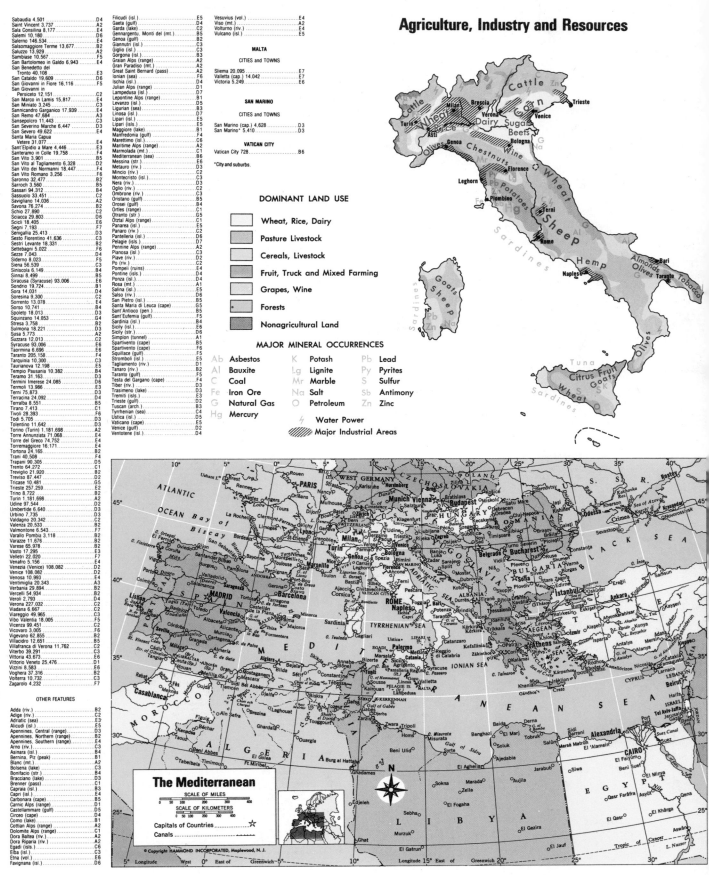

Agriculture, Industry and Resources

DOMINANT LAND USE

Wheat, Rice, Dairy

Pasture Livestock

Cereals, Livestock

Fruit, Truck and Mixed Farming

Grapes, Wine

Forests

Nonagricultural Land

MAJOR MINERAL OCCURRENCES

Ab Asbestos
Al Bauxite
C Coal
Fe Iron Ore
G Natural Gas
Hg Mercury
K Potash
Lg Lignite
Mr Marble
Na Salt
O Petroleum
Pb Lead
Py Pyrites
S Sulfur
Sb Antimony
Zn Zinc

Water Power
Major Industrial Areas

The Mediterranean

SCALE OF MILES
0 50 100 200 300 400

SCALE OF KILOMETERS
0 50 100 200 300 400

Capitals of Countries ....☆
Canals ....

© Copyright HAMMOND INCORPORATED, Maplewood, N.J.

SWITZERLAND

AREA 15,943 sq. mi. (41,292 sq. km.)
POPULATION 6,365,960
CAPITAL Bern
LARGEST CITY Zürich
HIGHEST POINT Dufourspitze
(Mte. Rosa) 15,203 ft. (4,634 m.)
MONETARY UNIT Swiss franc
MAJOR LANGUAGES German, French,
Italian, Romansch
MAJOR RELIGIONS Protestantism,
Roman Catholicism

LIECHTENSTEIN

AREA 61 sq. mi. (158 sq. km.)
POPULATION 25,220
CAPITAL Vaduz
LARGEST CITY Vaduz
HIGHEST POINT Grauspitze 8,527 ft.
(2,599 m.)
MONETARY UNIT Swiss franc
MAJOR LANGUAGE German
MAJOR RELIGION Roman Catholicism

SWITZERLAND

LIECHTENSTEIN

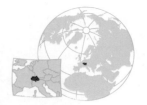

Languages

German
French
Italian
Romansch

Switzerland is a multilingual nation with four
official languages. 70% of the people speak
German, 19% French, 10% Italian and 1% Romansch.

Agriculture, Industry and Resources

DOMINANT LAND USE

Cereals, Dairy

Pasture Livestock

General Farming, Livestock

Fruit, Truck, Mixed Farming

Forests

Nonagricultural Land

⚡ Water Power

▨ Major Industrial Areas

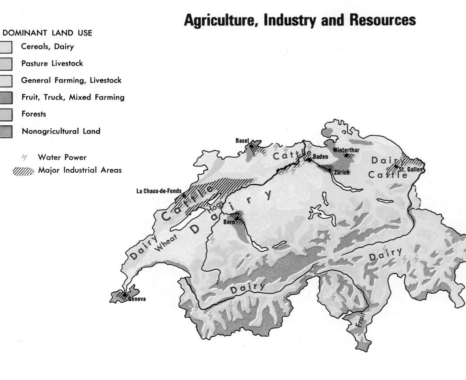

SWITZERLAND

CANTONS

Aargau 442,400 ....F2
Appenzell, Ausser
Rhoden 46,700 ....H2
Appenzell, Inner Rhoden 13,500 ....H2
Baselland 219,500 ....E2
Baselstadt 209,700 ....E1
Bern 920,900 ....D2
Fribourg 181,600 ....D3
Geneva (Genève) 338,600 ....B4
Glarus 35,700 ....H3
Graubünden (Grisons) 164,300 ....H3
Grisons (Graubünden) 164,300 ....H3
Jura 67,200 ....D2
Lucerne (Luzern) 292,900 ....F2
Luzern 292,900 ....F2
Neuchâtel 162,200 ....C3
Nidwalden 26,900 ....F3
Obwalden 25,400 ....F3
Sankt Gallen 385,000 ....H2
Schaffhausen 69,300 ....G1
Schwyz 93,100 ....G2
Soleure (Solothurn) 221,800 ....E2
Solothurn 221,800 ....E2
Thurgau 183,500 ....H1
Ticino 264,400 ....G4
Uri 34,000 ....G3
Valais 214,000 ....D4
Vaud 523,500 ....B3
Zug 73,600 ....G2
Zürich 1,117,300 ....F2

CITIES and TOWNS

Aadorf 3,022 ....G2
Aarau 16,881 ....F2
Aarau* 51,800 ....F2
Aarberg 3,122 ....D2
Aarburg 5,943 ....E2
Adelboden 3,326 ....E3
Adliswil 15,920 ....F2
Aeschi bei Spiez 1,402 ....E3
Affoltern am Albis 7,363 ....F2
Affoltern im Emmental 1,223 ....E2
Aigle 6,532 ....C4
Airolo 2,140 ....G3
Alle 1,615 ....D2
Allschwil 17,638 ....D1
Alpnach 3,277 ....F3
Altdorf 8,647 ....G3
Altstätten 9,084 ....J2
Amriswil 7,601 ....H1
Andelfingen 1,453 ....G1
Andermatt 1,589 ....G3
Appenzell 5,217 ....H2
Arbedo-Castione 2,456 ....G4
Arbon 12,227 ....H1
Arbon* 15,400 ....H1
Ardon 1,498 ....D4
Arosa 2,717 ....J3
Arth 7,580 ....F2
Ascona 4,086 ....G4
Attalens 1,116 ....C3
Au 4,944 ....J2
Aubonne 1,983 ....B4
Avenches 2,235 ....D3
Baar 14,074 ....F2
Baden 14,115 ....F2
Baden* 66,800 ....F2
Bad Ragaz 3,713 ....H2
Balerna 3,885 ....G5
Balsthal 5,607 ....E2
Bäretswil 2,733 ....G2
Basel 199,600 ....E1
Basel* 379,700 ....E1
Bassecourt 2,985 ....D2
Bätterkinden 1,757 ....E2
Bauma 3,159 ....G2
Beatenberg 1,263 ....E3
Beinwil am See 2,520 ....F2
Belfaux 1,075 ....D3
Bellinzona 16,979 ....H4
Bellinzona* 31,000 ....H4
Belp 6,981 ....D3
Berg 1,039 ....H1
Bern (cap.) 154,700 ....D3
Bern* 285,300 ....D3
Beromünster 1,552 ....F2
Bettlach 4,046 ....D2
Bex 5,069 ....D4
Biasca 4,696 ....H4
Biberist 7,769 ....D2
Biel 63,400 ....D2
Biel* 89,900 ....D2
Bière 1,252 ....B3
Binningen 15,344 ....D1
Bischofszell 4,233 ....H1
Blumenstein 1,049 ....E3
Bodio 1,425 ....G4
Bolligen 26,12* E3
Boltigen 1,519 ....D3
Bonaduz 1,289 ....H3
Boncourt 1,526 ....C2
Bönigen 1,738 ....E3
Boswil 1,904 ....F2
Boudry 4,372 ....C3
Bourg Saint-Pierre 236 ....D5
Breil-Brigels 1,215 ....H3
Breitenbach 2,455 ....E2
Bremgarten 4,873 ....F2
Brienz 2,796 ....F3
Brig 5,191 ....F4
Brissago 2,120 ....G4
Brittnau 2,888 ....E2
Broc 1,842 ....D3
Brugg 8,635 ....F2
Brusio 1,344 ....K4
Bubendorf 2,070 ....E2
Bubikon 3,244 ....G2
Buchs 8,454 ....H2
Bülach 11,043 ....G1
Bulle 7,556 ....D3
Buochs 3,232 ....F3
Büren an der Aare 3,085 ....D2
Burgdorf 15,888 ....E2
Burgdorf* 18,430 ....E2
Bürglen, Thurgau 1,920 ....H1
Bürglen, Uri 3,401 ....G3
Bussigny-près-Lausanne 4,509 ....B3
Bütschwil 3,270 ....H2
Carouge 14,055 ....B4
Castagnola 4,430 ....G4
Cazis 1,687 ....H3
Cernier 1,717 ....C3
Chalais 1,651 ....E4
Cham 8,209 ....F2
Chamoson 2,049 ....D4
Charmey 1,155 ....D3
Château-d'Oex 3,203 ....D4
Châtel-Saint-Denis 2,842 ....C3
Chêne-Bougeries 8,670 ....B4
Chavornay 1,521 ....C3
Chexbres 1,607 ....C3
Chiasso 8,868 ....G5
Chippis 1,561 ....E4
Chur 32,400 ....J3
Churwalden 1,052 ....J3
Claro 1,143 ....G4
Collombey-Muraz 2,279 ....C4
Collonge-Bellerive 3,541 ....B4
Conthey 4,259 ....D4
Coppet 1,097 ....B4
Corcelles-près-Payerne 1,256 ....C3
Corgémont 1,645 ....D2
Cossonay 1,529 ....B3
Courgenay 1,954 ....D2
Courrendlin 2,656 ....D2
Courroux 1,788 ....D2
Courtelary 1,462 ....C2
Courtételle 1,864 ....D2
Couvet 3,481 ....C3
Cully 1,535 ....C3
Davos 10,238 ....J3
Degersheim 3,400 ....H2
Delémont 11,797 ....D2
Derendingen 4,917 ....E2
Dielsdorf 2,691 ....F1
Diemtigen 1,913 ....D3
Diepoldsau 3,311 ....J2
Diessenhofen 2,532 ....G1
Dietikon 22,705 ....F2
Dietlikon 2,634 ....G2
Disentis-Mustér 2,319 ....G3
Domat-Ems 5,701 ....H3
Dombresson 1,109 ....C2
Dornach 5,258 ....D2
Döttingen 3,380 ....F1
Dübendorf 19,639 ....G2
Düdingen 4,932 ....D3
Dürnten 4,820 ....G2
Dürrenroth 1,084 ....E2
Ebnat-Kappel 5,131 ....H2
Echallens 1,643 ....C3
Ecublens 6,379 ....B3
Egg 5,250 ....G2
Eggiwil 2,391 ....E3
Eglisau 2,160 ....G1
Egnach 3,466 ....H1

(continued on following page)

Topography

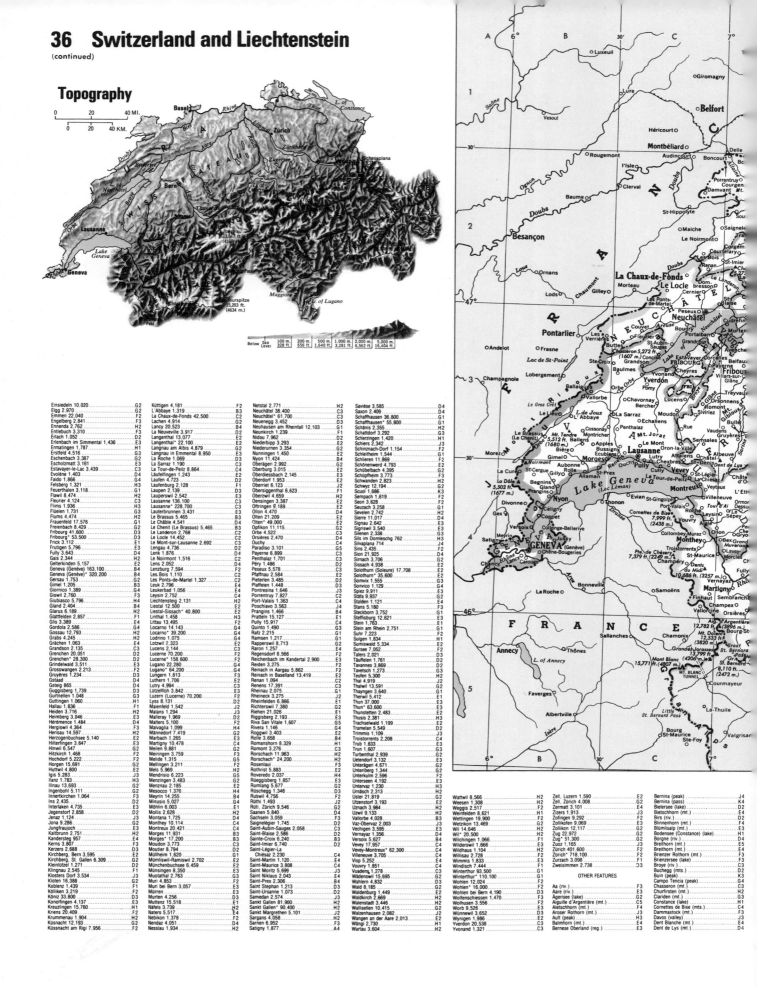

0   20   40 MI.
0   20   40 KM.

| Below Sea Level | 100 m. 328 ft. | 200 m. 656 ft. | 500 m. 1,640 ft. | 1,000 m. 3,281 ft. | 2,000 m. 6,562 ft. | 5,000 m. 16,404 ft. |

Einsiedeln 10,020 ...G2
Elgg 2,970 ...G2
Emmen 22,040 ...F2
Engelberg 2,841 ...F3
Ennenda 2,762 ...H2
Entlebuch 3,310 ...F3
Erlach 1,052 ...D2
Erlenbach im Simmental 1,436 ...E3
Ermatingen 1,787 ...H1
Erstfeld 4,516 ...G3
Eschenbach 3,387 ...G2
Escholzmatt 3,161 ...E3
Estavayer-le-Lac 3,439 ...C3
Évolène 1,403 ...D4
Faido 1,866 ...G4
Felsberg 1,321 ...H3
Feuerthalen 3,118 ...G1
Flawil 8,474 ...H2
Fleurier 4,124 ...C3
Flims 1,936 ...H3
Flüelen 1,731 ...G3
Flums 4,474 ...H2
Frauenfeld 17,576 ...G2
Freienbach 8,429 ...G2
Fribourg 41,600 ...D3
Fribourg* 53,500 ...D3
Frick 3,112 ...E1
Frutigen 5,796 ...E4
Fully 3,643 ...D4
Gais 3,344 ...H2
Gelterkinden 5,157 ...E2
Geneva (Genève) 163,100 ...B4
Geneva (Genève)* 320,200 ...B4
Gersau 1,753 ...G3
Gimel 1,205 ...B3
Giornico 1,389 ...G4
Giswil 2,760 ...F3
Giubiasco 5,796 ...H4
Gland 2,404 ...B4
Glarus 6,189 ...H2
Glattfelden 2,857 ...F1
Glis 3,389 ...E4
Gordola 2,586 ...G4
Gossau 12,793 ...H2
Gräbe 4,245 ...E4
Grächen 1,063 ...E4
Grandson 3,115 ...C3
Grenchen 20,051 ...D2
Grenchen* 28,300 ...D2
Grindelwald 3,511 ...E3
Grosswangen 2,213 ...F2
Gruyères 1,234 ...D3
Gstaad ...D4
Gsteig 865 ...D4
Guggisberg 1,739 ...D3
Gurtnellen 1,048 ...G3
Güttingen 1,060 ...H1
Hallau 1,836 ...F1
Heiden 3,716 ...H2
Heimberg 8,131 ...E3
Hérémence 1,484 ...D4
Hergiswil 4,364 ...F2
Herisau 14,597 ...H2
Herzogenbuchsee 5,140 ...E2
Hilterfingen 3,647 ...E3
Hinwil 6,547 ...G2
Hitzkirch 1,468 ...F2
Hochdorf 5,222 ...F2
Horgen 15,691 ...G2
Huttwil 4,800 ...E2
Igis 5,283 ...J3
Ilanz 1,783 ...H3
Illnau 13,410 ...G2
Ingenbohl 5,111 ...G2
Innertkirchen 1,064 ...F3
Ins 2,435 ...D2
Interlaken 4,735 ...E3
Jegenstorf 2,858 ...E2
Jenaz 1,124 ...J3
Jona 9,286 ...G2
Jungfraujoch ...E3
Kaltbrunn 2,751 ...G2
Kandersteg 957 ...E4
Kerns 3,807 ...F3
Kerzers 2,688 ...D3
Kirchberg, Bern 3,595 ...E2
Kirchberg, St. Gallen 6,309 ...H2
Kleinlützel 1,271 ...D2
Klingnau 2,545 ...F1
Klosters Dorf 3,534 ...J3
Kloten 16,388 ...G2
Koblenz 1,416 ...F1
Kölliken 3,219 ...E2
König 33,600 ...D3
Konolfingen 4,137 ...E3
Kreuzlingen 15,760 ...H1
Kriens 20,600 ...F2
Krumenau 1,904 ...H2
Küssnacht 12,193 ...G2
Küssnacht am Rigi 7,956 ...F2

Küttigen 4,181 ...F2
L'Abbaye 1,319 ...B3
La Chaux-de-Fonds 42,500 ...C2
Lachen 4,914 ...G2
Lancy 20,523 ...B4
La Neuveville 3,917 ...D2
Langenthal 13,077 ...E2
Langenthal* 22,100 ...E2
Langnau am Albis 4,879 ...G2
Langnau in Emmental 8,950 ...E3
La Roche 1,069 ...D3
La Sarraz 1,190 ...C3
La Tour-de-Peilz 8,864 ...C4
Läufelfingen 1,243 ...E2
Laufen 4,723 ...D2
Laufenburg 2,128 ...F1
Laupen 2,139 ...D3
Lauperswil 2,542 ...E3
Lausanne 136,100 ...C3
Lausanne* 228,700 ...C3
Lauterbrunnen 3,431 ...E3
Le Brassus 5,465 ...B3
Le Châble 4,541 ...D4
Le Landeron 2,768 ...C2
Le Locle 14,422 ...C2
Le Mont-sur-Lausanne 2,692 ...C3
Lengau 4,736 ...E3
Lenk 1,876 ...D4
Lens 2,052 ...D4
Lenzburg 7,594 ...F2
Les Bois 1,110 ...C2
Les Ponts-de-Martel 1,327 ...C2
Leuk 2,796 ...E4
Leukerbad 1,056 ...E4
Leysin 2,752 ...D4
Liechtenstein 2,131 ...H2
Liestal 12,500 ...E2
Liestal-Sissach 40,800 ...E2
Littau 13,495 ...F2
Locarno 14,143 ...G4
Locarno* 39,200 ...G4
Lodrino 1,075 ...G4
Lotzwil 2,323 ...E2
Lucens 2,144 ...C3
Lucerne 70,200 ...F2
Lucerne* 158,600 ...F2
Lugano 22,280 ...G4
Lugano* 64,200 ...G4
Lungern 1,813 ...F3
Luthern 1,706 ...E2
Lutry 4,736 ...C3
Lützelflüh 3,842 ...E3
Luzern (Lucerne) 70,200 ...F2
Lyss 8,131 ...D2
Maienfeld 1,542 ...J2
Malans 1,294 ...J3
Malleray 1,969 ...D2
Malters 5,100 ...F2
Malvaglia 1,099 ...H4
Männedorf 7,419 ...G2
Marbach 1,265 ...E3
Martigny 10,478 ...C4
Meilen 9,881 ...G2
Meiringen 3,759 ...F3
Melide 1,315 ...G5
Mellingen 3,211 ...F2
Mels 5,969 ...H2
Mendrisio 6,223 ...G5
Menzingen 3,483 ...G2
Menznau 1,620 ...F2
Meyrin 14,255 ...B4
Minusio 5,027 ...G4
Möhlin 6,003 ...E1
Mollis 2,628 ...H2
Monthey 10,114 ...C4
Montreux 20,421 ...C4
Morges 11,931 ...B3
Morges* 17,200 ...B3
Moudon 3,773 ...C3
Moutier 8,794 ...D2
Mümliswil-Ramiswil 2,702 ...E2
Münchenbuchsee 6,459 ...E2
Münsingen 8,350 ...E3
Muotathal 2,763 ...G3
Muri 6,953 ...F2
Muri bei Bern 3,057 ...E3
Mürren ...E3
Muttenz 15,518 ...E1
Näfels 3,739 ...H2
Naters 9,521 ...E4
Nendaz 4,051 ...D4
Nesslau 1,934 ...H2

Netstal 2,771 ...H2
Neuchâtel 38,400 ...C3
Neuchâtel* 61,700 ...C3
Neuenegg 3,452 ...D3
Neuhausen am Rheinfall 12,103 ...F1
Neunkirch 1,239 ...F1
Nidau 7,962 ...D2
Niederbipp 3,293 ...E2
Niederurnen 3,354 ...H2
Nunningen 1,450 ...E2
Nyon 11,424 ...B4
Oberägeri 2,992 ...G2
Oberdiessbach 3,015 ...E3
Oberdiessbach 2,145 ...E3
Oberdorf 1,953 ...E2
Oberriet 6,123 ...J2
Obersiggenthal 6,623 ...F1
Oberwil 4,659 ...H2
Oensingen 3,387 ...E2
Oftringen 9,189 ...E2
Ollon 4,470 ...D4
Olten 21,209 ...E2
Olten* 49,000 ...E2
Opfikon 11,115 ...G2
Orbe 4,522 ...C3
Orsières 2,470 ...C4
Ouchy ...C4
Paradiso 3,011 ...G5
Payerne 6,899 ...C3
Penthalaz 1,701 ...C3
Péry 1,486 ...D2
Peseux 5,578 ...C3
Pfäffikon 2,584 ...G2
Pieterlen 3,485 ...D2
Plaffeien 1,448 ...D3
Pontresina 1,646 ...J3
Porrentruy 7,827 ...C2
Port-Valais 1,363 ...C4
Poschiavo 3,563 ...J4
Prangins 1,466 ...B4
Pratteln 15,127 ...E1
Pully 15,917 ...C4
Quinto 1,490 ...G3
Rafz 2,215 ...G1
Ramsen 1,217 ...G1
Rapperswil 8,713 ...G2
Raron 1,257 ...E4
Regensdorf 8,566 ...F2
Reichenbach im Kandertal 2,900 ...E3
Reiden 3,275 ...E2
Reinach in Aargau 5,862 ...F2
Reinach in Baselland 13,419 ...E1
Renan 1,094 ...C2
Renens 17,391 ...C3
Rheinau 2,075 ...G1
Rheineck 3,275 ...J2
Rheinfelden 6,866 ...E1
Richterswil 7,380 ...G2
Riehen 21,026 ...E1
Riggisberg 2,193 ...E3
Riva San Vitale 1,607 ...G5
Rivera 1,146 ...G4
Roggwil 3,403 ...E2
Rolle 3,658 ...B4
Romanshorn 8,329 ...H1
Romont 3,276 ...C3
Rorschach 11,963 ...H2
Rorschach* 24,200 ...H2
Rosenlau ...F3
Rothrist 5,883 ...E2
Roveredo 2,037 ...H4
Rüeggisberg 1,857 ...E3
Rümlang 5,677 ...G2
Rüschegg 1,346 ...D3
Ruswil 4,756 ...F2
Rüti, Zürich 9,546 ...G2
Saanen 5,840 ...D4
Sachseln 3,059 ...F3
Saignelégier 1,745 ...C2
Saint-Aubin-Sauges 2,058 ...C3
Saint-Blaise 2,586 ...D2
Sainte-Croix 6,240 ...C3
Saint-Imier 6,740 ...C2
Saint-Légier-La Chiésaz 2,230 ...C4
Saint-Martin 1,120 ...D4
Saint-Maurice 3,808 ...C4
Saint Moritz 5,052 ...J3
Saint-Prex 2,306 ...B4
Saint Stephan 1,235 ...E4
Saint-Ursanne 1,073 ...D2
Sankt Gallen 81,900 ...H2
Sankt Gallen* 90,400 ...H2
Sankt Margrethen 5,101 ...J2
Sargans 4,058 ...H2
Sarnen 6,952 ...F3
Satigny 1,877 ...A4

Savièse 3,585 ...D4
Saxon 2,409 ...D4
Schaffhausen 36,800 ...G1
Schaffhausen* 55,800 ...G1
Schänis 2,355 ...H2
Schattdorf 3,292 ...G3
Scherzingen 1,420 ...H1
Schiers 2,342 ...J3
Schinznach-Dorf 1,154 ...F2
Schleitheim 1,554 ...G1
Schlieren 11,869 ...F2
Schönenwerd 4,793 ...E2
Schübelbach 4,395 ...G2
Schüpfheim 3,773 ...F3
Schwanden 2,823 ...H2
Schwyz 12,194 ...G2
Scuol 1,686 ...K3
Sempach 1,619 ...F2
Seon 3,628 ...E2
Seuzach 3,258 ...G1
Sevelen 2,742 ...H2
Sierre 11,017 ...D4
Signau 2,642 ...E3
Sigriswil 3,540 ...E3
Silenen 2,338 ...G3
Sils im Domleschg 762 ...H3
Silvaplana 714 ...J4
Sins 2,435 ...F2
Sion 21,925 ...D4
Sirnach 3,706 ...G2
Sissach 4,938 ...E2
Solothurn (Soleure) 17,708 ...E2
Solothurn* 35,600 ...E2
Somvix 1,665 ...H3
Sonvico 1,129 ...G4
Spiez 9,911 ...E3
Stäfa 9,937 ...G2
Stalden 1,121 ...E4
Stans 5,180 ...F3
Steckborn 3,752 ...G1
Steffisburg 12,621 ...E3
Stein 1,763 ...F1
Stein am Rhein 2,751 ...G1
Suhr 7,223 ...E2
Sulgen 1,834 ...H1
Sumiswald 5,334 ...E2
Sursee 7,922 ...F2
Tafers 2,021 ...D3
Täuffelen 1,761 ...D2
Tavanasa 3,869 ...H3
Tavetsch 1,273 ...G3
Teufen 5,307 ...H2
Thal 4,919 ...J2
Thalwil 13,591 ...G2
Thayngen 3,640 ...G1
Therwil 5,412 ...E1
Thun 37,000 ...E3
Thun* 63,600 ...E3
Thunstetten 2,483 ...E2
Thusis 2,381 ...H3
Trachselwald 1,199 ...E2
Tramelan 5,549 ...D2
Trimmis 1,609 ...J3
Troistorrents 2,208 ...C4
Trub 1,833 ...E3
Trun 1,607 ...H3
Turbenthal 2,939 ...G2
Uetendorf 3,132 ...E3
Unterägeri 4,671 ...G2
Unterkulm 2,924 ...E2
Unterseen 4,192 ...E3
Untervaz 2,313 ...H3
Uster 21,819 ...G2
Utzenstorf 3,193 ...E2
Uznach 3,984 ...H2
Vallorbe 4,028 ...B3
Vaz-Obervaz 2,003 ...H3
Vechigen 3,595 ...E3
Vernayaz 1,356 ...C4
Versoix 5,627 ...B4
Vevey 17,065 ...C4
Vevey-Montreux* 62,300 ...C4
Villeneuve 3,705 ...C4
Visp 5,252 ...E4
Vouvry 1,851 ...C4
Vuadens 1,270 ...D3
Wädenswil 15,695 ...G2
Wahlern 4,832 ...D3
Wald 6,188 ...G2
Waldenburg 1,449 ...E2
Waldkirch 2,669 ...H2
Walenstadt 3,556 ...H2
Wallisellen 10,415 ...G2
Walzenhausen 2,013 ...J2
Wangen an der Aare 2,013 ...E2
Wängi 2,730 ...G2
Wartau 3,604 ...H2

Wattwil 8,566 ...H2
Weesen 1,308 ...H2
Weggis 2,517 ...F2
Weinfelden 8,621 ...H1
Wettingen 19,900 ...F2
Wetzikon 13,469 ...G2
Wil 14,646 ...H2
Wil* 20,500 ...H2
Wichtrach 1,066 ...E3
Wilderswil 1,633 ...E3
Wildhaus 1,104 ...H2
Willisau 2,728 ...F2
Wimmis 1,833 ...E3
Windisch 7,444 ...F1
Winterthur 93,500 ...G1
Winterthur* 110,100 ...G1
Wohlen 12,024 ...F2
Wohlen* 16,000 ...F2
Wohlen bei Bern 4,190 ...D3
Wolhusen 3,556 ...F2
Wolfenschiessen 1,470 ...F3
Worb 9,526 ...E3
Wünnewil 3,652 ...D3
Wynigen 1,986 ...E2
Yverdon 20,538 ...C3
Yvonand 1,321 ...C3

Zell, Luzern 1,590 ...E2
Zell, Zürich 4,008 ...G2
Zermatt 3,101 ...E4
Zizers 1,913 ...J3
Zofingen 9,292 ...E2
Zollikofen 9,069 ...E3
Zollikon 12,117 ...G2
Zug 22,972 ...G2
Zug* 51,300 ...G2
Zuoz 1,165 ...J3
Zürich 401,600 ...F2
Zürich* 718,100 ...F2
Zurzach 3,098 ...F1
Zweisimmen 2,738 ...D3

OTHER FEATURES

Aa (riv.) ...F3
Aare (riv.) ...E3
Aegeri (lake) ...G2
Aiguille d'Argentière (mt.) ...C5
Aletschhorn (mt.) ...E4
Ault (peak) ...D4
Balmhorn (mt.) ...E4
Bernese Oberland (reg.) ...E3

Bernina (peak) ...J4
Bernina (pass) ...K4
Bielersee (lake) ...D2
Bietschhorn (mt.) ...E4
Birs (riv.) ...E2
Blinnenhorn (mt.) ...F4
Blümlisalp (mt.) ...E4
Bodensee (Constance) (lake) ...H1
Borgne (riv.) ...D4
Breithorn (mt.) ...E4
Breithorn (mt.) ...E4
Brienzer Rothorn (mt.) ...F3
Brienzersee (lake) ...E3
Broye (riv.) ...C3
Buchegg (riv.) ...K3
Campo Tencia (peak) ...G4
Chasseron (mt.) ...C3
Churfirsten (mt.) ...H2
Clariden (mt.) ...G3
Cornettes de Bise (mts.) ...C4
Dammastock (mt.) ...F3
Davos (valley) ...J3
Dent Blanche (mt.) ...D4
Dent de Lys (mt.) ...D3

Switzerland and Liechtenstein

CONIC PROJECTION

SCALE OF MILES

SCALE OF KILOMETERS

Capitals of Countries.................☆
Capitals of Cantons..................●
International Boundaries.............
Canals...................................

® Copyright HAMMOND INCORPORATED, Maplewood, N.J.

AUSTRIA

PROVINCES

Burgenland 272,119.............D3
Carinthia 525,728...............B3
Lower Austria 1,414,161........C2
Salzburg 401,766................B3
Styria 1,192,442................C3
Tirol 540,771...................A3
Upper Austria 1,223,444.........B2
Vienna (city) 1,614,841.........D2
Vorarlberg 271,473..............A3

CITIES and TOWNS†

Admont 3,126....................C2
Allentsteig 2,783...............C2
Altheim 4,766...................B2
Althofen 3,886..................C3
Amstetten 13,330................C2
Andau 3,058.....................D3
Arnoldstein 6,740...............B3
Aspang Markt 2,316..............D3
Attnang-Puchheim 7,837..........B2
Bad Aussee 5,039................B3
Baden 22,631....................D2
Badgastein 5,228................B3
Bad Goisern 6,360...............B3
Bad Hofgastein 5,525............B3
Bad Ischl 12,740................B3
Bad Leonfelden 2,712............C2
Bad Sankt-Leonhard im
  Lavanttal 4,882...............C3
Berndorf 8,371..................C3
Bischofshofen 9,417.............B3
Bludenz 12,050..................A3
Bramberg am Wildkogel 3,129.....B3
Braunau am Inn 16,432...........B2
Bregenz 22,839..................A3
Bruck an der Leitha 7,506.......D2
Bruck an der Mur 16,359.........C3
Deutsch Feistritz 3,820.........C3
Deutschkreutz 3,673.............D3
Deutsch Landsberg 6,614.........C3
Deutsch Wagram 4,481............D2
Dornbirn 33,810.................A3
Ebenfurth 2,272.................D3
Ebensee 9,413...................B3
Eferding 3,014..................B2
Eggenburg 3,730.................C2
Ehrwald 2,198...................A3

Eisenerz 11,563.................C3
Eisenkappel-Vellach 3,761.......C3
Eisenstadt 10,059...............D3
Enns 9,622......................C2
Feldbach 3,887..................C3
Feldkirch 21,214................A3
Feldkirchen in
  Kärnten 11,188................B3
Ferlach 7,621...................C3
Fieberbrunn 3,651...............B3
Fohnsdorf 11,189................C3
Frankenmarkt 2,960..............B2
Frauenkirchen 2,749.............D3
Freistadt 5,956.................C2
Freidberg 2,504.................C3
Friesach 7,257..................C3
Frohnleiten 5,081...............C3
Fulpmes 2,553...................A3
Fürstenfeld 6,054...............C3
Gaming 4,181....................C2
Gänserndorf 4,211...............D2
Gleisdorf 4,921.................C3
Gloggnitz 7,972.................C3
Gmünd, Carinthia 2,267..........B3
Gmünd, Lower Austria 6,323......C2
Gmunden 12,270..................B3
Golling an der Salzach 3,089....B3
Götzis 7,931....................A3
Gratwein 2,747..................C3
Graz 251,900....................C3
Graz* 314,200...................C3
Grein 2,767.....................C2
f21Grieskirchen 4,519...........B2
Grosssiegharts 3,288............C2
Grünburg 3,775..................C2
Güssing 3,675...................C3
Haag 5,060......................C2
Hainburg an der Donau 6,009.....D2
Hainfeld 3,897..................C2
Hallein 14,371..................B3
Hallstatt 1,303.................B3
Hartberg 5,702..................C3
Haslach an der Mühl 2,636.......C2
Heidenreichstein 4,340..........C2
Heiligenblut 1,324..............B3
Hermagor-Presegersee 7,531......B3
Herzogenburg 7,299..............C2
Hohenau an der March 3,591......D2
Hohenberg 2,016.................C3
Hohenems 11,487.................A3
Hollabrunn 6,563................C2
Hopfgarten in Nordtirol 4,784...B3

Horn 6,264......................C2
Hüttenberg 3,251................C3
Imst 5,855......................A3
Innsbruck 115,800...............A3
Innsbruck* 167,200..............A3
Jenbach 5,868...................A3
Jennersdorf 4,210...............C3
Judenburg 11,346................C3
Kaplenberg 26,001...............C3
Kapp 2,156......................A3
Kaprun 2,604....................B3
Kindberg 6,128..................C3
Kirchdorf an der Krems 3,471....C2
Kitzbühel 7,995.................B3
Klagenfurt 74,326...............C3
Klagenfurt* 112,600.............C3
Klosterneuburg 21,912...........D2
Knittelfeld 14,517..............C3
Köflach 12,612..................C3
Königswiesen 2,921..............C2
Korneuburg 8,892................D2
Kössen 2,764....................B3
Kötschach-Mauthen 3,740.........B3
Krems an der Donau 21,733.......C2
Kufstein 12,736.................B3
Kundl 3,020.....................A3
Laa an der Thaya 5,455..........D2
Laakirchen 7,664................B3
Lambach 3,301...................C2
Landeck 7,388...................A3
Langenfeld 2,838................A3
Langenlois 4,957................C2
Langenwang 4,071................C3
Lavamünd 4,120..................C3
Leibnitz 6,646..................C3
Lenzing 5,385...................B3
Leoben 35,153...................C3
Lienz 11,696....................B3
Liezen 6,244....................C3
Lilienfeld 3,126................C3
Linz 205,700....................C2
Linz* 356,500...................C2
Lustenau 15,239.................A3
Mannersdorf am
  Leithagebirge 4,012...........D3
Marchegg 2,678..................D2
Mariazell 2,298.................C3
Matrei in Osttirol 4,003........B3
Mattersburg 5,417...............D3
Mattighofen 4,344...............B2
Mauerkirchen 2,237..............B2
Mautern in Steiermark 2,536.....C3

Mauthausen 4,419................C2
Mauthen-Kötschach 3,750.........B3
Mayrhofen 3,174.................A3
Melk 5,108......................C2
Mistelbach an der Zaya 6,306....D2
Mittersill 4,361................B3
Mödling 18,712..................D2
Mondsee 2,141...................B3
Murau 2,710.....................C3
Mürzzuschlag 11,564.............C3
Neuberg an der Mürz 2,183.......C3
Neumarkt am Wallersee 3,267.....B3
Neunkirchen 10,922..............C3
Neusiedl am See 3,999...........D3
Neustift im Stubaital 2,789.....A3
Ober Grafendorf 4,989...........C2
Oberndorf bei Salzburg 3,293....B3
Oberndorf 2,420.................B3
Oberwart 5,661..................C3
Paternion 5,805.................B3
Perg 4,872......................C2
Peuerbach 2,161.................B2
Pfunds 2,043....................A3
Pinkafeld 4,639.................C3
Pöchlarn 3,199..................C2
Pörtschach am
  Wörthersee 2,511..............C3
Poysdorf 5,774..................D2
Pregarten 3,249.................C2
Raabs an der Thaya 4,194........C2
Radenthein 6,847................B3
Radkersburg 2,000...............C3
Radstadt 3,585..................B3
Rankweil 8,440..................A3
Rechnitz 3,412..................C3
Reichenau an der Rax 4,053......C3
Retz 4,780......................C2
Ried im Innkreis 10,534.........B2
Rottenmann 4,781................C3
Saalfelden am Steinernen
  Meer 10,172...................B3
Salzburg 122,100................B3
Salzburg* 213,430...............B3
Sankt Aegyd am Neuwalde 3,165...C3
Sankt Anton am Arlberg 2,086....A3
Sankt Johann in Tirol 5,942.....B3
Sankt Michael im Lungau 2,839...B3
Sankt Michael in
  Obersteiermark 3,717..........C3
Sankt Paul im Lavanttal 6,721...C3
Sankt Pölten 43,300.............C2

Sankt Valentin 8,715............C2
Sankt Veit an der Glan 11,047...C3
Sankt Wolfgang im
  Salzkammergut 2,746...........B3
Schärding 5,874.................B2
Scheibbs 4,419..................C2
Schladming 3,460................B3
Schrems 3,393...................C2
Schruns 3,607...................A3
Schwarzach im Pongau 3,616......B3
Schwaz 10,253...................A3
Schwechat 14,997................D2
Schwertberg 3,881...............C2
Sierning 8,162..................C2
Sillian 1,988...................B3
Solbad Hall in Tirol 12,335.....A3
Spital am Pyhrn 2,315...........C3
Spittal an der Drau 13,690......B3
Steinach 2,698..................A3
Steyr 40,578....................C2
Stockerau 12,634................D2
Strassburg 2,850................C3
Tamsweg 5,060...................B3
Telfs 6,589.....................A3
Ternitz 10,287..................C3
Traiskirchen 8,878..............D2
Traun 20,843....................C2
Trieben 4,639...................C3
Trofaiach 8,731.................C3
Tulln 7,705.....................C2
Velden am Wörthersee 7,306......C3
Vienna (cap.) 1,700,000.........D2
Vienna* 1,858,700...............D2
Villach 50,979..................B3
Vöcklabruck 10,627..............B2
Voitsberg 11,094................C3
Völkermarkt 10,772..............C3
Vorderberg 2,508................C3
Waidhofen an der Thaya 4,200....C2
Waidhofen an der Ybbs 5,218.....C3
Weitensfeld-Flattnitz 5,206.....B3
Weitra 3,250....................C2
Weiz 8,241......................C3
Wels 47,279.....................C2
Weyer Markt 2,518...............C3
Wien (Vienna) (cap.) 1,700,000..D2
Wiener Neustadt 34,774..........D3
Wildon 2,002....................C3
Wilhelmsburg 6,307..............C2
Wolfsberg 31,176................C3
Wörgl 7,811.....................A3
Ybbs an der Donau 6,422.........C2

Zams 3,120......................A3
Zell am See 7,456...............B3
Zell am Ziller 1,882............A3
Zeltweg 8,431...................C3
Zirl 4,157......................A3
Zistersdorf 3,412...............D2
Zwettl-Niederösterreich 11,624..C2

OTHER FEATURES

Allgäu Alps (mts.)..............A3
Bavarian Alps (mts.)............A3
Bodensee (Constance) (lake).....A3
Brenner (pass)..................A3
Carnic Alps (mts.)..............B3
Constance (lake)................A3
Danube (riv.)...................D2
Drau (riv.).....................B3
Enns (riv.).....................C3
Grossglockner (mt.).............B3
Hohe Tauern (range).............B3
Inn (riv.)......................A3
Karawanken (range)..............C3
March (riv.)....................D2
Mühlviertel (reg.)..............C2
Mur (riv.)......................C3
Neusiedler See (lake)...........D3
Niedere Tauern (range)..........B3
Ötztal Alps (mts.)..............A3
Raab (riv.).....................C3
Rhine (riv.)....................A3
Salzach (riv.)..................B3
Salzkammergut (reg.)............C2
Semmering (pass)................C3
Thaya (riv.)....................C2
Traun (riv.)....................C2
Wildspitze (mt.)................A3
Zugspitze (mt.).................A3

CZECHOSLOVAKIA

REPUBLICS

Czech Socialist Rep. 9,964,338...B1
Slovak Socialist Rep. 4,670,409..E2

REGIONS

Bratislava (city) 333,000.......D2
Jihočesky 662,002...............D2
Jihomoravsky 1,966,850..........D2
Praha (city) 1,161,200..........C1

Severočesky 1,122,035...........C1
Severomoravsky 1,849,286........D2
Středočesky 1,193,041...........C2
Stredoslovensky 1,436,351.......E2
Východočesky 1,214,581..........C1
Vychodoslovensky 1,298,481......F2
Západočesky 865,094.............C2
Západoslovensky 1,610,542.......D2

CITIES and TOWNS

Aš 120,000......................B1
Austerlitz (Slavkov)............D2
Bánovce nad Bebravou 11,400.....D2
Banská Bystrica 53,000..........E2
Banská Stiavnica 7,486..........E2
Bardejov 17,400.................F2
Benešov 11,100..................C2
Beroun 17,600...................B1
Bílina 17,800...................B1
Blansko 13,800..................D2
Boskovice 8,531.................D2
Brandys nad Labem-Stará
  Boleslav 333,000..............C1
Bratislava 333,000..............D2
Breclav 21,100..................D2
Brezno 14,800...................E2
Brno 335,700....................D2
Bruntál 12,300..................D1
Bystrice nad
  Pernštejnem 6,471.............D2
Bystrice pod
  Hostýnem 6,681................D2
Bytča 6,922.....................D2

Čadca 16,800....................E2
Čalovo 6,591....................D3
Čáslav 10,200...................C2
Česká Lípa 18,600...............C1
Česká Trebova 14,700............C2
České Budějovice 80,800.........C2
Český Brod 6,640................C2
Český Krumlov 12,000............C2
Český Těšín 17,200..............E2
Cheb 27,000.....................B1
Chocen 8,198....................C2
Chodov 14,400...................B1
Chomutov 44,200.................B1
Chotebor 6,692..................C2
Chrudim 18,800..................C2
Čierny Balog 6,435..............E2
Děčín 46,500....................C1
Detva 13,100....................E2
Dobřís 6,378....................C2
Dobruška 5,779..................D1
Dolní Kubín 9,900...............E2
Domažlice 9,100.................B2
Dubnica nad Váhom 11,300........D2
Duchcov 9,712...................B1
Dunajská Streda 13,000..........D3
Dvůr nad Žitavou 5,847..........E3
Dvůr Králové nad
  Labem 16,800..................C1
Falknov (Sokolov) 23,900........B1
Fil'akovo 7,822.................E2
Frenštat pod
  Radhoštěm 8,516...............E2
Frýdek-Mlstek 43,800............E2
Frýdlant v.
  Čechách 5,948.................C1

Frýdlant nad
  Ostravicí 6,250..............E2
Galanta 12,300.................D3
Gottwaldov 84,300.............E2
Handlova 16,200...............E2
Havlov 85,000.................E2
Havlíčkuv Brod 19,200.........C2
Hlinsko 8,890.................C2
Hlohovec 15,200...............D2
Hlučín 15,300.................E2
Hnúšt'a-Likier................E2
Hodonín 22,600................D2
Holešov 9,091.................E2
Holíc 7,602...................D2
Holice 6,151..................C2
Horažd'ovice..................B2
Hořice v
  Podkrkonoší 7,715...........C2
Horna Stubňa..................E2
Horní Benešov.................E2
Horní Libina..................E2
Hořovice 5,665................C2
Horšovský Tyn.................B2
Hostinné......................C1
Hradec Králové 85,600.........C1
Hranice 13,300................E2
Hrinova 7,800.................E2
Hronov 9,767..................C1
Hrušovany.....................D2
Humenné 22,200................F2
Humpolec 7,810................C2
Hurbanovo.....................D3
Hustopeče.....................D2
Ilava.........................D2
Ivančice 7,314................D2

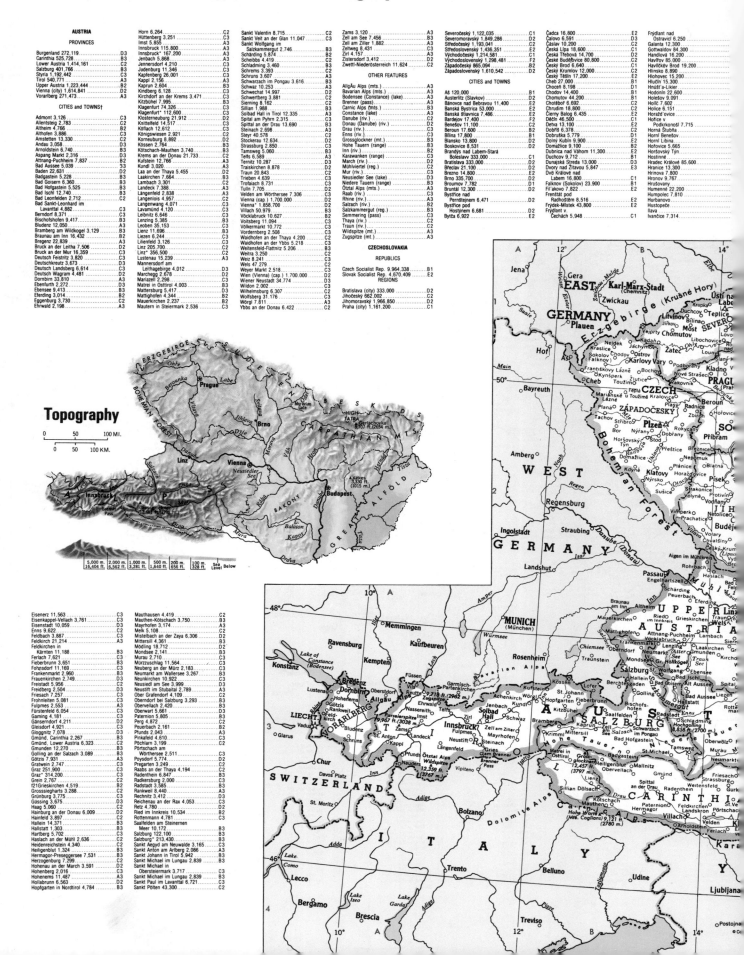

Topography

Sea Level Below
5,000 m.   2,000 m.   1,000 m.   500 m.   200 m.   100 m.
16,404 ft. 6,562 ft. 3,281 ft. 1,640 ft. 656 ft. 328 ft.

AREA 32,375 sq. mi. (83,851 sq. km.)
POPULATION 7,507,000
CAPITAL Vienna
LARGEST CITY Vienna
HIGHEST POINT Grossglockner
  12,457 ft. (3,797 m.)
MONETARY UNIT schilling
MAJOR LANGUAGE German
MAJOR RELIGION Roman Catholicism

AREA 49,373 sq. mi. (127,876 sq. km.)
POPULATION 15,276,799
CAPITAL Prague
LARGEST CITY Prague
HIGHEST POINT Gerlachovka 8,707 ft.
  (2,654 m.)
MONETARY UNIT koruna
MAJOR LANGUAGES Czech, Slovak
MAJOR RELIGIONS Roman Catholicism,
  Protestantism

AREA 35,919 sq. mi. (93,030 sq. km.)
POPULATION 10,709,536
CAPITAL Budapest
LARGEST CITY Budapest
HIGHEST POINT Kékes 3,330 ft.
  (1,015 m.)
MONETARY UNIT forint
MAJOR LANGUAGE Hungarian
MAJOR RELIGIONS Roman Catholicism,
  Protestantism

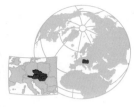

AUSTRIA   **CZECHOSLOVAKIA**   **HUNGARY**

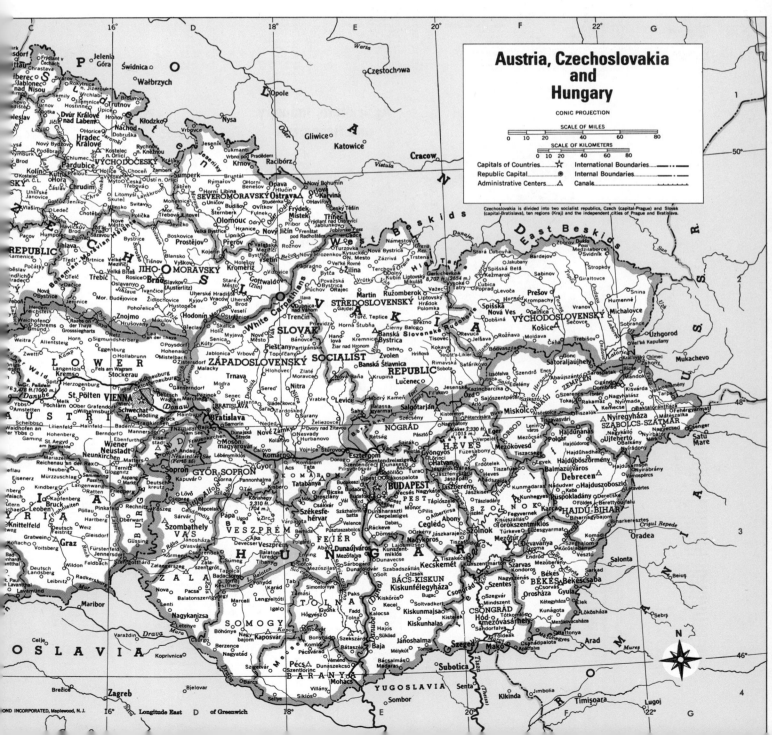

Austria, Czechoslovakia and Hungary

CONIC PROJECTION

SCALE OF MILES
0 10   20   40   60   80

SCALE OF KILOMETERS
0 10 20   40   60   80

Capitals of Countries..........☆   International Boundaries..........
Republic Capital..........⊛   Internal Boundaries..........
Administrative Centers..........△   Canals..........

Czechoslovakia is divided into two socialist republics, Czech (capital-Prague) and Slovak (capital-Bratislava), ten regions (Kraj) and the independent cities of Prague and Bratislava.

Jablonec nad Nisou 36,300 C1
Jablonica D2
Jablunkov 9,405 E2
Jáchymov B1
Jakubany F2
Jaroměř 11,600 C1
Jelšava F2
Jemnice C2
Jeseník 10,900 D1
Jesenské F2
Jevíčko D2
Jičín 13,200 C1
Jihlava 44,500 C2
Jilemnice C1
Jindřichův Hradec 15,700 C2
Jiřkov 11,400 B1
Kadaň 18,100 B1
Kamenice C2
Kaplice C2
Karlovy Vary 43,300 B1
Karviná 79,100 E2
Kdyně B2
Kežmarok 11,000 F2
Kladno 61,200 B1
Klatovy 18,500 B2
Kojetín 5,852 D2
Kokava nad Rimavicou 5,391 E2
Kolárovo 10,500 D3
Kolín 29,100 C1
Komárno 28,200 D3
Košice 169,100 F2
Kostelec nad Orlicí 5,575 D1
Král'ovský Chlmec 5,329 G2
Kralupy nad Vltavou 16,900 C1
Kraslice 6,733 B1
Kremnica 5,941 E2
Krnov 25,000 D1
Kroměříž 23,200 D2
Krompachy 6,332 F2
Krupina 6,627 E2
Krupka 8,301 B1
Kutná Hora 19,200 C2
Kyjov 10,700 D2
Kynšperk 5,524 B1
Kysucké Nové Mesto 11,700 E2
Lanškroun 8,683 D2
Levice 19,000 E2
Levoča 10,100 F2
Libáň C1
Liberec 75,600 C1
Moravě 6,581 D2
Nové Město nad Váhom 15,900 D2
Nové Strašecí B1
Nové Zámky 27,300 D3
Nový Bohumín 16,700 E2
Nový Bor 7,621 C1
Nový Bydžov 6,824 C1
Nový Hrozenkov E2
Nový Jičín 21,400 E2
Nymburk 13,600 C1
Nýřany 6,204 B2
Nýrsko B2
Odry D2
Olomouc 82,800 D2
Opava 53,800 E2
Orlová 25,500 E2
Ostrava 293,500 E2
Ostrov 18,200 B1
Pardubice 78,500 C1
Partizánske 15,100 E2
Pelhřimov 11,900 C2
Pezinok 13,100 D2
Piešt'any 25,400 D2
Písek 25,100 C2
Plzeň 155,000 B2
Počátky C2
Podbořany B1
Poděbrady 13,400 C1
Pohořelice D2
Polička 6,529 D2
Polná C2
Polomka E2
Poprad 25,800 F2
Považská Bystrica 19,300 E2
Prachatice 7,900 B2
Prague (Praha) (cap.) 1,161,200 C1
Přelouč 6,251 C1
Přerov 43,500 D2
Prešov 61,000 F2
Přeštice B2
Příbor 7,726 E2
Příbram 31,300 B2
Prievidza 30,900 E2
Prostějov 44,200 D2
Protivín C2
Púchov 9,306 E2
Radnice B2
Rajec E2
Rakovník 14,200 B1
Štúrovo 8,287 E3
Šumperk 25,900 D1
Šurany 6,693 E2
Sušice 10,300 B2
Svárov C1
Svidník 4,600 F2
Svitavy 15,000 D2
Tábor 28,100 C2
Tachov 11,400 B2
Telč 5,285 C2
Teplice 52,300 B1
Tišnov 8,263 D2
Topol'čany 17,500 D2
Třebíč 23,900 C2
Trebišov 13,700 F2
Třeboň 6,068 C2
Trenčín 38,800 E2
Třešt' 5,053 C2
Třinec 32,000 E2
Trnava 48,600 D2
Trutnov 24,500 D1
Turnov 13,600 C1
Turzovka 6,107 E2
Uherské Hradiště 32,100 D2
Uherský Brod 12,800 D2
Uničov 10,800 D2
Úpice 6,323 C1
Ústí nad Labem 74,900 C1
Ústí nad Orlicí 13,700 D2
Valašské Meziříčí 19,400 D2
Varnsdorf 14,700 C1
Važec E2
Vejprty B1
Velká Bíteš D2
Velká Bystřice D2
Vel'ké Kapušany G2
Velké Meziříčí 7,590 D2
Vel'ké Rovné E2
Veselí nad Lužnicí C2
Veselí nad Moravou 11,500 D2
Vimperk 5,749 B2
Vítkov 5,138 D2
Vizovice D2
Vlašim 8,873 C2
Vodňany 5,620 C2
Vojnice E3
Volary B2
Volyně B2
Votice C2
Jablunka (pass) E2
Jeseníky (mts.) D1
Jihlava (riv.) D2
Krušné Hory (Erzgebirge) (mts.) B1
Labe (riv.) C1
Lipno (res.) C2
Lužnice (riv.) C2
Moldau (Vltava) (riv.) C2
Morava (riv.) D2
Nitra (riv.) E2
Oder (Odra) (riv.) D2
Ohře (riv.) B1
Ondava (riv.) F2
Orava (riv.) E2
Orlická (res.) C2
Sázava (riv.) C2
Slovenské Rudohorie (mts.) E2
Sudeten (mts.) C1
Svitava (riv.) D2
Svratka (riv.) D2
Tatra, High (mts.) E2
Torysa (riv.) F2
Úhlava (riv.) B2
Váh (riv.) D2
Vltava (riv.) C2
White Carpathians (mts.) E2

HUNGARY

COUNTIES

Bács-Kiskun 568,532 E3
Baranya 434,030 E4
Békés 436,987 F3
Borsod-Abaúj-Zemplén 808,924 F2
Budapest (city) 2,060,170 E3
Csongrád 456,862 F3
Fejér 421,568 E3
Győr-Sopron 428,476 D3
Hajdú-Bihar 552,417 F3
Heves 350,874 F3
Komárom 321,579 E3
Nógrád 239,907 E3
Pest 973,486 E3
Somogy 360,308 D3
Szabolcs-Szatmár 593,746 G3
Szolnok 446,379 F3
Tolna 266,414 E3
Vas 285,527 D3
Csenger 4,792 G3
Csepel 71,693 E3
Csepreg 4,079 D3
Csongrád 22,202 E3
Csorna 12,131 D3
Csorvás 6,826 F3
Csurgó 5,463 D3
Dabas 13,075 E3
Debrecen 192,484 F3
Derecske 9,579 F3
Dévaványa 11,208 F3
Devecser 5,482 D3
Dombóvár 19,917 E3
Dombrád 6,328 F2
Dömsöd 6,545 E3
Dorog 10,754 E3
Dunaföldvár 10,318 E3
Dunaharaszti 15,788 E3
Dunakeszi 25,187 E3
Dunaszekcső 2,999 E3
Dunaújváros 60,694 E3
Dunavecse 4,521 E3
Edelény 9,559 F2
Eger 61,283 F3
Egyek 7,956 F3
Elek 6,032 F3
Enes 2,565 F2
Endrőd 8,136 F3
Enying 7,518 E3
Érd 41,210 E3
Erdőtelek 4,250 F3
Esztergom 30,476 E3
Fadd 4,805 E3
Fegyvernek 8,421 F3
Fehérgyarmat 6,729 G3
Földeák 3,855 F3
Földes 5,293 F2
Fonyód 3,957 D3
Füzesabony 6,965 F3
Füzesgyarmat 7,097 F3
Gödöllő 28,057 E3
Gönc 2,875 F2
Gyoma 10,392 F3
Gyöngyös 36,927 E3
Gyönk 2,507 E3
Győr 123,618 D3
Gyula 34,514 F3
Hajdúböszörmény 32,145 F3
Hajdúdorog 10,118 F3
Hajdúhadház 13,626 F3
Körmend 11,787 D3
Körösladány 6,565 F3
Kőszeg 12,705 D3
Kunágota 4,622 F3
Kunhegyes 10,116 F3
Kunmadaras 7,343 F3
Kunszentmárton 11,103 F3
Kunszentmiklós 7,952 E3
Lajosmizse 12,872 E3
Lébénymiklós 6,190 D3
Lengyeltóti 3,389 D3
Leninváros 18,667 F3
Lenti 8,106 D3
Létavértes 9,106 G3
Letenye 4,395 D3
Lőkösháza 2,514 F3
Lőrinci 10,679 E3
Madaras 4,519 E3
Makó 29,943 F3
Mándok 5,093 G2
Marcali 12,485 D3
Mátészalka 17,709 G3
Mélykút 7,640 E3
Mérk 3,211 G3
Mezőberény 12,702 F3
Mezőcsát 6,729 F3
Mezőfalva 5,008 E3
Mezőhegyes 8,631 F3
Mezőkovácsháza 7,473 F3
Mezőkövesd 18,435 F3
Mezőszilas 2,792 E3
Mezőtúr 22,018 F3
Mindszent 8,730 F3
Miskolc 206,727 F2
Mohács 21,385 E4
Monor 16,838 E3
Mór 12,066 E3
Mosonmagyaróvár 29,732 D3
Nádudvar 9,447 F3
Nagyatád 12,946 D3
Nagybajom 4,402 D3
Nagyecsed 8,225 G3
Nagyhalász 6,437 F2
Nagykálló 11,282 F3
Nagykanizsa 48,494 D3
Nagykáta 11,922 E3
Nagykőrös 27,900 E3
Nagyszénás 7,124 F3
Nyírábrány 4,509 G3
Nyíradony 7,146 G3
Szarvas 20,598
Szécsény 5,690
Százhalombatta 13,963
Szeged 171,342
Szeghalom 9,736
Szegvár 6,395
Székesfehérvár 103,197
Szekszárd 34,592
Szendrő 4,098
Szentendre 16,844
Szentes 35,326
Szentgotthárd 5,837
Szentlőrinc 3,926
Szerencs 8,612
Szigetvár 12,114
Szikszó 6,419
Szil 2,073
Szolnok 75,203
Szombathely 82,830
Tab 3,922
Tamási 7,602
Tápiószele 5,575
Tapolca 17,161
Tarpa 3,436
Tata 24,114
Tatabánya 75,942
Tét 4,441
Tiszacsege 6,263
Tiszaföldvár 12,560
Tiszafüred 12,259
Tiszakécske 12,378
Tiszalök 6,230
Tiszavasvári 13,292
Tokaj 4,845
Tolna 8,997
Tompa 5,365
Törökszentmiklós 25,551
Tótkomlós 8,803
Tura 8,235
Túrkeve 11,393
Újfehértó 14,412
Újpest 80,384
Újszász 7,098
Vác 34,837
Vál 2,488
Vámospércs 5,213
Várpalota 28,293
Vásárosnamény 8,637
Vasvár 4,275
Vecsés 19,193

Agriculture, Industry and Resources

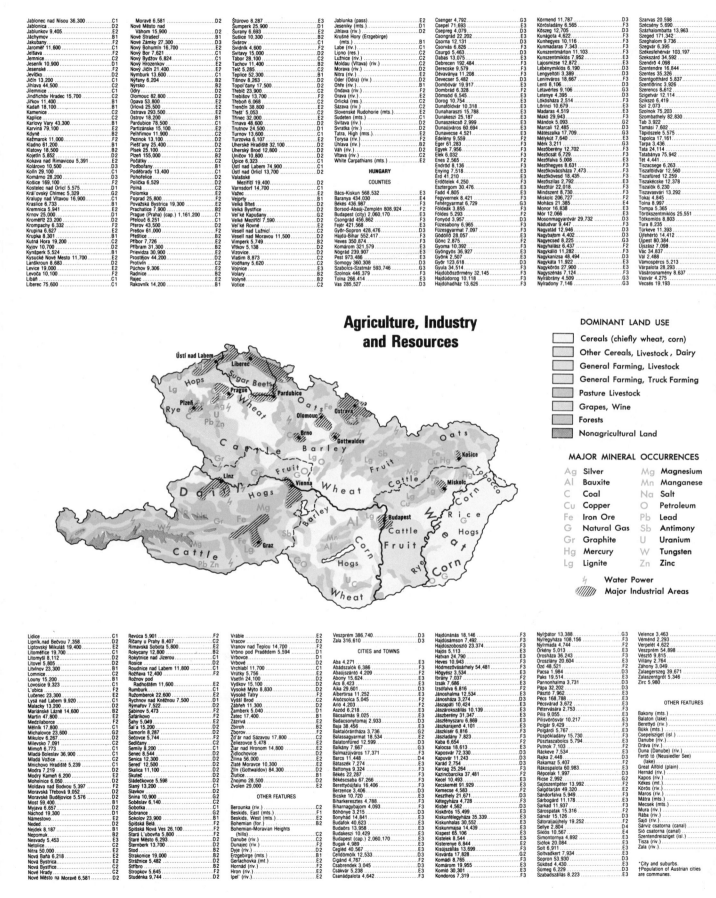

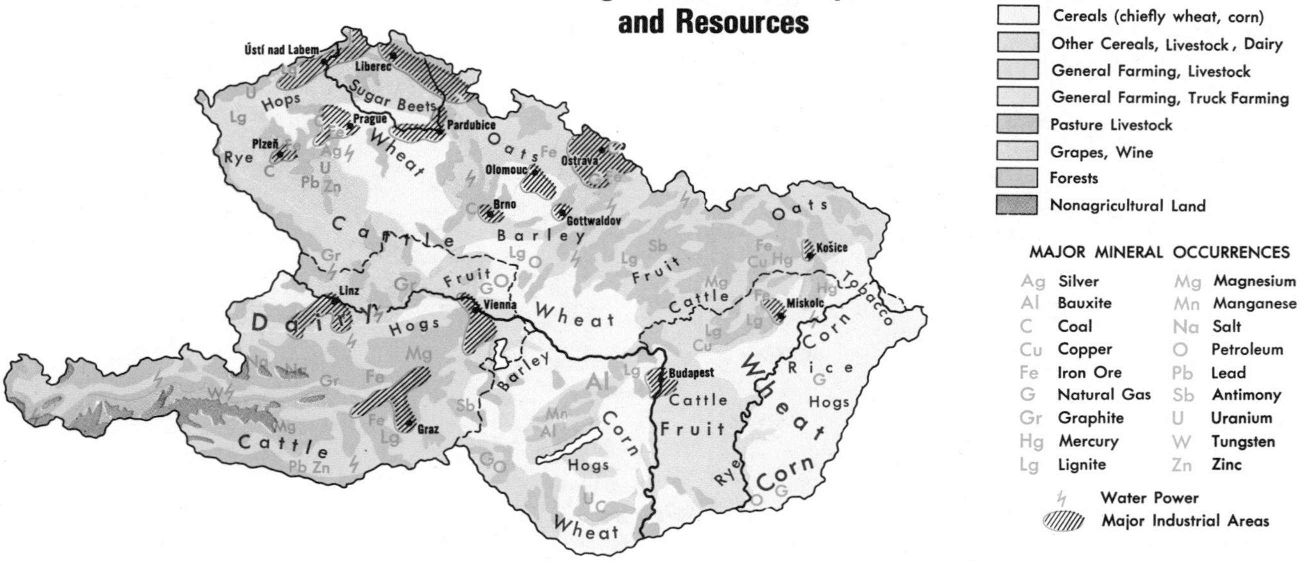
Ústí nad Labem
Liberec
Hops
Sugar Beets
Prague
Pardubice
Plzeň
Rye
Wheat
Oats
Olomouc
Ostrava
Brno
Gottwaldov
Cattle
Barley
Oats
Košice
Fruit
Linz
Vienna
Dairy
Hogs
Wheat
Cattle
Tobacco
Miskolc
Corn
Budapest
Rice
Cattle
Fruit
Hogs
Barley
Graz
Corn
Hogs
Rye
Wheat
DOMINANT LAND USE
Cereals (chiefly wheat, corn)
Other Cereals, Livestock, Dairy
General Farming, Livestock
General Farming, Truck Farming
Pasture Livestock
Grapes, Wine
Forests
Nonagricultural Land
MAJOR MINERAL OCCURRENCES
Ag Silver
Al Bauxite
C Coal
Cu Copper
Fe Iron Ore
G Natural Gas
Gr Graphite
Hg Mercury
Lg Lignite
Mg Magnesium
Mn Manganese
Na Salt
O Petroleum
Pb Lead
Sb Antimony
U Uranium
W Tungsten
Zn Zinc
Water Power
Major Industrial Areas

Lidice C1
Lipník nad Bečvou 7,358 D2
Liptovský Mikuláš 19,400 E2
Litoměřice 19,700 C1
Litomyšl 8,112 D2
Litovel 5,805 D2
Litvínov 23,300 B1
Lomnice C2
Louny 15,200 B1
Lovosice 9,323 C1
L'ubica F2
Lučenec 23,300 E2
Lysá nad Labem 9,920 C1
Malacky 13,200 D2
Mariánské Lázně 14,600 B2
Martin 47,800 E2
Medzilaborce F2
Mělník 17,800 C1
Michalovce 23,600 G2
Mikulov 6,267 D2
Milevsko 7,091 C2
Mimoň 6,773 C1
Mladá Boleslav 36,900 C1
Mladá Vožice C2
Mnichovo Hradiště 5,239 C1
Modra 7,219 D2
Modrý Kameň 6,200 E2
Mohelnice 6,050 D2
Moldava nad Bodvou 5,397 F2
Moravská Třebová 9,052 D2
Moravské Budějovice 5,576 D2
Most 59,400 B1
Myjava 6,657 D2
Náchod 19,300 D1
Námestovo E2
Neded D2
Nejdek 8,187 B1
Nepomuk B2
Nesvady 5,453 E3
Netolice C2
Nitra 50,000 E2
Nová Baňa 6,218 E2
Nová Bystrica E2
Nová Bystřice C2
Nové Hrady C2
Nové Město na Moravě 6,581 D2
Revúca 5,901 F2
Říčany u Prahy 8,407 C2
Rimavská Sobota 5,800 E2
Rokycany 12,800 B2
Rokytnice nad Jizerou C1
Rosice D2
Roudnice nad Labem 11,800 C1
Rožňava 12,400 F2
Rožnov pod Radhoštěm 11,600 E2
Rumburk C1
Ružomberok 22,600 E2
Rychnov nad Kněžnou 7,500 D1
Rýmařov 7,522 D2
Sabinov 5,473 F2
Šafárikovo F2
Šahy 5,049 E2
Šal'a 15,200 D2
Šamorín 8,287 D2
Sečovce 5,744 F2
Sedlčany C2
Semily 8,200 C1
Senec 8,544 D2
Senica 12,300 D2
Sereď 12,500 D2
Skalica 11,100 D2
Skuteč D2
Sládečkovce 5,598 D2
Slaný 13,200 C1
Slavkov D2
Snina 10,900 G2
Soběslav 6,140 C2
Sobotka C1
Sobrance G2
Sokolov 23,900 B1
Spišská Belá F2
Spišská Nová Ves 26,100 F2
Stará L'ubovňa 5,800 F2
Staré Město 6,293 D2
Šternberk 13,700 D2
Stod B2
Strakonice 19,000 B2
Strážnice 5,482 D2
Stříbro B2
Stropkov 5,645 F2
Studénka 9,744 D2
Vráble E2
Vracov D2
Vranov nad Teplou 14,700 F2
Vrbno pod Pradědem 5,594 D1
Vrbovce D1
Vrbové D2
Vrchlabí 11,700 C1
Vrútky 5,756 E2
Vsetín 24,100 D2
Vyškov 15,100 D2
Vysoké Mýto 8,830 D2
Vysoké Tatry F2
Vyšší Brod C2
Zábřeh 11,300 D2
Žamberk 5,040 D1
Žatec 17,400 B1
Zázrivá E2
Zbiroh B2
Zborov F2
Žd'ár nad Sázavou 17,800 C2
Želiezovce 5,478 E2
Žiar nad Hronom 14,800 E2
Židlochovice D2
Žilina 56,000 E2
Zlaté Moravce 10,300 E2
Zlín (Gottwaldov) 84,300 D2
Žlutice B1
Znojmo 28,500 D2
Zvolen 29,000 E2

OTHER FEATURES

Berounka (riv.) C2
Beskids, East (mts.) F1
Beskids, West (mts.) E2
Bohemian (for.) B2
Bohemian-Moravian Heights (hills) C2
Danube (riv.) C2
Dunajec (riv.) F2
Dyje (riv.) D2
Erzgebirge (mts.) B1
Gerlachovka (mt.) E2
Hornád (riv.) F2
Hron (riv.) E2
Ipel' (riv.) E2
Veszprém 386,740 D3
Zala 316,610 D3

CITIES and TOWNS

Aba 4,271 E3
Abádszalók 6,386 F3
Abaújszántó 4,209 F2
Abony 15,624 E3
Ács 8,423 E3
Ajka 29,601 D3
Albertirsa 11,252 E3
Alsózsolca 5,045 F2
Arló 4,203 F2
Aszód 6,218 E3
Bácsalmás 9,025 E3
Badacsonytomaj 2,933 D3
Baja 38,456 E3
Baktalórántháza 3,736 G2
Balassagyarmat 18,534 E2
Balatonfüred 12,599 D3
Balkány 7,667 G3
Balmazújváros 17,371 F3
Barcs 11,448 D4
Bátaszék 7,274 E3
Battonya 9,324 F3
Békés 22,287 F3
Békéscsaba 67,266 F3
Berettyóújfalu 16,406 F3
Berzence 3,406 D3
Bicske 10,720 E3
Biharkeresztes 4,788 F3
Biharnagybajom 4,093 F3
Böhönye 3,215 D3
Bonyhád 14,841 E3
Budafok 40,623 E3
Budaörs 13,958 E3
Budakeszi 10,429 E3
Budapest (cap.) 2,060,170 E3
Bugak 4,989 E3
Cegléd 40,567 E3
Celldömölk 12,533 D3
Cigánd 4,767 F2
Csabrendek 3,045 D3
Csákvár 5,238 E3
Csanádpalota 4,642 F3
Hajdúnánás 18,146 F3
Hajdúsámson 7,492 F3
Hajdúszoboszló 23,374 F3
Hajós 5,113 E3
Hatvan 24,790 E3
Heves 10,943 F3
Hódmezővásárhely 54,481 F3
Hőgyész 3,534 E3
Ibrány 7,037 F2
Izsák 7,686 E3
Izsófalva 6,816 F2
Jánoshalma 12,534 E3
Jánosháza 3,274 D3
Jászapáti 10,424 E3
Jászárokszállás 10,139 E3
Jászberény 31,347 E3
Jászfényszaru 6,869 E3
Jászkarajenő 4,101 E3
Jászkisér 6,816 F3
Jászladány 7,823 F3
Kaba 6,654 F2
Kalocsa 18,613 E3
Kaposvár 72,330 D3
Kapuvár 11,243 D3
Karád 2,754 D3
Karcag 25,264 F3
Kazincbarcika 37,481 F2
Kecel 10,493 E3
Kecskemét 91,929 E3
Kemecse 4,583 F2
Keszthely 21,671 D3
Kétegyháza 4,728 F3
Kisbér 4,562 D3
Kiskőrös 15,499 E3
Kiskunfélegyháza 35,339 E3
Kiskunhalas 30,552 E3
Kiskunmajsa 14,439 E3
Kispest 65,106 E3
Kistelek 8,544 E3
Kisterenye 6,844 E2
Kisújszállás 13,699 F3
Kisvárda 17,828 G2
Komádi 8,765 F3
Komárom 19,955 E3
Komló 30,301 E3
Kondoros 7,319 F3
Nyírbátor 13,388 G3
Nyíregyháza 108,156 F3
Nyírmada 4,744 F2
Örkény 5,013 E3
Orosháza 36,243 F3
Oroszlány 20,604 E3
Ózd 48,521 F2
Pacsa 1,984 D3
Paks 19,514 E3
Pannonhalma 3,731 D3
Pápa 32,202 D3
Pásztó 7,962 E3
Pécs 168,788 E3
Pécsvárad 3,672 E3
Pétervására 2,753 F3
Pilis 9,055 E3
Pilisvörösvár 10,217 E3
Polgár 9,429 F3
Polgárdi 5,767 E3
Püspökladány 15,730 F3
Pusztaszabolcs 5,794 E3
Putnok 7,103 F2
Ráckeve 7,534 E3
Rajka 2,448 D3
Rakamaz 5,407 F2
Rákospalota 60,983 E3
Répcelak 1,997 D3
Ricse 2,992 G2
Sajószentpéter 13,992 F2
Salgótarján 49,320 E2
Sándorfalva 5,949 F3
Sárbogárd 11,178 E3
Sarkad 11,937 F3
Sárospatak 15,316 F2
Sárvár 15,126 D3
Sátoraljaújhely 19,252 F2
Sellye 2,804 D4
Siklós 10,567 E4
Simontornya 4,892 E3
Siófok 20,084 E3
Solt 6,911 E3
Soltvadkert 7,934 E3
Sopron 53,930 D3
Sükösd 4,430 E3
Sümeg 6,229 D3
Szabadszállás 8,223 E3
Velence 3,463 [illegible]
Vémend 2,293 [illegible]
Verpelét 4,622 F2
Veszprém 54,898 D3
Vésztő 9,815 F3
Villány 2,764 E4
Záhony 3,049 G2
Zalaegerszeg 39,671 D3
Zalaszentgrót 5,346 D3
Zirc 5,980 D3

OTHER FEATURES

Bakony (mts.) D3
Balaton (lake) D3
Berettyó (riv.) F3
Bükk (mts.) F2
Csepelsziget (isl.) E3
Danube (riv.) E3
Dráva (riv.) D3
Duna (Danube) (riv.) E3
Fertő tó (Neusiedler See) (lake) D3
Great Alföld (plain) F3
Hernád (riv.) F2
Kapos (riv.) D3
Kékes (mt.) E3
Körös (riv.) F3
Maros (riv.) F3
Mátra (mts.) E3
Mecsek (mts.) D3
Mura (riv.) D3
Rába (riv.) D3
Sajó (riv.) F2
Sárviz csatorna (canal) E3
Sió csatorna (canal) E3
Szentendreisziget (isl.) E3
Tisza (riv.) F3
Zala (riv.) D3

*City and suburbs.
†Population of Austrian cities are communes.

YUGOSLAVIA
AREA 98,766 sq. mi. (255,804 sq. km.)
POPULATION 22,471,000
CAPITAL Belgrade
LARGEST CITY Belgrade
HIGHEST POINT Triglav 9,393 ft. (2,863 m.)
MONETARY UNIT Yugoslav dinar
MAJOR LANGUAGES Serbo-Croatian, Slovenian,
Macedonian, Montenegrin, Albanian
MAJOR RELIGIONS Eastern Orthodoxy,
Roman Catholicism, Islam

ALBANIA
AREA 11,100 sq. mi. (28,749 sq. km.)
POPULATION 2,590,600
CAPITAL Tiranë
LARGEST CITY Tiranë
HIGHEST POINT Korab 9,026 ft. (2,751 m.)
MONETARY UNIT lek
MAJOR LANGUAGE Albanian
MAJOR RELIGIONS Islam, Eastern Orthodoxy,
Roman Catholicism

ROMANIA
AREA 91,699 sq. mi. (237,500 sq. km.)
POPULATION 22,048,305
CAPITAL Bucharest
LARGEST CITY Bucharest
HIGHEST POINT Moldoveanul 8,343 ft.
(2,543 m.)
MONETARY UNIT leu
MAJOR LANGUAGES Romanian, Hungarian
MAJOR RELIGION Eastern Orthodoxy

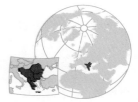

BULGARIA
AREA 42,823 sq. mi. (110,912 sq. km.)
POPULATION 8,862,000
CAPITAL Sofia
LARGEST CITY Sofia
HIGHEST POINT Musala 9,597 ft. (2,925 m.)
MONETARY UNIT lev
MAJOR LANGUAGE Bulgarian
MAJOR RELIGION Eastern Orthodoxy

GREECE
AREA 50,944 sq. mi. (131,945 sq. km.)
POPULATION 9,599,000
CAPITAL Athens
LARGEST CITY Athens
HIGHEST POINT Olympus 9,570 ft. (2,917 m.)
MONETARY UNIT drachma
MAJOR LANGUAGE Greek
MAJOR RELIGION Eastern (Greek) Orthodoxy

BULGARIA

GREECE

YUGOSLAVIA

ALBANIA

ROMANIA

Agriculture, Industry and Resources

DOMINANT LAND USE

- Cereals (chiefly wheat, corn)
- Mixed Farming, Horticulture
- Pasture Livestock
- Tobacco, Cotton
- Grapes, Wine
- Forests
- Nonagricultural Land

MAJOR MINERAL OCCURRENCES

Ab	Asbestos	Mg	Magnesium
Ag	Silver	Mn	Manganese
Al	Bauxite	Mr	Marble
C	Coal	Na	Salt
Cr	Chromium	Ni	Nickel
Cu	Copper	O	Petroleum
Fe	Iron Ore	Pb	Lead
G	Natural Gas	Sb	Antimony
Hg	Mercury	U	Uranium
Lg	Lignite	Zn	Zinc

⚡ Water Power
▨ Major Industrial Areas

ALBANIA

CITIES and TOWNS

Berat 25,700	D5
Çorovodë	E5
Burrel	D5
Delvinë 6,000	D6
Durrës (Durazzo) 53,800	D5
Elbasan 41,700	D5
Ersekë	E5
Fier 23,000	D5
Gjirokastër 17,100	E5
Kavajë 18,700	D5
Korçë 47,300	E5
Krujë 7,900	D5
Kuçovë (Stalin) 14,000	D5
Kukës 6,100	E4
Leskovik	E5
Lezhë	D5
Lushnjë 18,900	D5
Memaliaj	D5
Peqin	D5
Përmet	E5
Peshkopi 6,600	E5
Pogradec 10,100	E5
Pukë	D4
Sarandë 8,700	E6
Shëngjin	D5
Shijak 6,200	D5
Shkodër 55,300	D4
Stalin 14,000	D5
Tepelenë	D5
Tiranë (Tirana) (cap.) 171,300	E5
Vlorë 50,000	D5

OTHER FEATURES

Adriatic (sea)	B4
Drin (riv.)	D4
Korab (mt.)	E5
Ohrid (lake)	E5
Otranto (str.)	D5
Prespa (lake)	E5
Sazan (isl.)	D5
Scutari (lake)	D4
Vijosë (riv.)	D5

BULGARIA

CITIES and TOWNS

Akhtopol 1,265	H4
Alfatar 3,249	H4
Ardino 5,060	H5
Asenovgrad 43,049	G5
Aytos 20,967	H4
Balchik 11,070	H4
Bansko 10,011	F5
Belogradchik 6,892	F4
Berkovitsa 16,253	F4
Blagoevgrad 50,043	F5
Botevgrad 17,789	G4
Bregovo 5,567	F3
Breznik 4,699	F4
Burgas 144,449	H4
Byala 10,564	G4
Byala Slatina 15,788	G4
Chirpan 20,595	G4
Devin 7,120	G5
Dimitrovgrad 45,596	G4
Dobrich (Tolbukhin) 86,184	H4
Dryanovo 9,804	G4
Elena 7,008	G4
Elin Pelin 5,499	F4
Elkhovo 12,397	H4
Gabrovo 75,034	G4
General-Toshevo 8,928	H4
Godech 5,225	F4
Gorna Oryakhovitsa 34,157	G4
Gotse Delchev 17,015	F5
Grudovo 9,871	H4
Ikhtiman 11,482	F4
Isperikh 10,500	H4
Ivaylovgrad 3,900	H5
Karapelit	H4
Karlovo 25,472	G4
Karnobat 21,480	H4
Kavarna 10,872	H4
Kazanlŭk 53,607	G4
Kharmanli 19,240	H5
Khaskovo 75,031	G5
Kotel 8,229	H4
Krumovgrad 5,211	H5
Kubrat 9,826	H4
Kula 5,667	F4
Kŭrdzhali 47,757	G5
Kyustendil 48,239	F4
Lom 30,538	F4
Lovech 43,858	G4

Lukovit 10,400	G4
Malko Tŭrnovo 4,233	H4
Maritsa 8,664	H4
Michurin 4,434	H4
Mikhaylovgrad 40,064	F4
Momchilgrad 8,185	G5
Nesebŭr 6,768	H4
Nikopol 5,563	G4
Nova Zagora 21,872	H4
Novi Pazar 15,751	H4
Omurtag 9,067	H4
Oryakhovo 14,012	F4
Panagyurishte 20,649	F4
Pazardzhik 65,577	G4
Pernik 87,432	F4
Peshtera 16,882	G4
Petrich 24,381	F5
Pirdop 8,248	G4
Pleven 107,567	G4
Plovdiv 300,242	G4
Pomorie 11,960	H4
Popina	H4
Popovo 19,428	H4
Provadiya 15,143	H4
Radomir 10,436	F4
Razgrad 42,486	H4
Rŭzlog 13,690	F5
Rositsa	H4
Ruse 160,351	H4
Samokov 25,763	F4
Sandanski 19,003	F5
Sevlievo 24,421	G4
Shabla 4,471	J4
Shumen 83,525	H4
Silistra 58,270	H4
Simeonovgrad (Maritsa) 8,664	H4
Sliven 90,137	H4
Smolyan 29,032	G5
Smyadovo 5,020	H4
Sofia (cap.) 965,728	F4
Sozopol 3,877	H4
Stanke Dimitrov 42,034	F4
Stara Zagora 122,200	G4
Svilengrad 15,150	G5
Svishtov 29,412	G4
Tetevel 12,555	G4
Tolbukhin 86,184	H4
Topolovgrad 7,230	H4
Tryavna 23,692	G4
Trŭn 3,435	F4
Tŭrgovishte 38,796	H4
Tutrakan 11,447	H4
Varna 251,654	H4
Veliko Tŭrnovo 56,497	G4
Vidin 53,030	F4
Vratsa 61,265	F4
Yambol 75,861	H4
Zimnitsa	H4
Zlatograd 7,732	G5

OTHER FEATURES

Balkan (mts.)	G4
Black (sea)	J4
Danube (riv.)	H4
Dunav (Danube) (riv.)	H4
Emine (cape)	H4
Iskŭr (riv.)	G4
Kaliakra (cape)	J4
Maritsa (riv.)	G4
Mesta (riv.)	F5
Midzhur (mt.)	F4
Musala (mt.)	F4
Osŭm (riv.)	G4
Rhodope (mts.)	G5
Rujen (mt.)	F4
Struma (riv.)	F5
Timok (riv.)	F3
Tundzha (riv.)	H4
Vit (riv.)	G4

GREECE

REGIONS

Aegean Islands 417,813	G6
Athens, Greater 2,566,775	F7
Áyion Óros (aut. dist.) 1,732	G5
Central Greece and Euboea 966,543	F6
Crete 456,642	G8
Epirus 310,334	E6
Ionian Islands 184,443	D6
Macedonia 1,888,952	E5
Pelopónnisos 986,912	F7
Thessaly 659,913	F6
Thrace 329,582	H4

CITIES and TOWNS

Agrínion 30,973	E6
Aíyina 5,704	F7

Aíyion 18,829	F6
Alexandroúpolis 22,995	H5
Alivérion 4,414	G6
Almirós 5,680	F6
Amaliás 14,177	E7
Amfílokhía 4,668	E6
Ámfissa 6,605	F6
Andravídha 3,046	E6
Ándros 1,827	G7
Áno Viánnos 1,431	G8
Anóyia 2,750	G8
Ardhéa 3,555	F5
Areópolis 674	F7
Argalastí 1,621	F6
Árgos 18,890	F7
Argostólion 7,060	E6
Arkhángelos 3,015	J7
Árnaia 2,424	F5
Árta 19,498	E6
Astipálaia 787	H7
Ataláodi 4,581	F6
Athens (cap.) 867,023	F7
Athens* 2,566,775	F7
Ayiá 3,241	F6
Áyios Kírikos 1,083	H7
Áyios Matthaíos 1,596	D6
Áyios Nikólaos 5,002	G8
Candia (Iráklion) 77,506	G8
Canea (Khaniá) 40,564	G8
Corinth 20,773	F7
Delfí 1,185	F6
Delvinákion 1,067	E6
Dhidhimótikhon 8,388	H5
Dhíkaia 1,222	H5
Dhimitsána 996	F7
Dhomokós 1,991	F6
Dráma 29,692	G5
Édhessa 13,967	F5
Elassón 7,200	F6
Elevtheroúpolis 4,888	G5
Ermoúpolis 13,502	G7
Fársala 6,746	F6
Filiátes 2,579	E6
Filiátra 5,919	E7
Filippiás 3,248	E6
Flórina 11,164	E5
Gargaliánoi 5,888	E7
Grevená 8,106	E5
Ídhra 2,387	F7
Ierápetra 7,055	G8
Igoumenítsa 4,109	E6
Ioánnina 40,130	E6
Íos 1,270	G7
Iráklion 77,506	G8
Istiaía 4,059	F6
Itháki 2,293	E6
Kalámai 39,133	F7
Kalampáka 5,453	E6
Kalávrita 1,948	F6
Kálimnos 6,492	H7
Kándanos 403	F8
Kardhítsa 25,685	F6
Kariá 1,351	G8
Karíaí 301	G6
Káristos 3,550	G6
Kárpathos 1,363	H8
Karpenísion 4,414	E6
Kastéllion (Kíssamos) 2,996	F8
Kastéllion 1,152	G8
Kastoría 15,407	E5
Katákolon 690	E7
Kateríni 28,808	F5
Kavália 46,234	G5
Kéa 693	G7
Kérkira 28,630	D6
Khalkís 36,300	F6
Khaniá 40,564	G8
Khíos 24,084	G6
Khóra Sfakíon 246	G8
Kíaton 7,392	F6
Kilkís 10,538	F5
Kími 2,772	F6
Kiparissía 3,882	E7
Kíssamos 2,996	G8
Kíthira 349	F7
Komotiní 28,896	G5
Kónitsa 3,150	E5
Koropí 9,367	G7
Kos 7,828	H7
Kozáni 23,240	F5
Kranídhion 3,657	F7
Lagkadía 1,350	E7
Lamía 37,872	F6
Langadhás 6,707	F5
Langádhia	F7
Lárisa 72,336	F6
Lávrion 8,283	G7
Leonídhion 3,181	F7
Levádhia 15,445	F6
Levkás 6,818	E6
Limenária 1,507	G5

(continued on following page)

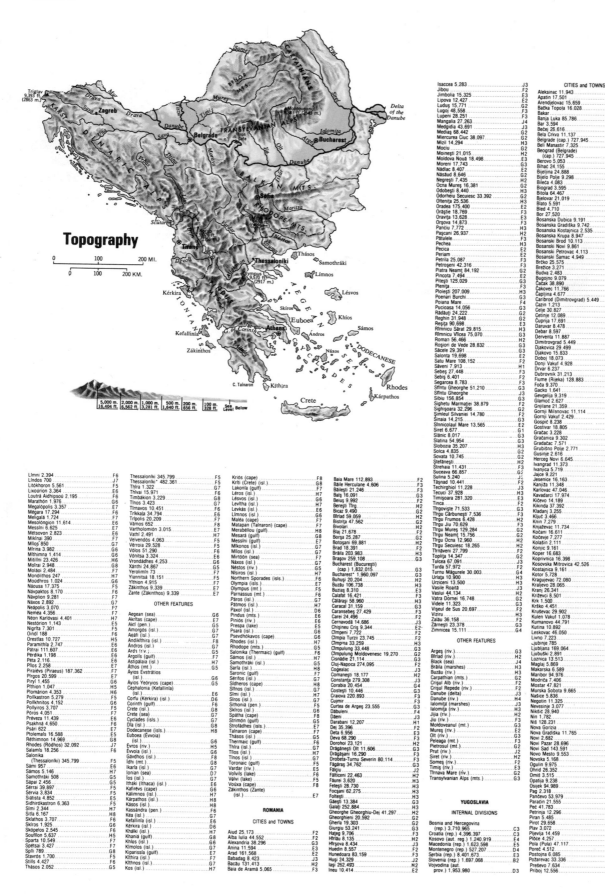

Topography

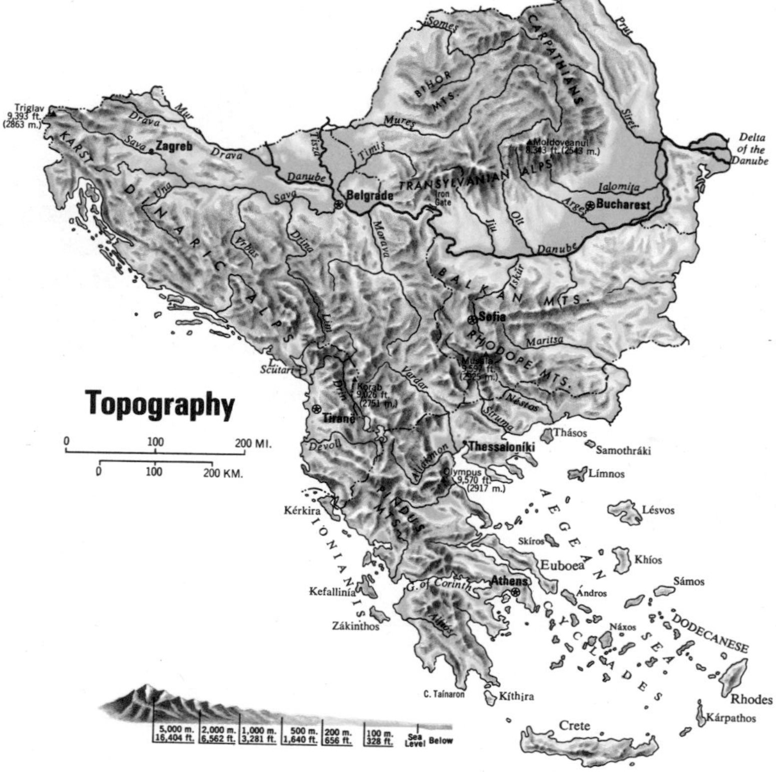
Triglav 9,393 ft. (2863 m.)
Zagreb
Drava
Sava
Mur
Mureș
Someș
Bihor Mts.
Carpathians
Siret
Prut
Delta of the Danube
Tisza
Timiș
Transylvanian Alps
Moldoveanul 8,343 ft. (2543 m.)
Ialomița
Argeș
Bucharest
Danube
Belgrade
Iron Gate
Jiu
Olt
Morava
Una
Vrbas
Drina
Karst
Dinaric Alps
Balkan Mts.
Iskur
Sofia
Maritsa
Rhodope Mts.
Scutari
Drin
Korab 9,026 ft. (2751 m.)
Vardar
Néstos
Struma
Tiranë
Devoli
Thessaloníki
Thásos
Samothráki
Olympus 9,570 ft. (2917 m.)
Límnos
Aliakmon
Pindus Mts.
Kérkira
Ionian Sea
Lésvos
Aegean Sea
Skíros
Euboea
Khíos
Sámos
G. of Corinth
Athens
Kefallinía
Ándros
Zákinthos
Náxos
Dodecanese
Cyclades Sea
C. Taínaron
Kíthira
Rhodes
Kárpathos
Crete
0 100 200 MI.
0 100 200 KM.
5,000 m. 16,404 ft.
2,000 m. 6,562 ft.
1,000 m. 3,281 ft.
500 m. 1,640 ft.
200 m. 656 ft.
100 m. 328 ft.
Sea Level
Below

Límni 2,394 F6
Líndos 700 J7
Litókhoron 5,561 F5
Lixoúrion 3,364 E6
Loutrá Aidhipsoú 2,195 F6
Marathón 1,976 G6
Megalópolis 3,357 E7
Mégara 17,294 F6
Meligalá 1,724 F7
Mesolóngion 11,614 E6
Messíni 6,625 E7
Métsovon 2,823 E6
Mikínai 390 F7
Mílos 850 G7
Mírina 3,982 G6
Míthimna 1,414 G6
Mitilíni 23,426 H6
Moîrai 2,948 G8
Moláoi 2,484 F7
Monólithos 247 H7
Moúdhros 1,024 G6
Náousa 17,375 F5
Návpaktos 8,170 F6
Návplion 9,281 F7
Náxos 2,892 G7
Neápolis 3,070 F7
Neméa 4,356 F7
Néon Karlóvasi 4,401 H7
Nestórion 1,143 E5
Nigríta 7,301 F5
Oinóî 188 F6
Orestías 10,727 H5
Paramithía 2,747 E6
Pátrai 111,607 E6
Pérdika 1,198 E6
Péta 2,116 E6
Pílos 2,258 E7
Piraiévs (Piraeus) 187,362 F7
Pírgos 20,599 E7
Piryí 1,455 G6
Píthion 1,047 H5
Plomárion 4,353 H6
Políkastron 5,279 F5
Políkhnitos 4,152 G6
Pollyíros 3,707 F5
Póros 4,051 F7
Préveza 11,439 E6
Psakhná 4,650 F6
Psári 622 E7
Ptolemaís 16,588 E5
Réthimnon 14,969 G8
Rhodes (Ródhos) 32,092 J7
Salamís 18,256 F6
Salonika
(Thessaloníki) 345,799 F5
Sámi 957 E6
Sámos 5,146 H7
Samothráki 508 G5
Sápai 2,456 G5
Sérrai 39,897 F5
Sérvia 3,834 F5
Siátista 4,852 E5
Sidhirókastron 6,363 F5
Sími 2,344 H7
Sitía 6,167 H8
Skíathos 3,707 F6
Skíros 1,925 G6
Skópelos 2,545 F6
Souflíon 5,637 H5
Sparta 10,549 F7
Spétsai 3,427 F7
Spíli 789 G8
Stavrós 1,700 F5
Stílis 4,427 F6
Thásos 2,052 G5
Thessaloníki 345,799 F5
Thessaloníki* 482,361 F5
Thíra 1,322 G7
Thívai 15,971 F6
Timbákion 3,229 G8
Tínos 3,423 G7
Tírnavos 10,451 F6
Tríkkala 34,794 E6
Trípolis 20,209 F7
Vámos 652 F8
Vartholomión 3,015 E7
Vathí 2,491 H7
Velvendós 4,063 F5
Véroia 29,528 F5
Vólos 51,290 F6
Vónitsa 3,324 E6
Vrondádhes 4,253 G6
Xánthi 24,867 G5
Yerolimín 73 F7
Yiannitsá 18,151 F5
Yíthion 4,915 F7
Zákinthos 9,339 E7
Zante (Zákinthos) 9,339 E7

OTHER FEATURES

Aegean (sea) G6
Akrítas (cape) E7
Aktí (pen.) G5
Amorgós (isl.) G7
Anáfi (isl.) G7
Andikíthira (isl.) F8
Ándros (isl.) G7
Arda (riv.) G5
Argolís (gulf) F7
Astipálaia (isl.) H7
Áthos (mt.) G5
Áyios Evstrátios
(isl.) G6
Áyios Yeóryios (cape) G5
Cephalonia (Kefallinía)
(isl.) E6
Corfu (Kérkira) (isl.) D6
Corinth (gulf) F6
Crete (isl.) G8
Crete (sea) G7
Cyclades (isls.) G7
Día (isl.) G8
Dodecanese (isls.) H8
Euboea (Évvoia)
(isl.) G6
Évros (riv.) H5
Évvoia (isl.) G6
Gávdhos (isl.) F8
Ídhi (mt.) G8
Ikaría (isl.) G7
Ionian (sea) D7
Íos (isl.) G7
Itháki (Ithaca) (isl.) E6
Kafirévs (cape) G6
Kálimnos (isl.) H7
Kárpathos (isl.) H8
Kásos (isl.) H8
Kassándra (pen.) F6
Kéa (isl.) G7
Kefallinía (isl.) E6
Kérkira (isl.) D6
Khálki (isl.) H7
Khaniá (gulf) G8
Khíos (isl.) G6
Kímolos (isl.) G7
Kiparissía (gulf) E7
Kíthira (isl.) F7
Kíthnos (isl.) G7
Kos (isl.) H7
Kriós (cape) F8
Kríti (Crete) (isl.) G8
Lakonía (gulf) F7
Léros (isl.) H7
Lésvos (isl.) G6
Levítha (isl.) H7
Levkás (isl.) E6
Límnos (isl.) G6
Maléa (cape) F7
Matapan (Taínaron) (cape) F7
Merabéllou (gulf) H8
Mesará (gulf) G8
Messíni (gulf) E7
Míkonos (isl.) G7
Mílos (isl.) G7
Mirtóön (sea) F7
Náxos (isl.) G7
Néstos (riv.) G5
Nísiros (isl.) H7
Northern Sporades (isls.) F6
Olympia (isls.) E7
Olympus (mt.) F5
Parnassus (mt.) F6
Páros (isl.) G7
Pátmos (isl.) H7
Paxoí (isl.) D6
Pindus (mts.) E6
Piniós (riv.) E6
Prespa (lake) E5
Psará (isl.) G6
Psevdhókavos (cape) G6
Rhodes (isl.) H7
Rhodope (mts.) G5
Salonika (Thermaic) (gulf) F6
Sámos (isl.) H7
Samothráki (isl.) G5
Saría (isl.) H8
Saronic (gulf) F7
Sérifos (isl.) G7
Sídheros (cape) H8
Sífnos (isl.) G7
Sími (isl.) H7
Síros (isl.) G7
Sithoniá (pen.) F5
Skíros (isl.) G6
Spátha (cape) F8
Strimón (gulf) G5
Strofádhes (isls.) E7
Taínaron (cape) F7
Thásos (isl.) G5
Thermaic (gulf) F6
Thíra (isl.) G7
Tílos (isl.) H7
Tínos (isl.) G7
Toronaic (gulf) F5
Vardar (riv.) E5
Voïvís (lake) F6
Vólvi (lake) F5
Voúxa (cape) F8
Zákinthos (Zante)
(isl.) E7

ROMANIA

CITIES and TOWNS

Aiud 25,173 F2
Alba Iulia 44,552 F2
Alexandria 38,296 G3
Anina 11,594 E3
Arad 161,568 E2
Babadag 8,423 J3
Bacău 131,413 H2
Baia de Aramă 5,065 F3
Baia Mare 112,893 F2
Băile Herculane 4,606 F3
Băilești 21,246 F3
Balș 16,091 G3
Beiuș 9,992 F2
Berești Tîrg H2
Bicaz 9,490 G2
Bîrlad 59,059 H2
Bistrița 47,562 G2
Bivolari H2
Blaj 21,678 F2
Borșa 25,287 G2
Botoșani 69,881 H2
Brad 18,391 F2
Brăila 203,983 H3
Brașov 259,108 G3
Bucharest (București)
(cap.) 1,832,015 G3
Bucharest* 1,960,097 G3
Buhuși 20,204 H2
Buzău 106,738 H3
Buziaș 8,310 E3
Calafat 16,421 F3
Călărași 58,960 H3
Caracal 31,159 G3
Caransebeș 27,429 F3
Carei 24,496 F2
Cernavodă 14,686 J3
Chișineu Criș 9,344 E2
Cîmpeni 7,722 F2
Cîmpia Turzii 23,745 F2
Cîmpina 33,259 H3
Cîmpulung 33,448 G3
Cîmpulung Moldovenesc 19,270 G2
Cisnădie 21,114 G3
Cluj-Napoca 274,095 F2
Cogealac J3
Comanești 18,177 H2
Constanța 279,308 J3
Corabia 20,454 G4
Costești 10,446 G3
Craiova 220,893 F3
Cujmir F3
Curtea de Argeș 23,555 G3
Dăbuleni F4
Dăeni J3
Darabani 12,207 H1
Dej 35,396 F2
Deta 6,956 E3
Deva 68,290 F3
Dorohoi 23,121 H2
Drăgănești Olt 11,606 G3
Drăgășani 16,290 F3
Drobeta-Turnu Severin 80,114 F3
Făgăraș 34,762 G3
Fălçiu J2
Fălticeni 22,463 H2
Făurei 3,620 H3
Fetești 28,730 H3
Focșani 62,275 H3
Foltești H3
Găești 13,384 G3
Galați 252,884 H3
Gheorghe Gheorghiu-Dej 41,297 H2
Gheorghieni 20,592 G2
Gherla 19,303 G2
Giurgiu 53,241 G3
Hațeg 9,706 F3
Hîrlău 8,135 H2
Hîrșova 8,434 J3
Huedin 8,557 F2
Hunedoara 83,159 F3
Huși 24,329 J2
Iași 262,493 H2
Ineu 10,414 E2
Isaccea 5,283 J3
Jibou F2
Jimbolia 15,325 E3
Lipova 12,427 E2
Luduș 15,771 G2
Lugoj 48,558 F3
Lupeni 28,251 F3
Mangalia 27,263 J4
Medgidia 43,691 J3
Mediaș 68,442 G2
Miercurea Ciuc 38,097 G2
Mizil 14,294 H3
Mociu G2
Moinești 21,015 H2
Moldova Nouă 18,498 E3
Moreni 17,743 G3
Nădlac 8,407 E2
Năsăud 8,646 G2
Negrești 7,435 H2
Ocna Mureș 16,381 G2
Odobești 8,440 H3
Odorheiu Secuiesc 33,392 G2
Oltenița 25,536 H3
Oradea 175,400 E2
Orăștie 18,769 F3
Oravița 13,628 E3
Orșova 14,873 F3
Panciu 7,772 H3
Pașcani 26,937 H2
Pătulele F3
Pechea H3
Pecica E2
Periam E2
Petrila 25,087 F3
Petroșeni 42,316 F3
Piatra Neamț 84,192 G2
Pincota 7,494 E2
Pitești 125,029 G3
Plenița F3
Ploiești 207,009 H3
Poenari Burchi G3
Poiana Mare F4
Pucioasa 14,056 G3
Rădăuți 24,222 G2
Reghin 31,948 G2
Reșița 90,698 E3
Rîmnicu Sărat 29,815 H3
Rîmnicu Vîlcea 75,070 G3
Roman 56,466 H2
Roșiori de Vede 28,832 G3
Săcele 29,391 G3
Salonta 19,698 E2
Satu Mare 108,152 F2
Săveni 7,913 H1
Sebeș 27,448 F3
Sebiș 6,401 F2
Segarcea 8,783 F3
Sfîntu Gheorghe 51,210 G3
Sfîntu Gheorghe J3
Sibiu 156,854 G3
Sighetu Marmației 38,879 F2
Sighișoara 32,296 G2
Șimleul Silvaniei 14,780 F2
Sinaia 14,215 G3
Sînnicolaul Mare 13,565 E2
Siret 6,677 G1
Slănic 8,017 G3
Slatina 54,954 G3
Slobozia 35,207 H3
Solca 4,835 G2
Sovata 10,745 G2
Ștefănești H2
Strehaia 11,431 F3
Suceava 66,857 G2
Sulina 5,240 J3
Tășnad 10,441 F2
Techirghiol 11,228 J3
Tecuci 37,928 H3
Timișoara 281,320 E3
Tinca F2
Tîrgoviște 71,533 G3
Tîrgu Cărbunești 7,536 F3
Tîrgu Frumos 6,428 H2
Tîrgu Jiu 70,629 F3
Tîrgu Mureș 129,284 G2
Tîrgu Neamț 15,756 G2
Tîrgu Ocna 12,960 H2
Tîrgu Secuiesc 18,265 H2
Tîrnăveni 27,799 F2
Toplița 14,347 G2
Tulcea 67,091 J3
Turda 57,972 F2
Turnu Măgurele 30,003 G4
Urlața 10,900 H3
Urziceni 13,500 H3
Vasile Roaită J3
Vaslui 44,134 H2
Vatra Dornei 16,748 G2
Videle 11,323 G3
Vișeul de Sus 20,697 F2
Viziru H3
Zalău 36,158 F2
Zărnești 23,378 G3
Zimnicea 15,111 G4

OTHER FEATURES

Argeș (riv.) G3
Bîrlad (riv.) H2
Black (sea) J4
Brăila (marshes) H3
Buzău (riv.) H3
Carpathian (mts.) G2
Crișul Alb (riv.) F2
Crișul Repede (riv.) F2
Danube (delta) J3
Danube (riv.) H4
Ialomiță (marshes) J3
Ialomița (riv.) H3
Jijia (riv.) H2
Jiu (riv.) F3
Moldoveanul (mt.) G3
Mureș (riv.) E2
Olt (riv.) G3
Peleaga (mt.) F3
Pietrosul (mt.) G2
Prut (riv.) J2
Siret (riv.) H2
Someș (riv.) F2
Timiș (riv.) E3
Tîrnava Mare (riv.) G2
Transylvanian Alps (mts.) G3

YUGOSLAVIA

INTERNAL DIVISIONS

Bosnia and Hercegovina
(rep.) 3,710,965 C3
Croatia (rep.) 4,396,397 C3
Kosovo (aut. reg.) 1,240,919 E4
Macedonia (rep.) 1,623,598 E5
Montenegro (rep.) 527,207 D4
Serbia (rep.) 8,401,673 E3
Slovenia (rep.) 1,697,068 B2
Vojvodina (aut.
prov.) 1,953,980 D3

CITIES and TOWNS

Aleksinac 11,943 E4
Apatin 17,501 D3
Arendjelovac 15,659 E3
Bačka Topola 16,028 D3
Bakar B3
Banja Luka 85,786 C3
Bar 3,594 D4
Bečej 26,616 E3
Bela Crkva 11,137 E3
Belgrade (cap.) 727,945 E3
Beli Manastir 7,325 D3
Beograd (Belgrade)
(cap.) 727,945 E3
Berovo 5,053 F5
Bihać 24,155 B3
Bijeljina 24,888 D3
Bijelo Polje 9,298 D4
Bileća 4,083 D4
Biograd 3,595 B4
Bitola 64,467 E5
Bjelovar 21,019 C3
Blato 5,591 C4
Bled 4,710 A2
Bor 27,520 E3
Bosanska Dubica 9,191 C3
Bosanska Gradiška 9,742 C3
Bosanska Kostajnica 2,535 B3
Bosanska Krupa 8,947 C3
Bosanski Brod 10,113 D3
Bosanski Novi 9,861 C3
Bosanski Petrovac 4,113 C3
Bosanski Šamac 4,949 D3
Brčko 25,575 D3
Brežice 3,271 B3
Budva 2,483 D4
Bugojno 9,079 C3
Čačak 38,890 E4
Čakovec 11,766 C2
Čapljina 4,677 C4
Caribrod (Dimitrovgrad) 5,449 F4
Cazin 1,213 B3
Celje 30,827 B2
Cetinje 12,089 D4
Ćuprija 17,691 E4
Daruvar 8,478 C3
Debar 8,597 E5
Derventa 11,887 C3
Dimitrovgrad 5,449 F4
Djakovica 29,499 E4
Djakovo 15,833 D3
Doboj 18,073 C3
Donji Vakuf 4,928 C3
Drvar 6,237 C3
Dubrovnik 31,213 C4
Fiume (Rijeka) 128,883 B3
Foča 9,370 D4
Gacko 1,641 D4
Gevgelija 9,319 F5
Glamoč 2,627 C3
Gnjilane 21,359 E4
Gornji Milanovac 11,114 D3
Gornji Vakuf 2,429 C4
Gospić 8,238 B3
Gostivar 18,805 E5
Gračac 3,228 B3
Gračanica 9,302 D3
Gradačac 7,571 D3
Grubišno Polje 2,771 C3
Gusinje 2,616 D4
Herceg Novi 6,645 D4
Ivangrad 11,373 E4
Ivanjica 5,719 E4
Jajce 9,221 C3
Jesenice 16,163 A2
Kanjiža 11,348 D2
Karlovac 47,046 B3
Kavadarci 17,974 E5
Kičevo 14,189 E5
Kikinda 37,392 E3
Kladanj 3,255 D3
Ključ 3,466 C3
Knin 7,279 C3
Knjaževac 11,734 F4
Kočani 16,611 F5
Kočevje 7,277 B3
Kolašin 2,111 D4
Konjic 9,161 D4
Koper 16,683 A3
Koprivnica 16,398 C2
Kosovska Mitrovica 42,526 E4
Kostajnica 9,161 C3
Kotor 5,728 D4
Kragujevac 72,080 E3
Kraljevo 28,065 E4
Kranj 26,341 B2
Križevci 8,501 C2
Krk 1,500 B3
Krško 4,451 B3
Kruševac 29,902 E4
Kulen Vakuf 1,078 B3
Kumanovo 44,791 E4
Kutina 10,892 C3
Leskovac 46,050 E4
Livno 7,223 C4
Ljubinje 785 D4
Ljubljana 169,064 B3
Ljubuški 2,891 C4
Loznica 13,513 D3
Maglaj 5,869 D3
Makarska 6,589 C4
Maribor 94,976 B2
Modriča 7,406 D3
Mostar 47,821 D4
Murska Sobota 9,665 C2
Našice 5,836 C3
Negotin 11,325 F3
Nevesinje 3,077 D4
Nikšić 28,940 D4
Nin 1,782 B3
Niš 128,231 F4
Nova Gorizia A2
Nova Gradiška 11,765 C3
Novi 2,682 B3
Novi Pazar 28,696 E4
Novi Sad 143,591 D3
Novo Mesto 9,553 B3
Novska 5,168 C3
Ogulin 9,975 B3
Ohrid 26,352 E5
Omiš 3,515 C4
Opatija 9,238 A3
Osijek 94,989 D3
Pag 2,318 B3
Pančevo 53,979 E3
Paraćin 21,555 E4
Peć 41,783 E4
Petrinja 12,296 B3
Piran 5,485 A3
Pirot 29,658 F4
Plav 3,072 D4
Pljevlja 14,459 D4
Ploče 4,257 C4
Pola (Pula) 47,117 A3
Poreč 4,512 A3
Postojna 6,085 B3
Požarevac 33,336 E3
Preševo 7,634 E4
Priboj 12,556 D4
Prijedor 22,379 C
Prijepolje 7,960 D
Prilep 48,045 E
Priština 71,264 E
Prizren 41,875 E
Prokuplje 20,617 E
Prozor 1,420 C
Ptuj 9,245 C
Pula 47,117 A
Rab 1,675 B
Radoviš 9,373 F
Ragusa (Dubrovnik) 31,213 C
Raška 3,935 E
Ravne na Koroškem 6,529 B2
Rijeka 128,883 B3
Rogatica 4,801 D4
Rovinj 8,998 A3
Rožaj E4
Ruma 24,180 D3
Šabac 43,539 D3
Samobor 7,821 B3
Sanski Most 8,718 C3
Sarajevo 245,058 D4
Senj 4,927 B3
Senta 24,694 D3
Šibenik 29,619 C4
Šid 11,867 D3
Sinj 4,705 C4
Sisak 37,215 C3
Sjenica 9,118 E4
Škofja Loka 4,971 A2
Skopje 308,117 E5
Skradin 893 B4
Slavonska Požega 18,160 C3
Slavonski Brod 38,829 D3
Smederevo 39,200 E3
Smederevska Palanka 18,837 E3
Sombor 44,210 D3
Split 150,739 C4
Srebrenica 3,101 D3
Sremska Mitrovica 32,569 D3
Štip 27,218 F5
Stolac 3,862 D4
Ston 407 C4
Struga 11,369 E5
Strumica 22,770 F5
Subotica 89,476 D2
Surdulica 7,048 F4
Svetozarevo 27,812 E4
Svilajnac 7,848 E3
Teslić 4,940 C3
Tetovo 35,293 E5
Titograd 54,639 D4
Titovo Užice 35,465 D4
Titov Veles 35,583 E5
Travnik 12,745 C3
Trbovlje 16,393 B2
Trebinje 3,553 D4
Trogir 6,162 C4
Trstenik 7,167 E4
Tržič 4,435 B2
Tuzla 53,836 D3
Ub 3,785 E3
Ulcinj 7,472 D5
Umag 3,228 A3
Uroševac E4
Valjevo 26,655 D3
Varaždin 34,662 B2
Vareš 7,632 D3
Velenje 11,225 B2
Velika Plana E3
Veliki Bečkerek
(Zrenjanin) 60,201 E3
Vinkovci 29,257 D3
Virovitica 16,389 C3
Višegrad 4,753 D4
Visoko 9,365 D4
Vlasenica 4,033 D3
Vranje 25,909 F4
Vrbas 22,502 D3
Vršac 33,573 E3
Vučitrn 11,701 E4
Vukovar 29,500 D3
Žabljak 1,023 D4
Zadar 43,588 B3
Zagreb 561,773 C3
Zaječar 27,724 E4
Zara (Zadar) 43,588 B3
Zenica 49,522 C3
Žepče 3,177 D3
Zrenjanin 60,201 E3
Zvornik 8,498 D3

OTHER FEATURES

Adriatic (sea) B4
Bobotov Kuk (mt.) D4
Bosna (riv.) D3
Brač (isl.) C4
Cazma (riv.) C3
Cres (isl.) B3
Čvrsnica (mt.) C4
Dalmatia (reg.) C4
Danube (riv.) E3
Dinaric Alps (mts.) B3
Drava (riv.) C3
Drina (riv.) D3
Dugi Otok (isl.) B3
Hvar (isl.) C4
Ibar (riv.) E4
Istria (pen.) A3
Kamenjak (cape) A3
Kladovo F3
Korab (mt.) E5
Korčula (isl.) C4
Kornat (isl.) B4
Krk (isl.) B3
Kupa (riv.) B3
Kvarner (gulf) B3
Lastovo (Lagosta) (isl.) C4
Lim (riv.) D4
Lošinj (isl.) B3
Midzhur (mt.) F4
Mljet (isl.) C4
Morava (riv.) E3
Mur (riv.) B2
Neretva (riv.) D4
Ohrid (lake) E5
Pag (isl.) B3
Palagruža (Pelagosa) (isl.) C4
Prespa (lake) E5
Rab (isl.) B3
Rujen (mt.) F4
Sava (riv.) D3
Scutari (lake) D4
Slavonia (reg.) C3
Šolta (isl.) C4
Tara (riv.) D4
Timok (riv.) F3
Tisa (riv.) E3
Triglav (mt.) A2
Una (riv.) C3
Vardar (riv.) E5
Vis (isl.) C4
Vrbas (riv.) C3
Žirje (isl.) B4

*City and suburbs.

The Balkan States

CONIC PROJECTION

SCALE OF MILES

0 25 50 75 100 125 150 175

SCALE OF KILOMETERS

0 25 50 75 100 125 150 175

Capitals of Countries ⎯⎯⎯⎯ ☆

Administrative Centers ⎯⎯⎯⎯ △

International Boundaries ⎯ ⎯ ⎯

Major Internal Boundaries ⎯ ⎯ ⎯

Minor Internal Boundaries ⎯⎯⎯⎯

Canals ⎯⎯⎯⎯

BULGARIA and GREECE are divided into counties and
departments, respectively. Because of the scale no
attempt has been made to delimit and name these subdivisions; their administrative centers have, however,
been designated.
  The larger divisions named in Greece are well-known
geographical regions, without administrative function.
ROMANIA consists of thirty-nine counties and
three cities of regional status, Bucharest, Constanța
and Petroșeni. Scale does not permit delimiting
these counties.
  ALBANIA is divided into twenty-seven districts. Scale
does not permit the delimitation of these divisions.
YUGOSLAVIA is a federation of six republics. The
Serbian republic includes an autonomous province
(Vojvodina), and an autonomous region (Kosovo).

© Copyright HAMMOND INCORPORATED, Maplewood, N. J.

Topography

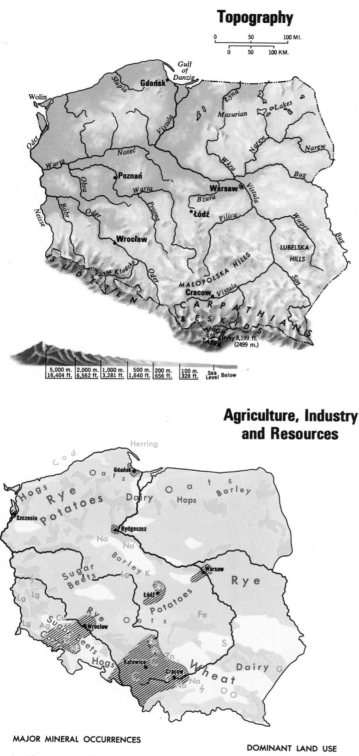

0   50   100 MI.

0   50   100 KM.

5,000 m.	2,000 m.	1,000 m.	500 m.	200 m.	100 m.	Sea	Below
16,404 ft.	6,562 ft.	3,281 ft.	1,640 ft.	656 ft.	328 ft.	Level	

Agriculture, Industry and Resources

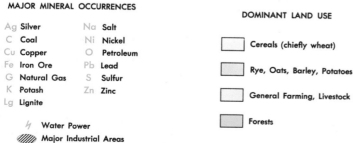

MAJOR MINERAL OCCURRENCES

Ag	Silver	Na	Salt
C	Coal	Ni	Nickel
Cu	Copper	O	Petroleum
Fe	Iron Ore	Pb	Lead
G	Natural Gas	S	Sulfur
K	Potash	Zn	Zinc
Lg	Lignite		

⚡ Water Power

▨ Major Industrial Areas

DOMINANT LAND USE

☐ Cereals (chiefly wheat)

▨ Rye, Oats, Barley, Potatoes

☐ General Farming, Livestock

▨ Forests

Poland 1938

0   50   100
MILES

Poland 1945

0   50   100
MILES

AREA 120,725 sq. mi. (312,678 sq. km.)
POPULATION 35,815,000
CAPITAL Warsaw
LARGEST CITY Warsaw
HIGHEST POINT Rysy 8,199 ft. (2,499 m.)
MONETARY UNIT zloty
MAJOR LANGUAGE Polish
MAJOR RELIGION Roman Catholicism

Braniewo 12,100	D1
Breslau (Wrocław) 461,900	C3
Brieg (Brzeg) 30,780	C3
Brodnica 17,300	D2
Brzeg 30,780	C3
Brzeg Dolny 10,800	C3
Brzesko 9,701	E3
Busko Zdrój 11,100	E3
Bydgoszcz 280,460	C2
Bytom 186,993	A3
Bytów 10,642	C1
Chełm 38,789	F3
Chełmno 17,906	D2
Chełmża 14,200	D2
Chodzież 14,100	C2
Chojnice 23,500	C2
Chojnów 11,000	B3
Chorzów 151,338	B4
Choszczno 9,800	B2
Chrzanów 29,300	B4
Ciechanów 28,500	E2
Cieplice Śląskie-Zdrój 15,400	B3
Cieszyn 25,234	D4
Cracow 651,300	E4
Czechowice-Dziedzice 25,400	D4
Czeladź 31,843	B4
Częstochowa 187,613	D3
Dąbrowa Górnicza 61,660	B3
Danzig (Gdańsk) 364,285	C1
Darłowo 11,200	C1
Dębica 22,900	E3
Dęblin 14,600	E3
Debno 10,700	A2
Działdowo 10,100	D2
Dzierżoniów 32,800	C3
Elbing (Elbląg) 89,835	D1
Ełk 27,188	F2
Gdańsk 364,285	C1
Gdynia 190,125	D1
Giżycko 18,200	E1
Gleiwitz (Gliwice) 170,912	A4
Głogów (Glogau) 20,226	C3
Głowno 12,800	D2
Głubczyce 11,300	C3
Głuchołazy 13,200	C3
Gniezno 50,643	C2
Goleniów 14,600	B2
Gorlice 15,200	E4
Gorzów Wielkopolski 74,267	B2
Gostyń 13,000	C3
Gostynin 12,000	D2
Grajewo 11,200	F2
Grodzisk Mazowiecki 20,400	E2
Grójec 10,300	E3
Grudziądz 75,511	D2
Grünberg (Zielona Góra) 59,700	B3
Gryfice 13,200	B2
Guben (Gubin) 14,600	B3
Hajnówka m4,345	F2
Hindenburg (Zabrze) 199,400	A4
Hirschberg (Jelenia Góra) 55,720	B3
Hrubieszów 14,999	F3
Iława 16,400	D2
Inowrocław 54,817	D2

Jarocin 18,100	C3
Jarosław 29,000	F4
Jasło 17,025	E4
Jastrzębie Zdrój 34,400	D3
Jaworzno 63,271	D3
Jędrzejów 13,264	E3
Jelenia Góra 55,720	B3
Kalisz 81,227	D3
Kamienna Góra 21,000	B3
Kartuzy 10,558	C1
Katowice 303,264	B4
Kępno 10,151	C3
Kętrzyn 19,300	E1
Kielce 125,952	E3
Kłobuck 12,600	D3
Kłodzko 26,000	C3
Kluczbork 18,000	D3
Knurów 28,400	A4
Kolberg (Kołobrzeg) 25,419	B1
Koło 13,100	D2
Kołobrzeg 25,419	B1
Konin 40,600	D2
Konstantynów Łódzki 12,800	D3
Kościan 18,700	C3
Kościerzyna 18,914	C1
Köslin (Koszalin) 64,414	C1
Kostrzyn 11,200	B2
Koszalin 64,414	C1
Kraków (Cracow) 651,300	E4
Krapkowice 13,800	D3
Kraśnik Fabryczny 14,600	F3
Krasnystaw 12,495	F3
Krosno 26,500	E4
Krotoszyn 21,900	C3
Krynica 10,200	E4
Ktistrin 11,200	B2
Kutno 30,000	D2
Kwidzyn 23,104	D2
Łańcut 12,049	F3
Landsberg (Gorzów Wielkopolski) 74,267	B2
Łaziska Górne 10,800	A4
Łebork 25,000	C1
Łęczyca 13,900	D2
Legionowo 20,800	E2
Legnica 75,843	C3
Leszczyny 12,200	A4
Leszno 33,890	C3
Libiąż 10,600	D3
Lidzbark Warmiński 12,900	E1
Liegnitz (Legnica) 75,843	C3
Lipno 10,900	D2
Łódź 777,800	D3
Łomża 25,500	F2
Łowicz 20,400	E2
Lubań 17,200	B3
Lubartów 10,000	F3
Lubin 28,400	C3
Lublin 235,937	F3
Lubliniec 19,800	D3
Lubin 16,400	C2
Lubsko 12,600	B3
Łuków 15,500	F3
Malbork (Marienburg) 30,900	D1

Międzyrzec Podlaski 13,500	F3
Międzyrzecz 14,900	B2
Mielec 26,800	E3
Mików 21,300	B4
Mińsk Mazowiecki 24,200	E2
Mława 20,007	E2
Mońki 9,560	F2
Morąg 9,681	E2
Mragowo 13,400	E2
Myślenice 12,100	E4
Myślowice 44,737	C4
Myszków 18,000	D3
Nakło nad Notecią 16,800	C2
Namysłów 11,700	C3
Neisse (Nysa) 31,837	C3
Nidzica 9,642	E2
Nisko 10,000	F3
Nowa Ruda 18,100	C3
Nowa Sól 33,300	B3
Nowy Dwór Mazowiecki 16,900	E2
Nowy Sącz 41,103	E4
Nowy Targ 21,900	E4
Nysa 31,837	C3
Oborniki 10,200	C2
Oława 17,746	C3
Oleśnica 27,500	C3
Olkusz 15,800	D3
Olsztyn 94,119	E2
Opoczno 12,168	E3
Opole 86,510	C3
Oppeln 86,510	C3
Oleszno 9,600	D2
Ostróda 21,300	D2
Ostrołęka 21,981	E2
Ostrów Mazowiecka 15,000	E2
Ostrów Wielkopolski 49,530	C3
Ostrowiec Świętokrzyski 49,958	E3
Oświęcim 39,600	D3
Otwock 39,863	E2
Ozorków 18,200	D3
Pabianice 62,275	D3
Piekary Śląskie 36,300	B4
Piła 43,778	C2

Pionki 13,600	E3
Piotrków Trybunalski 59,683	D3
Pisz 11,100	E2
Pleszew 13,348	C3
Płock 71,727	D2
Prudnik 11,619	C3
Police 12,700	B2
Poznań 469,085	C2
Prudnik 20,300	C3
Pruszcz Gdański 13,000	D1
Pruszków 44,737	E2
Przasnysz 11,100	E2
Przemyśl 53,228	F4
Puck 9,500	D1
Puławy 34,600	E3
Pułtusk 12,600	E2
Rabka 10,700	D4
Racibórz 40,418	C3
Radom 158,640	E3
Radomsko 31,179	D3
Ratibor (Racibórz) 40,418	C3
Rawa Mazowiecka 9,800	E3
Rawicz 18,300	C3
Ruda Śląska 142,407	B4
Rumia 23,300	D1
Rybnik 43,415	D3
Rypin 11,029	D2
Rzeszów 82,192	F4
Sandomierz 16,800	E3
Sanok 24,000	F4
Schneidemühl (Piła) 36,600	C2
Schweidnitz (Świdnica) 47,542	C3
Siedlce 38,983	F2
Siemianowice Śląskie 67,278	B4
Sieradz 18,500	D3
Sierpc 12,700	D2
Skarżysko-Kamienna 39,194	E3
Skawina 15,900	D3
Skierniewice 25,590	E2
Sławno 10,700	C1
Słubice 12,000	B2
Słupsk 68,311	C1

Sochaczew 20,500	E2
Sokółka 10,023	F2
Sokołów Podlaski 9,569	F2
Sopot 47,573	D1
Sosnowiec 144,652	B4
Śrem 65,000	C2
Środa Śląska 10,259	C3
Środa Wielkopolska 14,800	C2
Stalowa Wola 29,768	F3
Starachowice 42,807	E3
Stargard Szczeciński 44,400	B2
Starogard Gdański 33,400	D2
Stary Sącz 57,400	E4
Stettin (Szczecin) 337,294	B2
Stolp (Słupsk) 68,311	C1
Strzegom 14,000	C3
Strzelce Opolskie 14,700	D3
Strzelin 9,800	C3
Sulechów 10,300	B2
Suwałki 25,360	F1
Swarzędz 12,100	C2
Świdnica 47,542	C3
Świdnik 21,900	F3
Świdwin 12,500	B2
Świebodzice 18,500	C3
Świebodzin 14,900	B2
Świecie 17,900	D2
Świdwin 11,029	B4
Świętochłowice 57,633	A4
Świnoujście (Swinemünde) 27,900	B1
Szamotuły 14,600	C2
Szczecin 337,204	B2
Szczecinek 28,600	C2
Szczytno 17,371	E2
Szprotawa 11,200	B3
Tarnobrzeg 18,800	E3
Tarnów 85,514	E4
Tarnowskie Góry 34,200	A3
Tczew 40,794	D1
Tomaszów Lubelski 12,329	F3
Tomaszów Mazowiecki 54,911	E3
Toruń 129,152	D2
Trzcianka 10,900	C2
Trzebinia-Siersza	E2

Turek 18,500	D2
Tychy 71,384	B4
Ustka 9,900	C1
Wąbrzeźno 11,800	D2
Wadowice 11,700	D4
Wągrowiec 15,600	C2
Wałbrzych 125,048	C3
Wałcz 18,900	C2
Waldenburg (Wałbrzych) 125,048	C3
Warsaw (Warszawa) (cap.) 1,377,100	E2
Wejherowo 33,600	D1
Wieliczka 13,600	E4
Wieluń 14,300	D3
Wisła 9,800	D4
Włocławek 77,169	D2
Wodzisław Śląski 25,600	D4
Wolin 35,458	B2
Wołomin 24,000	E2
Wołów 10,500	C3
Woźniki 12,100	C2
Wrocław 523,318	C3
Września 17,800	C2
Wschowa 10,000	C3
Wyszków	E2
Ząbki 16,000	E2
Ząbkowice Śląskie 13,800	C3
Zabrze 197,214	A4
Żagań 21,400	B3
Zakopane 27,039	D4
Zambrów 14,082	F2
Zamość 34,734	F3
Żary 28,300	B3
Zawiercie 39,410	D3
Zduńska Wola 29,066	D3
Zgierz 42,838	D3
Zgorzelec 28,400	B3
Ziębice 9,900	C3
Zielona Góra 73,156	B3
Złocieniec 10,100	C2
Złotów 11,600	C2
Znin 9,600	C2
Żyrardów 33,196	E2

Żywiec 22,400	D4
OTHER FEATURES	
Baltic (sea)	B1
Beskids (range)	D4
Brda (riv.)	C2
Brynica (riv.)	B4
Bug (riv.)	F2
Danzig (Gdańsk) (gulf)	D1
Dukla (pass)	E4
Dunajec (riv.)	E4
Gwda (riv.)	C2
Hel (pen.)	D1
High Tatra (range)	D4
Kłodnica (riv.)	A4
Łyna (riv.)	E1
Mamry, Jezioro (lake)	E1
Narew (riv.)	E2
Neisse (riv.)	B3
Notec (riv.)	B2
Nysa Kłodzka (riv.)	C3
Nysa Łużycka (Neisse) (riv.)	B3
Oder (riv.)	B3
Orava (riv.)	D4
Pilica (riv.)	D3
Pomeranian (bay)	B1
Przemsza (riv.)	B4
Rysy (mt.)	F3
San (riv.)	F3
Słupia (riv.)	C1
Śniardwy, Jezioro (lake)	E2
Sudeten (range)	B3
Uznam (Usedom) (isl.)	B1
Vistula (riv.)	D1
Warmia (reg.)	D1
Warta (riv.)	B2
Wieprz (riv.)	F3
Wisła (Vistula) (riv.)	D2
Wkra (riv.)	E2
Wolin (Wollin) (isl.)	B2

© Copyright HAMMOND INCORPORATED, Maplewood, N.J.

Poland
CONIC PROJECTION

Capitals of Countries.......★
Other Capitals.......●
International Boundaries.......
Internal Boundaries.......
Canals.......

Poland is divided into 49 provinces (bearing the same name as their capitals) and the autonomous cities of Warsaw, Łódź and Cracow.

UNION REPUBLICS

Armenian S.S.R. 3,031,000	E6
Azerbaidzhan S.S.R. 6,028,000	E5
Estonian S.S.R. 1,466,000	C4
Georgian S.S.R. 5,015,000	E5
Kazakh S.S.R. 14,684,000	G5
Kirgiz S.S.R. 3,529,000	H5
Latvian S.S.R. 2,521,000	C4
Lithuanian S.S.R. 3,398,000	C4
Moldavian S.S.R. 3,947,000	C5
Russian S.F.S.R. 137,551,000	D4
Tadzhik S.S.R. 3,801,000	H6
Turkmen S.S.R. 2,759,000	F6
Ukrainian S.S.R. 49,755,000	C5
Uzbek S.S.R. 15,391,000	G5
White Russian S.S.R. 9,560,000	C4

INTERNAL DIVISIONS

Abkhaz A.S.S.R. 505,000	E5
Adygey Aut. Obl. 405,000	D5
Adzhar A.S.S.R. 354,000	E5
Aginsk Buryat Aut. Okr. 69,000	M4
Bashkir A.S.S.R. 3,849,000	F4
Buryat A.S.S.R. 900,000	M4
Chechen-Ingush A.S.S.R. 1,154,000	E5
Chukchi Aut. Okr. 133,000	R3
Chuvash A.S.S.R. 1,292,000	E4
Dagestan A.S.S.R. 1,628,000	E5
Evenki Aut. Okr. 16,000	K3
Gorno-Altay Aut. Obl. 172,000	J4
Gorno-Badakhshan Aut. Obl. 127,000	H6
Jewish Aut. Obl. 190,000	O5
Kabardin-Balkar	

A.S.S.R. 674,000	E5
Kalmuck A.S.S.R. 294,000	E5
Karachay-Cherkess Aut. Obl. 368,000	E5
Karakalpak A.S.S.R. 904,000	G5
Karelian A.S.S.R. 736,000	D3
Khakass Aut. Obl. 500,000	J4
Khanty-Mansi Aut. Okr. 569,000	H3
Komi A.S.S.R. 1,119,000	F3
Komi-Permyak Aut. Okr. 173,000	F4
Koryak Aut. Okr. 34,000	R3
Mari A.S.S.R. 703,000	E4
Mordvinian A.S.S.R. 991,000	E4
Nagorno-Karabakh Aut. Obl. 161,000	E6
Nakhichevan' A.S.S.R. 239,000	E6
Nenets Aut. Okr. 47,000	F3
North Ossetian A.S.S.R. 597,000	E5
South Ossetian Aut. Obl. 98,000	E5
Tatar A.S.S.R. 3,436,000	F4
Taymyr Aut. Okr. 44,000	K2
Tuvinian A.S.S.R. 267,000	K4
Udmurt A.S.S.R. 1,494,000	F4
Ust'-Ordynskiy Buryat Aut. Okr. 133,000	L4
Yakut A.S.S.R. 839,000	N3
Yamal-Nenets Aut. Okr. 158,000	H3

CITIES and TOWNS

Abakan 128,000	K4
Abay 34,245	H5
Abaza 15,202	J4
Achinsk 117,000	K4
Agata	K3
Aginskoye 7,922	M4
Akmolinsk (Tselinograd) 234,000	H4
Aksay 10,010	F4
Aktas	G5
Aktash	D3
Aktyubinsk 191,000	F4
Aldan 17,689	N4
Aleksandrovsk-Sakhalinskiy 20,342	P5
Alekseyevka 18,041	E4
Alga 12,000	F5
Aliskerovo	R3
Aliakh-Yun'	O3
Alma-Ata 910,000	H5
Almazny	M3
Ambarchik	R3
Amderma	E3
Amursk 24,010	O4
Anadyr' 7,703	S3
Andizhan 230,000	H5
Andropov 239,000	D4
Angarsk 239,000	L4
Angren	H5
Anzhero-Sudzhensk 105,000	J4
Aral'sk 37,722	G5
Archangel (Arkhangel'sk) 385,000	E3
Arkalyk 15,108	G4
Armavir 162,000	E5
Arsen'yev 60,000	O5
Artem 69,000	O5
Artemovskiy	G5
Arys 26,414	G5
Arzamas 93,000	E4
Asbest 79,000	G4

Ashkhabad 312,000	F6
Asino 29,395	J4
Astrakhan' 461,000	F5
Atbasar 37,229	H4
Atka	Q3
Ayaguz 35,827	J5
Ayan	O4
Aykhal	M3
Bagdarin	M4
Baku 1,022,000	F5
Baku' 1,550,000	F5
Balakovo 152,000	F4
Balashov 93,000	E4
Baley 27,215	M4
Balkhash 78,000	H5
Balykhty 22,397	H5
Bam	N2
Barabinsk 37,274	H4
Baranovichi 131,000	C4
Batagay 10,000	O3
Batumi 123,000	E5
Baykit	K3
Baykonyr	G5
Bayram-Ali 31,987	G6
Belgorod 240,000	D4
Belogorsk 63,000	N4
Belomorsk 16,595	D3
Beloretsk 71,000	F4
Belovo 112,000	J4
Berdichev 80,000	C5
Berdsk 67,000	J4
Bereznik 185,000	F4
Berezovo 6,000	G3
Beringovskiy	T3
Bikin 17,473	O5
Bira	O5

Birobidzhan 69,000	O5
Biruni	G5
Biysk 212,000	J4
Blagoveshchensk 172,000	N4
Bobruysk 192,000	C4
Bodaybo 19,000	M4
Borisoglebsk 68,000	E4
Bornya 27,815	M4
Bratsk 214,000	L4
Brest 177,000	C4
Brindakit	O4
Bryansk 394,000	D4
Bugul'ma 80,000	F4
Bukachacha 10,000	M4
Bukhara 185,000	G5
Bulun	N2
Buzuluk 76,000	F4
Chadan	K4
Chapayevsk 85,000	F4
Chara	M4
Chardzhou 140,000	G6
Charsk 10,100	J5
Cheboksary 308,000	E4
Chegdomyn 16,499	O4
Chelkar 19,377	F5
Chelyabinsk 1,030,000	G4
Cheremkhovo 77,000	L4
Cherepovets 266,000	D4
Cherkessk 91,000	E5
Chernigov 238,000	D4
Chernogorsk 71,000	K4
Chernovtsy 219,000	C5
Chernyshevsk 10,000	M4
Chersky	O3
Chimbay 18,899	G5
Chimkent 322,000	H5
Chirchik 132,000	H5

Chita 303,000	M4
Chokurdakh	P2
Chumikan	O4
Dal'negorsk 33,506	O5
Dal'nerechensk 28,224	O5
Daugavpils 116,000	C4
Denau	H6
Dikson	J2
Dimitrovgrad 106,000	F4
Dnepropetrovsk 1,066,000	D5
Donetsk 1,021,000	D5
Drogobych 66,000	C5
Druzhba	C5
Druzhina	P3
Dudinka 19,701	J3
Dushanbe 494,000	G6
Dzerzhinsk 257,000	E4
Dzhalal-Abad 55,000	H5
Dzhalinda	N4
Dzhambul 264,000	H5
Dzhelinda	M2
Dzhetygara 32,169	G4
Dzhezkazgan 89,000	G5
Dzhusaly 20,658	G5
Egvekinot	S3
Ekibastuz 66,000	H4
Ekimchan	O4
El'dikan	O3
Elista 70,000	E5
Emba 17,820	F5
Engel's 161,000	F4
Erivan 1,019,000	E6
Evensk	Q3
Fergana 176,000	H5
Fort-Shevchenko 12,000	F5
Frolovo 33,398	E4
Frunze 533,000	H5

Gasan-Kuli	F6
Gol'chikha	J3
Gomel 383,000	D4
Gor'kiy 1,344,000	E4
Gorno-Altaysk 34,413	J4
Gornyak 16,643	J4
Grodno 195,000	C4
Groznyy 375,000	E5
Gubakha 33,243	F4
Gulistan 30,879	H5
Gur'yev 131,000	F5
Gusinoozersk 10,000	L4
Gyda	H2
Igarka 15,624	J3
Igrim	G3
Ilanskiy 22,852	K4
Indiga	F3
Inta 51,000	F3
Iolotan' 10,000	G6
Irkutsk 550,000	L4
Ishim 63,000	G4
Isil'kul' 25,958	H4
Iul'tin	S3
Ivano-Frankovsk 150,000	C5
Ivanovo 465,000	E4
Ivdel 15,308	G3
Izhevsk (Ustinov) 549,000	F4
Izmail 83,000	C5
Kachug	L4
Kagan 34,117	G5
Kalachinsk 20,809	H4
Kalakan	M4
Kalinin 412,000	D4
Kaliningrad 355,000	B4
Kalmykovo	F5
Kaluga 265,000	D4
Kamen'-na-Obi 35,604	H4

Union of Soviet Socialist Republics
CONIC PROJECTION
SCALE OF MILES
0   100   200   300   400   500   600
SCALE OF KILOMETERS
0   100   200   300   400   500   600

Capitals
★ National
☆ Union Republic
◎ A.S.S.R.
⊚ Autonomous Oblast
⊙ Autonomous Okrug

Boundaries
National
Union Republic
A.S.S.R.
Autonomous Oblast
Autonomous Okrug

ADMINISTRATIVE DIVISIONS NOT NAMED ON MAP

Division	Ref.
1. Abkhaz A.S.S.R.	E5
2. Adygey Aut. Oblast	D5
3. Adzhar A.S.S.R.	E5
4. Aginsk Buryat Autonomous Okrug	M4
5. Chechen-Ingush A.S.S.R.	E5
6. Chuvash A.S.S.R.	E4
7. Gorno-Altay Aut. Oblast	J4
8. Gorno-Badakhshan Aut. Oblast	H6
9. Jewish Aut. Oblast	O5
10. Kabardin-Balkar A.S.S.R.	E5
11. Karachay-Cherkess Aut. Oblast	E5
12. Karakalpak A.S.S.R.	G5
13. Khakass Aut. Oblast	J4
14. Komi-Permyak Aut. Okrug	F4
15. Mari A.S.S.R.	E4
16. Mordvinian A.S.S.R.	E4
17. Nagorno-Karabakh Aut. Oblast	E5
18. Nakhichevan' A.S.S.R.	E5
19. North Ossetian A.S.S.R.	E5
20. South Ossetian Aut. Oblast	E5
21. Tatar A.S.S.R.	F4
22. Tuvinian A.S.S.R.	K4
23. Udmurt A.S.S.R.	F4
24. Ust'-Ordynsk Buryat Autonomous Okrug	L4

AREA 8,649,490 sq. mi. (22,402,179 sq. km.)
POPULATION 262,436,227
CAPITAL Moscow
LARGEST CITY Moscow
HIGHEST POINT Communism Peak 24,599 ft. (7,498 m.)
MONETARY UNIT ruble
MAJOR LANGUAGES Russian, Ukrainian, White Russian, Uzbek, Azerbaidzhani, Tatar, Georgian, Lithuanian, Armenian, Yiddish, Latvian, Mordvinian, Kirgiz, Tadzhik, Estonian, Kazakh, Moldavian (Romanian), German, Chuvash, Turkmenian, Bashkir
MAJOR RELIGIONS Eastern (Russian) Orthodoxy, Islam, Judaism, Protestantism (Baltic States)

UNION REPUBLICS

	AREA (sq. mi.)	AREA (sq. km.)	POPULATION	CAPITAL and LARGEST CITY
RUSSIAN S.F.S.R.	6,592,812	17,075,400	137,551,000	Moscow 7,831,000
KAZAKH S.S.R.	1,048,300	2,715,100	14,684,000	Alma-Ata 910,000
UKRAINIAN S.S.R.	233,089	603,700	49,755,000	Kiev 2,144,000
TURKMEN S.S.R.	188,455	488,100	2,759,000	Ashkhabad 312,000
UZBEK S.S.R.	173,591	449,600	15,391,000	Tashkent 1,780,000
WHITE RUSSIAN S.S.R.	80,154	207,600	9,560,000	Minsk 1,262,000
KIRGIZ S.S.R.	76,641	198,500	3,529,000	Frunze 533,000
TADZHIK S.S.R.	55,251	143,100	3,801,000	Dushanbe 494,000
AZERBAIDZHAN S.S.R.	33,436	86,600	6,028,000	Baku 1,022,000
GEORGIAN S.S.R.	26,911	69,700	5,015,000	Tbilisi 1,066,000
LITHUANIAN S.S.R.	25,174	65,200	3,398,000	Vilna 481,000
LATVIAN S.S.R.	24,595	63,700	2,521,000	Riga 835,000
ESTONIAN S.S.R.	17,413	45,100	1,466,000	Tallinn 430,000
MOLDAVIAN S.S.R.	13,012	33,700	3,947,000	Kishinev 503,000
ARMENIAN S.S.R.	11,506	29,800	3,031,000	Erivan 1,019,000

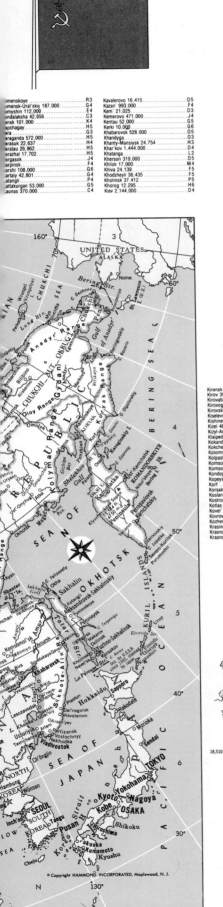

Topography

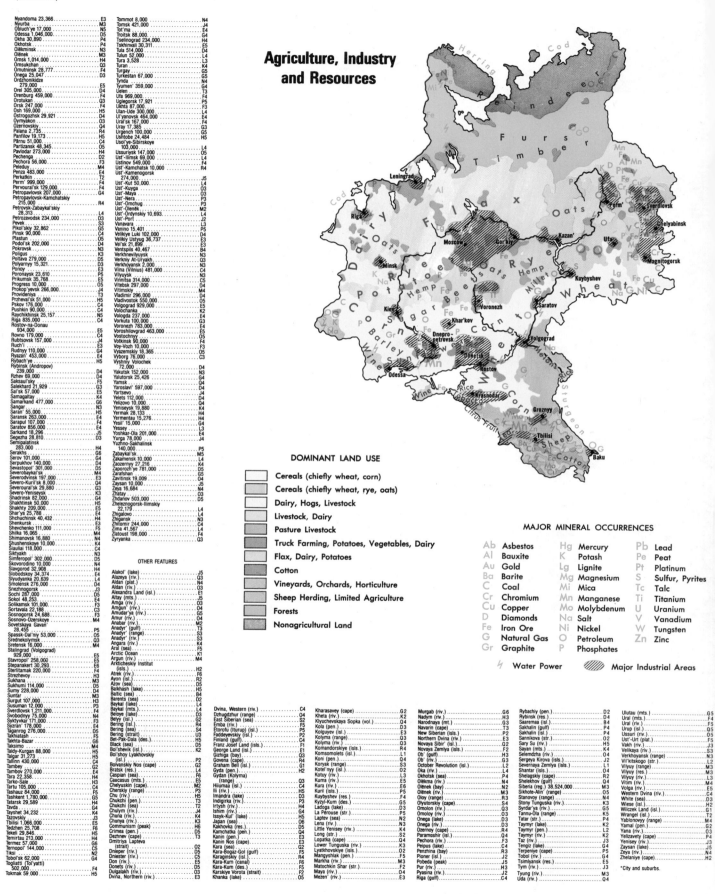

Agriculture, Industry and Resources

DOMINANT LAND USE

- Cereals (chiefly wheat, corn)
- Cereals (chiefly wheat, rye, oats)
- Dairy, Hogs, Livestock
- Livestock, Dairy
- Pasture Livestock
- Truck Farming, Potatoes, Vegetables, Dairy
- Flax, Dairy, Potatoes
- Cotton
- Vineyards, Orchards, Horticulture
- Sheep Herding, Limited Agriculture
- Forests
- Nonagricultural Land

MAJOR MINERAL OCCURRENCES

Ab	Asbestos	Hg	Mercury	Pb	Lead
Al	Bauxite	K	Potash	Pe	Peat
Au	Gold	Lg	Lignite	Pt	Platinum
Ba	Barite	Mg	Magnesium	S	Sulfur, Pyrites
Cr	Chromium	Mi	Mica	Tc	Talc
Cu	Copper	Mn	Manganese	Ti	Titanium
D	Diamonds	Mo	Molybdenum	U	Uranium
Fe	Iron Ore	Na	Salt	V	Vanadium
G	Natural Gas	Ni	Nickel	W	Tungsten
Gr	Graphite	O	Petroleum	Zn	Zinc
		P	Phosphates		

⚡ Water Power   ⬛ Major Industrial Areas

Agriculture, Industry and Resources

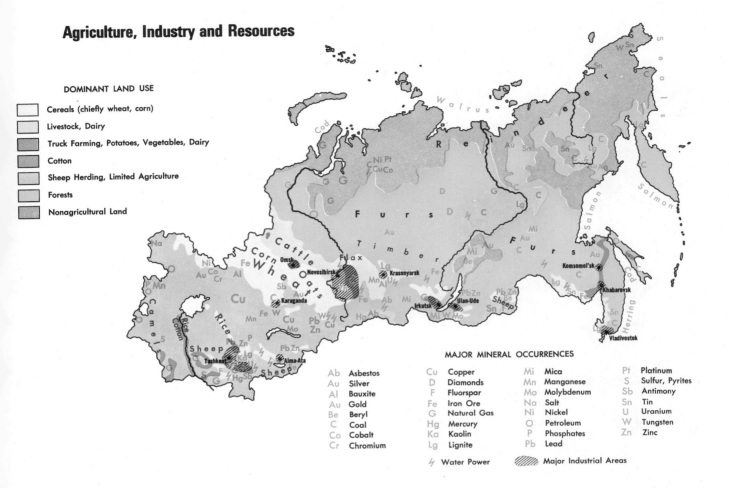

DOMINANT LAND USE

- Cereals (chiefly wheat, corn)
- Livestock, Dairy
- Truck Farming, Potatoes, Vegetables, Dairy
- Cotton
- Sheep Herding, Limited Agriculture
- Forests
- Nonagricultural Land

MAJOR MINERAL OCCURRENCES

Ab	Asbestos	Cu	Copper	Mi	Mica	Pt	Platinum
Au	Silver	D	Diamonds	Mn	Manganese	S	Sulfur, Pyrites
Al	Bauxite	F	Fluorspar	Mo	Molybdenum	Sb	Antimony
Au	Gold	Fe	Iron Ore	Na	Salt	Sn	Tin
Be	Beryl	G	Natural Gas	Ni	Nickel	U	Uranium
C	Coal	Hg	Mercury	O	Petroleum	W	Tungsten
Co	Cobalt	Ka	Kaolin	P	Phosphates	Zn	Zinc
Cr	Chromium	Lg	Lignite	Pb	Lead		

⚡ Water Power   ▨ Major Industrial Areas

U.S.S.R.—Railroads and Navigation

Principal Railroads ——
Navigable Rivers ......
Canals ......
Main Sea Routes - - - -
Major Russian Ports ‡

© Copyright HAMMOND INCORPORATED, Maplewood, N.J.

(continued on following page)

Union of Soviet Socialist Republics
European Part

CONIC PROJECTION

SCALE OF MILES

| 0 | 50 | 100 | 200 | 300 |

SCALE OF KILOMETERS

| 0 | 50 | 100 | 200 | 300 |

National Capitals .... ☆
Capitals of Union Republics .... ⌘
Administrative Centers .... △
International boundaries ....
Union Republic boundaries ....
A.S.S.R., Oblast, Kray boundaries ....
Autonomous Oblast boundaries ....
Autonomous Okrug boundaries ....

The government of the United States has not recognized the incorporation of Estonia, Latvia and Lithuania into the Soviet Union.

Administrative Divisions bear same names as their respective Capitals or Centers, except:

Abkhaz A.S.S.R.	Sukhumi	F6
Adygey Aut. Oblast	Maykop	F6
Adzhar A.S.S.R.	Batumi	F6
Bashkir A.S.S.R.	Ufa	J4
Chechen-Ingush A.S.S.R.	Groznyy	G6
Chuvash A.S.S.R.	Cheboksary	G3
Crimean Oblast	Simferopol'	D6
Dagestan A.S.S.R.	Makhachkala	G6
Kabardin-Balkar A.S.S.R.	Nal'chik	F6
Kalmuck A.S.S.R.	Elista	F5
Karachay-Cherkess Aut. Obl.	Cherkessk	F6
Karelian A.S.S.R.	Petrozavodsk	D2
Komi A.S.S.R.	Syktyvkar	H2
Komi-Permyak Aut. Okrug	Kudymkar	H3
Mari A.S.S.R.	Yoshkar-Ola	G3
Mordvinian A.S.S.R.	Saransk	G4
Nagorno-Karabakh Aut. Obl.	Stepanakert	G7
Nenets Aut. Okrug	Nar'yan-Mar	H1
North Ossetian A.S.S.R.	Ordzhonikidze	F6
South Ossetian Aut. Obl.	Tskhinvali	F6
Tatar A.S.S.R.	Kazan'	G3
Trans-Carpathian Oblast	Uzhgorod	B5
Udmurt A.S.S.R.	Ustinov	H3
Volyn Oblast	Lutsk	C4

© Copyright HAMMOND INCORPORATED, Maplewood, N.J.

U.S.S.R. — EUROPEAN

UNION REPUBLICS

ian S.S.R. 3,031,000 .... F6
aidzhan S.S.R. 6,028,000 .... G6
an S.S.R 1,466,000 .... C3
an S.S.R. 5,015,000 .... F6
n S.S.R 2,521,000 .... B3
nian S.S.R. 3,398,000 .... B3
vian S.S.R. 3,947,000 .... C5
an S.F.S.R. 137,551,000 .... F3
ian S.S.R. 49,755,000 .... D5
Russian S.S.R. 9,560,000 .... C4

INTERNAL DIVISIONS

az A.S.S.R. 505,000 .... F6
ey Aut. Obl. 405,000 .... F6
r A.S.S.R. 354,000 .... F6
kir A.S.S.R. 3,849,000 .... J4
hen-Ingush
S.S.R. 1,154,000 .... G6
ash A.S.S.R. 1,292,000 .... G3
ean Oblast 2,183,000 .... D6
stan A.S.S.R. 1,628,000 .... G6
rdin-Balkar
S.S.R. 674,000 .... F6
uck A.S.S.R. 294,000 .... F5
chay-Cherkess Aut. Obl. 368,000 .... F6
ian A.S.S.R. 736,000 .... D2
A.S.S.R. 1,119,000 .... H2
-Permyak Aut. Okr. 173,000 .... H3
A.S.S.R. 703,000 .... G3
dvinian A.S.S.R. 991,000 .... G4
rno-Karabakh Aut.
ol. 161,000 .... G7
ichevan' A.S.S.R. 239,000 .... F7
ets Aut. Okr. 47,000 .... H1
h Ossetian
.S.S.R. 597,000 .... F6
th Ossetian Aut.
bl. 98,000 .... F6
r A.S.S.R. 3,436,000 .... G3
ns-Carpathian
blast 1,155,000 .... B5
murt A.S.S.R. 1,494,000 .... H3
n Oblast 1,015,000 .... C4

CITIES and TOWNS

dulino 26,010 .... H4
lam 21,277 .... G6
yz 19,267 .... H3
altsikhe 18,972 .... F6
tubinsk 43,466 .... G5
nty G6
ntyrka 41,354 .... E4
kerman (Belgorod-
Dnestrovskiy) 32,928 .... D5
agir 18,161 .... F6
atyr' 43,499 .... G4
verdi 21,311 .... F6
ksandriya 82,000 .... D5
eksandrovsk 18,286 .... J3
ekseyevka 25,562 .... E4
eksin 67,000 .... E4
-Bayramly 33,828 .... G7
'met'yevsk 110,000 .... H3
ushta 22,016 .... D6
nderma K1
napa 29,900 .... E6
ndropov 239,000 .... E3
patity 62,000 .... D1
psheronsk 32,867 .... F6
rchangel (Arkhangel'sk)
385,000 .... F2
rmavir 162,000 .... F5
rzamas 93,000 .... F3
stara G7
strakhan' 461,000 .... G5
tkarsk 28,881 .... G4
zov 75,000 .... E5
akhchisaray 15,912 .... D6
aku 1,022,000 .... H6
alakhna 36,542 .... F3
alaklava D6
alakovo 152,000 .... G4
Balashov 93,000 .... F4
Baltiysk 20,300 .... A4
Baranovichi 131,000 .... C4
Barysh 20,792 .... G4
Bataysk 90,000 .... E5
Batumi 123,000 .... F6
Belaya Tserkov' 151,000 .... C5
Belebey 32,460 .... H4
Belev 17,733 .... E4
Belgorod 240,000 .... E4
Belgorod-Dnestrovskiy
32,928 .... D5
Belomorsk 16,595 .... D2
Belorechensk 35,970 .... E6
Beloretsk 71,000 .... J4
Belozersk E3
Bel'tsy 125,000 .... C5
Belush'ya Guba H1
Bendery 101,000 .... C5
Berdichev 80,000 .... C5
Berdyansk 122,000 .... E5
Beregovo 27,308 .... B5
Berezniki 185,000 .... J3
Beslan 26,893 .... F6
Bezhetsk 30,030 .... E3
Birsk 29,607 .... J3
Bobrov 17,977 .... F4
Bobruysk 192,000 .... C4
Bologoye 33,949 .... D3
Bor 63,000 .... F3
Borislav 33,800 .... B5
Borisoglebsk
68,000 .... F4
Borisov 112,000 .... C4
Borovichi 60,000 .... D3
Brest 177,000 .... B4
Brezhnev 301,000 .... H3
Bryansk 394,000 .... D4
Bugul'ma 80,000 .... H4
Buguruslan 54,000 .... H4
Buturlinovka 21,643 .... F4
Buy 29,946 .... F3
Buynaksk 37,946 .... G6
Buzuluk 76,000 .... H4
Bykhov 17,371 .... C4
Cēsis 17,696 .... C3
Chadyr-Lunga 20,474 .... C5
Chapayevsk 85,000 .... G4
Chaykovskiy 48,034 .... H3
Cheboksary 308,000 .... G3
Cherepovets 266,000 .... E3
Cherkassy 228,000 .... D5
Cherkessk 91,000 .... F6
Chernigov 238,000 .... D4
Chernovtsy 219,000 .... C5
Chernushka 21,106 .... J3
Chervonograd
55,000 .... B4
Chiatura 25,474 .... F6
Chistopol' 64,000 .... H3
Chortkov 19,183 .... B5
Chudovo D3
Chusovoy 56,000 .... J3
Danilov 17,500 .... E3
Dankov 20,030 .... E4
Daugavpils 116,000 .... C3
Davlekanovo 20,123 .... H4
Derbent 70,000 .... G6
Dimitrovgrad 106,000 .... G4
Dneprodzerzhinsk
250,000 .... D5
Dnepropetrovsk
1,066,000 .... D5
Dobrush 16,809 .... D4
Dobryanka 18,349 .... J3
Donetsk 1,021,000 .... E5
Drogobych 66,000 .... B5
Dubna 55,000 .... E3
Dubna E4
Dubno 25,442 .... C4
Dvinsk (Daugavpils)
116,000 .... C3
Dyat'kovo 26,825 .... D4
Dzerzhinsk 257,000 .... F3
Dzhankoy 43,459 .... D5
Dzhul'fa G7
Echmiadzin 31,819 .... F6
Elektrostal' 139,000 .... E3
Elista 70,000 .... F5
El'ton G5
Engel's 161,000 .... G4
Erivan 1,019,000 .... F6
Fastov 51,000 .... C4
Feodosiya 76,000 .... D5
Frolovo 33,398 .... F5
Furmanov 40,155 .... F3
Gagra 23,025 .... E6
Galich 19,374 .... F3
Gandzha (Kirovabad)
232,000 .... G6
Gatchina 75,000 .... C3
Gay 28,250 .... J4
Gaysin 23,741 .... C5
Gdov C3
Gelendzhik 29,086 .... E6
Genichesk 20,031 .... E5
Georgiu-Dezh 52,000 .... E4
Glazov 81,000 .... H3
Glubokoye C3
Glukhov 27,096 .... D4
Gomel' 383,000 .... D4
Gori 56,000 .... F6
Gorki 22,117 .... D4
Gor'kiy 1,344,000 .... F3
Gorlovka 336,000 .... E5
Gorodets 34,229 .... F3
Gremikha E1
Gremyachinsk 29,975 .... J3
Grodno 195,000 .... B4
Groznyy 375,000 .... G6
Gryazi 41,292 .... F4
Gubakha 33,243 .... J3
Gubkin 65,000 .... E4
Gudauta F6
Gudermes 32,445 .... G6
Gukovo 68,000 .... F5
Gus'-Khrustal'nyy 72,000 .... F3
Imishli 17,839 .... G7
Inta 51,000 .... K1
Inza 19,060 .... G4
Ishimbay 57,000 .... J4
Ivano-Frankovsk 150,000 .... B5
Ivanovo 465,000 .... E3
Izberbash 17,299 .... G6
Izhevsk (Ustinov)
549,000 .... H3
Izmail 83,000 .... C5
Izyum 61,000 .... E5
Jēkabpils 22,440 .... C3
Jelgava 68,000 .... B3
Jurmala 61,000 .... B3
Kadiyevka (Stakhanov)
108,000 .... E5
Kafan 29,916 .... G7
Kagul 26,249 .... C5
Kakhovka 28,472 .... D5
Kalach 18,475 .... F4
Kalach-na-Donu 20,795 .... F5
Kalinin 412,000 .... E3
Kaliningrad, Kaliningrad
355,000 .... B4
Kaliningrad, Moscow Oblast
133,000 .... E3
Kalinkovichi 23,918 .... C4
Kaluga 265,000 .... E4
Kalush 60,000 .... B5
Kamenets-Podol'skiy
81,000 .... C5
Kamenka 30,067 .... F4
Kamensk-Shakhtinskiy
72,000 .... F5
Kamyshin 112,000 .... F4
Kanash 40,682 .... G3
Kandalaksha 42,656 .... D1
Kapsukas 28,763 .... B4
Karachayevsk F6
Karachev 15,972 .... E4
Kashin 17,678 .... E3
Kasimov 33,066 .... F4
Kaspiysk 38,990 .... G6
Kaunas 370,000 .... B4
Kazan' 993,000 .... G3
Kazatin 26,649 .... C5
Kem' 21,025 .... D2
Kerch' 157,000 .... E5
Keret' D1
Khachmas 22,313 .... G6
Khadyzhensk 17,856 .... E6
Khar'kov 1,444,000 .... E5
Khasavyurt 65,000 .... G6
Khashuri 24,469 .... F6
Kherson 319,000 .... D5
Khmel'nitskiy 172,000 .... C5
Khotin 10,319 .... C5
Khust 23,810 .... B5
Khvalynsk 16,249 .... G4
Kiev 2,144,000 .... D4
Kiliya 24,276 .... C5
Kimovsk 44,490 .... E4
Kimry 58,000 .... E3
Kinel' 39,373 .... H4
Kineshma 101,000 .... F3
Kirishi 27,252 .... D3
Kirov, Kaluga 29,355 .... D4
Kirov, Kirov 390,000 .... G3
Kirovabad 232,000 .... G6
Kirovakan 146,000 .... G6
Kirovo-Chepetsk 71,000 .... H3
Kirovograd 237,000 .... D5
Kirovsk 38,484 .... D1
Kirsanov 21,795 .... F4
Kishinev 503,000 .... C5
Kislovodsk 101,000 .... F6
Kizel 46,264 .... J3
Kizlyar 29,745 .... G6
Klaipeda 176,000 .... B3
Klintsy 67,000 .... D4
Kobrin 24,935 .... B4
Kobuleti 18,051 .... F6
Kohtla-Järve 73,000 .... C3
Kolomiya 52,000 .... B5
Kolomna 147,000 .... E4
Kolpino 114,000 .... D3
Kommunarsk 120,000 .... E5
Komrat 21,369 .... C5
Komsomol'skiy 17,078 .... K1
Kondopoga 27,908 .... D2
Königsberg (Kaliningrad)
355,000 .... B4
Konotop 82,000 .... D4
Konstantinovka 112,000 .... E5
Korenovsk 26,323 .... E5
Korosten' 65,000 .... C4
Korostyshev 21,153 .... C4
Koryazhma 33,230 .... G2
Kostopol' 17,548 .... C4
Kostroma 255,000 .... F3
Kotel'nich 29,196 .... G3
Kotel'nikovo 19,063 .... F5
Kotlas 61,000 .... G2
Kotovo 20,553 .... G4
Kotovsk, Odessa
36,463 .... C5
Kotovsk, Tambov
33,347 .... F4
Kovel' 33,351 .... C4
Kovrov 143,000 .... F3
Kovylkino 17,300 .... F4
Kramatorsk 178,000 .... E5
Krasnoarmeysk 60,000 .... G4
Krasnodar 560,000 .... E6
Krasnograd 18,386 .... E5
Krasnokamsk 56,000 .... H3
Krasnoslobodsk
17,749 .... G5
Krasnovishersk J2
Krasnyy Kut 17,087 .... G4

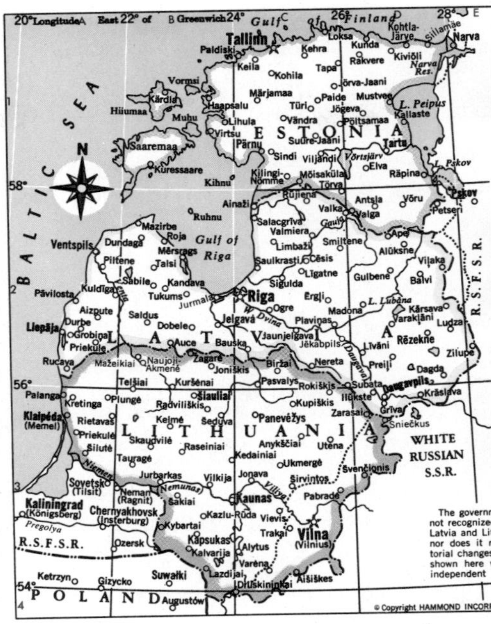

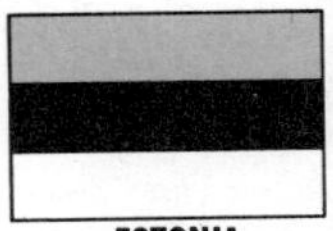
ESTONIA

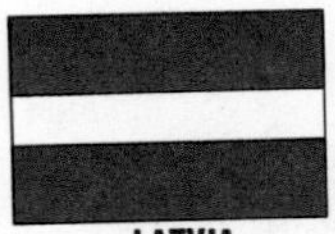
LATVIA

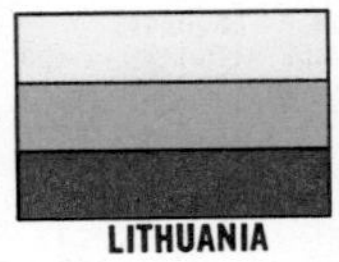
LITHUANIA

The government of the United States has not recognized the incorporation of Estonia, Latvia and Lithuania into the Soviet Union, nor does it recognize other post-war territorial changes shown on this map. The flags shown here were the official flags of the independent Baltic States prior to 1939.

The Baltic States

SCALE OF MILES 0 25 50 75 100
SCALE OF KILOMETERS 0 30 60 90 120 150 180

Capitals .... ☆
International Boundaries .... —··—
Union Republic Boundaries .... —·—
Prewar boundaries of the Baltic States where divergent from present boundaries ....

BALTIC STATES

Alytus 55,000 .... C3
Biržai 11,400 .... C2
Cēsis 17,696 .... C2
Daugava (Western Dvina)
(riv.) D2
Daugavpils 116,000 .... D3
Dobele 10,100 .... B2
Druskininkai 11,200 .... C3
Dvina Western (riv.) C2
Finland (gulf) D1
Gauja (riv.) C2
Haapsalu 11,483 .... B1
Hiiumaa (isl.) B1
Jēkabpils 22,400 .... C2
Jelgava 68,000 .... B2
Jonava 14,400 .... C3
Jurmala 61,000 .... B2
Kapsukas 28,763 .... B3
Kaunas 370,000 .... C3
Kedainiai 19,677 .... C3
Kihnu (isl.) B1
Kingisepp (Kuressaare) 12,140 .... B1
Kiviõli 11,153 .... D1
Klaipeda 176,000 .... A3
Kohtla-Järve 73,000 .... D1
Kretinga 13,000 .... A3
Kuldīga 12,300 .... A2
Kuressaare 12,140 .... B1
Kuršenai 11,500 .... B2
Liepāja 108,000 .... A2
Lubāna (lake) D2
Mažeikiai 13,400 .... A2
Memel (Klaipeda) 176,000 .... A3
Muhu (isl.) B1
Narva 73,000 .... E1
Naujoji-Akmene 10,200 .... B2
Niemen (riv.) A3
Ogre 15,708 .... C2
Panevežys 102,000 .... C3
Pärnu 51,000 .... C1
Peipus (lake) D1
Plunge 13,600 .... B3
Radviliškis 16,841 .... B3
Rakvere 17,891 .... D1
Rēzekne 30,803 .... D2
Riga (cap.), Latvia 835,000 .... C2
Riga (gulf) B2
Saaremaa (isl.) B1
Saldus 10,000 .... B2
Šiauliai 118,000 .... B3
Sillamäe 13,505 .... D1
Šilute 12,400 .... A3
Tallinn (cap.),
Estonia 430,000 .... C1
Tapa 10,037 .... C1
Tartu 105,000 .... D1
Taurage 19,461 .... B3
Telšiai 20,220 .... B2
Tukums 14,800 .... B2
Ukmerge 21,663 .... C3
Utena 13,300 .... C3
Valga 16,795 .... D2
Valmiera 20,331 .... C2
Venta (riv.) B2
Ventspils 40,467 .... A2
Viliya (riv.) C3
Viljandi 20,814 .... C1
Vilna (Vilnius) (cap.),
Lithuania 481,000 .... C3
Vormosi (isl.) B1
Võrtsjärv (lake) D1
Võru 15,398 .... D2
Western Dvina (riv.) C2

Krasnyy Luch 106,000 .... E5
Krasnyy Sulin 41,684 .... F5
Kremenchug 210,000 .... D5
Krichev 25,682 .... D4
Krivoy Rog 650,000 .... D5
Krolevets 18,307 .... D4
Kronshtadt 39,477 .... C3
Kropotkin 70,000 .... F5
Krymsk 41,430 .... E5
Kuba 18,871 .... G6
Kudymkar 26,350 .... H3
Kulebaki 46,252 .... F3
Kumertau 52,000 .... J4
Kunda C3
Kungur 80,000 .... J3
Kupyansk 30,055 .... E5
Kuressaare 12,140 .... B3
Kursk 375,000 .... E4
Kutaisi 194,000 .... F6
Kuvandyk 22,914 .... J4
Kuybyshev 1,216,000 .... H4
Kuznetsk 94,000 .... G4
Kuzomen' E1
Labinsk 54,000 .... F6
Lakhdenpokh'ya C2
Lebedin 29,240 .... D4
Leninakan 207,000 .... F6
Leningrad 4,073,000 .... C3
Leningrad* 4,588,000 .... C3
Leninogorsk 54,000 .... H4
Lenkoran' 35,505 .... G7
L'gov 25,110 .... E4
Lida 66,000 .... C4
Liepāja 108,000 .... B3
Likhoslavl' E3
Lipetsk 396,000 .... E4
Lisichansk 119,000 .... E5
Livny 37,290 .... E4
Lodeynoye Pole 19,632 .... D2
Lozovaya 53,000 .... E5
Lubny 54,000 .... D4
Luga 31,905 .... C3
Lutsk 137,000 .... B4
L'vov (Lwów) 667,000 .... B5
Lys'va 75,000 .... J3
Lyubertsy 160,000 .... E3
Lyubotin 33,324 .... E4
Lyudinovo 33,871 .... D4
Makeyevka 436,000 .... E5
Makhachkala 251,000 .... G6
Makharadze 21,679 .... F6
Malaya Vishera 15,381 .... D3
Malgobek 20,548 .... F6
Manturovo 21,510 .... F3
Marganets 50,000 .... E5
Mariupol' (Zhdanov) 503,000 .... E5
Marks 17,132 .... G4
Maykop 128,000 .... F6
Mednogorsk 38,024 .... J4
Medvezh'yegorsk 17,465 .... D2
Melenki 18,545 .... F3
Meleuz 24,851 .... J4
Melitopol' 161,000 .... D5
Memel (Klaipeda) 176,000 .... B3
Merefa 29,985 .... E5
Mezen' F1
Michurinsk 101,000 .... F4
Mikhaylovka 58,000 .... F4
Millerovo 34,627 .... F5
Mineral'nye Vody 67,000 .... F6
Mingechaur 60,000 .... G6
Minsk 1,262,000 .... C4
Minsk* 1,276,000 .... C4
Mirgorod 28,407 .... D5
Mogilev 290,000 .... C4
Mogilev-Podol'skiy 26,051 .... C5
Molodechno 73,000 .... C4
Molotov (Perm') 999,000 .... J3
Monchegorsk 51,000 .... D1
Morshansk 44,245 .... F4
Moscow (Moskva)
(cap.) 7,831,000 .... E3
Moscow* 8,011,000 .... E3
Mozhaysk 20,321 .... E3
Mozhga 38,930 .... H3
Mozyr' 73,000 .... C4
Mtsensk 27,833 .... E4
Mukachevo 72,000 .... B5
Murmansk 381,000 .... D1
Murom 114,000 .... F3
Mytishchi 141,000 .... E3
Nakhichevan' 33,279 .... F7
Nal'chik 207,000 .... F6
Narva 73,000 .... C3
Nar'yan-Mar 16,864 .... H1
Neftekamsk 70,000 .... J3
Nelidovo 29,813 .... D3
Nerekhta 25,722 .... F3
Nevel' 17,804 .... D3
Nevinnomyssk 104,000 .... F6
Nezhin 70,000 .... D4
Nikel' 21,299 .... C1
Nikolayev 440,000 .... D5
Nikol'sk 20,740 .... G4
Nikopol' 146,000 .... D5
Nizhnekamsk 134,000 .... H3
Nizhniy Lomov 17,460 .... F4
Nizhniy Novgorod
(Gor'kiy) 1,344,000 .... F3
Nosovka 19,430 .... D4
Novaya Kakhovka 52,000 .... D5
Novgorod 186,000 .... D3
Novgorod-Severskiy D4
Novoanninskiy 20,461 .... F4
Novocherkassk 183,000 .... F5
Novograd-Volynskiy 41,194 .... C4
Novogrudok 19,374 .... C4
Novokuybyshevsk 109,000 .... G4
Novomoskovsk 147,000 .... E4
Novopolotsk 67,000 .... C3
Novorossiysk 159,000 .... E6
Novoshakhtinsk 104,000 .... E5
Novotroitsk 95,000 .... J4
Novoukrainka 19,554 .... D5
Novouzensk G4
Novovolynsk 41,187 .... B4
Novovyatsk 26,408 .... G3
Novozybkov 34,433 .... D4
Nurlat 17,533 .... H4
Nyandoma 23,366 .... F2
Nytva 17,491 .... H3
Nyuvchim H2
Obninsk 73,000 .... E3
Ochamchira 18,718 .... F6
Odessa 1,046,000 .... D5
Oktyabr'sk 33,981 .... G4
Oktyabr'skiy 88,000 .... H4
Okulovka 19,194 .... D3
Olenegorsk 21,485 .... D1
Olonets D2
Omutninsk 28,777 .... H3
Onega 25,047 .... E2
Ordzhonikidze 279,000 .... F6
Orel 305,000 .... E4
Orenburg 459,000 .... J4
Orgeyev 25,798 .... C5
Orsha 112,000 .... C4
Orsk 247,000 .... J4
Osa 15,038 .... J3
Osipenko (Berdyansk) 122,000 .... E5
Osipovichi 19,705 .... C4
Ostashkov 23,419 .... D3
Ostrogozhsk 29,921 .... E4
Ostrov 22,369 .... C3
Otradnyy 44,426 .... H4
Panevežys 102,000 .... B3
Pärnu 51,000 .... C3
Pavlograd 107,000 .... E5
Pavlovo 68,000 .... F3
Pechenga D1
Pechora 56,000 .... J1
Penza 483,000 .... G4
Perm' 999,000 .... J3
Pervomaysk 72,000 .... D5
Petrokrepost' D3
Petrovsk 30,953 .... G4
Petrozavodsk 234,000 .... D2
Petsamo (Pechenga) D1
Pinsk 90,000 .... C4
Podol'sk 202,000 .... E3
Podporozh'ye 21,545 .... D2
Pokhvistnevo 26,125 .... H4
Polonnoye 22,484 .... C4
Polotsk 71,000 .... C3
Poltava 279,000 .... D5
Polyarnyy 15,321 .... D1
Ponoy F1
Poti 45,979 .... F6
Povenets E2
Povorino 20,591 .... F4
Prikumsk 35,768 .... F6
Priluki 65,000 .... D4
Primorsk C2
Primorsko-Akhtarsk 25,981 .... E5
Priozersk 16,652 .... D2
Privolzhskiy 23,041 .... G4
Priyutovo 21,051 .... H4
Prokhladnyy 40,074 .... F6
Pskov 176,000 .... C3
Pugachev 33,963 .... G4
Pushkin 90,000 .... C3
Pyatigorsk 110,000 .... F6
Rabocheostrovsk D1
Rakhov B5
Rakvere 17,891 .... C3
Rasskazovo 40,038 .... F4
Razdan 26,833 .... G6
Rechitsa 60,000 .... C4
Reni 19,625 .... C5
Revel (Tallinn) 430,000 .... B3
Rēzekne 30,803 .... C3
Riga 835,000 .... B3
Romny 53,000 .... D4
Roslavl' 56,000 .... D4
Rossosh' 36,438 .... E4
Rostov 30,815 .... E3
Rostov-na-Donu
934,000 .... F5
Rovno 179,000 .... C4
Rtishchevo 37,146 .... F4
Rubezhnoye 66,000 .... E5
Rustavi 129,000 .... G6
Ruzayevka 41,084 .... F4
Ryazan' 453,000 .... E4
Ryazhsk 25,425 .... F4
Rybinsk (Andropov)
239,000 .... E3
Rybnitsa 32,266 .... C5
Rzhev 69,000 .... D3
Safonovo 53,000 .... D3
Saki 24,208 .... D5
Salavat 137,000 .... H4
Sal'sk 57,000 .... F5
Sal'yany 24,228 .... G7
Samara (Kuybyshev)
1,216,000 .... H4
Sambor 29,253 .... B5
Saransk 263,000 .... G4
Sarapul 107,000 .... H3
Saratov 856,000 .... G4
Sasovo 27,228 .... F4
Segezha 28,810 .... D2
Semenov 23,633 .... F3
Semiluki 18,221 .... E4
Sengiley G4
Serdobol (Sortavala) 22,188 .... D2
Serdobsk 33,783 .... F4
Sergach 22,509 .... F3
Serpukhov 140,000 .... E4
Sevastopol' 301,000 .... D6
Severodonetsk 113,000 .... E5
Severodvinsk 197,000 .... E2
Severomorsk 50,000 .... D1
Shakhty 209,000 .... F5
Shakhun'ya 20,009 .... G3
Shar'ya 25,788 .... G3
Shchekino 70,000 .... E4
Shchigry 17,133 .... E4
Sheki 43,158 .... G6
Shemakha 17,986 .... G6
Shepetovka 38,707 .... C4
Shostka 82,000 .... D4
Shpola 19,806 .... D5
Shumerlya 33,816 .... G3
Shuya 72,000 .... F3
Šiauliai 118,000 .... B3
Sibay 37,656 .... J4
Simferopol' 302,000 .... D6
Skadovsk D5
Skopin 24,429 .... F4
Slantsy 41,146 .... C3
Slavuta 25,573 .... C4
Slavyansk 140,000 .... E5
Slavyansk-na-Kubani
54,000 .... E5
Slobodskoy 34,374 .... H3
Slonim 30,279 .... B4
Slutsk 35,609 .... C4
Smela 62,000 .... D5
Smolensk 276,000 .... D4
Sochi 287,000 .... E6
Sokol 48,243 .... F3
Soligorsk 65,000 .... C4
Solikamsk 101,000 .... J3
Sol'-Iletsk 22,227 .... J4
Sorochinsk 23,235 .... H4
Soroki 21,924 .... C5
Sortavala 22,188 .... D2
Sosnogorsk 24,688 .... H2
Sovetsk (Tilsit) 38,456 .... B4
Sovetsk 17,027 .... G3
Stakhanov 108,000 .... E5
Stalingrad (Volgograd)
929,000 .... F5
Staraya Russa 34,577 .... D3
Staryy Oskol 115,000 .... E4
Stavropol' 258,000 .... F5
Stepanakert 30,293 .... G7
Sterlitamak 220,000 .... J4
Stupino 70,000 .... E4
Sudak E6
Sukhumi 114,000 .... F6
Sumgait 190,000 .... G6
Sumy 228,000 .... E4
Svetlogorsk 55,000 .... C4
Svetlograd 40,265 .... F5
Syktyvkar 171,000 .... H2
Syzran' 178,000 .... G4
Taganrog 276,000 .... E5
Tallinn 430,000 .... B3
Tambov 270,000 .... F4
Tartu 105,000 .... C3
Taurage 19,461 .... B3
Tbilisi 1,066,000 .... F6
Telavi 21,179 .... G6
Telšiai 20,220 .... B3
Temryuk 23,172 .... E5
Ternopol' 144,000 .... C5
Teykovo 41,607 .... E3
Tiflis (Tbilisi) 1,066,000 .... F6
Tighina (Bendery)
101,000 .... C5
Tikhoretsk 64,000 .... F5
Tikhvin 59,000 .... D3
Tilsit (Sovetsk) 38,456 .... B4
Timashevsk 29,055 .... E5
Tiraspol' 139,000 .... D5
Togliatti (Tol'yatti)
502,000 .... G4
Tokmak 59,000 .... E5
Toropets 16,863 .... D3
Torzhok 45,443 .... D3
Troitsko-Pechorsk J2
Tskhinvali 30,311 .... F6
Tuapse 60,000 .... E6
Tula 514,000 .... E4
Tutayev 16,839 .... E3
Tuymazy 37,021 .... H4
Tver (Kalinin) 412,000 .... E3
Tyrnyauz 18,253 .... F6
Uchaly 21,808 .... J4
Ufa 969,000 .... J4
Uglich 35,463 .... E3
Ukmerge 21,663 .... C3
Ul'yanovsk 464,000 .... G4
Uman' 79,000 .... D5
Unecha 21,749 .... D4
Ungeny 17,228 .... C5
Uryupinsk 38,192 .... F4
Usinsk J1
Usman' 20,150 .... E4
Ustinov 549,000 .... H3
Uvarovo 24,946 .... F4
Uzhgorod 91,000 .... B5
Uzlovaya 65,000 .... E4
Valga 16,795 .... C3
Valmiera 20,331 .... C3
Valuyki 29,093 .... E4
Vasil'kov 26,741 .... D4
Velikiye Luki 102,000 .... D3
Velikiy Ustyug 36,737 .... F2
Vel'sk 21,899 .... F2
Ventspils 40,467 .... B3
Vereshchagino 23,585 .... H3
Vichuga 52,000 .... F3
Viipuri (Vyborg) 76,000 .... C2
Vileyka C4
Vilna (Vilnius) 481,000 .... C4
Vinnitsa 314,000 .... C5
Vinogradov 20,580 .... B5
Vitebsk 297,000 .... C3
Vladimir 296,000 .... F3
Vladimir-Volynskiy
28,412 .... B4
Volgodonsk 91,000 .... F5
Volgograd 929,000 .... F5
Volkhov 47,025 .... D3
Volkovysk 28,266 .... B4
Vologda 237,000 .... F3
Vol'sk 66,000 .... G4
Volzhsk 52,000 .... G3
Volzhskiy 209,000 .... G5
Vorkuta 100,000 .... K1
Voronezh 783,000 .... E4
Voroshilovgrad 463,000 .... E5
Voskresensk 76,000 .... E3
Votkinsk 90,000 .... H3
Voznesensk 36,457 .... D5
Vyatskiye Polyany
32,729 .... H3
Vyaz'ma 52,000 .... D3
Vyborg 76,000 .... C2
Vyksa 54,000 .... F3
Vyshniy Volochek
72,000 .... D3
Yalta 80,000 .... D6
Yanaul 20,115 .... J3
Yaroslavl' 597,000 .... E3
Yartsevo 36,662 .... D3
Yefremov 53,000 .... E4
Yelabuga 31,728 .... H3
Yelets 112,000 .... E4
Yenakiyevo 114,000 .... E5
Yershov 21,731 .... G4
Yessentuki 78,000 .... F6
Yevlakh 29,462 .... G6
Yevpatoria 93,000 .... D5
Yeysk 71,000 .... E5
Yoshkar-Ola 201,000 .... G3
Yur'yevets 20,144 .... F3
Zagorsk 107,000 .... E3
Zapolyarnyy 22,084 .... D1
Zaporozh'ye 781,000 .... E5
Zelenodol'sk 85,000 .... G3
Zelenokumsk 29,691 .... F6
Zernograd 20,324 .... F5
Zhdanov 503,000 .... E5
Zheleznodorozhnyy 76,000 .... H2
Zheleznogorsk 65,000 .... E4
Zhigulevsk 52,130 .... G4
Zhitomir 244,000 .... C4
Zhlobin 25,359 .... D4
Zhmerinka 36,195 .... C5
Zhodino 22,083 .... C4
Zhovtnevoye 31,102 .... D5
Znamenka 27,393 .... D5
Zolotonosha 27,639 .... D5
Zugdidi 39,896 .... F6
Zuyevka 17,001 .... H3

OTHER FEATURES

Apsheron (pen.) H6
Araks (riv.) G7
Azov (sea) E5
Baltic (sea) B3
Barents (sea) E1
Belaya (riv.) H3
Beloye (lake) E2
Black (sea) D6
Bug (riv.) B4
Bug (riv.) D5
Caspian (sea) G6
Caucasus (mts.) F6
Crimea (pen.) D5
Desna (riv.) D4
Dnieper (riv.) D5
Dniester (riv.) C5
Don (riv.) F5
Donets (riv.) E5
Dvina (bay) E2
Dvina, Northern (riv.) F2
Dvina, Western (riv.) C3
Dykh-Tau (mt.) F6
El'brus (mt.) F6
Finland (gulf) C3
Hiiumaa (isl.) B3
Il'men' (lake) D3
Imandra (lake) D1
Kakhovka (res.) D5
Kama (riv.) H2
Kandalaksha (gulf) D1
Kanin (pen.) G1
Kara (sea) K1
Karskiye Vorota (str.) J1
Kazbek (mt.) F6
Khoper (riv.) F4
Kola (pen.) E1
Kolguyev (isl.) G1
Kuban' (riv.) E5
Kura (riv.) G6
Kuybyshev (res.) G4
Ladoga (lake) D2
Lapland (reg.) D1
Mezen' (riv.) G1
Moksha (riv.) F4
Narodnaya (mt.) J1
Niemen (riv.) B4
Novaya Zemlya (isls.) H1
Oka (riv.) F4
Onega (bay) E2
Onega (lake) E2
Onega (riv.) E2
Pechora (riv.) H1
Peipus (lake) C3
Pripet (marshes) C4
Pripyat' (riv.) C4
Prut (riv.) C5
Riga (gulf) B3
Rybachiy (pen.) D1
Rybinsk (res.) E3
Saaremaa (isl.) B3
Samara (riv.) H4
Sevan (lake) G6
Seym (riv.) D4
Sura (riv.) G4
Svir' (riv.) D2
Timan (ridge) G1
Tsil'ma (riv.) H1
Tsimlyansk (res.) F5
Tuloma (riv.) D1
Ural (mts.) J2
Ural (riv.) J4
Usa (riv.) K1
Valday (hills) D3
Vaygach (isl.) K1
Velikaya (riv.) C3
Volga (riv.) G5
Volga-Don (canal) F5
Volgograd (res.) G5
Volkhov (riv.) D3
Vorskla (riv.) E4
Vyatka (riv.) H3
Vychegda (riv.) G2
Vyg (lake) E2
White (sea) E1
Yamantau (mt.) J4
Yugorskiy (pen.) K1

*City and suburbs.

ALGERIA
AREA 919,591 sq. mi. (2,381,740 sq. km.)
POPULATION 17,422,000
CAPITAL Algiers
LARGEST CITY Algiers
HIGHEST POINT Tahat 9,852 ft. (3,003 m.)
MONETARY UNIT Algerian dinar
MAJOR LANGUAGES Arabic, Berber,
French
MAJOR RELIGION Islam

ANGOLA
AREA 481,351 sq. mi. (1,246,700 sq. km.)
POPULATION 7,078,000
CAPITAL Luanda
LARGEST CITY Luanda
HIGHEST POINT Mt. Moco 8,593 ft.
(2,620 m.)
MONETARY UNIT kwanza
MAJOR LANGUAGES Mbundu, Kongo, Lunda,
Portuguese
MAJOR RELIGIONS Tribal religions, Roman
Catholicism

BENIN
AREA 43,483 sq. mi. (112,620 sq. km.)
POPULATION 3,338,240
CAPITAL Porto-Novo
LARGEST CITY Cotonou
HIGHEST POINT Atakora Mts. 2,083 ft.
(635 m.)
MONETARY UNIT CFA franc
MAJOR LANGUAGES Fon, Somba, Yoruba,
Bariba, French, Mina, Dendi
MAJOR RELIGIONS Tribal religions, Islam,
Roman Catholicism

BOTSWANA
AREA 224,764 sq. mi. (582,139 sq. km.)
POPULATION 819,000
CAPITAL Gaborone
LARGEST CITY Francistown
HIGHEST POINT Tsodilo Hill 5,922 ft.
(1,805 m.)
MONETARY UNIT pula
MAJOR LANGUAGES Setswana, Shona,
Bushman, English, Afrikaans
MAJOR RELIGIONS Tribal religions,
Protestantism

BURKINA FASO
AREA 105,869 sq. mi. (274,200 sq. km.)
POPULATION 6,908,000
CAPITAL Ouagadougou
LARGEST CITY Ouagadougou
HIGHEST POINT 2,352 ft. (717 m.)
MONETARY UNIT CFA franc
MAJOR LANGUAGES Mossi, Lobi, French,
Samo, Gourounsi
MAJOR RELIGIONS Islam, tribal religions,
Roman Catholicism

BURUNDI
AREA 10,747 sq. mi. (27,835 sq. km.)
POPULATION 4,021,910
CAPITAL Bujumbura
LARGEST CITY Bujumbura
HIGHEST POINT 8,858 ft. (2,700 m.)
MONETARY UNIT Burundi franc
MAJOR LANGUAGES Kirundi, French, Swahili
MAJOR RELIGIONS Tribal religions, Roman
Catholicism, Islam

CAMEROON
AREA 183,568 sq. mi.
(475,441 sq. km.)
POPULATION 8,503,000
CAPITAL Yaoundé
LARGEST CITY Douala
HIGHEST POINT Cameroon 13,350 ft.
(4,069 m.)
MONETARY UNIT CFA franc
MAJOR LANGUAGES Fang, Bamileke,
Fulani, Duala, French, English
MAJOR RELIGIONS Tribal religions,
Christianity, Islam

CAPE VERDE
AREA 1,557 sq. mi. (4,033 sq. km.)
POPULATION 324,000
CAPITAL Praia
LARGEST CITY Praia
HIGHEST POINT 9,281 ft. (2,829 m.)
MONETARY UNIT Cape Verde escudo
MAJOR LANGUAGE Portuguese
MAJOR RELIGION Roman Catholicism

CENTRAL AFRICAN REPUBLIC
AREA 242,000 sq. mi. (626,780 sq. km.)
POPULATION 2,284,000
CAPITAL Bangui
LARGEST CITY Bangui
HIGHEST POINT Gao 4,659 ft. (1,420 m.)
MONETARY UNIT CFA franc
MAJOR LANGUAGES Banda, Gbaya, Sangho,
French
MAJOR RELIGIONS Tribal religions,
Christianity, Islam

CHAD
AREA 495,752 sq. mi. (1,283,998 sq. km.)
POPULATION 4,309,000
CAPITAL N'Djamena
LARGEST CITY N'Djamena
HIGHEST POINT Emi Koussi 11,204 ft.
(3,415 m.)
MONETARY UNIT CFA franc
MAJOR LANGUAGES Arabic, Bagirmi, French,
Sara, Massa, Moudang
MAJOR RELIGIONS Islam, tribal religions

COMOROS
AREA 719 sq. mi. (1,862 sq. km.)
POPULATION 290,000
CAPITAL Moroni
LARGEST CITY Moroni
HIGHEST POINT Karthala 7,746 ft.
(2,361 m.)
MONETARY UNIT CFA franc
MAJOR LANGUAGES Arabic, French,
Swahili
MAJOR RELIGION Islam

CONGO
AREA 132,046 sq. mi. (342,000 sq. km.)
POPULATION 1,537,000
CAPITAL Brazzaville
LARGEST CITY Brazzaville
HIGHEST POINT Leketi Mts. 3,412 ft.
(1,040 m.)
MONETARY UNIT CFA franc
MAJOR LANGUAGES Kikongo, Bateke,
Lingala, French
MAJOR RELIGIONS Christianity, tribal
religions, Islam

DJIBOUTI
AREA 8,880 sq. mi. (23,000 sq. km.)
POPULATION 386,000
CAPITAL Djibouti
LARGEST CITY Djibouti
HIGHEST POINT Moussa Ali 6,768 ft.
(2,063 m.)
MONETARY UNIT Djibouti franc
MAJOR LANGUAGES Arabic, Somali,
Afar, French
MAJOR RELIGIONS Islam,
Roman Catholicism

EGYPT
AREA 386,659 sq. mi. (1,001,447 sq. km.)
POPULATION 41,572,000
CAPITAL Cairo
LARGEST CITY Cairo
HIGHEST POINT Jeb. Katherina 8,651 ft.
(2,637 m.)
MONETARY UNIT Egyptian pound
MAJOR LANGUAGE Arabic
MAJOR RELIGIONS Islam, Coptic Christianity

EQUATORIAL GUINEA
AREA 10,831 sq. mi. (28,052 sq. km.)
POPULATION 244,000
CAPITAL Malabo
LARGEST CITY Malabo
HIGHEST POINT 9,868 ft. (3,008 m.)
MONETARY UNIT ekuele
MAJOR LANGUAGES Fang, Bubi, Spanish
MAJOR RELIGIONS Tribal religions,
Christianity

ETHIOPIA
AREA 471,776 sq. mi. (1,221,900 sq. km.)
POPULATION 31,065,000
CAPITAL Addis Ababa
LARGEST CITY Addis Ababa
HIGHEST POINT Ras Dashan 15,157 ft.
(4,620 m.)
MONETARY UNIT birr
MAJOR LANGUAGES Amharic, Gallinya,
Tigrinya, Somali, Sidamo, Arabic, Ge'ez
MAJOR RELIGIONS Coptic Christianity, Islam

GABON
AREA 103,346 sq. mi. (267,666 sq. km.)
POPULATION 551,000
CAPITAL Libreville
LARGEST CITY Libreville
HIGHEST POINT Ibounzi 5,165 ft.
(1,574 m.)
MONETARY UNIT CFA franc
MAJOR LANGUAGES Fang and other Bantu
languages, French
MAJOR RELIGIONS Tribal religions,
Christianity, Islam

GAMBIA
AREA 4,127 sq. mi. (10,689 sq. km.)
POPULATION 601,000
CAPITAL Banjul
LARGEST CITY Banjul
HIGHEST POINT 100 ft. (30 m.)
MONETARY UNIT dalasi
MAJOR LANGUAGES Mandingo, Fulani,
Wolof, English, Malinke
MAJOR RELIGIONS Islam, tribal religions,
Christianity

GHANA
AREA 92,099 sq. mi. (238,536 sq. km.)
POPULATION 11,450,000
CAPITAL Accra
LARGEST CITY Accra
HIGHEST POINT Togo Hills 2,900 ft.
(884 m.)
MONETARY UNIT cedi
MAJOR LANGUAGES Twi, Fante, Dagbani,
Ewe, Ga, English, Hausa, Akan
MAJOR RELIGIONS Tribal religions,
Christianity, Islam

GUINEA
AREA 94,925 sq. mi. (245,856 sq. km.)
POPULATION 5,143,284
CAPITAL Conakry
LARGEST CITY Conakry
HIGHEST POINT Nimba Mts. 6,070 ft.
(1,850 m.)
MONETARY UNIT syli
MAJOR LANGUAGES Fulani, Mandingo,
Susu, French
MAJOR RELIGIONS Islam, tribal religions

GUINEA-BISSAU
AREA 13,948 sq. mi. (36,125 sq. km.)
POPULATION 777,214
CAPITAL Bissau
LARGEST CITY Bissau
HIGHEST POINT 689 ft. (210 m.)
MONETARY UNIT Guinea-Bissau escudo
MAJOR LANGUAGES Balante, Fulani,
Crioulo, Mandingo, Portuguese
MAJOR RELIGIONS Islam, tribal religions,
Roman Catholicism

IVORY COAST
AREA 124,504 sq. mi. (322,465 sq. km.)
POPULATION 7,920,000
CAPITAL Yamoussoukro
LARGEST CITY Abidjan
HIGHEST POINT 5,745 ft. (1,751 m.)
MONETARY UNIT CFA franc
MAJOR LANGUAGES Bale, Bete, Senufu,
French, Dioula
MAJOR RELIGIONS Tribal religions, Islam

KENYA
AREA 224,960 sq. mi. (582,646 sq. km.)
POPULATION 15,327,061
CAPITAL Nairobi
LARGEST CITY Nairobi
HIGHEST POINT Kenya 17,058 ft. (5,199 m.)
MONETARY UNIT Kenya shilling
MAJOR LANGUAGES Kikuyu, Luo, Kavirondo,
Kamba, Swahili, English
MAJOR RELIGIONS Tribal religions,
Christianity, Hinduism, Islam

LESOTHO
AREA 11,720 sq. mi. (30,355 sq. km.)
POPULATION 1,339,000
CAPITAL Maseru
LARGEST CITY Maseru
HIGHEST POINT 11,425 ft. (3,482 m.)
MONETARY UNIT loti
MAJOR LANGUAGES Sesotho, English
MAJOR RELIGIONS Tribal religions,
Christianity

LIBERIA
AREA 43,000 sq. mi. (111,370 sq. km.)
POPULATION 1,873,000
CAPITAL Monrovia
LARGEST CITY Monrovia
HIGHEST POINT Wutivi 5,584 ft.
(1,702 m.)
MONETARY UNIT Liberian dollar
MAJOR LANGUAGES Kru, Kpelle, Bassa,
Vai, English
MAJOR RELIGIONS Christianity, tribal
religions, Islam

LIBYA
AREA 679,358 sq. mi. (1,759,537 sq. km.)
POPULATION 2,856,000
CAPITAL Tripoli
LARGEST CITY Tripoli
HIGHEST POINT Bette Pk. 7,500 ft. (2,286 m.)
MONETARY UNIT Libyan dinar
MAJOR LANGUAGES Arabic, Berber
MAJOR RELIGION Islam

MADAGASCAR
AREA 226,657 sq. mi. (587,041 sq. km.)
POPULATION 8,742,000
CAPITAL Antananarivo
LARGEST CITY Antananarivo
HIGHEST POINT Maromokotro 9,436 ft.
(2,876 m.)
MONETARY UNIT Madagascar franc
MAJOR LANGUAGES Malagasy, French
MAJOR RELIGIONS Tribal religions,
Roman Catholicism, Protestantism

MALAWI
AREA 45,747 sq. mi. (118,485 sq. km.)
POPULATION 5,968,000
CAPITAL Lilongwe
LARGEST CITY Blantyre
HIGHEST POINT Mulanje 9,843 ft.
(3,000 m.)
MONETARY UNIT Malawi kwacha
MAJOR LANGUAGES Chichewa, Yao,
English, Nyanja, Tumbuka, Tonga,
Ngoni
MAJOR RELIGIONS Tribal religions, Islam,
Christianity

MALI
AREA 464,873 sq. mi. (1,204,021 sq. km.)
POPULATION 6,906,000
CAPITAL Bamako
LARGEST CITY Bamako
HIGHEST POINT Hombori Mts. 3,789 ft. (1,155 m.)
MONETARY UNIT Mali franc
MAJOR LANGUAGES Bambara, Senufu, Fulani, Soninke, French
MAJOR RELIGIONS Islam, tribal religions

MAURITANIA
AREA 419,229 sq. mi. (1,085,803 sq. km.)
POPULATION 1,634,000
CAPITAL Nouakchott
LARGEST CITY Nouakchott
HIGHEST POINT 2,972 ft. (906 m.)
MONETARY UNIT ouguiya
MAJOR LANGUAGES Arabic, Wolof, Tukolor, French
MAJOR RELIGION Islam

AFRICA
AREA 11,707,000 sq. mi. (30,321,130 sq. km.)
POPULATION 469,000,000
LARGEST CITY Cairo
HIGHEST POINT Kilimanjaro 19,340 ft. (5,895 m.)
LOWEST POINT Lake Assal, Djibouti -512 ft. (-156 m.)

MAURITIUS
AREA 790 sq. mi. (2,046 sq. km.)
POPULATION 959,000
CAPITAL Port Louis
LARGEST CITY Port Louis
HIGHEST POINT 2,711 ft. (826 m.)
MONETARY UNIT Mauritian rupee
MAJOR LANGUAGES English, French, French Creole, Hindi, Urdu
MAJOR RELIGIONS Hinduism, Christianity, Islam

MAYOTTE
AREA 144 sq. mi. (373 sq. km.)
POPULATION 47,300
CAPITAL Dzaoudzi

RÉUNION
AREA 969 sq. mi. (2,510 sq. km.)
POPULATION 491,000
CAPITAL St-Denis

MOROCCO
AREA 172,414 sq. mi. (446,550 sq. km.)
POPULATION 20,242,000
CAPITAL Rabat
LARGEST CITY Casablanca
HIGHEST POINT Jeb. Toubkal 13,665 ft. (4,165 m.)
MONETARY UNIT dirham
MAJOR LANGUAGES Arabic, Berber, French
MAJOR RELIGIONS Islam, Judaism, Christianity

MOZAMBIQUE
AREA 303,769 sq. mi. (786,762 sq. km.)
POPULATION 12,130,000
CAPITAL Maputo
LARGEST CITY Maputo
HIGHEST POINT Mt. Binga 7,992 ft. (2,436 m.)
MONETARY UNIT metical
MAJOR LANGUAGES Makua, Thonga, Shona, Portuguese
MAJOR RELIGIONS Tribal religions, Roman Catholicism, Islam

NAMIBIA (SOUTH-WEST AFRICA)
AREA 317,827 sq. mi. (823,172 sq. km.)
POPULATION 1,200,000
CAPITAL Windhoek
LARGEST CITY Windhoek
HIGHEST POINT Brandberg 8,550 ft. (2,606 m.)
MONETARY UNIT rand
MAJOR LANGUAGES Ovambo, Hottentot, Herero, Afrikaans, English
MAJOR RELIGIONS Tribal religions, Protestantism

NIGER
AREA 489,189 sq. mi. (1,267,000 sq. km.)
POPULATION 5,098,427
CAPITAL Niamey
LARGEST CITY Niamey
HIGHEST POINT Banguezane 6,234 ft. (1,900 m.)
MONETARY UNIT CFA franc
MAJOR LANGUAGES Hausa, Songhai, Fulani, French, Tamashek, Djerma
MAJOR RELIGIONS Islam, tribal religions

NIGERIA
AREA 357,000 sq. mi. (924,630 sq. km.)
POPULATION 82,643,000
CAPITAL Lagos
LARGEST CITY Lagos
HIGHEST POINT Dimlang 6,700 ft. (2,042 m.)
MONETARY UNIT naira
MAJOR LANGUAGES Hausa, Yoruba, Ibo, Ijaw, Fulani, Tiv, Kanuri, Ibibio, English, Edo
MAJOR RELIGIONS Islam, Christianity, tribal religions

RWANDA
AREA 10,169 sq. mi. (26,337 sq. km.)
POPULATION 4,819,317
CAPITAL Kigali
LARGEST CITY Kigali
HIGHEST POINT Karisimbi 14,780 ft. (4,505 m.)
MONETARY UNIT Rwanda franc
MAJOR LANGUAGES Kinyarwanda, French, Swahili
MAJOR RELIGIONS Tribal religions, Roman Catholicism, Islam

SÃO TOMÉ E PRÍNCIPE
AREA 372 sq. mi. (963 sq. km.)
POPULATION 85,000
CAPITAL São Tomé
LARGEST CITY São Tomé
HIGHEST POINT Pico 6,640 ft. (2,024 m.)
MONETARY UNIT dobra
MAJOR LANGUAGES Bantu languages, Portuguese
MAJOR RELIGIONS Tribal religions, Roman Catholicism

SENEGAL
AREA 75,954 sq. mi. (196,720 sq. km.)
POPULATION 5,508,000
CAPITAL Dakar
LARGEST CITY Dakar
HIGHEST POINT Futa Jallon 1,640 ft. (500 m.)
MONETARY UNIT CFA franc
MAJOR LANGUAGES Wolof, Peul (Fulani), French, Mende, Mandingo, Dida
MAJOR RELIGIONS Islam, tribal religions, Roman Catholicism

SEYCHELLES
AREA 145 sq. mi. (375 sq. km.)
POPULATION 63,000
CAPITAL Victoria
LARGEST CITY Victoria
HIGHEST POINT Morne Seychellois 2,993 ft. (912 m.)
MONETARY UNIT Seychellois rupee
MAJOR LANGUAGES English, French, Creole
MAJOR RELIGION Roman Catholicism

SIERRA LEONE
AREA 27,925 sq. mi. (72,325 sq. km.)
POPULATION 3,470,000
CAPITAL Freetown
LARGEST CITY Freetown
HIGHEST POINT Loma Mts. 6,390 ft. (1,947 m.)
MONETARY UNIT leone
MAJOR LANGUAGES Mende, Temne, Vai, English, Krio (pidgin)
MAJOR RELIGIONS Tribal religions, Islam, Christianity

SOMALIA
AREA 246,200 sq. mi. (637,658 sq. km.)
POPULATION 3,645,000
CAPITAL Mogadishu
LARGEST CITY Mogadishu
HIGHEST POINT Surud Ad 7,900 ft. (2,408 m.)
MONETARY UNIT Somali shilling
MAJOR LANGUAGES Somali, Arabic, Italian, English
MAJOR RELIGION Islam

SOUTH AFRICA
AREA 455,318 sq. mi. (1,179,274 sq. km.)
POPULATION 23,771,970
CAPITALS Cape Town, Pretoria
LARGEST CITY Johannesburg
HIGHEST POINT Injasuti 11,182 ft. (3,408 m.)
MONETARY UNIT rand
MAJOR LANGUAGES Afrikaans, English, Xhosa, Zulu, Sesotho
MAJOR RELIGIONS Protestantism, Roman Catholicism, Islam, Hinduism, tribal religions

SUDAN
AREA 967,494 sq. mi. (2,505,809 sq. km.)
POPULATION 18,691,000
CAPITAL Khartoum
LARGEST CITY Khartoum
HIGHEST POINT Jeb. Marra 10,073 ft. (3,070 m.)
MONETARY UNIT Sudanese pound
MAJOR LANGUAGES Arabic, Dinka, Nubian, Beja, Nuer
MAJOR RELIGIONS Islam, tribal religions

SWAZILAND
AREA 6,705 sq. mi. (17,366 sq. km.)
POPULATION 547,000
CAPITAL Mbabane
LARGEST CITY Manzini
HIGHEST POINT Emlembe 6,109 ft. (1,862 m.)
MONETARY UNIT lilangeni
MAJOR LANGUAGES siSwati, English
MAJOR RELIGIONS Tribal religions, Christianity

TANZANIA
AREA 363,708 sq. mi. (942,003 sq. km.)
POPULATION 17,527,560
CAPITAL Dar es Salaam
LARGEST CITY Dar es Salaam
HIGHEST POINT Kilimanjaro 19,340 ft. (5,895 m.)
MONETARY UNIT Tanzanian shilling
MAJOR LANGUAGES Nyamwezi-Sukuma, Swahili, English
MAJOR RELIGIONS Tribal religions, Christianity, Islam

TOGO
AREA 21,622 sq. mi. (56,000 sq. km.)
POPULATION 2,472,000
CAPITAL Lomé
LARGEST CITY Lomé
HIGHEST POINT Agou 3,445 ft. (1,050 m.)
MONETARY UNIT CFA franc
MAJOR LANGUAGES Ewe, French, Twi, Hausa
MAJOR RELIGIONS Tribal religions, Roman Catholicism, Islam

TUNISIA
AREA 63,378 sq. mi. (164,149 sq. km.)
POPULATION 6,367,000
CAPITAL Tunis
LARGEST CITY Tunis
HIGHEST POINT Jeb. Chambi 5,066 ft. (1,544 m.)
MONETARY UNIT Tunisian dinar
MAJOR LANGUAGES Arabic, French
MAJOR RELIGION Islam

UGANDA
AREA 91,076 sq. mi. (235,887 sq. km.)
POPULATION 12,630,076
CAPITAL Kampala
LARGEST CITY Kampala
HIGHEST POINT Margherita 16,795 ft. (5,119 m.)
MONETARY UNIT Ugandan shilling
MAJOR LANGUAGES Luganda, Acholi, Teso, Nyoro, Soga, Nkole, English, Swahili
MAJOR RELIGIONS Tribal religions, Christianity, Islam

WESTERN SAHARA
AREA 102,703 sq. mi. (266,000 sq. km.)
POPULATION 76,425
HIGHEST POINT 2,700 ft. (823 m.)
MAJOR LANGUAGE Arabic
MAJOR RELIGION Islam

ZAIRE
AREA 905,063 sq. mi. (2,344,113 sq. km.)
POPULATION 28,291,000
CAPITAL Kinshasa
LARGEST CITY Kinshasa
HIGHEST POINT Margherita 16,795 ft. (5,119 m.)
MONETARY UNIT zaire
MAJOR LANGUAGES Tshiluba, Mongo, Kikongo, Kingwana, Zande, Lingala, Swahili, French
MAJOR RELIGIONS Tribal religions, Christianity

ZAMBIA
AREA 290,586 sq. mi. (752,618 sq. km.)
POPULATION 5,679,808
CAPITAL Lusaka
LARGEST CITY Lusaka
HIGHEST POINT Sunzu 6,782 ft. (2,067 m.)
MONETARY UNIT Zambian kwacha
MAJOR LANGUAGES Bemba, Tonga, Lozi, Luvale, Nyanja, English
MAJOR RELIGIONS Tribal religions

ZIMBABWE
AREA 150,803 sq. mi. (390,580 sq. km.)
POPULATION 7,360,000
CAPITAL Harare
LARGEST CITY Harare
HIGHEST POINT Mt. Inyangani 8,517 ft. (2,596 m.)
MONETARY UNIT Zimbabwe dollar
MAJOR LANGUAGES English, Shona, Ndebele
MAJOR RELIGIONS Tribal religions, Protestantism

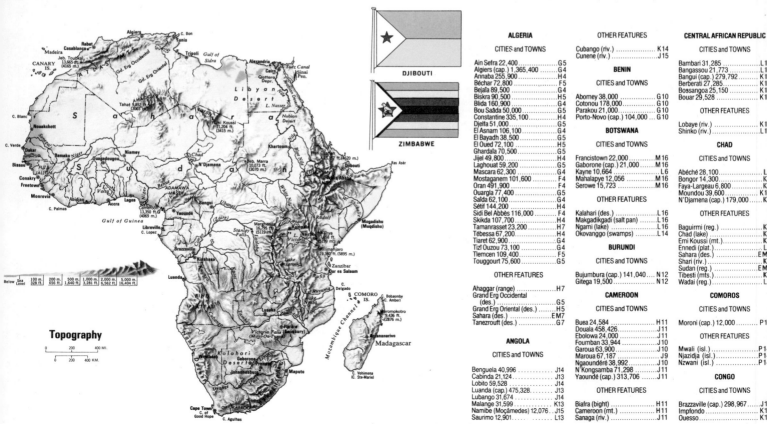

DJIBOUTI

ZIMBABWE

Topography

Below Sea Level 100 m. 328 ft. | 200 m. 656 ft. | 500 m. 1,640 ft. | 1,000 m. 3,281 ft. | 2,000 m. 6,562 ft. | 5,000 m. 16,404 ft.

0 200 400 MI.
0 200 400 KM.

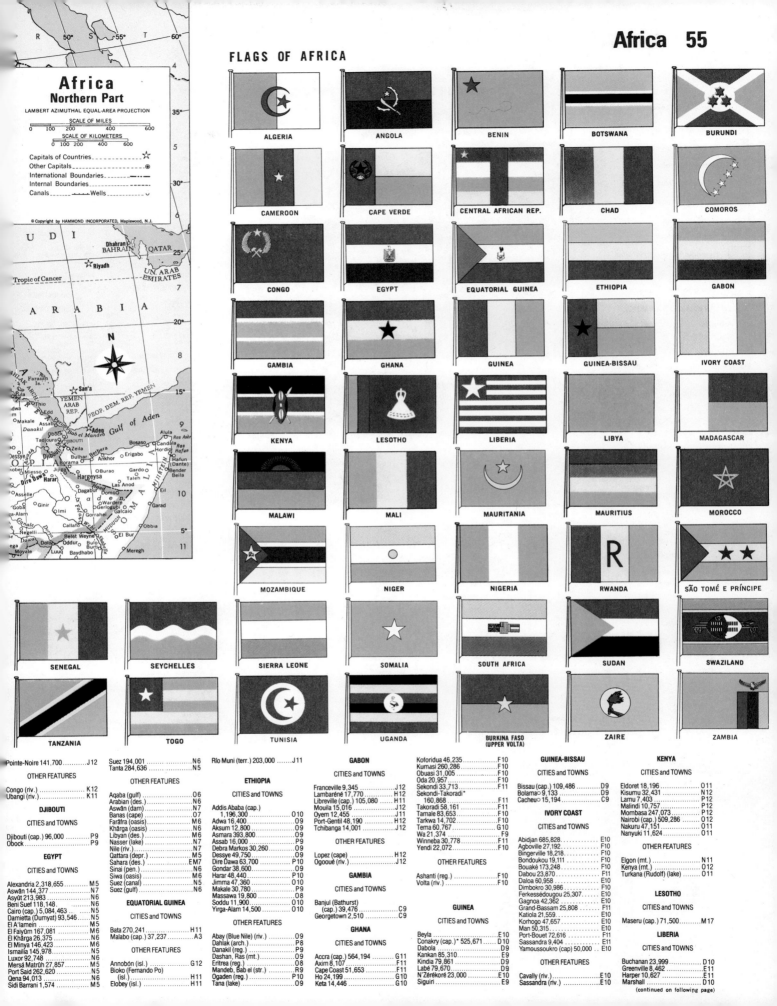

FLAGS OF AFRICA

ALGERIA · ANGOLA · BENIN · BOTSWANA · BURUNDI
CAMEROON · CAPE VERDE · CENTRAL AFRICAN REP. · CHAD · COMOROS
CONGO · EGYPT · EQUATORIAL GUINEA · ETHIOPIA · GABON
GAMBIA · GHANA · GUINEA · GUINEA-BISSAU · IVORY COAST
KENYA · LESOTHO · LIBERIA · LIBYA · MADAGASCAR
MALAWI · MALI · MAURITANIA · MAURITIUS · MOROCCO
MOZAMBIQUE · NIGER · NIGERIA · RWANDA · SÃO TOMÉ E PRÍNCIPE
SENEGAL · SEYCHELLES · SIERRA LEONE · SOMALIA · SOUTH AFRICA · SUDAN · SWAZILAND
TANZANIA · TOGO · TUNISIA · UGANDA · BURKINA FASO (UPPER VOLTA) · ZAIRE · ZAMBIA

Africa — Northern Part

LAMBERT AZIMUTHAL EQUAL-AREA PROJECTION

SCALE OF MILES
0   100   200   300   400   600

SCALE OF KILOMETERS
0   100   200   300   400   600

Capitals of Countries .... ☆
Other Capitals .... ◉
International Boundaries .... ━ ━ ━
Internal Boundaries .... ━ ━ ━
Canals .... Wells ⌣

© Copyright by HAMMOND INCORPORATED, Maplewood, N.J.

Pointe-Noire 141,700 ....J12

OTHER FEATURES

Congo (riv.) K12
Ubangi (riv.) K11

DJIBOUTI

CITIES and TOWNS

Djibouti (cap.) 96,000 ....P9
Obock P9

EGYPT

CITIES and TOWNS

Alexandria 2,318,655 ....M5
Aswān 144,377 ....N7
Asyût 213,983 ....N6
Beni Suef 118,148 ....N5
Cairo (cap.) 5,084,463 ....N5
Damietta (Dumyat) 93,546....N5
El A'iamein M5
El Faiyûm 167,081 ....M6
El Khârga 26,375 ....N6
El Minya 146,423 ....M6
Ismailia 145,978 ....N5
Luxor 92,748 ....N6
Mersâ Matrûh 27,857 ....M5
Port Said 262,620 ....N5
Qena 94,013 ....N6
Sidi Barrani 1,574 ....M5

Suez 194,001 ....N6
Tanta 284,636 ....N5

OTHER FEATURES

Aqaba (gulf) O6
Arabian (des.) N6
Aswân (dam) N7
Banas (cape) O7
Farâfra (oasis) M6
Khârga (oasis) N6
Libyan (des.) M6
Nile (riv.) N7
Nasser (lake) N7
Qattara (depr.) M5
Sahara (des.) EM7
Sinai (pen.) N6
Siwa (oasis) M6
Suez (canal) N5
Suez (gulf) N6

EQUATORIAL GUINEA

CITIES and TOWNS

Bata 270,241 ....H11
Malabo (cap.) 37,237 ....A3

OTHER FEATURES

Annobón (isl.) G12
Bioko (Fernando Po)
 (isl.) H11
Elobey (isl.) H11

Río Muni (terr.) 203,000 ....J11

GABON

CITIES and TOWNS

Franceville 9,345 ....J12
Lambaréné 17,770 ....H12
Libreville (cap.) 105,080 ......H11
Mouila 15,016 ....J12
Oyem 12,455 ....J11
Port-Gentil 48,190 ....H12
Tchibanga 14,001 ....J12

OTHER FEATURES

Lopez (cape) H12
Ogooué (riv.) J12

GAMBIA

CITIES and TOWNS

Banjul (Bathurst)
 (cap.) 39,476 ....C9
Georgetown 2,510 ....C9

GHANA

CITIES and TOWNS

Accra (cap.) 564,194 ....G11
Axim 8,107 ....F11
Cape Coast 51,653 ....F11
Ho 24,199 ....G10
Keta 14,446 ....G10

ETHIOPIA

CITIES and TOWNS

Addis Ababa (cap.)
 1,196,300 ....O10
Adwa 16,400 ....O9
Aksum 12,800 ....O9
Asmara 393,800 ....O9
Assab 16,000 ....P9
Debra Markos 30,260 ....O9
Dessye 49,750 ....O9
Dire Dawa 63,700 ....P10
Gondar 38,600 ....O9
Harar 48,440 ....P10
Jimma 47,360 ....O10
Makale 30,780 ....P9
Massawa 19,800 ....O8
Soddu 11,900 ....O10
Yirga-Alam 14,500 ....O10

OTHER FEATURES

Abay (Blue Nile) (riv.) O9
Dahlak (arch.) P8
Danakil (reg.) P9
Dashan, Ras (mt.) O9
Eritrea (reg.) O8
Mandeb, Bab el (str.) R9
Ogaden (reg.) P10
Tana (lake) O9

Koforidua 46,235 ....F10
Kumasi 260,286 ....F10
Obuasi 31,005 ....F10
Oda 20,957 ....F10
Sekondi 33,713 ....F11
Sekondi-Takoradi*
 160,868 ....F11
Takoradi 58,161 ....F11
Tamale 83,653 ....F10
Tarkwa 14,702 ....F10
Tema 60,767 ....G10
Winneba 30,778 ....F10
Yendi 22,072 ....F10

OTHER FEATURES

Ashanti (reg.) F10
Volta (riv.) F10

GUINEA

CITIES and TOWNS

Beyla E10
Conakry (cap.)* 525,671 .....D10
Dabola D9
Kankan 85,310 ....E9
Kindia 79,861 ....D9
Labé 79,670 ....D9
N'Zérékoré 23,000 ....E10
Siguiri E9

GUINEA-BISSAU

CITIES and TOWNS

Bissau (cap.) 109,486 ....D9
Bolama○ 9,133 ....D9
Cacheu○ 15,194 ....C9

IVORY COAST

CITIES and TOWNS

Abidjan 685,828 ....E10
Agboville 27,192 ....F10
Bingerville 18,218 ....F10
Bondoukou 19,111 ....F10
Bouaké 173,248 ....F10
Dabou 23,870 ....F11
Daloa 60,958 ....E10
Dimbokro 30,986 ....F10
Ferkéssédougou 25,307 ......E10
Gagnoa 42,362 ....E10
Grand-Bassam 25,808 ....F11
Katiola 21,559 ....E10
Korhogo 47,657 ....E10
Man 50,315 ....E10
Port-Bouet 72,616 ....F11
Sassandra 9,404 ....E11
Yamoussoukro (cap) 50,000 .E10

OTHER FEATURES

Cavally (riv.) E10
Sassandra (riv.) E10

KENYA

CITIES and TOWNS

Eldoret 18,196 ....O11
Kisumu 32,431 ....N12
Lamu 7,403 ....P12
Malindi 10,757 ....P12
Mombasa 247,073 ....P12
Nairobi (cap.) 509,286 ....O12
Nakuru 47,151 ....O11
Nanyuki 11,624 ....O11

OTHER FEATURES

Elgon (mt.) N11
Kenya (mt.) O12
Turkana (Rudolf) (lake) O11

LESOTHO

CITIES and TOWNS

Maseru (cap.) 71,500 ....M17

LIBERIA

CITIES and TOWNS

Buchanan 23,999 ....D10
Greenville 8,462 ....E11
Harper 10,627 ....E11
Marshall D10

(continued on following page)

Agriculture, Industry and Resources

DOMINANT LAND USE

- Cereals, Horticulture, Livestock
- Cash Crops, Mixed Cereals
- Cotton, Cereals
- Diversified Tropical Crops
- Plantation Agriculture
- Oases
- Pasture Livestock
- Nomadic Livestock Herding
- Forests
- Nonagricultural Land

MAJOR MINERAL OCCURRENCES

Ab	Asbestos	Mi	Mica
Ag	Silver	Mn	Manganese
Al	Bauxite	Na	Salt
Au	Gold	O	Petroleum
Be	Beryl	P	Phosphates
C	Coal	Pb	Lead
Co	Cobalt	Pt	Platinum
Cr	Chromium	Sb	Antimony
Cu	Copper	Sn	Tin
D	Diamonds	So	Soda Ash
Fe	Iron Ore	Ti	Titanium
G	Natural Gas	U	Uranium
Gp	Gypsum	V	Vanadium
Gr	Graphite	W	Tungsten
K	Potash	Zn	Zinc

⚡ Water Power

Major Industrial Areas

Monrovia (cap.) 166,507 ... D 10

OTHER FEATURES

Palmas (cape) ... E11

LIBYA

CITIES and TOWNS

Ajedabia○ 53,170 ... L5
Baida○ 59,765 ... L5
Benghazi○ 286,943 ... K5
Brak○ 12,507 ... J6
Derna○ 44,145 ... L5
El Azizia○ 34,077 ... J5
El Jauf○ 6,481 ... L7
El Marj (Barce)○ 55,444 ... L5
Ghadames○ 6,172 ... J6
Gharfan○ 65,224 ... J5
Ghat○ 6,924 ... J6
Homs○ 66,890 ... J5
Misurata○ 102,439 ... K5
Murzuk○ 22,185 ... J6
Nalut○ 23,535 ... J5
Sebha○ 35,879 ... K6
Shahat○ 17,157 ... L5
Syrte○ 22,797 ... K5
Tobruk○ 58,384 ... L5
Tripoli (cap.)○ 550,438 ... J5
Ubari○ 19,132 ... J6
Waddan○ 5,347 ... K6
Zella○ 72,092 ... K6
Zliten○ 58,981 ... K5
Zwara○ 15,078 ... J5

OTHER FEATURES

Cyrenaica (reg.) ... L6
Fezzan (reg.) ... J6
Idehan (des.) ... J6
Kufra (oasis) ... L7
Sahara (des.) ... EM7
Sidra (gulf) ... L5
Tripolitania (reg.) ... J5

MADAGASCAR

CITIES and TOWNS

Ambanja 12,258 ... R14
Ambatondrazaka 18,044 ... R15
Ambilobe 9,415 ... R14
Ambositra 16,780 ... R16
Antalaha 17,541 ... S14
Antananarivo 451,808 ... R15
Antsirabe 32,979 ... R16
Antsiranana
(Diego-Suarez) 40,443 ... R14
Arivonimamo 8,497 ... R15

Faradofay
(Fort-Dauphin) 13,805 ... R17
Farafangana 10,817 ... R16
Fenoarivo 7,696 ... R16
Fianarantsoa 68,054 ... R16
Maevatanana 7,197 ... R15
Maintirano 6,375 ... P15
Majunga 65,864 ... R15
Manakara 19,768 ... R16
Mananjary 14,638 ... R16
Marovoay 20,253 ... R15
Moramanga 10,806 ... R15
Morondava 19,061 ... P16
Sambava 6,215 ... S14
Tamatave 77,395 ... S15
Toliara 45,676 ... P16

OTHER FEATURES

Bobaomby (Amber) (cape) ... S15
Mozambique (chan.) ... O16
Nossi-Bé (isl.) ... R14
Tsiafajavona (mt.) ... R15
Vohimena (Ste Marie)
(cape) ... P17

MALAWI

CITIES and TOWNS

Blantyre 222,153 ... N15
Karonga 11,873 ... N13
Lilongwe (cap.) 102,924 ... N14
Nkhotakota 10,312 ... N14
Zomba 21,000 ... N15

OTHER FEATURES

Nyasa (lake) ... N14
Shire (riv.) ... N15

MALI

CITIES and TOWNS

Bamako (cap.) 404,022 ... E9
Bougouni 17,246 ... E9
Djenné 10,251 ... F9
Gao 30,714 ... G8
Goundam 10,262 ... F8
Kati 24,991 ... E9
Kayes 44,736 ... D9
Kita 17,538 ... E9
Koulikoro 16,376 ... E9
Koutiala 27,497 ... F9
Mopti 53,885 ... F9
Nioro 11,617 ... E8
San 22,962 ... F9
Ségou 64,890 ... E9
Sikasso 47,030 ... E9

Timbuktu 20,483 ... F8

OTHER FEATURES

Adrar des Iforas (plat.) ... G7
Niger (riv.) ... G9
Sahara (des.) ... EM7

MAURITANIA

CITIES and TOWNS

Atar 16,326 ... D7
Bir Mogrein ... D6
Bogué 8,056 ... D8
Boutilimit 7,261 ... D7
Fdérik 2,160 ... D7
Kaédi 20,248 ... D8
Kiffa 10,629 ... D8
Néma 8,232 ... E8
Nouadhibou 21,961 ... C7
Nouakchott (cap.) 134,986 ... C8
Rosso 16,466 ... C8
Tidjikja 7,870 ... D8

OTHER FEATURES

Adrar (reg.) ... D7
Blanc (cape) ... C7
Hodh (reg.) ... E8
Sahara (des.) ... EM7
Senegal (riv.) ... D8
Tagant (reg.) ... D8

MAURITIUS

CITIES and TOWNS

Curepipe 52,709 ... S19
Mahébourg 15,463 ... T19
Port Louis (cap.) 141,022 ... S19

MAYOTTE

CITIES AND TOWNS

Mamoutzou (cap.) 196 ... R14

MOROCCO

CITIES and TOWNS

Agadir 61,192 ... D5
Al Hoceima 18,686 ... F4
Casablanca 1,506,373 ... E5
El Jadida 55,501 ... D5
Essaouira 30,061 ... D5
Fès 325,327 ... F5
Kenitra 139,206 ... E5
Khenifra 25,526 ... F5

Larache 45,710 ... E4
Marrakech 332,741 ... E5
Meknès 248,369 ... E5
Ouezzane 33,267 ... E5
Oujda 175,532 ... F5
Rabat (cap.) 367,620 ... E5
Safi 129,113 ... E5
Salé 155,557 ... E5
Settat 42,325 ... E5
Tangier (Tanger) 187,894 ... E4
Taroudant 22,272 ... E5
Taza 55,157 ... F5
Tétouan 139,105 ... F4

OTHER FEATURES

Atlas (mts.) ... E5
Beddouza, Ras el (cape) ... D5
Draa, Wadi (dry riv.) ... E6
Juby (cape) ... D5

MOZAMBIQUE

CITIES and TOWNS

Bartolomeu Dias○ 6,102 ... O16
Beira 46,293 ... O15
Caia 1,363 ... N15
Chibuto 23,763 ... N16
Chimoio 4,507 ... N15
Homoíne 1,122 ... O16
Ibo 1,015 ... P14
Inhambane 4,975 ... O16
Magude 1,502 ... N16
Maniamba 7,634 ... O14
Maputo (cap.) 755,300 ... N17
Marromeu 1,330 ... O15
Massangena○ 3,301 ... N16
Meconta 1,051 ... O14
Moçambique 1,730 ... P15
Mocímboa da Praia 935 ... P14
Mocuba 2,293 ... O15
Nacala 4,601 ... P14
Nampula 23,072 ... P15
Pemba 3,629 ... P14
Quelimane 10,522 ... O15
Songo 1,350 ... N15
Tete 4,549 ... N15
Vila de Senao 21,074 ... N15
Xai-Xai 5,234 ... N16

OTHER FEATURES

Angoche (isl.) ... O16
Delagoa (bay) ... N17
Delgado (cape) ... P14
Mozambique (chan.) ... O16
Nyasa (chan.) ... N14
Rovuma (riv.) ... O14
Save (riv.) ... N16

NAMIBIA

CITIES and TOWNS

Bethanie 1,207 ... K17
Gobabis 4,428 ... K16
Grootfontein 4,627 ... K15
Karasburg 2,693 ... K17
Karibib 1,653 ... K16
Keetmanshoop 10,297 ... K17
Lüderitz 6,642 ... J17
Mariental 4,629 ... K16
Omaruru 2,783 ... K16
Oranjemund 2,594 ... K17
Otjiwarongo 8,018 ... K15
Outjo 2,545 ... K15
Rehoboth 5,363 ... K16
Swakopmund 5,681 ... J16
Tsumeb 12,338 ... K15
Usakos 2,334 ... K16
Windhoek (cap.) 61,369 ... K16

OTHER FEATURES

Caprivi Strip (reg.) ... L15
Cubango (riv.) ... K15
Cunene (riv.) ... J15
Damaraland (reg.) ... K16
Etosha Pan (salt pan) ... J15
Fish (riv.) ... K17
Fria (cape) ... J15
Great Namaland (reg.) ... K17
Kalahari (des.) ... L16
Namib (des.) ... J16
Okovanggo (riv.) ... K15
Orange (riv.) ... K17
Ovamboland (reg.) ... K15

NIGER

CITIES and TOWNS

Agadès 11,000 ... H8
Bilma ... J8
Birni-N'Konni 10,000 ... H9
Gaya 5,000 ... G9
Iférouane ... H8
Maradi 45,852 ... H9
N'Guigmi ... J9
Niamey (cap.) 225,314 ... G9
Tahoua 31,265 ... H9
Zinder 58,436 ... H9

OTHER FEATURES

Air (mts.) ... H8
Djado (plat.) ... J7
Niger (riv.) ... G9
Sahara (des.) ... EM7

Ténéré (des.) ... J8

NIGERIA

CITIES and TOWNS

Aba 177,000 ... H10
Abeokuta 253,000 ... G10
Benin City 136,000 ... H10
Bonny ... H11
Calabar 103,000 ... H10
Enugu 187,000 ... H10
Ibadan 847,000 ... G10
Ife 176,000 ... G10
Ilorin 282,000 ... G10
Kaduna 202,000 ... H9
Kano 399,000 ... H9
Katsina 109,424 ... H9
Lagos (cap.) 1,060,848 ... G10
Maiduguri 189,000 ... J9
Ogbomosho 432,000 ... H10
Onitsha 220,000 ... H10
Oshogbo 282,000 ... H10
Oyo 152,000 ... G10
Port Harcourt 242,000 ... H11
Sokoto ... H9
Yola ... J10
Zaria 224,000 ... H9

OTHER FEATURES

Adamawa (reg.) ... J10
Benin (bight) ... G11
Benue (riv.) ... H10
Chad (lake) ... K9
Gongola (riv.) ... J9
Kaduna (riv.) ... H9
Niger (riv.) ... G9

RÉUNION

CITIES and TOWNS

Le Port 21,564 ... P20
Le Tampon 17,089 ... P20
Saint-Denis (cap.) 80,075 ... P19
Saint-Louis 10,252 ... P20
Saint-Pierre 21,817 ... P20

OTHER FEATURES

Bassas da India (isl.) ... O16
Europa (isl.) ... P16
Glorioso (isls.) ... R14
Juan de Nova (isl.) ... P15
Piton des Neiges (mt.) ... P20

RWANDA

CITIES and TOWNS

Kigali (cap.) 117,749 ... N12

SÃO TOMÉ E PRÍNCIPE

CITIES and TOWNS

São Tomé (cap.) 7,681 ... H11

OTHER FEATURES

Príncipe (isl.) ... H11
São Tomé (isl.) ... H11

SENEGAL

CITIES and TOWNS

Dagana 10,506 ... C8
Dakar (cap.) 798,792 ... C9
Diourbel 50,618 ... C9
Kaolack 106,899 ... C9
Louga 35,063 ... C8
Matam 10,002 ... D8
M'Bour 37,663 ... C9
Saint-Louis 88,404 ... C8
Tambacounda 25,147 ... D9
Thiès 117,333 ... C9
Ziguinchor 72,726 ... C9

OTHER FEATURES

Senegal (riv.) ... D8
Verde (cape) ... C9

SEYCHELLES

OTHER FEATURES

Aldabra (isls.) ... P13
Assumption (isl.) ... R14
Cerf (isl.) ... S13
Cosmoledo (isls.) ... R13
Farquhar (isl.) ... S14
Providence (isl.) ... S13
Saint Pierre 47 ... —

SIERRA LEONE

CITIES and TOWNS

Bo 42,216 ... D10
Bonthe 6,230 ... D10
Freetown (cap.) 274,000 ... D10
Makeni 28,684 ... D10

OTHER FEATURES

Sherbro (isl.) ... D10

SOMALIA

CITIES and TOWNS

Afmadu 2,580 ... P11
Barawa (Brava) 6,167 ... P11

Baydhabo 14,962 ...
Belet Weyne 11,426 ...
Berbera 12,219 ...
Borama 3,244 ...
Bosaso ...
Brava 6,167 ...
Bulo Burti 5,247 ...
Burao 12,617 ...
Chisimayu 17,872 ...
Eil ...
Erigabo 4,279 ...
Galcaio ...
Giohar 13,156 ...
Hargeysa 40,254 ...
Jilib 3,232 ...
Las Anod 2,441 ...
Marka 17,708 ...
Mogadishu (cap.) 371,000 ...
Oddur ...
Zeila 1,226 ...

OTHER FEATURES

Asèr, Ras (cape) ...
Chiambone, Ras (cape) ...
Giuba (Juba) (riv.) ...
Mijirtein (reg.) ...
Mudugh (reg.) ...
Wabi Shabelle (riv.) ...

SOUTH AFRICA

INTERNAL DIVISIONS

Bophuthatswana (aut. rep.)
1,200,000 ...
Cape (prov.) 5,543,506 ...
Ciskei (aut. rep.) ...
Natal (prov.) 5,722,215 ...
Orange Free State (prov.)
1,833,216 ...
Transkei (aut. rep.)
2,000,000 ...
Transvaal (prov.) 10,673,033 ...
Venda (aut. rep.)
450,000 ...

CITIES and TOWNS

Aliwal North 12,311 ... M
Beaufort West 17,862 ... L
Bellville 49,026 ... G
Benoni□ 164,543 ... M
Bethlehem 29,918 ... M
Bisho ... M
Bloemfontein□ 182,329 ... L
Calvinia 6,386 ... K
Cape Town (cap.) □ 833,731 ... H
Ceres 9,230 ... H
Cradock 20,822 ... M
De Aar 18,057 ... L
Durban□ 975,494 ... N
East London□ 126,671 ... M
George 24,625 ... L
Germiston□ 293,257 ... M
Goodwood 31,592 ... G
Graaff-Reinet 22,392 ... L
Grahamstown 41,302 ... M
Johannesburg□ 1,417,818 ... M
Kimberley 105,258 ... L
King William's Town 15,798 ... M
Knysna 13,479 ... L
Kraaifontein 10,286 ... G
Kroonstad 51,988 ... M
Ladysmith 28,920 ... N
Louis Trichardt 8,906 ... M
Malmesbury 9,314 ... G
Messina 21,121 ... M
Middelburg, C. of
G.H. 11,121 ... M
Middelburg, Transv. 26,942 ... L
Mmabatho ... L
Moorreesburg 4,945 ... K
Mossel Bay 17,574 ... L
Newcastle 14,407 ... N
Oudtshoorn 26,907 ... L
Paarl 49,244 ... H
Parow 60,768 ... G
Pietermaritzburg□ 174,179 ... N
Pietersburg 27,174 ... M
Pinelands 11,769 ... G
Port Elizabeth□ 1,413,961 ... M
Port Nolloth 2,893 ... K
Port Shepstone 5,181 ... N
Potchefstroom 57,443 ... M
Pretoria (cap.)□ 573,283 ... M
Prieska 8,521 ... L
Queenstown 39,304 ... M
Richards Bay 598 ... N
Saldanha 4,994 ... K
Simonstown 12,137 ... F
Somerset West 11,828 ... G
Stellenbosch 29,955 ... G
Strand 24,503 ... G
Thohoyandou ... N
Uitenhage 70,517 ... M
Umtata 25,216 ... M
Upington 28,632 ... L
Vryburg 16,916 ... L
Walvis Bay 21,725 ... J
Wellington 17,092 ... H
Worcester 41,198 ... H

OTHER FEATURES

Agulhas (cape) ... K19
Algoa (bay) ... M18
Cape (pt.) ... F20
False (bay) ... G20
Good Hope (cape) ... F20
Hangkip (cape) ... G20
Kalahari (des.) ... L16
Limpopo (riv.) ... N16
Maclear (cape) ... F20
Molopo (riv.) ... L17
Nossob (riv.) ... L17
Orange (riv.) ... K17

*City and suburbs.
○Population of sub-district or division.
□Population of urban area.

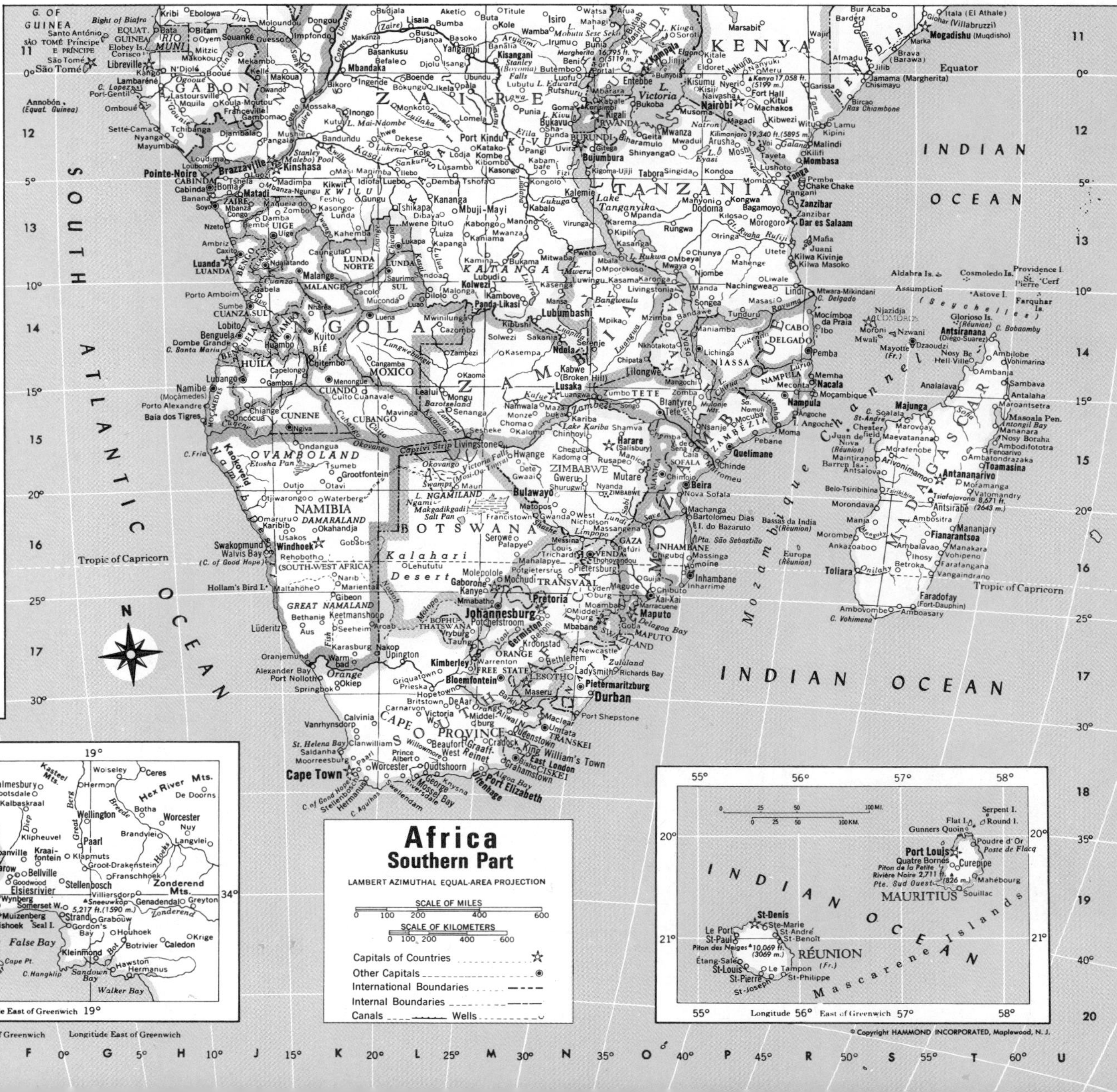

Africa
Southern Part

LAMBERT AZIMUTHAL EQUAL-AREA PROJECTION

SCALE OF MILES

0 100 200 300 400 500 600

SCALE OF KILOMETERS

0 100 200 300 400 500 600

Capitals of Countries	☆
Other Capitals	⊛
International Boundaries	— — —
Internal Boundaries	....
Canals ———— Wells	

© Copyright HAMMOND INCORPORATED, Maplewood, N.J.

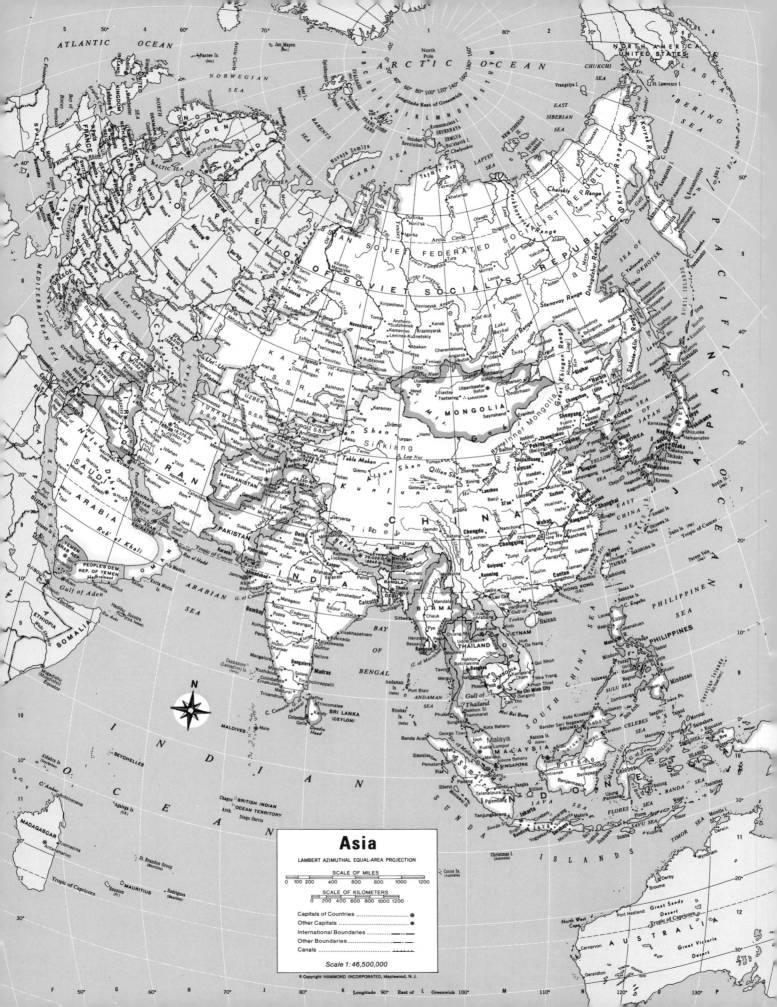

Asia

LAMBERT AZIMUTHAL EQUAL-AREA PROJECTION

SCALE OF MILES

0 100 200 400 600 800 1000 1200

SCALE OF KILOMETERS

0 200 400 600 800 1000 1200

Capitals of Countries .... ⊛
Other Capitals .... ⊛
International Boundaries .... ━━━
Other Boundaries .... ━ ‧ ━
Canals .... ━━━

Scale 1: 46,500,000

© Copyright HAMMOND INCORPORATED, Maplewood, N.J.

Population Distribution

AREA 17,128,500 sq. mi.
(44,362,815 sq. km.)
POPULATION 2,633,000,000
LARGEST CITY Tokyo
HIGHEST POINT Mt. Everest 29,028 ft.
(8,848 m.)
LOWEST POINT Dead Sea -1,296 ft.
(-395 m.)

Vegetation

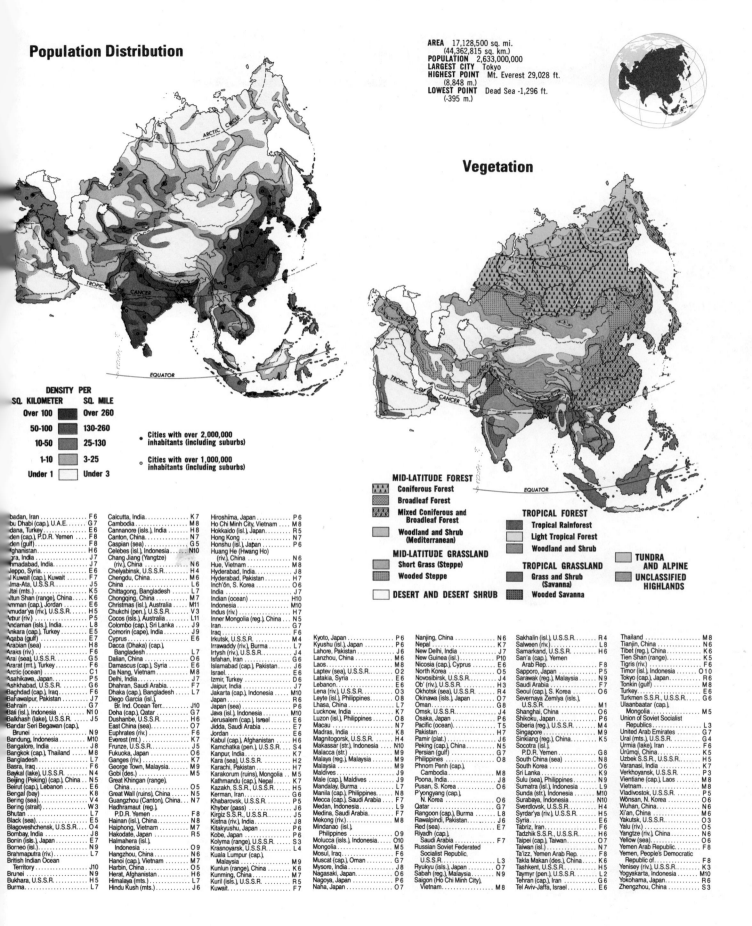

DENSITY PER

SQ. KILOMETER	SQ. MILE
Over 100	Over 260
50-100	130-260
10-50	25-130
1-10	3-25
Under 1	Under 3

• Cities with over 2,000,000 inhabitants (including suburbs)

○ Cities with over 1,000,000 inhabitants (including suburbs)

MID-LATITUDE FOREST
Coniferous Forest
Broadleaf Forest
Mixed Coniferous and Broadleaf Forest
Woodland and Shrub (Mediterranean)

MID-LATITUDE GRASSLAND
Short Grass (Steppe)
Wooded Steppe

DESERT AND DESERT SHRUB

TROPICAL FOREST
Tropical Rainforest
Light Tropical Forest
Woodland and Shrub

TROPICAL GRASSLAND
Grass and Shrub (Savanna)
Wooded Savanna

TUNDRA AND ALPINE

UNCLASSIFIED HIGHLANDS

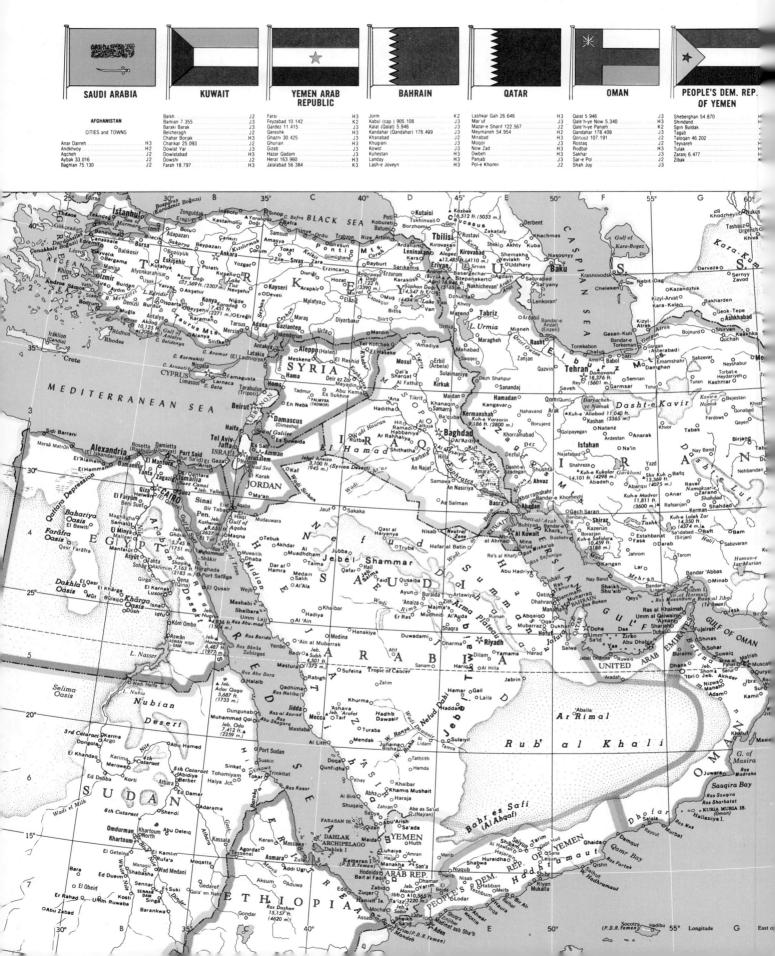

AFGHANISTAN

CITIES and TOWNS

Anar Darreh H3	Balkh J2	Farsi H3	Jorm K2	Lashkar Gah 26.646 .... H3	Qalat 5.946 .... J3	Sheberghan 54.870 .... J2
Andkhvoy H2	Bamian 7.355 .... J3	Feyzabad 10.142 .... K2	Kabul (cap.) 905.108 .... J3	Mar'uf J3	Qale'h-ye Now 5.340 .... H3	Shindand H3
Aqcheh J2	Baraki Barak J3	Gardez 11.415 .... J3	Kalat (Qalat) 5.946 .... J3	Mazar-e Sharif 122.567 .... J2	Qale'h-ye Panjeh K2	Spin Buldak J3
Aybak 33.016 .... J2	Belcheragh H3	Gereshk J3	Kandahar (Qandahar) 178.409 .... J3	Meymaneh 54.954 .... H2	Qandahar 178.409 .... J3	Tagab J2
Baghlan 75.130 .... J2	Chahar Borjak H3	Ghazni 30.425 .... J3	Khanabad J2	Mirabad H3	Qonuz 107.191 .... J2	Taloqan 46.202 .... J2
	Charikar 25.093 .... J3	Ghurian H3	Khugiani J3	Moqor J3	Rostaq J2	Teyvareh J3
	Dowlat Yar J3	Gizab J3	Kowst J3	Now Zad H3	Rudbar H3	Tulak H3
	Dowlatabad H3	Hazar Qadam J3	Kuhestan H3	Owbeh H3	Sakhar J3	Zarani 6.477 .... H3
	Dowshi J2	Herat 163.960 .... H3	Landay H3	Panjab J3	Sar-e Pol J2	Zibak J2
	Farah 18.797 .... H3	Jalalabad 56.384 .... K3	Lash-e Joveyn H3	Pol-e Khomri J2	Shah Juy J3	

UNITED ARAB EMIRATES

OTHER FEATURES

...h Rud (riv.)	H3
...d-e Zerreh (depr.)	H4
...rud (riv.)	H3
...mand (riv.)	J3
...du Kush (mts.)	J2
...ul (riv.)	K3
...ar (riv.)	K2
...ah (riv.)	J3

Margow, Dasht-e (des.)	H3
Murghab (riv.)	H2
Namaksar (salt lake)	H3
Paropamisus (mts.)	H3
Rigestan (reg.)	H3

BAHRAIN

CITIES and TOWNS

GAZA STRIP

CITIES and TOWNS

Gaza* 118,272 ... B3

Manama (cap.) 88,785	F4
Muharraq 37,732	F4

IRAN

CITIES and TOWNS

Abadan 296,081	E3
Abadeh 16,000	F3
Abarqu 8,000	F3
Ahvaz 329,006	E3

Amol 68,782	F2
Anar 463	G3
Anarak 2,038	F3
Arak 114,507	E3
Ardabil 147,404	E2
Ardestan 5,868	F3
Asterabad (Gorgan) 88,348	F2
Babol 67,790	F2
Bafq 5,000	G3
Baft 6,000	G4

(continued on following page)

SAUDI ARABIA

AREA 829,995 sq. mi.
(2,149,687 sq. km.)
POPULATION 8,367,000
CAPITAL Riyadh
MONETARY UNIT Saudi riyal
MAJOR LANGUAGE Arabic
MAJOR RELIGION Islam

YEMEN ARAB REPUBLIC

AREA 77,220 sq. mi. (200,000 sq. km.)
POPULATION 6,456,189
CAPITAL San'a
MONETARY UNIT Yemeni rial
MAJOR LANGUAGE Arabic
MAJOR RELIGION Islam

QATAR

AREA 4,247 sq. mi. (11,000 sq. km.)
POPULATION 220,000
CAPITAL Doha
MONETARY UNIT Qatari riyal
MAJOR LANGUAGE Arabic
MAJOR RELIGION Islam

PEOPLE'S DEM. REP. OF YEMEN

AREA 111,101 sq. mi. (287,752 sq. km.)
POPULATION 1,969,000
CAPITAL Aden
MONETARY UNIT Yemeni dinar
MAJOR LANGUAGE Arabic
MAJOR RELIGION Islam

KUWAIT

AREA 6,532 sq. mi. (16,918 sq. km.)
POPULATION 1,355,827
CAPITAL Al Kuwait
MONETARY UNIT Kuwaiti dinar
MAJOR LANGUAGE Arabic
MAJOR RELIGION Islam

BAHRAIN

AREA 240 sq. mi. (622 sq. km.)
POPULATION 358,857
CAPITAL Manama
MONETARY UNIT Bahraini dinar
MAJOR LANGUAGE Arabic
MAJOR RELIGION Islam

OMAN

AREA 120,000 sq. mi. (310,800 sq. km.)
POPULATION 891,000
CAPITAL Muscat
MONETARY UNIT Omani rial
MAJOR LANGUAGE Arabic
MAJOR RELIGION Islam

UNITED ARAB EMIRATES

AREA 32,278 sq. mi. (83,600 sq. km.)
POPULATION 1,040,275
CAPITAL Abu Dhabi
MONETARY UNIT dirham
MAJOR LANGUAGE Arabic
MAJOR RELIGION Islam

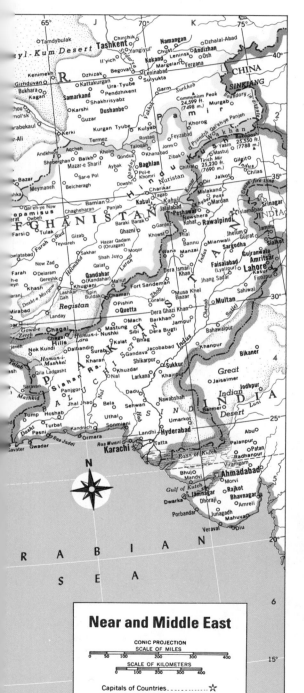

Near and Middle East

CONIC PROJECTION
SCALE OF MILES

SCALE OF KILOMETERS

Capitals of Countries .... ☆
International Boundaries _____

© Copyright HAMMOND INCORPORATED, Maplewood, N.J.

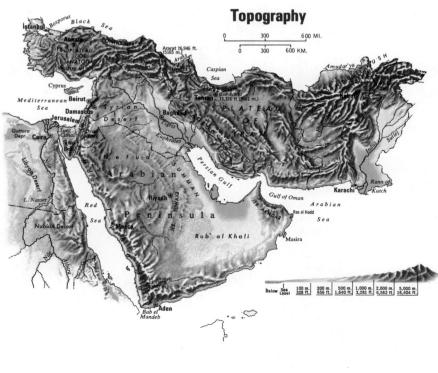

Topography

Agriculture, Industry and Resources

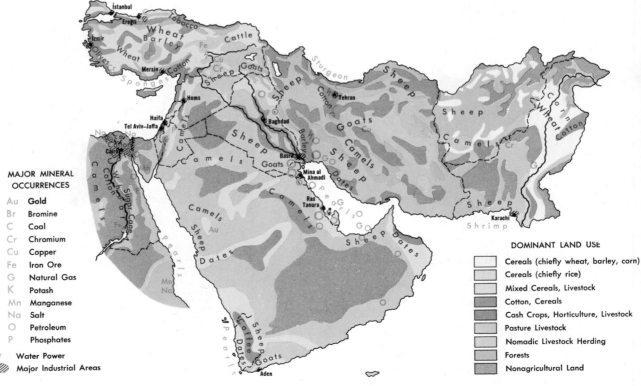

MAJOR MINERAL OCCURRENCES

Au   Gold
Br   Bromine
C   Coal
Cr   Chromium
Cu   Copper
Fe   Iron Ore
G   Natural Gas
K   Potash
Mn   Manganese
Na   Salt
O   Petroleum
P   Phosphates
⚡   Water Power
▨   Major Industrial Areas

DOMINANT LAND USE

Cereals (chiefly wheat, barley, corn)
Cereals (chiefly rice)
Mixed Cereals, Livestock
Cotton, Cereals
Cash Crops, Horticulture, Livestock
Pasture Livestock
Nomadic Livestock Herding
Forests
Nonagricultural Land

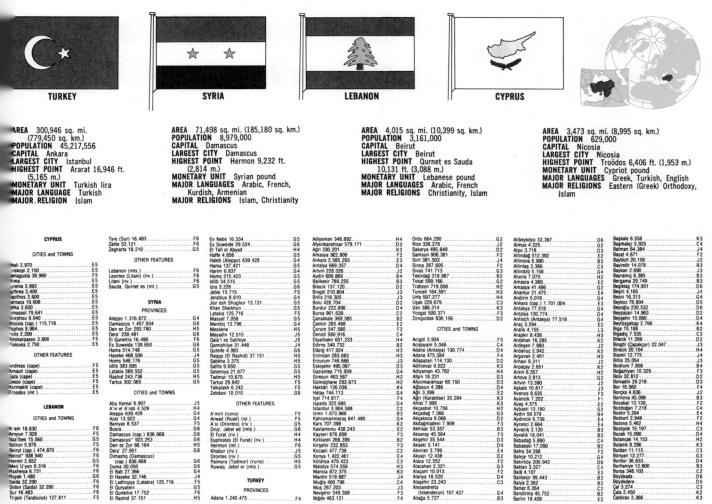

TURKEY

AREA 300,946 sq. mi. (779,450 sq. km.)
POPULATION 45,217,556
CAPITAL Ankara
LARGEST CITY Istanbul
HIGHEST POINT Ararat 16,946 ft. (5,165 m.)
MONETARY UNIT Turkish lira
MAJOR LANGUAGE Turkish
MAJOR RELIGION Islam

SYRIA

AREA 71,498 sq. mi. (185,180 sq. km.)
POPULATION 8,979,000
CAPITAL Damascus
LARGEST CITY Damascus
HIGHEST POINT Hermon 9,232 ft. (2,814 m.)
MONETARY UNIT Syrian pound
MAJOR LANGUAGES Arabic, French, Kurdish, Armenian
MAJOR RELIGIONS Islam, Christianity

LEBANON

AREA 4,015 sq. mi. (10,399 sq. km.)
POPULATION 3,161,000
CAPITAL Beirut
LARGEST CITY Beirut
HIGHEST POINT Qurnet es Sauda 10,131 ft. (3,088 m.)
MONETARY UNIT Lebanese pound
MAJOR LANGUAGES Arabic, French
MAJOR RELIGIONS Christianity, Islam

CYPRUS

AREA 3,473 sq. mi. (8,995 sq. km.)
POPULATION 629,000
CAPITAL Nicosia
LARGEST CITY Nicosia
HIGHEST POINT Troödos 6,406 ft. (1,953 m.)
MONETARY UNIT Cypriot pound
MAJOR LANGUAGES Greek, Turkish, English
MAJOR RELIGIONS Eastern (Greek) Orthodoxy, Islam

CYPRUS

CITIES and TOWNS

Khali 2,970 .... E5
Criskopi 2,150 .... E5
Famagusta 38,960 .... F5
Kima E5
Kyrenia 3,892 .... E5
Lythrea 3,400 .... E5
Lapithos 3,600 .... E5
Larnaca 19,608 .... E5
Lefka 3,650 .... E5
Limassol 79,641 .... E5
Morphou 9,040 .... E5
Nicosia (cap.) 115,718 .... E5
Paphos 8,984 .... E5
Polis 2,200 .... E5
Rizokarpasso 3,600 .... F5
Vatalousa 2,750 .... E5

OTHER FEATURES

Andreas (cape) F5
Arnauti (cape) E5
Gata (cape) E5
Greco (cape) F5
Kormakiti (cape) E5
Troodos (mt.) E5

LEBANON

CITIES and TOWNS

B'aleih 18,630 .... F6
Amyun 7,926 .... F6
Baa'lbek 15,560 .... G5
Batrun 5,976 .... F5
Beirut (cap.) 474,870 .... F6
Beirut* 938,940 .... F6
Hermil 2,652 .... G5
Merj U'yun 9,318 .... F6
Rasheiya 6,731 .... F6
Rayak 1,480 .... G6
Saida 32,200 .... F6
Sidon (Saida) 32,200 .... F6
Sur 16,483 .... F6
Tripoli (Tarabulus) 127,611 .... F5

Tyre (Sur) 16,483 .... F6
Zahle 53,121 .... F6
Zegharta 18,210 .... G5

OTHER FEATURES

Lebanon (mts.) F6
Leontes (Litani) (riv.) F6
Litani (riv.) F6
Sauda, Qurnet es (mt.) G5

SYRIA

PROVINCES

Aleppo 1,316,872 .... G4
Damascus 1,457,934 .... G6
Deir ez Zor 292,780 .... H5
El Quneitra 16,490 .... F6
Es Suweida 139,650 .... G6
Hama 514,748 .... G5
Haseke 468,506 .... J4
Homs 546,176 .... G5
Idlib 383,695 .... G5
Latakia 389,552 .... F5
Rashid 243,736 .... H5
Tartus 302,065 .... F5

CITIES and TOWNS

Abu Kemal 6,907 .... J5
A'in el A'rab 4,529 .... H4
Aleppo 639,428 .... G4
Azaz 13,923 .... G4
Baniyas 8,537 .... F5
Busra G6
Damascus (cap.) 836,668 .... G6
Damascus* 923,253 .... G6
Deir ez Zor 66,164 .... H5
Dera' 27,651 .... G6
Dimashq (Damascus) (cap.) 836,668 .... G6
Duma 30,050 .... G6
El Bab 27,366 .... G4
El Haseke 32,746 .... J4
El Ladhiqiya (Latakia) 125,716 .... F5
El Quryatein G5
El Quneitra 17,752 .... F6
El Rashid 37,151 .... H5

En Nebk 16,334 .... G5
Es Suweide 29,524 .... G6
Et Tell el Abyad H4
Haffe 4,656 .... G5
Haleb (Aleppo) 639,428 .... G4
Hama 137,421 .... G5
Harim 6,837 .... G4
Homs 215,423 .... G5
Idlib 34,515 .... G5
Izra 3,226 .... G6
Jeble 15,715 .... F5
Jerablus 8,610 .... G4
Jisr esh Shughur 13,131 .... G5
Khan Sheikhun G5
Latakia 125,716 .... F5
Masyaf 7,058 .... G5
Membij 13,796 .... G4
Meskene H5
Meyadin 12,515 .... H5
Qala't es Salihiye J5
Qamishliye 31,448 .... J4
Quteife 4,993 .... G6
Raqqa (El Rashid) 37,151 .... H5
Sabkha 3,375 .... H5
Safita 9,650 .... G5
Selemiya 21,677 .... G5
Tadmur 10,670 .... H5
Tartus 29,842 .... F5
Telkalakh 6,242 .... G5
Zebdani 10,010 .... G6

OTHER FEATURES

A'mrit (ruins) F5
Arwad (Ruad) (isl.) F5
A'si (Orontes) (riv.) G6
Druz, Jebel ed (mts.) G6
El Furat (riv.) H4
Euphrates (El Furat) (riv.) H4
Hermon (mt.) F6
Khabur (riv.) J5
Orontes (riv.) G5
Palmyra (Tadmor) (ruins) H5
Ruwaq, Jebel er (mts.) G6

TURKEY

PROVINCES

Adana 1,240,475 .... F4

Adiyaman 346,892 .... H4
Afyonkarahisar 579,171 .... D3
Agri 330,201 .... K3
Amasya 302,806 .... F2
Ankara 2,585,293 .... E3
Antalya 669,357 .... D4
Artvin 228,026 .... J2
Aydin 609,869 .... B4
Balikesir 789,255 .... B3
Bilecik 137,120 .... D2
Bingöl 210,804 .... J3
Bitlis 218,305 .... J3
Bolu 428,704 .... D2
Burdur 222,896 .... D4
Bursa 961,639 .... C2
Çanakkale 369,385 .... B2
Çankiri 265,468 .... F2
Çorum 547,580 .... F2
Denizli 560,916 .... C4
Diyarbakir 651,233 .... H4
Edirne 340,732 .... B2
Elazig 417,924 .... H3
Erzincan 283,683 .... H3
Erzurum 746,666 .... J3
Eskişehir 495,097 .... D3
Gaziantep 715,939 .... H4
Giresun 463,587 .... H2
Gümüşhane 293,673 .... H2
Hakkâri 126,036 .... K4
Hatay 744,113 .... G4
Içel 714,817 .... F4
Isparta 322,685 .... D4
Istanbul 3,904,588 .... C2
Izmir 1,673,966 .... B3
Kahramanmaraş 641,480 .... G4
Kars 707,398 .... K2
Kastamonu 438,243 .... E2
Kayseri 676,809 .... F3
Kirklareli 268,399 .... B2
Kirşehir 232,853 .... F3
Kocaeli 477,736 .... C2
Konya 1,422,461 .... E4
Kütahya 470,423 .... C3
Malatya 574,558 .... H3
Manisa 872,375 .... B3
Mardin 519,687 .... J4
Muğla 400,796 .... C4
Muş 262,203 .... J3
Nevşehir 249,308 .... F3
Niğde 463,121 .... F4

Ordu 664,290 .... G2
Rize 336,278 .... J2
Sakarya 495,649 .... D2
Samsun 906,381 .... F2
Siirt 381,503 .... J4
Sinop 267,605 .... F2
Sivas 741,713 .... G3
Tekirdağ 319,987 .... B2
Tokat 599,166 .... G2
Trabzon 719,008 .... H2
Tunceli 164,591 .... H3
Urfa 597,277 .... H4
Uşak 229,679 .... C3
Van 386,314 .... K3
Yozgat 500,371 .... F3
Zonguldak 836,156 .... D2

CITIES and TOWNS

Acigöl 3,934 .... F3
Acipayam 5,046 .... C4
Adalia (Antalya) 130,774 .... D4
Adana 475,384 .... F4
Adapazari 114,130 .... D2
Adilcevaz 9,022 .... K3
Adiyaman 43,782 .... H4
Afşin 18,231 .... G3
Afyonkarahisar 60,150 .... D3
Ağlasun 4,288 .... D4
Ağri 3,399 .... K3
Ağri (Karaköse) 35,284 .... K3
Ahlat 7,995 .... K3
Akçaabat 10,756 .... H2
Akçadağ 7,366 .... G3
Akçakoca 9,066 .... D2
Akdağmadeni 7,909 .... F3
Akhisar 53,357 .... B3
Aksaray 45,564 .... F3
Akşehir 35,544 .... D3
Akseki 5,141 .... D4
Akviran 3,799 .... E4
Akyazi 12,438 .... D2
Alaca 12,552 .... F2
Alacahan 2,321 .... G3
Alaçam 10,013 .... F2
Alanya 18,520 .... D4
Alaşehir 23,243 .... C3
Alexandretta (Iskenderun) 107,437 .... G4
Aliağa 5,727 .... B3

Alibeyköyü 33,387 .... D6
Almus 4,225 .... G2
Alpu 3,718 .... D3
Altindağ 512,392 .... E2
Altinova 6,980 .... B3
Altintaş 3,386 .... C3
Altinözü 5,158 .... G4
Alucra 7,070 .... H2
Amasra 4,369 .... E1
Amasya 41,496 .... G2
Anamur 21,475 .... E4
Andirin 5,018 .... G4
Ankara (cap.) 1,701,004 .... E2
Antakya 77,518 .... G4
Antalya 77,518 .... D4
Antalya 130,774 .... D4
Antioch (Antakya) 77,518 .... G4
Araç 3,594 .... E2
Aralik 4,155 .... K3
Arapkir 8,436 .... H3
Ardahan 16,285 .... K2
Ardeşen 7,980 .... J2
Arguvan 2,942 .... H3
Arguvan 2,461 .... H3
Arhavi 6,311 .... J2
Arpaçay 2,651 .... K2
Arsin 6,557 .... H2
Artova 2,813 .... G2
Artvin 13,390 .... J2
Aşkale 10,817 .... J3
Avanos 8,635 .... F3
Ayancik 7,202 .... F1
Ayaş 4,575 .... E2
Aybasti 13,180 .... G2
Aydin 59,579 .... B4
Aydincik 6,739 .... E4
Ayrancı 2,664 .... E3
Ayvacik 3,120 .... B3
Ayvalik 18,041 .... B3
Babadağ 5,890 .... C4
Babaeski 17,090 .... B2
Bafra 34,288 .... F2
Bahçe 10,212 .... G4
Bakirköy 200,942 .... C4
Baklan 3,327 .... C4
Balâ 4,107 .... E3
Balikesir 99,443 .... B3
Balya 2,362 .... B3
Banaz 6,254 .... C3
Bandirma 45,752 .... B2
Bartin 18,409 .... E2

Başkale 8,558 .... K3
Başmakçi 5,925 .... C4
Batman 64,384 .... J4
Bayat 4,671 .... F2
Bayburt 20,156 .... J2
Bayindir 14,078 .... B3
Baykan 2,690 .... J3
Bayramiç 6,385 .... B3
Bergama 29,749 .... B3
Beşiktaş 174,931 .... D6
Beşiri 4,165 .... J4
Besni 16,313 .... G4
Beykoz 76,804 .... D5
Beyoğlu 230,532 .... D6
Beypazari 14,963 .... D2
Beyşehir 15,186 .... D4
Beytüşşebap 2,766 .... K4
Biga 15,188 .... B2
Bigadiç 7,535 .... C3
Bilecik 11,269 .... D2
Birecik 20,104 .... H4
Bismil 12,775 .... J4
Bitlis 25,054 .... J3
Bodrum 7,858 .... B4
Boğazliyan 10,329 .... F3
Bolu 32,612 .... D2
Bolvadin 29,218 .... D3
Bor 16,560 .... F4
Borçka 4,636 .... J2
Bornova 45,096 .... B3
Boyabat 13,139 .... F2
Bozdoğan 7,218 .... C4
Bozkir 5,294 .... D4
Bozkurt 2,948 .... F2
Bozova 5,462 .... H4
Bozüyük 15,197 .... C3
Bucak 15,090 .... D4
Bulancak 14,153 .... H2
Bulanik 8,296 .... K3
Buldan 11,115 .... C3
Bünyan 12,277 .... F3
Burdur 36,633 .... D4
Burhaniye 12,800 .... B3
Bursa 346,103 .... C2
Büyükada D6
Büyükdere D5
Çal 3,274 .... C3
Çala 2,450 .... C3
Çaldiran 3,366 .... K3

(continued on following page)

Agriculture, Industry and Resources

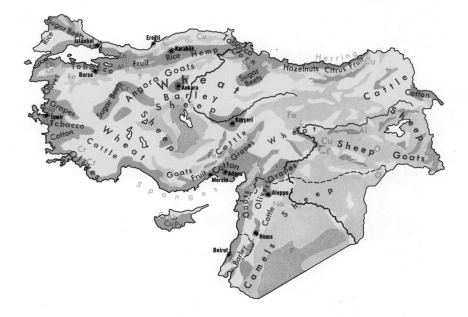

DOMINANT LAND USE

- Cereals (chiefly wheat, barley), Livestock
- Cash Crops, Horticulture, Livestock
- Pasture Livestock
- Nomadic Livestock Herding
- Forests
- Nonagricultural Land

MAJOR MINERAL OCCURRENCES

Ab	Asbestos	Na	Salt
Al	Bauxite	O	Petroleum
C	Coal	P	Phosphates
Cr	Chromium	Pb	Lead
Cu	Copper	Py	Pyrites
Fe	Iron Ore	Sb	Antimony
Hg	Mercury	Zn	Zinc
Mg	Magnesium		

⚡ Water Power
▨ Major Industrial Areas

Çalköy 3,002 ... C3	Demirkent 4,204 ... E4	Düzce 32,129 ... D2	Erzincan 60,351 ... H3	Gemerik 5,769 ... G3	Güdül 4,746 ... E2
Çamardi 2,419 ... F3	Demirköy 3,616 ... B2	Ecabat 3,642 ... B6	Erzurum 162,973 ... J3	Gemlik 20,704 ... C2	Gülnar 6,344 ... E4
Çameli 2,502 ... C4	Denizli 106,902 ... C4	Edirne 63,001 ... A2	Eskimalatya 10,182 ... H4	Genç 7,671 ... J3	Gülşehir 6,188 ... F3
Çamlidere 4,386 ... E2	Dereli 4,188 ... H2	Edremit 26,110 ... B3	Eskipazar 2,865 ... E2	Genezin 4,925 ... F3	Gümüş 3,066 ... F2
Çan 11,797 ... B2	Derik 13,292 ... J4	Eflâni 3,793 ... E2	Eskişehir 259,952 ... D3	Gerçüş 4,393 ... J4	Gümüşhacıköy 12,789 ... F2
Çanakkale 30,788 ... B6	Çiçekdağı 3,203 ... F3	Eğirdir 9,799 ... D4	Eşme 7,828 ... C3	Gerede 8,259 ... E2	Gümüşhane 11,166 ... H2
Çandir 6,986 ... E3	Cide 3,520 ... E2	Elazığ 131,415 ... H3	Eşme 8,168 ... H2	Gerger 2,773 ... H3	Güney 7,154 ... C4
Çankaya 895,005 ... E3	Çifteler 8,163 ... D3	Elbistan 26,048 ... G3	Eşme 6,081 ... J3	Germencik 10,558 ... B4	Gürün 9,138 ... G3
Çankiri 28,512 ... E2	Cihanbeyli 10,079 ... E3	Eldivan 3,302 ... E2	Eyüp 95,486 ... D6	Gerze 7,313 ... F2	Hacibektaş 5,032 ... F3
Çapakçur 22,047 ... J3	Çildir 2,260 ... K2	Eleşkirt 8,202 ... K3	Ezbider 3,631 ... H3	Gevaş 6,333 ... K3	Hacilar 15,622 ... G3
Çardak 4,232 ... C6	Cimin 5,341 ... H3	Elmali 10,184 ... D4	Ezine 9,359 ... B3	Geyve 7,806 ... D2	Hadim 10,467 ... E4
Çarşamba 23,973 ... G2	Cine 11,308 ... B4	Emet 6,239 ... C3	Gazi 1,824 ... —	Giresun 38,236 ... H2	Hafik 5,398 ... G3
Çatak 2,366 ... K4	Çivril 7,721 ... C3	Emirdağ 13,184 ... D3	Fatih 504,127 ... D6	Göksun 10,481 ... G3	Hakkâri
Çatalca 7,693 ... C2	Cizre 15,557 ... K4	Emirgazi 5,244 ... E4	Fatsa 19,758 ... G2	Gölbaşı 15,103 ... —	(Çölemerik) 11,735 ... K4
Çatalzeytin 2,271 ... F1	Çölemerik 11,735 ... K4	Enez 2,486 ... A2	Feke 5,576 ... G4	Gölcük 33,279 ... C2	Halfeti 3,689 ... G4
Çay 12,200 ... D3	Çorlu 40,134 ... B2	Erbaa 20,315 ... G2	Fethiye 12,700 ... C4	Göle 7,680 ... K2	Hamur 2,267 ... —
Çaycuma 8,118 ... E2	Çorum 64,852 ... F2	Erciş 22,351 ... K3	Fevzipaşa 5,495 ... G4	Gölhisar 7,095 ... C4	Hani 7,559 ... —
Çayeli 13,480 ... J2	Çubuk 13,793 ... E2	Erdek 8,685 ... B2	Findikli 5,008 ... J2	Gölköy 10,022 ... G2	Harput 3,231 ... —
Çayıralan 8,071 ... F3	Çukur 5,479 ... F3	Erdemli 19,936 ... F4	Finike 4,200 ... D4	Gölmarmara 11,982 ... B3	Haruniye 12,837 ... —
Çaykolu 4,580 ... E3	Çukurca 3,019 ... K4	Eregli 45,992 ... B3	Foça 4,829 ... B3	Göloşazı 5,002 ... —	Hassa 10,926 ... —
Cekerek 3,796 ... F2	Çumra 19,225 ... E4	Eregli 50,354 ... F4	Gallipoli 13,466 ... B5	Gönen 16,091 ... B2	Hatay (Antakya) 77,518 ... —
Çelikhan 5,066 ... H3	Doğubeyazıt 17,612 ... K3	Ergani 21,936 ... H3	Gaziantep 300,882 ... G4	Gördes 7,909 ... —	Havran 7,552 ... —
Çemişgezek 3,048 ... H3	Daday 2,528 ... E2	Erkilet 3,924 ... G3	Gazipaşa 6,696 ... E4	Gördes 8,079 ... —	Havsa 4,298 ... —
Çerkeş 3,780 ... E2	Darende 8,055 ... G3	Ermenak 13,464 ... E4	Gebze 33,110 ... C2	Göynücek 2,600 ... —	Havza 15,341 ... —
Çerkezköy 8,428 ... C2	Dazkiri 3,912 ... C4	Ermek 5,340 ... K4	Gediz 10,649 ... C3	Göynük 8,079 ... —	Haymana 6,123 ... —
Çermik 9,749 ... H3	Delice 3,462 ... E3	Erzin 15,314 ... G4	Gelibolu (Gallipoli) 13,466 ... C5	Göynük 2,519 ... D2	
	Demirci 15,016 ... C3	Duragan 3,259 ... F2			
	Dursunbey 8,615 ... C3				

...rabolu 12.331	B2	Islâhiye 20.683	G4
...o 4.896	J3	Isparta 62.870	D4
...imhan 11.818	D2	Ispir 3.929	J2
...dek 15.291	H4	Istanbul 2.547.364	D6
...s 10.226	J3	Ivrindi 3.730	B3
...arönü 4.485	K3	Izmir 636.834	B3
...an 2.545	J2	Izmit 165.483	C2
...s 9.089		Iznik 11.614	C2
...asan 7.724	K2	Kadiköy 354.957	D6
...at 5.796	H3	Kadinhani 11.802	E3
... 152.236	F4	Kadirli 34.779	F4
...4.862		Kağithane 164.448	D6
...at 29.542	K3	Kağizman 11.517	K2
...z 6 624	E2	Kâhta 15.602	H4
...n 11.830	D3	Kalan 11.637	H3
...8.947	J3	Kale 3.399	C4
...anli 5.667		Kalecik 4.707	E2
...esu 7.089	F3	Kaman 16.516	E3
...bolu 6.824		Kandira 10.187	D2
...öl 37.805	C2	Kangal 5.937	G3
...nü 4.152	D3	Karabük 69.182	E2
...ala 6.829	B2	Karacabey 21.648	C2
...le 2.328	G2	Karahalli 5.539	C3
...enderun 107.437	G4	Karaisali 2.316	F4
...lü 16.588	F2	Karaköçan 5.604	H3
		Karaköse (Ağri) 35.284	K3

Topography

Karaman 43.759	E4	Muğla 24.178	C4
Karamanli 5.904	C4	Muradiye 6.334	K3
Karapinar 19.589	E4	Muş 27.761	J3
Karasu 11.600	D2	Mustafakemalpaşa 27.706	C3
Karataş 5.598	F4	Mut 11.466	E4
Karayaka 4.242	G2	Mutki 2.815	J3
Karayazi 3.595	J3	Muttalip 3.917	D3
Kargi 5.021	F2	Nallihan 7.883	D2
Karliova 3.631	J3	Narman 4.607	J2
Kars 54.892	K2	Nazilli 52.176	C4
Karşiyaka 171.600	B3	Nevşehir 30.203	F3
Kartal 53.073	D6	Niğde 31.844	F4
Kaş 2.493	C4	Niksar 19.156	G2
Kastamonu 29.993	F2	Nizip 36.190	G4
Kavak, Çanakkale 3.932	C5	Nurhak 5.330	G4
Kavak, Samsun 3.964	F2	Nusaybin 23.684	J4
Kayseri 207.037	F3	Ödemiş 37.364	C3
Kazanli 4.461	F4	Of 10.376	J2
Kazimkarabekir 4.086	E4	Oğuzeli 7.194	G4
Keban 5.800	H3	Oltu 10.093	J2
Keçiborlu 7.096	C3	Ömerli 4.738	J4
Keles 2.423	C3	Ordu 47.481	G2
Kelkit 6.928	H2	Orhaneli 3.335	C3
Kemah 3.038	H3	Orhangazi 12.181	C2
Kemalpaşa 3.014	H3	Orta 3.596	E2
Kemalpaşa 7.572		Ortaca 8.604	C4
Kemerburgaz 7.234	D5	Ortakaravran 3.856	G4
Kemirhisar 6.205	F4	Ortaköy, Çorum 2.657	F2
Kepsut 4.704	C3	Ortaköy, Niğde 6.371	F3
Keşan 27.088	B2	Osmancik 11.921	F2
Keşap 5.264	H2	Osmaneli 4.789	C2
Keskin 10.540	E3	Osmaniye 61.581	G4
Kiği 5.598	J3	Ovacik, Tunceli 2.248	H3
Kilimli 26.649	D2	Özalp 4.188	K3
Kilis 54.055	G4	Palu 5.489	H3
Kinik 11.785	B3	Pasinler 14.267	J3
Kiraz 5.284	C3	Patnos 15.918	K3
Kirikhan 38.118	G4	Pazar, Rize 8.856	J2
Kirikkale 137.874	E3	Pazar, Tokat 4.337	G2
Kirkağaç 15.078	B3	Pazarcik 15.943	G4
Kirklareli 33.265	B2	Pazaryeri 5.633	C2
Kirşehir 41.415	F3	Pera (Beyoğlu) 230.532	D6
Kizilcahamam 7.050	E2	Perşembe 6.701	G2
Kizilhisar 11.119	C4	Pertek 4.176	H3
Kiziltepe 21.531	J4	Pervari 4.126	K4
Kiziliran 3.260	E4	Pinarbaşi 9.503	G3
Kocaeli (Izmit) 165.483	D2	Pinarhisar 10.523	B2
Koçarli 5.182	C4	Poiatli 35.267	E3
Konya 246.727	E4	Posof 2.209	K1
Korkuteli 10.334	C4	Pozanti 5.408	F4
Köyceğiz 4.612	C4	Pülümür 3.442	H3
Koyulhisar 3.861	G2	Pütürge 4.878	H3
Kozakli 6.200	F3	Refahiye 6.570	H3
Kozan 32.045	F4	Reşadiye 9.022	G2
Kozlu 27.322	D2	Reyhanli 25.749	G4
Kozluk 6.197	J3	Rize 36.044	J2
Küçükköy 56.411	C6	Şabanözü 3.442	E2
Kula 10.807	C3	Safranbolu 14.793	E2
Kulp 4.474	J3	Saimbeyli 3.622	F4
Kulu 11.707	E3	Sakarya (Adapazari) 114.130	D2
Kumkale 1.752	B6	Salihli 45.514	C3
Kumluca 7.704	D4	Samandağ 22.540	F4
Küre 2.378	E2	Samsat 2.083	H4
Kurşunlu 6.562	E2	Samsun 168.478	F2
Kurtalan 7.001	J3	Sandikli 13.181	D3
Kuşadasi 10.269	B4	Sapanca 9.040	D2
Kütahya 82.442	C3	Şaphane 3.919	C3
Kuyucak 6.039	C4	Sarayköy 10.513	C4
Ladik 6.785	F2	Sarayönü 8.946	E3
Lâpseki 3.727	C6	Sarigöl 6.979	C3
Lice 8.625	J3	Sarikamiş 21.262	K2
Lüleburgaz 32.401	B2	Sariköy 4.695	B2
Maden 15.151	H3	Sarioğlan 3.245	F3
Mağara 4.314	G3	Sariyer 79.329	D5
Mahmudiye 5.240	D3	Sariz 3.591	G3
Malatya 154.505	H3	Sarikaraağaç 4.772	D3
Malazgirt 13.094	K3	Sarikişla 12.763	G3
Malkara 14.399	B2	Şarköy 5.396	B2
Maltepe 66.343	D4	Sason 3.211	J3
Manavgat 10.804	D4	Savaştepe 7.179	B3
Manisa 78.114	B3	Şavşat 3.078	K1
Manyas 4.410	B3	Savur 4.983	J4
Maraş (Kahramanmaraş) 135.782	G4	Seben 2.471	D2
Mardin 36.629	J4	Selendi 5.092	C3
Marmaris 5.596	C4	Selçuk 12.251	B3
Mazgirt 3.141	H3	Selim 3.569	K2
Mazidaği 4.842	J4	Selimiye 2.989	B4
Mecitözü 6.066	F2	Senirkent 8.247	D3
Menemen 18.464	B3	Serik 14.161	D4
Mengen 2.459	D2	Seydişehir 25.651	D4
Meriç 3.922	B2	Seyitgazi 2.819	D3
Mersin 152.236	F4	Sğ 35.654	J4
Merzifon 30.801	F2	Şile 4.062	C2
Mesudiye 4.294	H4	Silifke 19.257	E4
Midyat 16.905	J4	Silivri 8.525	C2
Mihaliçcik 4.004	D3	Silopi 4.460	K4
Miláş 17.929	B4		
Mucur 9.398	F3		
Mudanya 8.399	C2		
Mudurnu 3.905	D2		

Silvan 29.599	J3	Yeşilyurt 7.451	H3
Simav 11.601	C3	Yildizeli 7.043	G3
Sincanli 3.847	D3	Yozgat 32.501	F3
Sindirgi 7.818	C3	Yüksekova 7.329	L4
Sinop 16.098	F1	Yumurtalik 2.442	F4
Şiran 5.048	H2	Yunak 6.187	D3
Şirnak 10.587	K4	Yusufeli 3.050	J2
Şirvan 5.166	K3	Zara 10.376	G3
Sivas 149.201	G3	Zeytinburnu 123.548	D6
Sivasli 4.394	C3	Zeytindağ 3.517	B3
Siverek 40.990	H4	Zile 32.157	F2
Sivrihisar 8.713	D3	Zivarik 2.703	E3
Smyrna (Izmir) 636.834	B3	Zonguldak 90.221	D2
Söğüt 5.329	D2		
Söke 35.407	B4	**OTHER FEATURES**	
Solhan 7.014	J3		
Soma 23.713	B3	Abydos (ruins)	B6
Sorgun 14.081	F3	Aci (lake)	D6
Suhut 8.154	D3	Adalar (isl.)	D6
Sulakyurt 4.311	E2	Aegean (sea)	A3
Sultandağ 4.017	D3	Ağri, Büyuk (Ararat) (mt.)	L3
Sultanhani 5.112	E4	Akdağ (mt.)	C4
Sulova 21.278	F2	Aladağ (mt.)	F4
Sungurlu 21.641	F2	Alexandretta (gulf)	F4
Sürmene 8.096	J2	Amanos (mts.)	G4
Suruç 20.395	H4	Anamur (cape)	E5
Suşehri 10.863	H2	Anatolia (reg.)	E3
Susurluk 14.000	C3	Ankara (riv.)	E2
Susuz 5.006	K2	Anti-Taurus (mts.)	G3
Sütçüler 2.721	D4	Antalya (gulf)	D4
Tarsus 102.186	F4	Araks (riv.)	L2
Taşkent 7.098	E4	Ararat (mt.)	L3
Taşköprü 8.146	F2	Arpa (riv.)	L2
Taşlicay 3.684	K3	Baba (cape)	A3
Taşova 9.516	F4	Bati Firat (riv.)	H3
Tatvan 29.271	K3	Beyşehir (lake)	D4
Tavas 9.728	C4	Black (sea)	E1
Tavşanli 19.575	C3	Bosporus (str.)	D6
Tefenni 4.280	C4	Bozcaada (isl.)	A3
Tekirdağ 41.257	B2	Burgaz (isl.)	D6
Tercan 6.068	J3	Büyük Ağri (Ararat) (mt.)	L3
Terme 15.660	G2	Çanakkale Boğazi (Dardanelles) (str.)	B6
Tire 30.694	B3	Çandarli (gulf)	B3
Tirebolu 7.385	H2	Çanik (mts.)	G2
Tokat 48.588	G3	Ceyhan (riv.)	F4
Tomarza 6.548	F3	Cilo Dağ (mt.)	L4
Tömük 7.660	F4	Çoruh (riv.)	J2
Tonya 10.544	J2	Dardanelles (str.)	B6
Torbali 17.237	B3	Dicle (riv.)	J4
Tortum 4.110	J2	Eastern Taurus (mts.)	J3
Torul 3.221	H2	Ephesus (ruins)	B3
Tosya 17.515	F2	Erciyas Daği (mt.)	F3
Trabzon 97.210	H2	Ergene (riv.)	B2
Trebizond (Trabzon) 97.210	H2	Euphrates (Firat) (riv.)	H3
Tunceli (Kalan) 11.637	H3	Firat (riv.)	G3
Turgutlu 47.009	B3	Gediz (riv.)	C3
Turhal 38.170	F2	Gelidonya (cape)	D4
Türkeli 2.194	F2	Gökçeada (isl.)	A3
Türkoğlu 9.207	G4	Göksu (riv.)	E4
Tutak 4.325	K3	Helles (cape)	B6
Tuzluca 5.209	K3	Heybeli (isl.)	D6
Tuzlukçu 4.613	D3	Ilium (ruins)	B6
Ula 5.117	C4	Imroz (Gökçeada) (isl.)	A2
Ulaş 5.186	G3	Ince (cape)	F1
Ulubey 4.214	C3	Istranca (mts.)	B2
Uluborlu 10.016	D3	Kaçkar Daği (mt.)	J2
Uludere 4.050	K4	Karadeniz Boğazi (Bosporus) (str.)	D6
Uluksla 6.336	F4	Karasu-Aras (riv.)	J3
Umurbey 2.754	D6	Kelkit (riv.)	G2
Ünye 23.366	G2	Kerme (gulf)	B4
Urfa 132.934	H4	Keşiş Tepesi (mt.)	H3
Ürgüp 6.758	F3	Kizilirmak (riv.)	F2
Urla 13.903	B3	Koca (riv.)	C2
Uşak 58.578	C3	Köroğlu (mts.)	E2
Üsküdar 202.957	D6	Küre (mts.)	F2
Üzümlü 4.365	H3	Mandalya (gulf)	B4
Uzunköprü 27.005	B2	Marmara (isl.)	C2
Vakfikebir 12.556	H2	Marmara (sea)	C2
Van 63.663	K3	Menderes, Büyük (riv.)	C4
Varto 5.572	J3	Meriç (riv.)	B2
Vezirköprü 11.705	F2	Murat (riv.)	H3
Viranşehir 26.244	H4	Pontic (mts.)	G2
Vize 8.203	B2	Porsuk (riv.)	D3
Yahyali 13.738	F3	Prinkipo (Adalar) (isl.)	D6
Yalova, Istanbul 27.289	C2	Sakarya (riv.)	D2
Yalvaç 18.305	D3	Saros (gulf)	B2
Yaprakli 3.020	E2	Seyhan (riv.)	F4
Yatağan 4.903	C4	Simav (riv.)	C3
Yayladaği 4.471	F5	Sinop (cape)	F1
Yenice, Çanakkale 4.004	B3	Sultan (mts.)	D3
Yenice. İçel 4.106	F4	Süphan Dağ (mt.)	K3
Yenice. Zonguldak 5.791	E2	Taurus (mts.)	D4
Yeniceoba 5.340	E3	Tigris (Dicle) (riv.)	J4
Yeniköy, Istanbul		Troy (Ilium) (ruins)	B6
Yenimahalle 198.643	E3	Tuz (lake)	E3
Yenişehir 15.188	C2	Van (lake)	K3
Yerkesek 2.387	F3	Yeşilirmak (riv.)	G2
Yerköy 19.927	F3		
Yeşilhisar 10.409	F3		
Yeşilköy	D6		
Yeşilova, Burdur 3.685	C3		
Yeşilova, Niğde 5.237	E3	*City and suburbs	

Turkey, Syria, Lebanon and Cyprus

© Copyright HAMMOND INCORPORATED, Maplewood, N.J.

SCALE OF MILES

0 25 50 75 100 125 150

SCALE OF KILOMETERS

0 25 50 75 100 125 150

Capitals of Countries ....☆   Capitals of Provinces ....△

Provincial Boundaries ....

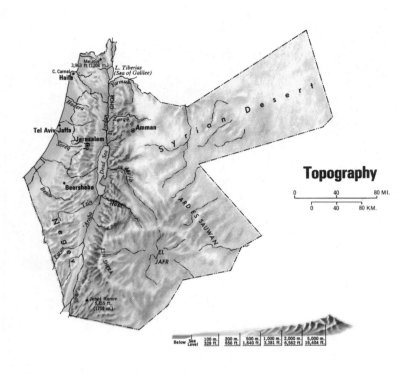

Topography

```
0    40    80 MI.
0    40    80 KM.
```

| Below Sea Level | 100 m. 328 ft. | 200 m. 656 ft. | 500 m. 1,640 ft. | 1,000 m. 3,281 ft. | 2,000 m. 6,562 ft. | 5,000 m. 16,404 ft. |

Archaeological Sites in Palestine
■ Major Excavations

```
0   10   20   30
    Miles
```

Mediterranean Sea

Dead Sea

Agriculture, Industry and Resources

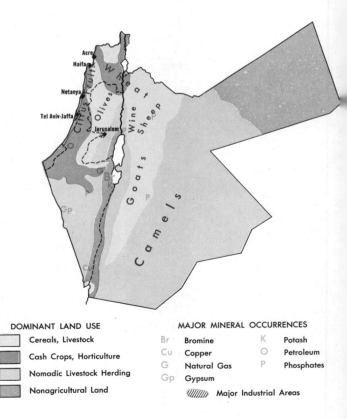

DOMINANT LAND USE

- Cereals, Livestock
- Cash Crops, Horticulture
- Nomadic Livestock Herding
- Nonagricultural Land

MAJOR MINERAL OCCURRENCES

Br	Bromine	K	Potash
Cu	Copper	O	Petroleum
G	Natural Gas	P	Phosphates
Gp	Gypsum		

///// Major Industrial Areas

© Copyright HAMMOND INCORPORATED

ISRAEL

DISTRICTS

Central 572,300	B3
Haifa 480,800	C2
Jerusalem 338,600	B4
Northern 473,700	C2
Southern 351,300	B5
Tel Aviv 905,100	B3

CITIES and TOWNS

Acre 34,400	C2
Afiqim 1,243	D2
'Afula 17,400	C2
Ahuzzam 407	B4
Akko (Acre) 34,400	C2
Arad 5,400	C5
'Arrabe 6,000	C2
Ashdot Yaa'qov 1,197	D2
Ashdod 40,500	B4
Ashqelon 43,100	A4
Atlit 1,516	B2
Avihayil 579	B3
Bat Shelomo 218	B2
Bat Yam 124,100	B3
Be'eri 300	A5
Be'er Menyha	
Beersheba (Be'er Sheva) 101,000	B5
Be'er Tuveya 602	B4
Beit Guvrin	B4
Bene Beraq 74,100	B3
Bet Qama 228	B5
Bet She'an 11,300	D3
Bet Shemesh 10,100	B4
Binyamina 2,701	B2
Carmel	C2
Dafna 577	D1
Dalyat al-Karmel 6,200	B2
Dan 498	D1
Dimona 23,700	C5
Dor 195	B2
E'in Gedi	C5
E'in Harod 1,372	C2
Elat	D6
Elath (Elat) 12,800	D6
El 'Auja	D5
Elyakim 568	B2
Elyashiv 435	B3
Even Yehuda 3,464	B3
Gal'on 356	B4
Gat 430	B4
Gedera 5,400	B4
Gerofit	D6
Gesher 360	C2
Gesher Haziv 238	C1
Gevara'm 283	B4
Gilat 561	B5
Ginnosar 473	C2
Giv'atayim 48,500	B3
Giva't Brenner 1,505	B4
Giv'at Hayyim 1,360	B3
Habonim 189	B2
Hadera 31,900	B3
Haifa 227,800	B2
Haifa* 367,400	B2
Hatseva	D5
Hazerim 127	B5

Hazor Hagelilit	D2
Helez 466	B4
Herzeliyya 41,200	B3
Hod Hasharon 13,500	B3
Hodiyya 400	B4
Holon 121,200	B3
Iksal 2,156	C2
Jerusalem (cap.) 376,000	C4
Jish 1 498	C1
Kafar Kanna 5,200	C2
Kafr Yasif 2,975	C2
Karkur-Pardes Hanna 13,600	C3
Kefar Blum 565	D1
Kefar Gila'di 701	C1
Kefar Ruppin 306	D3
Kefar Sava 26,500	B3
Kefar Vitkin 808	B3
Kefar Zekhariya 420	B4
Kinneret 909	D2
Lod (Lydda) 30,500	B4
Lydda 30,500	B4
Magen 149	A5
Maa'lot-Tarshiha	C1
Malkiya	C1
Mash 'Abbe Sade 238	B6
Mavqi'im 177	B4
Megiddo	C2
Metula 261	D1
Migdal 688	C2
Migdal Ha E'meq	C2
Mikhmoret 608	B3
Mishmar Hanegev 336	B5
Mishmar Hayarden	D1
Mivtahim 398	A5
Mizpe Ramon 331	D5
Moza Ilit 219	C4
Mughar 4,010	C2
Muqeble 459	C2
Nahariyya 24,000	C1
Nazareth 33,300	C2
Nazerat I'lit	C2
Negba 453	B4
Nes Ziyyona 11,700	B4
Netanya 70,700	B3
Netivot	B5
Nevatim 436	B5
Newe Yam 211	B2
Newe Zohar	C5
Nir Yitzhaq 209	A5
Nizzanim 479	B4
Ofaqim	B5
O'mer	B5
Oron	C6
Or Yehuda	B4
Pardes Hanna-Karkur 13,600	B2
Peduyim 361	B5
Petah Tiqwa 112,000	B3
Qadima 2,937	B3
Qalansuwa	B3
Qedma 157	B4
Qiryat Atta	C2
Qiryat Bialik 18,000	C2
Qiryat Gat 19,200	B4
Qiryat Mal'akhi	B4
Qiryat Motzkin 17,600	C2
Qiryat Shemona 15,200	C1
Qiryat Tivo'n 9,800	C2
Qiryat Yam 19,800	C2
Raa'nana 14,900	B3
Ramat Gan 120,900	B3

Ramat Hasharon 20,100	B3
Rame 2,986	C2
Ramla 34,100	B4
Rehovot 39,200	B4
Rei'm 155	A4
Revadim 175	B4
Revivim 258	B5
Rishon Le Ziyyon 51,900	B4
Rosh Ha 'Ayin	B3
Rosh Pinna 700	D2
Ruhama 497	B4
Saa'd 418	B4
Safad (Zefat) 13,600	C2
Sakhnin 8,400	C2
Sede Boqer	C5
Sederot	B4
Sedom	C5
Sedot Yam 511	B2
Shave Ziyyon 269	C1
Shefara'm 11,800	C2
Shefayim 614	B3
Shoval 393	B5
Tayibe 11,700	B3
Tel Aviv-Jaffa 343,300	B3
Tel Aviv-Jaffa* 1,219,900	B3
Tiberias 23,800	D2
Tirat Hakarmel 14,400	B2
Tirat Zevi 353	D3
Tur'an 2,304	C2
Umm el Fahm 13,300	C2
Urim 203	A5
Uzza 487	B4
Yad Mordekhai 416	A4
Yagur 1,266	C2
Yahav	D5
Yavne 10,100	B4
Yavne'el 1,580	C2
Yehud 8,900	B3
Yeruham 5,800	C5
Yesodot 293	B4
Yesud Hamaa'la 428	D1
Yiftah	C1
Yirka 2,715	C2
Yotvata	D6
Zavdi'el 396	B4
Ze'elim 148	B5
Zefat 13,600	C2
Zikhron Yaa'qov 6,500	B2
Zippori 241	C2

OTHER FEATURES

Aqaba (gulf)	D
'Araba, Wadi (valley)	B
Beer Sheva (dry riv.)	B
Besor (riv.)	B
Carmel (cape)	B
Carmel (mt.)	B
Dead (sea)	C
Galilee, Sea of (Tiberias) (lake)	C
Galilee (reg.)	C
Gerar (dry riv.)	B
Hadera (dry riv.)	B
Hanigra, Rosh (cape)	C
Jordan (riv.)	C
Judaea (reg.)	C
Lakhish (dry riv.)	B
Meiron (mt.)	C
Negev (reg.)	D

ISRAEL

ISRAEL
AREA 7,847 sq. mi. (20,324 sq. km.)
POPULATION 3,878,000
CAPITAL Jerusalem
LARGEST CITY Tel Aviv-Jaffa
HIGHEST POINT Meiran 3,963 ft.
(1,208 m.)
MONETARY UNIT shekel
MAJOR LANGUAGES Hebrew, Arabic
MAJOR RELIGIONS Judaism, Islam,
Christianity

JORDAN
AREA 35,000 sq. mi.
(90,650 sq. km.)
POPULATION 2,152,273
CAPITAL Amman
LARGEST CITY Amman
HIGHEST POINT Jeb. Ramm 5,755 ft.
(1,754 m.)
MONETARY UNIT Jordanian dinar
MAJOR LANGUAGE Arabic
MAJOR RELIGION Islam

JORDAN

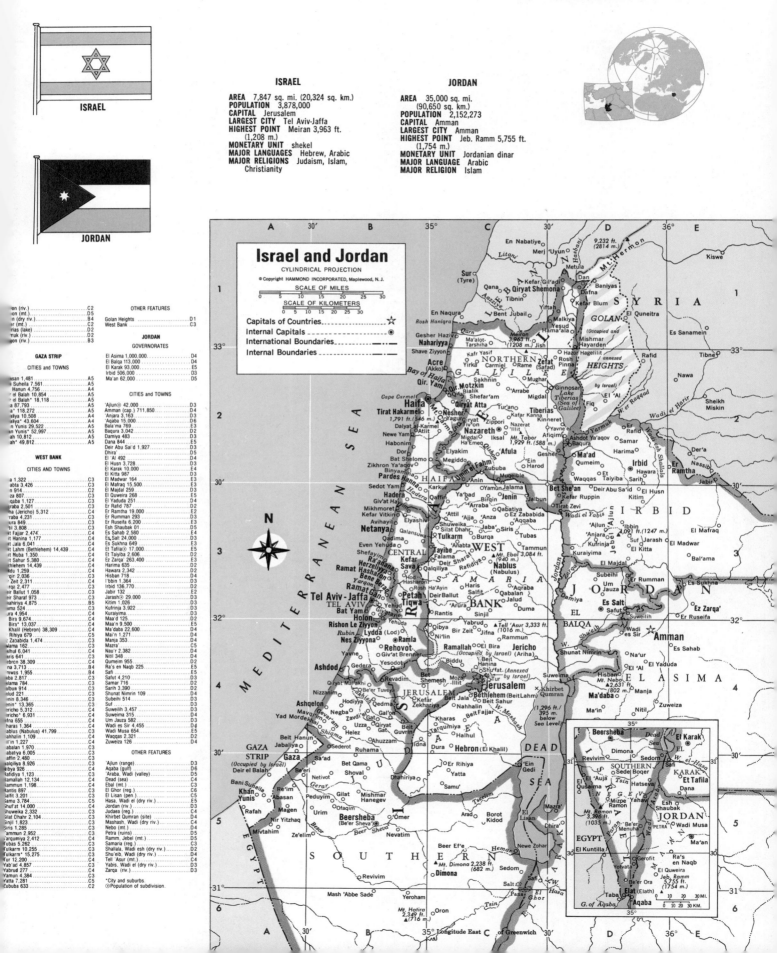

Israel and Jordan
CYLINDRICAL PROJECTION
© Copyright HAMMOND INCORPORATED, Maplewood, N. J.
SCALE OF MILES
SCALE OF KILOMETERS
Capitals of Countries
Internal Capitals
International Boundaries
Internal Boundaries

OTHER FEATURES
...on (riv.) C2
...on (mt.) D5
... (dry riv.) B4
...a (mt.) E2
...rias (lake) D2
...muk (riv.) D2
...on (riv.) B3

GAZA STRIP
CITIES and TOWNS
...asan 1,481 ....A5
...a Suheila 7,561 ....A5
...Hanun 4,756 ....A5
...el Balah 10,854 ....A5
...el Balah* 18,118 ....A5
...a 87,793 ....A5
...na 10,508 ....A4
...aliya* 43,604 ....A4
...n Yunis 29,522 ....A5
...n Yunis* 52,997 ....A5
...ah 10,812 ....A5
...ah* 49,812 ....A5

WEST BANK
CITIES AND TOWNS
...a 1,322 ....C3
...abta 3,426 ....C3
...a 914 ....C2
...za 807 ....C3
...qaba 2,501 ....C3
...ha (Jericho) 5,312 ....C4
...raba 4,231 ....C3
...ura 849 ....C3
...ti 3,808 ....C3
...ir* 118,272 ....C3
...Hanina 1,177 ....C4
...Lala 6,041 ....C4
...t Fajjar 2,474 ....C4
...t Hanina 1,350 ....C4
...t Sahur 5,380 ....C4
...thlehem 14,439 ....C4
...du 1,250 ....C3
...qir 2,036 ....C3
...Zeit 2,311 ....C4
...ir Ballut 1,058 ....C3
...ir Sharaf 973 ....C3
...ahiriya 4,875 ....B5
...ma 524 ....C3
...Bira 9,674 ....C4
...s 13,037 ....C4
...Khalil (Hebron) 38,309 ...C4
...Rihiya 679 ....C4
...Zababida 1,474 ....C3
...ama 162 ....C3
...alhul 6,041 ....C4
...is 641 ....C3
...hron 38,309 ....C4
...na 3,713 ....B4
...nwes 1,955 ....B4
...a 2,817 ....C3
...alama 784 ....C3
...albue 914 ....C3
...alud 221 ....C3
...nin 8,346 ....C3
...nin* 13,365 ....C3
...richo 6,931 ....C4
...richo* 5,312 ....C4
...fna 655 ....C4
...haras 1,364 ....C4
...ablus (Nablus) 41,799 ....C4
...ahhalin 1,109 ....C4
...il'in 1,227 ....C4
...abalan 1,970 ....C3
...abatya 6,905 ....C3
...affin 2,480 ....C3
...alqiliya 8,926 ....C3
...bya 926 ....C4
...aldiya 1,123 ....C4
...amallah 12,134 ....C4
...ammun 1,198 ....C4
...antis 897 ....C3
...ab 3,201 ....C3
...amu 3,784 ....C4
...huf'at 14,000 ....C4
...Shuweika 2,332 ....C3
...Silat Dhahr 2,104 ....C4
...Sinjil 1,823 ....C4
...Siris 1,285 ....C4
...arqumiya 2,412 ....C4
...ubas 5,262 ....C3
...ulkarm 10,255 ....C3
...ulkarm* 15,275 ....C3
...ar 12,200 ....C4
...abud 4,857 ....C3
...amun 381 ....C4
...atta 7,281 ....C5
...ububa 633 ....C2

OTHER FEATURES
'Ajlun (range) D3
Aqaba (gulf) D6
'Araba, Wadi (valley) D5
Dead (sea) C4
Ebal (mt.) C3
El Ghor (reg.) C4
El Lisan (pen.) C5
Hasa, Wadi el (dry riv.) E5
Jordan (riv.) D3
Judaea (reg.) C4
Mashash, Wadi (dry riv.) C4
Nebo (mt.) D4
Ramm, Jebel (mt.) D6
Samaria (reg.) C3
Shallala, Wadi (dry riv.) ...D2
Shu'eib, Wadi (dry riv.) D4
Yabis, Wadi (dry riv.) D3
Zarqa (riv.) D3

*City and suburbs.
⊙Population of subdivision.

OTHER FEATURES
Golan Heights D1
West Bank C3

JORDAN
GOVERNORATES
El Asima 1,000,000 ....D4
El Balqa 113,000 ....D4
El Karak 93,000 ....E5
Irbid 506,000 ....D3
Ma'an 62,000 ....D5

CITIES and TOWNS
'Ajlun ⊙ 42,000 ....D3
Amman (cap.) 711,850 ....D4
'Anjara 3,163 ....D3
'Aqaba 15,000 ....D6
Bala'ma 769 ....E3
Baqura 3,042 ....D3
Damiya 483 ....D3
Dana 844 ....D5
Dhira D5
El 'Al 492 ....D4
El Husn 3,728 ....D3
El Karak 10,000 ....E4
El Kitta 987 ....D3
El Madwar 164 ....E3
El Mafraq 15,500 ....E3
El Majdal 259 ....D3
El Quweira 268 ....D5
El Yaduda 251 ....D4
Er Rafid 787 ....D2
Er Ramtha 19,000 ....E3
Er Rumman 293 ....D3
Er Ruseifa 6,200 ....D4
Esh Shaubak 01 ....D5
Es Sahab 2,580 ....E4
Es Salt 24,000 ....D3
Es Sukhna 649 ....D3
Et Tafila 17,000 ....D5
Et Taiyiba 2,606 ....D2
Ez Zarqa 263,400 ....D3
Harima 635 ....D2
Hawara 2,342 ....D3
Hisban 718 ....D4
Ibbin 1,364 ....D3
Irbid 136,770 ....D3
Jabir 132 ....E2
Jarash ⊙ 29,000 ....D3
Kitim 1,026 ....D3
Kufrinja 3,922 ....D3
Kuraiyima D3
Maa'd 125 ....D3
Ma'daba 22,600 ....D4
Mai'n 1,271 ....D4
Manja 353 ....D4
Mazra' C5
Nau'r 2,382 ....D4
Nitil 348 ....D4
Qumeim 955 ....D3
Ra's en Naqb 225 ....E5
Safi C5
Salut 4,210 ....D3
Samar 716 ....D3
Sarih 3,390 ....D3
Suf D3
Suweilih 3,457 ....D3
Suweima 315 ....D4
Um Jauza 582 ....D4
Wadi es Sir 4,455 ....D4
Wadi Musa 644 ....E5
Waqqas 2,321 ....D2
Zuweiza 126 ....D4

OTHER FEATURES

IRAN

INTERNAL DIVISIONS

Azerbaijan, East
(prov.) 3,194,543 ....E1
Azerbaijan, West
(prov.) 1,404,875 ....D1
Bakhtiari
(governorate) 394,300 ....F4
Boyer Ahmediyeh and Kohkiluyeh
(governor 244,750 ....G5
Bushehr (prov.) 345,427 ......G6
Central (Markazi)
(prov.) 6,921,283 ....H4
Esfahan (Isfahan)
(prov.) 1,974,938 ....H4
Fars (prov.) 2,020,947 ....H4
Gilan (prov.) 1,577,800 ....F2
Hamadan (governorate) 1,086,512 ..F3
Hormozgan (prov.) 463,419 ...J7
Ilam (governorate) 244,222 ...F4
Isfahan (prov.) 1,974,938 .....H4
Kerman (prov.) 1,088,045 .....H4
Kermanshahan (prov.) 1,016,199 ..E3
Khorasan (prov.) 3,266,650 ...K3
Khuzestan (prov.) 2,176,612 ..F5
Kordestan (Kurdestan)
(prov.) 781,889 ....E3
Lorestan (Luristan)
(governorate) 924,848 ....F4
Mazandaran (prov.) 2,384,226 ..H2
Semnan (governorate) 485,875 ..J3
Sistan and Baluchestan
(prov.) 659,297 ....M6
Yazd (governorate) 356,218 ...J5
Zanjan (governorate) 579,000 ..F2

CITIES and TOWNS

Abadan 296,081 ....F5
Abadeh 16,000 ....H5
Abarqu 8,000 ....H5
Abhar 24,000 ....F2
Agha Jari 24,195 ....F5
Ahar 24,000 ....E1
Ahvaz (Ahwaz) 329,006 ......F5
Amol 68,782 ....H2
Anarak 2,038 ....H4
Andimeshk 16,000 ....F4
Aradan 8,978 ....H3
Arak 114,507 ....F4
Ardabil 147,404 ....F1
Ardestan 5,868 ....G4
Asadabad 7,000 ....F3
Asteradad (Gorgan) 88,348 ...J2
Azaran 3,153 ....E2
Babol 67,790 ....H2
Babol Sar 7,237 ....H2
Bafq 5,000 ....J5
Baft 6,000 ....K6
Bajgiran 1,151 ....K2
Bam 22,000 ....K6
Bampur 1,585 ....M7
Bandar A'bbas 89,103 ....J7
Bandar-e Anzali
(Enzeli) 55,978 ....F2
Bandar-e Deylam 3,691 ......G5
Bandar-e Khomeyni 6,000 ....F5
Bandar-e Lengeh 4,920 ....J7
Bandar-e Mas'har 17,000 .....F5
Bandar-e Rig 1,889 ....G5
Bandar-e Torkeman 13,000 ...H2
Bandar Shahpur 6,000 ....F5
Bastak 2,473 ....J7
Bastam 3,296 ....J2
Behbehan 39,874 ....G5

Behshahr 26,032 ....H2
Bejestan 3,823 ....K3
Bijar 12,000 ....E3
Birjand 25,854 ....L4
Bojnurd 31,248 ....L2
Borazjan 20,000 ....G6
Borujerd 100,103 ....F4
Bostan 4,619 ....F5
Bowkan 9,000 ....E2
Bushehr (Bushire) 57,681 ....G6
Chah Bahar 1,800 ....M8
Chalus 15,000 ....G2
Damavand 5,319 ....H3
Damghan 13,000 ....H2
Darab 13,000 ....H6
Daran 4,609 ....G4
Darreh Gaz 11,000 ....L2
Dasht-e-Azadegan 21,000 ....F5
Dehkhvaregan 6,000 ....D2
Delijan 6,000 ....G4
Dezful 110,287 ....F4
Dizful (Dezful) 110,287 .....F4
Duzdab (Zahedan) 92,628 ....M6
Emamshahr 30,767 ....J2
Esfahan (Isfahan) 671,820 ...G4
Elamabad 12,000 ....E3
Estahbanat 18,187 ....H6
Evaz 6,064 ....J7
Ezna 5,000 ....F4
Fahrej (Iranshahr) 5,000 ....M7
Fariman 8,000 ....L3
Farrashband 3,532 ....G6
Fasa 19,000 ....H6
Ferdows 11,000 ....K3
Firuzabad 8,718 ....H6
Firuzkuh 4,684 ....H3
Fowman 9,000 ....F2
Gach Saran G5

Ganaveh 9,000 ....G6
Garmsar 4,723 ....H3
Gavater M8
Ghaemshahr 63,289 ....H2
Golpayegan 20,515 ....G4
Golshan (Tabas) 10,000 .....K4
Gomishan 6,000 ....J2
Gonabad 8,000 ....L3
Gonbad-e Kavus 59,868 .....J2
Gonbadli 531 ....M2
Gorgan (Gurgan) 88,348 .....J2
Haft Gel 10,000 ....F5
Hamadan 155,846 ....F3
Haji Ibrahim E2
Hashtpar 5,000 ....F2
Huzgan 4,722 ....F5
Ilam 15,000 ....F4
Iranshahr 5,000 ....M7
Izlaian 671,825 ....G4
Izeh 1,983 ....F5
Jahrom 38,236 ....H6
Jajarm 3,641 ....K2
Jask 1,078 ....K8
Kakhk 4,043 ....L3
Kangan 2,682 ....G7
Kangavar 9,414 ....F3
Karaj 138,774 ....H3
Kangavar 84,545 ....G3
Kashmar 17,000 ....L3
Kazerun 51,309 ....G6
Kazvin (Qazvin) 138,527 ....F2
Kerman 140,309 ....K5
Kermanshah 290,861 ....E3
Khaf 5,000 ....L3
Khalkhal 5,422 ....F2
Khash 7,439 ....M7
Khiyav 9,000 ....E1
Khoman 3,054 ....F2
Khomeinishar 46,836 ....G4

Khorramabad 104,928 ....F4
Khorramshahr 146,709 ....F5
Khvaf 5,000 ....L3
Khvonsar 10,947 ....F4
Khvor 2,912 ....J4
Khvoy (Khoi) 70,040 ....D1
Kord Kuy 9,855 ....J2
Lahijan 25,725 ....G2
Lar 22,000 ....H7
Mahabad 28,610 ....D2
Mahallat 12,000 ....G4
Mahan 8,000 ....K5
Maku 7,000 ....D1
Malamir (Izeh) 1,983 ....F5
Malayer 28,434 ....F3
Maragheh 60,820 ....E2
Marand 24,000 ....D1
Marv Dasht 25,498 ....H6
Mashhad (Meshed) 670,180 ..L3
Masjed Soleyman 77,161 .....F5
Medishahr 9,000 ....H3
Mehran 664 ....F4
Meshed 670,180 ....L3
Meshed-i-Sar (Babol) H2
Meybod 15,000 ....H4
Miandowab 19,000 ....E2
Mianeh 28,447 ....E2
Minab 4,228 ....K7
Miriaveh 11,000 ....M6
Naft-e Shah 3,043 ....E3
Nahavand 24,000 ....F4
Na'in 5,925 ....H4
Najafabad 76,236 ....G4
Nasratabad (Zabol) 20,000 ..M5
Natanz 4,370 ....H4
Neyriz 16,114 ....J6
Neyshabur 59,101 ....L2

Nishapur (Neyshabur) 59,101 ..L2
Nosratabad 20,000 ....L6
Now Shahr 8,000 ....G2
Orumiyeh (Urmia) 163,991 ...D2
Oshnoviyeh 5,000 ....D2
Pahlevi (Enzeli) 55,978 ....F2
Pazanan 81 ....F5
Qasr-e-Shirin 15,094 ....E3
Qayen 6,000 ....L4
Qazvin 138,527 ....F2
Qom 246,831 ....G3
Qorveh 2,929 ....E3
Quchan 29,133 ....L2
Rafsanjan 21,000 ....K5
Ramhormoz 9,000 ....F5
Rasht 187,203 ....F2
Ravar 5,074 ....K5
Resht (Rasht) 187,203 .....F2
Reza'iyeh (Urmia) 163,991 ..D2
Rigan 8,255 ....L6
Rud Sar 7,460 ....G2
Sabzevar 69,174 ....K2
Sabzvaran 7,000 ....K6
Saeendey 4,195 ....L2
Sai'dabad 20,000 ....J6
Sakht-Sar 12,000 ....G2
Salmas 13,161 ....D1
Sanandaj 95,834 ....E3
Saqqez 17,000 ....E2
Sarab 16,000 ....E2
Sarakhs 3,461 ....M2
Saravan 4,012 ....N7
Sar Dasht 6,000 ....D2
Sari 70,936 ....H2
Savanat (Estahbanat) 18,187 ..J6
Saveh 17,565 ....G3
Semnan 31,058 ....H3

Shadegan 6,000 ....F5
Shahbad 2,777 ....F4
Shahistan (Saravan) 4,012 ...N7
Shahreza 34,220 ....G4
Shahr Kord 24,000 ....G4
Shahrud (Emamshahr) 30,767 ..J2
Sharafkhaneh 1,260 ....D1
Shiraz 416,408 ....H5
Shirvan 11,000 ....L2
Shush 1,433 ....F4
Shushtar 24,000 ....F4
Sinneh (Sanandaj) 95,834 ...E3
Sirjan (Sa'idabad) 20,000 ...J6
Sivand 1,811 ....H5
Songor 10,433 ....F3
Sufian 2,914 ....D1
Sultanabad (Kashmar) 17,000 ..L3
Tabas 10,000 ....K4
Tabriz 598,576 ....E1
Taft 7,000 ....J5
Tajrish 157,486 ....H3
Takestan 13,485 ....G3
Tehran (cap.) 4,496,159 ....H3
Tonekabon 12,000 ....G2
Torbat-e Heydariyeh 30,106 ..L3
Torbat-e Jam 13,000 ....M3
Tun (Ferdows) 11,000 ......K3
Tuysarkan 12,000 ....F4
Urmia 163,991 ....D2
Varamin 11,183 ....H3
Yazd (Yezd) 135,978 ....J5
Yazd-e Khvast 3,544 ....H5
Zabol 20,000 ....M5
Zahedan 92,628 ....M6
Zarand 5,000 ....K5
Zarqam 7,000 ....G3
Zenjan (Zanjan) 99,967 ....F2

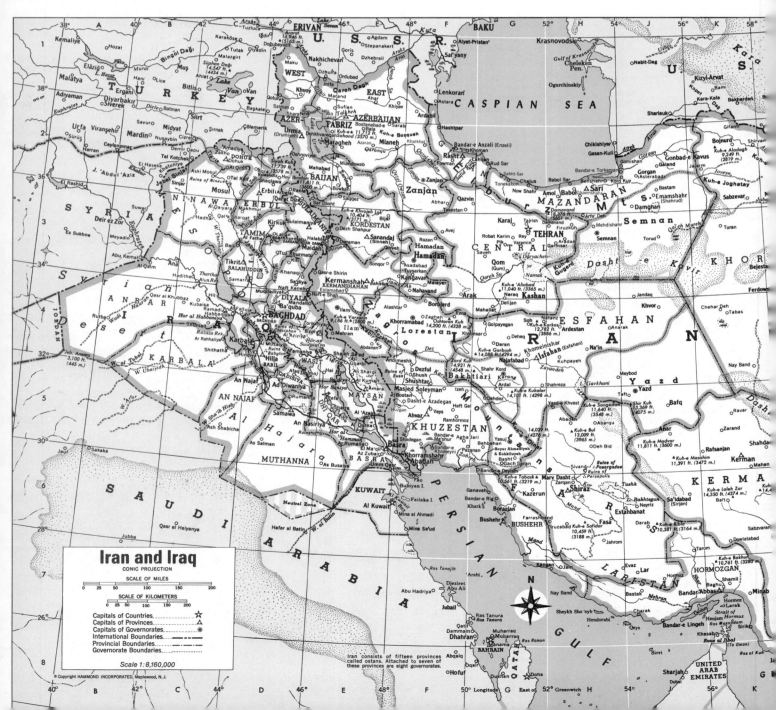

Iran and Iraq 69

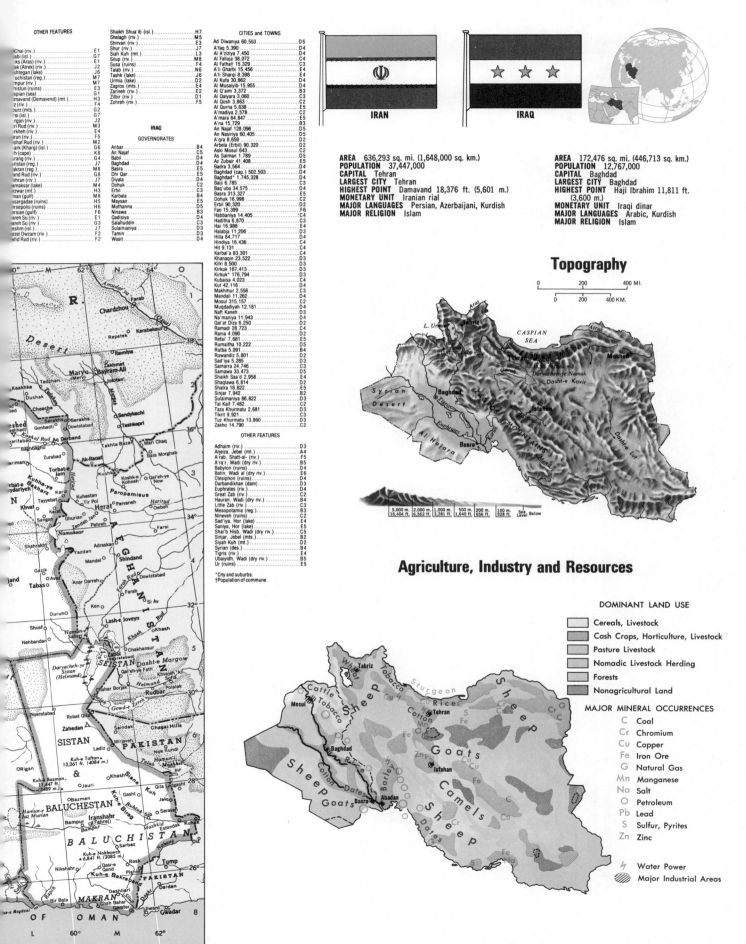

OTHER FEATURES

Chai (riv.)	E1
abi (isl.)	G7
aks (Aras) (riv.)	E1
ak (Atrek) (riv.)	J2
shtegan (lake)	J6
uchistan (reg.)	M7
mpur (riv.)	M7
histun (ruins)	E3
aspian (sea)	G1
mavand (Demavend) (mt.)	H3
z (riv.)	F4
burz (mts.)	G2
rsi (isl.)	G7
rgan (riv.)	J2
rkheh (riv.)	E4
run (riv.)	F5
ark (Kharg) (isl.)	G6
rang (riv.)	G4
ristan (reg.)	J7
akran (reg.)	M8
and Rud (riv.)	G6
hran (riv.)	J7
amaksar (lake)	M4
ezvar (mt.)	H3
zan (gulf)	H5
sargadae (ruins)	H5
ersepolis (ruins)	H6
ersian (gulf)	F6
areh Su (riv.)	E1
areh Su (riv.)	G3
eshm (isl.)	J7
ezel Owzam (riv.)	F2
afid Rud (riv.)	F2

Shaikh Shua'ib (isl.)	H7
Shelagh (riv.)	M5
Shirvan (riv.)	E3
Shur (riv.)	J7
Siah Kuh (mt.)	L3
Silup (riv.)	M8
Talab (riv.)	F4
Tashk (lake)	N6
Urmia (lake)	D2
Zagros (mts.)	E4
Zarineh (riv.)	E2
Zilbir (riv.)	D1
Zohreh (riv.)	F5

IRAQ

GOVERNORATES

Anbar	B4
An Najaf	C5
Babil	C4
Baghdad	D4
Basra	E5
Dhi Qar	D5
Diyala	D4
Dohuk	C2
Erbil	C2
Karbala	B4
Maysan	E5
Muthanna	D5
Ninawa	B3
Qadisiya	D4
Salahuddin	D3
Sulaimaniya	D3
Tamin	D3
Wasit	D4

CITIES and TOWNS

Ad Diwaniya 60,553	D5
A'faq 5,390	D4
Al A'ziziya 7,450	D4
Al Falluja 38,072	C4
Al Fathat 15,329	C3
Al Gharbi 15,456	E4
A'li Sharqi 8,398	E4
Al Kufa 30,862	D4
Al Musaiyib 15,955	D4
Al Qa'im 3,372	B3
Al Qaiyara 3,060	C3
Al Qosh 3,863	C2
Al Qurna 5,638	E5
A'madiya 2,578	C2
A'mara 64,847	E5
A'na 15,729	B3
An Najaf 128,096	D5
An Nasiriya 60,405	D5
A'qra 8,659	C2
Arbela (Erbil) 90,320	D2
Aski Mosul 643	C2
As Salman 1,789	D5
Badra 3,564	E4
Az Zubair 41,408	E5
Baghdad (cap.) 502,503	D4
Baghdad* 1,745,328	D4
Baiji 6,785	C3
Baq'uba 34,575	D4
Basra 313,327	E5
Dohuk 16,998	C2
Erbil 90,320	D2
Fao 15,399	F6
Habbaniya 14,405	C4
Haditha 6,870	C3
Hai 16,988	E4
Halabja 11,206	D4
Hilla 84,717	D4
Hindiya 16,436	C4
Hit 9,131	C4
Karbal'a 83,301	C4
Khanaqin 23,522	D3
Kifri 8,500	D3
Kirkuk 167,413	D3
Kirkuk* 176,794	D3
Kubaisa 4,023	C4
Kut 42,116	D4
Makhmur 2,556	C3
Mandali 11,262	D4
Mosul 315,157	C2
Muqdadiyah 12,181	D4
Naft Kaneh	D3
Na'maniya 11,943	D4
Qal'at Diza 6,250	D2
Ramadi 28,723	C4
Rania 4,090	D2
Refai 7,681	E5
Rumaitha 10,222	D5
Rutba 5,091	B4
Ruwandiz 5,801	D2
Sad'iya 5,285	D3
Samarra 24,746	C3
Samawa 33,473	D5
Shaikh Saa'd 2,958	E4
Shaqlawa 6,814	D2
Shatra 18,822	E5
Sinjar 7,942	B2
Sulaimaniya 86,822	D3
Tal Kaif 7,482	C2
Taza Khurmatu 2,681	D3
Tikrit 9,921	C3
Tuz Khurmatu 13,860	D3
Zakho 14,790	C2

OTHER FEATURES

Adhaim (riv.)	D3
Aneiza, Jebel (mt.)	A4
A'rab, Shatt-al- (riv.)	F5
A'ra'r, Wadi (dry riv.)	B5
Batin, Wadi al (dry riv.)	E6
Ctesiphon (ruins)	D4
Darbandikhan (dam)	D3
Euphrates (riv.)	C2
Great Zab (riv.)	C2
Hauran, Wadi (dry riv.)	B4
Little Zab (riv.)	C2
Mesopotamia (reg.)	B3
Nineveh (ruins)	C2
Sad'iya, Hor (lake)	E4
Saniya, Hor (lake)	E5
Shai'b Hisb, Wadi (dry riv.)	C5
Sinjar, Jebel (mts.)	B2
Siyah Kuh (mts.)	D2
Syrian (des.)	B4
Tigris (riv.)	E4
Ubaiyidh, Wadi (dry riv.)	B5
Ur (ruins)	E5

*City and suburbs.
†Population of commune.

IRAN

AREA 636,293 sq. mi. (1,648,000 sq. km.)
POPULATION 37,447,000
CAPITAL Tehran
LARGEST CITY Tehran
HIGHEST POINT Damavand 18,376 ft. (5,601 m.)
MONETARY UNIT Iranian rial
MAJOR LANGUAGES Persian, Azerbaijani, Kurdish
MAJOR RELIGION Islam

IRAQ

AREA 172,476 sq. mi. (446,713 sq. km.)
POPULATION 12,767,000
CAPITAL Baghdad
LARGEST CITY Baghdad
HIGHEST POINT Haji Ibrahim 11,811 ft. (3,600 m.)
MONETARY UNIT Iraqi dinar
MAJOR LANGUAGES Arabic, Kurdish
MAJOR RELIGION Islam

Topography

Agriculture, Industry and Resources

DOMINANT LAND USE

- Cereals, Livestock
- Cash Crops, Horticulture, Livestock
- Pasture Livestock
- Nomadic Livestock Herding
- Forests
- Nonagricultural Land

MAJOR MINERAL OCCURRENCES

C	Coal
Cr	Chromium
Cu	Copper
Fe	Iron Ore
G	Natural Gas
Mn	Manganese
Na	Salt
O	Petroleum
Pb	Lead
S	Sulfur, Pyrites
Zn	Zinc

Water Power
Major Industrial Areas

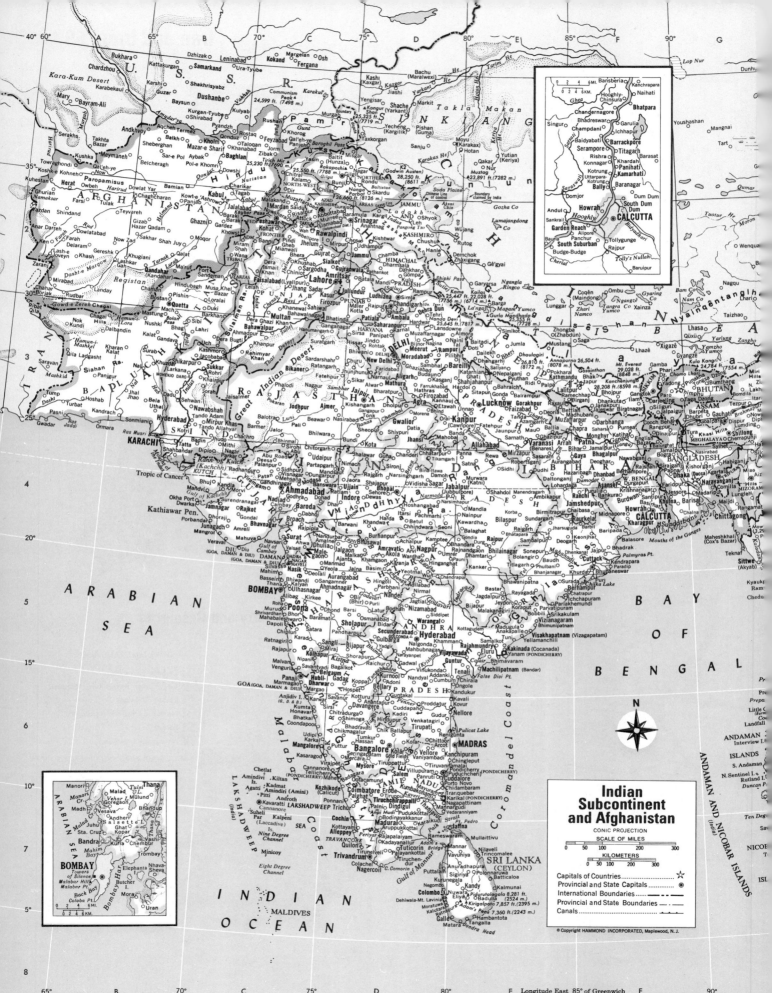

Indian Subcontinent and Afghanistan

CONIC PROJECTION

SCALE OF MILES

0   50   100   200   300

KILOMETERS

0 50 100   200   300

Capitals of Countries..............☆
Provincial and State Capitals.........◉
International Boundaries.......─ ─ ─ ─
Provincial and State Boundaries ─ · ─ ·
Canals..............................

© Copyright HAMMOND INCORPORATED, Maplewood, N.J.

BOMBAY
Towers of Silence
Malabar Hills
Malabar Pt.

Back Bay
Colaba Pt.

0 2 4 6 KM.

CALCUTTA

INDIA

AREA 1,269,339 sq. mi. (3,287,588 sq. km.)
POPULATION 683,810,051
CAPITAL New Delhi
LARGEST CITY Calcutta (greater)
HIGHEST POINT Nanda Devi 25,645 ft. (7,817 m.)
MONETARY UNIT Indian rupee
MAJOR LANGUAGES Hindi, English, Bihari, Telugu, Marathi, Bengali, Tamil, Gujarati, Rajasthani, Kanarese, Malayalam, Oriya, Punjabi, Assamese, Kashmiri, Urdu
MAJOR RELIGIONS Hinduism, Islam, Christianity, Sikhism, Buddhism, Jainism, Zoroastrianism, Animism

PAKISTAN

AREA 310,403 sq. mi. (803,944 sq. km.)
POPULATION 83,782,000
CAPITAL Islamabad
LARGEST CITY Karachi
HIGHEST POINT K2 (Godwin Austen) 28,250 ft. (8,611 m.)
MONETARY UNIT Pakistani rupee
MAJOR LANGUAGES Urdu, English, Punjabi, Pushtu, Sindhi, Baluchi, Brahui
MAJOR RELIGIONS Islam, Hinduism, Sikhism, Christianity, Buddhism

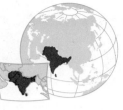

SRI LANKA (CEYLON)

AREA 25,332 sq. mi. (65,610 sq. km.)
POPULATION 14,850,001
CAPITAL Colombo
LARGEST CITY Colombo
HIGHEST POINT Pidurutalagala 8,281 ft. (2,524 m.)
MONETARY UNIT Sri Lanka rupee
MAJOR LANGUAGES Sinhala, Tamil, English
MAJOR RELIGIONS Buddhism, Hinduism, Christianity, Islam

AFGHANISTAN

AREA 250,775 sq. mi. (649,507 sq. km.)
POPULATION 15,540,000
CAPITAL Kabul
LARGEST CITY Kabul
HIGHEST POINT Nowshak 24,557 ft. (7,485 m.)
MONETARY UNIT afghani
MAJOR LANGUAGES Pushtu, Dari, Uzbek
MAJOR RELIGION Islam

NEPAL

AREA 54,663 sq. mi. (141,577 sq. km.)
POPULATION 14,179,301
CAPITAL Kathmandu
LARGEST CITY Kathmandu
HIGHEST POINT Mt. Everest 29,028 ft. (8,848 m.)
MONETARY UNIT Nepalese rupee
MAJOR LANGUAGES Nepali, Maithili, Tamang, Newari, Tharu
MAJOR RELIGIONS Hinduism, Buddhism

MALDIVES

AREA 115 sq. mi. (298 sq. km.)
POPULATION 143,046
CAPITAL Male
LARGEST CITY Male
HIGHEST POINT 20 ft. (6 m.)
MONETARY UNIT Maldivian rupee
MAJOR LANGUAGE Divehi
MAJOR RELIGION Islam

BHUTAN

AREA 18,147 sq. mi. (47,000 sq. km.)
POPULATION 1,298,000
CAPITAL Thimphu
LARGEST CITY Thimphu
HIGHEST POINT Kula Kangri 24,784 ft. (7,554 m.)
MONETARY UNIT ngultrum
MAJOR LANGUAGES Dzongka, Nepali
MAJOR RELIGIONS Buddhism, Hinduism

BANGLADESH

AREA 55,126 sq. mi. (142,776 sq. km.)
POPULATION 87,052,024
CAPITAL Dhaka
LARGEST CITY Dhaka
HIGHEST POINT Keokradong 4,034 ft. (1,230 m.)
MONETARY UNIT taka
MAJOR LANGUAGES Bengali, English
MAJOR RELIGIONS Islam, Hinduism, Christianity

INDIA
PAKISTAN
SRI LANKA (CEYLON)
BHUTAN
AFGHANISTAN
MALDIVES
BANGLADESH
NEPAL

AFGHANISTAN

CITIES and TOWNS

Bala Murghab 10,000	A1
Balkh 15,000	B1
Chahardeh	B2
Girishk 10,000	A2
Kabul (cap.) 318,094	B2
Kabul* 534,350	B2
Kuhsan	A2
Kushk 10,000	A1
Landi Muhammad Amin Khan 1,000	A2
Panjao 3,000	B2
Qaleh-i-Kang 17,400	A2
Sabzawar 5,000	A2
Shindand (Sabzawar) 5,000	A2
Taiwara 5,000	A2

OTHER FEATURES

Farah Rud (riv.)	A2
Hari Rud (riv.)	A1
Helmand (riv.)	B2
Hindu Kush (mts.)	B1
Jam (mt.)	A2
Kabul (riv.)	C2
Kunar (riv.)	C1
Kunduz (riv.)	B1
Lora (riv.)	B2
Margo, Dasht-i- (des.)	A2
Namaksar (salt lake)	A2
Paropamisus (range)	A2
Registan (reg.)	B2

BANGLADESH

CITIES and TOWNS

Chittagong 416,733	G4
Cox's Bazar (Maheshkhali)	G4
Dhaka (Dacca) (cap.) 1,310,976	G4
Dhaka (Dacca)□ 2,539,991	G4
Habiganj	G4
Jamalpur	F4
Khulna 436,000	F4
Kishorganj	G4
Madaripur	G4
Maheshkhali	G4
Narayanganj 176,879	G4
Nawabganj	F4
Noakhali 19,874	G4
Rangamati 6,416	G4

OTHER FEATURES

Bengal, Bay of (sea)	F5

Brahmaputra (riv.)	G3
Ganges (riv.)	F3
Sundarbans (reg.)	F4

BHUTAN

CITIES and TOWNS

Bumthang 10,000	G3
Punakha 12,000	G3
Taga Dzong 18,000	G3
Tongsa Dzong 2,500	G3

OTHER FEATURES

Chomo Lhari (mt.)	F3
Himalaya (mts.)	E2
Kula Kangri (mt.)	G3

INDIA

INTERNAL DIVISIONS

Andaman and Nicobar Isls. (terr.) 115,133	G6
Andhra Pradesh (state) 43,502,708	D5
Arunachal Pradesh (terr.) 467,511	G3
Assam (state) 14,625,152	G3
Bihar (state) 56,353,369	F4
Chandigarh (terr.) 257,251	D2
Dadra and Nagar Haveli (terr.) 74,170	C4
Delhi (terr.) 4,065,698	D3
Goa, Daman and Diu (terr.) 857,771	C4
Gujarat (state) 26,697,475	C4
Haryana (state) 10,036,808	D3
Himachal Pradesh (state) 3,460,434	D2
Jammu and Kashmir (state) 4,616,632	D2
Karnataka (state) 29,299,014	D6
Kerala (state) 21,347,375	D6
Lakshadweep (terr.) 31,810	C6
Madhya Pradesh (state) 41,654,119	D4
Maharashtra (state) 50,412,235	C5
Manipur (state) 1,072,753	G4
Meghalaya (state) 1,011,699	G3
Mizoram (terr.) 332,390	G4
Nagaland (state) 516,449	G3

(continued on following page)

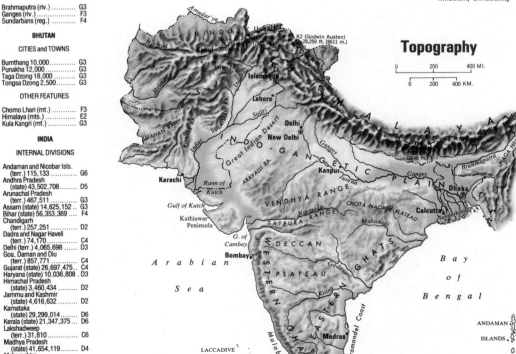

Topography

0 — 200 — 400 MI.
0 — 200 — 400 KM.

5,000 m. / 16,404 ft. 2,000 m. / 6,562 ft. 1,000 m. / 3,281 ft. 500 m. / 1,640 ft. 200 m. / 656 ft. 100 m. / 328 ft. Sea Level Below

Orissa (state) 21,944,615 ... E5
Pondicherry (terr.) 471,707 ... E6
Punjab (state) 13,551,060 ... D2
Rajasthan (state) 25,765,806 ... C3
Sikkim (state) 209,843 ... F3
Tamil Nadu (state) 41,199,168 ... D6
Tripura (state) 1,556,342 ... G4
Uttar Pradesh (state) 88,341,144 ... D3
West Bengal (state) 44,312,011 ... F4

CITIES and TOWNS

Abu 9,840 ... C4
Agra 591,917 ... D3
Agra□ 634,622 ... D3
Ahmadabad 1,591,832 ... C4
Ahmadabad□ 1,741,522 ... C4
Ajanta ... D4
Ajmer 262,851 ... C3
Akola 168,438 ... D4
Alibag 11,913 ... C5
Aligarh 252,314 ... D3
Allahabad 490,622 ... E3
Allahabad□ 513,036 ... E3
Alleppey 160,166 ... D7
Almora 19,671 ... D3
Ambikapur 23,087 ... E4
Amravati 193,800 ... D4
Amritsar 407,628 ... C2
Amritsar□ 458,029 ... C2
Asansol 155,968 ... F4
Aurangabad, Maharashtra 150,483 ... D5
Baltit ... C1
Bandra ... B7
Bangalore 1,540,741 ... D6
Bangalore□ 1,653,779 ... D6
Bareilly 296,248 ... D3
Baroda 466,696 ... C4
Baroda□ 467,487 ... C4
Barwani 22,099 ... D4
Belgaum 192,427 ... C5
Benares (Varanasi) 583,856 ... E3
Bhagalpur 172,202 ... F4
Bhatpara 204,750 ... F1
Bhavnagar 225,358 ... C4
Bhawanipatna 22,808 ... E5
Bhilai 157,173 ... E4
Bhopal 298,022 ... D4
Bikaner 188,518 ... C3
Bombay (Greater)* 5,970,575 ... B7
Bunji ... C1
Calcutta 3,148,746 ... F2
Calcutta□ 7,031,382 ... F2
Calicut (Kozhikode) 333,979 ... D6
Cawnpore (Kanpur) 1,154,388 ... E3
Chamba 11,814 ... D2
Chanderi 10,294 ... D4
Chandigarh 218,743 ... D2
Chembur ... B7
Chilas ... C1
Chushul ... D2
Cocanada (Kakinada) 164,200 ... E5
Cochin 439,066 ... D6
Coimbatore 356,368 ... D6
Coimbatore□ 736,203 ... D6
Colachel 18,819 ... D7
Cuttack 194,068 ... F4
Dehra Dun 166,073 ... D2
Delhi 3,287,883 ... D3
Delhi□ 3,647,023 ... D3
Dhanbad□ 434,031 ... F4
Dharmsala 10,939 ... D2
Dharwar-Hubli 379,166 ... C5
Diphu 10,200 ... G3
Dispur 1,725 ... G3
Dungarpur 19,773 ... C4
Durgapur 206,638 ... F4
Dwarka 17,801 ... B4
Gangtok 12,000 ... F3
Garden Reach 154,913 ... F2
Gaya 179,884 ... F4
Gilgit ... C1
Gorakhpur 230,911 ... E3
Goregaon ... B7
Guntur 269,991 ... D5
Gwalior 384,772 ... D3
Gwalior□ 406,140 ... D3
Haflong 5,197 ... G3
Honavar 12,444 ... C6
Howrah 737,877 ... F2
Hubli-Dharwar 379,166 ... C5
Hunza (Baltit) ... C1
Hyderabad 1,607,396 ... D5
Hyderabad□ 1,796,339 ... D5
Ichchapuram 15,850 ... F5
Indore 543,381 ... D4
Indore□ 560,936 ... D4
Itanagar⊙ 18,787 ... G3
Jabalpur 426,224 ... D4
Jabalpur□ 534,845 ... D4
Jaipur 615,258 ... D3
Jaipur□ 636,768 ... D3
Jaisalmer 16,578 ... C3
Jajpur 16,707 ... F4
Jalor 15,478 ... C3
Jammu 155,338 ... D2
Jamnagar 214,816 ... B4
Jamnagar□ 227,640 ... B4
Jamshedpur 341,576 ... F4
Jamshedpur□ 456,146 ... F4
Jhansi 173,292 ... D3
Jodhpur 317,612 ... C3
Jubbulpore (Jabalpur) 426,224 ... D4
Juhu ... B7
Jullundur 296,106 ... D2
Kakinada 164,200 ... E5
Kamarhati 169,404 ... F1
Kandla 17,995 ... C4
Kanpur 1,154,388 ... E3
Kanpur□ 1,275,242 ... E3
Kargil 2,390 ... D2
Katarnian Ghat ... E3
Kavaratti 4,420 ... C6
Kendrapara 20,079 ... F4
Kohima 21,545 ... G3
Kolhapur 259,050 ... C5
Koraput 21,505 ... E5
Kota 212,991 ... D3
Kozhikode 333,979 ... D6
Kumta 19,112 ... C6
Kurla ... B7
Leh 5,519 ... D2
Lucknow 749,239 ... E3
Lucknow□ 813,982 ... E3
Ludhiana 397,850 ... D2
Ludhiana□ 401,176 ... D2
Madras 2,469,449 ... E6
Madras□ 3,169,930 ... E6
Madurai 549,114 ... D7
Madurai□ 711,501 ... D7
Mahabaleshwar 7,318 ... C5
Mahe 8,972 ... D6
Malad ... B6
Malegaon 191,847 ... C4
Malvan 17,579 ... C5
Mandi 16,849 ... D2
Mandla 24,406 ... E4
Mangalore 165,174 ... C6
Meerut 270,993 ... D3
Mercara 19,357 ... D6
Mirpur ... C2
Moradabad 258,590 ... D3
Mulund ... B6
Muzaffarabad ... C2
Mysore 355,685 ... D6
Nagar ... D1
Nagpur 866,076 ... D4
Nagpur□ 930,459 ... D4
Nahan 16,017 ... D2
Naini Tal 23,986 ... D3
Nasik 176,091 ... C5
New Delhi (cap.) 301,801 ... D3
Okha Port 10,687 ... B4
Pachmarhi 1,212 ... D4
Panna 22,316 ... E4
Pasighat 5,116 ... G3
Patna 473,001 ... F3
Patna□ 491,217 ... F3
Poona 856,105 ... C5
Poona□ 1,135,034 ... C5
Porto Novo 17,412 ... E6
Raipur 174,518 ... E4
Rajahmundry 165,912 ... E5
Rajapur 9,017 ... C5
Rajkot 300,612 ... C4
Rameswaram 16,755 ... D7
Rampur, Uttar Pradesh 161,417 ... D3
Ranchi 175,934 ... F4
Raxaul 12,064 ... E3
Sadiya⊙ 64,252 ... H3
Saharanpur 225,396 ... D3
Salem 308,716 ... D6
Salem□ 416,440 ... D6
Santa Cruz ... B7
Sarnath ... E3
Secunderabad 250,636 ... D5
Seringapatam 14,100 ... D6
Sholapur 398,361 ... D5
Sidhi 8,341 ... E4
Silvassa ... C4
Sirohi 18,774 ... C4
Skardu ... D1
South Suburban 272,600 ... F2
Srinagar 403,413 ... D2
Srinagar□ 423,253 ... D2
Sundargarh 17,244 ... E4
Surat 471,656 ... C4
Surat□ 493,001 ... C4
Tehri 5,480 ... D2
Thana 170,675 ... B6
Tiruchchirappalli 307,400 ... D6
Tiruchchirappalli□ 464,624 ... D6
Tiruchendur 18,126 ... D7
Tollygunge ... F2
Tranquebar 17,318 ... E6
Trivandrum 409,627 ... D7
Trombay ... B7
Tura 15,489 ... G3
Tuticorin 155,310 ... D7
Udaypur 161,278 ... C4
Udhampur 16,392 ... D2
Ujjain 203,278 ... D4
Ulhasnagar 168,462 ... C5
Varanasi 583,856 ... E3
Varanasi□ 606,721 ... E3
Vellore□ 178,554 ... D6
Vengurla 11,805 ... C5
Vijayawada 317,258 ... D5
Visakhapatnam 352,504 ... E5
Vizagapatam (Visakhapatnam) 352,504 ... E5
Warangal 207,520 ... D5
Yanam 8,291 ... E5
Yasin ... C1

OTHER FEATURES

Abor (hills) ... G3
Adam's Bridge (sound) ... D7
Agatti (isl.) ... C6
Amindiri (isl.) ... C6
Amindivi (isls.) ... C6
Amini (Amindiri) (isl.) ... C6
Andaman (isls.) ... G6
Andaman (sea) ... G6
Androth (isl.) ... C6
Anjidiv (Angedeva) (isl.) ... C6
Arabian (sea) ... B5
Back (bay) ... B7
Baltistan (reg.) ... D1
Bengal, Bay of (sea) ... F5
Berar (reg.) ... D4
Brahmaputra (riv.) ... G3
Butcher (isl.) ... B7
Cambay (gulf) ... C4
Cannanore (isls.) ... C6
Car Nicobar (isl.) ... G7
Chambal (riv.) ... D3
Chenab (riv.) ... C2
Chetlat (isl.) ... C6
Chilka (lake) ... F5
Coco (chan.) ... G6
Colaba (pt.) ... B7
Comorin (cape) ... D7
Coromandel Coast (reg.) ... E6
Daman (dist.) ... C4
Damodar (riv.) ... F4
Deccan (plat.) ... D6
Diu (dist.) ... C4
Eastern Ghats (mts.) ... D6
Elephanta (isl.) ... B7
Ganga (Ganges) (riv.) ... F3
Ganges, Mouths of the (delta) ... F4
Ganges (riv.) ... F3
Ghaghra (riv.) ... E3
Goa (dist.) ... C5
Godavari (riv.) ... D5
Godwin Austen (K2) (mt.) ... D1
Golconda (ruins) ... D5
Great (chan.) ... G7
Great Indian (des.) ... C3
Great Nicobar (isl.) ... G7
Himalaya (mts.) ... D2
Hindu Kush (mts.) ... C1
Hooghly (riv.) ... F2
Indus (riv.) ... B3
Jhelum (riv.) ... C2
Jumna (riv.) ... E3
K2 (mt.) ... D1
Kachchh (gulf) ... B4
Kachchh (Kutch), Rann of (salt marsh) ... B4
Kadmat (isl.) ... C6
Kalpeni (isl.) ... C7
Kamet (mt.) ... D2
Kanchenjunga (mt.) ... F3
Karakoram (mts.) ... D1
Kaveri (riv.) ... D6
Khasi (hills) ... G3
Kiltan (isl.) ... C6
Kistna (Krishna) (riv.) ... D5
Krishna (Kistna) (riv.) ... D5
Kunlun (range) ... D1
Kutch (Kachchh) (gulf) ... B4
Kutch, Rann of (salt marsh) ... B4
Laccadive (Cannanore) (isls.) ... C6
Ladakh (reg.) ... D2
Little Andaman (isl.) ... G6
Little Nicobar (isl.) ... G7
Mahanadi (riv.) ... E4
Malabar (hill) ... B7
Malabar Coast (reg.) ... C6
Mannar (gulf) ... D7
Middle Andaman (isl.) ... G6
Minicoy (isl.) ... C7
Miri (hills) ... G3
Mishmi (hills) ... H3
Nancowry (isl.) ... G7
Nanda Devi (mt.) ... D2
Nanga Parbat (mt.) ... D1
Narmada (riv.) ... D4
Nicobar (isls.) ... G7
North Andaman (isl.) ... G6
Palk (strait) ... D7
Penganga (riv.) ... D5
Periyar (lake) ... D7
Pitti (isl.) ... C6
Pulicat (lake) ... E6
Rakaposhi (mt.) ... C1
Salsette (isl.) ... B7
Sambhar (lake) ... C3
Satpura (range) ... D4
Shipki (pass) ... D2
South Andaman (isl.) ... G6
Sundarbans (reg.) ... F4
Sutlej (riv.) ... C3
Ten Degree (chan.) ... G7
Towers of Silence ... B7
Travancore (reg.) ... D7
Tungabhadra (riv.) ... D5
Vindhya (range) ... D4
Western Ghats (mts.) ... C5
Zaskar (mts.) ... D2

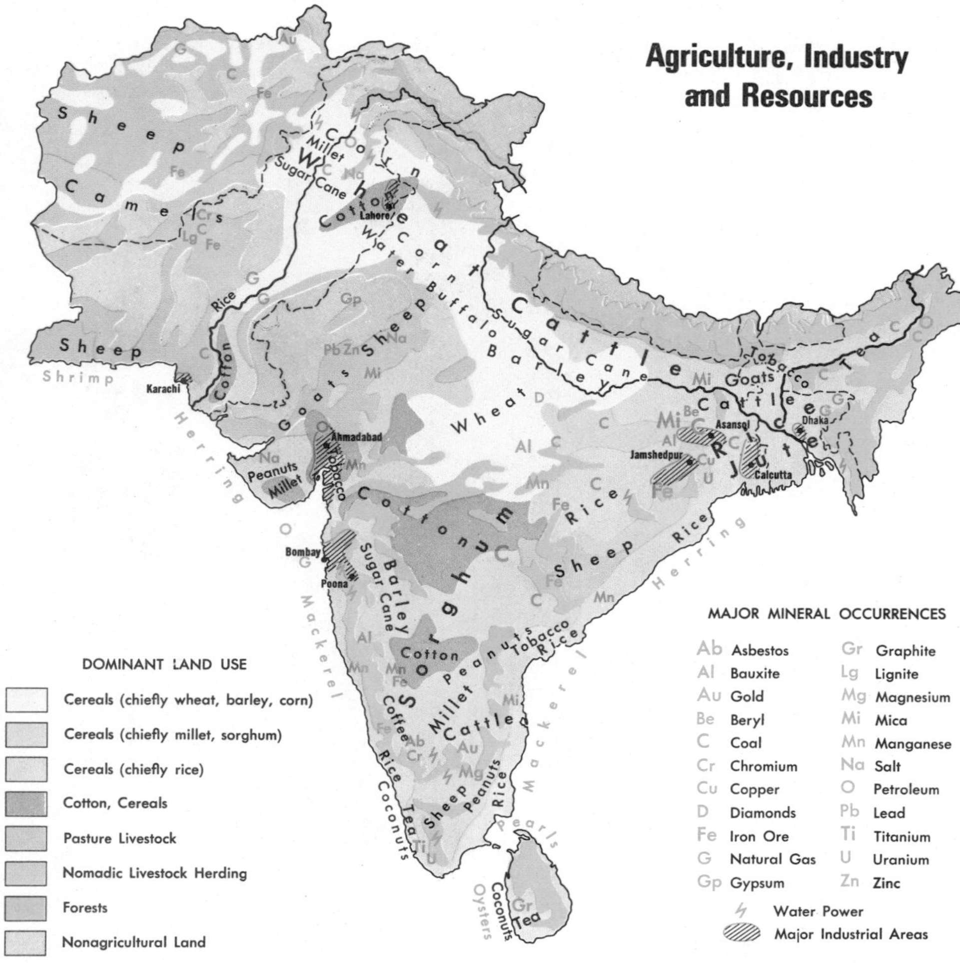
Agriculture, Industry and Resources
DOMINANT LAND USE
Cereals (chiefly wheat, barley, corn)
Cereals (chiefly millet, sorghum)
Cereals (chiefly rice)
Cotton, Cereals
Pasture Livestock
Nomadic Livestock Herding
Forests
Nonagricultural Land
MAJOR MINERAL OCCURRENCES
Ab Asbestos
Al Bauxite
Au Gold
Be Beryl
C Coal
Cr Chromium
Cu Copper
D Diamonds
Fe Iron Ore
G Natural Gas
Gp Gypsum
Gr Graphite
Lg Lignite
Mg Magnesium
Mi Mica
Mn Manganese
Na Salt
O Petroleum
Pb Lead
Ti Titanium
U Uranium
Zn Zinc
Water Power
Major Industrial Areas
Lahore
Karachi
Ahmadabad
Bombay
Poona
Asansol
Jamshedpur
Calcutta
Dhaka
Sheep
Camels
Wheat
Cotton
Millet
Sugar Cane
Corn
Water Buffalo
Goats
Cattle
Barley
Rice
Tobacco
Tea
Jute
Peanuts
Sorghum
Coffee
Coconuts
Shrimp
Herring
Mackerel
Pearls
Oysters

MALDIVES

Maldives 136,000 ... C7

NEPAL

CITIES and TOWNS

Dhangarhi ... E3
Jumla⊙ 122,753 ... E3
Kathmandu⊙ 353,752 ... E3
Lalitpur⊙ 154,998 ... E3
Mukhtinath ... E3
Mustang⊙ 26,944 ... E3
Nepalganj 23,523 ... E3
Pokhara 20,611 ... E3
Pyuthan⊙ 137,338 ... E3
Ridi ... E3
Sallyana⊙ 141,457 ... E3

OTHER FEATURES

Annapurna (mt.) ... E3
Bheri (riv.)
Dhaulagiri (mt.)
Everest (mt.)
Himalaya (mts.)
Kanchenjunga (mt.)

PAKISTAN

PROVINCES

Azad Kashmir
Baluchistan 2,409,000
Federal Administrated Tribal Areas
Islamabad District 235,000
Northern Areas
North-West Frontier 10,909,000
Punjab 37,374,000
Sind 13,965,000

CITIES and TOWNS

Abbottabad 47,011
Bahawalpur 133,956
Bahawalpur* 181,000
Baltit
Campbellpore 19,041
Chiniot 69,124
Dera Ghazi Khan 71,429
Dera Ismail Khan 59,892
Faisalabad 822,263
Gujranwala 360,419
Gujrat 100,581
Hunza (Baltit)
Hyderabad 628,310
Islamabad (cap.) 77,318
Jacobabad 57,292
Jhang Sadar 135,722
Jhelum 63,653
Karachi 3,498,634
Karachi* 3,650,000
Khanewal 67,617
Kohat 64,634
Lahore 2,165,372
Larkana 71,943
Lyallpur (Faisalabad) 822,263
Mardan 115,218
Mardan* 131,000
Multan 542,195
Multan* 723,000
Nagar
Nal
Nawabshah 80,779
Nowshera 56,117
Peshawar 268,366
Peshawar* 331,000
Quetta 156,000
Rahimyar Khan 74,407
Rahimyar Khan* 130,000
Rawalpindi 615,392
Sahiwal 106,213
Sargodha 201,407
Sargodha* 225,000
Shikarpur 70,301
Sialkot 203,779
Sukkur 158,876
Tando Adam 31,246

OTHER FEATURES

Arabian (sea) ... B5
Bolan (pass) ... B3
Chagai (hills) ... A3
Chenab (riv.) ... C2
Hindu Kush (mts.) ... B1
Indus (riv.) ... B3
Jhelum (riv.) ... C2
Khyber (pass) ... C2
Kunar (riv.) ... C1
Kutch, Rann of (salt marsh) ... B4
Mashkel (riv.) ... A3
Mohenjo Daro (ruins) ... B3
Muari, Ras (cape) ... B4
Ravi (riv.) ... C2
Siahan (range) ... A3
Sulaiman (range) ... C3
Sutlej (riv.) ... C3
Talab (riv.) ... A3
Taxila (ruins) ... C2
Tirich Mir (mt.) ... C1
Zhob (riv.) ... B2

SRI LANKA (CEYLON)

CITIES and TOWNS

Colombo (cap.) 618,000 ... D7
Colombo* 852,098 ... D7
Hambantota 6,908 ... E7
Kalmunai 19,176 ... E7
Mannar 11,157 ... E7
Mullaittivu 4,930 ... E7
Nuwara Eliya 16,347 ... E7
Polonnaruwa 9,551 ... E7
Puttalam 17,982 ... D7
Sigiriya 1,446 ... E7
Vavuniya 15,639 ... E7

OTHER FEATURES

Adam's (peak) ... E7
Adam's Bridge (shoals) ... D7
Dondra (head) ... E7
Kirigalpota (mt.) ... E7
Mannar (gulf) ... D7
Palk (str.) ... D7
Pedro (pt.) ... E6
Pidurutalagala (mt.) ... E7

*City and suburbs.
⊙Population of district.
□Population of urban areas.

AREA 145,730 sq. mi. (377,441 sq. km.)
POPULATION 117,057,485
CAPITAL Tokyo
LARGEST CITY Tokyo
HIGHEST POINT Fuji 12,389 ft. (3,776 m.)
MONETARY UNIT yen
MAJOR LANGUAGE Japanese
MAJOR RELIGIONS Buddhism, Shintoism

AREA 46,540 sq. mi. (120,539 sq. km.)
POPULATION 17,914,000
CAPITAL P'yŏngyang
LARGEST CITY P'yŏngyang
HIGHEST POINT Paektu 9,003 ft. (2,744 m.)
MONETARY UNIT won
MAJOR LANGUAGE Korean
MAJOR RELIGIONS Confucianism, Buddhism, Ch'ondogyo

AREA 38,175 sq. mi. (98,873 sq. km.)
POPULATION 37,448,836
CAPITAL Seoul
LARGEST CITY Seoul
HIGHEST POINT Halla 6,398 ft. (1,950 m.)
MONETARY UNIT won
MAJOR LANGUAGE Korean
MAJOR RELIGIONS Confucianism, Buddhism, Ch'ondogyo, Christianity

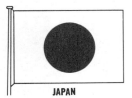

JAPAN

NORTH KOREA

SOUTH KOREA

JAPAN

PREFECTURES

...hi 5,923,569	H6
...ta 1,232,481	F6
...mori 1,468,646	K3
...ba 4,149,147	P2
...me 1,465,215	F7
...kui 773,599	G5
...kuoka 4,292,963	D7
...kushima 1,970,616	K5
...fu 1,867,978	H6
...mma 1,756,480	J5
...roshima 2,646,324	E6
...kkaido 5,338,206	K2
...yogo 4,992,140	H7
...raki 2,342,198	K5
...ikawa 1,069,872	H5
...ate 1,385,563	K4
...agawa 961,292	G6
...agoshima 1,723,902	E8
...anagawa 6,397,748	O2
...ochi 808,397	F7
...umamoto 1,715,273	E7
...yoto 2,424,856	J7
...ie 1,626,002	H6
...iyagi 1,955,267	K4
...iyazaki 1,085,055	E8
...agano 2,017,564	J5
...agasaki 1,571,912	D7
...ara 1,077,491	J8
...igata 2,391,938	J5
...ita 1,190,314	E7
...kayama 814,305	F6
...kinawa 1,042,572	N6
...saka 8,278,925	J8
...Saga 837,674	E7

Saitama 4,821,340	O2
Shiga 985,621	J7
Shimane 768,886	F6
Shizuoka 3,308,799	H6
Tochigi 1,698,003	K5
Tokushima 805,166	G7
Tokyo 11,673,554	O2
Tottori 581,311	G6
Toyama 1,070,791	H5
Wakayama 1,072,118	H6
Yamagata 1,220,302	K4
Yamaguchi 1,555,218	E6
Yamanashi 783,050	J6

CITIES and TOWNS

Abashiri 43,825	M1
Ageo 146,358	O2
Aikawa 13,546	H4
Aizuwakamatsu 108,650	J5
Ajigasawa 18,086	J3
Akashi 234,905	H8
Aki 24,480	J4
Akita 261,246	J4
Akkeshi 16,778	M2
Akune 30,295	D7
Amagasaki 545,783	H8
Amagi 42,725	E7
Anan 60,439	G7
Aomori 264,222	K4
Asahi 34,028	K6
Asahikawa 320,526	L2
Ashibetsu 36,520	L2
Ashikaga 162,359	J5
Ashiya 76,211	H8
Atami 51,437	J6
Atsugi 108,955	O2
Awaji 9,623	H8

Ayabe 43,490	G6
Beppu 133,894	E7
Bibai 38,416	L2
Biratori 9,331	L2
Chiba 659,356	P2
Chichibu 61,798	J5
Chigasaki 152,023	O3
Chitose 61,031	K2
Chofu 175,924	O2
Choshi 90,374	K6
Daito 110,829	J8
Ebetsu 77,624	K2
Eniwa 39,884	K2
Esashi, Hokkaido 10,172	L1
Esashi, Hokkaido 14,409	J3
Esashi, Iwate 36,336	K4
Fuchu, Hiroshima 50,217	F6
Fuchu, Tokyo 182,474	O2
Fuji 199,195	J6
Fujieda 90,358	J6
Fujisawa 265,975	O3
Fukagawa 36,000	L2
Fukuchiyama 60,003	G6
Fukue 32,018	D7
Fukui 231,364	G5
Fukuoka 1,002,201	D7
Fukushima 246,531	K5
Fukuyama 329,714	F6
Funabashi 423,101	P2
Furukawa 54,356	K4
Gifu 408,707	H6
Gobo 30,272	G7
Gose 37,554	J8
Gosen 39,376	J5
Goshogawara 49,040	K3
Gotsu 27,992	F6
Habikino 94,160	J8
Haboro 13,624	K1

Hachinohe 224,366	K3
Hachioji 322,580	O2
Hadano 103,663	O3
Hagi 52,724	E6
Hakodate 307,453	K3
Hakui 28,726	H5
Hamada 50,316	E6
Hamamatsu 468,884	H6
Hanamaki 65,826	K4
Hano 55,926	O2
Haramachi 43,483	K5
Hayama 24,026	O3
Higashiosaka 524,750	J8
Hikone 85,066	H6
Himeji 436,086	G6
Himi 61,789	H5
Hirado 126,847	D7
Hirakata 297,618	J7
Hirara 29,301	L2
Hirata 30,942	F6
Hiratsuka 195,635	O3
Hiroo 11,399	L2
Hirosaki 164,911	K3
Hiroshima 852,611	E6
Hitachi 202,383	K5
Hitachiota 35,322	K5
Hitoyoshi 41,118	E7
Hofu 105,540	E6
Hondo 40,432	E7
Honjo 40,488	J4
Hyuga 53,448	E7
Ibaraki 210,286	J7
Ibusuki 32,339	E8
Ichihara 194,068	P3
Ichikawa 319,291	P2
Ichinohe 21,433	J3
Ichinomiya 238,463	H6
Ichinoseki 59,122	K4

Ide 9,112	J7
Iida 77,112	H6
Iizuka 75,417	E7
Ikeda, Hokkaido 12,306	L2
Ikeda, Osaka 100,268	H7
Ikoma 48,848	J8
Ikuno 6,658	J6
Imabari 119,726	F6
Imari 60,913	D7
Imazu 11,519	G6
Ina 54,468	H6
Isahaya 73,341	D7
Ise 104,957	H6
Ishigaki 34,657	L7
Ishige 19,220	P2
Ishinomaki 115,085	K4
Ishioka 43,679	O3
Itami 171,978	H7
Ito 68,072	J6
Itoigawa 36,646	H5
Itoman 39,363	N6
Iwaizumi 20,219	K4
Iwaki 330,213	K5
Iwakuni 111,069	E6
Iwami 16,063	L2
Iwamizawa 72,305	L2
Iwanai 25,823	K2
Iwasaki 4,437	J3
Iwatsuki 83,825	O2
Izumi 118,237	J8
Izumiotsu 66,250	J8
Izumisano 86,139	G6
Izumo 71,568	F6
Joetsu 123,418	H5
Joyo 58,923	J7

Kadoma 143,238	J7
Kaga 61,599	H5
Kagoshima 456,827	E8
Kaizuka 79,506	H8
Kakogawa 169,293	G6
Kamaishi 68,981	L4
Kamakura 165,552	O3
Kameoka 58,184	J7
Kamisco 27,229	K3
Kaminoyama 37,858	J4
Kamiyaku 8,668	E8
Kamo 8,953	J7
Kanazawa 395,263	H5
Kanonji 44,131	F6
Kanoya 67,951	E8
Kanuma 81,799	J5
Karatsu 75,224	D7
Kaseda 24,969	D8
Kashihara 95,701	J8
Kashiwa 203,065	P2
Kashiwara 63,586	J8
Kashiwazaki 80,351	J5
Kasugai 213,857	H6
Kasukabe 121,639	O2
Katsuta 79,996	K6
Katsuura 26,755	K6
Kawachinagano 66,936	J8
Kawagoe 225,465	O2
Kawaguchi 345,538	J6
Kawanishi 115,773	H7
Kawasaki 1,014,951	O2
Kesennuma 66,616	K4
Kikonai 10,034	K3
Kimitsu 76,016	O3
Kiryu 134,239	J6
Kisarazu 96,840	P3
Kishiwada 174,952	J8
Kitaibaraki 44,332	K5

Kitakami 48,759	K4
Kitakata 37,471	J5
Kitakyushu 1,058,058	E6
Kitami 91,519	L2
Kizu 11,890	J7
Kobayashi 38,325	E8
Kobe 1,360,605	H7
Kochi 280,962	F7
Kodaira 156,181	O2
Kofu 193,879	J6
Koga 55,973	J5
Koganei 102,714	O2
Kokubu 31,660	E8
Komagane 30,318	H6
Komatsu 100,273	H5
Koriyama 264,628	K5
Koshigaya 195,917	O2
Koyama 16,394	E8
Kubohama 17,817	F7
Kuji 38,122	K3
Kuki 45,797	O2
Kumagaya 131,485	J5
Kumamoto 488,166	E7
Kumano 27,026	H7
Kunimi 13,540	J7
Kurashiki 392,755	F6
Kurayoshi 50,785	F6
Kure 242,655	F6
Kuroiso 42,349	K5
Kurume 204,474	E7
Kushikino 30,456	E8
Kushima 30,038	E8
Kushimoto 18,997	G7
Kushiro 206,840	M2
Kyonan 13,067	O3
Kyoto 1,461,059	J7
Machida 255,305	O2
Maebashi 250,241	J5
Maihara 12,845	G6
Maizuru 97,780	G6
Makubetsu 18,444	L2
Makurazaki 29,685	O3
Mashike 9,312	K1
Masuda 50,734	E6
Matsubara 132,662	H8
Matsue 127,440	F6
Matsumae 18,307	J3
Matsumoto 185,595	H5
Matsusaka 108,893	H6
Matsuto 36,170	H5
Matsuyama 367,323	F7
Mihara 83,679	F6
Miki 53,731	H7
Mikuni 21,600	G5
Minamata 36,782	E7
Minobu 10,345	J6
Minoo 79,621	J7
Misawa 37,437	K3
Mitaka 164,950	O2
Mito 197,953	K5
Mitsukaido 38,820	P2
Miura 47,888	O3
Miyako 61,912	L4
Miyakonojo 118,289	E8
Miyazaki 234,347	E8
Miyazu 30,194	G6
Miyoshi 37,193	F6
Mobara 52,266	K4
Mobara 64,942	K6
Mombetsu 32,825	L1
Monbetsu 15,029	L2
Mooka 47,345	K5
Mori 17,030	K2
Moriguchi 178,383	J7
Morioka 216,223	K4
Motobu 17,823	M6
Muko 45,886	J7
Murakami 32,939	J4
Muroran 158,715	K2
Muroto 26,660	G7
Musashino 139,508	O2
Mutsu 44,646	K3
Nachikatsuura 23,596	H7
Nagahama, Ehime 13,144	F7
Nagahama, Shiga 54,064	H6
Nagano 306,637	J5
Nagaoka, Kyoto 65,557	J7
Nagaoka, Niigata 171,742	J5
Nagaokakyo 65,557	J7
Nagasaki 450,194	D7
Nagato 27,327	E6
Nago 45,210	N6
Nagoya 2,079,740	N6
Naha 295,006	N6
Nakaminato 33,147	K5
Nakamura 34,437	F7
Nakasato 14,248	K3
Nakatsu 59,111	E7
Nanao 49,493	H5
Nankoku 42,832	F7
Nara 257,538	J8
Narashino 117,852	P2
Nayoro 35,145	L1
Naze 46,359	O5
Nemuro 45,817	M2
Neyagawa 254,311	J7
Nichinan 52,171	E8
Niigata 423,188	J5
Niihama 131,712	F6
Niimi 30,014	F6
Niitsu 58,970	J5
Nishinomiya 400,622	H8

(continued on following page)

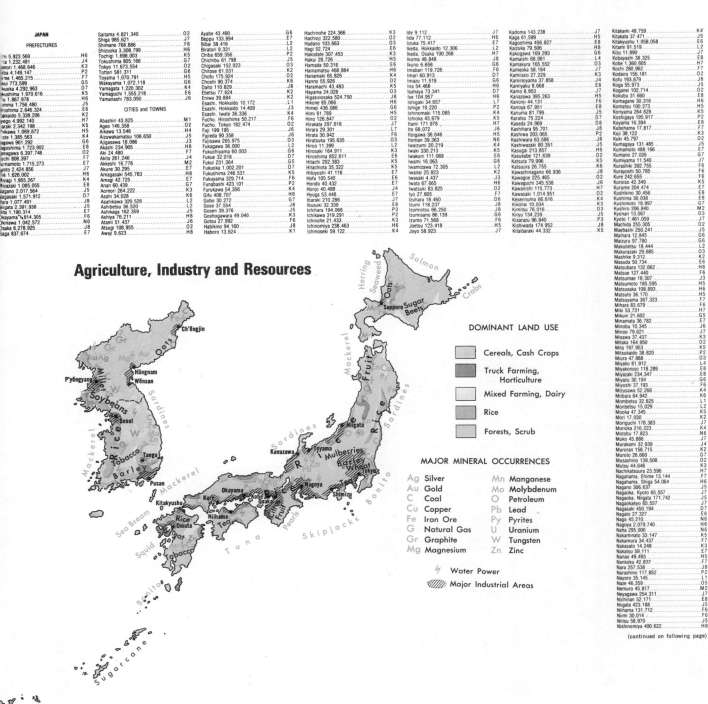

Agriculture, Industry and Resources

DOMINANT LAND USE

- Cereals, Cash Crops
- Truck Farming, Horticulture
- Mixed Farming, Dairy
- Rice
- Forests, Scrub

MAJOR MINERAL OCCURRENCES

Ag	Silver	Mn	Manganese
Au	Gold	Mo	Molybdenum
C	Coal	O	Petroleum
Cu	Copper	Pb	Lead
Fe	Iron Ore	Py	Pyrites
G	Natural Gas	U	Uranium
Gr	Graphite	W	Tungsten
Mg	Magnesium	Zn	Zinc

⚡ Water Power

▨ Major Industrial Areas

JAPAN is divided into prefectures bearing the same names as their capitals except:

Prefecture	Capital	Ref.
AICHI	NAGOYA	H 6
EHIME	MATSUYAMA	F 7
GUMMA	MAEBASHI	J 5
HOKKAIDO	SAPPORO	K 2
HYOGO	KOBE	H 7
IBARAKI	MITO	K 5
ISHIKAWA	KANAZAWA	H 5
IWATE	MORIOKA	K 4
KAGAWA	TAKAMATSU	F 6
KANAGAWA	YOKOHAMA	O 3
MIE	TSU	H 6
MIYAGI	SENDAI	K 4
OKINAWA	NAHA	N 6
SAITAMA	URAWA	O 2
SHIGA	OTSU	J 7
SHIMANE	MATSUE	F 6
TOCHIGI	UTSUNOMIYA	K 5
YAMANASHI	KOFU	J 6

Topography

Below Sea Level · 100 m. 328 ft. · 200 m. 656 ft. · 500 m. 1,640 ft. · 1,000 m. 3,281 ft. · 2,000 m. 6,562 ft. · 5,000 m. 16,404 ft.

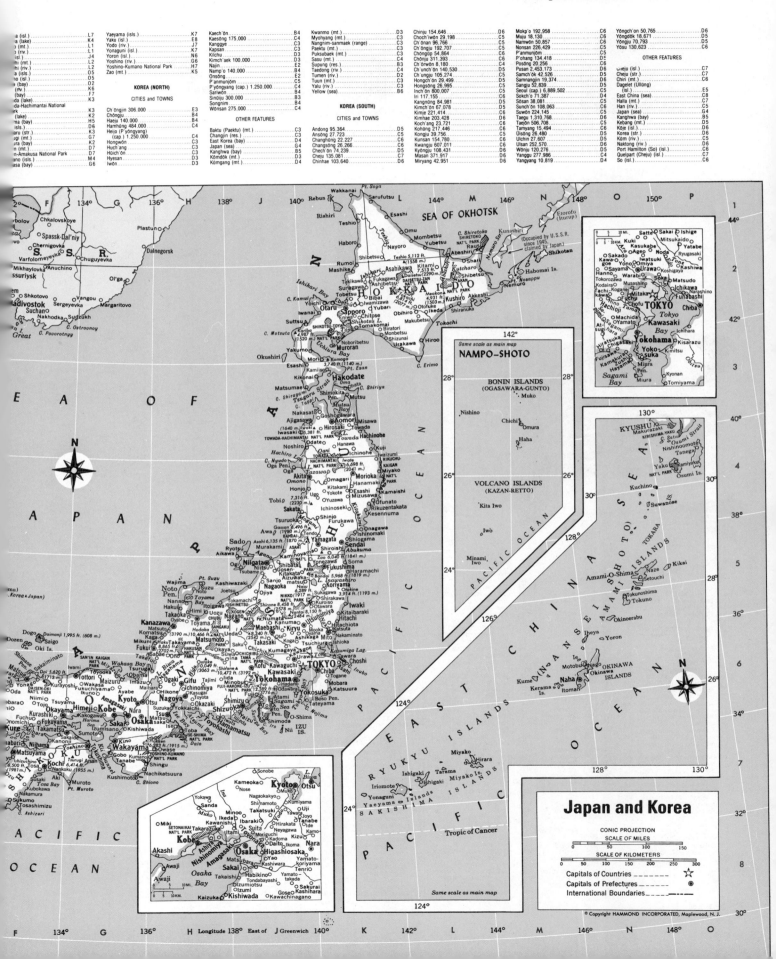

CHINA (MAINLAND)

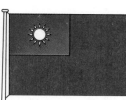

CHINA (TAIWAN)

MONGOLIA

CHINA (MAINLAND)
AREA 3,691,000 sq. mi. (9,559,690 sq. km.)
POPULATION 958,090,000
CAPITAL Peking (Beijing)
LARGEST CITY Shanghai
HIGHEST POINT Mt. Everest 29,028 ft. (8,848 m.)
MONETARY UNIT yuan
MAJOR LANGUAGES Chinese, Chuang, Uigur, Yi, Tibetan, Miao, Mongol, Kazakh
MAJOR RELIGIONS Confucianism, Buddhism, Taoism, Islam

Topography

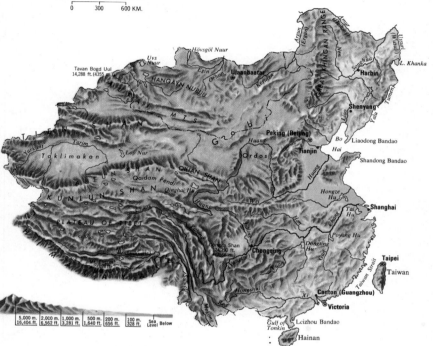

0   300   600 MI.
0   300   600 KM.

5,000 m. 2,000 m. 1,000 m. 500 m. 200 m. 100 m. Sea Level Below
16,404 ft. 6,562 ft. 3,281 ft. 1,640 ft. 656 ft. 328 ft.

CHINA†

PROVINCES

Anhui (Anhwei) 47,130,000 .... J5
Fujian (Fukien) 24,500,000 .... J6
Gansu (Kansu) 18,730,000 .... E3
Guangdong (Kwangtung)
  55,930,000 .... H7
Guangxi Zhuangzu (Kwangsi
  Chuang Autonomous Reg.)
  34,020,000 .... G7
Guizhou (Kweichow)
  26,860,000 .... G6
Heilongjiang
  (Heilungkiang) 33,760,000 .. K2
Hebei (Hopei) 50,570,000 .... J4
Henan (Honan) 70,660,000 ... H5
Hubei (Hupei) 45,750,000 .... H5
Hunan 51,660,000 .... H6
Jiangsu (Kiangsu) 58,340,000 . K5
Jiangxi (Kiangsi) 31,830,000 .. J6
Jilin (Kirin) 24,740,000 ...... L3
Liaoning 37,430,000 .... L3
Nei Monggol (Inner Mongolian
  Aut. Reg.) 8,900,000 ...... H3
Ningxia Huizu (Ningsia Hui Aut.
  Reg.) 3,660,000 .... F3
Qinghai (Tsinghai) 3,650,000 .. D4
Shaanxi (Shensi) 27,790,000 .. G5
Shanxi (Shansi) 24,340,000 ... H4
Shandong
  (Shantung) 71,600,000 ..... J4
Sichuan
  (Szechwan) 97,070,000 ..... F5
Taiwan 16,609,961 .... K7
Xinjiang Uygur (Sinkiang-Uigur
  Aut. Reg.) 12,330,000 ...... B3
Xizang (Tibet Aut.
  Reg.) 1,790,000 .... B5
Yunnan 30,920,000 .... F7
Zhejiang
  (Chekiang) 37,510,000 ...... K6

CITIES AND TOWNS

Aihui (Aigun) (Heihe) L1
Amoy (Xiamen) 400,000 ...... J7
Anqing (Anking) 160,000 ..... J5

Anshan 1,500,000 .... K3
Anyang 225,000 .... H4
Aqsu (Aksu) B3
Baoding (Paoting) 350,000 ... J4
Baoji (Paoki) 275,000 .... G5
Baoshan E7
Baotou (Paotow) 800,000 .... G3
Bei'an (Pehan) 130,000 ...... K2
Beihai (Pakhoi) 175,000 ..... G7
Beijing (Peking) (cap.)
  8,500,000 .... J3
Bengbu (Pengpu) 400,000 .... J5
Benxi (Penki) 750,000 .... K3
Canton (Guangzhou)
  2,300,000 .... H7
Chamdo (Qamdo) E5
Changchun 1,500,000 .... K3
Changde (Changteh) 225,000 .. H6
Changhua 137,236 .... K7
Changsha 850,000 .... H6
Changzhi (Changchih) H4
Changzhou (Changchow)
  400,000 .... K5
Chankiang (Zhanjiang)
  220,000 .... H7
Chao'an (Chaochow) J7
Charkhlia (Ruoqiang) C4
Chefoo (Yantai) 450,000 ..... K4
Chengchow (Zhengzhou)
  1,500,000 .... H5
Chengde (Chengteh) 200,000 .. J3
Chengdu (Chengtu)
  2,000,000 .... F5
Cherchen (Qiemo) C4
Chiai 238,713 .... K7
Chinchow (Jinzhou) 750,000 .. K3
Chinkiang (Zhenjiang)
  250,000 .... J5
Chinwangtao (Qinhuangdao)
  400,000 .... K4
Chongqing (Chungking)
  3,500,000 .... G6
Chüanchow (Quanzhou)
  130,000 .... J7
Chuchow (Zhuzhou) 350,000 .. H6
Chuguchak (Tacheng) B2
Chungshan (Zhongshan)
  135,000 .... H7

Dali E6
Dalian 1,480,240 .... K4
Dandong (Tantung) 450,000 .. K3
Datong (Tatung) 300,000 .... H3
Erenhot H3
Foshan (Fatshan) H7
Fushun 1,700,000 .... K3
Fuxin (Fusin) 350,000 .... K3
Fuzhou (Foochow) 900,000 ... J6
Ganzhou (Kanchow) 135,000 .. H6
Garyarsa (Gartok) B5
Gejiu (Kokiu) 250,000 .... F7
Golmud (Golmo) D4
Guangzhou (Canton)
  2,300,000 .... H7
Guilin (Kweilin) 225,000 ..... G6
Guiyang (Kweiyang) 1,500,000 . G6
Gulja (Yining) 160,000 .... B3
Gyangzê C6
Haikou (Hoihow) 500,000 .... H7
Hailar J2
Hami (Kumul) D3
Handan (Hantan) 500,000 .... H4
Hangzhou (Hangchow)
  1,100,000 .... J5
Hanzhong (Hanchung)
  120,000 .... G5
Harbin 2,750,000 .... L2
Hefei (Hofei) 400,000 .... J5
Hegang (Hokang) 350,000 .... L2
Heihe (Aihui) (Aigun) L1
Hengyang 310,000 .... H6
Hohhot (Huhehot) 700,000 ... H3
Horqin Youyi Qianqi (Ulanhot)
  110,000 .... K2
Hotan B4
Huainan 350,000 .... J5
Huangshi 200,000 .... J5
Ichang (Yichang) 150,000 .... H5
Ichun (Yichun) 200,000 ...... L2
Ipin (Yibin) 275,000 .... F6
Jiamusi (Kiamusze) 275,000 .. M2
Ji'an (Kian) 100,000 .... J6
Jiangmen (Kongmon)
  150,000 .... H7
Jiaozuo (Tsiaotso) 300,000 ... H4
Jilin (Kirin) 1,200,000 ...... L3
Jinan (Tsinan) 1,500,000 .... J4

Jingdezhen (Kingtehchen)
  300,000 .... J6
Jining (Tsining) 160,000 ..... H3
Jinshi (Tsingshih) 100,000 ... H6
Jinzhou (Chinchow) 750,000 .. K3
Jiujiang (Kiukiang) 120,000 ... J6
Jixi (Kisi) 350,000 .... M2
Juichin (Ruijin) J6
Kaifeng 330,000 .... H5
Kalgan (Zhangjiakou)
  1,000,000 .... J3
Kanchow (Ganzhou) 135,000 .. H6
Kaohsiung 1,028,334 .... J7
Karakax (Kara Kash) (Moyu) .. A4
Karghalik (Yecheng) A4
Kashi (Kashgar) 175,000 ..... A4
Kaxgar (Kashi) 175,000 ..... A4
Keelung 342,604 .... K6
Keriya (Yutian) B4
Khotan (Hotan) B4
Kiamusze (Jiamusi) 275,000 .. M2
Kian (Ji'an) 100,000 .... J6
Kingtehchen (Jingdezhen)
  300,000 .... J6
Kirin (Jilin) 1,200,000 ...... L3
Kisi (Jixi) 350,000 .... M2
Kiukiang (Jiujiang) 120,000 ... J6
Kokiu (Gejiu) 250,000 .... F7
Kongmoon (Jiangmen) 150,000 . H7
Kuldja (Yining) 160,000 ..... B3
Kunming 1,700,000 .... F6
Kwangchow (Canton)
  2,300,000 .... H7
Kweilin (Guilin) 225,000 ..... G6
Kweisui (Hohhot) 700,000 ... H3
Kweiyang (Guiyang) 1,500,000 . G6
Lanzhou (Lanchow) 1,500,000 . F4
Leshan (Loshan) 250,000 .... F6
Lhasa 175,000 .... D6
Lhazê (Lhatse) C6
Lianyungang (Lienyünkang)
  300,000 .... J5
Liaoyang 250,000 .... K3
Liaoyuan 300,000 .... K3
Linqing (Lintsing) J4
Liuzhou (Liuchow) 250,000 .. G7
Lopnur (Yuli) C3
Lüda (Dalian) 1,480,240 ..... K4

(continued on following page)

On this map Chinese place-names have been rendered according to the Pinyin spelling system within the area controlled by the People's Republic of China. Alphabetically listed below are selected Chinese place-names spelled in the traditional manner, followed by the equivalent Pinyin form.

Amoy (Hsiamen)	Xiamen	Kirin	Jilin	Sian	Xi'an
Anhwei	Anhui	Kiukiang	Jiujiang	Siangtan	Xiangtan
Canton		Kwangsi	Guangxi	Sining	Xining
(Kwangchow)	Guangzhou	Chuang	Zhuangzu	Sinkiang-	
Chefoo (Yentai)	Yantai	Kweichow	Guizhou	Sinkiang-	
Chekiang	Zhejiang	Kweilin	Guilin	Uighur	Xinjiang Uygur
Chengchow	Zhengzhou	Kweiyang	Guiyang	Soochow	Suzhou
Chengtu	Chengdu	Lanchow	Lanzhou	Suchow	Xuzhou
Chinchow	Jinzhou	Liuchow	Liuzhou	Swatow	Shantou
Chungking	Chongqing	Loyang	Luoyang	Szechwan	Sichuan
Foochow	Fuzhou	Lüta	Dalian	Tachai	Dazhai
Fukien	Fujian	Mutankiang	Mudanjiang	Tatung	Datong
Hangchow	Hangzhou	Nanking	Nanjing	Tibet	Xizang
Heilungkiang	Heilongjiang	Ningpo	Ningbo	Tientsin	Tianjin
Hofei	Hefei	Ningsia Hui	Ningxia Huizu	Tsinan	Jinan
Honan	Henan	Paoting	Baoding	Tsinghai	Qinghai
Huhehot	Hohhot	Paotow	Baotou	Tsingtao	Qingdao
Hupeh	Hubei	Penki	Benxi	Tsining	Jining
Hwainan	Huainan	Pengpu	Bengbu	Tsitsihar	Qiqihar
Inner Mongolia	Nei Monggol	Shansi	Shanxi	Tsunyi	Zunyi
Kansu	Gansu	Shantung	Shandong	Tungchwan	Tongchuan
Kiangsi	Jiangxi	Shensi	Shaanxi	Urumchi	Ürümqi
Kiangsu	Jiangsu	Shihkiachwang	Shijiazhuang	Wusih	Wuxi
Kingtehchen	Jingdezhen			Yenan	Yan'an
				Yinchwan	Yinchuan
				Zibo	Zibo

CHINA (TAIWAN)
A 13,971 sq. mi. (36,185 sq. km.)
ULATION 16,609,961
ITAL Taipei
GEST CITY Taipei
HEST POINT Yü Shan 13,113 ft. (3,997 m.)
NETARY UNIT new Taiwan yüan (dollar)
IOR LANGUAGES Chinese, Formosan
IOR RELIGIONS Confucianism, Buddhism, Taoism, Christianity, tribal religions

MONGOLIA
AREA 606,163 sq. mi. (1,569,962 sq. km.)
POPULATION 1,594,800
CAPITAL Ulaanbaatar
LARGEST CITY Ulaanbaatar
HIGHEST POINT Tabun Bogdo 14,288 ft. (4,355 m.)
MONETARY UNIT tughrik
MAJOR LANGUAGES Khalkha Mongolian, Kazakh (Turkic)
MAJOR RELIGION Buddhism

HONG KONG
AREA 403 sq. mi. (1,044 sq. km.)
POPULATION 5,022,000
CAPITAL Victoria
MONETARY UNIT Hong Kong dollar
MAJOR LANGUAGES Chinese, English
MAJOR RELIGIONS Confucianism, Buddhism, Christianity

MACAU
AREA 6 sq. mi. (16 sq. km.)
POPULATION 271,000
CAPITAL Macau
MONETARY UNIT pataca
MAJOR LANGUAGES Chinese, Portuguese
MAJOR RELIGIONS Confucianism, Buddhism, Taoism, Christianity

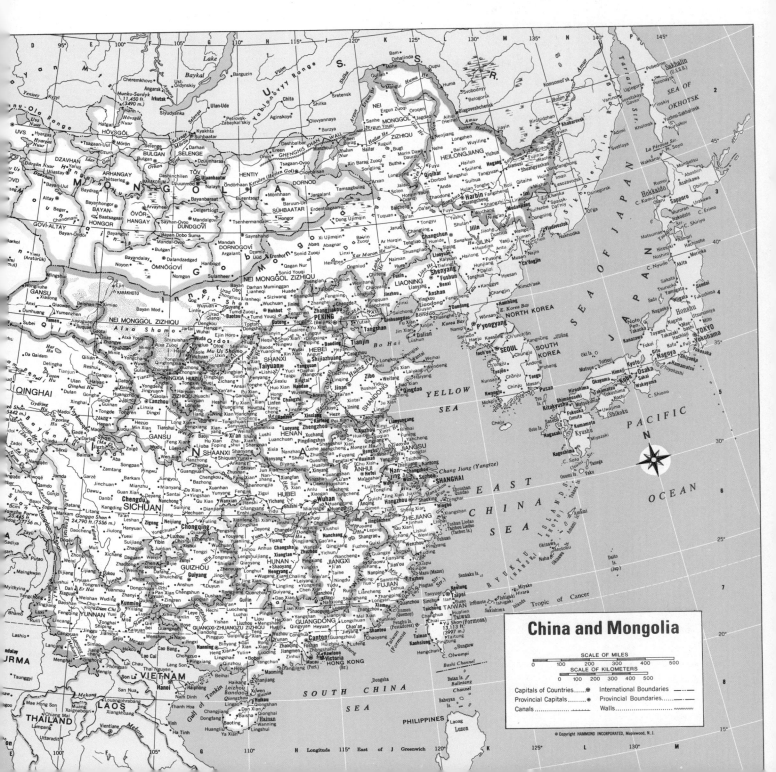

China and Mongolia

SCALE OF MILES
0 100 200 300 400 500

SCALE OF KILOMETERS
0 100 200 300 400 500

Capitals of Countries......⊛   International Boundaries ———
Provincial Capitals........◉   Provincial Boundaries......
Canals................   Walls.......................

© Copyright HAMMOND INCORPORATED, Maplewood, N.J.

(continued)

Luoyang (Loyang) 750,000 ..... H5
Lüshun K4
Luzhou (Luchol) 225,000 ..... G6
Ma'anshan J5
Manzhouli (Manchouli) J2
Maoming (Mowming) H7
Mengzi F7
Mianyang G5
Minfeng (Niya) B4
Moyu (Karakax) A4
Mudanjiang (Mutankiang) 400,000 ..... M3
Mukden (Shenyang) 3,750,000 K3
Nanchang 900,000 ..... J6
Nanchong (Nanchung) 275,000 G5
Nanjing (Nanking) 2,000,000 ... J5
Nanning 375,000 ..... G7
Nanping J6
Nantong 300,000 ..... K5
Nanyang H5
Neijiang (Neikiang) 240,000 ... G6
Nenjiang L2
Ningbo (Ningpo) 350,000 ..... K6
Ningsia (Yinchuan, Yinchwan) 175,000 ..... G4
Paicheng (Baicheng) K2
Pakhoi (Beihai) 175,000 ..... G7
Paoki (Baoji) 275,000 ..... G5
Paoting (Baoding) 350,000 ..... J4
Paotow (Baotou) 800,000 ..... G3
Pehan (Bei'an) 130,000 ..... L2
Peking (Beijing) (cap.)○8,500,000 ..... J3
Pengpu (Bengbu) 400,000 ..... J5
Penki (Benxi) 750,000 ..... K3
Pingdingshan H5
Pingliang G4
Pingtung 165,360 ..... K7
Pingxiang, Guangxi Zhuangzu G7
Pingxiang, Jiangxi H6
Piqan (Shanshan) D3
Qamdo E5
Qarkilik (Ruoqiang) C4
Qiemo (Qarqan) C4
Qingdao (Tsingtao) 1,900,000 . K4
Qingjiang 110,000 ..... J5
Qinhuangdao (Chinwangtao) 400,000 ..... K4
Qiqihar (Tsitsihar) 1,500,000 ..... K2
Qitai C3
Qoqek (Tacheng) B2
Quanzhou (Chüanchow) 130,000 ..... J7
Ruijin (Juichin) J6
Ruoqiang (Qarkilik) C4
Shache (Yarkand) A4
Shanghai○ 10,980,000 ..... K5
Shangqui (Shangkiu) 250,000 .. J5
Shangrao (Shangjao) 100,000 . J6
Shangshui 100,000 ..... J5
Shanshan (Piqan) D3
Shantou (Swatow) 400,000 ..... J7
Shaoguan (Shiukwan) 125,000 H7
Shaoxing (Shaohing) 225,000 .. K5
Shaoyang 275,000 ..... H6
Shashi 125,000 ..... H5
Shenyang (Mukden) 3,750,000 K3
Shigatse (Xigazê) C6
Shihezi (Shihhotzu) C3
Shijiazhuang (Shihkiachwang) 1,500,000 . J4
Shiyan H5
Shizuishan (Shihsuishan) G4
Shuangcheng L2
Shuangyashan 150,000 ..... M2
Siakwan (Xiaguan) E6
Sian (Xi'an) 1,900,000 ..... G5
Siangfan (Xiangfan) 150,000 ... H5
Siangtan (Xiangtan) 300,000 ... H6
Sienyang (Xianyang) 125,000 .. G5
Simao (Fusingchen) F7
Sinchu 208,038 ..... K7
Singtai (Xingtai) H4
Sining (Xining) 250,000 ..... F4
Sinsiang (Xinxiang) 300,000 ..... H4
Sinyang (Xinyang) 125,000 ..... H5
Siping (Szeping) 180,000 ..... K3
Soche (Shache) A4
Suao K7
Süchow (Xuzhou) 1,500,000 ... J5
Suifenhe M3
Suihua L2
Suining G5
Suzhou (Soochow) 1,300,000 . K5
Swatow (Shantou) 400,000 ..... J7
Tacheng (Qoqek) B2
Tai'an J4
Taichung 565,255 ..... K7
Tainan 541,390 ..... J7
Taipei 2,108,193 ..... K7
Taitung K7
Taiyuan 2,725,000 ..... H4
Taizhou (Taichow) 275,000 ..... K5
Tali (Dali) E6
Tangshan 1,200,000 ..... J4
Tantung (Dandong) 450,000 ... K3
Tao'an K2
Taoyuan 105,841 ..... K6
Tatung (Datong) 300,000 ..... H3
Tehchow (Dezhou) J4
Tianjin (Tientsin)○7,210,000 ... J4
Tianshui 100,000 ..... F5
Tieling K3
Tientsin (Tianjin)○7,210,000 ... J4
Tongchuan (Tungchwan) G5
Tonghua (Tunghwa) 275,000 ... L3
Tongjiang (Tungkiang) M2
Tongliao K3
Tongling J5
Tsiaotso (Jiaozuo) 300,000 ..... H4
Tsinan (Jinan) 1,500,000 ..... J4
Tsingkiang (Qingjiang) 110,000 ..... J5
Tsingshih (Jinshi) 100,000 ..... H6
Tsingtao (Qingdao) 1,900,000 . K4
Tsining (Jining) 160,000 ..... H3
Tsitsihar (Qiqihar) 1,500,000 ..... K2
Tsunyi (Zunyi) 275,000 ..... G6
Tumen M3
Tunxi (Tunki) J6
Turpan (Turfan) C3
Tzekung (Zigong) 350,000 ..... F6
Tzepo (Zibo) 1,750,000 ..... J4
Uch Turfan (Wushi) A3
Ulanhot (Horquin Youyi Qianqi) 100,000 ..... K2
Ulughchat (Wuqia) A4
Ürümqi (Urumchi) 500,000 ..... C3
Usu B3
Wanxian (Wanhsien) 175,000 .. G5
Weifang 260,000 ..... J4
Weihai (Weihaiwei) K4
Wenzhou 250,000 ..... J6
Wuda G4
Wuhan 4,250,000 ..... H5
Wuhu 300,000 ..... J5
Wuqi G4
Wuqia A4
Wushi A3
Wuxi (Wusih) 900,000 ..... K5
Wuxing (Wuhing) 160,000 ..... K5
Wuzhong (Wuchung) G4
Wuzhou (Wuchow) 150,000 ... H7
Xiaguan (Siakwan) E6
Xiamen (Amoy) 400,000 ..... J7
Xi'an (Sian) 1,900,000 ..... G5
Xiangfan (Siangfan) 150,000 ... H5
Xiangtan (Siangtan) 300,000 ... H6
Xianyang (Sienyang) 125,000 .. G5
Xiapu (Siapu) K6
Xichang (Sichang) F6
Xigazê (Shigatse) C6
Xingtai (Singtai) H4
Xining (Sining) 250,000 ..... F4
Xinxiang (Sinsiang) 300,000 ... H4
Xinyang (Sinyang) 125,000 ..... H5
Xuzhou (Süchow) 1,500,000 ... J5
Ya'an 100,000 ..... F6
Yadong C6
Yan'an (Yenan) G4
Yanji (Yenki) 130,000 ..... L3
Yangquan (Yangchüan) 350,000 ..... H4
Yangzhou (Yangchow) 210,000 ..... J5
Yantai (Chefoo) 180,000 ..... K4
Yarkand (Shache) A4
Ya Xian G8
Yecheng A4
Yenan (Yan'an) G4
Yibin (Ipin) 275,000 ..... F6
Yichang (Ichang) 150,000 ..... H5
Yichun 200,000 ..... L2
Yinchuan (Ningsia) 175,000 ... G4
Yingkou 215,000 ..... K3
Yining 160,000 ..... B3
Yiyang H6
Yuci (Yütze) H4
Yuli (Lopnur) C3
Yumen 325,000 ..... E4
Yungkia (Wenzhou) 250,000 ... J6
Yutian B4
Zhangjiakou (Kalgan) 1,000,000 ..... J3
Zhangzhou (Changchow) J7
Zhanjiang (Chankiang) 220,000 ..... H7
Zhaoqing H7
Zhengzhou (Chengchow) 1,500,000 ..... H5
Zhenjiang (Chinkiang) 250,000 ..... J5
Zhongshan (Chungshan) 135,000 ..... H7
Zhuzhou (Chuchow) 350,000 ... H6
Zibo (Tzepo) 1,750,000 ..... J4
Zigong (Tzekung) 350,000 ..... F6
Zunyi (Tsunyi) 275,000 ..... G6

OTHER FEATURES

Altun Shan (range) C4
Alxa Shamo (des.) F4
Amur (Heilong Jiang) (riv.) L2
A'nyêmaqên Shan (mts.) E5
Argun' (Ergun He) (riv.) K1
Bashi (chan.) K7
Bayan Har Shan (range) E5
Bo Hai (gulf) J4
Bosten (Bagrax) Hu (lake) C3
Chang Jiang (Yangtze) (riv.) ... K5
Da Hingan Ling (range) J3
Dian Chi (lake) F7
Dongsha (isl.) J7
Dongting Hu (riv.) H6
East China (sea) L6
Ergun He (Argun') (riv.) K1
Er Hai (lake) F6
Everest (mt.) C6
Formosa (Taiwan) (str.) J7
Gangdisê Shan (range) B5
Ghenghis Khan Wall (ruin) H2
Gobi (des.) G3
Grand (canal) J4
Great Wall (ruins) G4,J
Gurla Mandhada (mt.) B5
Hainan (isl.) H8
Hangzhou Wan (bay) K5
Heilong Jiang (Amur) (riv.) L2
Himalaya (mts.) C6
Hotan He (riv.) B4
Huang He (Yellow) (riv.) J4
Hulun Nur (lake) J2
Inner Mongolia (reg.) H3
Jinmen (Quemoy) (isl.) J7
Jinsha Jiang (Yangtze) (riv.) ... E5
Junggar Pendi (desert basin) C2
Karakhoto (ruins) F3
Karamiran Shankou (pass) C4
Keriya Shankou (pass) B4
Khanka (lake) M3
Kongur Shan (mt.) A4
Künes He (riv.) B3
Kunlun Shan (range) B4
Kuruktag Shan (range) C3
Lancang Jiang (riv.) F7
Leizhau Bandao (pen.) G7
Liaodong Bandao (pen.) K3
Liao He (riv.) K3
Lop Nor (Lop Nur) (lake) D3
Manas He (riv.) C3
Mazu (Matsu) (isl.) K6
Mekong (Lancang Jiang) (riv.) F7
Muztag (mt.) B4
Muztagata (mt.) A4
Nam Co (lake) D5
Namzha Parwa (mt.) E6
Nan Ling (mts.) H6
Nu Jiang (riv.) E6
Nyainqêntanglha Shan (range) D5
Olwampi (cape) K7
Ordos (reg.) G4
Penghu (Pescadores) (isls.) ... J7
Pobeda (peak) A3
Poyang Hu (lake) J6
Pratas (Dongsha) (isl.) J7
Qaidam Pendi (basin) (swamp) D4
Qarqan He (riv.) C4
Qilian Shan (range) E4
Qinghai Hu (lake) E4
Qiongzhou Haixia (str.) G7
Quemoy (Jinmen) (isl.) J7
Salween (Nu Jiang) (riv.) E6
Siling Co (lake) C5
Songhua Jiang (Sungari) (riv.) M2
South China (sea) J7
Tai Hu (lake) J5
Taiwan (Formosa) (str.) J7
Taizhou (Tachen) (isls.) K6
Takla Makan (Taklimakan Shamo) (des.) B4
Tanggula Shan (range) D5
Tangra Yumco (lake) C5
Tarim Pendi (basin) B4
Tian Shan (range) C3
Tibet (reg.) B5
Tongtian He (Zhi Qu) (riv.) E5
Tonkin (gulf) G7
Tumen (riv.) L3
Ulu Muztag (mt.) C4
Ussuri (Wusuli Jiang) (riv.) ... M2
Wei He (riv.) G5
Wusuli Jiang (Ussuri) (riv.) ... M2
Xiang Jiang (riv.) .....
Xi Jiang (riv.) .....
Yalong Jiang (riv.) .....
Yalu (riv.) .....
Yangtze (Chang Jiang) (riv.) ...
Yarkant He (riv.) .....
Yellow (Huang He) (riv.) .....
Yellow (sea) .....
Yü Shan (mt.) .....

HONG KONG

CITIES and TOWNS

Kowloon* 2,378,480 .....
Victoria (cap.)* 1,026,870 .....

MACAU (MACAO)

CITIES and TOWNS

Macau (Macao (cap.) 226,880 .

MONGOLIA

CITIES and TOWNS

Tamsagbulag .....
Ulaanbaatar (Ulan Bator) (cap.) 345,000 .....

OTHER FEATURES

Altai (mts.) C
Dzavhan Gol (riv.) ..... D
Hangayn Nuruu (mts.) ..... E
Har Us Nuur (lake) ..... D
Herlen Gol (Kerulen) (riv.) ..... H
Hovd Gol (riv.) ..... D
Hövsgöl Nuur (lake) ..... F
Hyargas Nuur (lake) ..... D
Karakorum (ruins) ..... F
Kerulen (riv.) ..... H
Munku-Sardyk (mt.) ..... F
Orhon Gol (riv.) ..... F
Selenge Mörön (riv.) ..... G
Tannu-Ola (range) ..... D
Tavan Bogd Uul (mt.) C
Uvs Nuur (lake) ..... D

○Population of municipality. *City and suburbs †Populations of mainland cities excluding Peking (Beijing), Shanghai and Tianjin (Tientsin), courtesy of Kingsley Davis, Office of Int'l Population and Urban Research, Institute of Int'l Studies, Univ. of California.

Agriculture, Industry and Resources

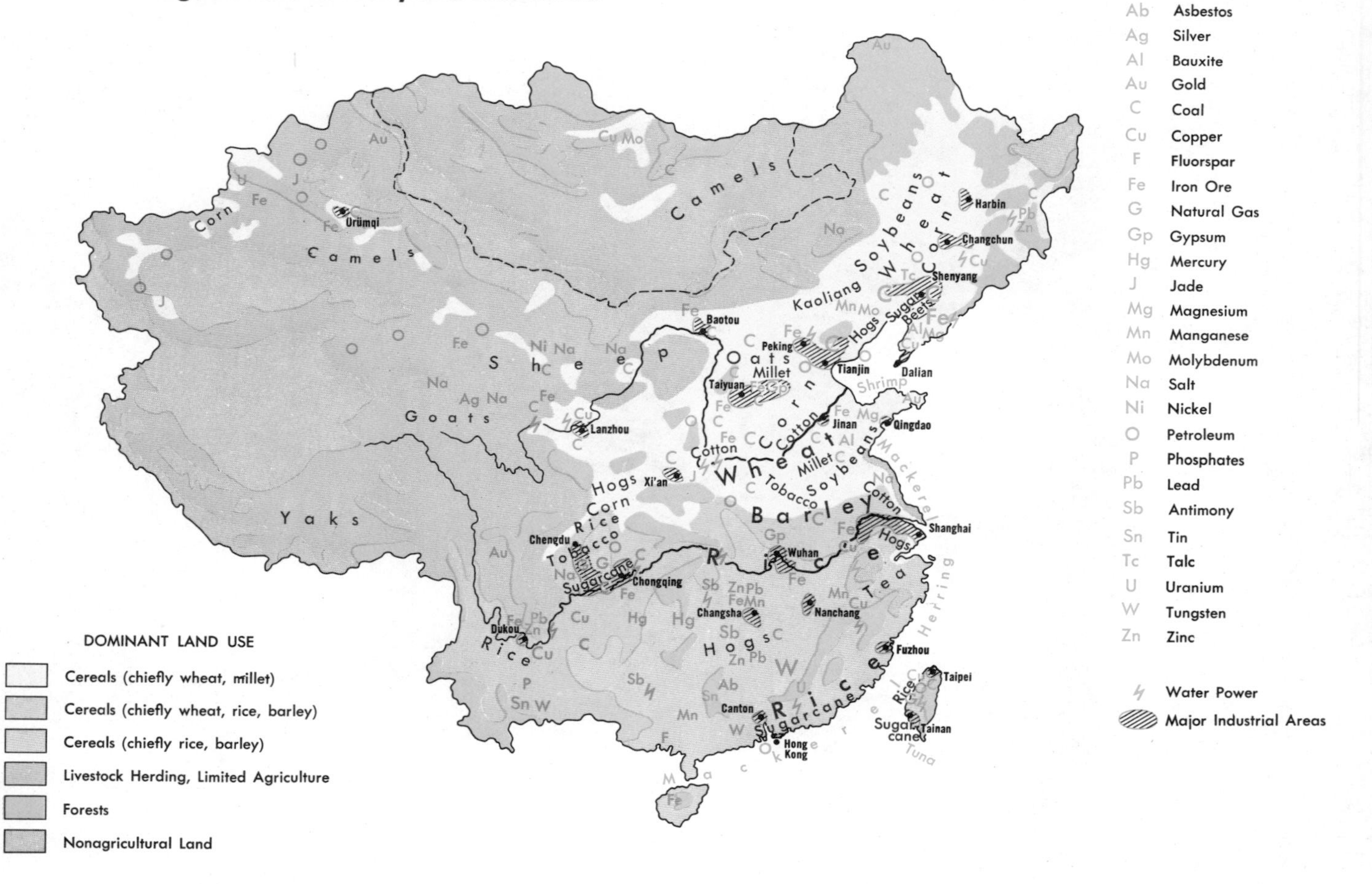
MAJOR MINERAL OCCURRENCES
Ab Asbestos
Ag Silver
Al Bauxite
Au Gold
C Coal
Cu Copper
F Fluorspar
Fe Iron Ore
G Natural Gas
Gp Gypsum
Hg Mercury
J Jade
Mg Magnesium
Mn Manganese
Mo Molybdenum
Na Salt
Ni Nickel
O Petroleum
P Phosphates
Pb Lead
Sb Antimony
Sn Tin
Tc Talc
U Uranium
W Tungsten
Zn Zinc
Water Power
Major Industrial Areas
DOMINANT LAND USE
Cereals (chiefly wheat, millet)
Cereals (chiefly wheat, rice, barley)
Cereals (chiefly rice, barley)
Livestock Herding, Limited Agriculture
Forests
Nonagricultural Land
Ürümqi
Harbin
Changchun
Shenyang
Baotou
Peking
Tianjin
Dalian
Taiyuan
Jinan
Qingdao
Lanzhou
Xi'an
Shanghai
Chengdu
Wuhan
Chongqing
Changsha
Nanchang
Dukou
Fuzhou
Taipei
Canton
Tainan
Hong Kong
Corn
Camels
Sheep
Goats
Yaks
Soybeans
Wheat
Kaoliang
Hogs
Sugar Beets
Oats
Millet
Cotton
Tobacco
Barley
Rice
Sugarcane
Tea
Shrimp
Mackerel
Herring
Tuna

BURMA

THAILAND

LAOS

CAMBODIA

VIETNAM

MALAYSIA

SINGAPORE

BURMA

AREA 261,789 sq. mi. (678,034 sq. km.)
POPULATION 32,913,000
CAPITAL Rangoon
LARGEST CITY Rangoon
HIGHEST POINT Hkakabo Razi 19,296 ft.
 (5,881 m.)
MONETARY UNIT kyat
MAJOR LANGUAGES Burmese, Karen, Shan,
 Kachin, Chin, Kayah, English
MAJOR RELIGIONS Buddhism, tribal religions

THAILAND

AREA 198,455 sq. mi. (513,998 sq. km.)
POPULATION 46,455,000
CAPITAL Bangkok
LARGEST CITY Bangkok
HIGHEST POINT Doi Inthanon 8,452 ft.
 (2,576 m.)
MONETARY UNIT baht
MAJOR LANGUAGES Thai, Lao, Chinese,
 Khmer, Malay
MAJOR RELIGIONS Buddhism, tribal religions

LAOS

AREA 91,428 sq. mi. (236,800 sq. km.)
POPULATION 3,721,000
CAPITAL Vientiane
LARGEST CITY Vientiane
HIGHEST POINT Phou Bia 9,252 ft. (2,820 m.)
MONETARY UNIT kip
MAJOR LANGUAGE Lao
MAJOR RELIGIONS Buddhism, tribal religions

CAMBODIA

AREA 69,898 sq. mi. (181,036 sq. km.)
POPULATION 5,200,000
CAPITAL Phnom Penh
LARGEST CITY Phnom Penh
HIGHEST POINT 5,948 ft. (1,813 m.)
MONETARY UNIT riel
MAJOR LANGUAGE Khmer (Cambodian)
MAJOR RELIGION Buddhism

VIETNAM

AREA 128,405 sq. mi. (332,569 sq. km.)
POPULATION 52,741,766
CAPITAL Hanoi
LARGEST CITY Ho Chi Minh City (Saigon)
HIGHEST POINT Fan Si Pan 10,308 ft.
 (3,142 m.)
MONETARY UNIT dong
MAJOR LANGUAGES Vietnamese, Thai,
 Muong, Meo, Yao, Khmer, French,
 Chinese, Cham
MAJOR RELIGIONS Buddhism, Taoism,
 Confucianism, Roman Catholicism,
 Cao-Dai

MALAYSIA

AREA 128,308 sq. mi. (332,318 sq. km.)
POPULATION 13,435,588
CAPITAL Kuala Lumpur
LARGEST CITY Kuala Lumpur
HIGHEST POINT Mt. Kinabalu 13,455 ft.
 (4,101 m.)
MONETARY UNIT ringgit
MAJOR LANGUAGES Malay, Chinese, English,
 Tamil, Dayak, Kadazan
MAJOR RELIGIONS Islam, Confucianism,
 Buddhism, tribal religions, Hinduism,
 Taoism, Christianity, Sikhism

SINGAPORE

AREA 226 sq. mi. (585 sq. km.)
POPULATION 2,413,945
CAPITAL Singapore
LARGEST CITY Singapore
HIGHEST POINT Bukit Timah 581 ft. (177 m.)
MONETARY UNIT Singapore dollar
MAJOR LANGUAGES Chinese, Malay, Tamil,
 English, Hindi
MAJOR RELIGIONS Confucianism, Buddhism,
 Taoism, Hinduism, Islam, Christianity

Topography

0   200   400 MI.
0   200   400 KM.

5,000 m. 2,000 m. 1,000 m. 500 m. 200 m. 100 m. Sea Below
16,404 ft. 6,562 ft. 3,281 ft. 1,640 ft. 656 ft. 328 ft. Level

BURMA

INTERNAL DIVISIONS

Arakan (state) 1,710,913	B3
Chin (state) 323,094	B2
Irrawaddy (div.) 4,152,521	B3
Kachin (state) 735,144	C1
Karen (state) 865,218	B3
Kayah (state) 126,492	C3
Magwe (div.) 2,632,144	B2
Mandalay (div.) 3,662,312	B2
Mon (state) 1,313,111	C3
Pegu (div.) 3,174,109	C3
Rangoon (div.) 3,186,886	C3
Sagaing (div.) 3,115,502	B1
Shan (state) 3,178,214	C2
Tenasserim (div.) 717,607	C4

CITIES and TOWNS

Akyab (Sittwe) 42,329	B2
Allanmyo 15,580	B3
Amarapura 11,268	B2
Amherst 6,000	C3
An	B3
Anin	C4
Bassein 126,045	B3
Bhamo 9,821	C1
Chauk 24,466	B2
Danubyu	B3
Falam	B2
Fort Hertz (Putao)	C1
Gawai	C1
Gokteik	C2
Gwa	B3
Gyobingauk 9,922	C3
Haka	B2
Henzada 61,972	B3
Hmawbi 23,032	C3
Homalin	B1
Hsenwi	C2
Hsipaw	C2
Htawgaw	C1
Insein 143,625	C3
Kamaing	C1
Karathuri	C5
Katha 7,648	C1
Kawludo	C3
Kawthaung 1,520	C5
Keng Hkam	C2
Keng Tung	C2
Koma	C2
Kunlong	C2
Kyaikto 13,154	C3
Kya-in Seikkyi	C3
Kyangin 6,073	B3
Kyaukme	C2
Kyaukpadaung 5,480	B2
Kyaukpyu 7,335	B2
Kyaukse 8,659	C2
Labutta 12,982	B3
Lai-hka	C2
Lamu	B3
Lashio	C2
Lenya	C5
Letpadan 15,896	B3
Lewe	B3
Loi-kaw	C3
Lonton	B1
Magwe 13,270	B2
Maingkwan	C1
Maliwun	C5
Mandalay 418,008	C2
Man Hpang	C2
Martaban 5,661	C3
Ma-ubin 23,362	B3
Maungdaw 3,772	B2
Mawkmai	C2
Mawlaik 2,993	B2
Mawlu	C1
Maymyo 22,287	C2
Meiktila 19,474	B2
Mergui 33,697	C4
Minbu 9,096	B2

Minhla 6,470	B3
Mogaung 2,920	C1
Mogok 8,334	C2
Mohnyin	C1
Möng Hsat	C2
Möng Maü	C3
Möng Mit	C2
Möng Pan	C2
Möng Si	C2
Möng Ton	C2
Möng Tung	C2
Monywa 26,279	B2
Moulmein 171,977	C3
Mudon 20,136	C3
Myanaung 11,155	B3
Myaungmya 24,532	B3
Myingyan 36,439	B2
Myitkyina 12,382	C1
Myohaung 6,534	B2
Naba	B1
Namhkam	C2
Namlan	C2
Namtu	C2
Natmauk	B2
Okkan 14,443	B3
Okpo 12,155	C3
Pakokku 30,943	B2
Palaw 5,596	C4
Paletwa	B2
Pantha	B2
Papun	C3
Pasawng	C3
Paungde 17,286	B3
Pegu 47,378	C3
Prome (Pye) 36,997	B3
Putao	C1
Pyapon 19,174	B3
Pye 36,997	B3
Pyinmana 22,025	C3
Pyu 10,443	C3
Rangoon (cap.) 1,586,422	C3
Rangoon* 2,055,365	C3
Rathedaung 2,969	B2
Sadon	C1
Sagaing 15,382	B2
Samka	C2
Sandoway 5,172	B3
Shingbwiyang	B1
Shwebo 17,827	B2
Shwenyaung	C2
Singkaling Hkamti	B1
Singu 4,027	C2
Sinlumkaba	C1
Sittwe 42,329	B2
Sumprabum	C1
Syriam 15,296	C3
Taungdwingyi 16,233	C2
Taunggyi	C2
Tavoy 40,312	C4
Tharrawaddy 8,977	C3
Thaton 38,047	C3
Thaungdut	B1
Thayetmyo 11,649	B3
Thazi 7,531	C2
Thongwa 10,829	C3
Toungoo 31,589	C3
Wakema 20,716	B3
Yamethin 11,167	C2
Yandoon 15,245	B3
Ye 12,852	C4
Yenangyaung 24,416	B2
Yesagyo 7,880	B2
Ye-u 5,307	B2
Ywathit	C3
Zadi	C4
Zalun 899	B3

OTHER FEATURES

Amya (pass)	C4
Andaman (sea)	B4
Arakan Yoma (mts.)	B3
Ataran (riv.)	C3
Bengal, Bay of (sea)	B3
Bentinck (isl.)	C5

(continued on following page)

(continued)

CAMBODIA (KAMPUCHEA)

CITIES and TOWNS

OTHER FEATURES

LAOS

CITIES and TOWNS

OTHER FEATURES

MALAYA, MALAYSIA*

STATES

CITIES and TOWNS

OTHER FEATURES

SINGAPORE

CITIES and TOWNS

OTHER FEATURES

THAILAND (SIAM)

CITIES and TOWNS

OTHER FEATURES

VIETNAM

CITIES and TOWNS

OTHER FEATURES

*See Southeast Asia, p. 84 for other part of Malaysia.

*City and suburbs.
⊙Population of district.

Agriculture, Industry and Resources

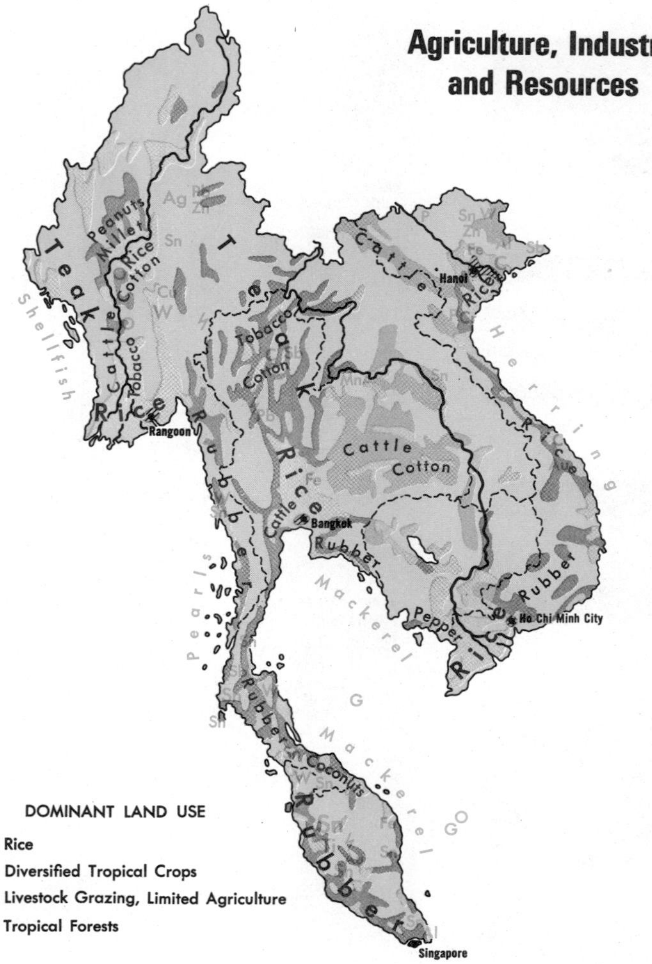

DOMINANT LAND USE

- Rice
- Diversified Tropical Crops
- Livestock Grazing, Limited Agriculture
- Tropical Forests

MAJOR MINERAL OCCURRENCES

Ag	Silver	Cu	Copper	O	Petroleum	Sn	Tin
Al	Bauxite	Fe	Iron Ore	P	Phosphates	Ti	Titanium
Au	Gold	G	Natural Gas	Pb	Lead	W	Tungsten
C	Coal	Mn	Manganese	Sb	Antimony	Zn	Zinc
Cr	Chromium						

Water Power

Major Industrial Areas

Burma, Thailand, Indochina and Malaya

CONIC PROJECTION

SCALE OF MILES

SCALE OF KILOMETERS

International Boundaries ———————
Division and State Boundaries ———·—·—
Capitals of Countries ————————☆
Division and State Capitals ————————◉

© Copyright HAMMOND INCORPORATED, Maplewood, N.J.

Longitude East 96° of Greenwich

PHILIPPINES

AREA 115,707 sq. mi. (299,681 sq. km.)
POPULATION 48,098,460
CAPITAL Manila
LARGEST CITY Manila
HIGHEST POINT Apo 9,692 ft. (2,954 m.)
MONETARY UNIT piso
MAJOR LANGUAGES Pilipino (Tagalog), English,
  Spanish, Bisayan, Ilocano, Bikol
MAJOR RELIGIONS Roman Catholicism, Islam,
  Protestantism, tribal religions

Topography

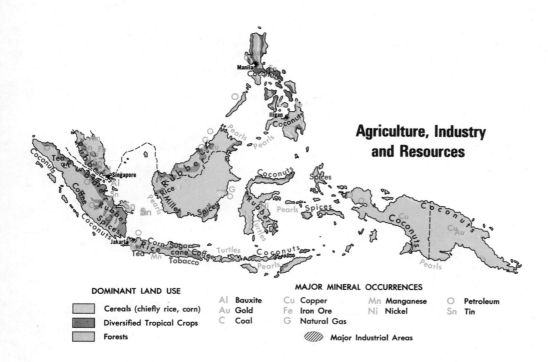

Agriculture, Industry and Resources

DOMINANT LAND USE

- Cereals (chiefly rice, corn)
- Diversified Tropical Crops
- Forests

MAJOR MINERAL OCCURRENCES

Al Bauxite	Cu Copper	Mn Manganese	O Petroleum
Au Gold	Fe Iron Ore	Ni Nickel	Sn Tin
C Coal	G Natural Gas		

///// Major Industrial Areas

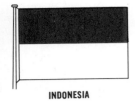

INDONESIA

BRUNEI

PAPUA NEW GUINEA

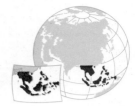

AREA 788,430 sq. mi. (2,042,034 sq. km.)
POPULATION 147,490,298
CAPITAL Jakarta
LARGEST CITY Jakarta
HIGHEST POINT Puncak Jaya 16,503 ft.
  (5,030 m.)
MONETARY UNIT rupiah
MAJOR LANGUAGES Bahasa Indonesia,
  Indonesian and Papuan languages,
  English
MAJOR RELIGIONS Islam, tribal religions,
  Christianity, Hinduism

AREA 2,226 sq. mi. (5,765 sq. km.)
POPULATION 192,832
CAPITAL Bandar Seri Begawan
LARGEST CITY Bandar Seri Begawan
HIGHEST POINT Pagon 6,070 ft. (1,850 m.)
MONETARY UNIT Brunei Dollar
MAJOR LANGUAGES Malay, English, Chinese
MAJOR RELIGIONS Islam, Buddhism,
  Christianity, tribal religions

AREA 183,540 sq. mi. (475,369 sq. km.)
POPULATION 3,010,727
CAPITAL Port Moresby
LARGEST CITY Port Moresby
HIGHEST POINT Mt. Wilhelm 15,400 ft.
  (4,694 m.)
MONETARY UNIT kina
MAJOR LANGUAGES pidgin English,
  Hiri Motu, English
MAJOR RELIGIONS Tribal religions,
  Christianity

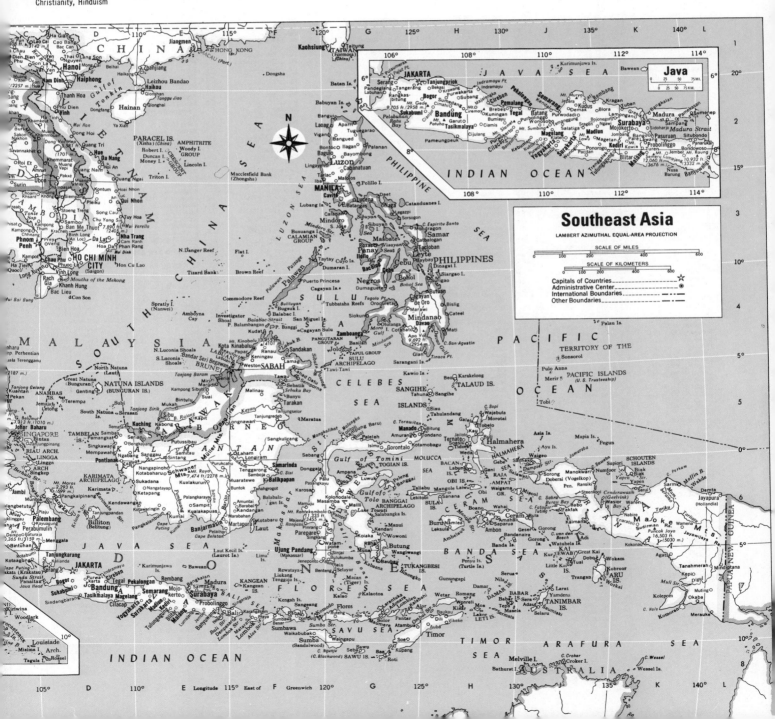

BRUNEI

CITIES and TOWNS

Bandar Seri Begawan 63,868 E 4
Seria 23,511 E 5

CHINA

OTHER FEATURES

Amphitrite (isls.) E 2
Crescent (isls.) E 2
Duncan (isls.) E 2
Lincoln (isl.) E 2
Money (isl.) E 2
Paracel (isls.) E 2
Robert (isl.) E 2
Triton (isl.) E 2
Xisha (isls.) E 2
Woody (isl.) E 2

INDONESIA

CITIES AND TOWNS

Agats K 7
Amahai H 6
Ambon (Amboina) 208,898 H 6
Ampana G 6
Amurang G 5
Atambua G 7
Auba H 7
Baa G 8
Babo K 7
Bagansiapiapi C 5
Balige B 5
Balikpapan 280,675 F 6
Banda Aceh 72,090 A 4
Bandanaira H 6
Bandung 1,462,637 H 2
Banggai G 6
Bangil •49,438 K 2
Bangkalan •41,639 K 2
Banjarmasin 381,286 E 6
Bantul •40,585 J 2
Banyumas J 2
Banyuwangi •76,596 L 2
Barabai •33,688 F 6
Barus •46,120 B 5
Batang •69,577 J 2
Batavia (Jakarta) (cap.) 6,503,449 H 1
Baturaja •48,350 C 6
Batusangkar C 6
Baubau G 7
Baukau H 7
Bekasi •123,264 H 2
Belawan B 5
Bengkalis •14,072 C 5
Bengkayang •15,404 E 5
Bengkulu 64,783 C 6
Benteng F 7
Beo H 5
Biak K 6
Binjai 76,464 B 5
Bintuhan C 6
Bireuen B 4
Bitung •59,507 H 5
Blitar 78,503 K 2
Blora •67,853 K 2
Bogor 247,409 H 2
Bojonegoro •74,241 J 2
Bondowoso •50,317 L 2
Bonthain •30,377 F 7
Brebes •87,918 H 2
Bukittinggi 70,771 B 6
Bula J 6
Buli H 5
Bulukumba •63,932 G 7
Bumiayu •65,403 H 2
Buntok F 6
Buol G 5
Calang B 5
Ciamis •105,434 H 2
Cianjur •132,058 H 2
Cijulang •44,487 H 2
Cilacap •118,815 H 2
Cimahi •157,222 H 2
Cirebon 223,776 H 2
Curup •71,965 C 6
Demak •57,676 J 2
Demta L 6
Denpasar •98,005 E 7
Dili H 7
Djambi (Jambi) 230,373 C 6
Djokjakarta (Yogyakarta) 398,727 J 2
Dobo J 7
Dompu •14,103 F 7
Donggala F 6
Ende G 7
Fakfak J 6
Galela •11,554 H 5
Garut •93,340 H 2
Genting D 5
Gorontalo 97,628 G 5
Gresik •48,561 K 2
Hollandia (Jayapura) •45,786 K 6
Indramayu •69,441 H 2
Isimu G 5
Jailolo •17,243 H 5
Jakarta (cap.) 6,503,449 H 1
Jambi 230,373 C 6
Jayapura •45,786 L 6
Jember •115,201 K 2
Jeneponto •6,883 F 7
Jepara •75,124 J 2
Jogjakarta (Yogyakarta) 398,727 J 2
Jombang •80,643 K 2
Kaimana J 6
Kayuagung •37,319 D 6
Kalianda •42,609 D 7
Kampung Baru (Tolitoli) •10,071 G 5
Karangasem •15,177 F 7
Karosa F 6
Kau H 5
Kebumen •81,571 J 2
Kediri 221,830 K 2
Kendal •32,544 J 2
Kendari •28,628 G 6
Kepi K 7
Ketapang E 6
Klaten •58,870 J 2
Kokonau K 6
Kolaka •10,384 G 6
Kolonodale G 6
Kotaagung •20,154 C 7
Kotabaharu E 6
Kotabaru •23,443 F 6
Kotabumi C 7
Kotawaringin E 6
Kragan •33,389 K 2
Krawang •99,552 H 2
Kualakapuas E 6
Kudus •79,186 J 2
Kumai E 6
Kumai •13,564 E 6
Kuningan •105,255 H 2
Kupang •49,354 G 8
Kutaraja (Banda Aceh) 72,090 A 4
Kutoarjo •52,989 J 2
Labuha H 6
Labuhan •34,274 G 2
Laham F 5
Lahat •48,136 C 6
Laiwui H 6
Lamongan •38,897 K 2
Langsa •58,060 B 5
Larantuka G 7
Lawang •59,071 K 2
Lekitobi G 6
Letong D 5
Longiram F 5
Longnawan F 5
Lubuklinggau •43,011 C 6
Lubuksikaping •24,244 B 5
Lumajang •79,641 K 2
Madiun 150,562 K 2
Majalengka •80,999 H 2
Magelang 123,484 J 2
Magetan •59,507 K 2
Makassar (Ujung Pandang) 709,038 F 7
Malang 511,780 K 2
Malili G 6
Malinau •14,130 F 5
Mamuju •17,345 F 6
Manado 217,159 G 5
Manokwari J 6
Maros F 6
Martapura •55,011 F 6
Masamba •16,571 G 6
Mataram •46,846 F 7
Maumere G 7
Medan 1,378,955 B 5
Menggala •20,878 D 6
Merauke •21,366 K 7
Mindiptana L 7
Mojokerto 68,849 K 2
Muarabungo •26,304 C 6
Muarasiberut B 6
Muaratewe F 6
Muntok •31,719 D 6
Nabire K 6
Nangapinoh •19,983 E 6
Nangatayap E 6
Negara •65,762 E 7
Ngabang •33,190 D 5
Ngawi K 2
Okaba K 7
Pacitan •51,993 J 2
Padang 480,922 B 6
Padangpanjang 34,517 B 6
Padangsidempuan •134,611 B 5
Painan C 6
Pakanbaru 186,262 C 5
Palangkaraya 60,447 E 6
Palaumerak •58,655 G 1
Paleleh •7,603 G 5
Palembang 787,187 D 6
Palopo F 6
Pamangkat •62,402 D 5
Pamekasan •55,409 L 2
Pameungpeuk •41,449 H 2
Panarukan •37,482 K 2
Pandeglang •35,550 G 1
Pangkalanberandan •60,299 B 5
Pangkalanbuun E 6
Pangkalpinang 90,096 D 6
Pare •107,806 K 2
Parepare 86,450 F 6
Pariaman •44,428 B 6
Pasangkayu F 6
Pasuruan 95,864 K 2
Pati •75,397 J 2
Payakumbuh 78,836 C 6
Pekalongan 132,558 J 2
Pemalang •110,206 J 2
Pematangsiantar 150,376 B 5
Perabumulih •88,031 C 6
Pinrang F 6
Piru H 6
Plaju D 6
Ponorogo •58,321 J 2
Pontianak 304,778 D 6
Poso G 6
Prapat •7,723 B 5
Praya •89,266 F 7
Probolinggo 100,296 K 2
Purbolinggo •41,031 J 2
Purwakarta •93,016 H 2
Purwodadi •75,713 J 2
Purwokerto •125,464 H 2
Purworejo •28,663 J 2
Putussibau •12,408 E 5
Raha G 6
Rangkasbitung •78,685 G 2
Ransiki J 6
Rantauprapat C 5
Rembang •33,610 K 2
Rengat •33,559 C 6
Ruteng •12,294 G 7
Sabang, Celebes F 5
Sabang, Weh 23,821 B 4
Salatiga 85,849 J 2
Samarinda 264,718 F 6
Sambas •48,253 D 5
Samboja F 6
Sampang •60,136 K 2
Sampit E 6
Sanggau •7040 E 5
Sangkulirang •8,769 F 5
Saparua H 6
Sarmi K 6
Saumlaki J 7
Sawahlunto 13,561 C 6
Seba G 8
Semarang 1,026,671 J 2
Semitau •7,165 E 5
Serang •79,675 G 1
Serui K 6
Siaksriinderapura C 5
Sibolga 59,897 B 5
Sidoharjo •59,942 K 2
Sigli •10,623 B 4
Sinabang B 5
Sindangbarang •70,603 D 7
Singaraja F 7
Singkawang •93,650 D 5
Sinjai G 7
Sintang •24,842 E 5
Situbondo •36,094 L 2
Soe G 7
Solo (Surakarta) 469,888 J 2
Solok 31,724 C 6
Sorong •23,763 J 6
Sragen •50,515 J 2
Subang •35,077 H 2
Sukabumi 109,994 H 2
Sukadana •9,741 E 6
Sumbawa Besar F 7
Sumedang H 2
Sumenep •46,659 L 2
Surabaya 2,027,913 K 2
Surakarta 469,888 J 2
Takalar F 7
Takingeun B 5
Talangbetutu C 6
Tanahgrogot F 6
Tanahmerah K 7
Tangerang G 1
Tanjungbalai 41,894 C 5
Tanjungkarang 284,275 D 7
Tanjungpandan •61,225 D 6
Tanjungpinang C 5
Tanjungpriok •147,824 H 1
Tanjungpura •30,992 B 5
Tanjungredeb F 5
Tanjungselor F 5
Tapaktuan B 5
Tarakan •31,118 F 5
Tarutung B 5
Tasikmalaya •135,919 H 2
Tebingtinggi 92,087 B 5
Tegal 131,728 J 2
Telukbayur C 6
Temanggung •85,492 J 2
Tenggarong •15,081 F 6
Tepa H 7
Terempa D 5
Ternate •34,539 H 5
Tjilatjap (Cilacap) •118,815 H 2
Tjirebon (Cirebon) 223,776 H 2
Tobelo H 5
Tolitoli •10,071 G 5
Tondano •35,978 H 5
Trenggalek •49,065 K 2
Tual J 7
Tuban •54,212 K 2
Tulungagung •53,880 K 2
Turen •76,018 K 2
Ujung Pandang 709,038 F 7
Vikeke H 7
Wahai H 6
Waikabubak F 7
Waingapu G 7
Wajabula H 5
Waren K 6
Wasior K 6
Watampone G 6
Weda H 5
Wonogiri •56,435 J 2
Wonosobo •47,650 J 2
Wonreli H 7
Yogyakarta 398,727 J 2

OTHER FEATURES

Adi (isl.) J 6
Adonara (isl.) 71,462 G 7
Alas (str.) F 7
Alor (isl.) 86,136 G 7
Ambelau (isl.) H 6
Anambas (isls.) 29,572 D 5
Arafura (sea) J 8
Aru (isls.) 34,195 K 7
Asahan (riv.) B 5
Asia (isls.) J 5
Ayu (isls.) J 5
Babar (isl.) H 7
Babar (isls.) 28,636 H 7
Bacan (isls.) 29,137 H 6
Balabalagan (isls.) F 6
Bali (isl.) 2,074,438 F 7
Bali (sea) F 7
Bali (str.) E 7
Banda (isls.) 13,638 H 6
Banda (sea) H 7
Banggai (arch.) 169,025 G 6
Bangka (isl.) 298,017 D 6
Bangka (str.) C 6
Banyak (isls.) 1,980 B 5
Barbar (isls.) J 7
Barisan (mts.) C 6
Barito (riv.) E 6
Batu (isls.) 16,390 B 6
Bawean (isl.) 64,551 K 1
Belitung (Billiton) (isl.) 128,694 D 6
Benggala (str.) A 4
Berau (bay) J 6
Berhala (str.) C 6
Biak (isl.) K 6
Billiton (isl.) 128,694 D 6
Binongko (isl.) 11,549 G 7
Bintan (isl.) 102,644 C 5
Blackwood (Ngundju) (cape) F 8
Boano (isl.) H 6
Bone (gulf) G 7
Borneo (isl.) E 5
Bosch, van den (cape) J 6
Bungalaut (chan.) B 6
Bunguran (Great Natuna) (isl.) D 5
Bunguran (Natuna) (isls.) D 5
Bunyu (isl.) F 5
Buru (isl.) 23,034 H 6
Buru (sea) H 6
Butung (isl.) 188,173 G 6
Celebes (Sulawesi) (isl.) 7,732,383 G 5
Celebes (sea) G 5
Cenderawasih (bay) K 6
Ceram (isl.) 158,591 H 6
Ciremay (mt.) H 2
Damar (isl.) H 7
Damar (isls.) H 7
Dampier (str.) J 6
Dempo (mt.) C 6
Digul (riv.) K 7
Doberai (pen.) J 6
Enggano (isl.) 1,082 C 7
Ewab (Kai) (isls.) 108,328 J 7
Fatagar Tuting (cape) J 6
Flores (isl.) 860,328 G 7
Flores (sea) F 7
Frederik Hendrik (Kolepom) (isl.) K 7
Gebe (isl.) 8,607 H 6
Gede (mt.) H 2
Geelvink (Cenderawasih) (bay) K 6
Gorong (isl.) J 6
Gorong (isls.) J 6
Great Kai (isl.) 38,748 J 7
Great Natuna (isl.) D 5
Gunungapi (isl.) H 7
Halmahera (isl.) 122,521 H 5
Halmahera (sea) H 5
Hari (riv.) C 6
Indian Ocean E 8
Indramayu (pt.) H 1
Irian Jaya (reg.) 923,440 J 6
Jambuair (cape) B 4
Jamursba (cape) J 5
Java (head) C 7
Java (isl.) 73,712,411 J 2
Java (sea) D 6
Jaya, Puncak (mt.) K 6
Jayawijaya (range) K 6
Jemaja (isl.) 5,628 D 5
Kabaena (isl.) G 7
Kahayan (riv.) E 6
Kai (isls.) 108,328 J 7
Kalao (issl.) G 7
Kalaotoa (isl.) G 5
Kalimantan (reg.) 4,956,865 E 5
Kampar (riv.) C 5
Kangean (isl.) F 7
Kangean (isls.) 89,060 F 7
Kapuas (riv.) D 6
Karakelong (isl.) H 5
Karimata (arch.) 9,398 D 6
Karimata (isl.) D 6
Karimata (str.) D 6
Karimunjawa (isls.) 5,025 J 1
Kawi (mt.) K 2
Kawio (isls.) G 5
Kayan (riv.) F 5
Kelasa (str.) D 6
Kengah (isls.) F 7
Kerinci (mt.) C 6
Kisar (isl.) H 7
Kobroor (isl.) K 7
Kolepom (isl.) K 7
Komodo (isl.) 30,407 F 7
Komoran (isl.) K 7
Krakatau (Rakata) (isl.) C 7
Kur (isl.) J 7
Lakor (isl.) H 7
Larat (isl.) J 7
Laurot (Laut Kecil) (isls.) E 7
Laut (isl.) 55,711 F 6
Laut (North Natuna) (isl.) D 5
Laut Kecil (isls.) E 7
Lawu (mt.) J 2
Leti (isls.) H 7
Leuser (mt.) B 5
Lima (isls.) F 7
Lingga (arch.) 46,658 D 5
Lingga (isl.) 18,027 D 6
Little Kai (isl.) J 7
Liukang Tenggaja (isls.) F 7
Lomblen (isl.) 62,572 G 7
Lombok (isl.) 1,581,193 F 7
Lombok (str.) E 7
Macan (isls.) G 7
Madura (isl.) 1,509,774 K 2
Madura (str.) K 2
Maffin (bay) K 6
Mahakam (riv.) F 6
Makassar (str.) F 6
Malacca (str.) C 5
Malangka (cape) G 5
Mamberamo (riv.) K 6
Mandar (cape) F 6
Mangkalihat (cape) F 5
Mangole (isl.) H 6
Manipa (str.) H 6
Manui (isl.) G 6
Maoke (mts.) K 6
Mapia (isls.) J 5
Maras (mt.) D 6
Maratua (isl.) F 5
Masela (isl.) H 7
Mega (isl.) C 6
Mentawai (isls.) 30,107 B 6
Misool (isl.) J 6
Moa (isl.) H 7
Molucca (sea) H 6
Moluccas (isls.) 944,240 H 6
Morotai (isl.) 27,333 H 5
Muli (str.) K 7
Müller (mts.) E 5
Muna (isl.) 156,186 G 7
Muryo (mt.) J 2
Musi (riv.) C 6
Natuna (isls.) 23,893 D 5
Ngunju (cape) F 8
Nias (isl.) 356,093 B 5
Nila (isl.) H 7
North Natuna (isl.) D 4
North Pagai ((isl.) C 6
Numfoor (isl.) J 6
Nusa Barung (isl.) K 3
Obi (isl.) H 6
Obi (isls.) 12,437 H 6
Ombai (str.) H 7
Panaitan (isl.) C 7
Pantar (isl.) 28,259 G 7
Patuha (mt.) H 2
Pegun (isl.) J 5
Pelabuhan Ratu (bay) G 2
Peleng (isl.) G 6
Pembuang (riv.) E 6
Penyu (isls.) H 7
Perkam (cape) K 6
Pujut (pt.) G 1
Puting, Borneo (cape) E 6
Puting, Sumatra (cape) C 7
Raja Ampat Group (isls.) H 6
Rakata (isl.) C 7
Rangasa (cape) F 6
Rantekombola (mt.) F 6
Raung (mt.) L 2
Raya (mt.) E 6
Rewataya (reef) F 7
Riau (arch.) 483,230 C 5
Rokan (riv.) C 5
Romang (isl.) H 7
Roti (isl.) 76,270 G 8
Rupat (isl.) 17,672 C 5
Sabra (cape) J 6
Salabangka (isls.) G 6
Salawati (isl.) J 6
Sandalwood (Sumba) (isl.) 291,190 F 7
Sanding (isl.) C 6
Sangeang (isl.) F 7
Sanggabuwana (mt.) G 2
Sangihe (isl.) H 5
Sangihe (isls.) 183,000 G 5
Saweba (cape) J 6
Sawu (isl.) G 8
Sawu (isls.) 51,002 G 8
Sawu (sea) G 7
Schouten (isls.) 110,148 K 6
Schwaner (mts.) E 6
Sebatik (isll.) F 5
Sebuku (bay) F 5
Selaru (isl.) J 7
Selatan (cape) E 6
Selayar (isl.) 92,342 G 7
Semeru (mt.) K 2
Sera (isl.) J 7
Serasan (isl.) 5,024 D 5
Sermata (isl.) H 7
Serua (isl.) H 7
Siak (riv.) C 5
Siau (isl.) 46,801 H 5
Siberut (isl.) 14,732 B 6
Siberut (str.) B 6
Simeulue (isl.) 29,147 A 5
Singkep (isl.) 28,631 D 6
Sipura (isl.) 6,051 B 6
Sisi (cape) F 6
Slamet (mt.) J 2
Solor (isl.) 24,586 G 7
Sopi (cape) H 5
Sorikmerapi (mt.) B 5
South China (sea) D 4
South Natuna (isls.) D 5
South Pagai (isl.) C 6
Subi Besar (isl.) D 5
Sudirman (range) K 6
Sula (isls.) 36,922 H 6
Sulawesi (isl.) 7,732,383 G 6
Sumatra (isl.) 19,360,400 B 5
Sumba (isl.) 291,190 F 7
Sumba (str.) F 7
Sumbawa (isl.) 621,140 F 7
Sumbing (mt.) J 2
Sunda (str.) C 7
Supiori (isl.) K 6
Tahulandang (isl.) 21,493 H 5
Talaud (isls.) 46,395 H 5
Taliabu (isl.) 18,303 G 6
Tambelan (isls.) 4,032 D 5
Tanimbar (isls.) 55,405 J 7
Tariku (riv.) K 6
Taritatu (riv.) K 6
Tidore (isl.) 28,655 H 5
Tiger (Macan) (isls.) G 7
Timor (reg.) 1,435,527 H 7
Timor (sea) H 7
Toba (lake) B 5
Togian (isls.) 13,913 G 6
Tolo (gulf) G 6
Tomini (gulf) G 6
Torawitan (cape) G 5
Towuti (lake) G 6
Trangan (isl.) J 7
Tukangbesi (isls.) 73,106 G 7
Turtle (Penju) (isls.) H 7
Vals (cape) K 7
Vogelkop (Doberai) (pen.) J 6
Waigeo (isl.) J 5
Wakde (isl.) K 6
Wangiwangi (isl.) 28,469 G 7
Watubela (isls.) J 6
We (isl.) B 4
Wetar (isl.) H 7
Wokam (isl.) K 7
Workai (isl.) K 7
Wowoni (isl.) G 6
Yamdena (isl.) J 7
Yapen (isl.) 50,888 K 6
Yapen (str.) K 6

MALAYSIA

STATES

Labuan 26,453 F 4
(North Borneo) Sabah 1,002,608 F 3
Sarawak 1,294,753 E 5

CITIES and TOWNS

Beaufort 2,709 F 4
Bintulu 4,424 E 5
Kabong E 5
Kampong Sibuti E 5
Kapit 1,929 E 5
Keningau 2,037 F 4
Kota Kinabalu 40,939 F 4
Kuching 63,535 E 5
Kudat 5,089 F 4
Labuan 7,216 E 4
Lahad Datu 5,169 F 5
Lamag F 4
Marudi 4,700 E 5
Miri 35,702 E 5
Mukah 1,717 E 5
Papar 1,855 F 4
Ranau 2,024 F 4
Sandakan 42,413 F 4
Sematan D 5
Semporna 3,371 F 5
Serian 2,209 E 5
Sibu 50,635 E 5
Simanggang 8,445 E 5
Suai E 5
Tawau 24,247 F 5
Weston F 4

OTHER FEATURES

Balambangan (isl.) F 4
Banggi (isl.) F 4
Barut, Tanjong (cape) E 5
Borneo (isl.) E 5
Iran (mts.) E 5
Kinabalu (mt.) F 4
Labuan (isl.) 17,189 E 4
Labuk (bay) F 4
Malay (pen.) B 4
Rajang (riv.) E 5
Sebatik (isl.) F 5
Sirik (cape) E 5
South China (sea) D 4

PAPUA NEW GUINEA

CITIES and TOWNS

Abau C 7
Aitape 3,368 B 6
Ambunti 1,035 B 6
Angoram 1,846 B 6
Baniara C 7
Bogia 755 B 6
Bulolo 6,730 B 7
Buna C 7
Daru 7,127 B 7
Finschhafen 756 C 7
Gaima B 7
Gehua C 8
Gona C 7
Goroka 18,511 B 7
Ihu 541 B 7
Ioma C 7
Kaiapit 515 B 7
Kairuku B 7
Kerema 3,389 B 7
Kikori 763 B 7
Kiunga 1,407 B 7
Kokoda C 7
Kundiawa 4,299 B 7
Lae 61,617 B 7
Madang 21,335 B 7
Marienberg B 6
Mendi 4,130 B 7
Morobe C 7
Mount Hagen 13,441 B 7
Popondetta 6,429 C 7
Port Moresby (cap.) 123,624 B 7
Rigo C 7
Rouka B 7
Saidor 500 B 7
Samarai 864 C 8
Telefomin B 7
Tufi C 7
Vanimo 3,071 B 6
Wau 2,349 B 7
Wedau C 7
Wewak 19,890 B 6

OTHER FEATURES

Coral (sea) B 7
Dampier (str.) C 7
D'Entrecasteaux (isls.) C 7
Fly (riv.) A 7
Huon (gulf) C 7
Karkar (isl.) B 6
Kiriwina (isl.) C 7
Long (isl.) B 7
Louisiade (arch.) D 8
Milne (bay) C 8
Misima (isl.) C 8
Murray (lake)
New Britain (isl.) 148,773
Ramu (riv.)
Rossel (isl.)
Schouten (isls.)
Sepik (riv.)
Solomon (sea)
Tagula (isl.)
Torres (str.)
Trobriand (isls.)
Vitiaz (str.)
Wilhelm (mt.)
Woodlark (isl.)

PHILIPPINES

CITIES and TOWNS

Aparri 45,070
Bacolod 262,415
Baguio 119,009
Bangued 28,666
Bangui 11,122
Batangas 143,570
Baybay 74,640
Bayombong 32,066
Bislig 81,615
Bontoc 17,091
Butuan 172,489
Cabanatuan 138,298
Cagayan de Oro 227,312
Calapan 67,370
Catbalogan 58,737
Cateel 20,084
Cavite 87,666
Cebu 490,281
Cotabato 83,871
Daet 54,785
Davao 610,375
Dumaguete 63,411
Glan 48,882
Iba 22,791 F
Iloilo 244,827 G
Laoag 69,648 F
Legazpi 99,766 G
Lingayen 65,187 F
Lucena 107,880 G
Manila (cap.) 1,630,485 G
Marawi 53,812 G
Mati 78,178 H
Mondragon 20,423 H
Naga 90,712 G
Oroquieta 47,328 G
Palanan 10,295 G
Puerto Princesa 60,234 F
Roxas 81,183 G
San Jose 66,262 G
Siocon (Siokun) 29,515 G
Sorsogon 60,574 G
Surigao 79,745 H
Tacloban 102,523 H
Tarlac 175,691 G
Taytay 22,980 G
Tuguegarao 73,507 G
Vigan 33,483 F
Zamboanga 343,722 G

OTHER FEATURES

Babuyan (isls.) G
Balabac (isl.) F
Balabac (str.) F
Basilan (isl.) G 4
Batan (isls.) G 1
Bohol (isl.) G 4
Bugsuk (isl.) F 4
Buliluyan (cape) F 4
Busuanga (isl.) F 3
Cagayan (isls.) F 4
Cagayan Sulu (isl.) F 4
Calamian Group (isls.) F 3
Catanduanes (isl.) H 3
Cebu (isl.) G 3
Cuyo (isls.) G 3
Davao (gulf) H 4
Dinagat (isl.) H 3
Dumaran (isl.) G 3
Espiritu Santo (cape) H 3
Jolo (isl.) G 4
Leyte (isl.) H 3
Lubang (isls.) F 3
Luzon (isl.) G 2
Masbate (isl.) G 3
Matutum (mt.) G 4
Mindanao (isl.) H 4
Mindanao (sea) G 4
Mindoro (isl.) G 3
Mindoro (str.) F 3
Moro (gulf) G 4
Negros (isl.) G 4
Olutanga (isl.) G 4
Palawan (isl.) F 4
Palawan (passg.) F 4
Panay (isl.) G 3
Pangutaran Group (isls.) G 4
Philippine (sea) G 2
Polillo (isl.) G 3
Samar (isl.) H 3
San Agustin (cape) H 4
San Miguel (isls.) F 4
Sarangani (isls.) G 4
Siargao (isl.) H 4
Sibutu (passg.) F 4
Sibuyan (isl.) G 3
Sibuyan (sea) G 3
South China (sea) D 4
Sulu (arch.) G 4
Sulu (sea) G 4
Tagolo (pt.) G 4
Tapul Group (isls.) G 4
Tawitawi Group (isls.) G 4
Tinaca (pt.) H 4
Tubbataha (reefs) G 4
Visayan (sea) G 3

•Population of district, sub-district or division.

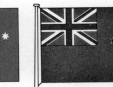

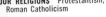

AUSTRALIA

AREA 2,966,136 sq. mi. (7,682,300 sq. km.)
POPULATION 14,576,330
CAPITAL Canberra
LARGEST CITY Sydney
HIGHEST POINT Mt. Kosciusko 7,310 ft. (2,228 m.)
LOWEST POINT Lake Eyre -39 ft. (-12 m.)
MONETARY UNIT Australian dollar
MAJOR LANGUAGE English
MAJOR RELIGIONS Protestantism, Roman Catholicism

NEW ZEALAND

AREA 103,736 sq. mi. (268,676 sq. km.)
POPULATION 3,175,737
CAPITAL Wellington
LARGEST CITY Auckland
HIGHEST POINT Mt. Cook 12,349 ft. (3,764 m.)
MONETARY UNIT New Zealand dollar
MAJOR LANGUAGES English, Maori
MAJOR RELIGIONS Protestantism, Roman Catholicism

AUSTRALIA

STATES and TERRITORIES

Ashmore and Cartier Is., Terr. of..........C 2
Australian Capital Territory 221,609...........H 7
Coral Sea Islands Territory..H 2
New South Wales 5,126,217..H 6
Norfolk Island 2,175.........L 5
Northern Territory 123,324..E 3
Queensland 2,295,123........G 4
South Australia 1,285,033...F 6
Tasmania 418,957...........H 8
Victoria 3,832,443..........G 7
Western Australia 1,273,624.B 5

CITIES and TOWNS

Adelaide (cap.), S. Aust. 882,520.........D 8
Albany, W. Aust. 15,222....B 6
Albury, N.S.W. 35,072.......H 7
Alice Springs, N. Terr. 18,395.E 4
Altona, Vic. 30,909.........J 3
Ararat, Vic. 8,336..........G 7
Armidale, N.S.W. 18,922....J 6
Ashfield, N.S.W. 41,253.....K 4
Auburn, N.S.W. 46,622......K 4
Ayr, Queens. 8,787.........H 3
Bairnsdale, Vic. 9,459.......H 7
Ballarat, Vic. 35,681.......G 7
Bankstown, N.S.W. 152,636..K 4
Bathurst, N.S.W. 19,640....H 6
Bega, Vic. 4,388............G 7
Bendigo, Vic. 31,841........G 7
Blackall, Queens. 1,609.....H 4
Blacktown, N.S.W. 181,139..K 4

Blue Mountains, N.S.W. 55,877.............J 6
Bordertown, S. Aust. 2,138..F 7
Botany, N.S.W. 34,703......L 4
Boulder-Kalgoorlie, W. Aust. 19,848..............C 6
Bourke, N.S.W. 3,326.......H 6
Bowen, Queens. 7,663.......H 3
Box Hill, Vic. 47,579........J 2
Brighton, S. Aust. 19,441...D 8
Brighton, Vic. 33,697.......K 3
Brisbane (cap.), Queens. 942,836.............K 3
Brisbane Water, N.S.W. 71,984............J 4
Broadmeadows, Vic. 103,540.J 2
Broken Hill, N.S.W. 26,913..G 6
Broome, W. Aust. 3,666.....C 3
Brunswick, Vic. 44,464......K 2
Bunbury, W. Aust. 21,749...B 6
Bundaberg, Queens. 32,560..J 4
Burnie-Somerset, Tas. 19,994............H 8
Burnside, S. Aust. 37,593...E 8
Burwood, Vic. 26,896.......K 4
Busselton, W. Aust. 6,463...A 6
Cairns, Queens. 48,557......H 3
Camberwell, Vic. 85,883....K 2
Campbelltown, S. Aust. 43,084............E 8
Canberra (cap.), A.C.T. *220,822..........H 7
Canterbury, N.S.W. 126,741.K 4
Carnarvon, W. Aust. 5,053..A 4
Casino, N.S.W. 9,743.......J 5
Caulfield, Vic. 69,922.......K 2
Ceduna, S. Aust. 2,794.....F 6
Cessnock-Bellbird, N.S.W. 16,916............J 6
Charleville, Queens. 3,523...H 5

Charters Towers, Queens. 6,823.............H 4
Chelsea, Vic. 26,034........H 4
Clermont, Queens. 1,659....H 4
Cloncurry, Queens. 1,961...G 4
Cobar, N.S.W. 3,583........H 6
Coburg, Vic. 55,035........K 2
Coffs Harbour, N.S.W. 16,020.J 6
Collie, W. Aust. 2,667......B 6
Collinsville, Queens. 2,756..H 4
Concord, N.S.W. 23,926....K 4
Condobolin, N.S.W. 3,355...H 6
Coober Pedy, S. Aust. 2,078.E 5
Cooma, N.S.W. 7,978.......H 7
Coonamble, N.S.W. 3,090...H 6
Cootamundra, N.S.W. 6,540.H 6
Cowra, N.S.W. 7,900........H 6
Croydon, Vic. 36,210.......L 2
Cunnamulla, Queens. 1,627.H 5
Dalby, Queens. 8,784.......J 5
Dandenong, Vic. 54,962....L 3
Darwin (cap.), N. Terr. 56,482.E 2
Deniliquin, N.S.W. 7,354....G 7
Derby, W. Aust. 2,933......C 3
Devonport, Tas. 21,424.....H 8
Doncaster and Templestowe, Vic. 90,660..........K 2
Drummoyne, N.S.W. 30,961..K 4
Dubbo, N.S.W. 23,986......H 6
Echuca, Vic. 7,943.........G 7
Elizabeth, S. Aust. 32,608..E 7
Eltham, Vic. 34,648........K 2
Enfield, S. Aust. 66,797....D 7
Esperance, W. Aust. 6,375..C 6
Essendon, Vic. 56,380......J 2
Fairfield, N.S.W. 129,557...K 4
Footscray, Vic. 49,756.....J 2
Forbes, N.S.W. 8,029.......H 6
Fremantle, W. Aust. 22,484..B 6
Gawler, S. Aust. 9,433......F 6

Geelong, Vic. 14,471.......G 7
Geraldton, W. Aust. 20,895..A 5
Gladstone, Queens. 22,083..J 4
Glen Innes, N.S.W. 6,052...J 5
Glenorchy, Tas. 41,019.....H 8
Gold Coast, Queens. 135,437............J 5
Goondiwindi, Queens. 3,576.H 5
Goulburn, N.S.W. 21,755....J 6
Grafton, N.S.W. 17,005.....J 5
Griffith, N.S.W. 13,187.....H 6
Gunnedah, N.S.W. 8,909....H 6
Gympie, Queens. 10,768....J 5
Hamilton, Vic. 9,751........G 7
Hawthorne, Vic. 30,689....K 2
Hay, N.S.W. 2,958..........H 6
Heidelberg, Vic. 64,757.....K 2
Hindmarsh, S. Aust. 7,593..D 8
Hobart (cap.), Tas. 128,603.H 8
Holyroyd, N.S.W. 80,116....K 4
Home Hill, Queens. 3,138...H 3
Hornsby, N.S.W. 111,081....K 3
Horsham, Vic. 12,034.......G 7
Hughenden, Queens. 1,657..G 4
Hurstville, N.S.W. 64,910...K 4
Ingham, Queens. 5,598......H 3
Innisfail, Queens. 7,933.....H 3
Inverell, N.S.W. 9,734......J 5
Kadina, S. Aust. 2,943......F 6
Kalgoorlie, W. Aust. 9,145..C 6
Katanning, W. Aust. 4,413..B 6
Katherine, N. Terr. 3,737...E 2
Keilor, Vic. 81,762..........J 2
Kempsey, N.S.W. 9,037.....J 6
Kensington and Norwood, S. Aust. 8,950.........E 8
Kew, Vic. 28,870...........K 2
Kingaroy, Queens. 5,134....J 5
Knox, Vic. 88,902..........L 2
Kogarah, N.S.W. 46,322....K 4

Kwinana-Newtown, W. Aust. 12,355...........B 2
Lane Cove, N.S.W. 29,113...L 4
Launceston, Tas. 31,273....H 8
Leichhardt, N.S.W. 57,332..L 4
Leigh Creek, S. Aust. 1,635.............F 6
Leonora, W. Aust. 524......C 5
Lismore, N.S.W. 24,033.....J 5
Lithgow, N.S.W. 12,793.....H 6
Liverpool, N.S.W. 92,715...K 4
Longreach, Queens. 2,971...G 4
Mackay, Queens. 35,361....H 4
Maitland, N.S.W. 38,865....J 6
Malvern, Vic. 43,211........K 2
Mandurah, W. Aust. 10,978..B 3
Maralinga, S. Aust..........E 6
Mareeba, Queens. 6,309....G 3
Marion, S. Aust. 66,580....D 8
Maroochydore-Mooloolaba, Queens. 17,460.......J 5
Marrickville, N.S.W. 83,448.L 4
Maryborough, Queens. 20,111............J 5
Maryborough, Vic. 7,858....G 7
Meekatharra, W. Aust. 989..B 5
Melbourne (cap.), Vic. 2,578,759.........K 2
Merredin, W. Aust. 3,520...B 6
Mildura, Vic. 15,763........G 6
Mingenew, W. Aust. 368....B 5
Mitcham, S. Aust. 60,309...D 8
Moora, W. Aust. 1,677......B 6
Moorabbin, Vic. 97,810.....K 3
Mordialloc, Vic. 27,869.....K 3
Moree, N.S.W. 10,459.......H 5
Mossman, Queens. 1,614....G 3
Mount Gambier, S. Aust. 18,193............G 7
Mount Isa, Queens. 23,679..F 4

Mount Morgan, Queens. 2,974.............J 4
Mudgee, N.S.W. 6,015......J 6
Murray Bridge, S. Aust. 8,664.F 7
Murwillumbah, N.S.W. 7,807.J 5
Muswellbrook, N.S.W. 8,548.J 6
Naracoorte, S. Aust. 4,758..F 7
Narrabri, N.S.W. 7,296.....J 6
Narrandera, N.S.W. 5,813...H 6
Narrogin, W. Aust. 4,969...B 6
Narromine, N.S.W. 2,994...H 6
Nedlands, W. Aust. 20,257..B 2
Newcastle, N.S.W. 135,207..J 6
New Norfolk, Tas. 6,243....H 8
Northam, W. Aust. 6,791....B 6
Northampton, W. Aust. 750..A 5
Northcote, Vic. 51,235......K 2
North Sydney, N.S.W. 48,500.L 4
Nowra-Bomaderry, N.S.W. 17,887............J 6
Nunawading, Vic. 97,052....K 2
Nyngan, N.S.W. 2,485......H 6
Oakleigh, Vic. 55,612.......K 2
Orange, N.S.W. 27,626.....H 6
Orbost, Vic. 2,586..........H 7
Parkes, N.S.W. 9,047.......H 6
Parramatta, N.S.W. 130,943..K 4
Penrith, N.S.W. 108,720....K 4
Perth (cap.), W. Aust. 809,035.B 2
Peterborough, S. Aust. 2,575.F 6
Port Adelaide, S. Aust. 35,407............D 7
Port Augusta, S. Aust. 15,566.F 6
Port Hedland, W. Aust. 12,948............B 3
Portland, Vic. 9,353.........G 7
Port Lincoln, S. Aust. 9,846..E 6
Port Melbourne, Vic. 8,585..J 6
Port Macquarie, N.S.W. 19,581............J 6

Port Pirie, S. Aust. 14,695..F 6
Prahan, Vic. 45,018.........K 2
Preston, Vic. 84,519........K 2
Proserpine, Queens. 3,058..H 4
Queenstown, Tas. 3,714....H 8
Randwick, N.S.W. 116,202..L 4
Red Cliffe, Queens. 42,223..J 5
Renmark, S. Aust. 3,475....G 6
Richmond, Vic. 24,506......K 2
Ringwood, Vic. 38,665......K 2
Rockdale, N.S.W. 83,719....K 4
Rockhampton, Queens. 50,146............H 4
Rockingham, W. Aust. 24,932.B 2
Roebourne, W. Aust. 1,688..B 4
Roma, Queens. 5,706.......H 5
Ryde, N.S.W. 88,948.......K 4
Saint George, Queens. 2,204.H 5
Saint Kilda, Vic. 49,366....K 2
Sale, Vic. 12,968...........H 7
Salisbury, S. Aust. 86,451..E 7
Sandringham, Vic. 31,175...K 3
Sarina, Queens. 2,815.......H 4
Seymour, Vic. 6,494........H 7
Shepparton-Mooroopna, Vic. †27,373............G 7
South Sydney, N.S.W. 30,776.L 4
Stanthorpe, Queens. 3,966..J 5
Stirling, W. Aust. 161,858...B 2
Strathfield, N.S.W. 25,882..K 4
Sunshine, Vic. 94,419......J 2
Sutherland, N.S.W. 165,336..K 5
Swan Hill, Vic. 8,398.......G 7
Sydney (cap.), N.S.W. 2,876,508.........L 4
Tamworth, N.S.W. 29,657...J 6
Taree, N.S.W. 14,697.......J 6
Tea Tree Gully, S. Aust. 67,237............E 7

(continued on following page)

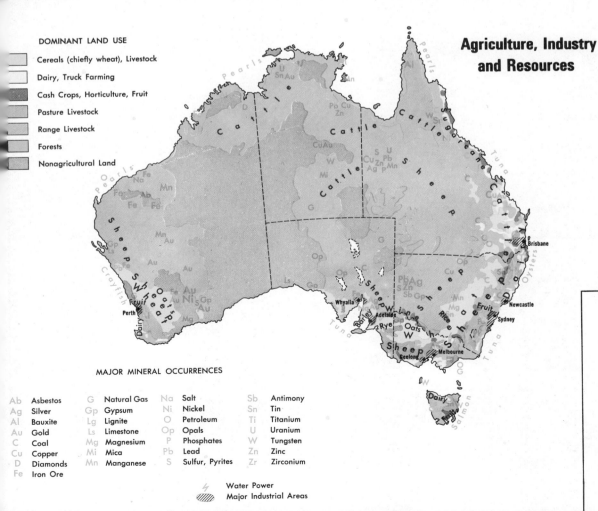

Agriculture, Industry and Resources

DOMINANT LAND USE

Cereals (chiefly wheat), Livestock
Dairy, Truck Farming
Cash Crops, Horticulture, Fruit
Pasture Livestock
Range Livestock
Forests
Nonagricultural Land

MAJOR MINERAL OCCURRENCES

Ab	Asbestos	G	Natural Gas	Na	Salt	Sb	Antimony
Ag	Silver	Gp	Gypsum	Ni	Nickel	Sn	Tin
Al	Bauxite	Lg	Lignite	O	Petroleum	Ti	Titanium
Au	Gold	Ls	Limestone	Op	Opals	U	Uranium
C	Coal	Mg	Magnesium	P	Phosphates	W	Tungsten
Cu	Copper	Mi	Mica	Pb	Lead	Zn	Zinc
D	Diamonds	Mn	Manganese	S	Sulfur, Pyrites	Zr	Zirconium
Fe	Iron Ore						

Water Power
Major Industrial Areas

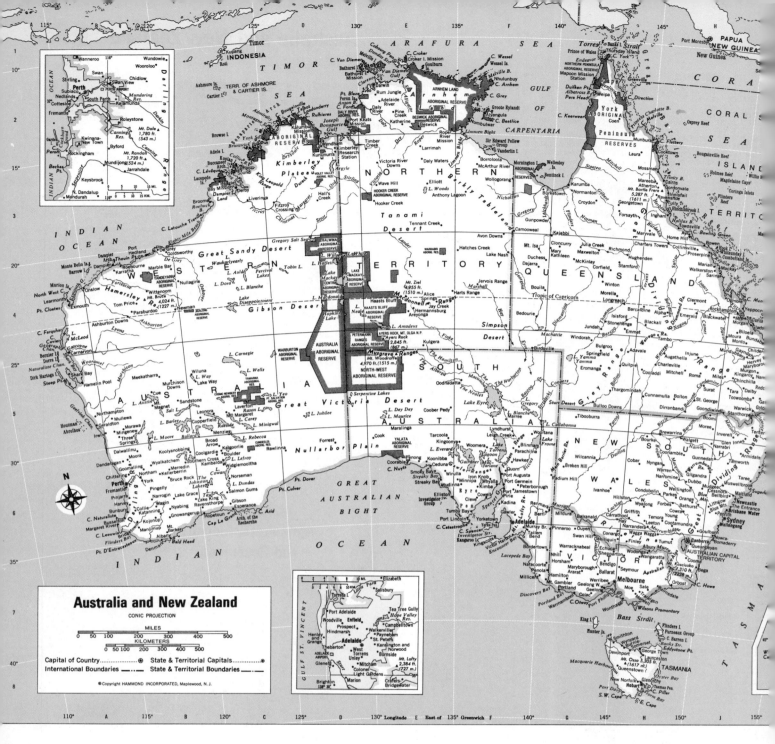

Australia and New Zealand

CONIC PROJECTION

MILES
0 50 100 200 300 400 500
KILOMETERS
0 50 100 200 300 400 500

Capital of Country................⊛   State & Territorial Capitals.............⊛
International Boundaries .—.—.   State & Territorial Boundaries .—.—.

® Copyright HAMMOND INCORPORATED, Maplewood, N.J.

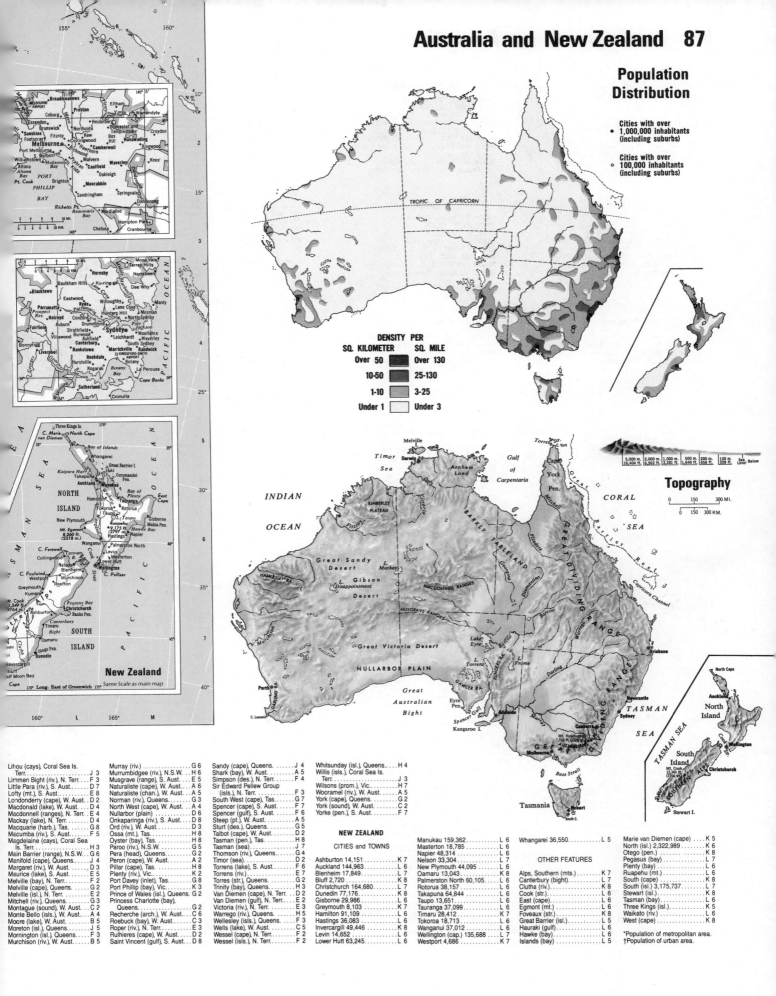

Population Distribution

- Cities with over 1,000,000 inhabitants (including suburbs)
- Cities with over 100,000 inhabitants (including suburbs)

DENSITY PER	
SQ. KILOMETER	SQ. MILE
Over 50	Over 130
10-50	25-130
1-10	3-25
Under 1	Under 3

Topography

Melbourne inset

MELBOURNE AIRPORT, Broadmeadows, Coburg, Preston, Eltham, Warrandyte, Essendon, Brunswick, Northcote, Heidelberg, Templestowe, Croydon, Sunshine, Fitzroy, Collingwood, Doncaster, Box Hill, Nunawading, Ringwood, Footscray, Kew, Camberwell, Port Melbourne, Richmond, Malvern, Waverley, Knox, Williamstown, St. Kilda, Caulfield, Oakleigh, Altona, Holbrook, Brighton, Moorabbin, Springvale, Altona Bay, PORT PHILLIP BAY, Sandringham, Dandenong, Pt. Cook, Ricketts Pt., Beaumaris, Mordialloc, Hampton Park, Chelsea, Cranbourne

Sydney inset

Terrey Hills, Mona Vale, Hornsby, Narrabeen, Baulkham Hills, Ku-ring-gai, Dee Why, Blacktown, Eastwood, Willoughby, Manly, Parramatta, Ryde, Lane Cove, Prospect Res., Holroyd, Concord, Hunters Hill, Mosman, Fairfield, Auburn, Strathfield, North Sydney, Burwood, Leichhardt, Port Jackson, Liverpool, Ashfield, Woollahra, Canterbury, South Sydney, Waverley, Bankstown, Marrickville, Randwick, KINGSFORD-SMITH AIRPORT, Rockdale, Kogarah, Botany, Hurstville, Botany Bay, La Perouse, Cape Banks, Sutherland, Cronulla

New Zealand inset

Three Kings Is., C. Maria van Diemen, North Cape, Bay of Islands, Whangarei, Great Barrier I., Kaipara Har., Takapuna, Coromandel Pen., NORTH ISLAND, Auckland, Manukau, Bay of Plenty, Hamilton, Tauranga, East Cape, New Plymouth, Tokoroa, Rotorua, Gisborne, L. Taupo, Mahia Pen., Mt. Egmont 8,260 ft. (2518 m.), Ruapehu 9,175 m. (2797 m.), Hawke Bay, Hastings, Napier, Wanganui, Palmerston North, C. Farewell, Levin, Tasman B., Masterton, Collingwood, Nelson, Lower Hutt, Cook Str., Westport, Blenheim, Wellington, Greymouth, Murchison, C. Palliser, Kumara, Reefton, Southern Alps, Mt. Cook 12,349 ft. (3764 m.), Ashburton, Banks Pen., Christchurch, Pegasus Bay, Timaru, Canterbury Bight, Oamaru, Otago Pen., SOUTH ISLAND, Invercargill, Dunedin, Bluff, Half Moon Bay

New Zealand Same Scale as main map

Topography main map

Melville, Timor Sea, Darwin, Arnhem Land, Gulf of Carpentaria, Cape York, Torres Str., C. York, KIMBERLEY PLATEAU, Victoria, BARKLY TABLELAND, Mitchell, Great Barrier Reef, INDIAN OCEAN, Fitzroy, HAMERSLEY RA., Great Sandy Desert, L. Mackay, MACDONNELL RANGES, Georgina, Flinders, CORAL SEA, Capricorn Channel, L. Disappointment, Gibson Desert, Diamantina, MUSGRAVE RANGES, Barcoo, GREAT DIVIDING RANGE, Murchison, Great Victoria Desert, Lake Eyre, L. Torrens, L. Frome, Brisbane, NULLARBOR PLAIN, GAWLER RA., Darling, Perth, DARLING RA., FLINDERS RA., Eyre Pen., Spencer Gulf, Murray, Newcastle, C. Leeuwin, Great Australian Bight, Adelaide, Canberra, Sydney, Kangaroo I., Mt. Kosciusko 7,310 ft. (2228 m.), TASMAN SEA, GREAT DIVIDING RANGE, Melbourne, Bass Strait, Tasmania, Hobart, South C., North Cape, Auckland, North Island, TASMAN SEA, South Island, Mt. Cook 12,349 ft. (3764 m.), SOUTHERN ALPS, Wellington, Cook Str., Christchurch, Stewart I.

FIJI

AREA 7,055 sq. mi. (18,272 sq. km.)
POPULATION 588,068
CAPITAL Suva
LARGEST CITY Suva
HIGHEST POINT Tomaniivi 4,341 ft. (1,323 m.)
MONETARY UNIT Fijian dollar
MAJOR LANGUAGES Fijian, Hindi, English
MAJOR RELIGIONS Protestantism, Hinduism

KIRIBATI

AREA 291 sq. mi. (754 sq. km.)
POPULATION 56,213
CAPITAL Bairiki (Tarawa)
HIGHEST POINT (on Banaba I.) 285 ft. (87 m.)
MONETARY UNIT Australian dollar
MAJOR LANGUAGES I-Kiribati, English
MAJOR RELIGIONS Protestantism, Roman Catholicism

NAURU

AREA 7.7 sq. mi. (20 sq. km.)
POPULATION 7,254
CAPITAL Yaren (district)
MONETARY UNIT Australian dollar
MAJOR LANGUAGES Nauruan, English
MAJOR RELIGION Protestantism

SOLOMON ISLANDS

AREA 11,500 sq. mi. (29,785 sq. km.)
POPULATION 221,000
CAPITAL Honiara
HIGHEST POINT Mount Popomanatseu 7,647 ft. (2,331 m.)
MONETARY UNIT Solomon Islands dollar
MAJOR LANGUAGES English, pidgin English, Melanesian dialects
MAJOR RELIGIONS Tribal religions, Protestantism, Roman Catholicism

TONGA

AREA 270 sq. mi. (699 sq. km.)
POPULATION 90,128
CAPITAL Nuku'alofa
LARGEST CITY Nuku'alofa
HIGHEST POINT 3,389 ft. (1,033 m.)
MONETARY UNIT pa'anga
MAJOR LANGUAGES Tongan, English
MAJOR RELIGION Protestantism

TUVALU

AREA 9.78 sq. mi. (25.33 sq. km.)
POPULATION 7,349
CAPITAL Fongafale (Funafuti)
HIGHEST POINT 15 ft. (4.6 m.)
MONETARY UNIT Australian dollar
MAJOR LANGUAGES English, Tuvaluan
MAJOR RELIGION Protestantism

Abaiang (atoll) 3,296 . . . . H 5
Abemama (atoll) 2,300 . . . . H 5
Adamstown (cap.), Pitcairn Is. 54 . . . . N 8
Admiralty (isls.) . . . . E 6
Agaña (cap.), Guam 896 . . . . . . E 4
Agrihan (isl.) . . . . E 4
Ailinglapalap (atoll) 1,385 . . . . . G 5
Ailuk (atoll) 413 . . . . H 4
Aitutaki (atoll) 2,348 . . . . K 7
Alofi (cap.), Niue 960 . . . . K 7
Alotau 4,310 . . . . E 7
Ambrym (isl.) 6,324 . . . . G 7
American Samoa 32,297 . . . . . . J 7
Anaa (atoll) 444 . . . . M 7
Angaur (isl.) 243 . . . . D 5
Apataki (atoll) . . . . M 7
Apia (cap.), W. Samoa 33,100 . . J 7
Arorae (atoll) 1,626 . . . . H 6
Atafu (atoll) 577 . . . . J 6
Atiu (isl.) 1,225 . . . . L 8
Austral (isls.) 5,208 . . . . L 8
Avarua (cap.), Cook Is. . . . . L 8
Babelthuap (isl.) 10,391 . . . . . . D 5
Bairiki (cap.), Kiribati 1,777 . . . . H 5
Baker (isl.) . . . . J 5
Banaba (isl.) 2,314 . . . . G 6
Banks (isls.) 3,158 . . . . G 7
Belau (Palau) 12,116 . . . . D 5
Belep (isls.) 624 . . . . G 7
Bellona (reefs) . . . . G 8
Beru (atoll) 2,318 . . . . H 6
Bikini (atoll) . . . . G 4
Bismarck (arch.) 218,339 . . . . . . E 6
Bonin (isls.) 1,879 . . . . E 3
Bora-Bora (isl.) 2,572 . . . . L 7
Bougainville (isl.) 71,761 . . . . . . F 6
Bounty (isls.) . . . . H 10
Bourail 3,149 . . . . G 8
Butaritari (atoll) 2,971 . . . . H 5
Canton (isl.) . . . . J 6
Capitol Hill (cap.), No. Marianas 592 . . . . E 4
Caroline (isl.) . . . . M 7
Caroline (isls.) . . . . E 5
Chichi (isl.) 1,879 . . . . E 3
Choiseul (isl.) 10,349 . . . . F 6
Christmas (Kiritimati) (isl.) 674 . . . . L 5
Cook (isls.) 17,695 . . . . K 7
Coral (sea) . . . . F 7
Danger (Pukapuka) (atoll) 797 . . . . K 7
Daru 7,127 . . . . E 6
Disappointment (isls.) 373. . . . . . N 7
Ducie (isl.) . . . . O 8
Easter (isl.) 1,598 . . . . Q 8
Ebon (atoll) 887. . . . . G 5
Efate (isl.) 18,038 . . . . G 7
Enderbury (isl.) . . . . J 6
Enewetak (Eniwetok) (atoll) 542 . . . . G 4
Erromanga (isl.) 945. . . . . H 7
Espíritu Santo (isl.) 16,220 . . . . G 7
Fais (isl.) 207 . . . . E 5
Fakaofo (atoll) 654 . . . . J 6
Fanning (Tabuaeran) (isl.) 340 L 5
Faraulep (atoll) 132 . . . . E 5
Fatuhiva (isl.) 386 . . . . N 7
Fiji 588,068 . . . . H 8
Flint (isl.) . . . . L 6
Fly (riv.) . . . . E 6
Fongafale (cap.), Tuvalu . . . . . . H 6
French Polynesia 137,382. . . . . . L 8
Funafuti (atoll) 2,120 . . . . H 6
Futuna (Hoorn) (isls.) 3,173 . . J 7
Gambier (isls.) 556 . . . . N 8
Gardner (Nukumaroro)(isl.). . . . . J 6
Gilbert (isls.) 47,711 . . . . H 6
Greenwich (Kapingamarangi) (atoll) 508 . . . . F 5
Guadalcanal (isl.) 46,619 . . . . . F 7
Guam (isl.) 105,979 . . . . E 4
Hall (isls.) 647 . . . . F 5
Hawaiian (isls.) 964,691. . . . . . . J 3
Henderson (isl.) . . . . O 8
Hivaoa (isl.) 1,159 . . . . N 6
Honiara (cap.), Solomon Is. 14,942 . . . . F 6
Hoorn (isls.) 3,173 . . . . J 7
Howland (isl.) . . . . J 5
Huahine (isl.) 3,140 . . . . L 7
Hull (Orona) (atoll) . . . . J 6
Huon (gulf) . . . . E 6
Ifalik (atoll) 389 . . . . E 5
Iwo (isl.) . . . . E 3
Jaluit (atoll) 1,450 . . . . G 5
Jarvis (isl.) . . . . K 5
Johnston (atoll) 327 . . . . K 4
Kadavu (Kandavu) (isl.) 8,699 H 7
Kapingamarangi (atoll) 508. . . . . F 5
Kavieng 4,633 . . . . E 6
Kermadec (isls.) 5. . . . . J 9
Kieta 3,491 . . . . F 6
Kimbe 4,662. . . . . E 6
Kimbe (reef) . . . . K 5
Kiribati 57,500 . . . . H 5
Kiritimati (isl.) 674. . . . . L 5
Kolonia (cap.), Micronesia 5,549 . . . . F 5
Koror (cap.), Belau 6,222 . . . . . D 5
Kosrae (isl.) 5,491 . . . . G 5
Kwajalein (atoll) 6,624 . . . . G 5
Lae 61,617. . . . . E 6
Lau Group (isls.) 14,452 . . . . . . J 7
Lavongai (isl.) . . . . F 6
Lifu (isl.) 7,585. . . . . G 8
Line (isls.) . . . . K 5
Little Makin (atoll) 1,445 . . . . . . H 5
Lord Howe (Ontong Java) (isl.) 1,082 . . . . G 6
Lord Howe (isl.) 287 . . . . G 9
Lorengau 3,986. . . . . E 6
Louisiade (arch.) . . . . F 7
Loyalty (isls.) 14,518 . . . . G 8
Luganville 4,935 . . . . G 7
Madang 21,335. . . . . E 6

Majuro (atoll) (cap.), Marshall Is. 8,583. . . . . H 5
Makin (Butaritari) (atoll) 2,971 H 5
Malaita (isl.) 50,912 . . . . G 6
Malden (isl.) . . . . L 6
Malekula (isl.) 15,931 . . . . G 7
Maloelap (atoll) 763 . . . . H 5
Mangaia (isl.) 1,364 . . . . L 8
Mangareva (isl.) 556. . . . . N 8
Manihiki (atoll) 405 . . . . K 7
Manra (isl.) . . . . K 6
Manua (isls.) 1,459 . . . . K 7
Manus (isl.) 25,844. . . . . E 6
Marcus (isl.) . . . . F 3
Maré (isl.) 4,156 . . . . G 8
Marianas, Northern 16,780. . . . . E 4
Mariana Trench . . . . E 4
Marquesas (isls.) 5,419 . . . . . . N 6
Marshall Islands 30,873. . . . . . . G 4
Marutea (atoll) . . . . N 8
Mata Utu (cap.), Wallis and Futuna 558 . . . . J 7
Mauke (isl.) 684 . . . . L 8
Melanesia (reg.) . . . . E 5
Micronesia (reg.) . . . . E 4
Micronesia, Federated States of 73,160 . . . . F 5
Midway (isls.) 453 . . . . J 3
Mili (atoll) 763 . . . . H 5
Moen (isl.) 10,351. . . . . F 5

Moorea (isl.) 5,788 . . . . L 8
Mururoa (isl.) . . . .
Nadi 6,938 . . . .
Namonuito (atoll) 783. . . . .
Namorik (atoll) 617. . . . .
Nanumea (atoll) 844. . . . .
Nauru 7,254 . . . .
Ndeni (isl.) 4,854. . . . .
New Britain (isl.) 148,773 . . . . . .
New Caledonia 133,233 . . . .
New Caledonia (isl.) 118,715 . . . .
New Georgia (isl.) 16,472 . . . . . .
New Guinea (isl.) . . . .
New Ireland (isl.) 65,657 . . . .
Ngatik (atoll) 560. . . . .
Ngulu (atoll) 21 . . . .
Niuatoputapu (isl.) 1,650 . . . .
Niue (isl.) 3,578. . . . .
Niutao (atoll) 866 . . . .
Nomoi (isls.) 1,879 . . . .
Nonouti (atoll) 2,223. . . . .
Norfolk Island (terr.) 2,175.. . . . .
Northern Marianas 116,780 . . . . .
Nouméa (cap.), New Caled. 56,078 . . . .
Nui (atoll) 603 . . . .
Nuku'alofa (cap.), Tonga 18,356 . . . . J
Nukuhiva (isl.) 1,484. . . . .

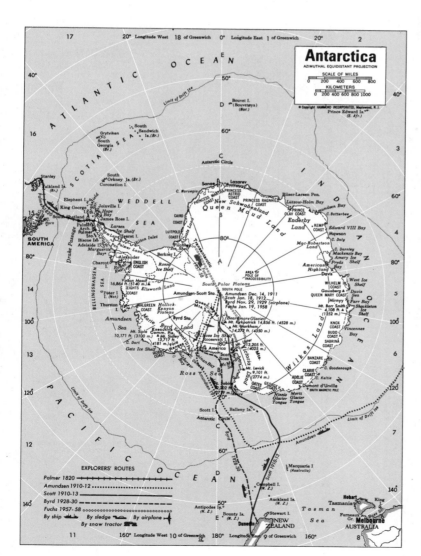

VANUATU

AREA 5,700 sq. mi. (14,763 sq. km.)
POPULATION 112,596
CAPITAL Vila
HIGHEST POINT Mt. Tabwemasana 6,165 ft. (1,879 m.)
MONETARY UNIT vatu
MAJOR LANGUAGES Bislama, English, French
MAJOR RELIGIONS Christian, animist

WESTERN SAMOA

AREA 1,133 sq. mi. (2,934 sq. km.)
POPULATION 158,130
CAPITAL Apia
LARGEST CITY Apia
HIGHEST POINT Mt. Silisili 6,094 ft. (1,857 m.)
MONETARY UNIT tala
MAJOR LANGUAGES Samoan, English
MAJOR RELIGIONS Protestantism, Roman Catholicism

*City and suburbs.
●Population of urban area.

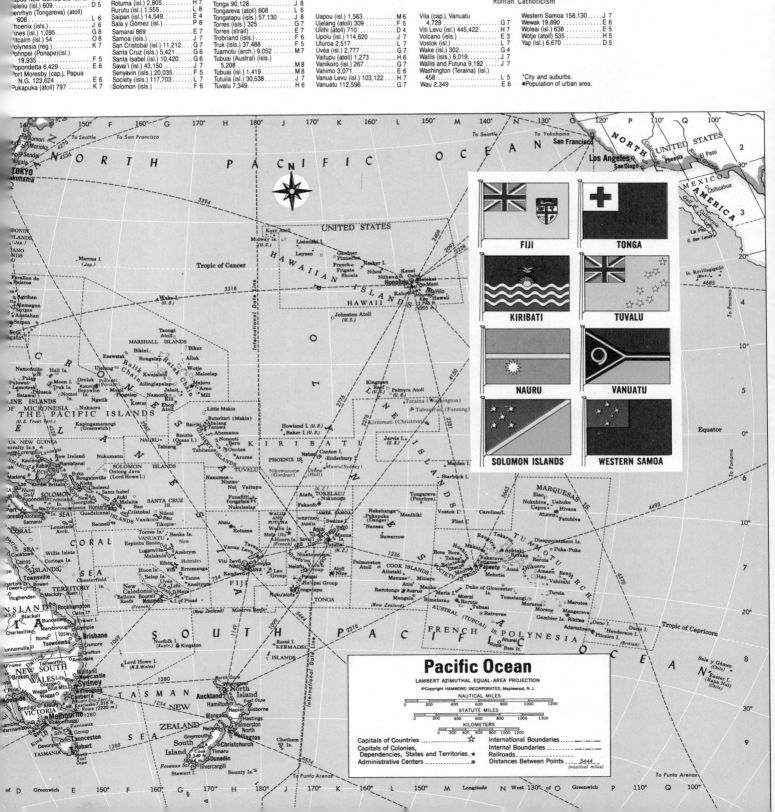

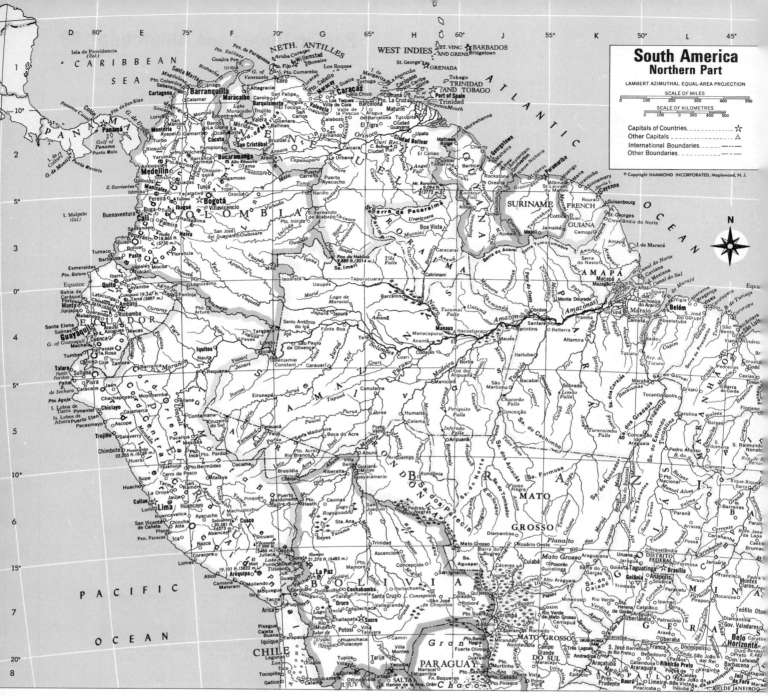

South America — Northern Part

ARGENTINA	Bell Ville 26,559	H 10	Miramar 15,473	J 11	San Rafael 7,047	G 10	Salado (riv.)	H 9	Real, Cordillera (mts.)	G 7	CITIES and TOWNS
PROVINCES	Bolívar 16,382	H 11	Necochea 50,939	J 11	Santa Cruz 2,353	G 14	San Antonio (cape)	J 11	Titicaca (lake)	F 7	
	Buenos Aires (cap.)		Neuquén 90,037	G 11	Santa Fe 287,240	H 10	San Martín (lake)	F 13			Alagoinhas 76,377	N 6
Buenos Aires 10,796,036	H 11	*9,927,404	H 10	Olavarría 63,686	H 11	Santa Rosa 51,689	H 11	San Matías (gulf)	H 12	BRAZIL	Alcobaça 3,430	
Catamarca 206,204	G 9	Campana 51,498	J 10	Paraná 159,581	J 10	Santiago del Estero 148,357	H 9	Staten (Los Estados) (isl.)	H 14	STATES	Alegrete 54,786	
Chaco 692,410	H 9	Catamarca *88,432	H 9	Pehuajó 25,613	H 11	Tandil 78,821	J 9	Tierra del Fuego (isl.)	G 14		Amapá 2,676	
Chubut 262,196	6 12	Chivilcoy 43,779	H 11	Pergamino 68,989	H 10	Tartagal 31,367	H 8	Tres Puntas (cape)	G 13	Acre 301,605	F 5	Amarante 6,848	
Córdoba 2,407,135	H 10	Comodoro Rivadavia 96,865	G 13	Plaza Huincul 7,988	G 11	Trelew 52,073	G 12	Uruguay (riv.)	J 9	Alagoas 1,987,581	N 5	Anápolis 160,520	L 7
Corrientes 657,716	J 9	Concepción del Uruguay		Posadas 139,941	J 9	Trenque Lauquen 22,504	H 11	Valdés (pen.)	H 12	Amapá (terr.) 175,634	K 3	Andradina 42,036	
Distrito Federal 2,908,001	J 10	46,065	J 10	Presidencia Roque Sáenz		Tres Arroyos 42,118	J 11			Amazonas 1,432,066	G 5	Aracaju 288,106	
Entre Ríos 902,241	J 10	Concordia 93,618	J 10	Peña 49,261	J 9	Ushuaia 10,988	G 14	BOLIVIA	Bahia 9,474,263	M 6	Araçatuba 1,113,486	
Formosa 292,479	H 8	Córdoba *982,018	G 10	Puerto Madryn 20,709	G 12	Valcheta 2,994	G 12		Ceará 5,294,876	N 5	Araguari 73,302	
Jujuy 408,514	G 8	Corrientes 179,590	J 9	Punta Alta 54,375	H 11	Venado Tuerto 46,775	H 10	CITIES and TOWNS	Distrito Federal 1,177,393	L 7	Arapiraca 84,133	
La Pampa 207,132	G 11	Cruz del Eje 23,473	H 10	Rafaela 53,152	H 10	Viedma 24,338	H 12		Espírito Santo 2,023,821	M 8	Araraquara 77,202	
La Rioja 163,342	G 9	Curuzú Cuatiá 24,955	J 9	Rawson 12,981	H 12	Villa Dolores 21,508	G 10	Cochabamba 204,684	G 7	Goiás 3,865,482	L 6	Araxá 51,339	
Mendoza 1,187,305	G 10	Embarcación 9,016	G 8	Reconquista 32,442	H 9	Villa María *67,400	H 10	Guaqui 2,266	G 7	Maranhão 4,002,599	L 5	Bacabal 43,229	
Misiones 579,579	K 9	Esperanza 22,838	H 10	Resistencia *218,438	J 9			Guayamerín 1,470	G 6	Mato Grosso 1,141,661	J 6	Bahia (Salvador) 1,496,276	N 6
Neuquén 241,904	G 11	Formosa 95,067	J 9	Rinconada	G 8	OTHER FEATURES	Huanchaca	G 7	Mato Grosso do Sul		Barbacena 69,675	
Río Negro 383,896	G 12	Gaimán 2,651	G 12	Río Cuarto 110,148	H 10			La Paz (cap.) 635,283	G 7	1,370,333	J 8	Barcelos 1,846	
Salta 662,369	G 8	Gastre	G 12	Río Gallegos 43,479	G 14	Aconcagua (mt.)	G 10	Oruro 124,213	G 7	Minas Gerais 13,390,805	M 7	Barra do Garças	
San Juan 469,973	G 10	General Alvear 21,250	G 11	Río Grande 13,271	G 14	Andes de Patagonia (mts.)	F 14	Potosí 77,397	G 7	Pará 3,411,868	K 4	Barretos 65,294	
San Luis 212,837	G 10	General Pico 30,180	H 11	Rivadavia	H 8	Argentino (lake)	F 14	Puerto Suárez 1,159	J 7	Paraíba 2,772,600	N 5	Bauru 178,861	
Santa Cruz 114,479	G 13	General Roca 38,296	G 11	Rosario *954,606	H 10	Bermejo (riv.)	H 9	Santa Cruz 254,682	H 7	Paraná 7,630,466	K 8	Bebedouro 39,070	
Santa Fe 2,457,188	H 9	Godoy Cruz 141,553	G 10	Rosario de la Frontera 13,531	H 9	Colorado (riv.)	H 11	Sucre (cap.) 63,625	H 7	Pernambuco 6,147,102	N 5	Belém 758,117	
Santiago del Estero 652,318	H 9	Goya 47,357	J 9	Salta 260,323	G 8	Estados, Los (isl.)	H 14	Tarija 38,916	H 8	Piauí 2,140,066	M 5	Belo Horizonte †2,541,788	N 7
Tierra del Fuego, Antártida,		Jáchal 8,832	G 10	San Antonio de los Cobres		Gran Chaco (reg.)	H 8			Rio de Janeiro 11,297,327	M 8	Benjamin Constant 6,563	
e Islas del Atlántico		Jujuy 124,487	G 8	2,357	G 8	Iguassú (falls)	K 9	OTHER FEATURES	Rio Grande do Norte		Blumenau 144,819	
Sur 29,451	G 14	La Plata *560,341	J 11	San Carlos de Bariloche		Magellan (str.)	G 14		1,899,720	N 5	Boa Vista 43,131	
Tucumán 968,066	G 9	La Rioja 66,826	G 10	48,222	F 12	Maipo (mt.)	G 10	Abuná (riv.)	G 6	Rio Grande do Sul		Borba 5,366	
		Liberador General San Martín		San Francisco *58,616	H 10	Nahuel Huapi (lake)	F 12	Beni (riv.)	G 7	7,777,212	K 9	Botucatu 56,316	
CITIES and TOWNS		30,814	G 8	San Juan *290,479	G 10	Negro (riv.)	H 11	Desaguadero (riv.)	G 7	Rondônia 492,810	H 6	Bragança 1,208	
		Lincoln 19,009	H 10	San Julián 4,278	G 13	Ojos del Salado (mt.)	G 9	Grande (riv.)	H 7	Roraima (terr.) 79,153	H 3	Brasiléia 4,835	
Azul 43,582	H 11	Maquinchao 1,295	G 12	San Luis 70,632	G 10	Pampas (plain)	H 11	Guaporé (riv.)	H 7	Santa Catarina 3,628,751	K 9	Brasília (cap.) 411,305	L 7
Bahía Blanca *220,765	H 11	Mar del Plata 407,024	J 11	San Miguel de Tucumán		Paraná (riv.)	F 12	Illampu (mt.)	G 7	São Paulo 25,040,698	L 8	Brejo 5,859	
Balcarce 28,985	J 11	Mercedes 50,856	G 10	*496,914	H 9	Plata, Río de la (est.)	J 11	Mamoré (riv.)	H 6	Sergipe 1,141,834	N 6	Brumado 24,663	
				San Nicolás 96,313	J 10	Salado (riv.)	G 11	Poopó (lake)	G 7			(continued on following p...)

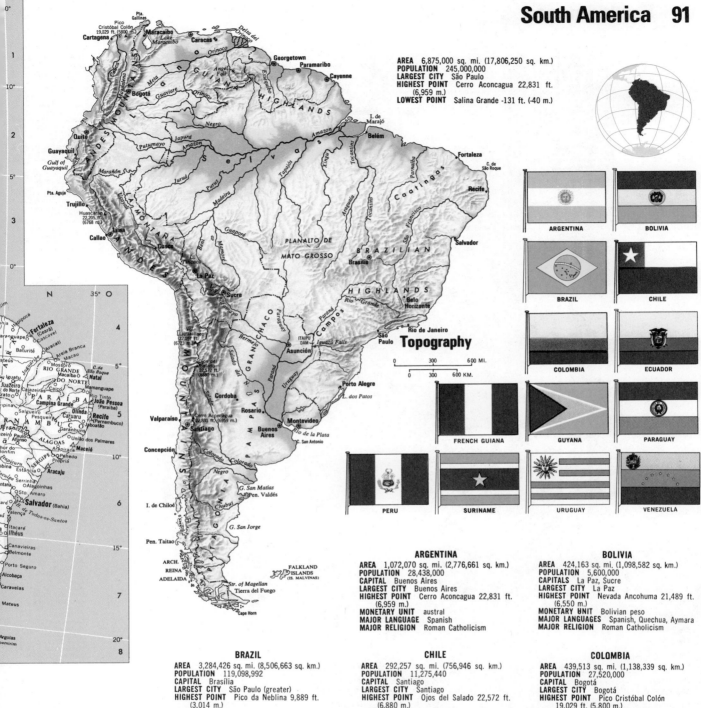

AREA 6,875,000 sq. mi. (17,806,250 sq. km.)
POPULATION 245,000,000
LARGEST CITY São Paulo
HIGHEST POINT Cerro Aconcagua 22,831 ft.
(6,959 m.)
LOWEST POINT Salina Grande -131 ft. (-40 m.)

Topography

0   300   600 MI.
0   300   600 KM.

Flags: ARGENTINA, BOLIVIA, BRAZIL, CHILE, COLOMBIA, ECUADOR, FRENCH GUIANA, GUYANA, PARAGUAY, PERU, SURINAME, URUGUAY, VENEZUELA

ARGENTINA
AREA 1,072,070 sq. mi. (2,776,661 sq. km.)
POPULATION 28,438,000
CAPITAL Buenos Aires
LARGEST CITY Buenos Aires
HIGHEST POINT Cerro Aconcagua 22,831 ft.
(6,959 m.)
MONETARY UNIT austral
MAJOR LANGUAGE Spanish
MAJOR RELIGION Roman Catholicism

BOLIVIA
AREA 424,163 sq. mi. (1,098,582 sq. km.)
POPULATION 5,600,000
CAPITALS La Paz, Sucre
LARGEST CITY La Paz
HIGHEST POINT Nevada Ancohuma 21,489 ft.
(6,550 m.)
MONETARY UNIT Bolivian peso
MAJOR LANGUAGES Spanish, Quechua, Aymara
MAJOR RELIGION Roman Catholicism

BRAZIL
AREA 3,284,426 sq. mi. (8,506,663 sq. km.)
POPULATION 119,098,992
CAPITAL Brasília
LARGEST CITY São Paulo (greater)
HIGHEST POINT Pico da Neblina 9,889 ft.
(3,014 m.)
MONETARY UNIT cruzeiro
MAJOR LANGUAGE Portuguese
MAJOR RELIGION Roman Catholicism

CHILE
AREA 292,257 sq. mi. (756,946 sq. km.)
POPULATION 11,275,440
CAPITAL Santiago
LARGEST CITY Santiago
HIGHEST POINT Ojos del Salado 22,572 ft.
(6,880 m.)
MONETARY UNIT Chilean escudo
MAJOR LANGUAGE Spanish
MAJOR RELIGION Roman Catholicism

COLOMBIA
AREA 439,513 sq. mi. (1,138,339 sq. km.)
POPULATION 27,520,000
CAPITAL Bogotá
LARGEST CITY Bogotá
HIGHEST POINT Pico Cristóbal Colón
19,029 ft. (5,800 m.)
MONETARY UNIT Colombian peso
MAJOR LANGUAGE Spanish
MAJOR RELIGION Roman Catholicism

ECUADOR
AREA 109,483 sq. mi. (283,561 sq. km.)
POPULATION 8,354,000
CAPITAL Quito
LARGEST CITY Guayaquil
HIGHEST POINT Chimborazo 20,561 ft.
(6,267 m.)
MONETARY UNIT sucre
MAJOR LANGUAGES Spanish, Quechua
MAJOR RELIGION Roman Catholicism

FRENCH GUIANA
AREA 35,135 sq. mi. (91,000 sq. km.)
POPULATION 73,022
CAPITAL Cayenne
LARGEST CITY Cayenne
HIGHEST POINT 2,723 ft. (830 m.)
MONETARY UNIT French franc
MAJOR LANGUAGE French
MAJOR RELIGIONS Roman Catholicism,
Protestantism

GUYANA
AREA 83,000 sq. mi. (214,970 sq. km.)
POPULATION 820,000
CAPITAL Georgetown
LARGEST CITY Georgetown
HIGHEST POINT Mt. Roraima 9,094 ft.
(2,772 m.)
MONETARY UNIT Guyana dollar
MAJOR LANGUAGES English, Hindi
MAJOR RELIGIONS Christianity, Hinduism,
Islam

PARAGUAY
AREA 157,047 sq. mi. (406,752 sq. km.)
POPULATION 2,973,000
CAPITAL Asunción
LARGEST CITY Asunción
HIGHEST POINT Amambay Range
2,264 ft. (690 m.)
MONETARY UNIT guaraní
MAJOR LANGUAGES Spanish, Guaraní
MAJOR RELIGION Roman Catholicism

PERU
AREA 496,222 sq. mi. (1,285,215 sq. km.)
POPULATION 17,031,221
CAPITAL Lima
LARGEST CITY Lima
HIGHEST POINT Huascarán 22,205 ft.
(6,768 m.)
MONETARY UNIT sol
MAJOR LANGUAGES Spanish, Quechua, Aymara
MAJOR RELIGION Roman Catholicism

SURINAME
AREA 55,144 sq. mi. (142,823 sq. km.)
POPULATION 354,860
CAPITAL Paramaribo
LARGEST CITY Paramaribo
HIGHEST POINT Julianatop 4,200 ft. (1,280 m.)
MONETARY UNIT Suriname guilder
MAJOR LANGUAGES Dutch, Hindi, Indonesian
MAJOR RELIGIONS Christianity, Islam,
Hinduism

URUGUAY
AREA 72,172 sq. mi. (186,925 sq. km.)
POPULATION 2,899,000
CAPITAL Montevideo
LARGEST CITY Montevideo
HIGHEST POINT Mirador Nacional 1,644 ft.
(501 m.)
MONETARY UNIT Uruguayan peso
MAJOR LANGUAGE Spanish
MAJOR RELIGION Roman Catholicism

VENEZUELA
AREA 352,143 sq. mi. (912,050 sq. km.)
POPULATION 14,313,000
CAPITAL Caracas
LARGEST CITY Caracas
HIGHEST POINT Pico Bolívar 16,427 ft.
(5,007 m.)
MONETARY UNIT Bolívar
MAJOR LANGUAGE Spanish
MAJOR RELIGION Roman Catholicism

Agriculture, Industry and Resources

MAJOR MINERAL OCCURRENCES

Al	Bauxite
Ag	Silver
Au	Gold
Be	Beryl
C	Coal
Cr	Chromium
Cu	Copper
D	Diamonds
Em	Emeralds
Fe	Iron Ore
G	Natural Gas
Hg	Mercury
Id	Iodine
Mi	Mica
Mn	Manganese
Mo	Molybdenum
N	Nitrates
Na	Salt
Ni	Nickel
O	Petroleum
P	Phosphates
Pb	Lead
Pt	Platinum
Q	Quartz Crystal
S	Sulfur
Sb	Antimony
Sn	Tin
U	Uranium
V	Vanadium
W	Tungsten
Zn	Zinc

⚡ Water Power

▨ Major Industrial Areas

DOMINANT LAND USE

- Wheat, Livestock
- Wheat, Corn, Livestock
- Cereals, Livestock
- Diversified Tropical Crops (chiefly plantation agriculture)
- Truck Farming, Horticulture, Special Crops
- Upland Cultivated Areas
- Intensive Livestock Ranching
- Upland Livestock Grazing, Limited Agriculture
- Extensive Livestock Ranching
- Forests
- Nonagricultural Land

(riv.) . . . . F 8
. . llan (str.) . . . . E 14
. . rino (isl.) . . . . O 10
. . o (mt.) . . . . G 14
. . gins (lake) . . . . G 13
. . del Salado (mt.) . . . . G 9
. . s (gulf) . . . . E 13
. . (pen.) . . . . E 13
. . a del Fuego (isl.) . . . . . . G 14

COLOMBIA

CITIES and TOWNS

. . ca 7,613 . . . . F 2
. . ancabermeja 87,191 . . . . . F 2
. . anquilla 661,009 . . . . F 1
. . otá (cap.) 2,696,270 . . . . . F 3
. . ar . . . . E 3
. . aramanga 291,661 . . . . . . F 2
. . aventura 115,770 . . . . E 3
. . a 71,016 . . . . E 3
. . 898,253 . . . . E 3
. . agena 292,512 . . . . E 1
. . quinquirá 21,727 . . . . F 2
. . aga 42,546 . . . . F 1
. . uta 219,772 . . . . F 2
. . anco 20,756 . . . . F 2
. . atativá 27,892 . . . . F 3
. . encia 31,817 . . . . E 3
. . ué 176,223 . . . . F 3
. . es 30,871 . . . . E 3
. . cia 6,285 . . . . F 4
. . angué 34,396 . . . . E 2
. . izales 199,904 . . . . E 2
. . ellín 1,070,924 . . . . E 2
. . 1,637 . . . . F 3
. . oca 6,221 . . . . E 3
. . tería 89,583 . . . . F 2
. . va 105,476 . . . . F 3
. . ña 38,352 . . . . F 2
. . mira 140,481 . . . . E 3
. . aplona 31,817 . . . . E 2
. . eira 119,339 . . . . E 3
. . eira 174,128 . . . . E 3
. . ayán 77,669 . . . . E 3
. . rto Carreño 2,172 . . . . . . G 2
. . o Wilches 5,282 . . . . E 2
. . bdó 28,040 . . . . E 2
. . Marcos 26,542 . . . . F 1
. . nta Marta 102,484 . . . . . . F 1
. . celejo 68,797 . . . . F 2
. . gamoso 48,891 . . . . F 2
. . aco 38,742 . . . . E 3
. . a 51,620 . . . . F 2
. . avicencio 82,869 . . . . . . F 3
. . rumal 21,333 . . . . E 2

OTHER FEATURES

. . o Ritacuva (mt.) . . . . F 2
. . aporis (riv.) . . . . F 3
. . auca (riv.) . . . . G 2
. . aquetá (riv.) . . . . F 4
. . asanare (riv.) . . . . E 2
. . auca (riv.) . . . . E 2
. . entral, Cordillera (mts.) . . . E 2
. . uainía (riv.) . . . . G 3
. . uajira (pen.) . . . . F 1
. . aviare (riv.) . . . . F 3
. . uila (mt.) . . . . E 3
. . érida (riv.) . . . . G 3
. . eta (riv.) . . . . G 2
. . ccidental, Cordillera (mts.) . E 3
. . riental, Cordillera (mts.) . . . E 2
. . rinoco (riv.) . . . . F 2
. . utumayo (riv.) . . . . F 3
. . olima (mt.) . . . . E 3
. . aupés (riv.) . . . . F 3
. . ichada (riv.) . . . . F 3

ECUADOR

CITIES and TOWNS

. . mbato 77,955 . . . . E 4
. . abahoyo 28,914 . . . . D 4
. . aquerizo Moreno 1,311 . . D 7
. . uenca 104,470 . . . . E 4
. . smeraldas 60,364 . . . . . . D 3
. . uayaquil 823,219 . . . . . . D 4
. . barra 41,335 . . . . E 3
. . ipijapa 19,996 . . . . D 4
. . atacunga 21,921 . . . . E 4
. . acas 1,934 . . . . E 4
. . achala 69,170 . . . . D 4
. . anta 64,519 . . . . D 4
. . asaje 20,790 . . . . D 4
. . ortoviejo 59,550 . . . . . . D 4
. . uerto Villamil . . . . D 7
. . uito (cap.) 599,828 . . . . . E 4
. . iobamba 58,087 . . . . E 4
. . anta Elena 7,687 . . . . . . D 4
. . anta Rosa 19,696 . . . . . . D 4
. . ena . . . . E 4
. . ulcán 24,398 . . . . E 3

OTHER FEATURES

. . Chimborazo (mt.) . . . . . . E 4
. . Cotopaxi (mt.) . . . . E 4
. . Guayaquil (gulf) . . . . D 4
. . Morona (riv.) . . . . E 4
. . Napo (riv.) . . . . E 4
. . Occidental, Cordillera (mts.) E 4
. . Pastaza (riv.) . . . . E 4
. . Real, Cordillera (mts.) . . . . E 4
. . Santiago (riv.) . . . . E 4

FALKLAND ISLANDS

CITIES and TOWNS

Stanley (cap.) . . . . J 14

OTHER FEATURES

East Falkland (isl.) . . . . J 14
Falkland (sound) . . . . H 14
West Falkland (isl.) . . . . H 14

FRENCH GUIANA

CITIES and TOWNS

Cayenne (cap.) 37,097 . . . . K 2
Guisanbourg . . . . K 3
Iracoubo 483 . . . . K 2
Mana 623 . . . . K 2
Saint-Georges 921 . . . . K 3
St-Laurent du Maroni 5,042 . . K 2

OTHER FEATURES

Devils (isl.) . . . . K 2
Maroni (riv.) . . . . K 3
Oyapock (riv.) . . . . K 3

GUYANA

CITIES and TOWNS

Corriverton ●10,502 . . . . J 2
Georgetown (cap.) 63,184 . . J 2
Morawhanna ●292 . . . . J 2
New Amsterdam 17,782 . . . . J 2

OTHER FEATURES

Courantyne (riv.) . . . . J 3
Cuyuni (riv.) . . . . H 2
Essequibo (riv.) . . . . J 2
Kaieteur (falls) . . . . J 3
Mazaruni (riv.) . . . . H 2
Roraima (mt.) . . . . H 2
Rupununi (riv.) . . . . J 3

PARAGUAY

CITIES and TOWNS

Asunción (cap.) 387,676 . . . J 9
Concepción 19,392 . . . . J 8
Encarnación 23,343 . . . . . . J 9
Fuerte Olimpo 3,063 . . . . . . J 8
Mariscal Estigarribia 3,150 . . H 8
Puerto Casado 4,078 . . . . . . J 8
Puerto Guaraní 302 . . . . . . J 8
Puerto Sastre 160 . . . . J 8
Villarrica 17,687 . . . . J 9

OTHER FEATURES

Gran Chaco (reg.) . . . . H 8
Itaipú (res.) . . . . K 8
Paraguay (riv.) . . . . J 8
Paraná (riv.) . . . . K 9
Pilcomayo (riv.) . . . . H 8

PERU

CITIES and TOWNS

Arequipa 447,431 . . . . F 7
Ayacucho 68,535 . . . . E 6
Cajamarca 60,280 . . . . E 5
Callao 441,374 . . . . E 6
Cañete 15,277 . . . . E 6
Catacaos 30,927 . . . . D 5
Cerro de Pasco 71,558 . . . . E 6
Chiclayo 280,244 . . . . E 5
Chimbote 216,406 . . . . E 5
Chincha Alta 37,475 . . . . . . E 6
Coracora 4,598 . . . . F 7
Cusco 181,604 . . . . F 6
Huacho 43,402 . . . . E 6
Huancavelica 20,889 . . . . . . E 6
Huancayo 165,132 . . . . F 6
Huánuco 52,628 . . . . E 6
Huaráz 45,116 . . . . E 5
Ica 111,087 . . . . E 6
Iquitos 173,629 . . . . F 4
Jauja 14,630 . . . . E 6
Juliaca 77,976 . . . . F 7
La Oroya 33,305 . . . . E 6
Lima (cap.) 375,957 . . . . . . E 6
Machupicchu 544 . . . . F 6
Matarani . . . . F 7
Mollendo 21,206 . . . . F 7
Moquegua 21,488 . . . . F 7
Nazca 22,862 . . . . F 7
Pacasmayo 17,588 . . . . D 5
Paita 18,749 . . . . D 5
Pisco 53,414 . . . . E 6
Piura 186,354 . . . . D 5
Pucallpa 91,953 . . . . F 5
Puerto Maldonado 12,609 . . G 6
Puno 66,477 . . . . F 7
Sullana 68,947 . . . . D 4
Supe 10,061 . . . . E 6
Tacna 92,862 . . . . F 7
Talara 55,122 . . . . D 4
Tarma 34,369 . . . . E 6
Trujillo 354,557 . . . . E 5
Tumbes 48,187 . . . . D 4

OTHER FEATURES

Aguja (pt.) . . . . D 5
Altiplano (plat.) . . . . F 7
Apurímac (riv.) . . . . F 6
Central, Cordillera (mts.) . . . . E 5
Huascarán (mt.) . . . . E 5
Madre de Dios (riv.) . . . . . . G 6
Marañón (riv.) . . . . E 4
Misti, El (mt.) . . . . F 7
Montaña, La (reg.) . . . . F 5
Napo (riv.) . . . . F 4

Occidental, Cordillera (mts.) . . F 6
Oriental, Cordillera (mts.) . . . E 5
Paracas (pen.) . . . . E 6
Putumayo (riv.) . . . . F 4
Real, Cordillera (mts.) . . . . . F 6
Sechura (bay) . . . . D 5
Titicaca (lake) . . . . F 7
Ucayali (riv.) . . . . E 5
Urubamba (riv.) . . . . F 6
Vilcanota (mt.) . . . . F 6

SURINAME

CITIES and TOWNS

Albina 1,000 . . . . K 3
Groningen 600 . . . . J 2
Moengo 2,100 . . . . K 3
Nieuw-Nickerie 7,400 . . . . . J 2
Paramaribo ●67,905 . . . . . . J 2
Totness 1,300 . . . . J 2

OTHER FEATURES

Coeroeni (riv.) . . . . J 3
Tapanahoni (riv.) . . . . J 3

URUGUAY

CITIES and TOWNS

Artigas 29,256 . . . . J 10
Canelones 15,938 . . . . J 10
Colonia 16,895 . . . . J 10
Durazno 25,811 . . . . J 10
Florida 25,030 . . . . J 10
Fray Bentos 19,569 . . . . . . J 10
Maldonado 22,159 . . . . K 11
Melo 38,260 . . . . K 10
Mercedes 34,667 . . . . J 10
Minas 35,433 . . . . K 10

Montevideo (cap.) 1,173,254 . J 11
Paysandú 62,412 . . . . J 10
Rivera 49,013 . . . . J 10
Rocha 21,612 . . . . K 10
Salto 72,948 . . . . J 10
San José 28,427 . . . . J 10
Tacuarembó 34,152 . . . . . . J 10
Treinta y Tres 25,757 . . . . . K 10
Trinidad 17,598 . . . . J 10

OTHER FEATURES

Mirim (lag.) . . . . K 10
Negro (riv.) . . . . J 10
Plata, Río de la (est.) . . . . . J 11
Uruguay (riv.) . . . . J 9

VENEZUELA

CITIES and TOWNS

Barcelona 78,201 . . . . H 2
Barinas 56,329 . . . . G 2
Barquisimeto 330,815 . . . . . F 2
Bruzual 941 . . . . G 2
Calabozo 37,282 . . . . G 2
Caracas (cap.) 1,035,499 . . G 1
Carora 36,115 . . . . F 1
Carúpano 50,935 . . . . H 1
Ciudad Bolívar 103,728 . . . . H 2
Ciudad Piar 3,965 . . . . H 2
Coro 68,701 . . . . G 1
Cumaná 119,751 . . . . H 1
El Tigre 49,801 . . . . H 2
El Tocuyo 19,351 . . . . G 2
Guanare 34,148 . . . . G 2
La Guaira 20,344 . . . . G 1
Los Teques 63,106 . . . . G 1
Maracaibo 651,574 . . . . . . F 1
Maracay 255,134 . . . . G 1
Maturín 98,188 . . . . H 2

Mérida 74,214 . . . . F 2
Puerto Ayacucho 10,417 . . . G 2
Puerto Cabello 72,103 . . . . G 1
Puerto La Cruz 63,276 . . . . H 1
San Carlos 21,029 . . . . F 2
San Cristóbal 151,717 . . . . F 2
San Felipe 43,801 . . . . G 1
San Fernando 38,960 . . . . . G 2
Trujillo 25,921 . . . . F 2
Tucacas 4,780 . . . . G 1
Tucupita 21,417 . . . . H 2
Valencia 367,171 . . . . G 2
Valera 76,740 . . . . G 2
Valle de la Pascua 36,809 . . G 2
Villa de Cura 27,832 . . . . . . G 2

OTHER FEATURES

Angel (fall) . . . . H 2
Arauca (riv.) . . . . G 2
Apure (riv.) . . . . F 2
Bolívar (mt.) . . . . F 2
Caroní (riv.) . . . . H 3
Casiquiare, Brazo (riv.) . . . . G 3
Maracaibo (lake) . . . . F 2
Margarita (isl.) . . . . H 1
Mérida (mts.) . . . . G 2
Orinoco (riv.) . . . . G 2
Paraguaná (pen.) . . . . F 1
Paria (gulf) . . . . H 1
Serpents Mouth (str.) . . . . . H 2
Tortuga, La (isl.) . . . . G 1
Venezuela (gulf) . . . . F 1

*City and suburb.
†Population of metropolitan area.
△Population of commune.
●Population of district, sub-district
or division.

South America 93 map, *Southern Part*, LAMBERT AZIMUTHAL EQUAL-AREA PROJECTION

© Copyright HAMMOND INCORPORATED, Maplewood, N.J.

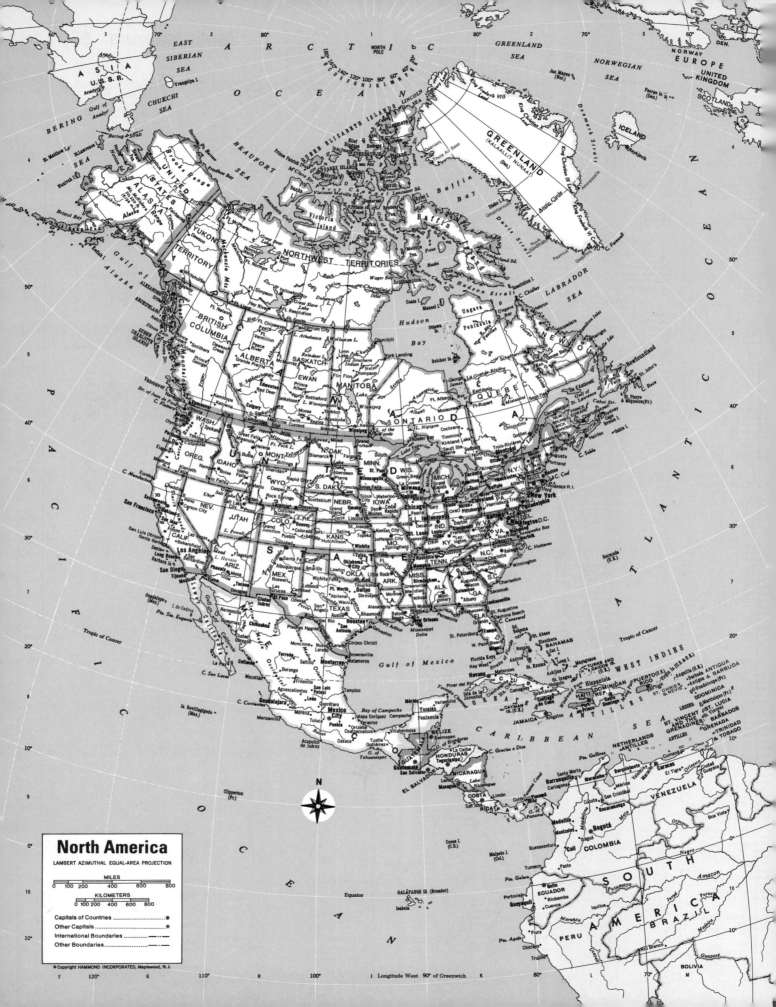

North America

LAMBERT AZIMUTHAL EQUAL-AREA PROJECTION

MILES
0 100 200 400 600 800

KILOMETERS
0 100 200 400 600 800

Capitals of Countries .... ⦿
Other Capitals .... ⊛
International Boundaries ....
Other Boundaries ....

© Copyright HAMMOND INCORPORATED, Maplewood, N.J.

Population Distribution

AREA 9,363,000 sq. mi.
(24,250,170 sq. km.)
POPULATION 370,000,000
LARGEST CITY New York
HIGHEST POINT Mt. McKinley 20,320 ft.
(6,194 m.)
LOWEST POINT Death Valley -282 ft.
(-86 m.)

DENSITY PER

SQ. KILOMETER	SQ. MILE
Over 100	Over 260
50-100	130-260
10-50	25-130
1-10	3-25
Under 1	Under 3

• Cities with over 2,000,000 inhabitants (including suburbs)

○ Cities with over 1,000,000 inhabitants (including suburbs)

Vegetation

MID-LATITUDE FOREST
- Coniferous Forest
- Broadleaf Forest
- Mixed Coniferous and Broadleaf Forest
- Woodland and Shrub (Mediterranean)

MID-LATITUDE GRASSLAND
- Short Grass (Steppe)
- Tall Grass (Prairie)

TROPICAL FOREST
- Tropical Rainforest
- Light Tropical Forest

TROPICAL GRASSLAND
- Wooded Savanna

DESERT AND DESERT SHRUB

TUNDRA AND ALPINE

PERMANENT ICE

Canada

CONIC PROJECTION

SCALE OF MILES
0 50 100   200   300

SCALE OF KILOMETERS
0 50 100   200   300   400   500

Capitals of Countries .... ☆
Provincial & Territorial Capitals ...... △
Administrative Centers .... ◉
International Boundaries ....
Provincial Boundaries ....
Regional Boundaries ....

Scale 1:19,600,000

© Copyright HAMMOND INCORPORATED, Maplewood, N. J.

AREA 3,851,787 sq. mi. (9,976,139 sq. km.)
POPULATION 24,343,181
CAPITAL Ottawa
LARGEST CITY Montréal
HIGHEST POINT Mt. Logan 19,524 ft. (5,951 m.)
MONETARY UNIT Canadian dollar
MAJOR LANGUAGES English, French
MAJOR RELIGIONS Protestantism, Roman Catholicism

Population Distribution

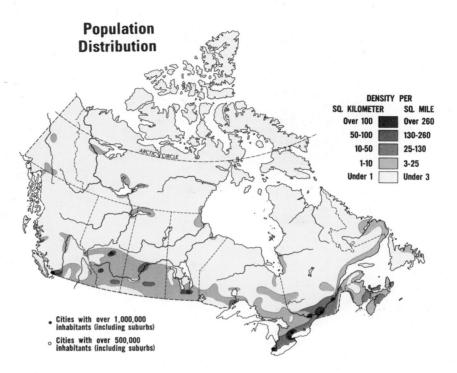

| DENSITY PER | |
SQ. KILOMETER	SQ. MILE
Over 100	Over 260
50-100	130-260
10-50	25-130
1-10	3-25
Under 1	Under 3

• Cities with over 1,000,000 inhabitants (including suburbs)

○ Cities with over 500,000 inhabitants (including suburbs)

Vegetation

MID-LATITUDE FOREST
Coniferous Forest
Broadleaf Forest
Mixed Coniferous and Broadleaf Forest

MID-LATITUDE GRASSLAND
Short Grass (Steppe)
Tall Grass (Prairie)

DESERT AND DESERT SHRUB
TUNDRA AND ALPINE
PERMANENT ICE

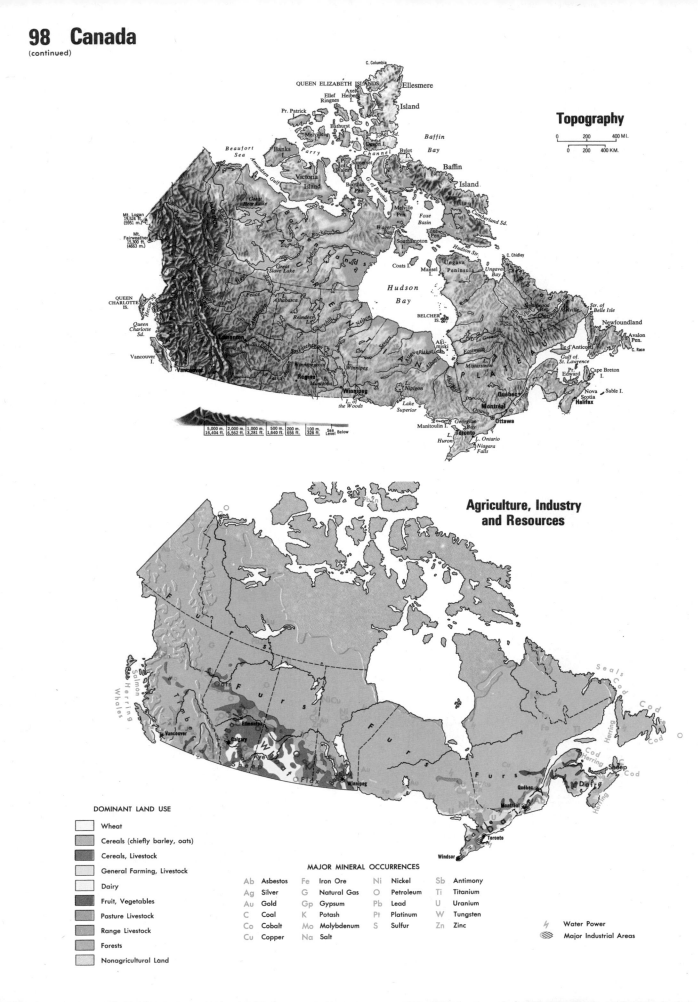

Topography

0   200   400 MI.

0   200   400 KM.

C. Columbia

QUEEN ELIZABETH ISLANDS — Ellesmere
Axel
Ellef Heiberg Island
Ringnes I.

Pr. Patrick   Baffin
Bathurst   Bay

Melville   John
Baffin

Beaufort   Banks Parry   Bylot   Island
Sea   I.   Channel

Pr. of   Somerset   Cumberland Sd.
Wales

Victoria   G. of Boothia   Melville
Island   Boothia   Pen.   Foxe
Pen.   Basin

Mt. Logan   Wager   Foxe
19,524 ft.   Great   Bay   Pen.
(5951 m.)   Bear Lake   Southampton   C. Chidley
Mt.   Hudson Str.
Fairweather   Great   Coats I.   Ungava
15,300 ft.   Slave Lake   Mansel   Ungava Bay
(4663 m.)   Reindeer   I.   Peninsula

QUEEN   Peace   Athabasca   Belcher   Smallwood   Newfoundland
CHARLOTTE   IS.   Nelson   HUDSON   IS.   Res.   Melville   Str. of
Belle Isle

Queen   BAY   Akimiski   Eastmain   Avalon
Charlotte   Churchill   Nelson   Mistassini   Gulf of   Pen.
Sd.   Edmonton   Saskatchewan   Attawapiskat   St. Lawrence   C. Race
Vancouver   Albany   Île d'Anticosti
I.   Saskatchewan   Pr.   Cape Breton
Regina   Winnipeg   Edward   I.
Vancouver   L.   Severn   Nova   Sable I.
Manitoba   PLATEAU   Scotia
Winnipeg   L.   Québec   Halifax
L. of   Winnipeg   Nipigon
the Woods   Lake   Montréal   Ottawa
Superior   Georgian   Ottawa
Manitoulin I.   Bay   Toronto
L. Ontario
L.   Niagara
Huron   Falls

5,000 m. 2,000 m. 1,000 m. 500 m. 200 m. 100 m. Sea
16,404 ft. 6,562 ft. 3,281 ft. 1,640 ft. 656 ft. 328 ft. Level Below

Agriculture, Industry and Resources

Salmon
Herring
Whales
Oats
Furs
Ni Cu
Vancouver   Tribe
Edmonton   Furs
Calgary   Furs
Rye
Wheat   Seals
Cod   Cod
Sheep   Furs
Flax   Cu
Winnipeg   Herring
Cod
Herring
Sheep   Cod
Québec   Dairy
Ni
Montreal   Herring
Toronto
Windsor

DOMINANT LAND USE

- Wheat
- Cereals (chiefly barley, oats)
- Cereals, Livestock
- General Farming, Livestock
- Dairy
- Fruit, Vegetables
- Pasture Livestock
- Range Livestock
- Forests
- Nonagricultural Land

MAJOR MINERAL OCCURRENCES

Ab	Asbestos	Fe	Iron Ore	Ni	Nickel	Sb	Antimony
Ag	Silver	G	Natural Gas	O	Petroleum	Ti	Titanium
Au	Gold	Gp	Gypsum	Pb	Lead	U	Uranium
C	Coal	K	Potash	Pt	Platinum	W	Tungsten
Co	Cobalt	Mo	Molybdenum	S	Sulfur	Zn	Zinc
Cu	Copper	Na	Salt				

⚡ Water Power

〰 Major Industrial Areas

AREA 156,184 sq. mi. (404,517 sq. km.)
POPULATION 567,681
CAPITAL St. John's
LARGEST CITY St. John's
HIGHEST POINT in Torngat Mountains
5,420 ft. (1,652 m.)
SETTLED IN 1610
ADMITTED TO CONFEDERATION 1949
PROVINCIAL FLOWER Pitcher Plant

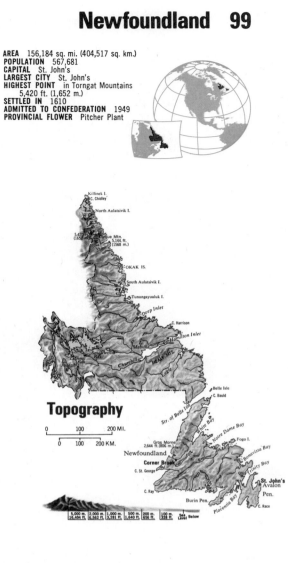

Topography

Newfoundland

Corner Brook

5,000 m.	2,000 m.	1,000 m.	500 m.	200 m.	100 m.	Sea Level Below
16,404 ft.	6,562 ft.	3,281 ft.	1,640 ft.	656 ft.	328 ft.	

Agriculture, Industry and Resources

DOMINANT LAND USE

- General Farming, Dairy
- General Farming, Livestock
- Forests
- Nonagricultural Land

MAJOR MINERAL OCCURRENCES

Ab	Asbestos
Ag	Silver
Au	Gold
Cu	Copper
F	Fluorspar
Fe	Iron Ore
Gp	Gypsum
O	Petroleum
Pb	Lead
Zn	Zinc

⚡ Water Power
▨ Major Industrial Areas

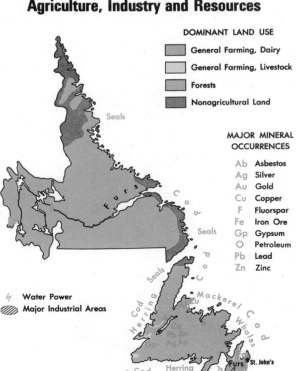

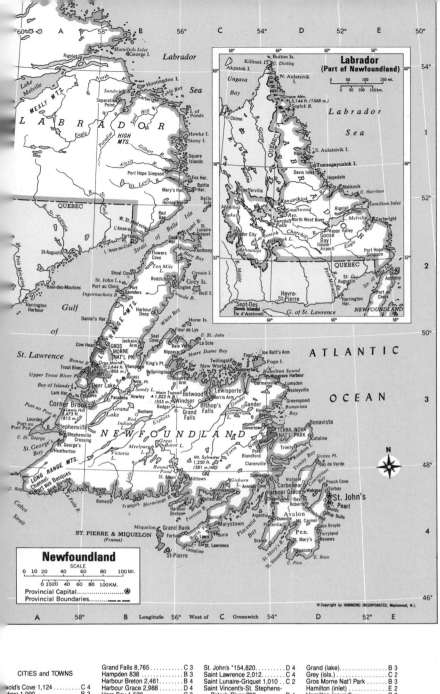

Newfoundland
SCALE

0 10 20 40 60 80 100 MI.

0 1020 40 60 80 100 KM.

Provincial Capital.................⊛
Provincial Boundaries.............

© Copyright by HAMMOND INCORPORATED, Maplewood, N.J.

NOVA SCOTIA

COUNTIES

Annapolis 22,522 .... C 4
Antigonish 18,110 .... F 3
Cape Breton 127,035 .... H 3
Colchester 43,224 .... D 3
Cumberland 35,231 .... D 3
Digby 21,689 .... C 4
Guysborough 12,752 .... F 3
Halifax 288,126 .... E 4
Hants 33,121 .... D 3
Inverness 22,337 .... G 2
Kings 49,739 .... D 4
Lunenburg 45,746 .... D 4
Pictou 50,350 .... F 3
Queens 13,126 .... D 4
Richmond 12,284 .... H 3
Shelburne 17,328 .... C 5
Victoria 8,432 .... H 2
Yarmouth 26,290 .... C 5

CITIES and TOWNS

Alder Point 651 .... H 2
Aldershot .... D 3
Amherst⊙ 9,684 .... D 3
Annapolis Royal⊙ 631 .... C 4
Antigonish⊙ 5,205 .... F 3
Arichat 824 .... H 3
Aylesford 744 .... D 3
Baddeck⊙ 972 .... H 2
Barrington Passage 722 ..... C 5
Bear River-Sissiboo 854 .... C 4
Beaverbank 1,322 .... E 4
Berwick 1,699 .... D 4
Bridgetown 1,047 .... C 4
Bridgewater 6,669 .... D 4
Brookfield 619 .... E 3
Brooklyn 1,269 .... D 4
Cambridge Station 799 ...... D 3
Canning 763 .... D 3
Canso 1,255 .... H 3
Centreville 765 .... D 3
Chéticamp 1,022 .... G 2
Chester 1,131 .... D 4
Chester Basin 639 .... D 4
Church Point 318 .... B 4
Clark's Harbour 1,059 ...... C 5
Coldbrook Station 617 ...... D 4
Cow Bay 670 .... E 4
Dartmouth 62,277 .... E 4
Debert 618 .... E 3
Digby⊙ 2,558 .... C 4
Dominion 2,856 .... J 2
Donkin 873 .... J 2
Ellershouse-Hartville 662 .. D 4
Elmsdale 1,172 .... E 4
Enfield 1,510 .... E 4
Fall River 1,897 .... E 4
Falmouth 1,110 .... D 3
Glace Bay 21,466 .... J 2
Guysborough⊙ 496 .... G 3
Halifax (cap.)⊙ 114,594 .... E 4
Halifax 277,727 .... E 4
Hantsport 1,395 .... D 3
Herring Cove 1,323 .... E 4
Hilden 1,262 .... E 3

Ingonish 471 .... H 2
Inverness 2,013 .... G 2
Judique 925 .... G 3
Kentville⊙ 4,974 .... D 3
Kingston 1,612 .... D 4
Lakeside 936 .... E 4
Lantz 1,172 .... E 4
Liverpool⊙ 3,304 .... D 4
Lockeport 929 .... C 5
Louisbourg 1,410 .... J 3
Louisdale 979 .... H 3
Lower West Pubnico 790 ..... C 5
Lunenburg⊙ 3,014 .... D 4
Mahone Bay 1,228 .... D 4
Meteghan 890 .... B 4
Middleton 1,834 .... C 4
Milford Station 748 .... E 3
Milton 1,678 .... D 4
Mount Uniacke 1,145 .... E 4
Mulgrave 827 .... G 3
Musquodoboit Harbour 936 ... E 4
New Glasgow 10,464 .... F 3
New Victoria 1,374 .... H 2

New Waterford 8,808 .... J 2
North Sydney 7,820 .... H 2
Oxford 1,470 .... E 3
Parrsboro 1,799 .... D 3
Pictou⊙ 4,628 .... F 3
Port Hastings 312 .... G 3
Port Hawkesbury 3,850 ...... G 3
Port Hood⊙ 701 .... G 2
Port Morien 717 .... J 2
Port Williams 1,227 .... D 3
Prospect 693 .... E 4
Pugwash 648 .... E 3
Reserve Mines 2,472 .... H 2
River Hébert 835 .... D 3
Saint Peters 669 .... H 3
Sandy Point 691 .... C 5
Scotchtown 2,037 .... H 2
Sheet Harbour 819 .... F 4
Shelburne⊙ 2,303 .... C 5
Springhill 4,896 .... E 3
Stellarton 5,435 .... F 3

Stewiacke 1,174 .... E 3
Sydney⊙ 29,444 .... H 2
Sydney Mines 8,501 .... H 2
Terence Bay 960 .... E 4
Thorburn 1,014 .... F 3
Three Mile Plains 1,355 .... D 4
Timberlea 1,159 .... E 4
Trenton 3,154 .... F 3
Truro⊙ 12,552 .... E 3
Waterville 687 .... D 3
Waverley 1,699 .... E 4
Wedgeport 827 .... C 5
Western Shore 1,712 .... D 4
Westmount 3,097 .... H 2
Westville 4,522 .... F 3
Wileville 766 .... D 4
Windsor⊙ 3,646 .... D 3
Wolfville 3,235 .... D 3
Yarmouth⊙ 7,475 .... B 5

OTHER FEATURES

Advocate (bay) .... D 3

Ainslie (lake) ....
Amet (sound) ....
Andrew (isl.) ....
Annapolis (basin) ....
Annapolis (riv.) ....
Antigonish (harb.) ....
Argos (bay) ....
Asgy (bay) ....
Avon (riv.) ....
Baccaro (pt.) ....
Baddeck (riv.) ....
Barachois (pt.) ....
Barren (isl.) ....
Barrington (bay) ....
Bedford (basin) ....
Berry (head) ....
Boularderie (isl.) ....
Bras d'Or (lake) ....
Breton (cape) ....
Brier (isl.) ....
Canso (cape) ....
Canso (str.) ....
Cap d'Or (cape) ....

PRINCE EDWARD ISLAND

AREA 2,184 sq. mi. (5,657 sq. km.)
POPULATION 122,506
CAPITAL Charlottetown
LARGEST CITY Charlottetown
HIGHEST POINT 465 ft. (142 m.)
SETTLED IN 1720
ADMITTED TO CONFEDERATION 1873
PROVINCIAL FLOWER Lady's Slipper

NOVA SCOTIA

AREA 21,425 sq. mi. (55,491 sq. km.)
POPULATION 847,442
CAPITAL Halifax
LARGEST CITY Halifax
HIGHEST POINT Cape Breton Highlands 1,747 ft. (532 m.)
SETTLED IN 1605
ADMITTED TO CONFEDERATION 1867
PROVINCIAL FLOWER Trailing Arbutus or Mayflower

Topography

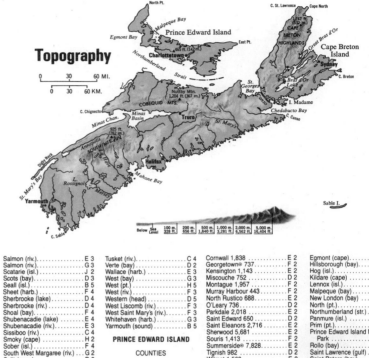

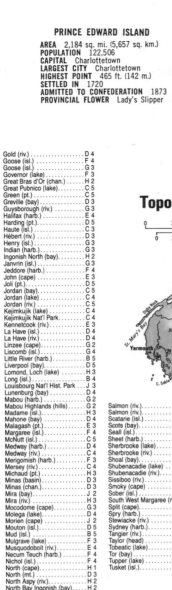

⊛County seat.
*Population of metropolitan area.

Agriculture, Industry and Resources

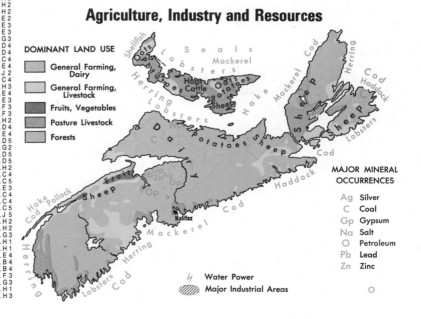

DOMINANT LAND USE

- General Farming, Dairy
- General Farming, Livestock
- Fruits, Vegetables
- Pasture Livestock
- Forests

MAJOR MINERAL OCCURRENCES

Ag	Silver
C	Coal
Gp	Gypsum
Na	Salt
O	Petroleum
Pb	Lead
Zn	Zinc

⚡ Water Power

▨ Major Industrial Areas

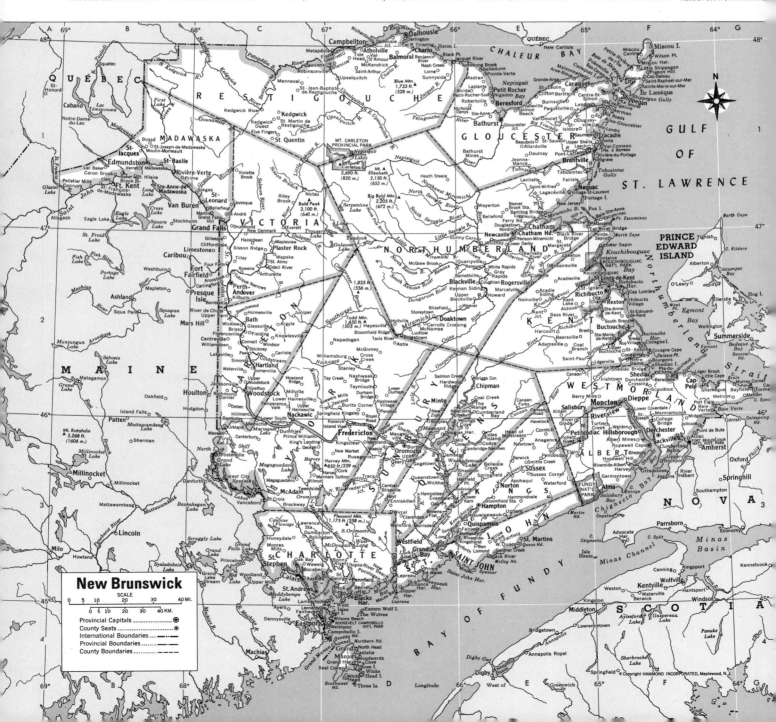

AREA 28,354 sq. mi. (73,437 sq. km.)
POPULATION 696,403
CAPITAL Fredericton
LARGEST CITY Saint John
HIGHEST POINT Mt. Carleton 2,690 ft. (820 m.)
SETTLED IN 1611
ADMITTED TO CONFEDERATION 1867
PROVINCIAL FLOWER Purple Violet

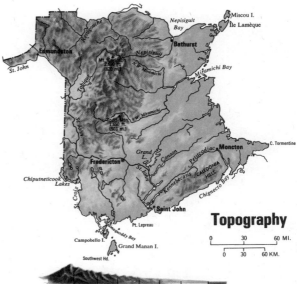

Topography

0   30   60 MI.
0   30   60 KM.

5,000 m. | 2,000 m. | 1,000 m. | 500 m. | 200 m. | 100 m. | Sea Level | Below
16,404 ft. | 6,562 ft. | 3,281 ft. | 1,640 ft. | 656 ft. | 328 ft.

Agriculture, Industry and Resources

DOMINANT LAND USE

- Cereals, Livestock
- Dairy
- Potatoes
- General Farming, Livestock
- Pasture Livestock
- Forests

MAJOR MINERAL OCCURRENCES

Ag Silver
C Coal
Cu Copper
Pb Lead
Sb Antimony
Zn Zinc

⚡ Water Power
▨ Major Industrial Areas

Topography

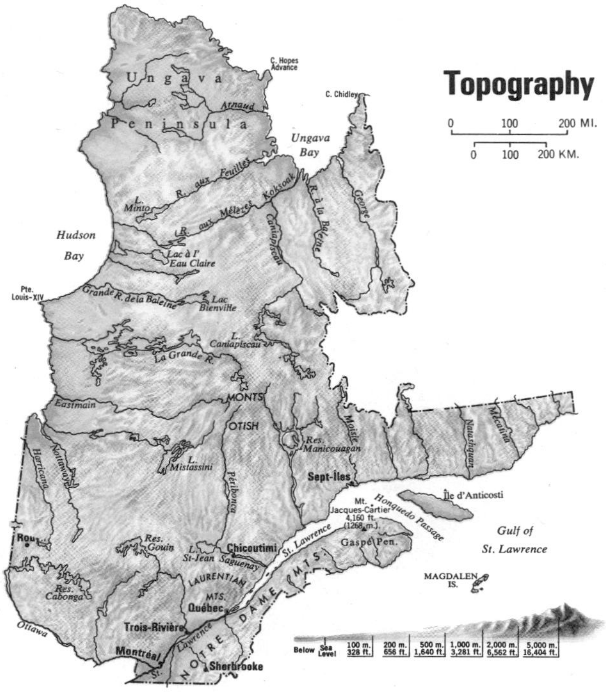
0 100 200 MI.
0 100 200 KM.
Ungava Peninsula
Ungava Bay
Hudson Bay
C. Hopes Advance
C. Chidley
Gulf of St. Lawrence
Île d'Anticosti
Sept-Îles
Chicoutimi
Québec
Trois-Rivière
Montréal
Sherbrooke
MAGDALEN IS.
Below Sea Level
100 m. 328 ft.
200 m. 656 ft.
500 m. 1,640 ft.
1,000 m. 3,281 ft.
2,000 m. 6,562 ft.
5,000 m. 16,404 ft.

COUNTIES

Argenteuil 32,454 . . . . . C 4
Arthabaska 59,277 . . . . . E 4
Bagot 26,840 . . . . . E 4
Beauce 73,427 . . . . . G 3
Beauharnois 54,034 . . . . . C 4
Bellechasse 23,559 . . . . . G 3
Berthier 31,096 . . . . . C 3
Bonaventure 40,487 . . . . . C 2
Brome 17,436 . . . . . E 4
Chambly 307,090 . . . . . J 4
Champlain 119,595 . . . . . E 2
Charlevoix-Est 17,448 . . . . . G 2
Charlevoix-Ouest 14,172 . . . . . G 2
Châteauguay 59,968 . . . . . D 4
Chicoutimi 174,441 . . . . . G 1
Compton 20,536 . . . . . F 4
Deux-Montagnes 71,252 . . . . . C 4
Dorchester 33,949 . . . . . C 3
Drummond 69,770 . . . . . E 4
Frontenac 26,814 . . . . . G 4
Gaspé-Est 41,173 . . . . . D 1
Gaspé-Ouest 18,943 . . . . . C 1
Gatineau 54,229 . . . . . B 3
Hull 131,213 . . . . . B 4
Huntingdon 16,953 . . . . . C 4
Iberville 23,180 . . . . . D 4
Île-de-Montréal 1,760,122 . . . . . H 4
Île-Jésus 268,335 . . . . . H 4
Joliette 60,384 . . . . . C 3
Kamouraska 28,642 . . . . . H 2
Labelle 34,395 . . . . . B 3
Lac-Saint-Jean-Est 47,891 . . . . . F 1
Lac-Saint-Jean-Ouest 62,952 . E 1
Laprairie 105,962 . . . . . H 4
L'Assomption 109,705 . . . . . D 4
Lévis 94,104 . . . . . J 3
L'Islet 22,062 . . . . . G 2
Lotbinière 29,653 . . . . . F 3
Maskinongé 20,763 . . . . . D 3
Matane 29,955 . . . . . B 1
Matapédia 23,715 . . . . . B 2
Mégantic 57,892 . . . . . F 3
Missisquoi 36,161 . . . . . D 4
Montcalm 27,557 . . . . . C 3
Montmagny 25,622 . . . . . G 3
Montmorency No. 1 23,048 . . . F 2
Montmorency No. 2 6,436 . . . . G 3
Napierville 13,562 . . . . . D 4
Nicolet 33,513 . . . . . E 3
Papineau 37,975 . . . . . B 4
Pontiac 20,283 . . . . . A 3
Portneuf 58,843 . . . . . E 3
Québec 458,980 . . . . . F 3
Richelieu 53,058 . . . . . D 4
Richmond 40,871 . . . . . E 4
Rimouski 69,099 . . . . . J 1
Rivière-du-Loup 41,250 . . . . . H 2
Rouville 42,391 . . . . . D 4
Saguenay 115,881 . . . . . H 1
Saint-Hyacinthe 55,888 . . . . . D 4
Saint-Jean 55,576 . . . . . D 4
Saint-Maurice 107,703 . . . . . D 3
Shefford 70,733 . . . . . E 4
Sherbrooke 115,983 . . . . . E 4
Soulanges 15,429 . . . . . C 4
Stanstead 38,186 . . . . . F 4
Témiscouata 52,570 . . . . . J 2
Terrebonne 193,865 . . . . . H 4
Vaudreuil 50,043 . . . . . C 4
Verchères 63,353 . . . . . J 4
Wolfe 15,635 . . . . . F 4
Yamaska 14,797 . . . . . E 3

CITIES and TOWNS

Acton Vale 4,371 . . . . . E 4
Albanel 992 . . . . . E 1
Alma◎ 26,322 . . . . . F 1
Amqui◎ 4,048 . . . . . B 2
Ancienne-Lorette 12,935 . . . . . H 3
Angers . . . . . B 4
Anjou 37,346 . . . . . H 4
Annaville 712 . . . . . E 3
Armagh 878 . . . . . G 3
Arthabaska◎ 6,827 . . . . . F 3
Arvida . . . . . F 1
Asbestos 7,967 . . . . . F 4
Ascot Corner 847 . . . . . F 4
Audet 760 . . . . . G 4
Ayer's Cliff◎ 810 . . . . . E 4
Aylmer 26,695 . . . . . B 4
Baie-Comeau 12,866 . . . . . A 1
Baie-d'Urfé 3,674 . . . . . G 4
Baie-Saint-Paul◎ 3,961 . . . . . G 2
Baie-Trinité 749 . . . . . B 1
Beaconsfield 19,613 . . . . . H 4
Beauceville 4,302 . . . . . G 3
Beauharnois◎ 7,025 . . . . . D 4
Beaumont 791 . . . . . F 3
Beauport 60,447 . . . . . J 3
Beaupré 2,740 . . . . . G 2
Bécancour◎ 10,247 . . . . . E 3
Bedford◎ 2,832 . . . . . E 4
Beebe Plain 1,072 . . . . . E 4
Bélair (Val-Bélair) 12,695 . . . . H 3
Beloeil 17,540 . . . . . D 4
Bernierville 2,120 . . . . . F 3
Berthier-en-Bas 562 . . . . . G 3
Berthierville◎ 4,049 . . . . . D 3
Bic 2,994 . . . . . J 1
Biencourt 824 . . . . . J 2
Black Lake 5,148 . . . . . F 3
Blainville 14,682 . . . . . H 4
Boischatel 3,345 . . . . . J 3
Bois-des-Filion 4,943 . . . . . H 4
Bolduc 1,565 . . . . . G 4
Bonaventure 1,371 . . . . . C 2
Boucherville 29,704 . . . . . J 4
Bromont 2,731 . . . . . E 4
Bromptonville 3,035 . . . . . F 4
Brossard 52,232 . . . . . H 4
Brownsburg 2,875 . . . . . C 4
Buckingham 7,992 . . . . . B 4
Cabano 3,291 . . . . . J 2
Cacouna 1,160 . . . . . H 2
Calumet 729 . . . . . C 4
Candiac 8,502 . . . . . J 4
Cap-à-l'Aigle 819 . . . . . G 2
Cap-Chat 3,464 . . . . . B 1
Cap-de-la-Madeleine 32,626 . E 3
Caplan-Rivière Caplan 1,139 . C 2
Cap-Saint-Ignace 1,485 . . . . . G 2
Cap-Santé◎ 671 . . . . . F 3
Carignan 4,544 . . . . . J 4
Carleton 2,710 . . . . . C 2
Causapscal 2,501 . . . . . B 2
Chambly 12,190 . . . . . J 4
Chambord 961 . . . . . E 1
Chandler 3,946 . . . . . D 2
Charlemagne 4,827 . . . . . H 4
Charlesbourg 68,326 . . . . . J 3
Charny 8,240 . . . . . J 3
Châteauguay 36,928 . . . . . H 4
Château-Richer◎ 3,628 . . . . . F 3
Chénéville 633 . . . . . B 4
Chicoutimi◎ 60,064 . . . . . G 1
Chicoutimi-Jonquière
  *135,172 . . . . . G 1
Chute-aux-Outardes 2,280 . . . A 1
Clermont 3,621 . . . . . G 2
Coaticook 6,271 . . . . . F 4
Coleraine 1,660 . . . . . F 4
Compton 728 . . . . . F 4
Contrecoeur 5,449 . . . . . D 4
Cookshire◎ 1,480 . . . . . F 4
Coteau-du-Lac 1,247 . . . . . C 4
Coteau-Landing◎ 1,386 . . . . . C 4
Côte-Saint-Luc 27,531 . . . . . H 4
Courcelles 608 . . . . . G 4
Courville . . . . . J 3
Cowansville 12,240 . . . . . E 4
Crabtree 1,950 . . . . . D 4
Danville 2,200 . . . . . E 4
Daveluyville 1,257 . . . . . E 3
Deauville 942 . . . . . E 4
Dégelis 3,477 . . . . . J 2
Delisle 4,011 . . . . . F 1
Delson 4,935 . . . . . H 4
Desbiens 1,541 . . . . . E 1
Deschaillons-sur-Saint-
  Laurent 950 . . . . . E 3
Deschambault 977 . . . . . E 3
Deschênes . . . . . B 4
Deux-Montagnes 9,944 . . . . . H 4
Didyme 667 . . . . . E 1
Disraëli 3,181 . . . . . F 4
Dolbeau 8,766 . . . . . E 1
Dollard-des-Ormeaux 39,940 . H 4
Donnacona 5,731 . . . . . F 3
Dorion 5,749 . . . . . C 4
Dorval 17,727 . . . . . H 4
Dosquet 703 . . . . . F 3
Douville . . . . . D 4
Drummondville◎ 27,347 . . . . . E 4
Drummondville-Sud 9,220 . . . . E 4
Dunham 2,887 . . . . . E 4
Durham-Sud 1,045 . . . . . E 4
East Angus 4,016 . . . . . F 4
East Broughton 1,397 . . . . . F 3
East Broughton Station 1,302 . F 3
Eastman 612 . . . . . E 4
Entrelacs 1,735 . . . . . C 3
Farnham 6,498 . . . . . E 4
Ferme-Neuve 2,266 . . . . . B 3
Forestville 4,271 . . . . . H 1
Frampton 684 . . . . . G 3
Francoeur 1,422 . . . . . F 3
Gaspé 17,261 . . . . . D 1
Gatineau 74,988 . . . . . B 4
Giffard . . . . . J 3
Girardville 1,128 . . . . . E 1
Gracefield 869 . . . . . A 3
Granby 38,069 . . . . . E 4
Grand'Mère 15,442 . . . . . E 3
Grande-Rivière 4,420 . . . . . D 2
Grandes-Bergeronnes 748 . . . H 1
Grande-Vallée 700 . . . . . D 1
Greenfield Park 18,527 . . . . . J 4
Grenville 1,417 . . . . . C 4
Gros-Morne 672 . . . . . C 1
Hampstead 7,598 . . . . . H 4
Ham-Sud◎ 62 . . . . . F 4
Hauterive 13,995 . . . . . A 1
Hébertville 2,515 . . . . . F 1
Hébertville-Station 1,442 . . . . . F 1
Hemmingford 737 . . . . . D 4
Henryville 595 . . . . . D 4
Howick 639 . . . . . D 4
Hudson 4,414 . . . . . C 4
Hull◎ 56,225 . . . . . B 4
Huntingdon◎ 3,018 . . . . . C 4
Île-Perrot 5,945 . . . . . G 4
Iberville◎ 8,587 . . . . . D 4
Inverness◎ 329 . . . . . F 3
Joliette◎ 16,987 . . . . . D 3
Jonquière 60,354 . . . . . F 1
Jonquière-Chicoutimi
  *135,172 . . . . . F 1
Kingsey Falls 818 . . . . . E 4
Kirkland 10,476 . . . . . H 4
Knowlton (Lac-Brome)◎
  4,316 . . . . . E 4
La Baie 20,935 . . . . . G 1
Labelle 1,534 . . . . . C 3
Lac-à-la-Croix 1,017 . . . . . F 1
Lac-Alouette-Lac-Brière 1,356 D 4
Lac-au-Saumon 1,332 . . . . . B 2
Lac-aux-Sables 838 . . . . . E 3
Lac-Beaufort . . . . . F 3
Lac-Bouchette 1,703 . . . . . E 1
Lac-Carré 717 . . . . . C 3
Lac-des-Écorces 766 . . . . . B 3
Lac-Drolet 1,120 . . . . . G 4
Lac-Etchemin 2,729 . . . . . G 3
Lachenaie 8,631 . . . . . D 4
Lachine 37,521 . . . . . H 4
Lachute◎ 11,729 . . . . . C 4
Lac-Mégantic◎ 6,119 . . . . . G 4
Lacolle 1,319 . . . . . D 4
Lac-Saint-Charles 5,837 . . . . . H 3
Lafontaine 4,799 . . . . . C 4
La Guadeloupe 1,692 . . . . . F 4
La Malbaie◎ 4,030 . . . . . G 2
Lambton 1,559 . . . . . F 4
L'Annonciation 2,384 . . . . . C 3
Lanoraie (Lanoraie-d'Autry)
  1,613 . . . . . D 4
La Pêche 4,977 . . . . . B 4
La Pérade 1,039 . . . . . E 3
La Pocatière 4,560 . . . . . H 2
La Prairie◎ 10,627 . . . . . J 4
La Providence . . . . . E 4
Larouche 662 . . . . . F 1
La Salle 76,299 . . . . . H 4
L'Ascension 1,287 . . . . . F 1
L'Assomption◎ 4,844 . . . . . D 4
La Station-du-Coteau 892 . . . . C 4
Laterrière 788 . . . . . F 1
La Tuque 11,556 . . . . . E 2
Laurentides 1,947 . . . . . D 4
Laurier-Station 1,123 . . . . . F 3
Laurierville 939 . . . . . F 3
Lauzon 13,362 . . . . . J 3
Laval 268,335 . . . . . H 4
Lavaltrie 2,053 . . . . . D 4
L'Avenir 1,116 . . . . . E 4
Lawrenceville 562 . . . . . E 4
Le Moyne 6,137 . . . . . J 4
L'Épiphanie 2,971 . . . . . D 4
Léry 2,239 . . . . . H 4
Lévis 17,895 . . . . . J 3
Lennoxville 3,922 . . . . . F 4
Les Méchins 803 . . . . . B 1
Linière 1,168 . . . . . G 3
L'Islet 1,070 . . . . . G 2
L'Islet-sur-Mer 774 . . . . . G 2
L'Isle-Verte 1,142 . . . . . G 1
Longueuil◎ 124,320 . . . . . J 4
Loretteville◎ 15,060 . . . . . H 3
Lorraine 6,881 . . . . . H 4
Louiseville◎ 3,735 . . . . . E 3
Luceville 1,524 . . . . . J 1
Lyster 830 . . . . . F 3
Magog 13,604 . . . . . E 4
Maniwaki◎ 5,424 . . . . . B
Manseau 626 . . . . . E
Maple Grove 2,009 . . . . . H
Maria 1,178 C
Marieville◎ 4,877 . . . . . D
Mascouche 20,345 . . . . . H
Maskinongé 1,005 . . . . . E
Masson 4,264 . . . . . B
Massueville 671 . . . . . E
Matane◎ 13,612 . . . . . B
Matapédia 586 . . . . . B
Melocheville 1,892 C
Mercier 6,352 . . . . . H
Metabetchouan 3,406 . . . . . F
Mirabel◎ 14,080 . . . . . H
Mistassini 6,682 . . . . . E
Montauban 557 . . . . . E
Mont-Carmel 807 . . . . . H
Montcerf 570 . . . . . A
Montebello 1,229 . . . . . B
Mont-Joli 6,359 . . . . . J
Mont-Laurier◎ 8,405 . . . . . B
Mont-Louis 756 C
Montmagny◎ 12,405 . . . . . G
Montréal◎ 980,354 . . . . . H
Montréal *2,828,349 . . . . . H
Montréal-Est 3,778 . . . . . J
Montréal-Nord 94,914 . . . . . H
Mont-Rolland 1,517 C
Mont-Royal 19,247 . . . . . H
Mont-Saint-Hilaire 10,066 . . . . D
Morin Heights 592 C
Murdochville 3,396 C
Nantes 1,167 . . . . . F

Agriculture, Industry and Resources

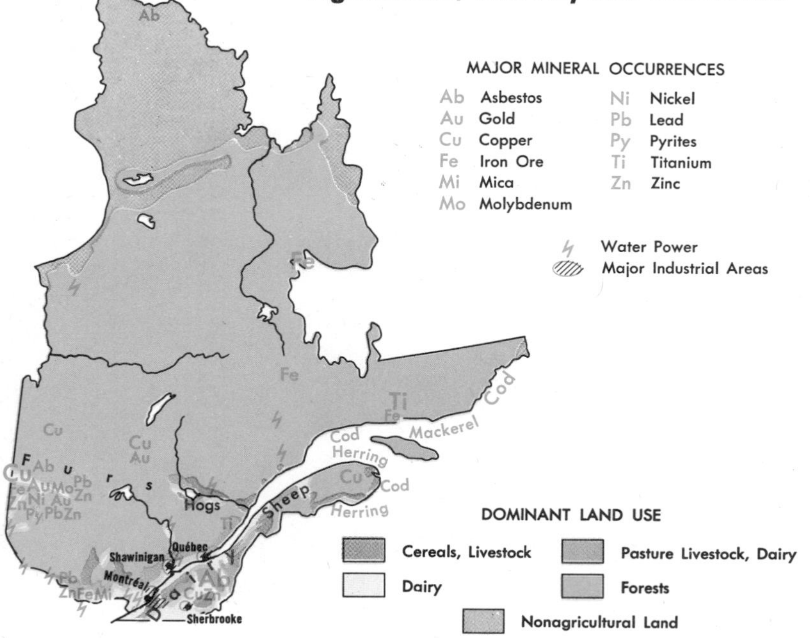
MAJOR MINERAL OCCURRENCES
Ab Asbestos
Au Gold
Cu Copper
Fe Iron Ore
Mi Mica
Mo Molybdenum
Ni Nickel
Pb Lead
Py Pyrites
Ti Titanium
Zn Zinc
Water Power
Major Industrial Areas
DOMINANT LAND USE
Cereals, Livestock
Pasture Livestock, Dairy
Dairy
Forests
Nonagricultural Land
Cod
Herring
Mackerel
Sheep
Hogs
Shawinigan
Québec
Montréal
Sherbrooke

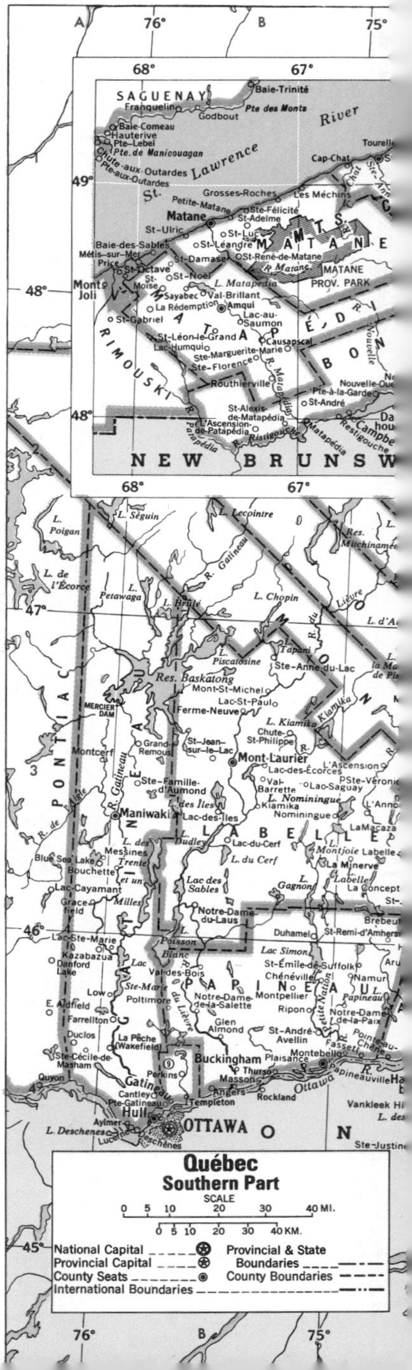
Québec
Southern Part
SCALE
0 5 10 20 30 40 MI.
0 5 10 20 30 40 KM.
National Capital
Provincial Capital
County Seats
International Boundaries
Provincial & State Boundaries
County Boundaries
OTTAWA
Hull
Gatineau
Buckingham
Maniwaki
Mont-Laurier
Matane
Amqui
Mont Joli
NEW BRUNSWICK

AREA 594,857 sq. mi. (1,540,680 sq. km.)
POPULATION 6,438,403
CAPITAL Québec
LARGEST CITY Montréal
HIGHEST POINT Mont D'Iberville 5,420 ft. (1,652 m.)
SETTLED IN 1608
ADMITTED TO CONFEDERATION 1867
PROVINCIAL FLOWER White Garden Lily

Internal divisions represent Municipal Counties

Longitude 72° West of Greenwich

Saint-Eustache 29,716......H 4
Saint-Fabien 1,361.........J 1
Saint-Félicien 9,058.......E 1
Saint-Félix-de-Valois 1,462..D 3
Saint-Ferréol-les-Neiges
　1,758..................G 2
Saint-Flavien 734.........F 3
Saint-François-de-Sales 831..E 1
Saint-François-du-Lac® 942...E 3
Saint-Fulgence 950.........G 1
Saint-Gabriel 3,161........D 3
Saint-Gabriel-de-Rimouski
　779....................J 1
Saint-Gédéon, Frontenac
　1,569..................G 4
Saint-Gédéon, Lac-St-Jean-E.
　1,000..................F 1
Saint-Georges, Beauce
　10,342.................G 3
Saint-Georges, Champlain
　3,344..................E 3
Saint-Georges-Ouest 6,378..G 3
Saint-Germain-de-Grantham
　1,373..................E 4
Saint-Gervais 973.........G 3
Saint-Gilles 912..........F 3
Saint-Grégoire (Mont-St-
　Grégoire) 740...........D 4
Saint-Henri 1,970.........J 3
Saint-Honoré, Beauce 1,116..G 4
Saint-Honoré, Chicoutimi
　1,790..................F 1
Saint-Hubert 60,573.......J 4
Saint-Hubert-de-Témiscouata
　871....................J 2
Saint-Hyacinthe 38,246....D 4
Saint-Isidore 811.........J 4
Saint-Isidore-de-Laprairie 769 D 4
Saint-Jacques 2,152.......D 4
Saint-Jacques-le-Mineur
　1,203..................H 4
Saint-Jean-Chrysostome
　6,930..................J 3
Saint-Jean-de-Dieu 1,377...J 1
Saint-Jean-de-Matha 931...D 3
Saint-Jean-Port-Joli® 1,813..G 2
Saint-Jean-sur-Richelieu®
　35,640.................D 4
Saint-Jérôme 25,123.......H 4
Saint-Joachim 1,139.......G 2
Saint-Joseph-de-Beauce
　3,216..................G 3
Saint-Joseph-de-Sorel 2,545..D 3
Saint-Jovite 3,841........C 3
Saint-Lambert 20,557......J 4

Saint-Lazare 731..........G 3
Saint-Léonard 79,429......H 4
Saint-Léonard-d'Aston 992...E 3
Saint-Léon-de-Chicoutimi 749 F 1
Saint-Léon-de-Standon 816...G 3
Saint-Léon-le-Grand 722....B 2
Saint-Liboire® 746........E 3
Saint-Louis-de-Gonzague
　615....................D 4
Saint-Louis-de-Terrebonne
　14,172.................H 4
Saint-Louis-du-Ha! Ha! 809...H 2
Saint-Luc 8,815...........H 4
Saint-Luc-de-Matane 598....B 1
Saint-Marc-des-Carrières
　2,822..................F 3
Saint-Méthode-de-Frontenac
　925....................F 3
Saint-Michel-de-Bellechasse
　963....................G 3
Saint-Michel-des-Saints
　1,584..................D 3
Saint-Nazaire-de-Chicoutimi
　962....................F 1
Saint-Nérée 970...........G 3
Saint-Nicolas 5,074.......H 3
Saint-Noël 666............B 1
Saint-Odilon 580..........G 3
Saint-Omer 718............C 2
Saint-Ours 625............D 4
Saint-Pacôme 1,996........G 2
Saint-Pamphile 3,428......H 3
Saint-Pascal® 2,763.......H 2
Saint-Paul-de-Montminy 602..G 3
Saint-Paulin 663..........D 3
Saint-Paul-l'Ermite (Le
　Gardeur) 8,312..........J 4
Saint-Philippe-de-Néri 715...H 2
Saint-Pie 1,725...........E 4
Saint-Pierre 5,305........H 4
Saint-Pierre-d'Orléans 880...J 3
Saint-Polycarpe 602.......C 4
Saint-Prime 2,522.........E 1
Saint-Prosper-de-Dorchester
　2,150..................G 3
Saint-Raphaël 1,346.......G 3
Saint-Raymond 3,605.......F 3
Saint-Rédempteur 4,463....J 3
Saint-Régis 1,370.........C 4
Saint-Rémi 5,146..........D 4
Saint-Roch-de-l'Achigan
　1,160..................D 4
Saint-Roch-de-Richelieu
　1,650..................D 4
Saint-Romuald-d'Etchemin®
　9,849..................J 3

Saint-Sauveur-des-Monts
　2,348..................C 4
Saint-Siméon 1,152........C 4
Saint-Simon 602...........H 1
Saint-Stanislas 1,443.....E 3
Saint-Sylvère 1,006.......E 3
Saint-Timothée 2,113......D 4
Saint-Tite 3,031..........E 3
Saint-Tite-des-Caps 626....F 4
Saint-Ubald 1,605.........E 3
Saint-Ulric 792...........B 1
Saint-Urbain-de-Charlevoix
　1,079..................G 2
Saint-Victor 1,104........G 3
Saint-Zacharie 1,284......G 3
Saint-Zotique 1,774.......C 4
Sault-au-Mouton 828.......H 1
Sawyerville 939...........F 4
Sayabec 1,721............B 2
Scotstown 762............F 4
Senneville 1,221.........G 4
Shannon 3,488............F 3
Shawbridge 942...........C 4
Shawinigan 23,011........E 3
Shawinigan-Sud 11,325.....E 3
Shawville 1,608..........A 4
Sherbrooke® 74,075.......E 4
Sherrington 614..........D 4
Sillery 12,825...........J 3
Sorel® 20,347............D 4
Squatec 1,000............J 2
Stanstead Plain 1,093....E 4
Sutton 1,599.............E 4
Tadoussac® 900...........H 1
Templeton................B 4
Terrebonne 11,769........H 4
Thetford Mines 19,965....F 3
Thurso 2,780.............B 4
Tourelle (Tourelle-Grand-
　Tourelle) 942...........C 1
Tourville 659............H 2
Tracy 12,843.............D 4
Tring-Jonction 1,315.....F 3
Trois-Pistoles 4,445.....H 1
Trois-Rivières 50,466....E 3
Trois-Rivières® 111,453...E 3
Trois-Rivières-Ouest 13,107 E 3
Upton 926................E 4
Val-Barrette 609.........B 3
Val-Brillant 687.........B 1
Valcourt 2,601...........E 4
Val-David 2,336..........C 3
Vallée-Jonction 1,200....G 3
Valleyfield (Salaberry-de-
　Valleyfield) 29,574.....C 4
Vanier 10,725............J 3

Varennes 8,764...........J 4
Vaudreuil® 7,608.........C 4
Verchères 4,473..........J 4
Verdun 61,287............H 4
Victoriaville 21,838.....F 3
Villeneuve...............J 3
Warwick 2,847............E 4
Waterloo® 4,664..........E 4
Waterville 1,397.........E 4
Weedon-Centre 1,263......F 4
Westmount 20,480.........H 4
Wickham 2,043............E 4
Windsor 5,233............E 4
Wottonville 673..........E 4
Yamachiche® 1,258........E 3

OTHER FEATURES

Alma (isl.)..............F 1
Aylmer (lake)............F 4
Baskatong (res.).........B 3
Batiscan (riv.)..........E 2
Bécancour (riv.).........F 3
Bonaventure (isl.).......D 1
Bonaventure (riv.).......C 1
Brome (lake).............E 4
Brompton (lake)..........E 4
Cascapedia (riv.)........C 1
Chaleur (bay)............C 2
Champlain (lake).........D 4
Chaudière (riv.).........G 4
Chic-Chocs (mts.)........C 1
Chicoutimi (riv.)........F 2
Coudres (isl.)...........G 2
Deschênes (lake).........A 4
Deux Montagnes (lake)....C 4
Ditton (riv.)............F 4
Forillon Nat'l Park......D 1
Fort Chambly Nat'l Hist. Park J 4
Gaspé (bay)..............D 1
Gaspé (cape).............D 1
Gaspé (pen.).............D 2
Gaspésie Prov. Park......C 1
Gatineau (riv.)..........B 3
Îles (lake)..............B 3
Jacques-Cartier (mt.)....C 1
Jacques-Cartier (riv.)...F 2
Kénogami (lake)..........F 1
Kiamika (lake)...........B 3
La Maurice Nat'l Park....D 3
Laurentides Prov. Park...F 2
Lièvre (riv.)............B 3
Lièvres (isl.)...........H 2
Maskinongé (riv.)........D 3
Matane (riv.)............B 1
Matane Prov. Park........B 1

Matapédia (riv.).........B 2
Mégantic (lake)..........G 4
Memphremagog (lake)......E 4
Mercier (dam)............A 3
Métabetchouane (riv.)....F 1
Mille Îles (riv.)........H 4
Montmorency (riv.).......F 4
Mont-Tremblant Prov. Park...C 3
Nicolet (riv.)...........E 3
Nominingue (lake)........B 3
Nord (riv.)..............C 4
Orléans (isl.)...........F 3
Ottawa (riv.)............B 4
Ouareau (riv.)...........C 4
Ouelle (riv.)............H 2
Patapédia (riv.).........B 2
Péribonca (riv.).........F 1
Petite Nation (riv.).....B 4
Prairies (riv.)..........H 4
Rimouski (riv.)..........J 1
Ristigouche (riv.).......B 2
Saguenay (riv.)..........G 1
Sainte-Anne (riv.).......F 3
Sainte-Anne (riv.).......H 4
Saint-François (lake)....F 4
Saint-François (riv.)....E 3
Saint-Jean (lake)........E 1
Saint Lawrence (gulf)....D 2
Saint Lawrence (riv.)....H 1
Saint-Louis (lake).......H 4
Saint-Maurice (riv.).....E 2
Saint-Pierre (lake)......E 3
Shawinigan (riv.)........E 3
Shipshaw (riv.)..........F 1
Soeurs (isl.)............H 4
Témiscouata (lake).......H 2
Tremblant (lake).........C 3
Trente et un Milles (lake)..B 3
Verte (isl.).............H 1
York (riv.)..............D 1

® County seat.
*Population of metropolitan area.

QUÉBEC, NORTHERN
INTERNAL DIVISIONS

Abitibi (county) 93,529....B 2
Abitibi (terr.)..........B 3
Berthier (county) 31,096...C 3
Bonaventure (county) 40,487 D 3
Champlain (county) 119,595..C 3
Charlevoix-Est (co.) 17,448..C 3

Charlevoix-Ouest (county)
　14,172.................C 3
Chicoutimi (county) 174,441..C 2
Gaspé-Est (county) 41,173...E 3
Gaspé-Ouest (county) 18,943 D 3
Gatineau (county) 54,229....B 3
Joliette (county) 60,384....B 3
Lac-Saint-Jean-Est (county)
　47,891.................C 3
Lac-Saint-Jean-Ouest
　(county) 62,952.........C 2
Maskinongé (county) 20,763..C 3
Matane (county) 29,955.....D 3
Matapédia (county) 23,715...D 3
Mistassini (terr.)........C 2
Montcalm (county) 27,557....B 3
Montmorency No. 1 (county)
　23,048.................E 1
Nouveau-Québec (terr.).....E 1
Pontiac (county) 20,283....A 3
Portneuf (county) 58,843...C 3
Québec (county) 458,980....C 3
Rimouski (county) 69,099...D 3
Saguenay (county) 115,881..C 3
Saint-Maurice (co.) 107,703..C 3
Témiscamingue (co.) 52,570..B 3

CITIES and TOWNS

Alma® 26;322.............C 3
Amos® 9,421..............C 3
Baie-Comeau 12,866.......D 3
Baie-du-Poste 1,690......D 3
Chicoutimi® 60,064.......C 3
Gaspé 17,261.............E 3
Hauterive 13,995.........D 3
Jonquière 60,354.........C 3
Lévis 17,895.............C 3
La Tuque 11,556..........C 3
Manicouagan.............D 3
Maniwaki® 5,424.........B 3
Matane® 13,612..........D 3
Mistassini (Baie-du-Poste)
　1,690..................C 2
Mont-Laurier 8,405.......B 3
Montmagny® 12,405.......C 3
New Carlisle® 781........E 3
Nouveau-Comptoir........C 2
Percé® 4,839............E 3
Port-Cartier-Ouest.......D 3
Port-Menier® 275........D 3
Povungnituk 745.........E 1
Québec (cap.)® 166,474...C 3
Rimouski 29,120..........D 3
Rivière-au-Tonnerre 480...D 2
Rivière-du-Loup 13,459...D 3

Rouyn 17,224.............C 3
Sept-Îles 29,262.........D 3
Seven Islands (Sept-Îles)
　29,262.................D 3
Shawinigan 23,011........C 3
Tadoussac 900............D 3
Val d'Or 21,371..........C 3
Ville-Marie 2,651........C 3

OTHER FEATURES

Allard (riv.)............D 3
Anticosti (isl.).........D 3
Baleine, Grande Rivière de la
　(riv.).................C 2
Bell (riv.)..............C 3
Betsiamites (riv.).......D 3
Bienville (lake).........C 2
Broadback (riv.).........C 3
Cabonga (res.)...........B 3
Caniapiscau (riv.).......D 2
Eastmain (riv.)..........C 3
Eau Claire (lake)........C 2
Feuilles (riv.)..........C 1
Gaspésie Prov. Park......E 3
George (riv.)............D 1
Gouin (res.).............C 3
Grande Rivière, La (riv.)..C 2
Honguedo (passage).......D 3
Hudson (bay).............B 2
Hudson (str.)............C 1
Jacques-Cartier (passage)..D 3
James (bay)..............B 2
Koksoak (riv.)...........D 1
Laurentides Prov. Park...C 3
Louis-XIV (pt.)..........C 2
Manicouagan (res.).......D 3
Minto (lake).............C 1
Mistassibi (riv.)........C 3
Mistassini (lake)........C 3
Moisie (riv.)............D 3
Natashquan (riv.)........D 2
Nottaway (riv.)..........C 3
Nouveau-Québec (crater)...D 1
Otish (mts.).............C 3
Ottawa (riv.)............B 3
Péribonca (riv.).........C 3
Plétipi (lake)...........C 3
Saguenay (riv.)..........C 3
Saint-Jean (lake)........C 3
Saint Lawrence (gulf)....D 3
Saint Lawrence (riv.)....D 3
Ungava (pen.)............D 1

® County seat.
*Population of metropolitan are

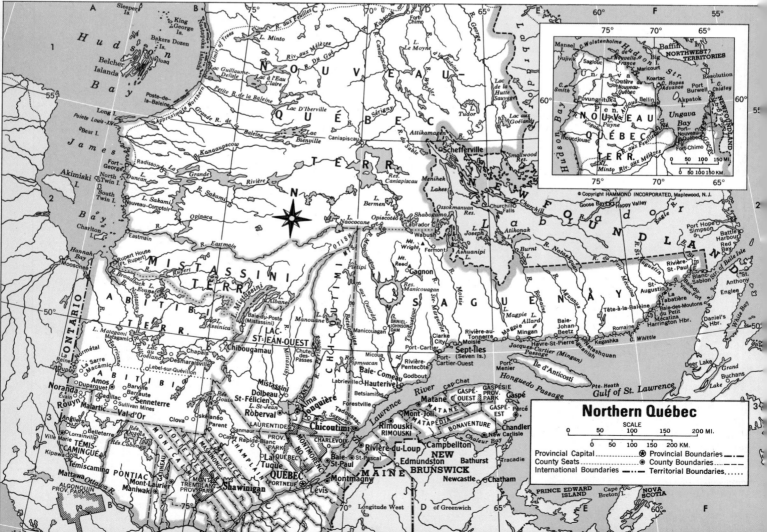

ONTARIO, NORTHERN

INTERNAL DIVISIONS

...ma (terr. dist.) 133,553	D 3
...hrane (terr. dist.) 96,875	D 2
...ora (terr. dist.) 59,421	C 2
...itoulin (terr. dist.) 11,001	D 3
...issing (terr. dist.) 80,268	E 3
...y Sound (terr. dist.)	
...,528	E 3
...59,779	D 3
...bury (terr. dist.) 27,068	D 3
...nder Bay (terr. dist.)	
...53,997	C 3
...iskaming (terr. dist.)	
...1,288	D 3

CITIES and TOWNS

...alk River 1,010	E 3
...t Lake 16,723	D 3
...t Albany 482	D 2
...t Frances® 8,906	B 3
...puskasing 12,014	D 2
...ora® 9,817	B 3
...kland Lake 12,219	D 3
...ose Factory 1,452	D 2
...osonee 1,433	D 2
...kel Centre 12,318	D 3
...rth Bay® 51,268	E 3
...mbroke® 14,026	E 3
...ault Sainte Marie® 82,697	D 3
...dbury 91,829	D 3
...under Bay® 112,486	C 3
...mmins 46,114	D 3
...bley East 20,433	D 3

OTHER FEATURES

...bitibi (lake)	E 3
...bitibi (riv.)	D 2
...bany (riv.)	C 2
...gonquin Prov. Park	E 3
...sheweig (lake)	C 2
...tawapiskat (lake)	C 2
...tawapiskat (riv.)	C 2
...asswood (lake)	A 3
...erens (riv.)	A 2
...g Trout (lake)	B 2
...lack Duck (riv.)	C 1
...loodvein (riv.)	A 2
...aribou (isl.)	C 3

Cobham (riv.)	A 2
Eabamet (lake)	C 2
Ekwan (riv.)	C 2
English (riv.)	B 2
Fawn (riv.)	C 2
Finger (lake)	B 2
Georgian (bay)	D 3
Hannah (bay)	D 2
Henrietta Maria (cape)	D 1
Hudson (bay)	D 1
Huron (lake)	D 3
James (bay)	D 2
Kapiskau (riv.)	D 2
Kapuskasing (riv.)	C 2
Kenogami (riv.)	D 2
Kesagami (riv.)	E 2
Lake of the Woods (lake)	B 3
Lake Superior Prov. Park	C 2
Little Current (riv.)	C 2
Long (lake)	C 2
Manitoulin (isl.)	D 3
Mattagami (riv.)	D 2
Michipicoten (isl.)	C 3
Mille Lacs (lake)	B 3
Missinaibi (lake)	D 2
Missinaibi (riv.)	D 2
Missisa (lake)	D 2
Nipigon (lake)	C 3
Nipissing (lake)	E 3
North (chan.)	D 3
North Caribou (lake)	B 2
Nungesser (lake)	B 2
Ogidaki (mt.)	D 3
Ogoki (riv.)	C 2
Opazatika (riv.)	D 2
Opinnagau (riv.)	D 2
Otoskwin (riv.)	C 2
Pipestone (riv.)	B 2
Polar Bear Prov. Park	D 1
Pukaskwa Prov. Park	C 3
Quetico Prov. Park	B 3
Rainy (lake)	B 3
Red (lake)	B 2
Sachigo (riv.)	B 2
Saganaga (lake)	B 3
Saint Ignace (isl.)	C 3
Saint Joseph (lake)	B 2
Sandy (lake)	B 2
Savant (lake)	B 2
Seine (riv.)	B 3
Seul (lake)	B 2
Severn (lake)	B 2
Severn (riv.)	B 2
Shamattawa (riv.)	C 2
Shibogama (lake)	C 2

Sibley Prov. Park	C 3
Slate (isls.)	C 3
Stout (lake)	B 2
Superior (lake)	D 2
Sutton (lake)	D 2
Sutton (riv.)	D 2
Timagami (lake)	E 3
Timiskaming (lake)	E 3
Trout (lake)	B 2
Wabuk (pt.)	D 1
Winisk (lake)	C 2
Winisk (riv.)	C 2
Winnipeg (riv.)	A 2
Woods (lake)	B 3

ONTARIO

INTERNAL DIVISIONS

Algoma (terr. dist.) 133,553	J 5
Brant (county) 104,427	D 4
Bruce (county) 60,020	C 3
Cochrane (terr. dist.) 96,875	J 4
Dufferin (county) 31,145	D 3
Dundas (county) 18,946	J 2
Durham (reg. munic.) 283,639	F 3
Elgin (county) 69,707	C 5
Essex (county) 312,467	B 5
Frontenac (county) 108,133	H 3
Glengarry (county) 20,254	K 2
Grenville (county) 27,176	J 3
Grey (county) 73,824	C 3
Haldimand-Norfolk (reg. munic.) 89,456	E 5
Haliburton (county) 11,361	F 2
Halton (reg. munic.) 253,883	E 4
Hamilton-Wentworth (reg. munic.) 411,445	D 4
Hastings (county) 106,883	G 3
Huron (county) 56,127	C 4
Kenora (terr. dist.) 59,421	G 5
Kent (county) 107,022	B 5
Lambton (county) 123,445	B 5
Lanark (county) 45,676	H 3
Leeds (county) 53,765	H 3
Lennox and Addington (county) 33,040	G 3
Manitoulin (terr. dist.) 11,001	H 4
Middlesex (county) 318,184	C 4
Muskoka (dist. munic.) 38,370	E 3
Niagara (reg. munic.) 368,288	E 4
Nipissing (terr. dist.) 80,268	F 2
Northumberland (county) 64,966	G 3

Ottawa-Carleton (reg. munic.) 546,849	J 2
Oxford (county) 85,920	D 4
Parry Sound (terr. dist.) 33,528	D 2
Peel (reg. munic.) 490,731	E 4
Perth (county) 66,096	C 4
Peterborough (county) 102,452	F 3
Prescott (county) 30,365	K 2
Prince Edward (county) 22,336	G 3
Rainy River (terr. dist.) 22,798	G 5
Renfrew (county) 87,484	G 2
Russell (county) 22,412	J 2
Simcoe (county) 225,071	E 3
Stormont (county) 61,927	K 2
Sudbury (reg. munic.) 159,779	K 6
Sudbury (terr. dist.) 27,068	J 5
Thunder Bay (terr. dist.) 153,997	H 5
Timiskaming (terr. dist.) 41,288	K 5
Toronto (metro. munic.) 2,137,395	K 4
Victoria (county) 47,854	F 3
Waterloo (reg. munic.) 305,496	D 4
Wellington (county) 129,432	D 4
York (reg. munic.) 252,053	E 4

CITIES and TOWNS

Ailsa Craig 765	C 4
Ajax 25,475	E 4
Alexandria 3,271	K 2
Alfred 1,057	K 2
Alliston 4,712	E 3
Almonte 3,855	H 2
Alvinston 736	B 5
Amherstburg 5,685	A 5
Amherst View 6,110	H 3
Ancaster 14,428	D 4
Angus 3,085	E 3
Appsley 264	F 3
Armstrong 378	H 4
Arnprior 5,828	H 2
Aroland 291	H 4
Arthur 1,700	D 4
Astorville 340	E 1
Athens 948	J 3
Atherley 366	E 3
Atikokan 4,452	G 5

Atwood 723	D 4
Aurora 16,267	J 3
Avonmore 273	K 2
Aylmer 5,254	C 5
Ayr 1,295	D 4
Ayton 424	D 3
Baden 945	D 4
Bala 577	E 2
Bancroft 2,329	G 2
Barrie® 38,423	E 3
Barry's Bay 1,216	G 2
Batawa 430	G 3
Bath 1,071	H 3
Bayfield 649	C 4
Beachburg 682	H 2
Beachville 917	D 4
Beardmore 583	H 5
Beaverton 1,952	E 3
Beeton 1,989	E 3
Belle River 3,568	B 5
Belleville® 34,881	G 3
Belmont 831	C 5
Bethany 365	F 3
Bewdley 508	F 3
Binbrook 306	D 4
Blackstock 720	F 3
Blenheim 4,044	C 5
Blind River 3,444	J 5
Bloomfield 718	G 3
Blyth 926	C 4
Bobcaygeon 1,625	F 3
Bonfield 540	E 1
Bothwell 915	C 5
Bourget 1,057	J 2
Bracebridge® 9,063	E 2
Bradford 7,370	E 3
Braeside 492	H 2
Brampton® 149,030	J 4
Brantford® 74,315	D 4
Bridgenorth 1,633	F 3

Brigden 635	B 5
Brighton 3,147	G 3
Britt 419	D 2
Brockville® 19,896	J 3
Bruce Mines 635	J 5
Brussels 962	C 4
Burford 1,461	D 4
Burgessville 302	D 4
Burk's Falls 922	E 2
Burlington 114,853	E 4
Cache Bay 665	E 1
Caesarea 551	F 3
Calabogie 256	H 2
Caledon 26,645	E 4
Callander 1,158	E 1
Cambridge 77,183	D 4
Campbellford 3,409	G 3
Cannington 1,623	F 3
Capreol 3,845	K 5
Caramat 265	C 4
Cardinal 1,753	J 3
Carleton Place 5,626	H 2
Carlisle 781	D 4
Carlsbad Springs 616	J 2
Carp 707	H 2
Cartier 590	J 5
Casselman 1,675	J 2
Castleton 346	F 3
Chalk River 1,010	G 1
Chapleau 3,243	J 5
Charing Cross 443	B 5
Chatham® 40,952	B 5
Chatsworth 383	D 3
Cherry Valley 289	G 3
Chesley 1,840	C 3
Chesterville 1,430	J 2
Chute-à-Blondeau 365	K 2
City View	J 2
Clarence Creek 796	J 2
Clarksburg 508	C 3

Clifford 645	D 4
Clinton 3,081	C 4
Cobalt 1,759	K 5
Cobden 997	H 2
Coboconk 426	F 3
Cobourg® 11,385	F 4
Cochrane® 4,848	K 5
Colborne 1,796	G 4
Colchester 711	B 6
Coldwater 964	E 3
Collingwood 12,064	D 3
Comber 667	B 5
Conseccon 295	G 3
Cookstown 918	E 3
Cornwall® 46,144	K 2
Cottam 404	B 5
Courtland 647	D 5
Courtright 1,024	B 5
Crediton 971	C 4
Creemore 1,182	D 3
Crysler 540	J 2
Cumberland 518	J 2
Cumberland Beach-Bramshot- Buena Vista 679	E 3
Dashwood 426	C 4
Deep River 5,095	G 1
Delaware 481	C 5
Delhi 4,043	D 5
Delta 360	H 3
Deseronto 1,740	G 3
Douglas 303	H 2
Drayton 809	D 4
Dresden 2,550	B 5
Drumbo 476	D 4
Dryden 6,640	G 4
Dublin 295	C 4
Dubreuilville △988	J 5
Dundalk 1,250	D 3
Dundas 19,586	D 4
Dungannon 284	C 4
Dunnville 11,353	E 5
Durham 2,458	D 3
Dutton 1,115	C 5
Earlton 1,028	K 5
East York 101,974	J 4
Echo Bay 786	J 5
Eden Mills 318	D 4
Eganville 1,245	G 2
Egmondville 465	C 4
Elgin 327	H 3
Elk Lake 526	K 5
Elliot Lake 16,723	B 1
Elmira 7,063	D 4
Elmvale 1,183	E 3
Elmwood 364	C 3
Elora 2,666	D 4
Embro 727	C 4
Embrun 1,883	J 2
Emeryville-Puce 1,611	B 5
Emo 762	F 5
Englehart 1,689	K 5
Enterprise 357	H 3
Erieau 430	C 5
Erin 2,313	D 4
Espanola 5,836	J 5
Essex 6,295	B 5
Etobicoke 298,713	J 4
Everett 366	E 3
Exeter 3,732	C 4
Fauquier 561	J 5
Fenelon Falls 1,701	F 3
Fergus 6,064	D 4
Field 462	E 1
Finch 353	J 2
Fingal 380	C 5
Fitzroy Harbour 446	H 2
Flesherton 565	D 3
Foleyet 484	J 5
Fordwich 365	C 4
Forest 2,671	C 4
Formosa 393	C 4
Fort Erie 24,096	E 5
Fort Frances® 8,906	F 5
Foxboro 597	G 3
Frankford 1,919	G 3
Fraserdale 303	J 5
Freelton 307	D 4
Gananoque 4,863	H 3
Garden Village 270	E 1
Geraldton 2,956	H 5
Glencoe 1,694	C 5
Glen Miller 639	G 3
Glen Robertson 378	K 2
Glen Walter 710	K 2
Goderich® 7,322	C 4
Gogama 652	J 5
Goodwood 335	E 3
Gore Bay 777	B 2
Gorrie 468	C 4
Grafton 409	C 4
Grand Bend 680	C 4
Grand Valley 1,226	D 3
Granton 315	C 4
Gravenhurst 8,532	E 3
Greely 567	J 2
Green Valley 459	K 2
Grimsby 15,797	E 5
Guelph® 71,207	D 4

(continued on following page)

AREA and FACTS

AREA 412,580 sq. mi. (1,068,582 sq. km.)
POPULATION 8,625,107
CAPITAL Toronto
LARGEST CITY Toronto
HIGHEST POINT in Timiskaming Dist. 2,275 ft. (693 m.)
SETTLED IN 1749
ADMITTED TO CONFEDERATION 1867
PROVINCIAL FLOWER White Trillium

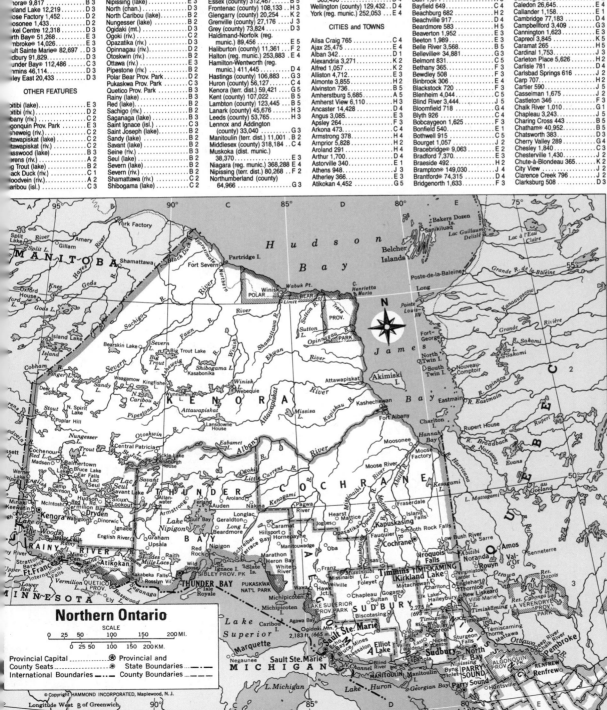

Northern Ontario

SCALE
0 25 50 100 150 200 MI.
0 25 50 100 150 200 KM.

Provincial Capital	®
County Seats	® Provincial and State Boundaries
International Boundaries	County Boundaries

© Copyright HAMMOND INCORPORATED, Maplewood, N. J.

Longitude West B of Greenwich

Topography

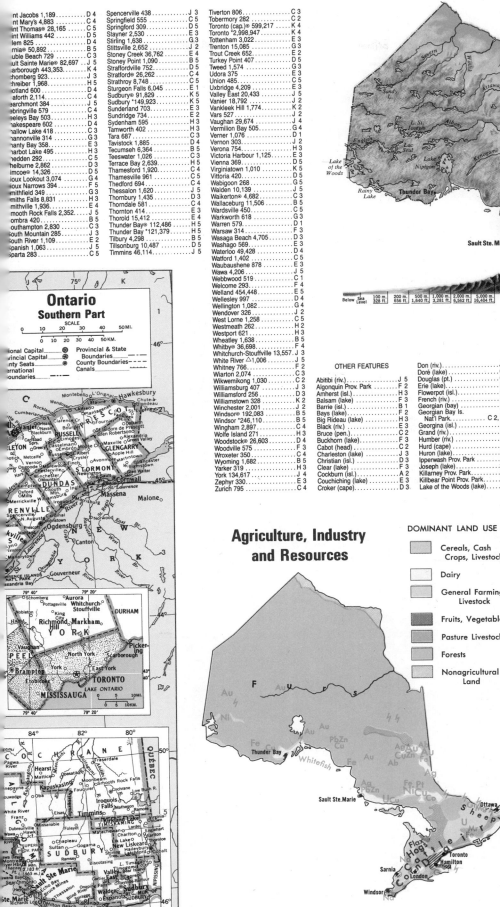

Ontario
Southern Part

SCALE
0 10 20 30 40 50 MI.
0 10 20 30 40 50 KM.

National Capital ® Provincial & State
vincial Capital ® Boundaries
nty Seats ® County Boundaries
ernational Canals
oundaries

Agriculture, Industry and Resources

DOMINANT LAND USE

Cereals, Cash Crops, Livestock
Dairy
General Farming, Livestock
Fruits, Vegetables
Pasture Livestock
Forests
Nonagricultural Land

MAJOR MINERAL OCCURRENCES

Ab	Asbestos	Mg	Magnesium
Ag	Silver	Mr	Marble
Au	Gold	Na	Salt
Co	Cobalt	Ni	Nickel
Cu	Copper	Pb	Lead
Fe	Iron Ore	Pt	Platinum
G	Natural Gas	U	Uranium
Gr	Graphite	Zn	Zinc

⚡ Water Power
〰 Major Industrial Areas

® County seat.
*Population of metropolitan area.
△Population of town or township.

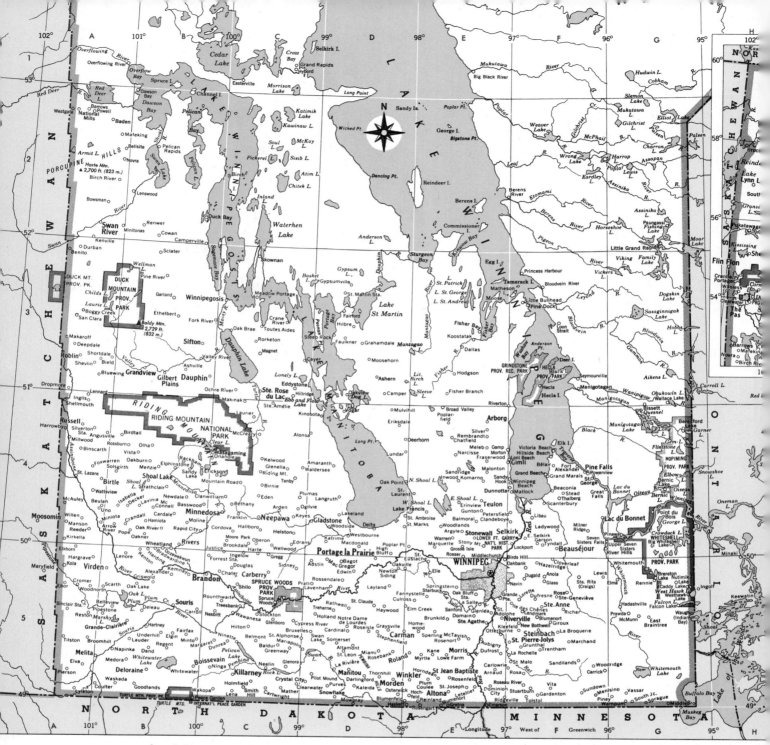

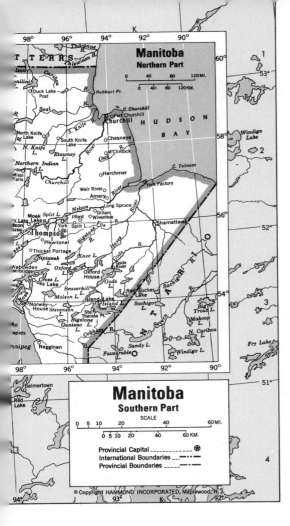

Manitoba
Northern Part

0 40 80 120 MI.
0 40 80 120 KM.

Manitoba
Southern Part

SCALE

0 5 10 20 40 60 MI.
0 5 10 20 40 60 KM.

Provincial Capital ············ ⊛
International Boundaries ···—··—··—
Provincial Boundaries ···———

© Copyright HAMMOND INCORPORATED, Maplewood, N.J.

The Pas 6,390 .... H 3
Thicket Portage 195 .... J 3
Thompson 14,288 .... J 2
Treherne 743 .... D 5
Tyndall 421 .... F 4
Virden 2,940 .... A 5
Vita 364 .... F 5
Wabowden 655 .... J 3
Wallace Lake ●2,044 .... G 3
Wanless 193 .... H 3
Warren 459 .... E 4
Waskada 239 .... B 5
Wawanesa 492 .... C 5
Whitemouth 320 .... G 5
Whitewater ●856 .... B 5
Winkler 5,046 .... E 5
Winnipeg (cap.) 564,473 ..... E 5
Winnipeg *584,842 .... E 5
Winnipeg Beach 565 .... F 4
Winnipegosis 855 .... B 3
Woodlands 185 .... E 4
Woodridge 170 .... G 5
York Landing 229 .... J 2

OTHER FEATURES

Aikens (lake) .... G 3
Anderson (lake) .... D 2
Anderson (pt.) .... F 3
Armit (lake) .... A 2
Assapan (lake) .... G 2
Assiniboine (riv.) .... C 5
Assinika (lake) .... G 3
Assinika (riv.) .... G 2
Atim (lake) .... C 2
Baldy (mt.) .... B 3
Basket (lake) .... C 3
Beaverhill (lake) .... J 3
Berens (isl.) .... E 2
Berens (riv.) .... F 2
Bernic (lake) .... G 4
Big Sand (lake) .... H 2
Bigstone (lake) .... J 3
Bigstone (pt.) .... E 2
Bigstone (riv.) .... J 3
Birch (isl.) .... C 2
Black (isl.) .... F 3
Black (riv.) .... F 4
Bloodvein (riv.) .... G 4
Bonnet (lake) .... G 4
Buffalo (bay) .... G 5
Burntwood (riv.) .... J 2
Caribou (riv.) .... J 1
Carroll (lake) .... G 3
Cedar (lake) .... B 1
Channel (isl.) .... B 2
Charron (lake) .... G 2
Childs (lake) .... A 3
Chitek (lake) .... C 2
Churchill (cape) .... K 2
Churchill (riv.) .... J 2
Clear (lake) .... C 4
Clearwater Lake Prov. Park .. H 3
Cobham (riv.) .... G 1
Cochrane (riv.) .... H 2
Commissioner (isl.) .... E 2
Cormorant (lake) .... H 3
Cross (bay) .... C 1
Cross (lake) .... J 3
Crowduck (lake) .... G 4
Dancing (pt.) .... D 2
Dauphin (lake) .... C 3
Dauphin (riv.) .... D 3
Dawson (bay) .... B 2
Dog (lake) .... D 3
Dogskin (lake) .... G 3
Duck Mountain Prov. Park .... B 3
Eardley (lake) .... F 2

East Shoal (lake) .... E 4
Ebb and Flow (lake) .... C 3
Egg (isl.) .... E 3
Elbow (lake) .... F 4
Elk (isl.) .... F 4
Elliot (lake) .... G 2
Etawney (lake) .... J 2
Etomami (riv.) .... F 2
Falcon (lake) .... G 5
Family (lake) .... G 3
Fisher (bay) .... E 3
Fisher (riv.) .... E 3
Fishing (lake) .... C 3
Flintstone (lake) .... G 4
Fox (riv.) .... K 2
Gammon (riv.) .... G 3
Garner (lake) .... G 4
Gem (lake) .... G 4
George (isl.) .... E 2
George (lake) .... G 4
Gilchrist (creek) .... F 2
Gilchrist (lake) .... G 3
Gods (lake) .... K 3
Gods (riv.) .... K 3
Granville (lake) .... H 2
Grass (riv.) .... J 3
Grass River Prov. Park ...... H 3
Grindstone Prov. Rec. Park .. F 3
Gunisao (lake) .... D 3
Gypsum (lake) .... D 3
Harrop (lake) .... G 2
Harte (mt.) .... A 2
Hayes (riv.) .... K 3
Hecla (isl.) .... F 3
Hecla Prov. Park .... F 3
Hobbs (lake) .... G 3
Horseshoe (lake) .... G 2
Hubbart (pt.) .... K 2
Hudson (bay) .... K 2
Hudwin (lake) .... G 1
Inland (lake) .... C 2
International Peace Garden .. B 5
Island (lake) .... K 3
Katimik (lake) .... C 2
Kawinaw (lake) .... C 2
Kinwow (bay) .... E 2
Kississing (lake) .... H 2
Knee (lake) .... J 3
Lake of the Woods (lake) .... H 5
La Salle (riv.) .... E 5
Laurie (lake) .... A 3
Leaf (riv.) .... F 2
Lewis (lake) .... G 2
Leyond (riv.) .... F 3
Little Birch (lake) .... E 3
Lonely (lake) .... C 3
Long (lake) .... G 4
Long (pt.) .... D 1
Long (pt.) .... D 4
Manigotagan (lake) .... G 4

Manigotagan (riv.) .... G 3
Manitoba (lake) .... D 4
Mantagao (riv.) .... E 3
Marshy (lake) .... B 5
McKay (lake) .... C 2
McPhail (riv.) .... F 2
Minnedosa (riv.) .... B 4
Moar (lake) .... G 2
Molson (lake) .... J 3
Moose (isl.) .... E 3
Morrison (lake) .... C 1
Mossy (riv.) .... C 3
Mukutawa (lake) .... G 2
Mukutawa (riv.) .... E 1
Muskeg (bay) .... G 6
Nejanilini (lake) .... J 1
Nelson (riv.) .... J 2
Nopiming Prov. Park .... G 4
Northern Indian (lake) ...... J 2
North Knife (lake) .... J 2
North Seal (riv.) .... H 2
North Shoal (lake) .... E 4
Nueltin (lake) .... H 1
Oak (lake) .... B 5
Obukowin (lake) .... G 3
Oiseau (lake) .... G 4
Oiseau (riv.) .... G 4
Overflow (bay) .... A 1
Overflowing (riv.) .... A 1
Owl (riv.) .... K 2
Oxford (lake) .... J 3
Paint (lake) .... G 2
Palsen (riv.) .... G 2
Pelican (bay) .... B 2
Pelican (lake) .... B 2
Pelican (lake) .... C 5
Pembina (hills) .... D 5
Pembina (riv.) .... C 5
Peonan (pt.) .... D 3
Pickerel (lake) .... C 2
Pigeon (riv.) .... F 2
Pipestone (creek) .... A 5
Plum (creek) .... B 5
Plum (lake) .... B 5
Poplar (riv.) .... E 2
Porcupine (hills) .... A 2
Portage (bay) .... D 3
Punk (isl.) .... F 3
Quesnel (lake) .... G 4
Rat (riv.) .... F 5
Red (riv.) .... F 4
Red Deer (lake) .... A 2
Red Deer (riv.) .... A 2
Reindeer (isl.) .... E 2
Reindeer (lake) .... H 2
Riding (mt.) .... B 4
Riding Mountain Nat'l Park .. B 4
Rock (lake) .... C 5
Ross (isl.) .... J 3
Sagemace (bay) .... B 3

Saint Andrew (lake) .... E 3
Saint George (lake) .... E 3
Saint Martin (lake) .... D 3
Saint Patrick (lake) .... E 3
Sale (riv.) .... E 5
Sandy (isls.) .... D 2
Sasaginnigak (lake) .... G 3
Seal (riv.) .... J 2
Selkirk (isl.) .... C 1
Setting (lake) .... H 3
Shoal (lake) .... G 5
Shoal (riv.) .... B 2
Sipiwesk (lake) .... J 3
Sisib (lake) .... C 2
Sleeve (lake) .... E 3
Slemon (lake) .... G 1
Snowshoe (lake) .... G 4
Soul (lake) .... C 2
Souris (riv.) .... B 5
Southern Indian (lake) ...... H 2
South Knife (riv.) .... J 2
South Seal (riv.) .... J 2
Split (lake) .... J 2
Spruce (isl.) .... B 1
Spruce Woods Prov. Park ..... C 5
Stevenson (lake) .... J 3
Sturgeon (bay) .... B 2
Swan (lake) .... D 5
Swan (lake) .... A 3
Swan (riv.) .... A 3
Tadoule (lake) .... J 2
Tamarack (lake) .... F 3
Tatnam (cape) .... K 2
Traverse (bay) .... F 4
Turtle (mts.) .... B 5
Turtle (riv.) .... B 4
Turtle Mountain Prov. Park .. B 5
Valley (lake) .... B 3
Vickers (lake) .... F 3
Viking (lake) .... G 3
Wanipigow (riv.) .... G 3
Washow (bay) .... F 3
Waterhen (lake) .... C 2
Weaver (lake) .... F 2
Wellman (lake) .... B 3
West Hawk (lake) .... G 5
West Shoal (lake) .... E 4
Whitemouth (lake) .... G 5
Whitemouth (riv.) .... G 5
Whiteshell Prov. Park .... G 4
Whitewater (lake) .... B 5
Wicked (pt.) .... D 2
Winnipeg (lake) .... E 2
Winnipeg (riv.) .... G 4
Winnipegosis (lake) .... C 2
Woods (lake) .... H 5
Wrong (lake) .... F 2

*Population of metropolitan area.
●Population of rural municipality.

AREA 250,999 sq. mi. (650,087 sq. km.)
POPULATION 1,026,241
CAPITAL Winnipeg
LARGEST CITY Winnipeg
HIGHEST POINT Baldy Mtn. 2,729 ft. (832 m.)
SETTLED IN 1812
ADMITTED TO CONFEDERATION 1870
PROVINCIAL FLOWER Prairie Crocus

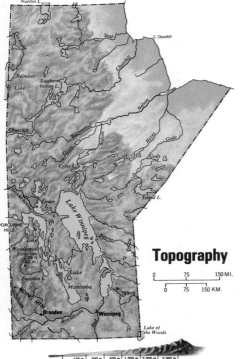

Topography

0 75 150 MI.
0 75 150 KM.

Below Sea Level | 100 m. 328 ft. | 200 m. 656 ft. | 500 m. 1,640 ft. | 1,000 m. 3,281 ft. | 2,000 m. 6,562 ft. | 5,000 m. 16,404 ft.

Agriculture, Industry and Resources

DOMINANT LAND USE

▨ Cereals (chiefly barley, oats)
▨ Cereals, Livestock
☐ Dairy
▨ Livestock
▨ Forests
▨ Nonagricultural Land

MAJOR MINERAL OCCURRENCES

Au Gold
Co Cobalt
Cu Copper
Na Salt
Ni Nickel
O Petroleum
Pb Lead
Pt Platinum
Zn Zinc

⚡ Water Power
▧ Major Industrial Areas

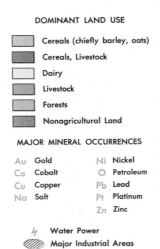

Topography

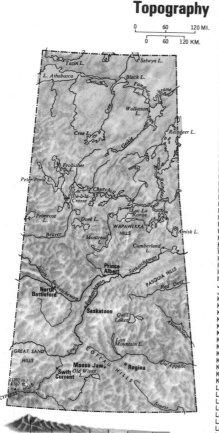

0   60   120 MI.

0   60   120 KM.

5,000 m. | 2,000 m. | 1,000 m. | 500 m. | 200 m. | 100 m. | Sea
16,404 ft. | 6,562 ft. | 3,281 ft. | 1,640 ft. | 656 ft. | 328 ft. | Level Below

CITIES and TOWNS

Abbey 218 .... C 5
Aberdeen 496 .... E 3
Abernethy 300 .... H 5
Air Ronge 557 .... M 3
Alameda 318 .... J 6
Alida 169 .... K 6
Allan 871 .... E 4
Alsask 652 .... B 4
Annaheim 209 .... G 3
Antelope ●231 .... C 5
Arborfield 439 .... H 2
Archerwill 286 .... H 3
Arcola 493 .... J 6
Arlington Beach ●432 ...... F 4
Asquith 507 .... D 3
Assiniboia 2,924 .... F 6
Avonlea 442 .... G 5
Baildon ●799 .... F 5
Balcarres 739 .... H 5
Balgonie 777 .... G 5
Batoche .... E 3
Battleford 3,565 .... C 3
Beauval 606 .... L 3
Beechy 279 .... D 5
Bengough 536 .... F 6
Bethune 369 .... F 5
Bienfait 835 .... J 6
Biggar 2,561 .... C 3
Big River 819 .... D 2
Birch Hills 957 .... F 3
Bjorkdale 269 .... H 3
Blaine Lake 653 .... D 3
Borden 197 .... D 3
Brabant Lake 245 .... M 3
Bradwell 168 .... E 4
Bredenbury 467 .... K 5
Briercrest 151 .... F 5
Broadview 840 .... J 5
Brock 184 .... C 4
Browning ●687 .... J 6
Bruno 772 .... F 3
Buchanan 392 .... J 4
Buffalo Gap ●598 .... F 6
Buffalo Narrows 1,088 ... L 3
Burstall 550 .... B 5
Cabri 632 .... C 5
Cadillac 173 .... D 6
Calder 164 .... K 4
Cana ●1,238 .... J 5
Candle Lake 219 .... F 2
Cando 163 .... D 3
Canoe Lake 182 .... L 3
Canora 2,667 .... J 4
Canwood 340 .... E 2
Carievale 246 .... K 6
Carlyle 1,074 .... J 6
Carnduff 1,043 .... K 6
Carrot River 1,169 ...... H 2

Central Butte 548 .... E 5
Ceylon 184 .... G 6
Chaplin 389 .... E 5
Chitek Lake 170 .... D 2
Choiceland 543 .... G 2
Christopher Lake 227 ... F 2
Churchbridge 972 .... J 5
Clavet 234 .... E 4
Climax 293 .... C 6
Cochin 221 .... C-2
Codette 236 .... H 2
Coleville 383 .... B 4
Colonsay 594 .... F 4
Connaught Heights ●982 . G 3
Conquest 256 .... D 4
Consul 153 .... B 6
Coronach 1,032 .... F 6
Craik 565 .... F 4
Craven 206 .... G 5
Creelman 184 .... H 6
Creighton 1,636 .... N 4
Cudworth 947 .... F 3
Cumberland House 831 .. J 2
Cupar 669 .... G 5
Cut Knife 624 .... B 3
Dalmeny 1,064 .... E 3
Davidson 1,166 .... E 4
Debden 403 .... E 2
Delisle 980 .... D 4
Denare Beach 592 .... M 4
Denzil 199 .... B 3
Deschambault Lake 386 . M 3
Dinsmore 398 .... D 4
Dodsland 272 .... C 4
Domremy 209 .... F 3
Drake 211 .... G 4
Duck Lake 699 ...... E 3
Dundurn 531 .... E 4
Dysart 275 .... H 5
Earl Grey 303 ..... G 5
Eastend 723 ...... C 6
Eatonia 528 ...... B 4
Ebenezer 164 .... J 4
Edam 384 .... C 2
Edenwold 143 .... G 5
Elbow 313 .... E 4
Eldorado 229 .... L 2
Elfros 199 ...... H 4
Elrose 624 ...... D 4
Elstow 143 ...... E 4
Endeavour 199 ... J 3
Englefeld 271 ... F 3
Enwood 149 ..... J 3
Esterhazy 3,065 . J 5
Eston 1,413 ..... C 4
Estevan 9,174 ... H 6
Eyebrow 168 .... E 5
Fillmore 396 .... H 6
Fleming 141 .... K 5
Flin Flon 367 ... N 4

Foam Lake 1,452 .... H 4
Fond du Lac 494 .... L 2
Fort Qu'Appelle 1,827 ... H 5
Fox Valley 380 .... B 5
Francis 182 .... H 5
Frobisher 166 .... J 6
Frontier 619 .... C 6
Gainsborough 308 ..... K 6
Gerald 197 .... K 5
Glaslyn 430 .... D 2
Glenavon 284 .... J 5
Glen Ewen 168 ...... K 6
Goodsoil 263 .... L 4
Govan 394 .... G 4
Grand Coulee 208 ... G 5
Gravelbourg 1,338 ... E 6
Grayson 264 .... J 5
Green Acres 139 .... F 2
Green Lake 634 ..... L 4
Grenfell 1,307 ...... J 5
Guernsey 198 ...... F 4
Gull Lake 1,095 .... C 5
Hafford 557 .... D 3
Hague 625 .... E 3
Hanley 484 .... E 4
Harris 259 .... D 4
Hawarden 137 .... E 4
Hearts Hill ●552 .. B 3
Hepburn 411 ..... E 3
Herbert 1,019 .... D 5
Hodgeville 329 .... E 5
Holdfast 297 ..... F 5
Hudson Bay 2,361 . J 3
Humboldt 4,705 ... F 3
Hyas 165 .... J 4
Ile-à-la-Crosse 1,035 . L 3
Imperial 501 ..... F 4
Indian Head 1,889 . H 5
Invermay 353 .... J 4
Ituna 870 .... H 4
Jansen 223 ..... F 4
Jasmin ●14 ..... H 4
Kamsack 2,688 .. K 4
Kelliher 397 .... H 4
Kelvington 1,054 . H 3
Kenaston 345 ... E 4
Kennedy 275 ... J 5
Kerrobert 1,141 . C 4
Kincaid 256 .... D 6
Kindersley 3,969 . B 4
Kinistino 783 ... F 3
Kipling 1,016 ... J 5
Kisbey 228 .... J 6
Kronau 154 .... G 5
Kyle 516 ...... C 5
Lac Pelletier ●586 . C 6
Lafleche 583 .... E 6
Laird 233 .... E 3
Lake Lenore 361 . G 3
La Loche 1,632 .. L 2
Lampman 651 ... J 6
Lancer 156 ..... C 5
Landis 277 ..... C 3
Lang 219 ...... G 5
Langenburg 1,324 . K 5
Langham 1,151 ... E 3
Lanigan 1,732 .... F 4
La Ronge 2,579 ... L 3
Lashburn 813 .... B 2
Leader 1,108 .... B 5
Leask 478 .... E 2
Lebret 274 ...... H 5
Lemberg 414 .... H 5
Leoville 393 ..... D 2
Leroy 504 ...... G 4
Lestock 402 ..... G 4
Limerick 164 .... E 6
Lintlaw 234 ..... H 3

Lipton 364 .... H 5
Lloydminster 6,034 .... A 2
Loon Lake 369 .... B 1
Loreburn 201 .... E 4
Lucky Lake 333 ...... D 5
Lumsden 1,303 ...... G 5
Luseland 704 .... B 3
Macdowall 171 ...... E 2
Macklin 976 .... A 3
Macoun 190 .... H 6
Maidstone 1,001 .... B 2
Mankota 375 .... D 6
Manor 368 .... K 6
Maple Creek 2,470 .. B 6
Marcelin 208 ...... E 3
Margo 153 .... H 4
Marriott ●627 ..... D 4
Marsden 229 ...... B 3
Marshall 453 ..... A 2
Martensville 1,966 . E 3
Maryfield 431 .... K 6
Maymont 212 .... D 3
McLean 189 ..... G 5
Meacham 178 ... F 3
Meadow Lake 3,857 . C 1
Meath Park 262 ... F 2
Medstead 163 .... C 2
Melfort 6,010 .... G 3
Melville 5,092 ... J 5
Meota 235 ...... C 2
Mervin 155 ..... C 2
Midale 564 ..... H 6
Middle Lake 275 . F 3
Milden 251 ..... D 4
Milestone 602 ... G 5
Montmartre 544 .. H 5
Montreal Lake 448 . F 1
Moose Jaw 33,941 . F 5
Moose Range ●679 . H 2
Moosomin 2,579 ... K 5
Morse 416 .... D 5
Mortlach 293 .... E 5
Mossbank 464 ... E 6
Muenster 385 ... F 3
Naicam 886 .... G 3
Neilburg 354 ... B 3
Neuanlage 144 .. E 3
Neudorf 425 ... J 5
Neuhorst 146 .. E 3
Nipawin 4,376 . H 2
Nokomis 524 .. F 4
Norquay 552 .. J 4
North Battleford 14,030 . C 3
North Portal 164 ... J 6
Odessa 232 ..... H 5
Ogema 441 ..... G 6
Osler 527 .... E 3
Outlook 1,976 ... E 4
Oxbow 1,191 .... J 6
Paddockwood 211 . F 2
Pangman 227 .... G 6
Paradise Hill 421 . B 2
Patuanak 173 .... L 3
Paynton 210 ..... B 2
Pelican Narrows 331 . N 3
Pelly 391 .... K 4
Pennant 202 .... C 5
Pense 472 ...... G 5
Perdue 407 ..... D 3
Pierceland 425 .. K 4
Pilger 150 ...... F 3
Pilot Butte 1,255 . G 5
Pine House 612 .. M 3
Plenty 175 ...... C 4
Plunkett 150 .... F 4
Ponteix 769 ..... D 6
Porcupine Plain 937 . J 3
Preeceville 1,243 .. J 4

Prelate 317 .... B 5
Prince Albert 31,380 ..... F 3
Prud'homme 222 .... F 3
Punnichy 394 .... G 4
Qu'Appelle 653 .... H 5
Quill Lake 514 .... G 3
Quinton 169 .... G 4
Rabbit Lake 159 ...... D 2
Radisson 439 .... D 3
Radville 1,012 ...... G 6
Rama 133 .... H 4
Raymore 635 ...... G 4
Redvers 859 ...... K 6
Regina (cap.) 162,613 . G 5
Regina *164,313 ...... G 5
Regina Beach 603 ... F 5
Rhein 271 .... J 4
Richmound 188 .... B 5
Riverhurst 193 .... E 5
Rocanville 934 .... K 5
Roche Percé 142 ... J 6
Rockglen 511 ..... F 6
Rosetown 2,664 ... D 4
Rose Valley 538 ... H 3
Rosthern 1,609 .... E 3
Rouleau 443 .... F 5
Saint Benedict 157 . F 3
Saint Brieux 401 ... G 3
Saint Louis 448 .... F 3
Saint Philips ●538 .. K 4
Saint Walburg 802 .. B 2
Saltcoats 549 ...... J 4
Sandy Bay 756 .... N 3
Saskatoon 154,210 .. E 3
Saskatoon *154,210 . E 3
Sceptre 169 .... B 5
Scott 203 .... C 3
Sedley 373 .... H 5
Semans 344 ...... G 4
Shaunavon 2,112 .. C 6
Sheho 285 .... H 4
Shell Lake 220 ... D 2
Shellbrook 1,228 . E 2
Simpson 231 .... F 4
Sintaluta 215 ... H 5
Smeaton 246 .... G 2
Southey 697 .... G 5
Spalding 337 .... G 3
Spiritwood 926 .. D 2
Springside 533 .. J 4
Spy Hill 354 .... K 5
Star City 527 ... G 3
Stenen 143 ..... J 4
Stockholm 391 .. J 5
Stonehenge ●701 . F 6
Storthoaks 142 .. K 6
Stoughton 716 .. H 6
Strasbourg 842 . G 4
Sturgis 789 .... J 4
Swift Current 14,747 . D 5
Tantallon 196 ... K 5
Theodore 473 ... J 4
Timber Bay 152 .. F 1
Tisdale 3,107 ... H 3
Togo 181 ...... K 4
Tompkins 275 .. C 5
Torch River ●2,440 . G 2
Torquay 311 .... H 6
Tramping Lake 178 . B 3
Tugaske 175 .... E 5
Turnor Lake 166 . L 3
Turtleford 505 .. B 2
Unity 2,408 ..... B 3
Uranium City 2,507 . L 2
Val Marie 236 ... D 6
Vanguard 287 ... D 6
Vanscoy 298 .... D 4
Vibank 369 ..... H 5

Viscount 386 .... F 4
Vonda 313 .... F 3
Wadena 1,495 .... H 4
Wakaw 1,030 .... F 3
Waldeck 292 .... D 5
Waldheim 758 .... E 3
Walpole ●711 .... K 6
Wapella 487 .... K 5
Warman 2,076 ..... E 3
Waseca 169 ...... B 2
Waskesiu Lake 176 . E 2
Watrous 1,830 .... F 4
Watson 901 ...... G 3
Wawota 622 ..... J 6
Weldon 279 ..... F 3
Welwyn 170 .... K 5
Weyburn 9,523 .. H 6
White City 602 .. G 5
White Fox 394 .. H 2
Whitewood 1,003 . J 5
Wilcox 202 ..... G 5
Wilkie 1,501 .... C 3
Willow Bunch 494 . F 6
Willow Creek ●1,218 . B 6
Windthorst 254 ... J 5
Wiseton 195 ..... D 4
Wishart 212 ..... G 4
Wolfe Lake 248 ... N 2
Wolseley 904 .... H 5
Wymark 162 ..... D 5
Wynyard 2,147 ... G 4
Yarbo 158 ...... K 5

Yellow Grass 477 ...... H 5
Yorkton 15,339 .... J
Young 456 .... F 3
Zenon Park 273 .... H

OTHER FEATURES

Allan (hills) .... E
Amisk (lake) .... M
Antelope (lake) C
Antler (riv.) .... K
Arm (riv.) L
Assiniboine (riv.) ...... A
Athabasca (lake) L
Bad (lake) C
Bad (hills) C
Basin (lake) .... G
Batoche Nat'l Hist. Site . E
Battle (creek) .... A
Battle (riv.) C
Bear (hills) C
Beaver (hills) .... H
Beaver (riv.) L
Beaverlodge (lake) ... L
Big Muddy (lake) .... G
Bigstick (lake) ...... B
Birch (lake) .... B
Bitter (lake) .... M
Black (lake) .... M
Boundary (plat.) ... B
Brightsand (lake) .. B
Bronson (lake) .... B

Agriculture, Industry and Resources

DOMINANT LAND USE

▢ Wheat
▢ Cereals (chiefly barley, oats)
▢ Cereals, Livestock
▢ Livestock
▢ Forests

MAJOR MINERAL OCCURRENCES

Au Gold
Cu Copper
G   Natural Gas
He Helium
K   Potash
Lg Lignite
Na Salt
O   Petroleum
S   Sulfur
U   Uranium
Zn Zinc

⚡ Water Power
▨ Major Industrial Areas

AREA 251,699 sq. mi. (651,900 sq. km.)
POPULATION 968,313
CAPITAL Regina
LARGEST CITY Regina
HIGHEST POINT Cypress Hills 4,567 ft. (1,392 m.)
SETTLED IN 1774
ADMITTED TO CONFEDERATION 1905
PROVINCIAL FLOWER Prairie Lily

*Population of metropolitan area.
●Population of rural municipality.

Saskatchewan
Northern Part

Saskatchewan

SCALE
0 5 10   20   40   60 MI.
0 5 10 20 40 60 KM.

Provincial Capital .... ⊛
International Boundaries ....
Provincial Boundaries ....

© Copyright HAMMOND INCORPORATED, Maplewood, N.J.

Alberta
Southern Part

SCALE

| 0 10 20 40 60 80 MI. |
| 0 10 20 40 60 80 KM. |

Provincial Capital .... ✷
International Boundaries _____
Provincial Boundaries ------------------

Alberta
Northern Part

0 20 40 60 80 MI.
0 20 40 60 80KM.

© Copyright HAMMOND INCORPORATED, Maplewood, N.J.

Alberta 115

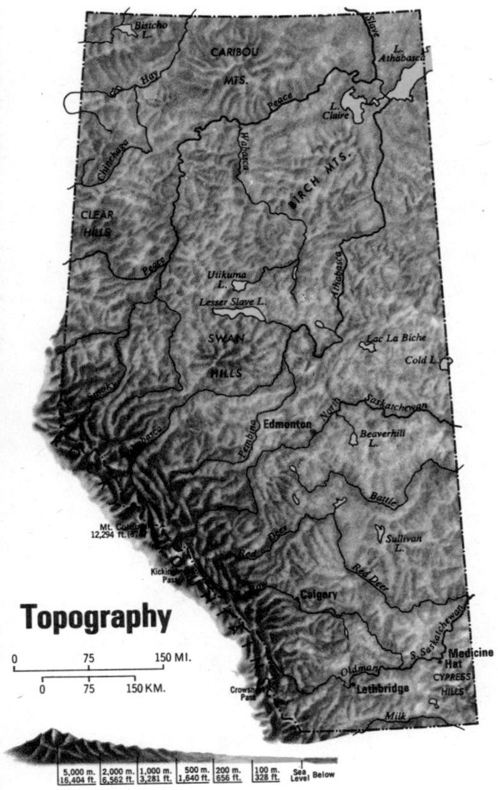
Bistcho L.
Slave
CARIBOU MTS.
L. Athabasca
Hay
Peace
L. Claire
Chinchaga
Wabasca
BIRCH MTS.
CLEAR HILLS
Utikuma L.
Athabasca
Lesser Slave L.
SWAN HILLS
Lac La Biche
Cold L.
Smoky
North Saskatchewan
Edmonton
Beaverhill L.
Pembina
Battle
Mt. Columbia 12,294 ft.
Sullivan L.
Red Deer
Calgary
Medicine Hat
Oldman
Lethbridge
CYPRESS HILLS
Milk
0 75 150 MI.
0 75 150 KM.
5,000 m. 16,404 ft.
2,000 m. 6,562 ft.
1,000 m. 3,281 ft.
500 m. 1,640 ft.
200 m. 656 ft.
100 m. 328 ft.
Sea Level
Below

Topography

AREA 255,285 sq. mi. (661,185 sq. km.)
POPULATION 2,237,724
CAPITAL Edmonton
LARGEST CITY Edmonton
HIGHEST POINT Mt. Columbia 12,294 ft. (3,747 m.)
SETTLED IN 1861
ADMITTED TO CONFEDERATION 1905
PROVINCIAL FLOWER Wild Rose

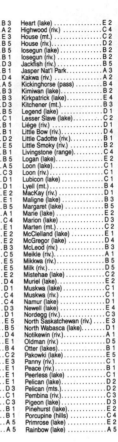

CITIES and TOWNS

ne 457 . . . . D 4
rie 8,414 . . . . C 4
erta Beach 485 . . . . C 3
837 . . . . D 3
drew 548 . . . . D 3
ler Lake 334 . . . . D 3
more 224 . . . . E 2
owwood 156 . . . . D 4
abasca 1,731 . . . . D 2
nff 4,208 . . . . C 4
rnwell 359 . . . . D 5
rons 315 . . . . D 4
rrhead 3,736 . . . . C 2
shaw 875 . . . . D 3
ssano 1,200 . . . . D 4
wlf 350 . . . . D 3
aumont 2,638 . . . . D 3
averlodge 1,937 . . . . A 2
iseker 580 . . . . D 4
ntley 823 . . . . C 3
rwyn 557 . . . . B 1
g Valley 360 . . . . D 3
ack Diamond 1,444 . . . . C 4
ackfalds 1,488 . . . . D 3
ackfoot 220 . . . . E 3
ackie 298 . . . . D 4
on Accord 1,376 . . . . D 3
onnyville 4,454 . . . . E 2
owden 989 . . . . C 4
ow Island 1,491 . . . . E 5
oyle 638 . . . . D 2
agg Creek 505 . . . . C 4
eton 552 . . . . C 3
rooks 9,421 . . . . E 4
uce 88 . . . . E 3
uderheim 1,136 . . . . D 3
urdett 220 . . . . E 5
algary 592,743 . . . . C 4
algary *592,743 . . . . C 4
almar 1,003 . . . . D 3
amrose 12,570 . . . . D 3
anmore 3,484 . . . . C 4
arbon 434 . . . . D 4
ardston 3,267 . . . . D 5
armangay 266 . . . . D 4
aroline 436 . . . . C 3
arseland 484 . . . . D 4
arstairs 1,587 . . . . D 4
astor 1,123 . . . . D 3
ereal 249 . . . . E 4
Champion 339 . . . . D 4
Chauvin 298 . . . . E 3
Chipman 266 . . . . D 3
Clairmont 469 . . . . A 2
Claresholm 3,493 . . . . D 4
Clive 364 . . . . D 3
Clyde 364 . . . . D 2
Coaldale 4,579 . . . . D 5
Coalhurst 882 . . . . D 5
Cochrane 3,544 . . . . C 4
Cold Lake 2,110 . . . . E 2
College Heights 267 . . . . D 3
Consort 632 . . . . E 3
Cooking Lake 218 . . . . D 3
Coronation 1,309 . . . . E 3
Coutts 400 . . . . D 5
Cowley 304 . . . . D 5
Cremona 382 . . . . C 4
Crossfield 1,217 . . . . C 4
Daysland 679 . . . . D 3
Delburne 574 . . . . D 3
Desmarais 260 . . . . D 2
Devon 3,885 . . . . D 3
Didsbury 3,095 . . . . C 4
Donalda 280 . . . . D 3
Donnelly 336 . . . . B 2
Drayton Valley 5,042 . . . . C 3
Drumheller 6,508 . . . . D 4
Duchess 429 . . . . E 4
East Coulee 218 . . . . D 4
Eckville 870 . . . . C 3
Edgerton 387 . . . . E 3
Edmonton (cap.) 532,246 . . . . D 3
Edmonton *657,057 . . . . D 3
Edmonton Beach 280 . . . . C 3
Edson 5,835 . . . . B 3
Elk Point 1,022 . . . . E 3
Elnora 249 . . . . D 3
Entwistle 462 . . . . C 3
Erskine 259 . . . . D 3
Evansburg 779 . . . . C 3
Exshaw 353 . . . . C 4
Fairview 2,869 . . . . A 1
Falher 1,102 . . . . B 2
Faust 399 . . . . C 2
Foremost 568 . . . . E 5
Forestburg 924 . . . . E 3
Fort Assiniboine 207 . . . . C 2
Fort Chipewyan 944 . . . . C 5
Fort Macleod 3,139 . . . . D 5
Fort McKay 267 . . . . E 1
Fort McMurray 31,000 . . . . E 1
Fort Saskatchewan 12,169 . . . . D 3
Fort Vermilion 752 . . . . B 5
Fox Creek 1,978 . . . . B 2
Fox Lake 634 . . . . B 5
Gibbons 2,276 . . . . D 3
Gift Lake 428 . . . . C 2
Girouxville 325 . . . . B 2
Gleichen 381 . . . . D 4
Glendon 430 . . . . E 2
Glenwood 259 . . . . D 5
Grand Centre 3,146 . . . . E 2
Grande Cache 4,523 . . . . A 3
Grande Prairie 24,263 . . . . A 2
Granum 399 . . . . D 5
Grimshaw 2,316 . . . . B 1
Grouard Mission 221 . . . . C 2
Hanna 2,806 . . . . E 4
Hardisty 641 . . . . E 3
Hay Lakes 302 . . . . D 3
Heisler 212 . . . . D 3
High Level 2,194 . . . . A 5
High Prairie 2,506 . . . . B 2
High River 4,792 . . . . D 4
Hines Creek 575 . . . . A 1
Hinton 8,342 . . . . B 3
Holden 430 . . . . D 3
Hughenden 267 . . . . E 3
Hythe 639 . . . . A 2
Innisfail 5,247 . . . . D 3
Innisfree 255 . . . . E 3
Irma 474 . . . . E 3
Irricana 558 . . . . D 4
Irvine 360 . . . . E 5
Jasper 3,269 . . . . B 3
John d'Or Prairie 437 . . . . B 5
Joussard 330 . . . . B 2
Killam 1,005 . . . . E 3
Kinuso 285 . . . . C 2
Kitscoty 497 . . . . E 3
Lac La Biche 2,007 . . . . E 2
Lacombe 5,591 . . . . D 3
La Crete 479 . . . . B 5
Lake Louise 355 . . . . B 4
Lamont 1,563 . . . . D 3
Leduc 12,471 . . . . D 3
Legal 1,022 . . . . D 3
Lethbridge 54,072 . . . . D 5
Linden 407 . . . . D 4
Little Buffalo Lake 253 . . . . B 1
Lloydminster 8,997 . . . . E 3
Longview 301 . . . . C 4
Lougheed 226 . . . . E 3
Lundbreck 244 . . . . C 5
Magrath 1,576 . . . . D 5
Manning 1,173 . . . . B 1
Mannville 788 . . . . E 3
Marlboro 211 . . . . B 3
Marwayne 500 . . . . E 3
Mayerthorpe 1,475 . . . . C 3
McLennan 1,125 . . . . B 2
Medicine Hat 40,380 . . . . E 4
Milk River 894 . . . . D 5
Millet 1,120 . . . . D 3
Mirror 507 . . . . D 3
Monarch 212 . . . . D 5
Morinville 4,657 . . . . D 3
Morrin 244 . . . . D 4
Mundare 604 . . . . D 3
Myrnam 397 . . . . E 3
Nacmine 369 . . . . D 4
Nampa 334 . . . . B 1
Nanton 1,641 . . . . D 4
New Norway 291 . . . . D 3
New Sarepta 417 . . . . D 3
Nobleford 534 . . . . D 5
North Calling Lake 234 . . . . D 2
Okotoks 3,847 . . . . C 4
Olds 4,813 . . . . D 4
Onoway 621 . . . . C 3
Oyen 975 . . . . E 4
Peace River 5,907 . . . . B 1
Penhold 1,531 . . . . D 3
Picture Butte 1,404 . . . . D 5
Pincher Creek 3,757 . . . . D 5
Plamondon 259 . . . . D 2
Pollockville 19 . . . . E 4
Ponoka 5,221 . . . . D 3
Provost 1,645 . . . . E 3
Rainbow Lake 504 . . . . A 5
Ralston 357 . . . . E 4
Raymond 2,837 . . . . D 5
Redcliff 3,876 . . . . E 4
Red Deer 46,393 . . . . D 3
Redwater 1,932 . . . . D 3
Rimbey 1,685 . . . . C 3
Robb 230 . . . . B 3
Rockyford 329 . . . . D 4
Rocky Mountain House 4,698 . C 3
Rosemary 328 . . . . E 4
Rycroft 649 . . . . A 2
Ryley 483 . . . . D 3
Saint Albert 31,996 . . . . D 3
Saint Paul 4,884 . . . . E 3
Sangudo 398 . . . . C 3
Sedgewick 879 . . . . E 3
Sexsmith 1,180 . . . . A 2
Shaughnessy 270 . . . . D 5
Sherwood Park 29,285 . . . . D 3
Slave Lake 4,506 . . . . C 2
Smith 216 . . . . D 2
Smoky Lake 1,074 . . . . D 2
Spirit River 1,104 . . . . A 2
Spruce Grove 10,326 . . . . D 3
Standard 379 . . . . D 4
Stavely 504 . . . . D 4
Stettler 5,136 . . . . D 3
Stirling 688 . . . . D 5
Stony Plain 4,839 . . . . C 3
Strathmore 2,986 . . . . D 4
Strome 281 . . . . E 3
Sundre 1,742 . . . . C 4
Swan Hills 2,497 . . . . C 2
Sylvan Lake 3,779 . . . . C 3
Taber 5,988 . . . . E 5
Thorhild 576 . . . . D 2
Thorsby 737 . . . . C 3
Three Hills 1,787 . . . . D 4
Tilley 345 . . . . E 4
Tofield 1,504 . . . . D 3
Trochu 880 . . . . D 4
Turner Valley 1,311 . . . . C 4
Two Hills 1,193 . . . . E 3
Valleyview 2,061 . . . . B 2
Vauxhall 1,049 . . . . D 4
Vegreville 5,251 . . . . E 3
Vermilion 3,766 . . . . E 3
Veteran 314 . . . . E 3
Viking 1,232 . . . . E 3
Vilna 345 . . . . E 2
Vulcan 1,489 . . . . D 4
Wabamun 662 . . . . C 3
Wabasca 701 . . . . D 2
Wainwright 4,266 . . . . E 3
Warburg 501 . . . . C 3
Warner 477 . . . . D 5
Waskatenau 290 . . . . D 2
Wembley 1,169 . . . . A 2
Westlock 4,424 . . . . C 2
Wetaskiwin 9,597 . . . . D 3
Whitecourt 5,585 . . . . C 2
Wildwood 441 . . . . C 3
Willingdon 366 . . . . E 3
Youngstown 297 . . . . E 4

OTHER FEATURES

Abraham (lake) . . . . B 3
Alberta (mt.) . . . . B 3
Assiniboine (mt.) . . . . C 4
Athabasca (lake) . . . . C 5
Athabasca (riv.) . . . . D 1
Banff Nat'l Park . . . . B 4
Battle (riv.) . . . . D 3
Bear (lake) . . . . A 2
Beaver (riv.) . . . . E 2
Beaverhill (lake) . . . . D 3
Behan (lake) . . . . E 2
Belly (riv.) . . . . D 5
Berland (riv.) . . . . A 3
Berry (creek) . . . . E 4
Biche (lake) . . . . E 2
Big (isl.) . . . . B 5
Big Horn (dam) . . . . B 3
Bighorn (range) . . . . B 3
Birch (hills) . . . . A 2
Birch (lake) . . . . E 3
Birch (mts.) . . . . B 5
Birch (riv.) . . . . B 5
Bison (lake) . . . . B 1
Bittern (lake) . . . . D 3
Botha (riv.) . . . . B 1
Bow (riv.) . . . . D 4
Boyer (riv.) . . . . A 5
Brazeau (mt.) . . . . B 3
Brazeau (riv.) . . . . B 3
Buffalo (lake) . . . . D 3
Buffalo Head (hills) . . . . B 5
Burnt (lakes) . . . . C 1
Cadotte (lake) . . . . B 1
Cadotte (riv.) . . . . B 1
Calling (lake) . . . . D 2
Canal (creek) . . . . E 5
Cardinal (lake) . . . . B 1
Caribou (mts.) . . . . B 5
Chinchaga (riv.) . . . . A 5
Chip (lake) . . . . C 3
Chipewyan (lake) . . . . D 1
Chipewyan (riv.) . . . . D 1
Christina (lake) . . . . E 2
Christina (riv.) . . . . E 1
Claire (lake) . . . . B 5
Clear (hills) . . . . A 1
Clearwater (riv.) . . . . C 4
Clearwater (riv.) . . . . E 1
Clyde (lake) . . . . E 2
Cold (lake) . . . . E 2
Columbia (mt.) . . . . B 3
Crowsnest (pass) . . . . C 5
Cypress (hills) . . . . E 5
Cypress Hills Prov. Park . . . . E 5
Dillon (riv.) . . . . E 2
Dowling (lake) . . . . D 4
Dunkirk (riv.) . . . . D 1
Eisenhower (mt.) . . . . C 4
Elbow (riv.) . . . . C 4
Elk Island Nat'l Park . . . . D 3
Ells (riv.) . . . . D 1
Etzikom Coulee (riv.) . . . . E 5
Eva (lake) . . . . B 5
Farrell (lake) . . . . D 4
Firebag (riv.) . . . . E 1
Forbes (mt.) . . . . B 4
Freeman (riv.) . . . . C 2
Frog (lake) . . . . E 3
Garson (lake) . . . . E 1
Gipsy (lake) . . . . E 1
Gordon (lake) . . . . E 1
Gough (lake) . . . . D 3
Graham (lake) . . . . C 1
Gull (lake) . . . . C 3
Haig (lake) . . . . B 1
Hawk (hills) . . . . B 1
Hay (lake) . . . . A 5
Hay (riv.) . . . . A 5
Heart (lake) . . . . E 2
Highwood (riv.) . . . . C 4
House (mt.) . . . . C 2
House (riv.) . . . . D 2
Iosegun (lake) . . . . B 2
Iosegun (riv.) . . . . B 2
Jackfish (riv.) . . . . B 5
Jasper Nat'l Park . . . . A 3
Kakwa (riv.) . . . . A 2
Kickinghorse (pass) . . . . B 4
Kimiwan (lake) . . . . B 2
Kirkpatrick (lake) . . . . E 4
Kitchener (mt.) . . . . B 3
Legend (lake) . . . . D 1
Lesser Slave (lake) . . . . C 2
Liége (riv.) . . . . D 1
Little Bow (riv.) . . . . D 4
Little Cadotte (riv.) . . . . B 1
Little Smoky (riv.) . . . . B 2
Livingstone (range) . . . . C 4
Logan (lake) . . . . E 2
Loon (lake) . . . . C 1
Loon (riv.) . . . . C 1
Lubicon (lake) . . . . C 1
Lyell (mt.) . . . . B 4
MacKay (riv.) . . . . D 1
Maligne (lake) . . . . B 3
Margaret (lake) . . . . B 5
Marie (lake) . . . . E 2
Marion (lake) . . . . D 3
Marten (mt.) . . . . C 2
McClelland (lake) . . . . E 1
McGregor (lake) . . . . D 4
McLeod (riv.) . . . . B 3
Meikle (riv.) . . . . A 1
Mikkwa (riv.) . . . . B 5
Milk (riv.) . . . . D 5
Mistehae (lake) . . . . C 2
Muriel (lake) . . . . E 2
Muskwa (lake) . . . . C 1
Muskwa (riv.) . . . . C 1
Namur (lake) . . . . D 1
Newell (lake) . . . . E 4
Nordegg (riv.) . . . . C 3
North Saskatchewan (riv.) . . . . E 3
North Wabasca (lake) . . . . D 1
Notikewin (riv.) . . . . A 1
Oldman (riv.) . . . . D 5
Otter (lakes) . . . . B 1
Pakowki (lake) . . . . E 5
Panny (riv.) . . . . C 1
Peace (riv.) . . . . B 1
Peerless (lake) . . . . C 1
Pelican (lake) . . . . D 2
Pelican (mts.) . . . . D 2
Pembina (riv.) . . . . C 3
Pigeon (lake) . . . . D 3
Pinehurst (lake) . . . . E 2
Porcupine (hills) . . . . C 4
Primrose (lake) . . . . E 2
Rainbow (lake) . . . . A 5
Red Deer (lake) . . . . D 3
Red Deer (riv.) . . . . D 4
Richardson (riv.) . . . . C 5
Rocky (mts.) . . . . B-C 4
Rosebud (riv.) . . . . D 4
Russell (lake) . . . . C 1
Saddle (hills) . . . . A 2
Sainte Anne (lake) . . . . C 3
Saint Mary (res.) . . . . D 5
Saint Mary (riv.) . . . . D 5
Saulteaux (riv.) . . . . C 2
Seibert (lake) . . . . E 2
Simonette (riv.) . . . . A 2
Slave (riv.) . . . . C 5
Smoky (riv.) . . . . A 2
Snake Indian (riv.) . . . . A 3
Snipe (lake) . . . . B 2
Sounding (creek) . . . . E 4
South Saskatchewan (riv.) . . . . E 4
South Wabasca (lake) . . . . D 2
Spencer (lake) . . . . E 2
Spray (mts.) . . . . C 4
Sturgeon (lake) . . . . B 2
Sullivan (lake) . . . . D 3
Swan (hills) . . . . C 2
Swan (riv.) . . . . C 2
Temple (mt.) . . . . B 4
The Twins (mt.) . . . . B 3
Thickwood (hills) . . . . D 1
Touchwood (lake) . . . . E 2
Travers (res.) . . . . D 4
Trout (mt.) . . . . C 1
Trout (riv.) . . . . C 1
Utikuma (lake) . . . . C 2
Utikuma (riv.) . . . . C 1
Utikumasis (lake) . . . . C 2
Vermilion (riv.) . . . . E 3
Wabasca (riv.) . . . . C 1
Wallace (mt.) . . . . C 2
Wapiti (riv.) . . . . A 2
Wappau (lake) . . . . E 2
Watchusk (lake) . . . . E 1
Waterton-Glacier Int'l Peace Park . . . . C 5
Waterton Lakes Nat'l Park . . . . C 5
Whitemud (riv.) . . . . A 1
Wildhay (riv.) . . . . B 3
Willmore Wilderness Prov. Park . . . . A 3
Winagami (lake) . . . . B 2
Winefred (lake) . . . . E 2
Winefred (riv.) . . . . E 2
Wolf (lake) . . . . E 2
Wolverine (riv.) . . . . B 1
Wood Buffalo Nat'l Park . . . . B 5
Yellowhead (pass) . . . . A 3
Zama (lake) . . . . A 5

*Population of metropolitan area.

Agriculture, Industry and Resources

DOMINANT LAND USE

- Wheat
- Cereals (chiefly barley, oats)
- Cereals, Livestock
- Dairy
- Pasture Livestock
- Range Livestock
- Forests
- Nonagricultural Land

MAJOR MINERAL OCCURRENCES

- C Coal
- O Petroleum
- G Natural Gas
- S Sulfur
- Na Salt

- Water Power
- Major Industrial Areas

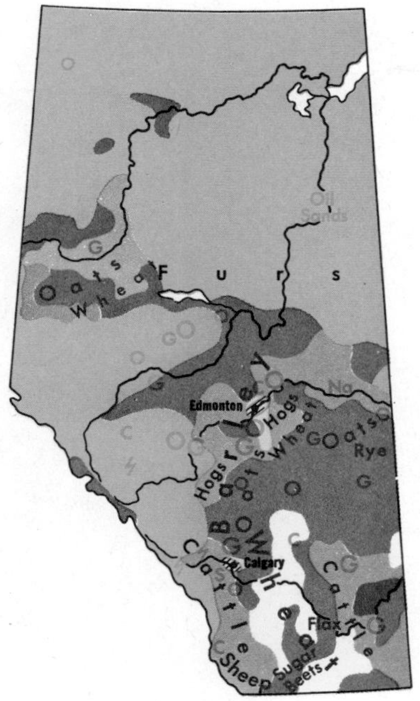
Oil Sands
Furs
Oats
Wheat
Edmonton
Hogs
Barley
Rye
Calgary
Cattle
Flax
Sheep
Sugar Beets

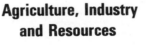

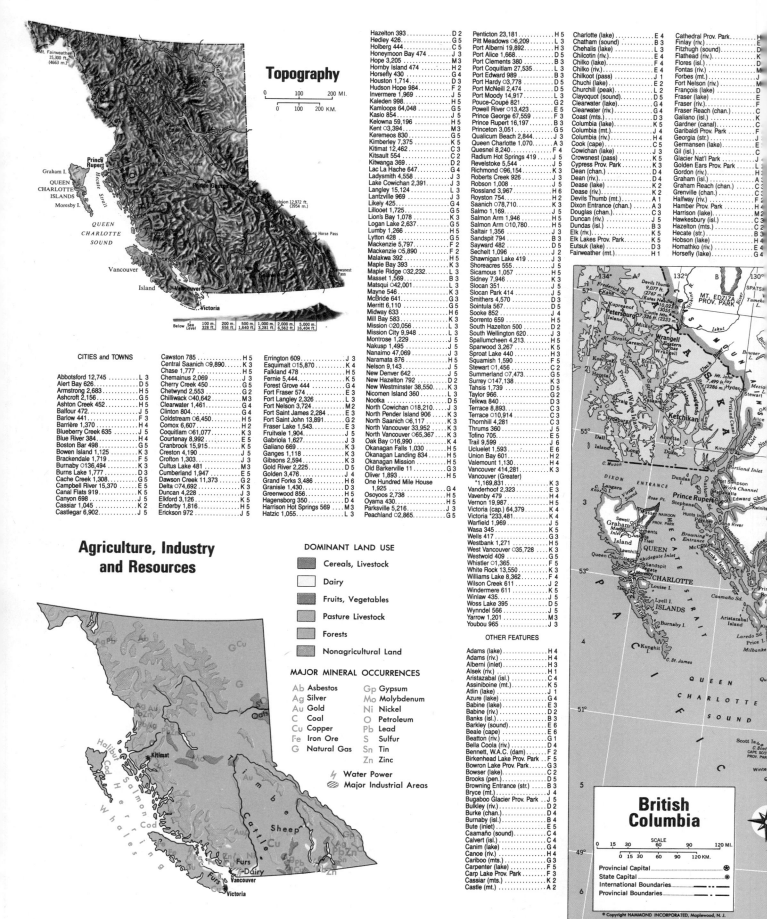

116 British Columbia

Topography

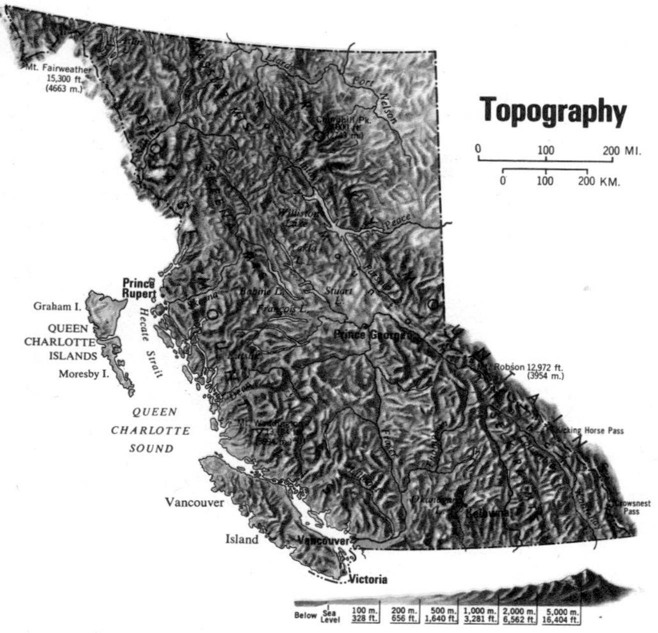
Mt. Fairweather 15,300 ft. (4663 m.)
Prince Rupert
Graham I.
QUEEN CHARLOTTE ISLANDS
Moresby I.
Hecate Strait
QUEEN CHARLOTTE SOUND
Prince George
Robson 12,972 ft. (3954 m.)
Kicking Horse Pass
Crowsnest Pass
Vancouver Island
Vancouver
Victoria
0 100 200 MI.
0 100 200 KM.
Below Sea Level
100 m. 328 ft.
200 m. 656 ft.
500 m. 1,640 ft.
1,000 m. 3,281 ft.
2,000 m. 6,562 ft.
5,000 m. 16,404 ft.

CITIES and TOWNS

Abbotsford 12,745 .... L 3
Alert Bay 626.............. D 5
Armstrong 2,683............ H 5
Ashcroft 2,156............. G 5
Ashton Creek 452........... H 5
Balfour 472................ J 5
Barlow 441................. F 3
Barrière 1,370 .... H 4
Blueberry Creek 635 .... J 5
Blue River 384............. H 4
Boston Bar 498............. G 5
Bowen Island 1,125 .... K 3
Brackendale 1,719 .... F 5
Burnaby ○136,494 .... K 3
Burns Lake 1,777 .... D 3
Cache Creek 1,308.......... G 5
Campbell River 15,370 ..... E 5
Canal Flats 919............ K 5
Canyon 698 .... J 5
Cassiar 1,045 .... K 2
Castlegar 6,902............ J 5
Cawston 785 .... H 5
Central Saanich ○9,890..... K 3
Chase 1,777 .... H 5
Chemainus 2,069 .... J 3
Cherry Creek 450 .... G 5
Chetwynd 2,553 .... G 2
Chilliwack ○40,642 .... M 3
Clearwater 1,461........... G 4
Clinton 804................ G 4
Coldstream ○6,450.......... H 5
Comox 6,607................ H 2
Coquitlam ○61,077.......... K 3
Courtenay 8,992............ E 5
Cranbrook 15,915........... K 5
Creston 4,190 .... J 5
Crofton 1,303.............. J 3
Cultus Lake 481 .... M 3
Cumberland 1,947 .... E 5
Dawson Creek 11,373 .... G 2
Delta ○74,692 .... K 3
Duncan 4,228 .... J 3
Elkford 3,126.............. K 5
Enderby 1,816.............. H 5
Erickson 972 .... J 5
Errington 609.............. J 3
Esquimalt ○15,870 .... K 4
Falkland 478 .... H 5
Fernie 5,444............... K 5
Forest Grove 444 .... G 4
Fort Fraser 574 .... E 3
Fort Langley 2,326 .... L 3
Fort Nelson 3,724.......... M 2
Fort Saint James 2,284 .... E 3
Fort Saint John 13,891..... G 2
Fraser Lake 1,543.......... E 3
Fruitvale 1,904............ J 5
Gabriola 1,627............. J 3
Galiano 669 .... K 3
Ganges 1,118 .... K 3
Gibsons 2,594.............. K 3
Gold River 2,225........... D 5
Golden 3,476............... J 4
Grand Forks 3,486 .... H 6
Granisle 1,430............. D 3
Greenwood 856.............. H 5
Hagensborg 350............. D 4
Harrison Hot Springs 569 .... M 3
Hatzic 1,055............... L 3
Hazelton 393............... D 2
Hedley 426................. G 5
Holberg 444................ C 5
Honeymoon Bay 474 .... J 3
Hope 3,205 .... M 3
Hornby Island 474 .... H 2
Horsefly 430 .... G 4
Houston 1,714.............. D 3
Hudson Hope 984............ F 2
Invermere 1,969 .... J 5
Kaleden 998................ H 5
Kamloops 64,048 .... G 5
Kaslo 854.................. J 5
Kelowna 59,196 .... H 5
Kent ○3,394................ M 3
Keremeos 830............... G 5
Kimberley 7,375 .... K 5
Kitimat 12,462............. C 3
Kitsault 554 .... C 2
Kitwanga 369............... D 2
Lac La Hache 647........... G 4
Ladysmith 4,558 .... J 3
Lake Cowichan 2,391........ J 3
Langley 15,124 .... L 3
Lantzville 969 .... J 3
Likely 425................. G 4
Lillooet 1,725............. G 5
Lion's Bay 1,078 .... K 3
Logan Lake 2,637........... G 5
Lumby 1,266 .... H 5
Lytton 428 .... G 5
Mackenzie 5,797............ F 2
Mackenzie ○5,890 .... F 2
Malakwa 392 .... H 5
Maple Bay 393 .... K 3
Maple Ridge ○32,232........ L 3
Masset 1,569............... B 3
Matsqui ○42,001............ L 3
Mayne 546.................. K 3
McBride 641................ G 3
Merritt 6,110 .... G 5
Midway 633 .... H 6
Mill Bay 583............... K 3
Mission ○20,056 .... L 3
Mission City 9,948 .... L 3
Montrose 1,229............. J 5
Nakusp 1,495 .... J 5
Nanaimo 47,069 .... J 3
Naramata 876 .... H 5
Nelson 9,143............... J 5
New Denver 642 .... J 5
New Hazelton 792 .... D 2
New Westminster 38,550..... K 3
Nicomen Island 360 .... L 3
Nootka .... D 5
North Cowichan ○18,210..... J 3
North Pender Island 906 ..... K 3
North Saanich ○6,117 ...... K 3
North Vancouver 33,952 ..... K 3
North Vancouver ○65,367 .... K 3
Oak Bay ○16,990 .... K 4
Okanagan Falls 1,030 ...... H 5
Okanagan Landing 834 ...... H 5
Okanagan Mission .... H 5
Old Barkerville 11 .... G 3
Oliver 1,893............... H 5
One Hundred Mile House 1,925 .... G 4
Osoyoos 2,738 .... H 5
Oyama 430.................. H 5
Parksville 5,216........... J 3
Peachland ○2,865........... G 5
Penticton 23,181........... H 5
Pitt Meadows ○6,209 .... L 3
Port Alberni 19,892........ H 3
Port Alice 1,668........... D 5
Port Clements 380 .... B 3
Port Coquitlam 27,535...... L 3
Port Edward 989 .... B 3
Port Hardy ○3,778 .... D 5
Port McNeill 2,474 .... D 5
Port Moody 14,917 .... L 3
Pouce-Coupé 821............ G 2
Powell River ○13,423....... E 5
Prince George 67,559 ...... F 3
Prince Rupert 16,197....... B 3
Princeton 3,051............ G 5
Qualicum Beach 2,844....... J 3
Queen Charlotte 1,070...... A 3
Quesnel 8,240.............. F 4
Radium Hot Springs 419 ..... J 5
Revelstoke 5,544 .... J 5
Richmond ○96,154........... K 3
Roberts Creek 926 .... J 3
Robson 1,008 .... J 5
Rossland 3,967............. H 6
Royston 754................ H 2
Saanich ○78,710............ K 3
Salmo 1,169................ J 5
Salmon Arm 1,946 .... H 5
Salmon Arm ○10,780......... H 5
Saltair 1,356 .... J 3
Sandspit 794 .... B 3
Sayward 482 .... D 5
Sechelt 1,096 .... J 2
Shawnigan Lake 419 .... J 3
Shoreacres 555............. J 5
Sicamous 1,057 .... H 5
Sidney 7,946 .... K 3
Slocan 351................. J 5
Slocan Park 414 .... J 5
Smithers 4,570 .... D 3
Sointula 567............... D 5
Sooke 852 .... J 4
Sorrento 659 .... H 5
South Hazelton 500 .... D 2
South Wellington 620....... J 3
Spallumcheen 4,213......... H 5
Sparwood 3,267 .... K 5
Sproat Lake 440 .... H 3
Squamish 1,590 .... F 5
Stewart ○1,456 .... C 2
Summerland ○7,473.......... G 5
Surrey ○147,138............ K 3
Tahsis 1,739 .... D 5
Taylor 966................. G 2
Telkwa 840................. D 3
Terrace 8,893.............. C 3
Terrace ○10,914 .... C 3
Thornhill 4,281 .... C 3
Thrums 360 .... J 5
Tofino 705................. E 5
Trail 9,599 .... J 6
Ucluelet 1,593............. E 6
Union Bay 601.............. H 2
Valemount 1,130............ H 4
Vancouver 414,281.......... K 3
Vancouver (Greater) *1,169,831 .... K 3
Vanderhoof 2,323........... E 3
Vavenby 479 .... H 4
Vernon 19,987.............. H 5
Victoria (cap.) 64,379..... K 4
Victoria *233,481.......... K 4
Warfield 1,969............. J 5
Wasa 345................... K 5
Wells 417 .... G 3
Westbank 1,271 .... H 5
West Vancouver ○35,728 .... K 3
Westwold 409 .... G 5
Whistler ○1,365............ F 5
White Rock 13,550.......... K 3
Williams Lake 8,362........ F 4
Wilson Creek 611 .... J 2
Windermere 611 .... K 5
Winlaw 435................. J 5
Woss Lake 395 .... D 5
Wynndel 566 .... J 5
Yarrow 1,201 .... M 3
Youbou 965 .... J 3

OTHER FEATURES

Adams (lake)............... H 4
Adams (riv.) .... H 4
Alberni (inlet)............ H 3
Alsek (riv.) .... H 1
Aristazabal (isl.) .... C 4
Assiniboine (mt.).......... K 5
Atlin (lake) .... J 1
Azure (lake) .... G 4
Babine (lake).............. E 3
Babine (riv.) .... D 2
Banks (isl.)............... B 3
Barkley (sound)............ E 6
Beale (cape) .... E 6
Beatton (riv.) .... G 1
Bella Coola (riv.) .... D 4
Bennett, W.A.C. (dam)...... F 2
Birkenhead Lake Prov. Park .. F 5
Bowron Lake Prov. Park..... G 3
Bowser (lake).............. C 2
Brooks (pen.).............. D 5
Browning Entrance (str.) ..... B 3
Bryce (mt.)................ J 4
Bugaboo Glacier Prov. Park .. J 5
Bulkley (riv.) .... D 2
Burke (chan.).............. D 4
Burnaby (isl.)............. B 4
Bute (inlet)............... E 5
Caamaño (sound)............ C 4
Calvert (isl.) .... C 4
Canim (lake) .... G 4
Canoe (riv.) .... H 4
Cariboo (mts.)............. G 3
Carpenter (lake) .... F 5
Carp Lake Prov. Park ...... F 3
Cassiar (mts.) .... K 2
Castle (mt.) .... A 2
Charlotte (lake) .... E 4
Chatham (sound) .... B 3
Chehalis (lake) .... L 3
Chilcotin (riv.)........... E 4
Chilko (lake).............. F 4
Chilko (riv.).............. E 4
Chilkoot (pass) .... J 1
Chuchi (lake).............. E 2
Churchill (peak)........... L 2
Clayoquot (sound).......... D 5
Clearwater (lake).......... G 4
Clearwater (riv.).......... G 4
Coast (mts.)............... D 3
Columbia (lake)............ K 5
Columbia (mt.)............. J 4
Columbia (riv.)............ H 4
Cook (cape)................ C 5
Cowichan (lake) .... J 3
Crowsnest (pass) .... K 5
Cypress Prov. Park .... K 3
Dean (chan.) .... D 4
Dean (riv.)................ D 4
Dease (lake) .... K 2
Dease (riv.)............... K 2
Devils Thumb (mt.)......... A 1
Dixon Entrance (chan.) ...... A 3
Douglas (chan.)............ C 3
Duncan (riv.) .... J 5
Dundas (isl.) .... B 3
Elk (riv.)................. K 5
Elk Lakes Prov. Park....... K 5
Eutsuk (lake) .... D 3
Fairweather (mt.).......... H 1
Cathedral Prov. Park....... H
Finlay (riv.) .... E
Fitzhugh (sound)........... D
Flathead (riv.)............ K
Flores (isl.).............. D
Fontas (riv.) .... M
Forbes (mt.)............... J
Fort Nelson (riv.) .... M
François (lake) .... D
Fraser (lake) .... E
Fraser (riv.).............. F
Fraser Reach (chan.) C
Galiano (isl.) .... K
Gardner (canal)............ C
Garibaldi Prov. Park ...... F
Georgia (str.)............. J
Germansen (lake)........... E
Gil (isl.)................. C
Glacier Nat'l Park .... J
Golden Ears Prov. Park L
Gordon (riv.).............. H
Graham (isl.) .... A
Graham Reach (chan.) C
Grenville (chan.) C
Halfway (riv.) .... F
Hamber Prov. Park .... H 4
Harrison (lake)............ M 2
Hawkesbury (isl.) .... C 3
Hazelton (mts.) .... C 2
Hecate (str.).............. B 3
Hobson (lake) .... H 4
Homathko (riv.) .... E 4
Horsefly (lake)............ G 4

Agriculture, Industry and Resources

DOMINANT LAND USE

- Cereals, Livestock
- Dairy
- Fruits, Vegetables
- Pasture Livestock
- Forests
- Nonagricultural Land

MAJOR MINERAL OCCURRENCES

Ab	Asbestos	Gp	Gypsum
Ag	Silver	Mo	Molybdenum
Au	Gold	Ni	Nickel
C	Coal	O	Petroleum
Cu	Copper	Pb	Lead
Fe	Iron Ore	S	Sulfur
G	Natural Gas	Sn	Tin
		Zn	Zinc

- Water Power
- Major Industrial Areas

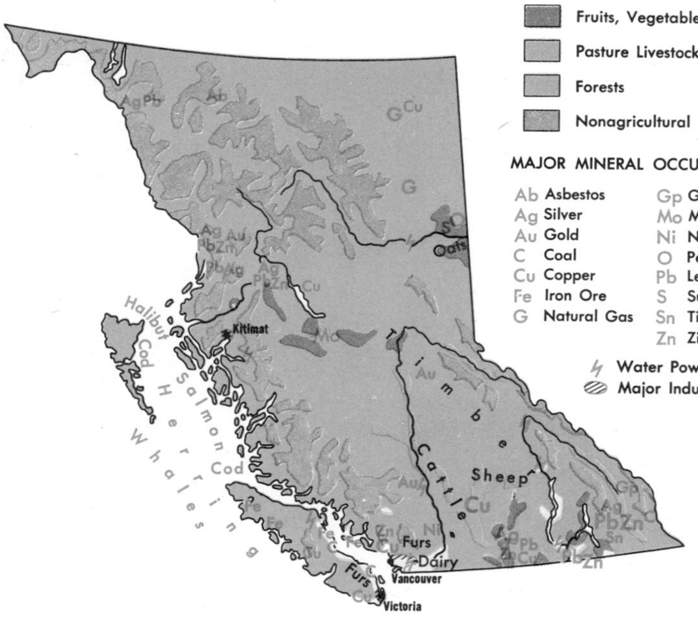
Kitimat
Halibut
Cod
Salmon
Herring
Whales
Timber
Cattle
Sheep
Oats
Furs
Dairy
Vancouver
Victoria

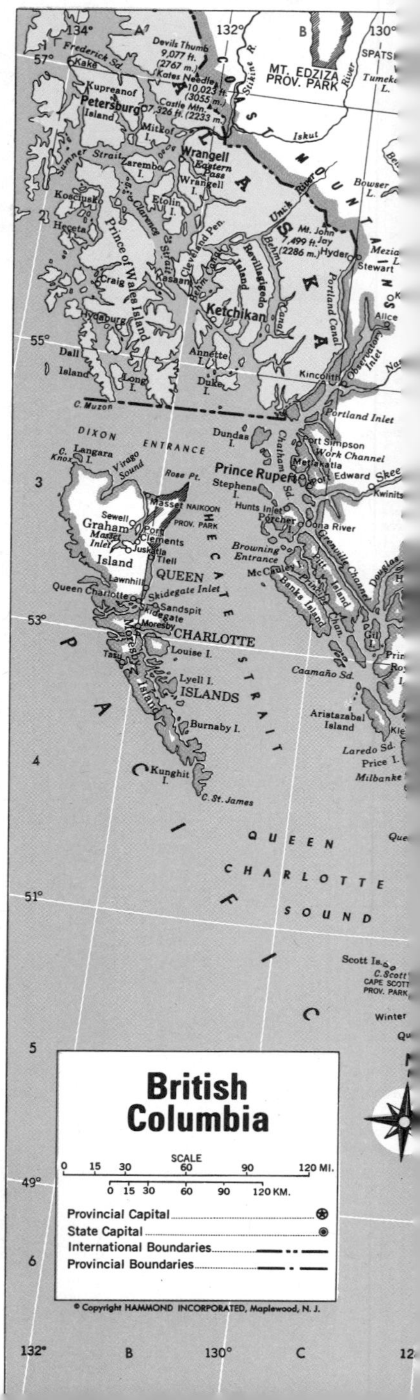
British Columbia
SCALE
0 15 30 60 90 120 MI.
0 15 30 60 90 120 KM.
Provincial Capital
State Capital
International Boundaries
Provincial Boundaries
Prince Rupert
Ketchikan
Wrangell
Petersburg
DIXON ENTRANCE
QUEEN CHARLOTTE ISLANDS
QUEEN CHARLOTTE SOUND
MT. EDZIZA PROV. PARK
© Copyright HAMMOND INCORPORATED, Maplewood, N. J.

AREA 366,253 sq. mi. (948,596 sq. km.)
POPULATION 2,744,467
CAPITAL Victoria
LARGEST CITY Vancouver
HIGHEST POINT Mt. Fairweather 15,300 ft.
(4,663 m.)
SETTLED IN 1806
ADMITTED TO CONFEDERATION 1871
PROVINCIAL FLOWER Dogwood

*Population of metropolitan area.
○Population of municipality.

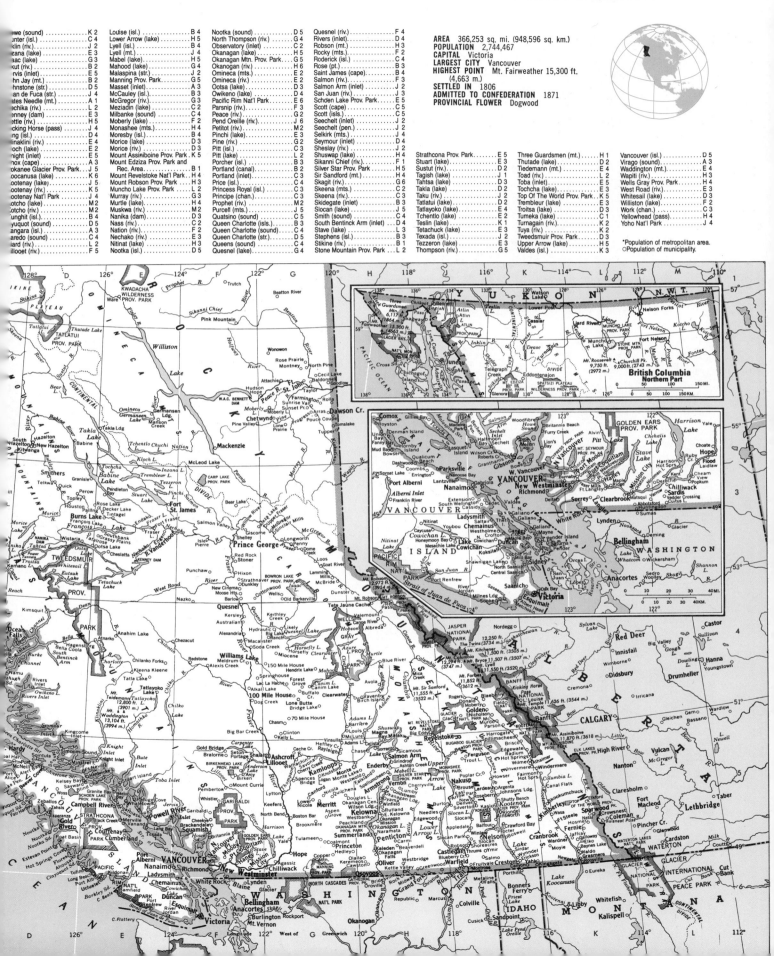

Topography

5,000 m.	2,000 m.	1,000 m.	500 m.	200 m.	100 m.
16,404 ft.	6,562 ft.	3,281 ft.	1,640 ft.	656 ft.	328 ft.	Sea Level Below

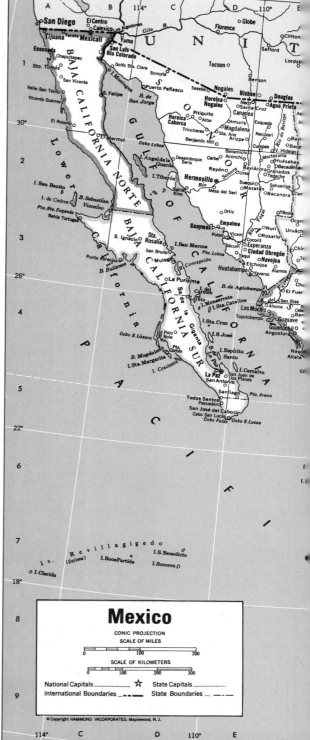

Mexico
CONIC PROJECTION
SCALE OF MILES

SCALE OF KILOMETERS

National Capitals ★
International Boundaries — · — · —
State Capitals
State Boundaries — — —

© Copyright HAMMOND INCORPORATED, Maplewood, N.J.

(continued on following page)

AREA 761,601 sq. mi. (1,972,546 sq. km.)
POPULATION 67,395,826
CAPITAL Mexico City
LARGEST CITY Mexico City
HIGHEST POINT Citlaltépetl 18,855 ft.
  (5,747 m.)
MONETARY UNIT Mexican peso
MAJOR LANGUAGE Spanish
MAJOR RELIGION Roman Catholicism

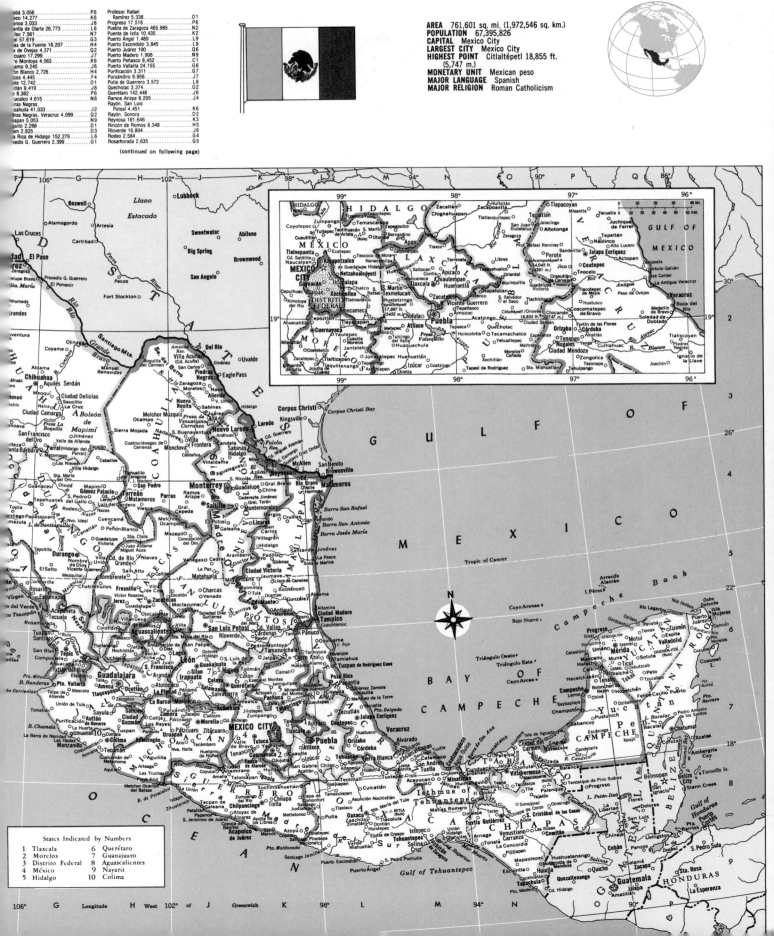

120 Mexico

(continued)

Rosario, Sinaloa 10,276 ..... G5
Rosario, Sonora 1,887 ..... E3
Ruiz 8,954 ..... G6
Sabancuy 1,819 ..... O7
Sabinas 20,538 ..... J3
Sabinas Hidalgo 17,439 ..... J3
Sahuaripa 4,710 ..... E2
Sahuayo de Díaz 28,727 ..... H7
Sain Alto 3,628 ..... H5
Salamanca 61,039 ..... J6
Salina Cruz 22,004 ..... M9
Salinas 7,471 ..... J5
Saltillo 200,712 ..... J4
Salvatierra 18,975 ..... J6
San Andrés Tuxtla 24,267 ..... M7
San Blas, Nayarit 3,443 ..... G6
San Blas, Sinaloa 6,222 ..... E3
San Buenaventura 9,188 ..... J3
San Carlos, Coahuila 1,960 ..... J2
San Cristóbal de las Casas 25,700 ..... N8
San Felipe, Baja California 160 ..... B1
San Felipe, Guanajuato 10,129 ..... J6
San Fernando, Tamaulipas 27,656 ..... L4
San Francisco del Oro 12,116 ..... F3
San Francisco del Rincón 27,079 ..... H6
San Gabriel Chilac 6,707 ..... K7
San Ignacio, Sinaloa 1,804 ..... F5
San Jerónimo de Juárez 5,204 ..... J8
San José del Cabo 2,571 ..... D5
San Juan 15,422 ..... K6
San Juan de los Lagos 19,570 ..... H6
San Juan Xiutetelco 3,306 ..... O1
San Luis de la Paz 12,654 ..... J6
San Luis del Cordero 2,203 ..... H4
San Luis Potosí 271,123 ..... J5
San Luis Río Colorado 49,990 ..... B1
San Marcos 5,861 ..... K8
San Martín de las Pirámides 4,575 ..... M1
San Martín Texmelucan 23,355 ..... M1
San Miguel de Allende 24,286 ..... J6
San Nicolás de los Garza 28,803 ..... J3
San Pedro de las Colonias 26,882 ..... H4
San Pedro Pochutla 4,395 ..... L9
San Rafael 8,974 ..... M1
San Salvador el Seco 7,729 ..... O1
Santa Ana 7,020 ..... D1
Santa Ana Chiautempan (Chiautempan) 12,327 ..... N1
Santa Bárbara 16,978 ..... F3
Santa Clara 3,449 ..... H4
Santa María del Oro 4,231 ..... G3
Santa María del Río 4,972 ..... J6
Santa María del Tule 1,674 ..... L8
Santander Jiménez 3,586 ..... K4
Santa Rosalía 7,356 ..... C3
Santiago Ixcuintla 17,321 ..... G6
Santiago Jamiltepec 5,280 ..... K8
Santiago Juxtlahuaca 2,923 ..... K8
Santiago Miahuatlán 4,917 ..... O2
Santiago Papasquiaro 6,636 ..... F4
Santiago Pinotepa Nacional 9,382 ..... K8
Santiago Tuxtla 9,426 ..... M7
Saucillo 8,467 ..... G2
Sayula 14,339 ..... H7
Sayula de Alemán 4,896 ..... M8
Seybaplaya 4,439 ..... O7
Silao 31,825 ..... J6
Simojovel de Allende 3,779 ..... N8
Sinaloa de Leyva 1,998 ..... E4
Soledad de Doblado 6,612 ..... Q2
Soledad Díez Gutiérrez 9,622 ..... J5
Sombrerete 11,077 ..... H5
Sonoyta 2,463 ..... C1
Sotuta 3,772 ..... P6
Tabasco 3,197 ..... H6
Tacámbaro de Codallos 9,695 ..... J7
Tacotalpa 2,019 ..... N8
Tala 15,744 ..... H6
Talpa de Allende 4,264 ..... G6
Tamazulapan del Progreso 2,870 ..... L8
Tamazunchale 12,302 ..... K6
Tamiahua 6,264 ..... L6
Tampico 212,188 ..... L5
Tamuín 7,251 ..... K6
Tantoyuca 11,902 ..... L6
Tapachula 60,620 ..... N9
Taxco de Alarcón 27,089 ..... K7
Tayoltita 2,697 ..... G4
Teapa 6,534 ..... N8
Tecamachalco 3,319 ..... O2
Tecate 14,738 ..... A1
Tecomán 31,625 ..... H7
Tecpan de Galeana 8,095 ..... J8
Tecuala 12,461 ..... G5
Tehuacán 47,497 ..... L7
Tehuantepec 16,179 ..... M8
Tekax de Álaro Obregón 10,326 ..... P6
Teloloapan 10,335 ..... J7
Temax 4,915 ..... P6
Temósachic 1,738 ..... E2
Tenabo 3,278 ..... P6
Tenancingo de Degollado 12,807 ..... K7
Tenango de Río Blanco 12,302 ..... O2
Tenosique de Pino Suárez 11,393 ..... O8
Teocaltiche 13,745 ..... H6
Teocelo 4,572 ..... P1
Teotihuacán de Arista 2,238 ..... L1
Teotitlán del Camino 3,106 ..... L8
Tepache 1,591 ..... E2
Tepalcingo 5,968 ..... M2
Tepatitlán de Morelos 29,292 ..... H6
Tepeaca 7,466 ..... N2
Tepeapulco 7,027 ..... M1
Tepehuanes 2,531 ..... G4
Tepeji del Río 10,365 ..... L1
Tepexi de Rodríguez 2,618 ..... N2
Tepic 108,924 ..... G6
Tepoztlán 6,851 ..... L1
Tequixquitla 4,825 ..... O1
Terán 5,215 ..... N8
Terrenate 1,515 ..... N1
Texcoco de Mora 18,044 ..... M1
Teziutlán 23,948 ..... O1
Tezonapa 3,506 ..... P2
Tezontepec 2,762 ..... M1
Ticul 14,341 ..... P6
Tierra Blanca 22,727 ..... L7
Tila 2,633 ..... N8
Tijuana 363,154 ..... A1
Tixtla de Guerrero 10,334 ..... K8
Tizayuca 6,262 ..... L1
Tizimín 18,343 ..... Q6
Tlachichuca 3,721 ..... O1
Tlacolula de Matamoros 8,300 ..... L8
Tlacotepec de Mejiá 1,595 ..... P1
Tlahualilo de Zaragoza 8,951 ..... H3
Tlalancaneca 5,090 ..... M1
Tlalixcoyan 3,211 ..... Q2
Tlalmanalco de Velásquez 5,744 ..... L1
Tlalnepantla de Comonfort 45,575 ..... L1
Tlalpan 130,719 ..... L1
Tlaltenango de Sánchez Román 7,698 ..... H6
Tlaltizapan 6,384 ..... L2
Tlapacoyan 13,172 ..... P1
Tlapa de Comonfort 6,676 ..... K8

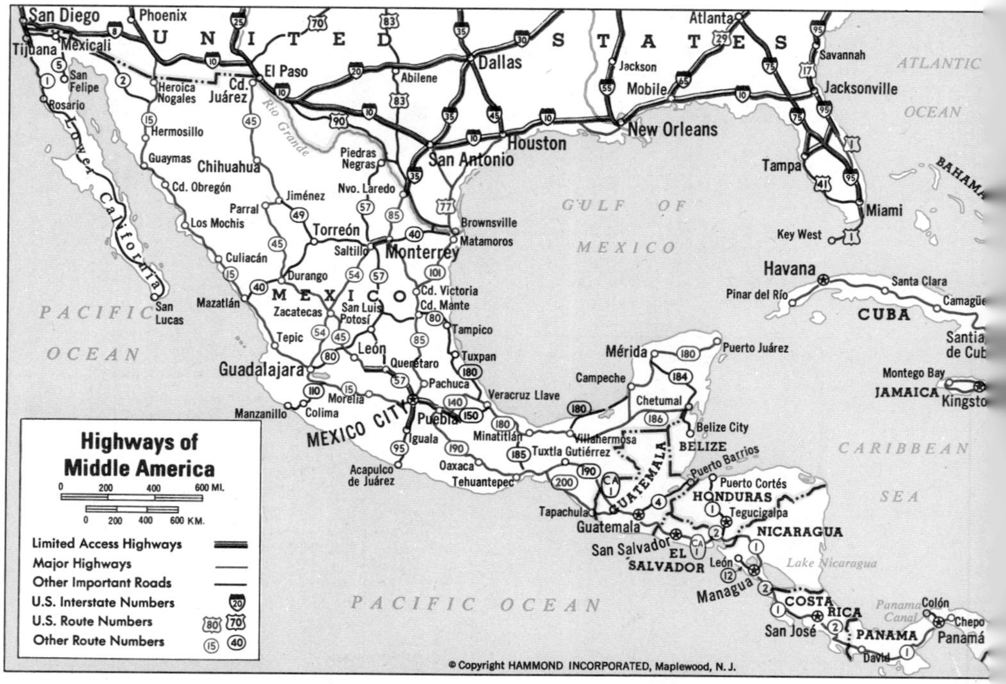

Highways of Middle America
0 200 400 600 MI.
0 200 400 600 KM.
Limited Access Highways
Major Highways
Other Important Roads
U.S. Interstate Numbers
U.S. Route Numbers
Other Route Numbers
UNITED STATES
San Diego
Phoenix
Tijuana
Mexicali
El Paso
Cd. Juárez
Abilene
Dallas
Atlanta
Jackson
Mobile
Savannah
Jacksonville
ATLANTIC OCEAN
New Orleans
Houston
San Antonio
Tampa
Miami
Key West
San Felipe
Rosario
Heroica Nogales
Hermosillo
Guaymas
Chihuahua
Cd. Obregón
Los Mochis
Parral
Jiménez
Piedras Negras
Nvo. Laredo
Torreón
Saltillo
Monterrey
Brownsville
Matamoros
GULF OF MEXICO
Havana
Santa Clara
Pinar del Río
CUBA
Camagüey
Culiacán
Durango
Mazatlán
San Lucas
MEXICO
Zacatecas
San Luis Potosí
Cd. Victoria
Cd. Mante
Tampico
Tepic
León
Querétaro
Tuxpan
Guadalajara
Pachuca
PACIFIC OCEAN
Manzanillo
Colima
Morelia
MEXICO CITY
Puebla
Veracruz Llave
Mérida
Puerto Juárez
Campeche
Chetumal
Belize City
BELIZE
Minatitlán
Villahermosa
Tuxtla Gutiérrez
Iguala
Oaxaca
Acapulco de Juárez
Tehuantepec
Tapachula
GUATEMALA
Guatemala
Puerto Barrios
Puerto Cortés
HONDURAS
Tegucigalpa
San Salvador
EL SALVADOR
NICARAGUA
León
Managua
Lake Nicaragua
COSTA RICA
San José
Panama Canal
Colón
Chepo
PANAMA
Panamá
David
Montego Bay
JAMAICA
Kingston
CARIBBEAN SEA
PACIFIC OCEAN
© Copyright HAMMOND INCORPORATED, Maplewood, N. J.

Tlaquepaque 59,760 ..... G6
Tlatlauquitepec 4,272 ..... O1
Tlaquiltenango 8,625 ..... L2
Tlaxcala de Xicotencatl 9,972 ..... M1
Tlaxco 4,969 ..... N1
Tlaxiaco 4,477 ..... L8
Tlayacapan 3,538 ..... L1
Tochimilco 3,190 ..... M2
Todos Santos 2,400 ..... D5
Toluca de Lerdo 136,092 ..... K7
Tomatlán 2,695 ..... G6
Tonalá 15,611 ..... N8
Topolobampo 4,685 ..... E4
Torreón 244,309 ..... H4
Tula, Tamaulipas 5,407 ..... K5
Tula de Allende 10,720 ..... K6
Tulancingo 35,799 ..... K7
Tulcingo del Valle 2,983 ..... M2
Tultepec 8,321 ..... L1
Tuxpan, Jalisco 14,693 ..... H7
Tuxpan, Nayarit 20,322 ..... G6
Tuxpan de Rodríguez Cano 33,901 ..... L6
Tuxtepec 17,701 ..... L7
Tuxtla Gutiérrez 66,851 ..... N8
Tzucabab 4,876 ..... P7
Umán 8,371 ..... P6
Unión de Tula 6,399 ..... G7
Unión Hidalgo 8,658 ..... M8
Ures 3,681 ..... D2
Ursulo Galván 2,637 ..... Q1
Uruapan del Progreso 108,124 ..... H7
Valladolid 14,663 ..... P6
Valle de Allende 4,973 ..... G3
Valle de Bravo 7,628 ..... J7
Valle Hermoso 19,278 ..... L4
Vanegas 2,042 ..... J5
Venado 2,790 ..... J5
Venustiano Carranza 23,624 ..... N8
Veracruz 255,646 ..... Q1
Vicam 4,104 ..... D3
Vicente Guerrero, Durango 8,451 ..... G5
Victor Rosales 7,629 ..... H5
Viesca 2,923 ..... H4
Villa Acuña 30,276 ..... J2
Villa Cuauhtémoc 6,611 ..... L5
Villa de Cos 1,850 ..... H5
Villa de Guadelupe Hidalgo 88,537 ..... L1
Villa Frontera 25,761 ..... J3
Villa García 2,765 ..... J5
Villahermosa 133,181 ..... N8
Villa Hidalgo 2,126 ..... E1
Villaldama 2,350 ..... J3
Villa Matamoros 1,998 ..... G3
Villanueva 5,895 ..... H5
Villa Unión, Coahuila 4,058 ..... J2
Villa Unión, Durango 4,042 ..... H5
Villa Unión, Sinaloa 6,789 ..... F5
Villa Vicente Guerrero 18,280 ..... N1
Xaltocan 2,524 ..... N1
Xicoténcatl 6,374 ..... K5
Xicotepec de Juárez 12,656 ..... L6
Xochihuehuetlán 3,268 ..... K8
Xochimilco 116,493 ..... L1
Xochitlán 3,312 ..... N2
Yajalón 4,506 ..... N8
Yanga 3,843 ..... P2
Yaqui 8,061 ..... D3
Yautepec 13,952 ..... L2
Yavaros 1,959 ..... E3
Yécora E2
Yecuatla 2,816 ..... P1
Yehualtepec 2,558 ..... O2
Zaachila 7,270 ..... L8
Zacapoaxtla 4,527 ..... O1
Zacapu 31,989 ..... J7
Zacatepec 16,839 ..... L2
Zacatecas 50,251 ..... H5
Zacatelco 14,117 ..... N1
Zacatlán 7,909 ..... N1
Zacoalco de Torres 11,343 ..... H6
Zamora de Hidalgo 5,775 ..... H7
Zaragoza, Coahuila 6,797 ..... J2
Zaragoza, Chihuahua 3,984 ..... F1
Zaragoza, Puebla 4,754 ..... O1
Zempoala 5,064 ..... Q1
Zihuatenejo 4,879 ..... J8
Zimatlán de Álvarez 5,746 ..... L8
Zitácuaro 36,911 ..... J7
Zongolica 2,378 ..... P2
Zumpango de Ocampo 12,923 ..... L1
Zumpango del Río 8,162 ..... J8

OTHER FEATURES

Agiobampo (bay) E3
Aguanaval (riv.) H4
Amistad (res.) J2
Ángel de la Guarda (isl.) C2
Antigua (riv.) Q1
Arena (pt.) E5
Arenas (cay) O5
Atoyac (riv.) N2
Atoyac (riv.) Q2
Babia (riv.) J2
Bacalar (lake) P7
Ballenas (bay) C3
Balsas (riv.) J7
Banderas (bay) G6
Bavispe, Río de (riv.) E1
Blanco (riv.) Q2
Bravo (Grande) (riv.) G2
Burro (mts.) J2
California (gulf) D3
Campeche (bank) O6
Campeche (bay) N7
Candelaria (riv.) O8
Carmen (isl.) D3
Casas Grandes (riv.) F1
Catoche (cape) Q6
Cedros (isl.) B2
Cerralvo (isl.) E4
Chamela (bay) G7
Chapala (lake) H6
Chetumal (bay) P8
Chichén-Itzá (ruin) P6
Citlaltépetl (mt.) O2
Clarión (isl.) B7
Colorado (riv.) B1
Conchos (riv.) G2
Corrientes (cape) F6
Coyuca (riv.) O1
Creciente (isl.) D5
Cuitzeo (lake) J7
Delgada (pt.) L7
Dzibichaltún (ruin) P6
El Azúcar (res.) K3
Espíritu Santo (isl.) D4
Falcón (res.) .....
Falso (cape) .....
Fuerte (riv.) .....
Giganta, Sierra de la (mts.) .....
Grande (riv.) .....
Grande (riv.) .....
Grande de Santiago (riv.) .....
Grijalva (riv.) .....
Guzmán (lake) .....
Herrero (pt.) .....
Hondo (riv.) .....
Jesús María (reef) .....
La Boquilla (res.) .....
La Paz (bay) .....
Lobos (cape) .....
Lobos (pt.) .....
Lower California (pen.) .....
Madre (lag.) .....
Madre del Sur, Sierra (mts.) .....
Madre Occidental, Sierra (mts.) .....
Madre Oriental, Sierra (mts.) .....
Magdalena (bay) .....
Maldonado (pt.) .....
Mapimí (depr.) .....
María Cleófas (isl.) .....
María Madre (isl.) .....
María Magdalena (isl.) .....
Mexico (gulf) .....
Mezquital (riv.) .....
Mita (pt.) .....
Mitla (ruin) .....
Moctezuma (riv.) .....
Monserrate (isl.) .....
Montague (isl.) .....
Muerto, Mar (lag.) .....
Nauhcampatépetl (mt.) .....
Nayarit, Sierra (mts.) .....
Nazas (riv.) .....
Nuevo, Bajo (reef) .....
Orizaba (Citlaltépetl) (mt.) .....
Palenque (ruin) .....
Palmito de la Virgen (isl.) .....
Palmito del Verde (isl.) .....
Pánuco (riv.) .....
Paricutín (vol.) .....
Pátzcuaro (lake) .....
Pérez (isl.) .....
Petacalco (bay) .....
Popocatépetl (mt.) .....
Ramos (riv.) .....
Revillagigedo (isls.) .....
Roca Partida (isl.) .....
Sabinas (riv.) .....
San Antonio (reef) .....
San Benedicto (isl.) .....
San Benito (isl.) .....
San Jorge (bay) .....
San José (isl.) .....
San Lázaro (cape) .....
San Lucas (cape) E5
San Marcos (isl.) D3
San Rafael (reef) L4
Santa Ana (reef) N7
Santa Catalina (isl.) D4
Santa Cruz (isl.) D4
Santa Eugenia (pt.) B3
Santa Margarita (isl.) C4
Santa María (lake) F1
Santa María (riv.) F1
Santiaguillo (lake) G4
Sebastián Vizcaíno (bay) B2
Socorro (isl.) D7
Sonora (riv.) D2
Superior (lag.) M9
Teacapán (inlet) F5
Tehuantepec (gulf) M9
Tehuantepec (isth.) M8
Teotihuacán (ruin) M1
Términos (lag.) O7
Tiburón (isl.) C2
Triángulo Este (isl.) N6
Triángulo Oeste (isl.) N6
Tula (riv.) L1
Urique (riv.) F3
Usumacinta (riv.) O8
Uxmal (ruins) P6
Valsequillo (res.) N2
Verde (riv.) F3
Verde (riv.) L8
Yaqui (riv.) E2

*City and suburbs.

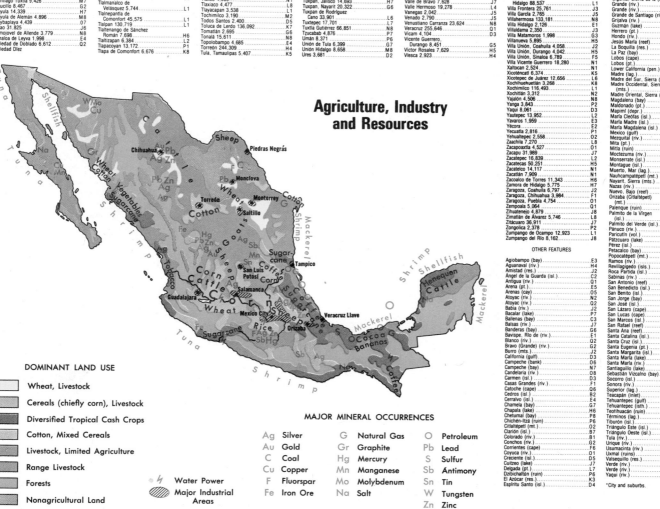

Agriculture, Industry and Resources

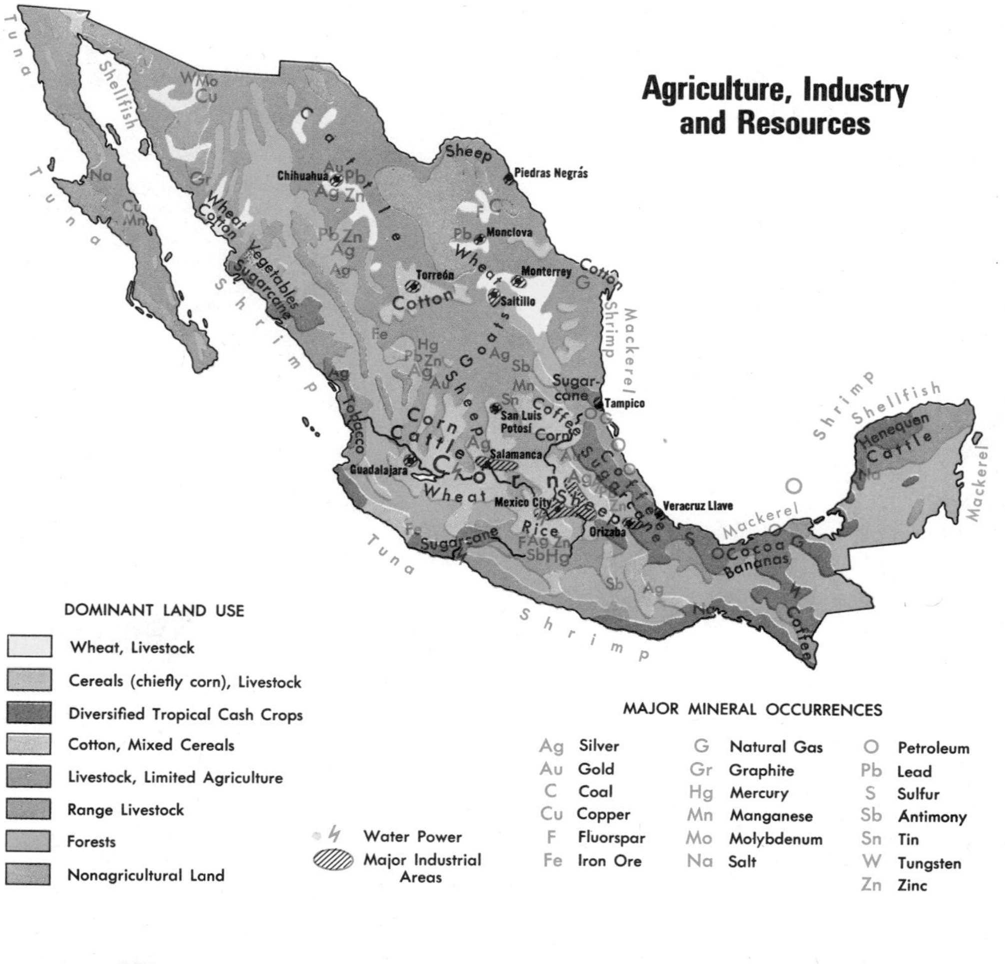

Chihuahua
Piedras Negras
Monclova
Torreón
Monterrey
Saltillo
Tampico
San Luis Potosí
Salamanca
Guadalajara
Mexico City
Veracruz Llave
Orizaba
Cattle
Sheep
Wheat
Cotton
Goats
Corn
Coffee
Sugarcane
Vegetables
Tobacco
Rice
Cocoa
Bananas
Henequen
Tuna
Shellfish
Shrimp
Mackerel
DOMINANT LAND USE
Wheat, Livestock
Cereals (chiefly corn), Livestock
Diversified Tropical Cash Crops
Cotton, Mixed Cereals
Livestock, Limited Agriculture
Range Livestock
Forests
Nonagricultural Land
Water Power
Major Industrial Areas
MAJOR MINERAL OCCURRENCES
Ag Silver
Au Gold
C Coal
Cu Copper
F Fluorspar
Fe Iron Ore
G Natural Gas
Gr Graphite
Hg Mercury
Mn Manganese
Mo Molybdenum
Na Salt
O Petroleum
Pb Lead
S Sulfur
Sb Antimony
Sn Tin
W Tungsten
Zn Zinc

GUATEMALA
EA 42,042 sq. mi. (108,889 sq. km.)
PULATION 7,262,419
PITAL Guatemala
RGEST CITY Guatemala
GHEST POINT Tajumulco 13,845 ft.
(4,220 m.)
ONETARY UNIT quetzal
AJOR LANGUAGES Spanish, Quiché
AJOR RELIGION Roman Catholicism

BELIZE
AREA 8,867 sq. mi. (22,966 sq. km.)
POPULATION 144,857
CAPITAL Belmopan
LARGEST CITY Belize City
HIGHEST POINT Victoria Peak 3,681 ft. (1,122 m.)
MONETARY UNIT Belize dollar
MAJOR LANGUAGES English, Spanish, Mayan
MAJOR RELIGIONS Roman Catholicism, Protestantism

EL SALVADOR
AREA 8,260 sq. mi. (21,393 sq. km.)
POPULATION 4,813,000
CAPITAL San Salvador
LARGEST CITY San Salvador
HIGHEST POINT Santa Ana 7,825 ft.
(2,385 m.)
MONETARY UNIT colón
MAJOR LANGUAGE Spanish
MAJOR RELIGION Roman Catholicism

HONDURAS
REA 43,277 sq. mi. (112,087 sq. km.)
OPULATION 3,691,000
APITAL Tegucigalpa
ARGEST CITY Tegucigalpa
IGHEST POINT Las Minas 9,347 ft.
(2,849 m.)
ONETARY UNIT lempira
AJOR LANGUAGE Spanish
AJOR RELIGION Roman Catholicism

NICARAGUA
AREA 45,698 sq. mi. (118,358 sq. km.)
POPULATION 2,703,000
CAPITAL Managua
LARGEST CITY Managua
HIGHEST POINT Cerro Mocotón 6,913 ft.
(2,107 m.)
MONETARY UNIT córdoba
MAJOR LANGUAGE Spanish
MAJOR RELIGION Roman Catholicism

COSTA RICA
AREA 19,575 sq. mi. (50,700 sq. km.)
POPULATION 2,245,000
CAPITAL San José
LARGEST CITY San José
HIGHEST POINT Chirripó Grande
12,530 ft. (3,819 m.)
MONETARY UNIT colón
MAJOR LANGUAGE Spanish
MAJOR RELIGION Roman Catholicism

PANAMA
AREA 29,761 sq. mi. (77,082 sq. km.)
POPULATION 1,830,175
CAPITAL Panamá
LARGEST CITY Panamá
HIGHEST POINT Vol. Baru 11,401 ft.
(3,475 m.)
MONETARY UNIT balboa
MAJOR LANGUAGE Spanish
MAJOR RELIGION Roman Catholicism

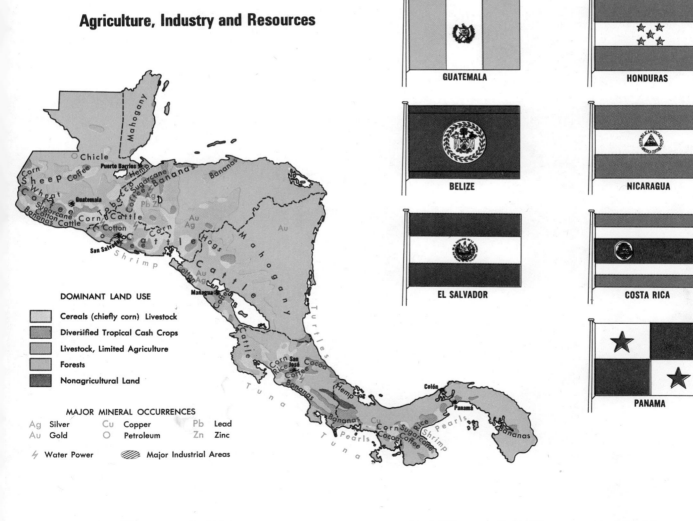

Agriculture, Industry and Resources

DOMINANT LAND USE

- Cereals (chiefly corn) Livestock
- Diversified Tropical Cash Crops
- Livestock, Limited Agriculture
- Forests
- Nonagricultural Land

MAJOR MINERAL OCCURRENCES

Ag Silver Cu Copper Pb Lead
Au Gold O Petroleum Zn Zinc

⚡ Water Power ▨ Major Industrial Areas

GUATEMALA
HONDURAS
BELIZE
NICARAGUA
EL SALVADOR
COSTA RICA
PANAMA

(continued on following page)

OTHER FEATURES

Blanca (pt.) F5
Blanco (cape) E6
Blanco (peak) F6
Burica (pt.) F6
Cahuita (pt.) F6
Caño (isl.) F6
Carreta (pt.) F6
Chirripó Grande (mt.) F6
Coronado (bay) F6
Cuilapa Miravalles (vol.) E5
Dulce (gulf) F6
Góngora (mt.) F5
Guionas (pt.) E5
Irazú (mt.) E6
Judas (pt.) E6
Llerena (pt.) F6
Matapalo (cape) F6
Nicoya (gulf) E6
Nicoya (pen.) E5
Papagayo (gulf) E5
Salinas (bay) D5
San Juan (riv.) E5
Santa Elena (cape) D5

Talamanca (range) F6
Velas (cape) D5

EL SALVADOR

CITIES and TOWNS

Acajutla 8,598 .... B4
Ahuachapán 17,242 .... B4
Alquizaya 7,035 .... C3
Chalatenango 7,633 .... C4
Chinameca 6,303 .... C4
Cojutepeque 20,615 .... C4
Estanzuelas 2,548 .... C4
Ilobasco 6,572 .... C4
Intipucá 3,469 .... D4
Jucuarán 1,443 .... C4
La Libertad C4
La Palma 1,998 .... C3
La Unión 17,207 .... D4
Metapán 7,704 .... C3
Nueva San Salvador 35,106 .... C4
Puerto de la Concordia C4
San Francisco Gotera 4,725 .... C4

San Miguel 59,304 .... D4
San Salvador (cap.) 337,171 .... C4
Santa Ana 96,306 .... C4
Santa Rosa de Lima 5,707 .... C4
San Vicente 18,872 .... C4
Sensuntepeque 7,226 .... C4
Sonsonate 33,562 .... C4
Suchitoto 5,540 .... C4
Texistepeque 1,722 .... C3
Usulután 19,616 .... C4
Zacatecoluca 15,718 .... C4

OTHER FEATURES

Fonseca (gulf) D4
Güija (lake) C3
Lempa (riv.) C3
Remedios (pt.) B4
Santa Ana (mt.) C4

GUATEMALA

CITIES and TOWNS

Amatitlán 15,251 .... B3

Antigua 17,994 .... B3
Asunción Mita 7,477 .... C3
Cabañón 1,344 .... C3
Chajul 4,329 .... A3
Champerico 5,722 .... A3
Chichicastenango 2,635 .... A3
Chimaltenango 12,860 .... B3
Chiquimula 16,126 .... C3
Coatepeque 15,979 .... A3
Cobán 11,418 .... B3
Comalapa 10,980 .... B3
Cubulco 2,021 .... B3
Cuilapa 4,287 .... B3
Cuilco 862 .... B3
Dolores 973 .... C2
El Estor 2,324 .... C3
El Progreso 4,009 .... B3
Escuintla 33,205 .... B3
Flores 1,477 .... C2
Gualán 5,169 .... C3
Guatemala (cap.)
    700,538 .... B3
Huehuetenango 12,570 .... B3
Ipala 3,386 .... C3
Iztapa 1,237 .... B4

Jacaltenango 4,517 .... B3
Jalapa 13,788 .... B3
Jutiapa 8,210 .... B3
La Gomera 2,394 .... B3
La Libertad 908 .... B2
Livingston 2,898 .... C3
Los Amates 1,383 .... C3
Masagua 1,178 .... B3
Mazatenango 23,285 .... B3
Momostenango 5,210 .... B3
Morales 2,113 .... C3
Ocós 741 .... A3
Panzós 1,643 .... C3
Puerto Barrios 22,598 .... C3
Quezaltenango 53,021 .... B3
Quezaltepeque 2,222 .... C3
Rabinal 4,625 .... B3
Retalhuleu 19,060 .... B3
Río Hondo 1,416 .... C3
Sacapulas 1,439 .... B3
Salamá 5,529 .... B3
San Andrés 1,066 .... B2
San Felipe 3,210 .... B3
San José 9,402 .... B4
San Luis 1,136 .... C2

San Luis Jilotepeque 6,055 .... C3
San Marcos 5,700 .... B3
San Martín Jilotepeque 3,770 .... B3
San Mateo Ixtatán 1,834 .... B3
San Pedro Carchá 4,465 .... C3
Santa Cruz del Quiché 7,651 .... B3
Santa Rosa de Lima 1,161 .... B3
Solóla 3,960 .... B3
Tacaná 1,280 .... A3
Tejutla 1,205 .... B3
Tikal C2
Totonicapán 8,568 .... B3
Zacapa 12,688 .... C3

HONDURAS

CITIES and TOWNS

Amapala 2,274 .... C3
Brus Laguna 933 .... D2
Catacamas 9,134 .... D3
Cedros 917 .... C3
Choloma 961 .... C2
Choluteca 26,152 .... C3
Comayagua 15,941 .... C3
Corquín 2,629 .... B3
Danlí 10,825 .... C3
El Dulce Nombre 1,297 .... C3

OTHER FEATURES

Pasión (riv.) B3
Petén-Itzá (lake) C2
San Pedro (riv.) B2
Sarstún (riv.) C3
Tacaná (vol.) A3
Tajumulco (vol.) A3
Tres Puntas (cape) C3
Usumacinta (riv.) A3

Atitlán (lake) B3
Atitlán (vol.) B3
Azul (riv.) C2
Chixoy (riv.) B2
Güija (lake) C3
Honduras (gulf) D2
Izabal (lake) C3
Minas (mts.) C3
Motagua (riv.) C3

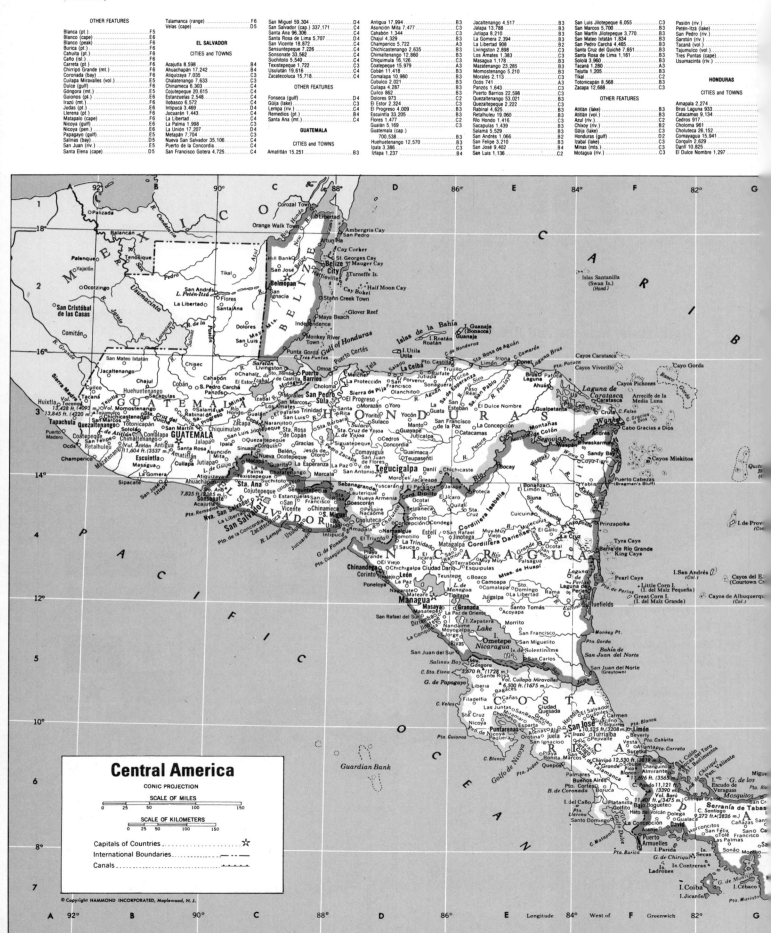

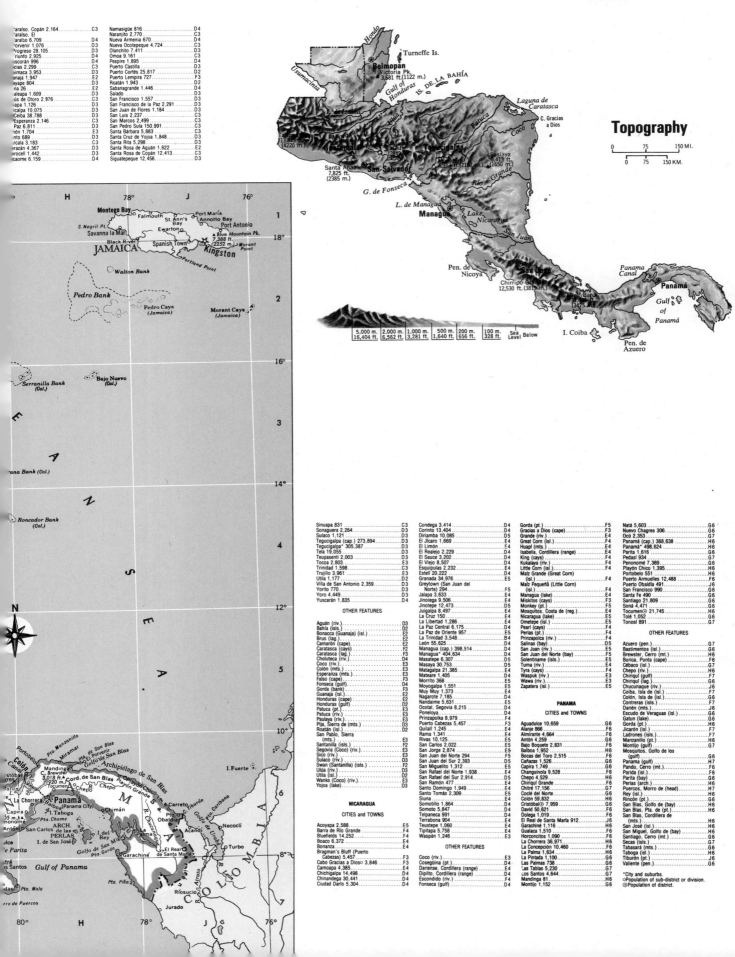

Topography

0 75 150 MI.
0 75 150 KM.

| 5,000 m. 16,404 ft. | 2,000 m. 6,562 ft. | 1,000 m. 3,281 ft. | 500 m. 1,640 ft. | 200 m. 656 ft. | 100 m. 328 ft. | Sea Level | Below |

BAHAMAS

CUBA

HAITI

DOMINICAN REPUBLIC

JAMAICA

BAHAMAS

AREA 5,382 sq. mi. (13,939 sq. km.)
POPULATION 209,505
CAPITAL Nassau
LARGEST CITY Nassau
HIGHEST POINT Mt. Alvernia 206 ft. (63 m.)
MONETARY UNIT Bahamian dollar
MAJOR LANGUAGE English
MAJOR RELIGIONS Roman Catholicism,
Protestantism

CUBA

AREA 44,206 sq. mi. (114,494 sq. km.)
POPULATION 9,706,369
CAPITAL Havana
LARGEST CITY Havana
HIGHEST POINT Pico Turquino
6,561 ft. (2,000 m.)
MONETARY UNIT Cuban peso
MAJOR LANGUAGE Spanish
MAJOR RELIGION Roman Catholicism

JAMAICA

AREA 4,411 sq. mi. (11,424 sq. km.)
POPULATION 2,161,000
CAPITAL Kingston
LARGEST CITY Kingston
HIGHEST POINT Blue Mountain Peak
7,402 ft. (2,256 m.)
MONETARY UNIT Jamaican dollar
MAJOR LANGUAGE English
MAJOR RELIGIONS Protestantism,
Roman Catholicism

GRENADA

AREA 133 sq. mi. (344 sq. km.)
POPULATION 103,103
CAPITAL St. George's
LARGEST CITY St. George's
HIGHEST POINT Mt. St. Catherine
2,757 ft. (840 m.)
MONETARY UNIT East Caribbean dollar
MAJOR LANGUAGES English, French patois
MAJOR RELIGIONS Roman Catholicism,
Protestantism

DOMINICA

AREA 290 sq. mi. (751 sq. km.)
POPULATION 74,089
CAPITAL Roseau
HIGHEST POINT Morne Diablotin
4,747 ft. (1,447 m.)
MONETARY UNIT Dominican dollar
MAJOR LANGUAGES English, French patois
MAJOR RELIGIONS Roman Catholicism,
Protestantism

SAINT VINCENT AND THE GRENADINE

AREA 150 sq. mi. (388 sq. km.)
POPULATION 124,000
CAPITAL Kingstown
HIGHEST POINT Soufrière 4,000 ft. (1,
MONETARY UNIT East Caribbean dollar
MAJOR LANGUAGE English
MAJOR RELIGIONS Protestantism,
Roman Catholicism

HAITI

AREA 10,694 sq. mi. (27,697 sq. km.)
POPULATION 5,009,000
CAPITAL Port-au-Prince
LARGEST CITY Port-au-Prince
HIGHEST POINT Pic La Selle 8,793 ft. (2,680 m.)
MONETARY UNIT gourde
MAJOR LANGUAGES Creole French, French
MAJOR RELIGION Roman Catholicism

TRINIDAD AND TOBAGO

AREA 1,980 sq. mi. (5,128 sq. km.)
POPULATION 1,067,108
CAPITAL Port of Spain
LARGEST CITY Port of Spain
HIGHEST POINT Mt. Aripo 3,084 ft. (940 m.)
MONETARY UNIT Trinidad and Tobago dollar
MAJOR LANGUAGES English, Hindi
MAJOR RELIGIONS Roman Catholicism,
Protestantism, Hinduism, Islam

DOMINICAN REPUBLIC

AREA 18,704 sq. mi. (48,443 sq. km.)
POPULATION 5,647,977
CAPITAL Santo Domingo
LARGEST CITY Santo Domingo
HIGHEST POINT Pico Duarte
10,417 ft. (3,175 m.)
MONETARY UNIT Dominican peso
MAJOR LANGUAGE Spanish
MAJOR RELIGION Roman Catholicism

BARBADOS

AREA 166 sq. mi. (430 sq. km.)
POPULATION 248,983
CAPITAL Bridgetown
LARGEST CITY Bridgetown
HIGHEST POINT Mt. Hillaby 1,104 ft.
(336 m.)
MONETARY UNIT Barbadian dollar
MAJOR LANGUAGE English
MAJOR RELIGION Protestantism

SAINT LUCIA

AREA 238 sq. mi. (616 sq. km.)
POPULATION 115,783
CAPITAL Castries
HIGHEST POINT Mt. Gimie 3,117 ft. (9
MONETARY UNIT East Caribbean dollar
MAJOR LANGUAGES English, French p
MAJOR RELIGIONS Roman Catholicism,
Protestantism

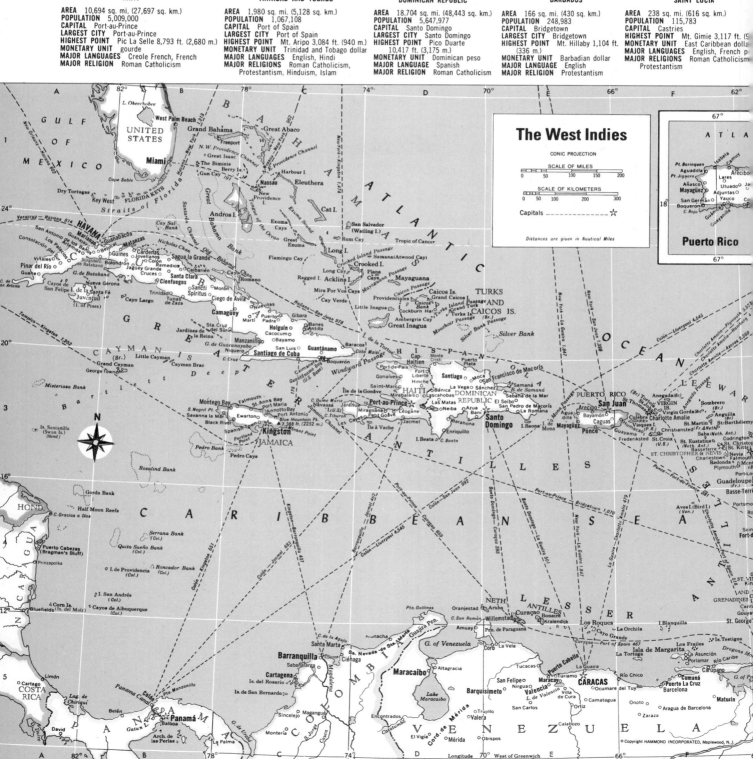

The West Indies

CONIC PROJECTION

SCALE OF MILES

SCALE OF KILOMETERS

Capitals

Distances are given in Nautical Miles

Puerto Rico

© Copyright HAMMOND INCORPORATED, Maplewood, N.J.

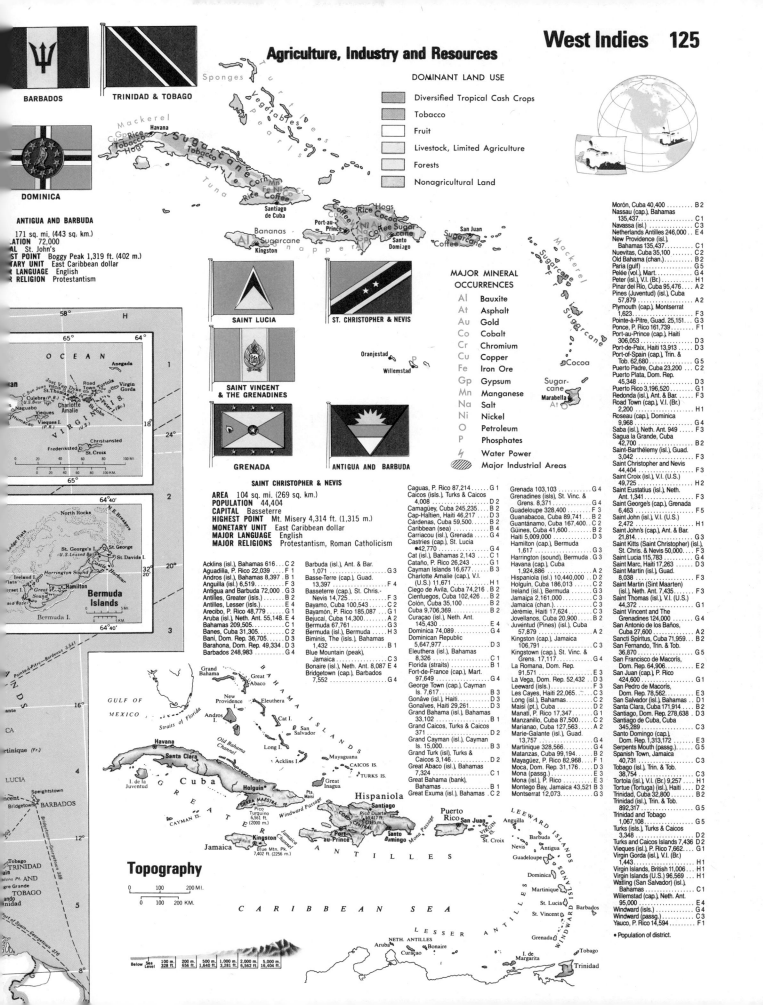

AREA 3,623,420 sq. mi.
(9,384,658 sq. km.)
POPULATION 226,504,825
CAPITAL Washington
LARGEST CITY New York
HIGHEST POINT Mt. McKinley 20,320 ft.
(6,194 m.)
MONETARY UNIT U.S. dollar
MAJOR LANGUAGE English
MAJOR RELIGIONS Protestantism,
Roman Catholicism, Judaism

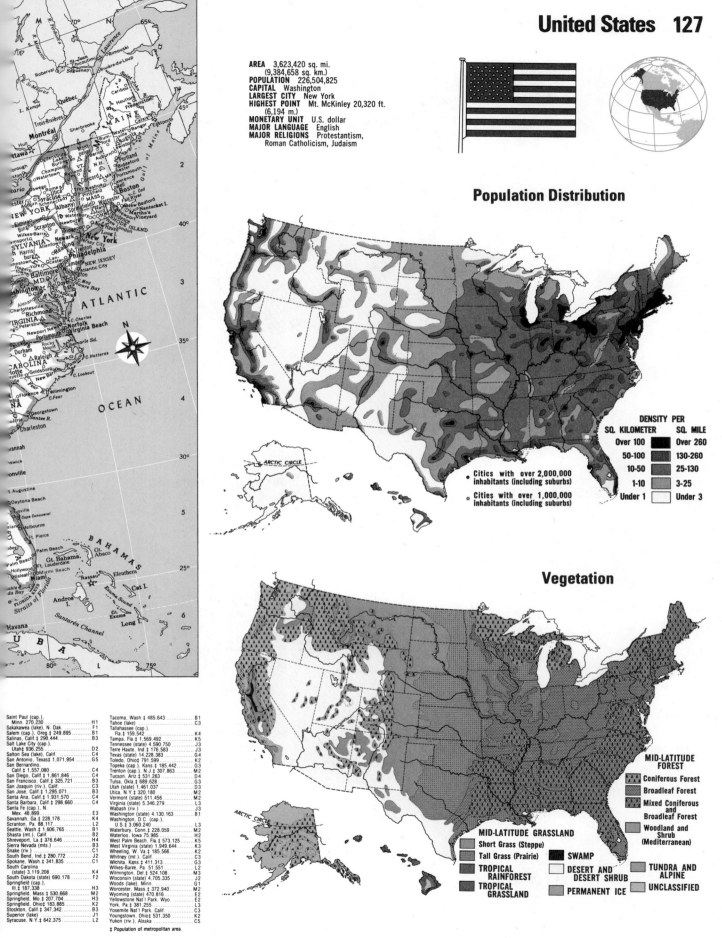

Population Distribution

DENSITY PER	
SQ. KILOMETER	SQ. MILE
Over 100	Over 260
50-100	130-260
10-50	25-130
1-10	3-25
Under 1	Under 3

● Cities with over 2,000,000 inhabitants (including suburbs)
○ Cities with over 1,000,000 inhabitants (including suburbs)

Vegetation

MID-LATITUDE FOREST
Coniferous Forest
Broadleaf Forest
Mixed Coniferous and Broadleaf Forest
Woodland and Shrub (Mediterranean)

MID-LATITUDE GRASSLAND
Short Grass (Steppe)
Tall Grass (Prairie)
SWAMP
DESERT AND DESERT SHRUB
TROPICAL RAINFOREST
TROPICAL GRASSLAND
PERMANENT ICE
TUNDRA AND ALPINE
UNCLASSIFIED

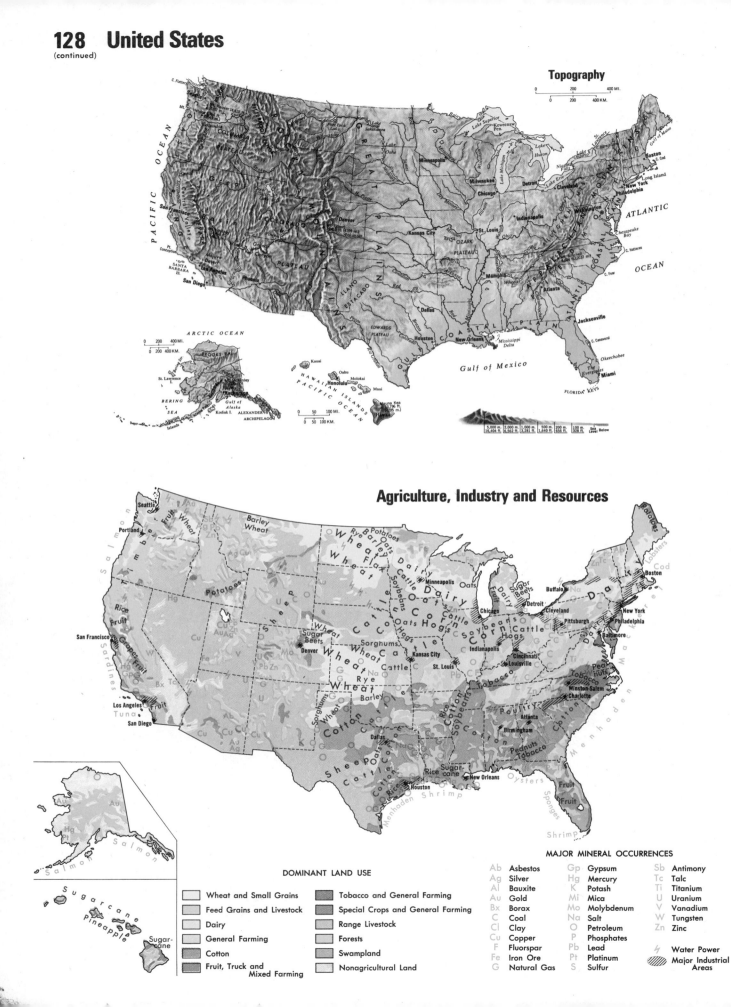

Topography

Agriculture, Industry and Resources

DOMINANT LAND USE

Wheat and Small Grains
Feed Grains and Livestock
Dairy
General Farming
Cotton
Fruit, Truck and Mixed Farming
Tobacco and General Farming
Special Crops and General Farming
Range Livestock
Forests
Swampland
Nonagricultural Land

MAJOR MINERAL OCCURRENCES

Ab	Asbestos	Gp	Gypsum	Sb	Antimony
Ag	Silver	Hg	Mercury	Tc	Talc
Al	Bauxite	K	Potash	Ti	Titanium
Au	Gold	Mi	Mica	U	Uranium
Bx	Borax	Mo	Molybdenum	V	Vanadium
C	Coal	Na	Salt	W	Tungsten
Cl	Clay	O	Petroleum	Zn	Zinc
Cu	Copper	P	Phosphates		
F	Fluorspar	Pb	Lead		Water Power
Fe	Iron Ore	Pt	Platinum		Major Industrial Areas
G	Natural Gas	S	Sulfur		

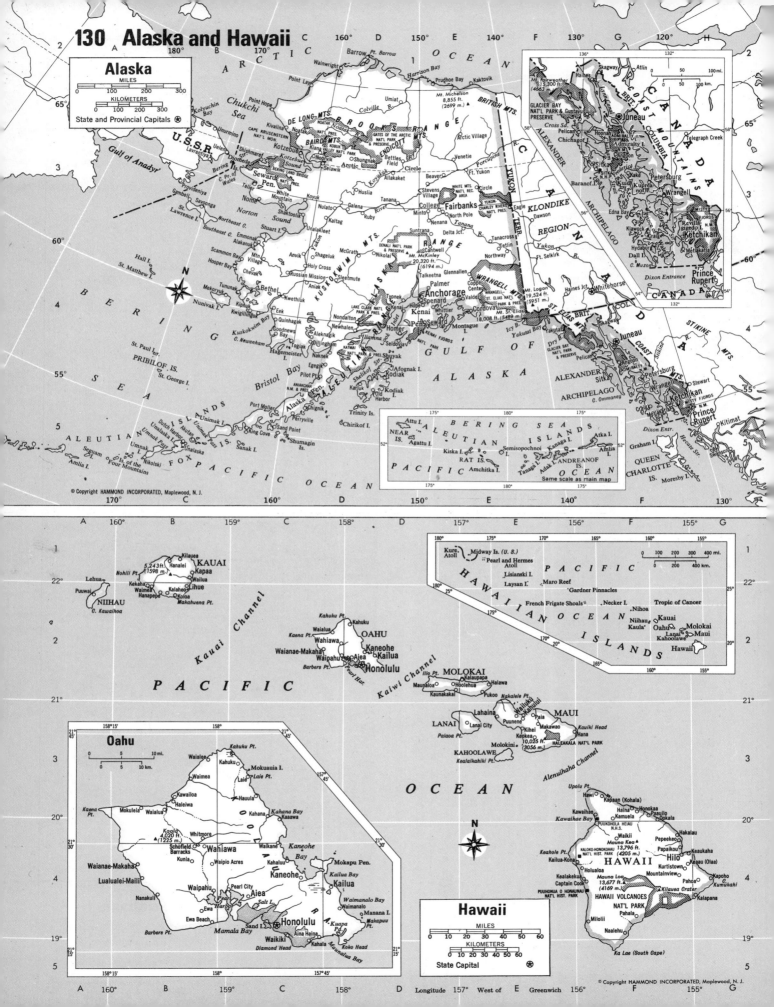

130 Alaska and Hawaii

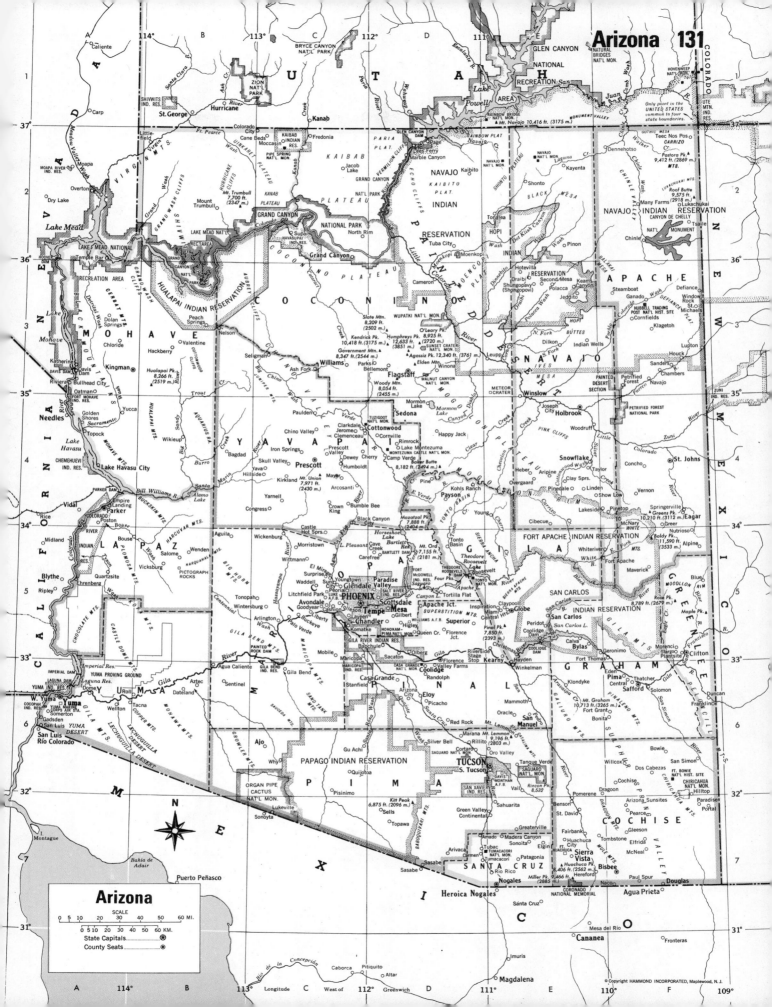

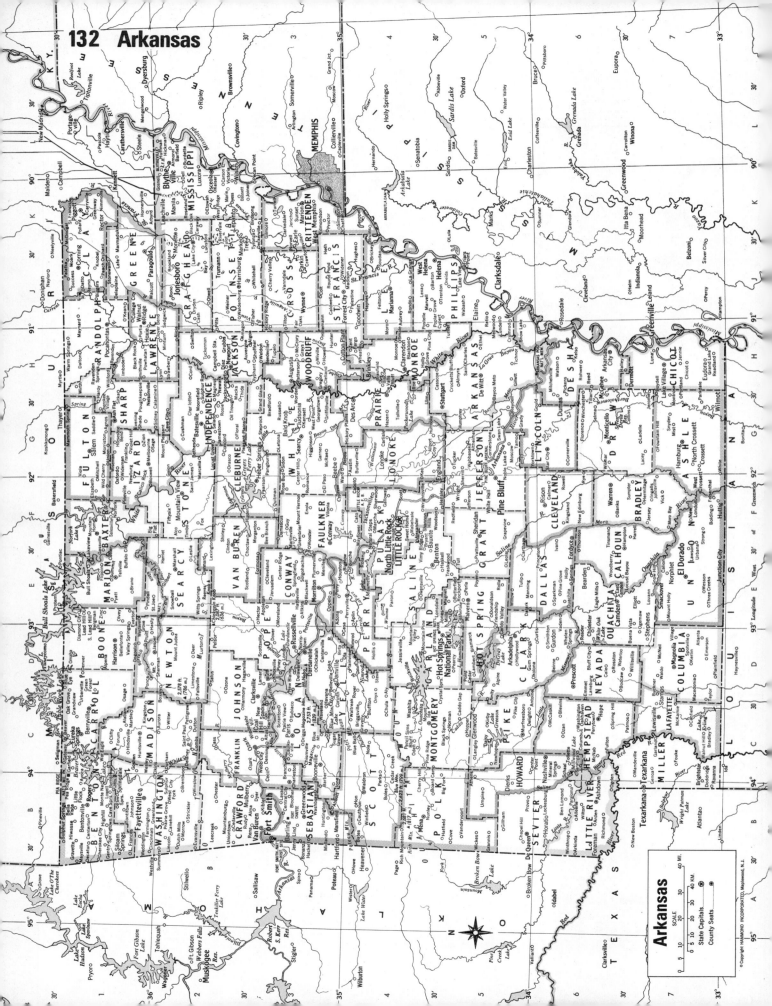

Arkansas

SCALE

State Capitals .... ⊛

County Seats .... ⊛

California

SCALE

State Capitals

County Seats

Canals

San Francisco
and Vicinity

Sacramento
and Vicinity

Los Angeles
and Vicinity

© Copyright HAMMOND INCORPORATED, Maplewood, N.J.

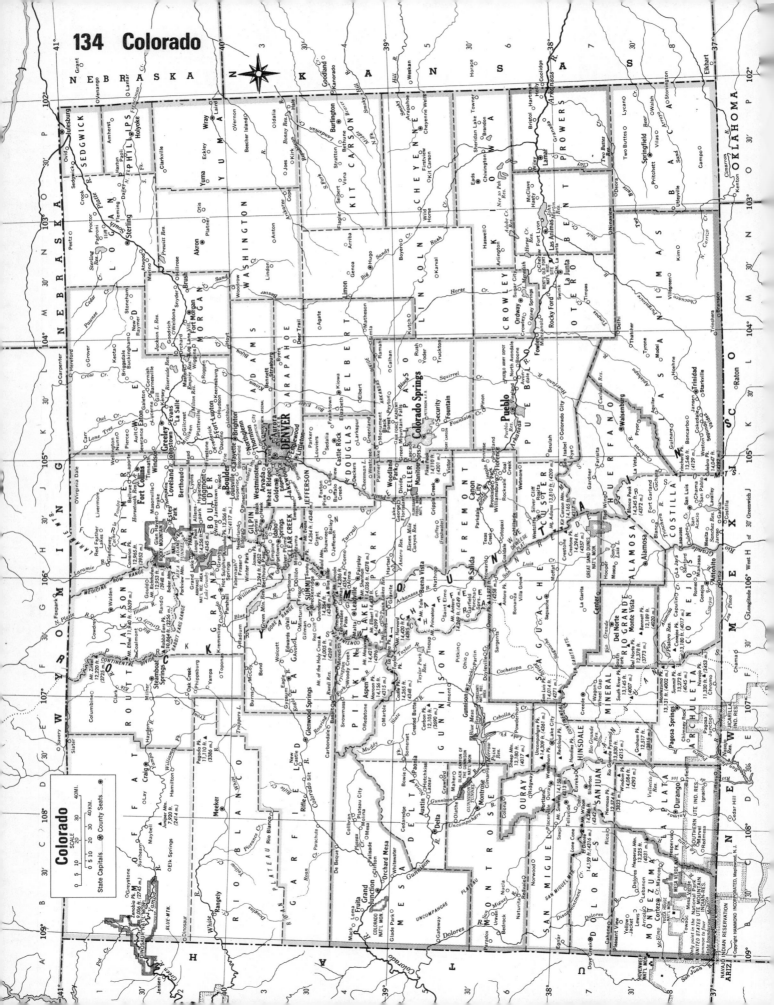

136 Florida

Florida
SCALE

State Capitals.............. ⊛
County Seats.............. ◉
Canals...................

Western Part of
Florida
Same scale as main map

© Copyright HAMMOND INCORPORATED, Maplewood, N.J.

Georgia

SCALE

0 5 10   20   30   40 MI.

0 5 10   20   30 40 KM.

State Capitals .... ⊛

County Seats .... ⊛

® Copyright HAMMOND INCORPORATED, Maplewood, N.J.

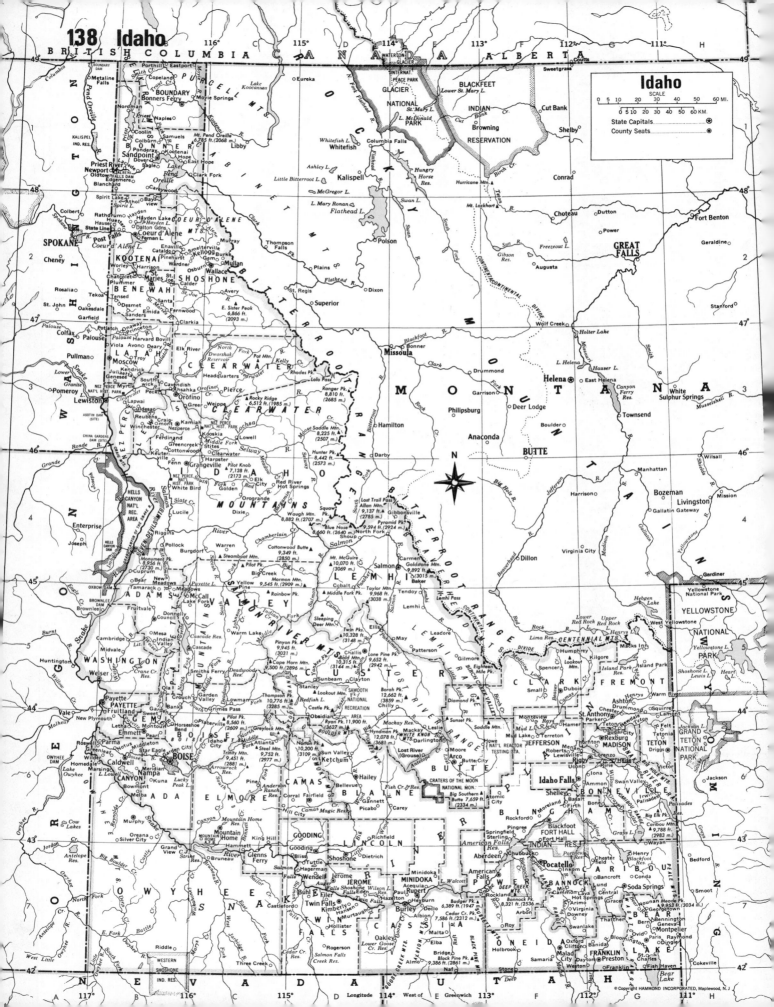

Illinois

SCALE

State Capitals ⊛
County Seats ⊙
Canals

Chicago and Vicinity

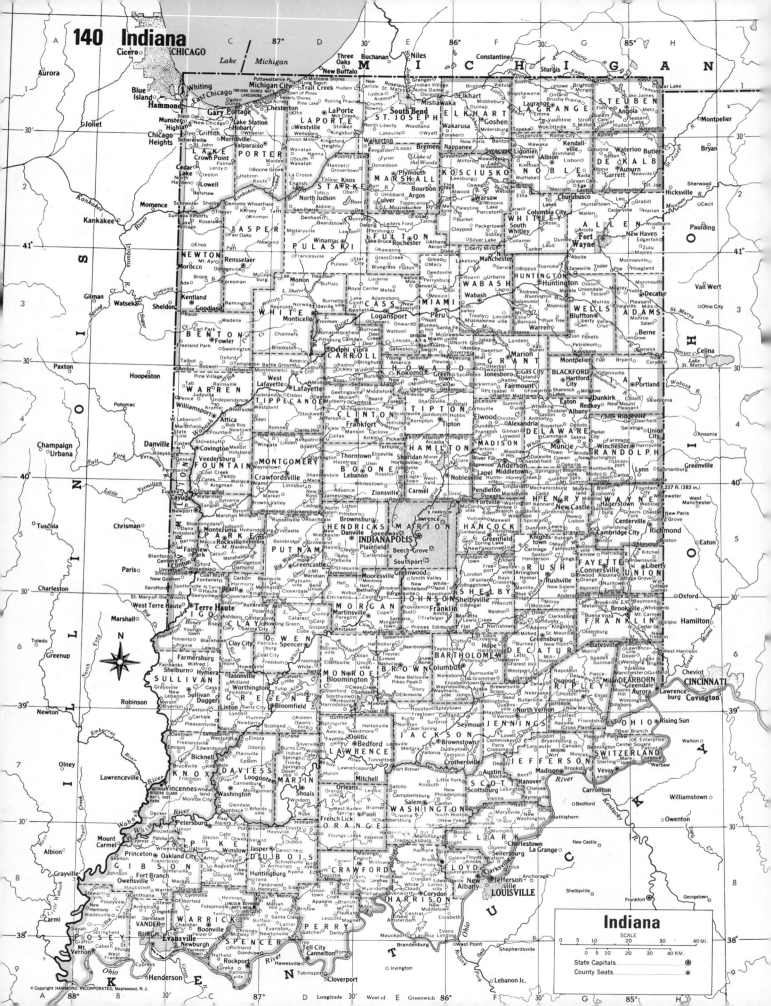

140 Indiana

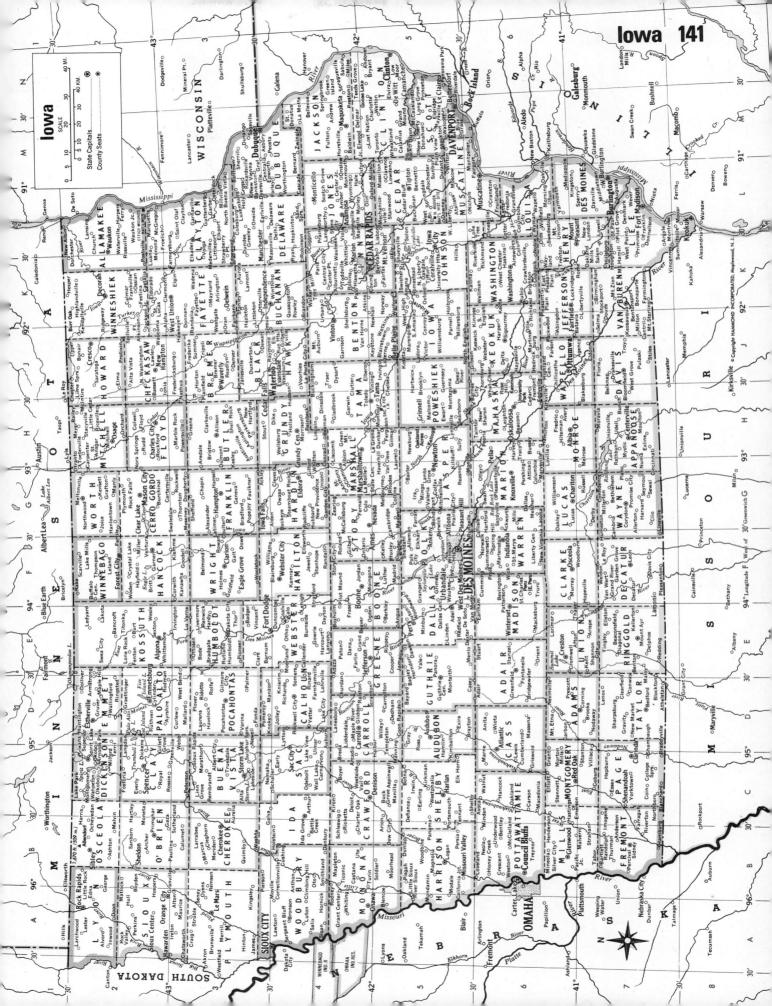

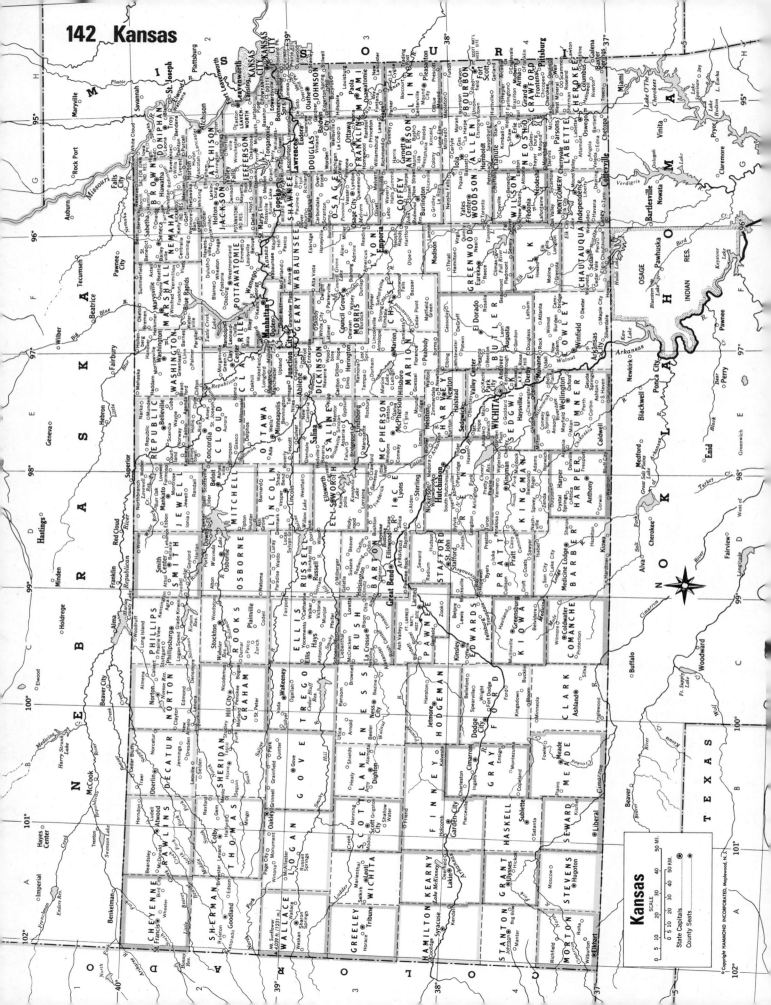

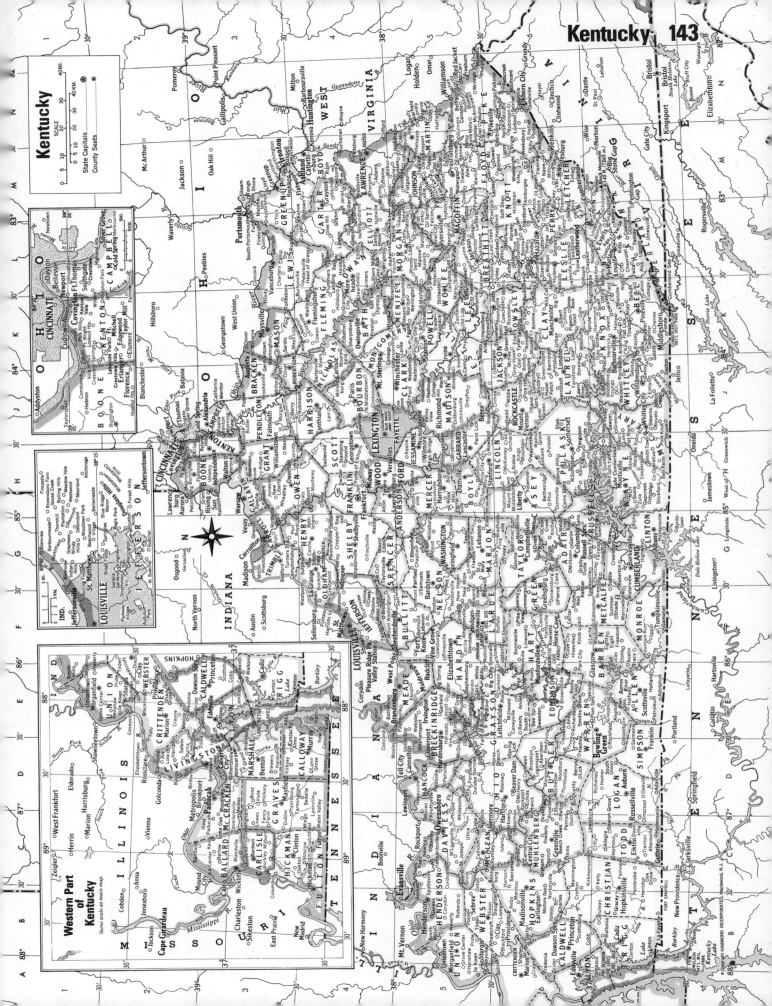

New Orleans, Baton Rouge and Vicinity

Louisiana

SCALE
State Capitals ⊛
Parish Seats ⊙
Canals

© Copyright HAMMOND INCORPORATED, Maplewood, N.J.

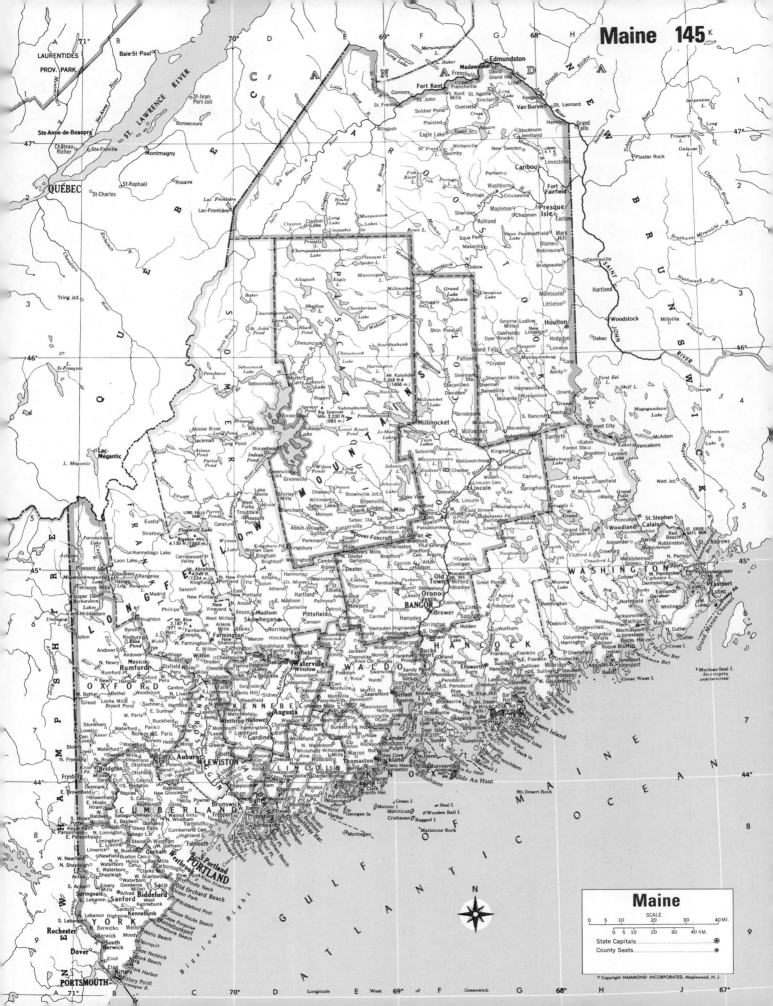

Maine 145 K

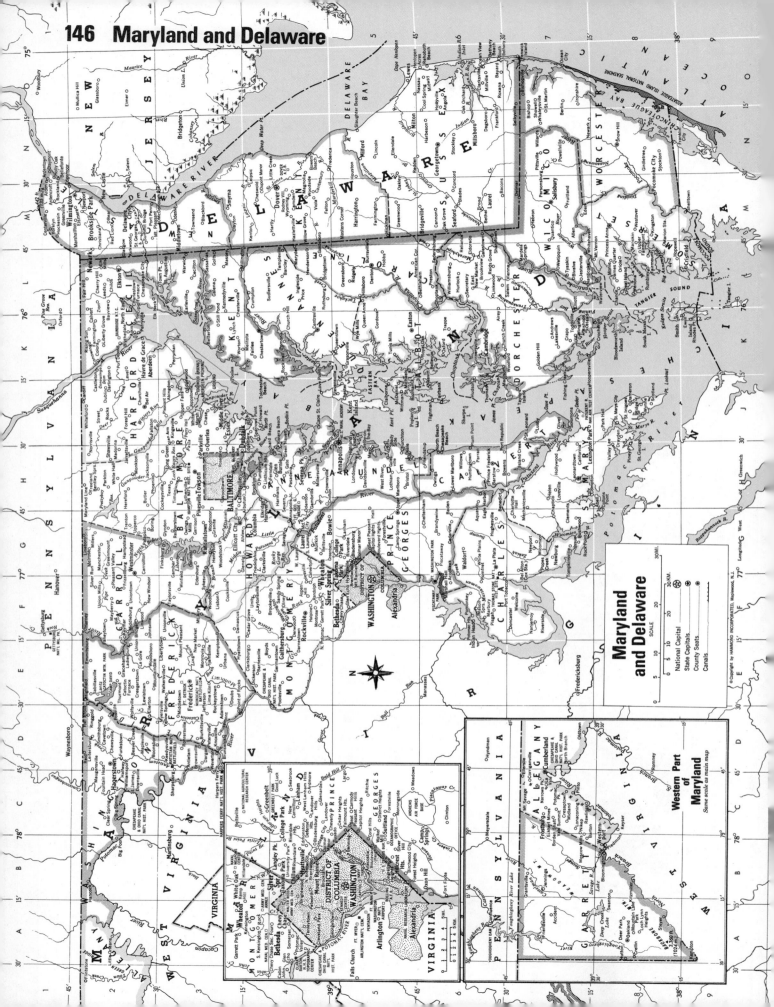

Maryland
and Delaware

SCALE

National Capital
State Capitals
County Seats
Canals

© Copyright by HAMMOND INCORPORATED, Maplewood, N.J.

Western Part
of
Maryland
Same scale as main map

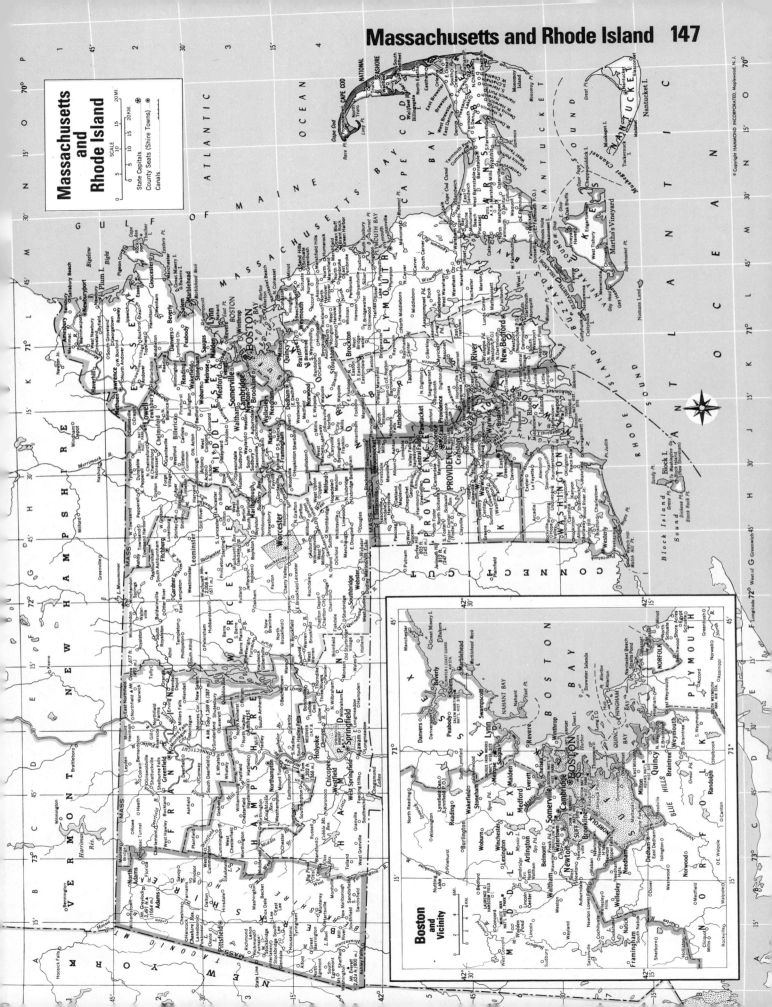

Northeastern Part of Minnesota

Minnesota

SCALE

State Capitals.................⊛
County Seats..................◉

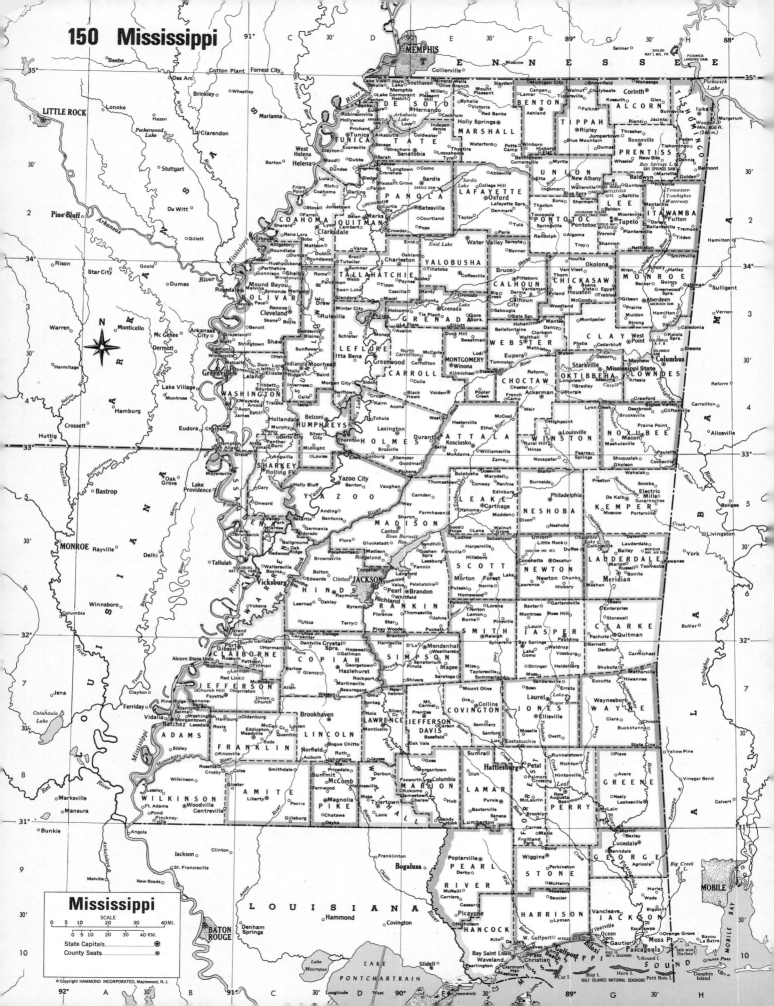

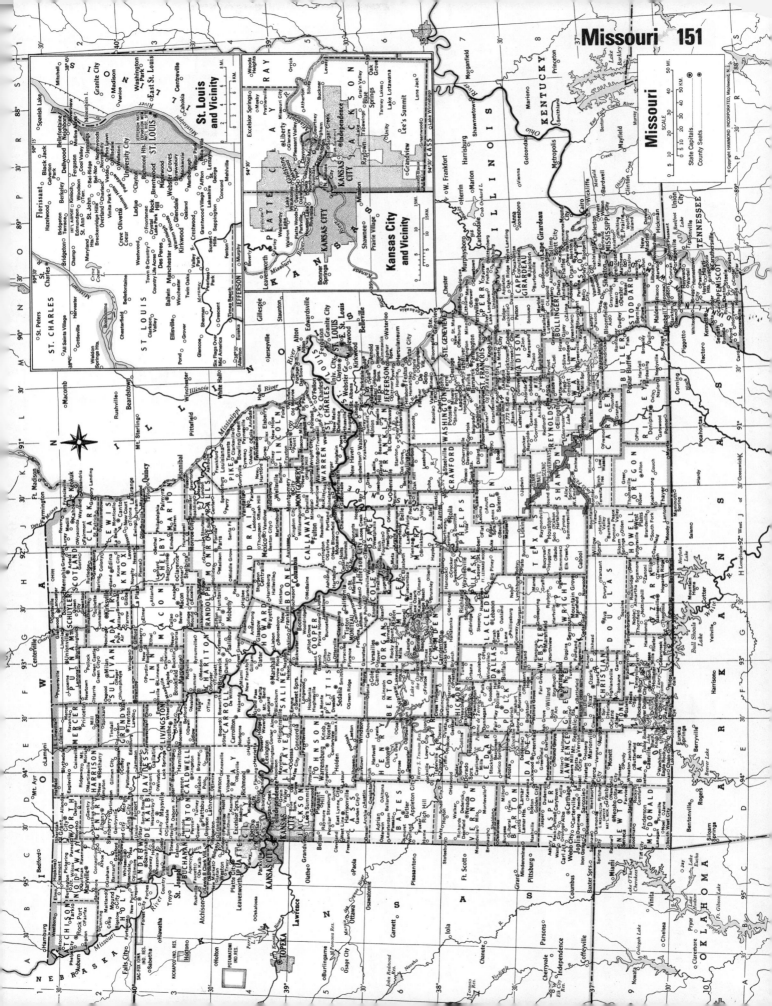

Montana

SCALE
0 5 10 20   40   60   80 MI.
0 5 10 20   40   60   80 KM.

State Capitals ⊛
County Seats ⊙

© Copyright HAMMOND INCORPORATED, Maplewood, N.J.

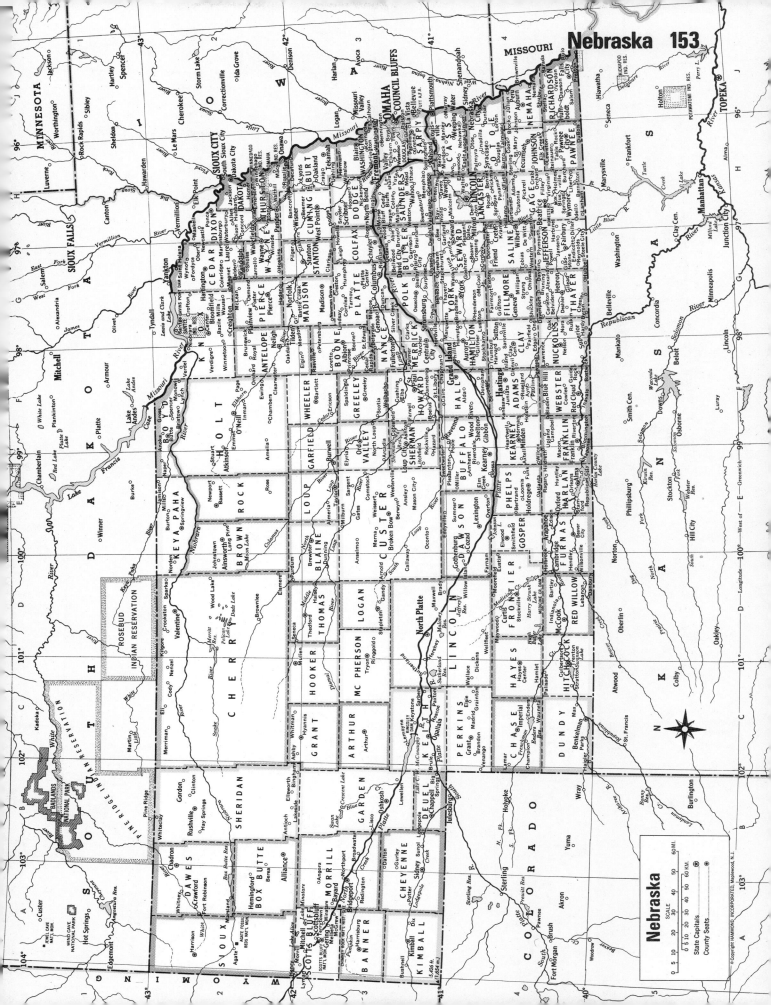

154 Nevada

Nevada

SCALE

0 5 10   20   30   40   50   60 MI.

0 5 10 20 30 40 50 60 KM.

State Capitals ⊛

County Seats ⊙

© Copyright HAMMOND INCORPORATED, Maplewood, N.J.

New Hampshire
and Vermont

SCALE
0 5 10 15 20 25MI.
0 5 10 15 20 25KM.

State Capitals..............⊛
County Seats...............◉

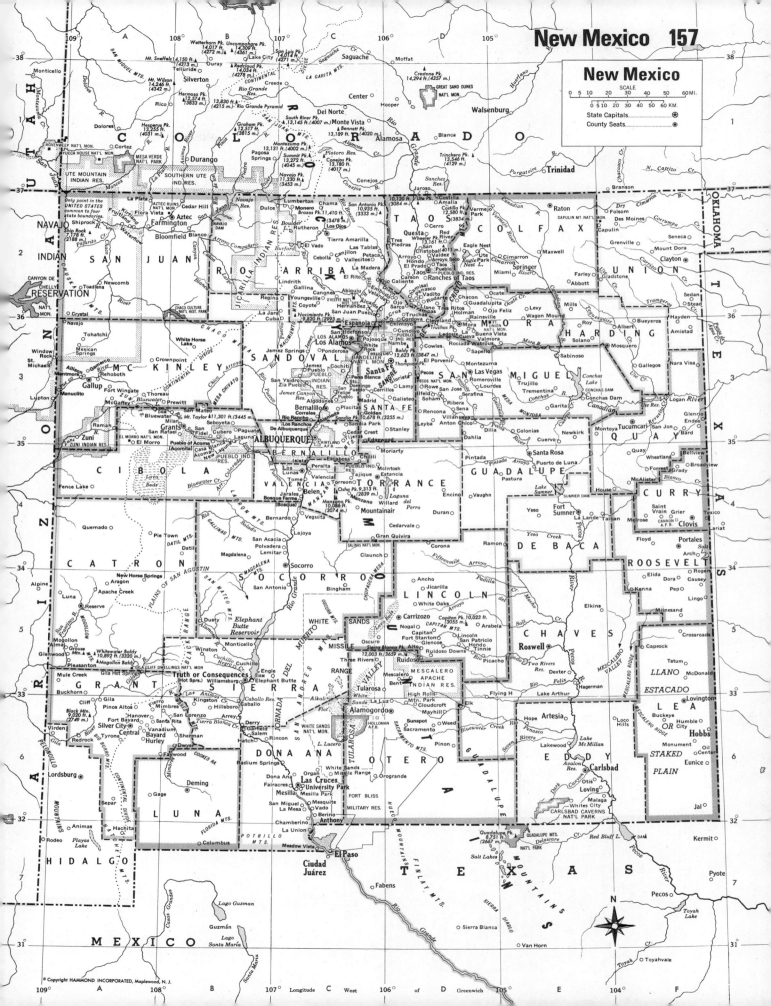

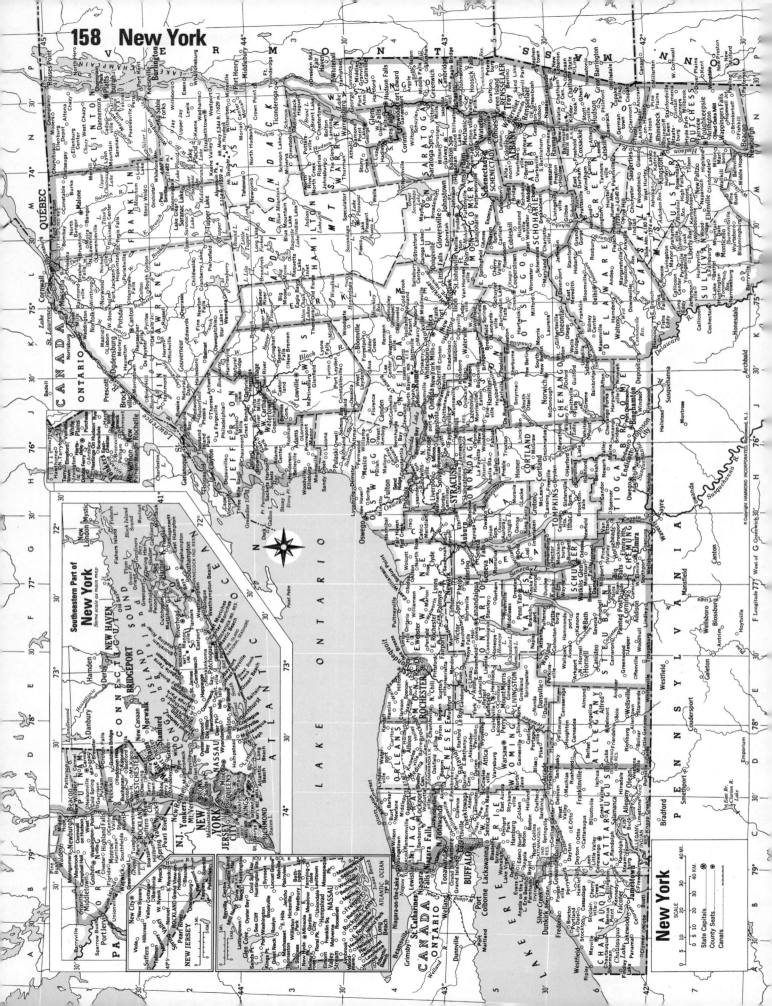

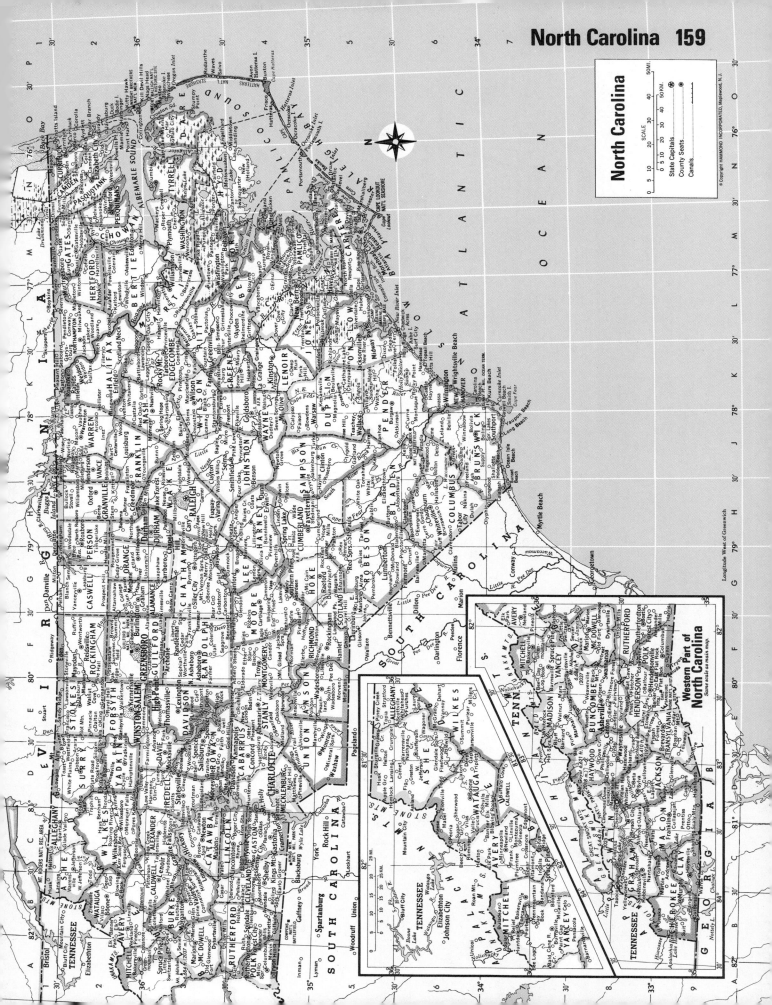

North Carolina

SCALE

State Capitals ⊛
County Seats ⊛
Canals.

© Copyright HAMMOND INCORPORATED, Maplewood, N.J.

Western Part of
North Carolina
Same scale as main map.

North Dakota

SCALE

0 5 10 20 30 MI.

0 5 10 20 30 KM.

State Capitals .... ⊛

County Seats .... ⊙

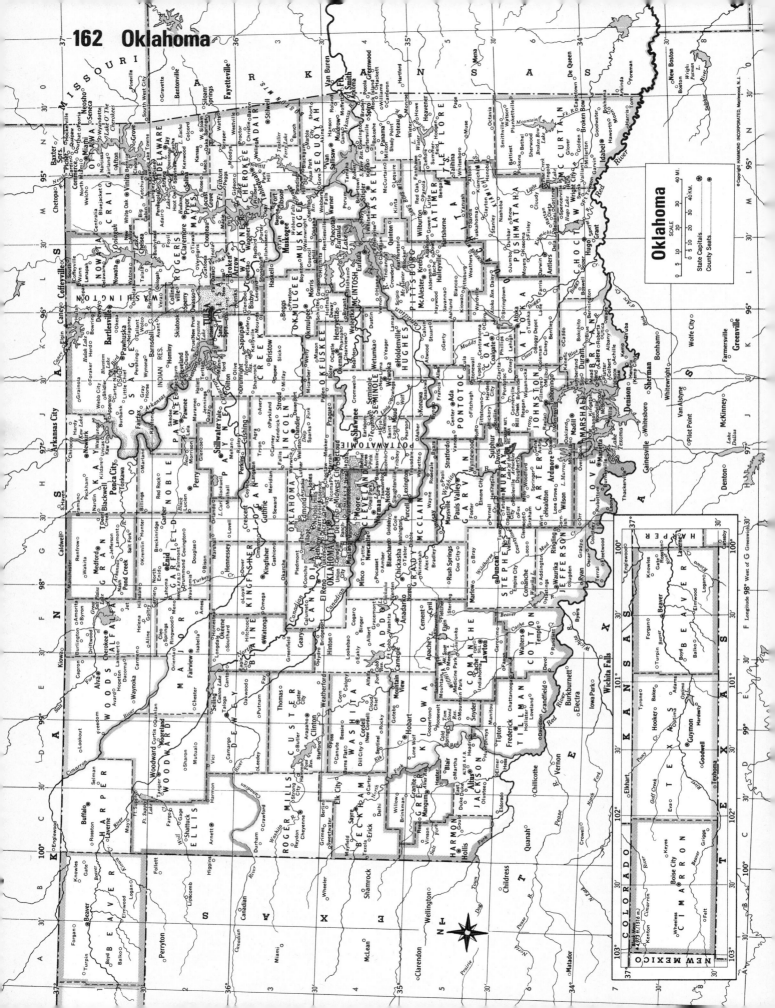

Oklahoma

SCALE
0 5 10 20   30   40 MI.
0 5 10 20 30 40 KM.

State Capitals ⊛
County Seats ◉

© Copyright HAMMOND INCORPORATED, Maplewood, N.J.

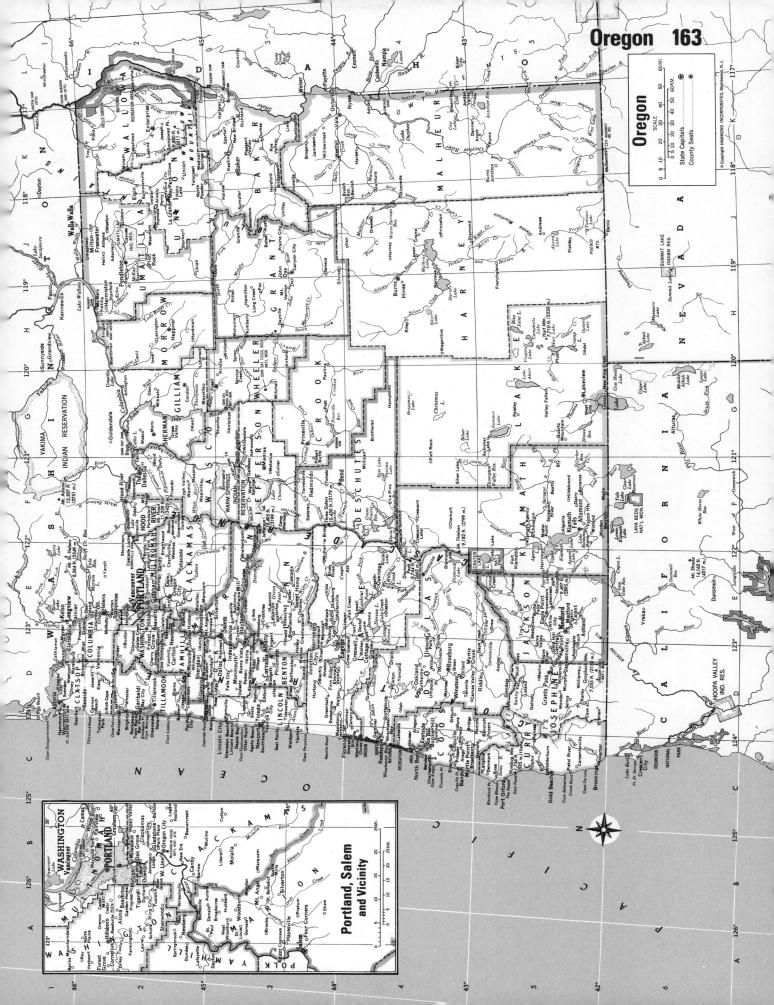

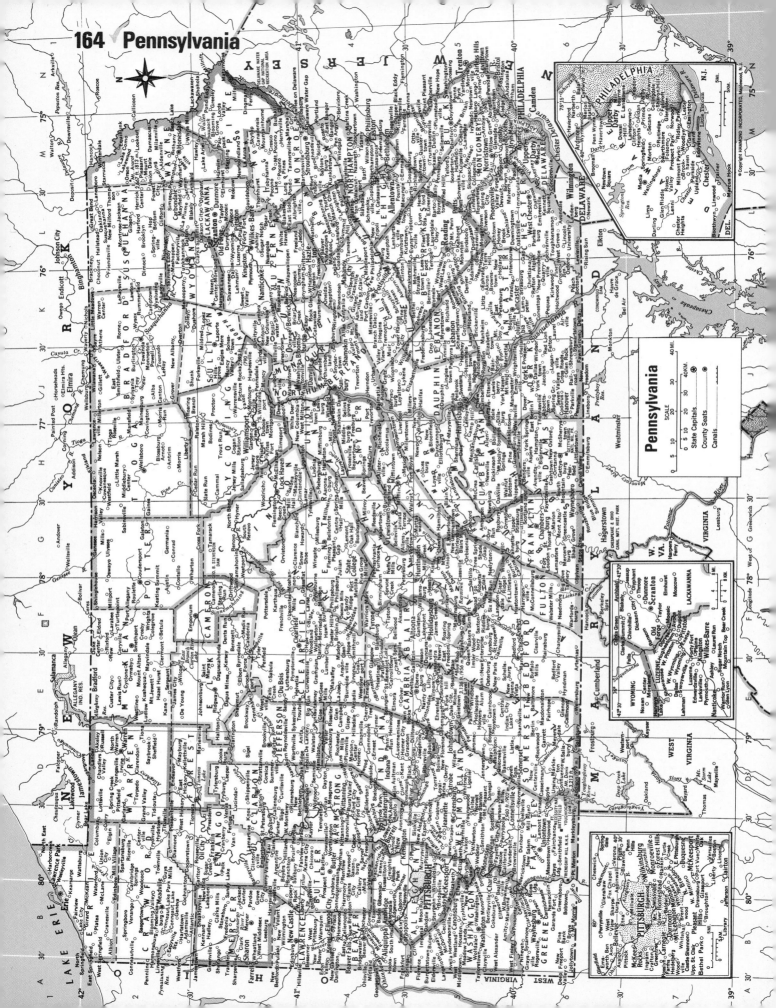

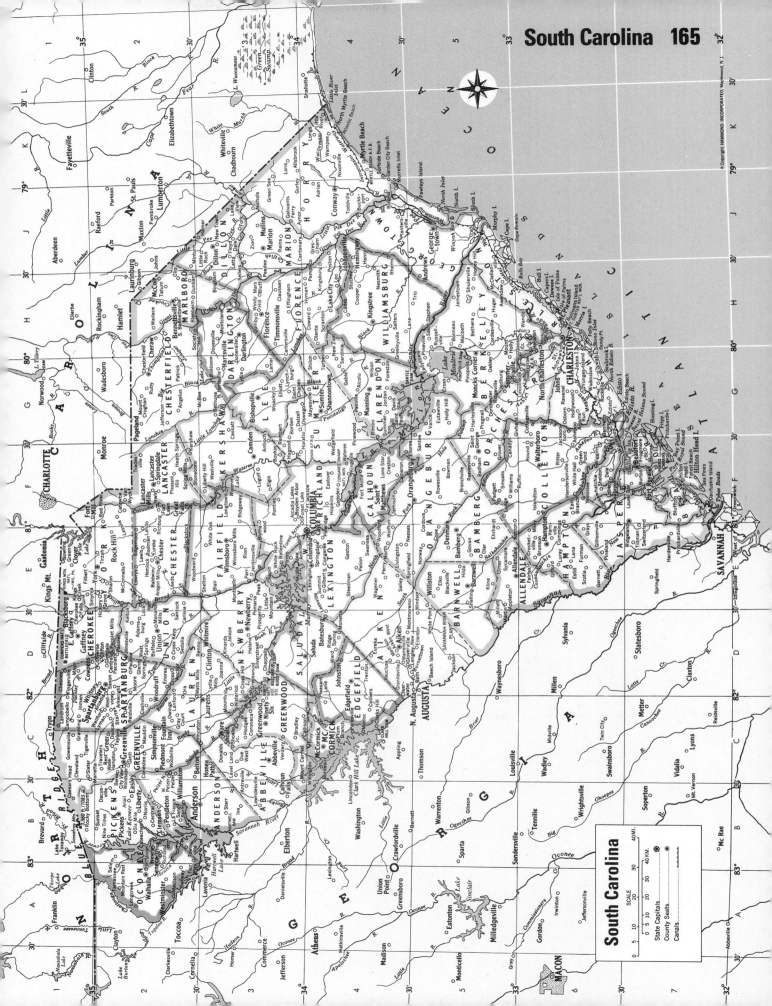

South Carolina

SCALE

		40MI.
0 5 10 20 30 40KM.		

⊛ State Capitals..............
◉ County Seats..............
Canals..............

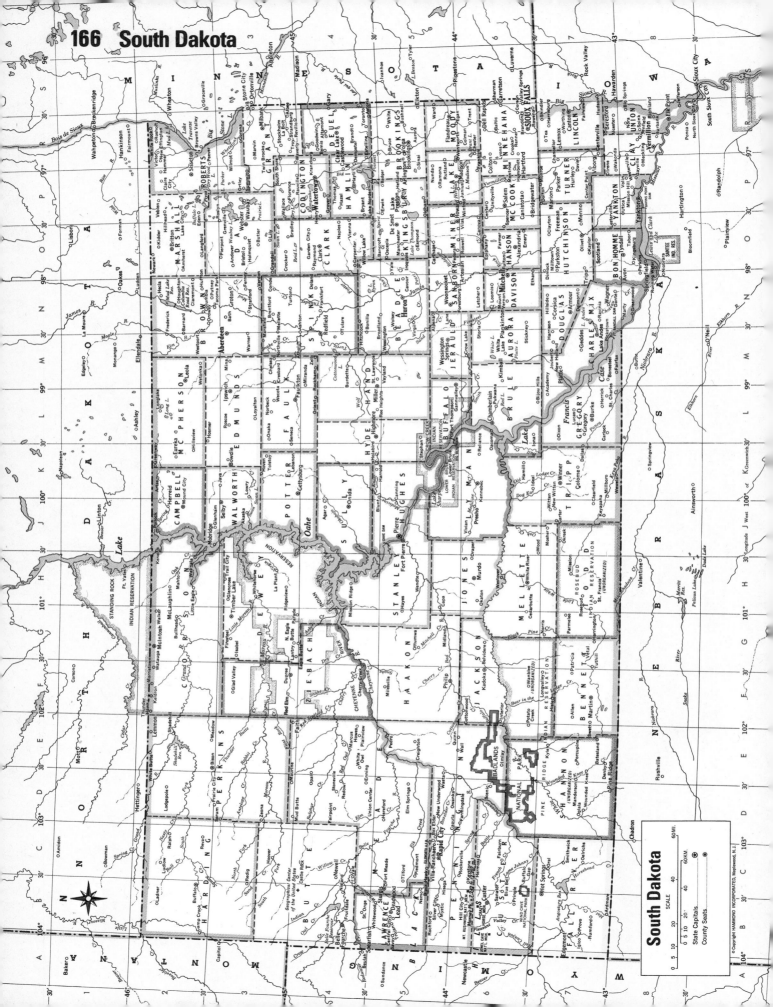

South Dakota

SCALE

0 5 10 20 30 40 50 60 MI.
0 10 20 30 40 50 60 KM.

State Capitals... ⊛
County Seats... ⊛

Utah

SCALE

0 5 10 20 30 40 50 MI.

0 5 10 20 30 40 50 KM.

State Capitals............⊛
County Seats.............◉

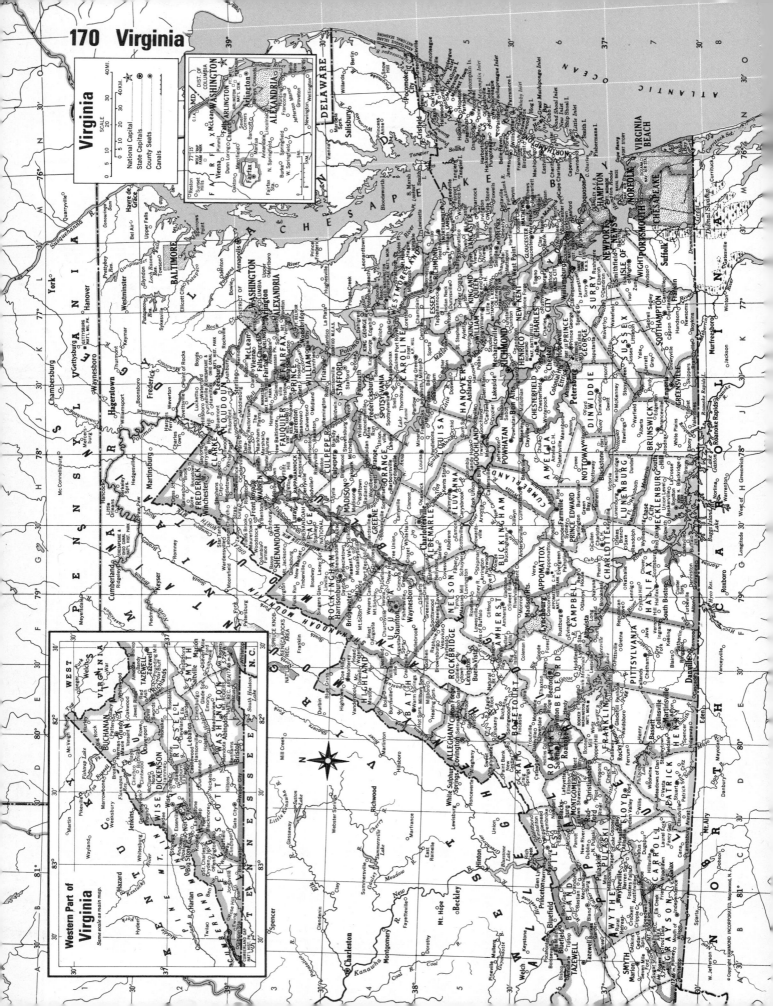

Virginia

SCALE
National Capitals
State Capitals
County Seats
Canals

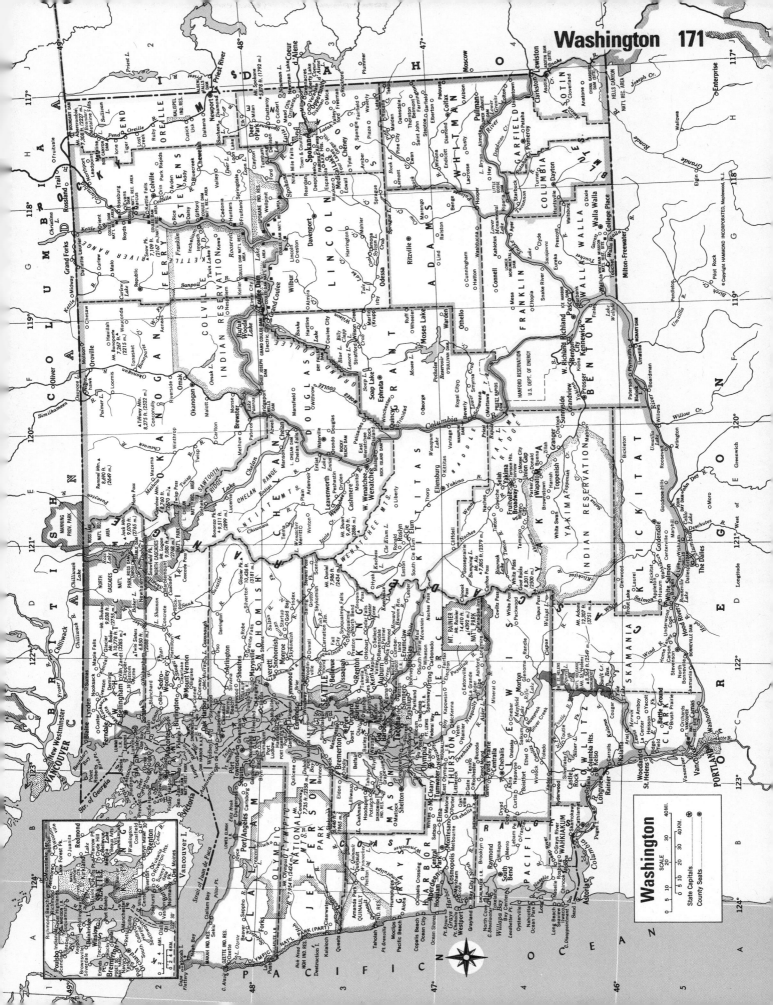

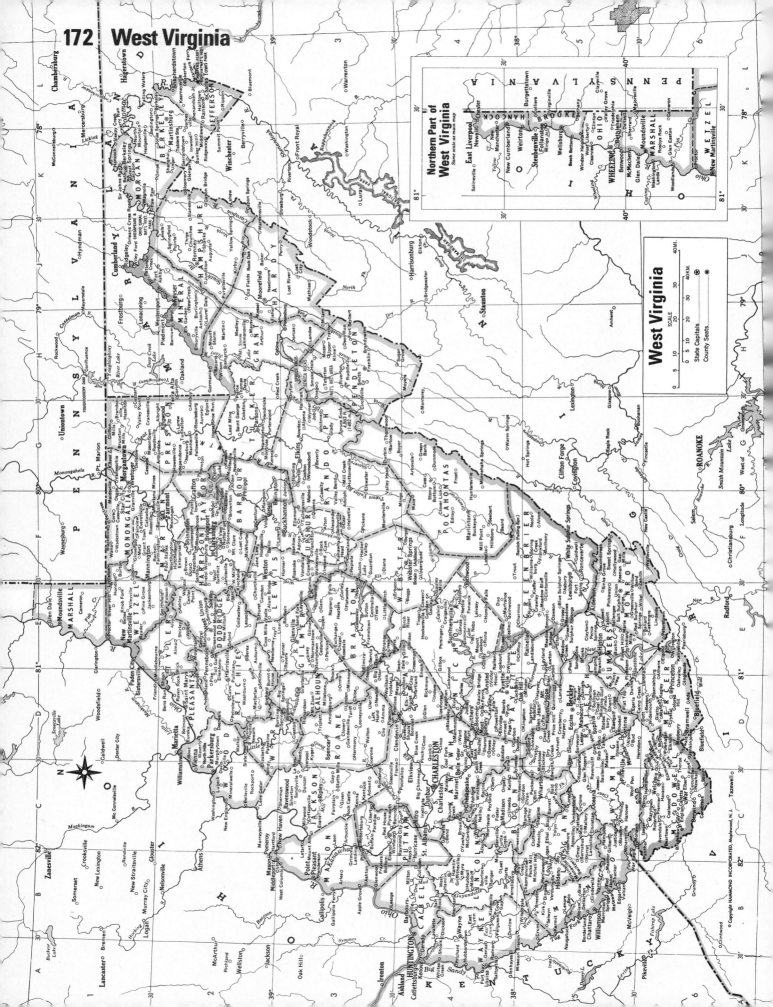

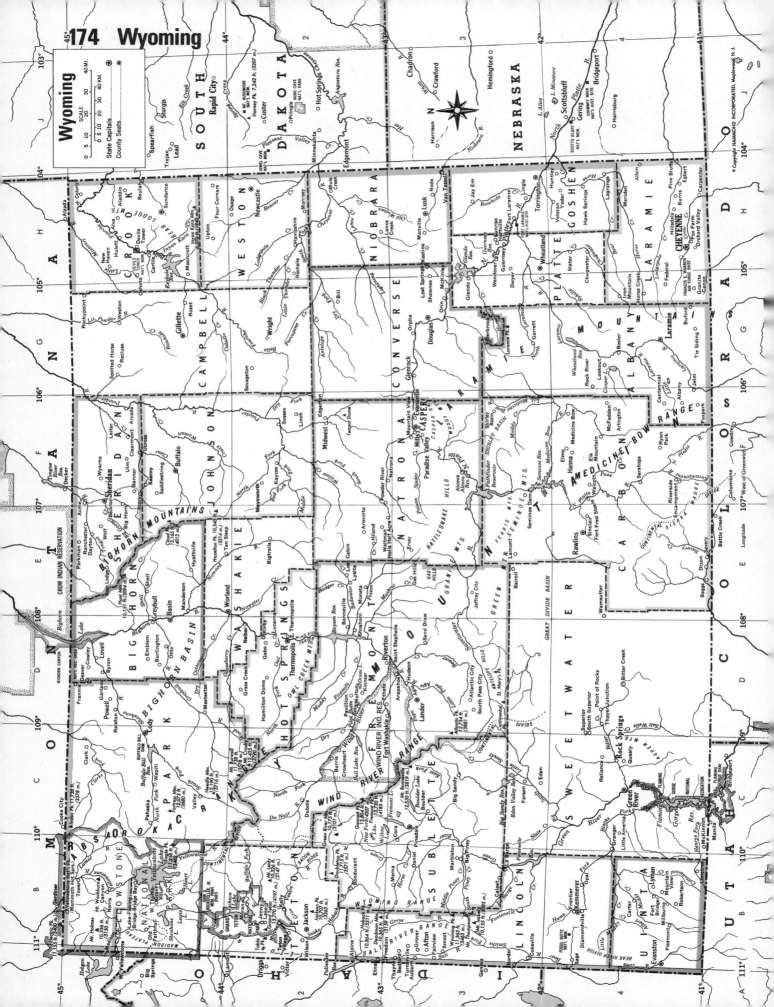

	LAND AREA IN SQUARE MILES	POPULATION 1980	CAPITAL	LARGEST CITY	STATE FLOWER	STATE BIRD
Alabama	51,705	3,893,888	Montgomery	Birmingham	Camellia	Yellowhammer
Alaska	591,004	401,851	Juneau	Anchorage	Forget-me-not	Willow Ptarmigan
Arizona	114,000	2,718,425	Phoenix	Phoenix	Saguaro Cactus Blossom	Cactus Wren
Arkansas	53,187	2,286,435	Little Rock	Little Rock	Apple Blossom	Mockingbird
California	158,706	23,667,565	Sacramento	Los Angeles	Golden Poppy	California Valley Quail
Colorado	104,091	2,889,735	Denver	Denver	Rocky Mountain Columbine	Lark Bunting
Connecticut	5,018	3,107,576	Hartford	Bridgeport	Mountain Laurel	Robin
Delaware	2,044	594,317	Dover	Wilmington	Peach Blossom	Blue Hen Chicken
Florida	58,664	9,746,342	Tallahassee	Jacksonville	Orange Blossom	Mockingbird
Georgia	58,910	5,463,105	Atlanta	Atlanta	Cherokee Rose	Brown Thrasher
Hawaii	6,471	964,691	Honolulu	Honolulu	Hibiscus	Nene (Hawaiian Goose)
Idaho	83,564	944,038	Boise	Boise	Syringa	Mountain Bluebird
Illinois	56,345	11,426,596	Springfield	Chicago	Native Violet	Cardinal
Indiana	36,185	5,490,260	Indianapolis	Indianapolis	Peony	Cardinal
Iowa	56,275	2,913,808	Des Moines	Des Moines	Wild Rose	Eastern Goldfinch
Kansas	82,277	2,364,236	Topeka	Wichita	Sunflower	Western Meadowlark
Kentucky	40,409	3,660,257	Frankfort	Louisville	Goldenrod	Cardinal
Louisiana	47,752	4,206,312	Baton Rouge	New Orleans	Magnolia	Eastern Brown Pelican
Maine	33,265	1,125,027	Augusta	Portland	White Pine Cone and Tassel	Chickadee
Maryland	10,460	4,216,975	Annapolis	Baltimore	Black-eyed Susan	Baltimore Oriole
Massachusetts	8,284	5,737,037	Boston	Boston	Mayflower	Chickadee
Michigan	58,527	9,262,078	Lansing	Detroit	Apple Blossom	Robin
Minnesota	84,402	4,075,970	St. Paul	Minneapolis	Pink and White Lady's-Slipper	Common Loon
Mississippi	47,689	2,520,638	Jackson	Jackson	Magnolia	Mockingbird
Missouri	69,697	4,916,759	Jefferson City	St. Louis	Hawthorn	Bluebird
Montana	147,046	786,690	Helena	Billings	Bitterroot	Western Meadowlark
Nebraska	77,355	1,569,825	Lincoln	Omaha	Goldenrod	Western Meadowlark
Nevada	110,561	800,493	Carson City	Las Vegas	Sagebrush	Mountain Bluebird
New Hampshire	9,279	920,610	Concord	Manchester	Purple Lilac	Purple Finch
New Jersey	7,787	7,364,823	Trenton	Newark	Purple Violet	Eastern Goldfinch
New Mexico	121,593	1,302,981	Santa Fe	Albuquerque	Yucca	Road Runner
New York	49,108	17,558,072	Albany	New York	Rose	Bluebird
North Carolina	52,669	5,881,813	Raleigh	Charlotte	Flowering Dogwood	Cardinal
North Dakota	70,702	652,717	Bismarck	Fargo	Wild Prairie Rose	Western Meadowlark
Ohio	41,330	10,797,624	Columbus	Cleveland	Scarlet Carnation	Cardinal
Oklahoma	69,956	3,025,290	Oklahoma City	Oklahoma City	Mistletoe	Scissor-tailed Flycatcher
Oregon	97,073	2,633,149	Salem	Portland	Oregon Grape	Western Meadowlark
Pennsylvania	45,308	11,863,895	Harrisburg	Philadelphia	Mountain Laurel	Ruffed Grouse
Rhode Island	1,212	947,154	Providence	Providence	Violet	Rhode Island Red
South Carolina	31,113	3,121,833	Columbia	Columbia	Carolina (Yellow) Jessamine	Carolina Wren
South Dakota	77,116	690,768	Pierre	Sioux Falls	Pasqueflower	Ring-necked Pheasant
Tennessee	42,144	4,591,120	Nashville	Memphis	Iris	Mockingbird
Texas	266,807	14,229,288	Austin	Houston	Bluebonnet	Mockingbird
Utah	84,899	1,461,037	Salt Lake City	Salt Lake City	Sego Lily	Sea Gull
Vermont	9,614	511,456	Montpelier	Burlington	Red Clover	Hermit Thrush
Virginia	40,767	5,346,818	Richmond	Norfolk	Dogwood	Cardinal
Washington	68,139	4,132,180	Olympia	Seattle	Western Rhododenaron	Willow Goldfinch
West Virginia	24,231	1,950,279	Charleston	Charleston	Big Rhododendron	Cardinal
Wisconsin	56,153	4,705,521	Madison	Milwaukee	Wood Violet	Robin
Wyoming	97,809	469,557	Cheyenne	Casper	Indian Paintbrush	Meadowlark

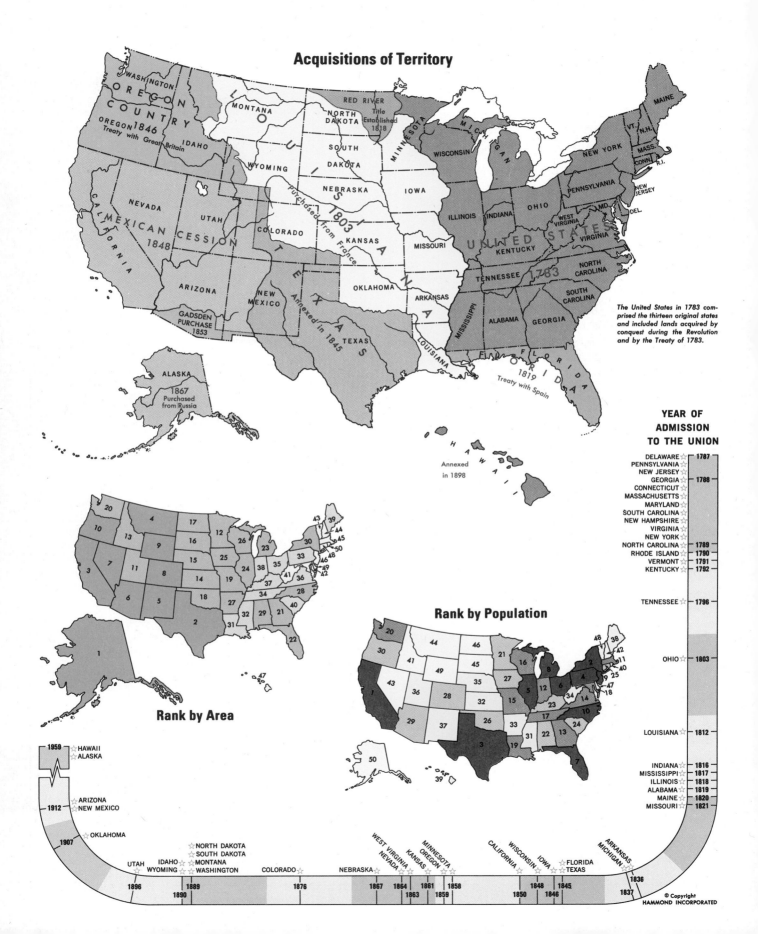

Acquisitions of Territory

WASHINGTON
OREGON COUNTRY
OREGON 1846
Treaty with Great Britain
IDAHO
MONTANA
LOUISIANA
RED RIVER
Title Established 1818
NORTH DAKOTA
SOUTH DAKOTA
MINNESOTA
MICHIGAN
MAINE
VT.
N.H.
NEW YORK
MASS.
CONN.
R.I.
WYOMING
WISCONSIN
PENNSYLVANIA
NEW JERSEY
NEVADA
UTAH
MEXICAN CESSION
1848
CALIFORNIA
COLORADO
NEBRASKA
IOWA
ILLINOIS
INDIANA
OHIO
WEST VIRGINIA
MD.
DEL.
UNITED STATES
KANSAS
MISSOURI
KENTUCKY
VIRGINIA
ARIZONA
NEW MEXICO
Purchased from France 1803
OKLAHOMA
ARKANSAS
TENNESSEE
1783
NORTH CAROLINA
SOUTH CAROLINA
GADSDEN PURCHASE 1853
TEXAS
Annexed in 1845
MISSISSIPPI
ALABAMA
GEORGIA
LOUISIANA
FLORIDA
1819
Treaty with Spain

ALASKA
1867
Purchased from Russia

HAWAII
Annexed in 1898

The United States in 1783 comprised the thirteen original states and included lands acquired by conquest during the Revolution and by the Treaty of 1783.

Rank by Area

Rank by Population

YEAR OF ADMISSION TO THE UNION

DELAWARE ☆	1787
PENNSYLVANIA ☆	
NEW JERSEY ☆	
GEORGIA ☆	1788
CONNECTICUT ☆	
MASSACHUSETTS ☆	
MARYLAND ☆	
SOUTH CAROLINA ☆	
NEW HAMPSHIRE ☆	
VIRGINIA ☆	
NEW YORK ☆	
NORTH CAROLINA ☆	1789
RHODE ISLAND ☆	1790
VERMONT ☆	1791
KENTUCKY ☆	1792
TENNESSEE ☆	1796
OHIO ☆	1803
LOUISIANA ☆	1812
INDIANA ☆	1816
MISSISSIPPI ☆	1817
ILLINOIS ☆	1818
ALABAMA ☆	1819
MAINE ☆	1820
MISSOURI ☆	1821

1959 ☆ HAWAII
☆ ALASKA
1912 ☆ ARIZONA
☆ NEW MEXICO
1907 ☆ OKLAHOMA

☆ NORTH DAKOTA
☆ SOUTH DAKOTA
WEST VIRGINIA
MINNESOTA
KANSAS
OREGON
CALIFORNIA
WISCONSIN
IOWA
ARKANSAS
MICHIGAN
☆ IDAHO ☆ MONTANA
UTAH
WYOMING ☆ WASHINGTON
COLORADO ☆
NEBRASKA ☆
NEVADA
☆ FLORIDA
TEXAS

1896
1890
1889
1876
1867
1864
1863
1861
1859
1858
1850
1848
1846
1845
1836
1837

© Copyright
HAMMOND INCORPORATED

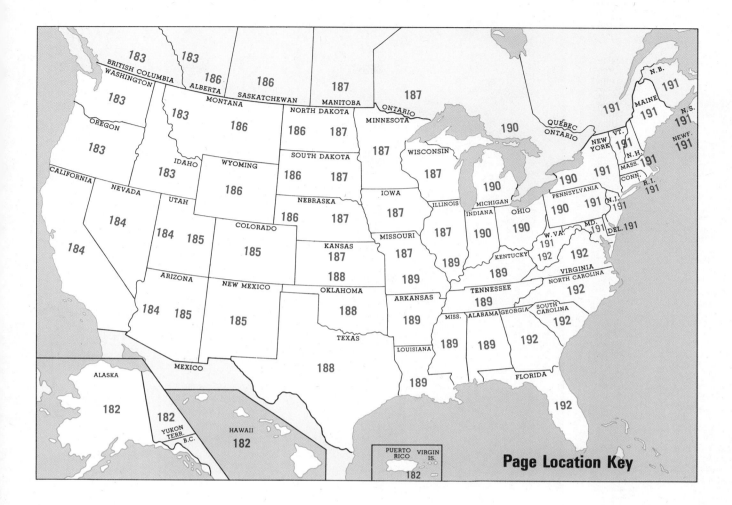

Page Location Key

Legend

National Capitals	⊛	State and Provincial Capitals	⊛	
Limited Access Highways	▬▬	National Parkways	══	
Major Through Routes	▬	Other Important Roads	▬	
Ferries	FY.	Mileage Between Dots	•⊢ 72 ⊣•	
Canals	▭			
U.S. Interstate Route Numbers	95	Federal Route Numbers	23 23	
Trans-Canada Highway	⬢	State and Other Route Numbers	② ②	
International Boundaries	▬ ▪ ▪	State and Provincial Boundaries	▬ ▪▪	

Points of Interest

National Park/Preserve	▣	National Forest/Forest Reserve	▣	
National Monument	▣	National Recreation Area	▢	
National Historical Park	▲	National Seashore/Lakeshore	▢ ≈	
National Historic Site	△	National Military Park	⊗	
National Memorial Park	●	National Battlefield Park	⊠	
National Memorial	◉	National Battlefield/Site	✕	
State/Provincial Park	▣	Other Points of Interest	▢	

NATIONAL PARKS

UNITED STATES

Acadia ....Maine
Arches ....Utah
Badlands ....South Dakota
Big Bend ....Texas
Biscayne ....Florida
Bryce Canyon ....Utah
Canyonlands ....Utah
Capitol Reef ....Utah
Carlsbad Caverns ......New Mexico
Channel Islands ....California
Crater Lake ....Oregon
Denali ....Alaska
Everglades ....Florida
Gates of the Arctic ....Alaska
Glacier ....Montana
Glacier Bay ....Alaska
Grand Canyon ....Arizona
Grand Teton ....Wyoming
Great Smoky Mts. .....N.C.-Tenn.
Guadalupe Mts. ....Texas
Haleakala ....Hawaii
Hawaii Volcanoes ....Hawaii
Hot Springs ....Arkansas
Isle Royale ....Michigan
Katmai ....Alaska
Kenai Fjords ....Alaska
Kings Canyon ....California
Kobuk Valley ....Alaska
Lake Clark ....Alaska
Lassen Volcanic ....California
Mammoth Cave ....Kentucky
Mesa Verde ....Colorado
Mount Rainier ....Washington
North Cascades ....Washington
Olympic ....Washington
Petrified Forest ....Arizona
Redwood ....California
Rocky Mountain ....Colorado
Sequoia ....California
Shenandoah ....Virginia
Theodore Roosevelt ......N. Dakota
Virgin Islands ....Virgin Islands
Voyageurs ....Minnesota
Wind Cave ....South Dakota
Wrangell-St. Elias ....Alaska
Yellowstone ....Wyo., Mont., Idaho
Yosemite ....California
Zion ....Utah

CANADA

Auyuittuq ....N. W. Terrs.
Banff ....Alberta
Cape Breton
   Island ....Nova Scotia
Elk Island ....Alberta
Forillon ....Quebec
Fundy ....New Brunswick
Georgian Bay Islands ....Ontario
Glacier ....Br. Columbia
Grasslands ....Saskatchewan
Gros Morne ....Newfoundland
Jasper ....Alberta
Kejimkujik ....Nova Scotia
Kluane ....Yukon Terr.
Kootenay ....Br. Columbia
Kouchibouguac ....New Brunswick
La Mauricie ....Quebec
Mount Revelstoke ....Br. Columbia
Nahanni ....N. W. Terrs.
Pacific Rim ....Br. Columbia
Point Pelee ....Ontario
Prince Albert ....Saskatchewan
Prince Edward Island .........P.E.I.
Pukaskwa ....Ontario
Riding Mountain ....Manitoba
St. Lawrence Islands ....Ontario
Terra Nova ....Newfoundland
Waterton Lakes ....Alberta
Wood Buffalo ...Alta., N.W. Terrs.
Yoho ....Br. Columbia

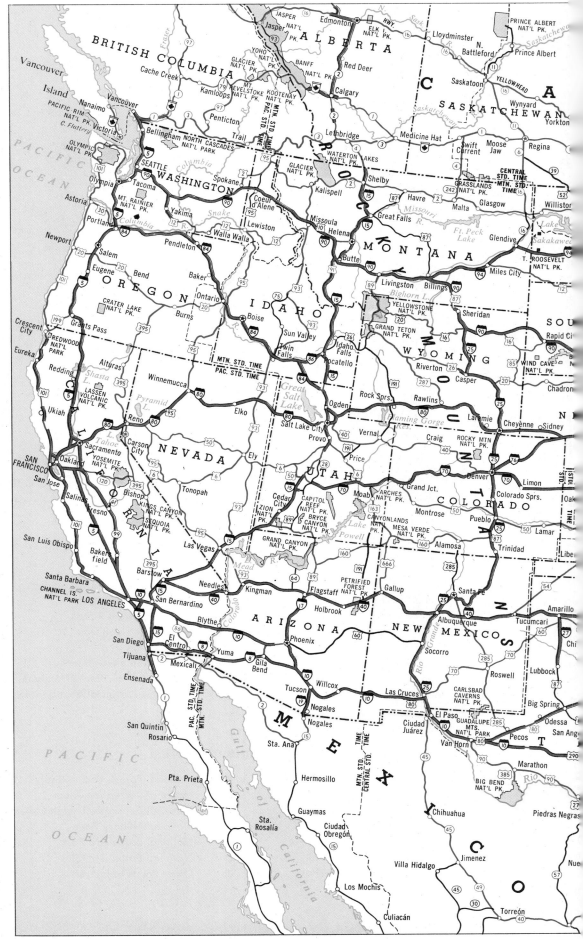

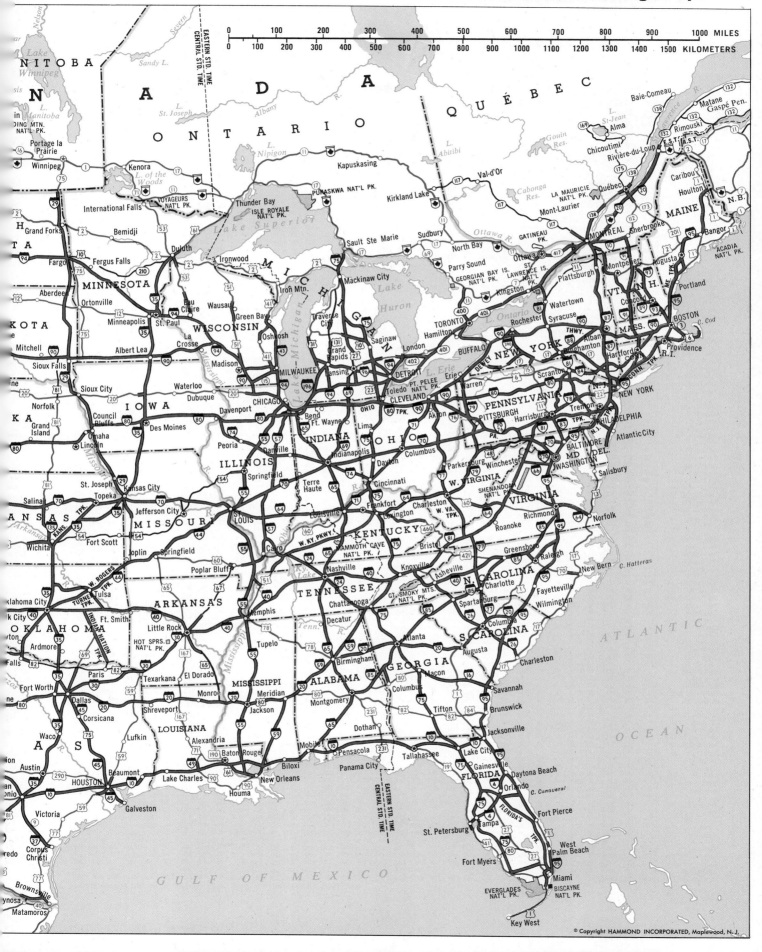

© Copyright HAMMOND INCORPORATED, Maplewood, N.J.

	Albuquerque, N. Mex.	Amarillo, Tex.	Atlanta, Ga.	Baltimore, Md.	Bangor, Maine	Birmingham, Ala.	Boise, Idaho	Boston, Mass.	Buffalo, N.Y.	Butte, Mont.	Charlotte, N. C.	Chicago, Ill.	Cincinnati, Ohio	Cleveland, Ohio	Dallas, Tex.	Denver, Colo.	Detroit, Mich.	El Paso, Tex.	Fargo, N. Dak.	Houston, Tex.	Jacksonville, Fla.	Kansas City, Mo.	Little Rock, Ark.	Los Angeles, Calif.	Louisville, Ky.	Memphis, Tenn.	Miami, Fla.	Milwaukee, Wis.	Minn.-St. Paul, Minn.	New Orleans, La.	New York, N.Y.	Oklahoma City, Okla.	Omaha, Nebr.
Albany, N.Y.	2114	1825	988	321	366	1091	2584	170	283	2344	750	807	707	466	1702	1844	536	2168	1462	1824	1117	1268	1360	2930	827	1217	1468	894	1223	1476	147	1569	1295
Albuquerque, N. Mex.	•	289	1429	1884	2433	1276	980	2232	1781	1040	1669	1285	1405	1516	650	432	1580	270	1310	844	1662	791	901	805	1328	1032	1986	1390	1223	1145	2056	545	892
Amarillo, Tex.	289	•	1143	1595	2144	985	1279	1963	1524	1237	1380	1071	1123	1319	361	422	1295	417	1056	604	1373	577	612	1091	1039	743	1697	1144	979	859	1756	263	648
Atlanta, Ga.	1429	1143	•	671	1215	155	2292	1070	876	2158	259	707	467	692	820	1431	726	1429	1343	841	315	823	541	2254	428	366	665	804	1114	517	863	880	1006
Austin, Tex.	774	485	938	1571	2221	783	1749	2012	1571	1814	1187	1140	1133	1383	197	907	1372	592	1307	161	1085	727	507	1385	1042	646	1403	1224	1161	519	1771	480	884
Baltimore, Md.	1884	1595	671	•	632	800	2440	400	366	2151	421	690	497	348	1393	1625	510	2025	1367	1452	794	1062	1102	2669	602	951	1143	772	1100	1153	192	1339	1153
Bangor, Maine	2433	2144	1315	632	•	1407	2900	233	652	2642	1049	1174	1094	827	2019	2189	892	2573	1828	2107	1426	1630	1718	3238	1198	1594	1773	1271	1589	1747	450	1902	1639
Billings, Mont.	1024	1001	1875	1924	2406	1782	607	2213	1754	237	2037	1234	1528	1579	1352	579	1503	1291	621	1595	2190	1065	1474	1300	1564	1532	2547	1171	831	1853	2062	1195	857
Birmingham, Ala.	1276	985	155	800	1407	•	2201	1210	932	2018	415	661	499	742	660	1327	743	1288	1308	673	427	716	386	2073	362	247	765	748	1069	359	988	741	926
Boise, Idaho	980	1279	2292	2440	2900	2201	•	2722	2268	452	2433	1726	1963	2082	1637	867	2011	1267	1228	1825	2615	1446	1833	887	1993	1913	2901	1763	1446	2140	2568	1489	1267
Boston, Mass.	2232	1967	1070	400	233	1210	2722	•	458	2442	821	974	861	640	1815	2012	707	2401	1631	1874	1201	1436	1492	3037	964	1340	1539	1060	1387	1556	211	1733	1467
Buffalo, N.Y.	1781	1524	876	366	652	932	2268	458	•	1988	733	520	428	186	1406	1537	249	1950	1177	1502	1080	980	1066	2586	537	924	1431	610	937	1248	367	1249	990
Butte, Mont.	1040	1237	2158	2151	2642	2018	452	2442	1988	•	2266	1468	1783	1813	1586	815	1737	1310	858	1829	2427	1302	1711	1158	1790	1769	2784	1408	1068	2077	2317	1413	1086
Charleston, W. Va.	1594	1325	519	391	1018	589	2197	781	439	2327	303	483	202	268	1119	1369	357	1670	1119	1201	671	796	752	2341	266	615	1043	561	880	936	566	988	905
Charlotte, N.C.	1669	1380	259	421	1049	415	2433	821	733	2266	•	765	475	578	1055	1609	664	1688	1419	1139	388	987	776	2474	467	637	746	854	1180	781	613	1119	1180
Chattanooga, Tenn.	1356	1067	118	662	1282	145	2140	1063	775	1972	320	590	343	592	807	1317	605	1439	1234	838	441	694	456	2197	275	317	788	686	995	514	854	811	886
Cheyenne, Wyo.	545	533	1468	1656	2147	1374	766	1954	1501	711	1644	967	1192	1320	880	101	2515	809	823	1143	1899	657	1053	1182	1187	1127	2240	1019	821	1376	1782	702	491
Chicago, Ill.	1285	1071	707	690	1174	661	1726	974	520	1468	765	•	294	345	936	1018	269	1466	657	1092	1017	505	652	2106	304	548	1377	87	418	929	828	826	465
Cincinnati, Ohio	1405	1123	467	497	1094	492	1963	861	428	1783	475	294	•	244	984	1171	251	1505	956	1081	783	600	625	2226	108	487	1133	385	717	820	635	901	700
Cleveland, Ohio	1596	1319	692	348	827	742	2082	640	186	1813	578	345	244	•	1219	1351	168	1754	999	1335	971	789	884	2427	351	737	1322	433	760	1060	486	1096	818
Columbia, S.C.	1655	1366	215	509	1140	371	2558	910	806	2278	94	759	527	664	1045	1687	733	1644	1416	1040	294	1045	749	2486	512	607	645	898	1226	713	694	1137	1205
Columbus, Ohio	1472	1220	563	392	994	592	2023	757	332	1789	503	311	108	140	1080	1228	186	1619	968	1205	867	668	762	2292	218	618	1213	404	737	959	546	937	765
Dallas, Tex.	650	361	820	1393	2019	660	1637	1815	1406	1568	1055	936	984	1219	•	784	1182	624	1110	243	1029	498	330	1410	876	468	1327	1063	964	500	1642	212	672
Denver, Colo.	432	422	1431	1625	2189	1327	867	2012	1537	815	1609	1018	1171	1351	784	•	1305	668	901	1028	1790	613	962	1162	1143	1058	2100	1039	845	1284	1788	616	537
Des Moines, Iowa	1032	786	916	1013	1520	854	1397	1328	866	1189	1085	330	584	688	704	674	614	1160	491	948	1255	207	581	1788	585	627	1598	358	254	1028	1165	566	139
Detroit, Mich.	1580	1295	726	510	892	743	2011	707	249	1737	664	269	251	168	1182	1305	•	1716	926	1307	1039	750	859	2419	363	726	1387	357	690	1077	626	1068	744
Duluth, Minn.	1380	1141	1193	1179	1585	1150	1540	1392	933	1109	1244	487	787	836	1113	1000	757	1506	251	1357	1518	608	996	2088	795	980	1870	406	152	1382	1315	968	518
El Paso, Tex.	270	417	1429	2025	2573	1288	1267	2401	1950	1310	1688	1466	1505	1754	624	668	1716	•	1453	753	1641	946	961	793	1513	1092	1994	1557	1351	1119	2175	682	1027
Fargo, N. Dak.	1310	1056	1343	1367	1828	1308	1228	1631	1177	858	1419	657	956	999	1110	901	926	1453	•	1364	1684	636	1045	1935	951	1061	2008	573	239	1479	1485	900	436
Fort Wayne, Ind.	1395	1181	633	528	1026	606	1882	845	394	1624	629	156	154	199	1035	1179	159	1559	819	1147	943	604	681	2224	207	568	1287	251	580	962	670	907	629
Fort Worth, Tex.	616	340	859	1367	2038	696	1615	1847	1438	1543	1087	968	1011	1248	31	759	125	588	1110	261	1061	534	371	1441	919	512	1398	1082	964	531	1667	212	701
Grand Forks, N. Dak.	1387	1133	1287	1415	1897	1385	1305	1705	1254	913	1496	734	1033	1076	1187	978	1003	1530	77	1441	1751	713	1122	1990	1028	1138	2085	650	316	1039	1552	984	513
Grand Rapids, Mich.	1462	1248	781	631	1017	736	1903	840	381	1645	857	167	306	278	1160	1207	148	1755	834	1278	1106	663	829	2355	364	694	1439	262	601	1124	763	1003	659
Great Falls, Mont.	1227	1224	2097	2113	2595	2026	610	2375	1923	158	2458	1423	1717	1768	1586	803	1692	1497	744	1831	2412	1301	1698	1316	1991	1768	2757	1322	988	2086	2247	1419	1035
Greensboro, N.C.	1762	1473	352	328	1316	507	2408	718	640	2292	93	749	469	485	1148	1626	571	1764	1425	1232	481	1030	824	2537	492	687	839	836	1167	874	520	1174	1156
Hartford, Conn.	2169	1869	966	297	332	1108	2634	101	387	2376	711	908	753	582	1755	1901	648	2288	1565	1791	1092	1327	1396	2947	866	1242	1440	995	1324	1464	113	1632	1373
Houston, Tex.	844	604	841	1452	2107	673	1825	1874	1502	1829	1139	1092	1081	1335	243	1028	1307	753	1364	•	924	744	439	1554	981	572	1242	1163	1211	358	1678	458	917
Indianapolis, Ind.	1313	1034	539	565	1136	492	1853	931	486	1674	586	188	104	300	921	1057	277	1425	840	1031	852	491	571	2131	114	444	1197	276	601	839	716	778	591
Jackson, Miss.	1062	777	400	998	1635	243	2063	1446	1115	1968	668	747	678	924	411	1219	931	1040	1271	433	597	613	257	1864	573	210	920	826	1062	182	1232	587	882
Jacksonville, Fla.	1662	1373	315	794	1426	427	2615	1201	1080	2427	388	1017	783	971	1029	1790	1039	1641	1684	924	•	1138	821	2427	766	672	345	1123	1440	568	979	1195	1349
Kansas City, Mo.	791	577	823	1062	1630	716	1446	1436	980	1302	987	505	600	789	498	613	750	946	636	744	1138	•	409	1620	523	467	1491	564	461	846	1214	357	208
Las Vegas, Nev.	587	876	2015	2478	3074	1861	688	2841	2396	877	2268	1876	1996	2221	1238	901	2140	716	1656	1445	2249	1416	1488	287	1939	1631	2628	1902	1708	1733	2630	1140	1401
Lincoln, Nebr.	834	590	1005	1211	1697	938	1240	1550	1048	1080	1211	576	758	876	635	613	845	1017	459	885	1360	222	631	1662	745	689	1713	557	289	1068	1304	430	58
Little Rock, Ark.	901	612	541	1102	1718	386	1833	1492	1066	1711	776	652	625	884	330	962	859	961	1045	439	821	409	•	1698	531	139	1161	727	833	434	1283	350	623
Los Angeles, Calif.	805	1091	2254	2669	3238	2073	887	3037	2586	1158	2474	2106	2226	2427	1410	1162	2419	793	1935	1554	2427	1620	1698	•	2161	1823	2737	2145	1996	1916	2823	1353	1698
Louisville, Ky.	1328	1039	428	602	1198	362	1993	964	537	1790	467	304	108	351	876	1143	363	1513	951	981	766	523	531	2161	•	365	1078	392	712	719	759	808	707
Madison, Wis.	1312	1091	842	834	1318	805	1685	1127	664	1330	909	144	443	493	1007	975	417	1508	506	1194	1178	493	747	2101	449	636	1507	78	267	1065	990	875	423
Memphis, Tenn.	1032	743	366	951	1594	247	1913	1340	924	1769	637	548	487	737	468	1058	726	1092	1061	572	672	467	139	1823	365	•	1017	632	852	399	1142	482	671
Miami, Fla.	1986	1697	665	1143	1773	765	2901	1539	1431	2784	746	1377	1133	1322	1327	2100	1387	1994	2008	1242	345	1491	1161	2737	1078	1017	•	1463	1771	878	1327	1518	1671
Milwaukee, Wis.	1390	1144	804	772	1271	748	1763	1060	610	1408	854	87	385	433	1063	1039	357	1557	573	1163	1123	564	727	2145	392	632	1463	•	334	1034	922	905	501
Minn.-St. Paul, Minn.	1223	979	1114	1100	1589	1069	1446	1387	937	1068	1180	413	717	760	964	845	690	1351	239	1211	1440	461	833	1996	712	852	1771	334	•	1251	1246	818	364
Mobile, Ala.	1277	988	369	1040	1672	235	2270	1439	1167	2148	628	896	734	977	627	1399	978	1263	1411	510	405	846	437	2037	597	350	687	983	1402	140	1232	787	1021
Montréal, Que.	2161	1876	1268	597	363	1324	2592	321	383	2309	1018	841	821	577	1759	1881	576	2331	1502	1883	1384	1326	1435	2995	828	1302	1732	941	1263	1637	395	1662	1320
Nashville, Tenn.	1247	972	251	732	736	201	2002	1126	717	1907	422	452	289	532	700	1187	544	1320	1092	810	577	556	359	2047	180	220	916	542	853	536	929	702	761
New Orleans, La.	1145	859	517	1153	1747	359	2140	1556	1248	2077	780	929	820	1060	500	1284	1077	1119	1479	358	568	846	434	1916	719	399	878	1034	1251	•	1353	684	1065
New York, N.Y.	2056	1756	863	192	450	988	2568	211	367	2317	613	828	635	486	1642	1788	626	2175	1485	1678	979	1214	1283	2823	759	1142	1327	922	1246	1353	•	1519	1293
Norfolk, Va.	1962	1673	592	249	881	753	2561	543	561	2342	321	874	600	531	1433	1892	699	2009	1531	1460	661	1193	1097	2795	693	958	1013	961	1287	1101	441	1535	1311
Oklahoma City, Okla.	545	263	880	1339	1902	741	1489	1733	1249	1413	1119	826	901	1096	210	616	1068	682	900	458	1195	357	350	1353	808	482	1518	905	818	648	1519	•	477
Omaha, Nebr.	892	646	1006	1153	1639	926	1267	1467	990	1086	1180	465	700	818	672	537	744	1027	436	917	1349	208	623	1698	707	671	1671	501	364	1065	1293	477	•
Philadelphia, Pa.	1915	1694	771	99	541	897	2450	303	360	2226	521	758	571	425	1540	1726	578	2091	1415	1589	889	1121	1197	2741	682	1057	1230	853	1176	1239	91	1436	1219
Phoenix, Ariz.	449	727	1888	2310	2882	1697	1020	2703	2348	1141	2126	1753	1854	2061	1021	826	2027	401	1726	1158	2053	1238	1337	389	1776	1470	2388	1833	1671	1527	2479	989	1325
Pittsburgh, Pa.	1636	1379	737	230	819	763	2156	576	220	1927	523	459	278	127	1260	1427	287	1803	1116	1364	893	850	914	2194	398	786	1237	550	877	1113	363	1145	918
Portland, Oreg.	1461	1737	2735	2847	3295	2658	435	3039	2671	653	2880	2131	2413	2519	2057	1285	2425	1709	1590	2282	3070	1901	2284	994	2437	2367	3414	2069	1721	2591	2959	1926	1700
Providence, R.I.	2232	1932	1037	368	276	1176	2757	44	456	2444	777	976	811	642	1818	1964	705	2351	1633	1854	1155	1390	1459	2999	935	1318	1503	1066	1389	1529	176	1695	1441
Québec, Que.	2333	2048	1426	765	228	1496	2764	390	533	2470	1176	1002	1027	738	1911	2043	738	2492	1764	2045	1542	1488	1597	3157	1058	1475	1897	1089	1420	1810	544	1806	1482
Rapid City, S. Dak.	831	799	1575	1605	2089	1498	952	1982	1493	552	1714	915	1231	1278	1108	401	1225	1080	536	1352	1932	743	1164	1399	1238	1245	2284	858	576	1573	1764	873	534
Reno, Nev.	1036	1324	2471	2641	3147	2416	427	2978	2512	842	2649	1970	2187	2323	1695	1040	2249	1167	1639	1888	2560	1665	2030	476	2213	2083	3021	2003	1797	2199	2818	1529	1500
Richmond, Va.	1877	1586	545	144	773	697	2473	543	473	2254	292	786	512	443	1333	1754	611	1937	1443	1353	646	1105	984	2709	575	845	994	877	1204	1057	330	1345	1223
Sacramento, Calif.	1117	1406	2611	2781	3287	2556	545	3118	2652	982	2789	2110	2327	2463	1835	1180	2389	1267	1779	2020	2700	1805	2170	387	2353	2223	3161	2143	1937	2339	2958	1669	1640
St. Louis, Mo.	1057	783	553	804	1379	503	1701	1188	723	1536	738	291	338	540	651	863	513	1167	812	801	881	254	357	1862	267	294	1222	371	553	699	961	523	453
Salt Lake City, Utah	612	908	1976	2110	2616	1857	363	2419	1965	428	2121	1443	1661	1784	1262	512	1719	880	1215	1453	2237	1118	1444	730	1656	1570	2603	1502	1246	1773	2278	1112	953
San Antonio, Tex.	719	512	1023	1649	2299	861	1704	2099	1651	1749	1254	1223	1230	1470	275	947	1448	568	1378	197	1141	773	578	1380	1124	711	1439	1314	1234	575	1863	477	943
San Diego, Calif.	815	1087	2172	2668	3240	2043	963	3061	2637	1212	2450	2118	2241	2446	1291	1201	2416	742	1943	1491	2320	1605	1695	122	2143	1829	2618	2191	2046	1864	2851	1349	1716
San Francisco, Calif.	1132	1420	2563	2884	3371	2409	654	3182	2728	1069	2835	2183	2424	2527	1773	1267	2482	1196	1873	1955	2787	1893	2032	403	2425	2162	3193	2203	2001	2278	3054	1692	1720
Savannah, Ga.	1683	1380	254	640	1269	409	2546	1048	971	2345	240	951	660	818	1017	1717	914	1653	1597	1029	154	1112	795	2482	640	657	506	1038	1352	641	830	1156	1298
Seattle, Wash.	1511	1800	2843	2733	3205	2703	529	3095	2629	615	2992	2031	2451	2511	2136	1377	2444	1785	1505	2354	3115	1904	2273	1177	2427	2362	3451	2045	1673	2645	2944	1975	1657
Shreveport, La.	836	547	637	1296	1940	477	1844	1736	1308	1796	892	867	879	1127	186	981	1078	813	1212	239	829	567	216	1631	751	322	1180	970	1386	316	1486	366	776
Sioux Falls, S. Dak.	1082	838	1196	1215	1699	1116	1295	1499	1045	895	1370	525	890	870	844	655	794	1217	230	1110	1539	390	799	1817	897	858	1861	507	221	1265	1353	644	187
Spokane, Wash.	1336	1559	2531	2515	2990	2420	391	2804	2390	318	2584	1716	2159	2176	1928	1067	2085	1617	1208	2164	2818	1617	2018	1249	2167	2082	3191	1751	1386	2383	2671	1651	1513
Springfield, Ill.	1086	861	652	753	1316	602	1688	1134	675	1507	749	196	302	489	766	832	443	1284	857	915	946	295	464	1982	282	390	1317	280	481	796	914	637	421
Tampa, Fla.	1738	1449	464	986	1620	552	2753	1383	1263	2551	583	1187	948	1166	1106	1928	1201	1746	1807	1007	194	1280	939	2607	865	782	248	1268	1578	644	1176	1264	1493
Topeka, Kans.	801	551	898	1133	1701	787	1433	1510	1051	1279	1058	568	688	862	509	557	841	947	604	759	1203	71	479	1549	593	538	1562	633	532	929	1288	342	168
Toronto, Ont.	1815	1530	975	465	683	1031	2246	462	99	1972	832	495	540	296	1391	1540	235	1951	1161	1542	1275	985	1094	2654	598	961	1530	582	913	1347	486	1303	979
Tucson, Ariz.	454	674	1746	2380	2887	1605	1191	2686	2235	1245	2005	1739	1842	2037	951	845	2005	317	1746	1070	1958	1255	1278	512	1749	1417	2311	1819	1677	1456	2517	941	1341
Tulsa, Okla.	658	374	832	1230	1791	680	1569	1597	1143	1498	1066	702	753	953	277	691	930	791	840	522	1123	247	291	1458	687	426	1461	792	779	706	1374	110	399
Vancouver, B.C.	1660	1949	2992	2882	3303	2852	674	3168	2878	764	3141	2247	2541	2504	2259	1526	2505	1934	1654	2503	3264	2053	2422	1328	2576	2511	3600	1612	1822	2794	3023	2121	1803
Walla Walla, Wash.	1208	1527	2570	2566	3045	2430	260	2938	2449	390	2670	1871	2187	2234	1858	1104	2181	1476	1248	2049	2833	1631	2000	1092	2194	2162	3204	1814	1458	2369	2720	1708	1384
Washington, D.C.	1904	1591	640	39	673	767	2440	440	372	2153	383	687	497	362	1403	1640	516	2040	1357	1448	754	1057	1058	2739	605	917	1105	784	1105	1150	226	1330	1149
Wichita, Kans.	620	359	978	1293	1832	830	1663	1673	1206	1327	1186	711	817	1012	386	512	969	744	731	629	1309	202	472	1384	744	549	1206	792	650	840	1436	168	309
Winnipeg, Man.	1658	1444	1587	1570	1803	1541	1443	1812	1377	875	1622	857	1151	1227	1328	1065	1149	1621	215	1611	1896	851	1260	2033	1161	1428	2212	786	462	1713	1683	1208	643

DISTANCES ARE APPROXIMATE AND HAVE BEEN COMPUTED OVER MAJOR THROUGH ROUTES

	Philadelphia, Pa.	Phoenix, Ariz.	Pittsburgh, Pa.	Portland, Oreg.	Rapid City, S. Dak.	Reno, Nev.	Richmond, Va.	St. Louis, Mo.	• Salt Lake City, Utah	San Antonio, Tex.	San Diego, Calif.	San Francisco, Calif.	Savannah, Ga.	Seattle, Wash.	Spokane, Wash.	Tampa, Fla.	Washington, D.C.
Albany, N.Y.	233	2536	457	2999	1784	2798	472	1016	2251	1962	2894	3009	981	2928	2623	1331	367
Albuquerque, N. Mex.	1915	449	1636	1461	831	1036	1877	1057	612	719	815	1132	1683	1511	1336	1738	1904
Amarillo, Tex.	1694	727	1379	1737	799	1324	1586	783	908	512	1087	1420	1380	1800	1559	1449	1591
Atlanta, Ga.	771	1888	737	2735	1575	2471	545	553	1976	1023	2172	2563	254	2843	2531	464	640
Austin, Tex.	1681	993	1411	2301	1257	1759	1479	876	1386	78	1334	1787	1160	2274	1974	1168	1563
Baltimore, Md.	99	2310	230	2847	1605	2641	144	804	2110	1649	2668	2884	640	2733	2515	986	39
Bangor, Maine	541	2882	819	3295	2089	3147	773	1379	2616	2299	3240	3371	1269	3205	2990	1620	673
Billings, Mont.	1992	1258	1693	890	323	982	2040	1307	570	1513	1354	1208	2029	835	553	2314	1919
Birmingham, Ala.	897	1697	763	2658	1498	2416	697	503	1857	861	2043	2409	409	2703	2420	552	767
Boise, Idaho	2450	1020	2156	435	952	427	2473	1701	363	1704	963	654	2546	525	391	2753	2440
Boston, Mass.	303	2703	576	3039	1982	2978	543	1188	2419	2099	3061	3182	1048	3095	2804	1383	440
Buffalo, N.Y.	360	2348	220	2671	1493	2512	473	723	1964	1651	2637	2728	971	2629	2390	1263	372
Butte, Mont.	2226	1141	1927	653	552	842	2254	1536	428	1749	1212	1069	2345	615	318	2551	2153
Charleston, W. Va.	481	2042	233	2619	1457	2389	309	538	1865	1363	2409	2615	536	2618	2265	884	355
Charlotte, N.C.	513	2126	523	2880	1714	2649	292	738	2121	1254	2450	2835	240	2992	2584	583	383
Chattanooga, Tenn.	757	1808	618	2668	1420	2359	545	433	1829	1022	2146	2515	373	2598	2290	586	611
Cheyenne, Wyo.	1727	924	1427	1211	300	995	1708	910	457	1068	1257	1209	1722	1279	1032	1992	1658
Chicago, Ill.	758	1753	459	2131	915	1970	786	291	1443	1223	2118	2183	951	2031	1716	1187	687
Cincinnati, Ohio	571	1854	278	2413	1231	2187	512	338	1661	1230	2241	2424	660	2451	2159	948	497
Cleveland, Ohio	425	2061	127	2519	1278	2328	443	540	1784	1473	2446	2547	818	2511	2176	1166	362
Columbia, S.C.	604	2086	599	2995	1726	2697	362	742	2166	1250	2448	2771	142	2985	2676	492	412
Columbus, Ohio	472	1929	184	2478	1239	2269	473	413	1716	1372	2307	2475	720	2445	2117	1058	390
Dallas, Tex.	1540	1021	1260	2057	1108	1695	1333	651	1262	275	1291	1773	1017	2136	1928	1106	1403
Denver, Colo.	1726	826	1427	1285	401	1040	1754	863	512	947	1201	1267	1717	1377	1067	1928	1640
Des Moines, Iowa	1088	1449	799	1819	637	1638	1105	349	1089	983	1835	1851	1217	1766	1574	1403	1041
Detroit, Mich.	578	2027	287	2425	1225	2249	611	513	1719	1448	2416	2482	914	2444	2085	1201	516
Duluth, Minn.	1254	1830	954	1771	688	1956	1273	676	1395	1389	2188	2084	1435	1677	1385	1681	1179
El Paso, Tex.	2091	401	1803	1709	1080	1167	1937	1167	880	568	742	1196	1653	1785	1617	1746	2040
Fargo, N. Dak.	1415	1726	1116	1590	536	1639	1443	812	1215	1378	1943	1873	1597	1505	1208	1807	1357
Fort Wayne, Ind.	595	1842	302	2287	1071	2126	614	356	1572	1269	2200	2339	814	2187	1872	1099	528
Fort Worth, Tex.	1593	1044	1305	2078	1235	1663	1364	701	1239	268	1358	1734	752	2148	1903	1138	1434
Grand Forks, N. Dak.	1492	1803	1193	1645	613	1694	1520	889	1649	1455	1920	1928	1674	1459	1162	1884	1434
Grand Rapids, Mich.	738	1975	442	2308	1092	2147	750	478	1626	1412	2364	2389	966	2208	1893	1281	643
Great Falls, Mont.	2181	1273	1882	779	558	1000	2209	1533	585	1736	1370	1226	2351	701	413	2561	2108
Greensboro, N.C.	420	2219	430	2973	1807	2742	452	831	2224	1347	2543	2928	333	3085	2677	676	290
Hartford, Conn.	201	2592	474	3039	1823	2818	445	1070	2351	1976	2932	3091	937	2939	2624	1287	340
Houston, Tex.	1589	1158	1364	2282	1352	1888	1353	801	1453	197	1491	1955	1029	2354	2164	1007	1448
Indianapolis, Ind.	639	1750	355	2307	1122	2074	620	239	1544	1176	2134	2331	766	2312	1959	1005	567
Jackson, Miss.	1153	1456	972	2506	1453	2104	944	505	1685	614	1789	2203	603	2601	2263	678	1000
Jacksonville, Fla.	889	2053	893	3070	1932	2697	646	881	2237	1141	2320	2787	154	3115	2818	194	754
Kansas City, Mo.	1121	1238	850	1901	743	1665	1105	254	1118	773	1605	1893	1112	1904	1617	1280	1057
Las Vegas, Nev.	2537	338	2274	1016	1129	446	2514	1677	449	1319	337	583	2256	1193	1070	2325	2429
Lincoln, Nebr.	1213	1293	918	1712	569	1460	1270	473	931	930	1658	1683	1259	1790	1461	1465	1207
Little Rock, Ark.	1197	1337	914	2284	1164	2030	984	357	1444	578	1695	2032	795	2273	2018	939	1058
Los Angeles, Calif.	2741	389	2194	994	1399	476	2709	1862	730	1380	122	403	2482	1177	1249	2607	2739
Louisville, Ky.	682	1776	398	2437	1238	2213	575	267	1656	1124	2143	2425	640	2427	2167	865	605
Madison, Wis.	908	1748	602	2034	780	1925	930	361	1387	1282	2139	2145	1095	1956	1673	1306	835
Memphis, Tenn.	1057	1470	786	2367	1245	2083	845	294	1570	711	1829	2162	657	2362	2082	782	917
Miami, Fla.	1230	2388	1237	3414	2284	3021	994	1222	2603	1439	2618	3193	506	3451	3191	248	1105
Milwaukee, Wis.	853	1833	550	2069	858	2003	877	371	1502	1314	2191	2203	1038	2045	1751	1268	784
Minn.-St. Paul, Minn.	1176	1671	877	1721	576	1797	1204	553	1246	1234	2046	2001	1352	1673	1386	1578	1105
Mobile, Ala.	1140	1648	1106	2705	1601	2316	914	644	1881	707	1918	2400	506	2710	2455	522	1031
Montréal, Que.	480	2603	603	2830	1756	2825	725	1073	1295	2024	2942	3029	1225	2774	2486	1571	601
Nashville, Tenn.	838	1690	568	2457	1295	2227	625	295	1674	949	2051	2409	508	2495	2173	908	697
New Orleans, La.	1239	1527	1113	2591	1573	2199	1057	699	1773	575	1864	2278	641	2645	2383	644	1150
New York, N.Y.	91	2479	363	2959	1764	2818	330	961	2278	1863	2851	3054	830	2944	2671	1176	226
Norfolk, Va.	348	2437	400	3012	1859	2734	88	930	2352	1575	2733	3059	507	3024	2775	859	195
Oklahoma City, Okla.	1436	989	1145	1926	873	1529	1345	523	1112	477	1349	1692	1156	1975	1651	1264	1330
Omaha, Nebr.	1219	1325	918	1700	534	1500	1223	453	453	943	1716	1720	1298	1657	1513	1493	1149
Philadelphia, Pa.	•	2430	294	2921	1703	2724	240	881	2188	1772	2769	2951	736	2862	2624	1083	136
Phoenix, Ariz.	2430	•	2085	1273	1238	762	2332	1492	688	978	358	794	2046	1510	1419	2134	2331
Pittsburgh, Pa.	294	2085	•	2599	1395	2427	312	599	1902	1521	2493	2645	745	2511	2267	1045	229
Portland, Oreg.	2921	1273	2599	•	1237	566	2924	2113	807	2190	1115	669	3051	173	366	3225	2904
Providence, R.I.	267	2655	539	3135	1891	2941	506	1137	2419	2039	3013	3168	1006	3007	2692	1352	402
Québec, Que.	635	2765	735	2994	1937	2987	869	1251	2457	2168	3120	3190	1368	2934	2646	1720	762
Rapid City, S. Dak.	1703	1238	1395	1237	•	1224	1771	984	686	1263	1466	1454	1828	1183	870	2011	1624
Reno, Nev.	2724	762	2427	566	1224	•	2737	1906	531	1744	565	227	2703	760	779	2798	2666
Richmond, Va.	240	2332	312	2924	1771	2646	•	842	2264	1579	2638	2964	499	2936	2687	842	107
Sacramento, Calif.	2864	902	2567	544	1364	140	2877	2046	671	1758	509	87	2792	717	834	2896	2806
St. Louis, Mo.	881	1492	599	2113	984	1879	842	•	1381	927	1906	2133	841	2102	1868	1030	804
Salt Lake City, Utah	2188	688	1902	807	686	531	2264	1381	•	1341	784	755	2236	869	738	2416	2123
San Antonio, Tex.	1772	978	1521	2190	1263	1744	1579	927	1341	•	1306	1779	1227	2265	2113	1229	1641
San Diego, Calif.	2769	358	2493	1115	1466	565	2638	1906	784	1306	•	526	2381	1292	1343	2457	2737
San Francisco, Calif.	2951	794	2645	669	1454	227	2964	2133	755	1779	526	•	2792	858	921	2943	2886
Savannah, Ga.	736	2046	745	3051	1828	2703	499	841	2236	1227	2381	2792	•	3063	2772	352	604
Seattle, Wash.	2862	1510	2511	173	1183	760	2936	2102	869	2265	1292	858	3063	•	288	3250	2752
Shreveport, La.	1394	1221	1161	2226	1309	1885	1183	582	1460	389	1549	1990	831	2344	2129	923	1246
Sioux Falls, S. Dak.	1283	1481	984	1580	343	1472	1311	632	941	1119	1865	1696	1473	1526	1213	1683	1212
Spokane, Wash.	2624	1419	2267	366	870	779	2687	1868	738	2113	1343	921	2772	288	•	2942	2500
Springfield, Ill.	841	1533	551	2121	955	1872	810	99	1374	1062	1900	2133	906	2133	1825	1154	765
Tampa, Fla.	1083	2134	1045	3225	2011	2798	842	1030	2416	1229	2457	2943	352	3250	2942	•	947
Topeka, Kans.	1214	1250	921	1863	727	1645	1176	321	1086	794	1534	1847	1183	1833	1658	1351	1128
Toronto, Ont.	460	2262	320	2626	1410	2465	572	748	1954	1683	2613	2678	976	2600	2312	1424	477
Tucson, Ariz.	2377	123	2486	1396	1246	912	2286	1457	820	881	422	921	1970	1666	1523	2063	2360
Tulsa, Okla.	1304	1113	1010	2037	932	1713	1288	412	1194	554	1475	1790	1106	2026	1830	1213	1214
Vancouver, B.C.	3008	1656	2657	319	1329	906	3082	2250	1015	2411	1438	995	3209	146	288	3396	2881
Walla Walla, Wash.	2659	1222	2318	281	956	622	2643	1832	596	1992	1214	849	2821	273	157	2977	2479
Washington, D.C.	136	2331	229	2904	1624	2666	107	804	2123	1641	2737	2886	604	2752	2488	947	•
Wichita, Kans.	1361	1040	1070	1854	729	1542	1318	460	1020	634	1410	1730	2821	1842	1642	1386	1283
Winnipeg, Man.	1615	1941	1316	1523	751	1854	1643	1105	1430	1602	2260	2088	1808	1444	1156	2014	1541

	AVERAGE TEMPERATURE IN °F				AVERAGE RAINFALL IN INCHES			
CITY	JAN	APR	JUL	OCT	JAN	APR	JUL	OCT
Albany, N.Y.	23	46	72	51	2.5	2.8	3.5	2.8
Albuquerque, N. Mex.	35	56	79	58	0.4	0.5	1.2	0.8
Amarillo, Texas	36	56	78	59	0.6	1.5	3.0	2.2
Anchorage, Alaska	12	37	58	36	0.8	0.4	1.9	1.9
Atlanta, Ga.	45	60	79	62	4.4	4.5	4.7	2.4
Augusta, Maine	20	43	70	49	3.5	3.3	3.4	3.4
Birmingham, Ala.	47	63	82	66	5.0	4.5	5.2	3.0
Boise, Idaho	29	50	75	52	1.3	1.2	0.2	0.8
Boston, Mass.	30	48	74	55	3.9	3.8	2.9	3.1
Buffalo, N.Y.	25	44	70	51	2.8	3.0	2.6	3.0
Butte, Mont.	15	38	63	42	0.4	0.9	1.2	0.7
Charleston, S.C.	50	65	81	66	2.5	2.9	7.7	2.8
Charlotte, N.C.	43	60	79	63	3.5	3.4	4.8	2.7
Cheyenne, Wyo.	25	43	70	48	0.6	1.7	1.9	0.9
Chicago, Ill.	26	49	76	55	1.9	3.0	3.4	2.8
Cincinnati, Ohio	34	54	77	58	3.7	3.5	3.5	2.2
Cleveland, Ohio	28	47	72	53	2.7	3.4	3.3	2.4
Dallas. Texas	46	65	85	68	2.3	4.0	1.9	2.7
Denver, Colo.	29	46	73	51	0.6	2.1	1.5	1.0
Detroit, Mich.	27	48	74	54	1.9	3.1	2.7	2.6
El Paso, Texas	43	63	82	64	0.5	0.2	1.6	0.9
Fargo, N. Dak.	6	43	71	47	0.5	1.7	3.5	1.1
Great Falls, Mont.	22	44	69	48	0.7	1.0	1.3	0.8
Honolulu, Hawaii	73	74	79	78	3.8	1.3	0.4	1.8
Houston, Texas	54	69	83	71	3.8	3.2	4.3	3.8
Jacksonville, Fla.	56	69	83	71	2.5	3.6	7.7	5.2
Juneau, Alaska	25	38	55	42	4.0	2.9	4.5	8.3
Kansas City, Mo.	32	56	82	60	1.4	3.6	3.2	2.9
Las Vegas, Nev.	44	65	90	67	0.6	0.2	0.5	0.3
Los Angeles, Calif.	56	62	73	67	3.1	1.2	.01	0.4
Memphis, Tenn.	42	61	81	63	6.1	4.6	3.5	2.7
Mexico City, D.F.	54	64	62	59	0.2	0.5	4.9	1.4
Miami, Fla.	67	74	82	78	2.0	3.9	6.8	8.2
Milwaukee, Wis.	21	44	69	50	1.8	2.5	3.0	2.1
Minneapolis, Minn.	12	44	72	49	0.7	1.9	3.3	1.6
Montréal, Que.	16	43	71	49	1.2	2.8	4.0	3.2
New Orleans, La.	55	68	82	70	3.8	4.6	6.7	2.8
New York, N.Y.	33	51	77	58	3.3	3.4	3.7	3.1
Oklahoma City, Okla.	37	60	83	63	1.3	3.1	2.4	2.5
Omaha, Nebr.	22	52	79	56	0.8	2.6	3.4	1.7
Philadelphia, Pa.	32	52	76	56	3.3	3.4	4.2	2.8
Phoenix, Ariz.	50	67	90	71	0.7	0.3	0.8	0.5
Pittsburgh, Pa.	29	49	72	53	3.0	3.1	3.9	2.5
Portland, Oreg.	38	52	67	54	5.4	2.1	0.4	3.6
Rapid City, S. Dak.	24	45	72	50	0.4	1.9	2.3	1.0
Reno, Nev.	30	48	68	49	1.2	0.5	0.3	0.5
Richmond, Va.	39	58	78	59	3.5	3.2	5.6	3.0
St. Louis, Mo.	32	55	78	58	2.0	3.7	3.3	2.9
Salt Lake City, Utah	27	50	77	52	1.4	1.8	0.6	1.2
San Antonio, Texas	52	68	84	71	1.7	2.8	2.1	2.5
San Diego, Calif.	55	62	70	66	2.0	0.8	.01	0.5
San Francisco, Calif.	51	56	59	61	4.0	1.3	.01	0.7
San Juan, P. Rico	74	77	80	80	4.7	3.7	6.3	5.8
Seattle, Wash.	38	49	65	52	5.7	2.4	0.8	4.0
Spokane, Wash.	25	47	71	49	2.4	0.9	0.4	1.6
Tampa, Fla.	61	71	82	75	2.1	2.8	8.6	2.8
Toronto, Ont.	25	45	72	51	1.3	2.3	2.9	2.4
Vancouver, Br. Col.	37	48	64	50	6.6	2.8	1.4	5.4
Washington, D.C.	37	56	78	59	3.0	3.2	4.2	3.1
Winnipeg, Man.	0	38	68	43	.01	0.8	2.7	1.2

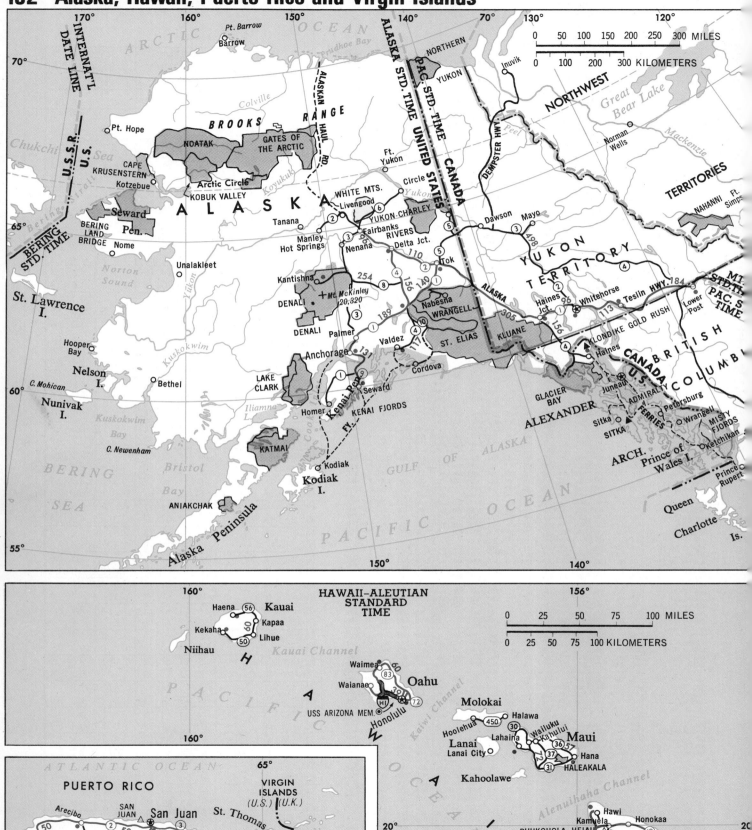

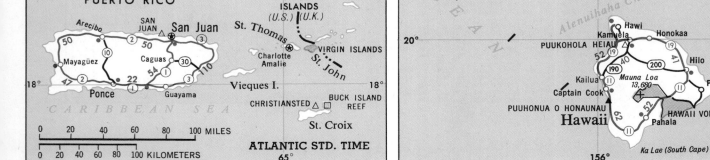

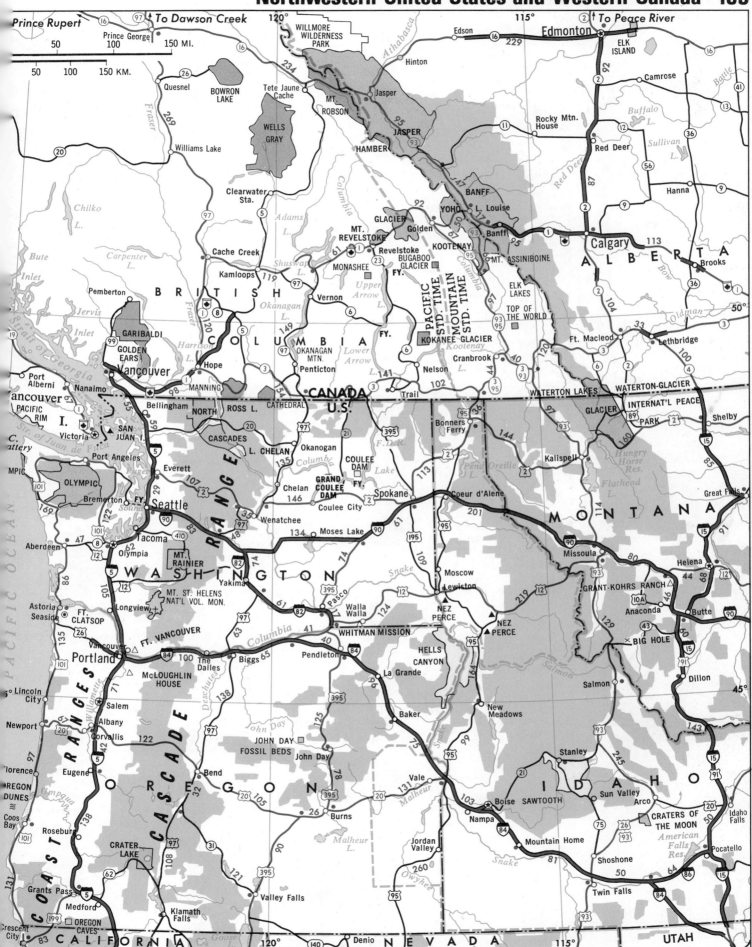

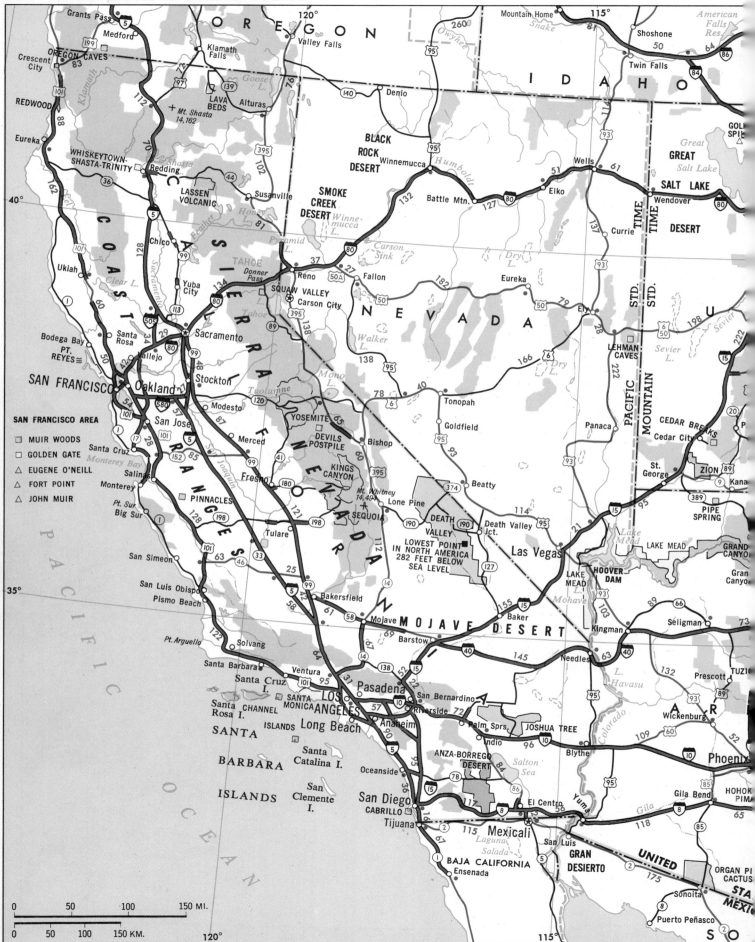

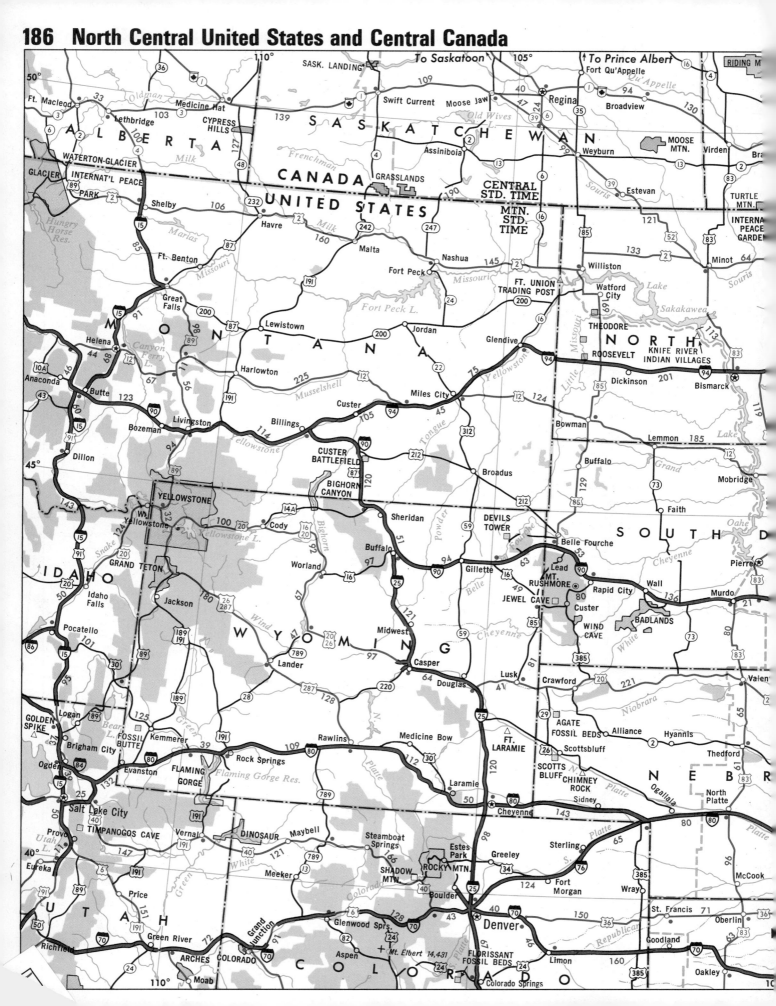

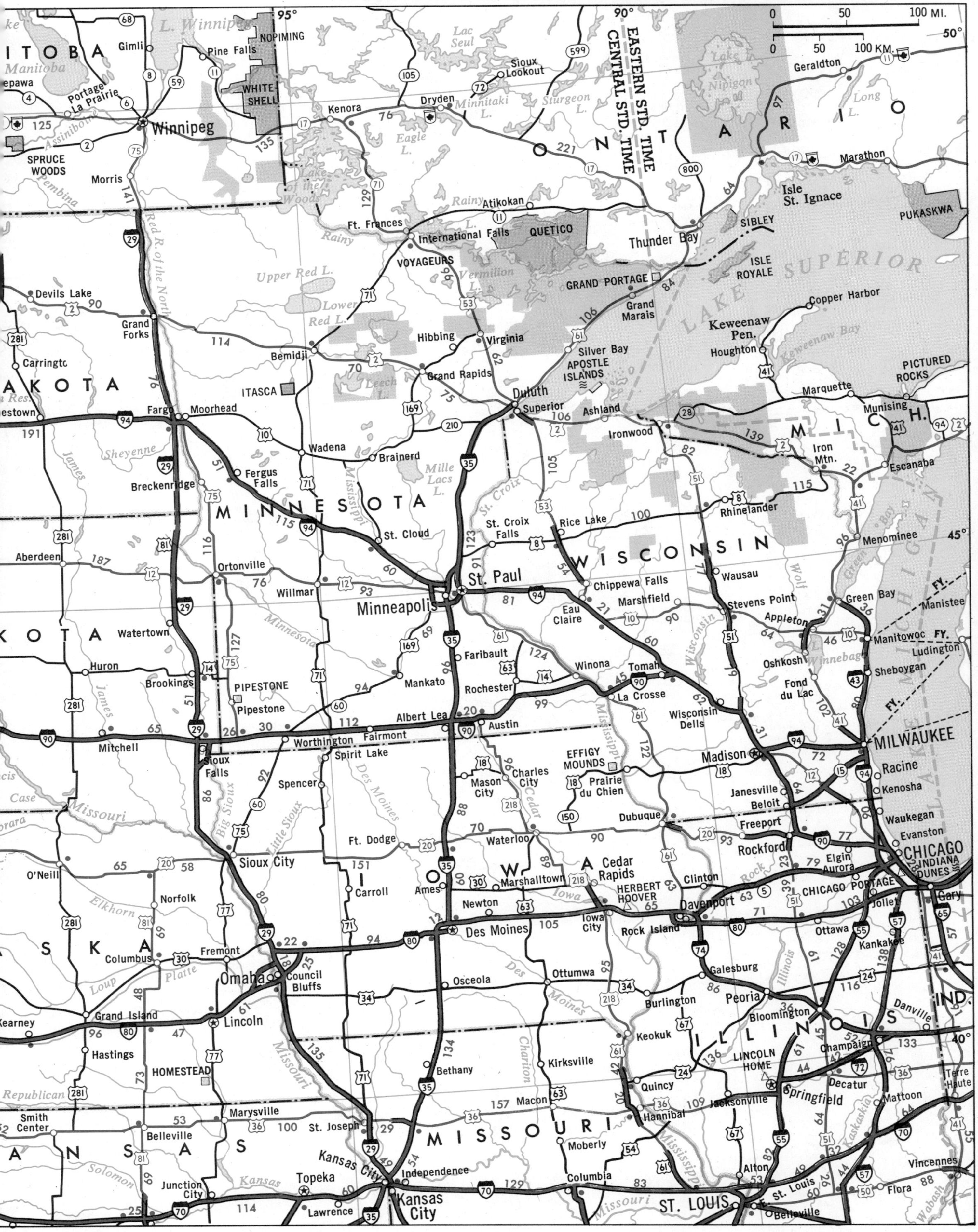

0 50 100 MI.

0 50 100 KM.

50°

MANITOBA
Gimli
Pine Falls
NOPIMING
L. Winnipeg
95°
90°
Lac Seul
Sioux Lookout
599
Geraldton
11
pepawa
Portage La Prairie
WHITE SHELL
Lake Nipigon
4
6
8
59
11
105
72
Kenora
76
Dryden
Minnitaki L.
Sturgeon L.
97
Long L.
125
Winnipeg
Assiniboine
17
Eagle L.
221
17
ONTARIO
64
17
Marathon
Isle St. Ignace
2
75
135
Lake of the Woods
Rainy L.
Ft. Frances
800
Thunder Bay
SIBLEY
PUKASKWA
SPRUCE WOODS
Morris
141
129
71
Atikokan
11
QUETICO
ISLE ROYALE
Pembina
International Falls
VOYAGEURS
Vermilion L.
GRAND PORTAGE
84
LAKE SUPERIOR
Upper Red L.
96
53
106
Grand Marais
Copper Harbor
Devils Lake
2
90
Red R. of the North
Lower Red L.
71
Hibbing
Virginia
62
61
Silver Bay
APOSTLE ISLANDS
Keweenaw Pen.
Houghton
Keweenaw Bay
Grand Forks
114
Bemidji
Leech L.
Grand Rapids
75
Duluth
PICTURED ROCKS
281
Carringto
ITASCA
169
Superior
106
Ashland
28
Marquette
Munising
MICH.
estown
Fargo
Moorhead
10
210
Ironwood
139
2
41
94
2
191
94
Sheyenne
Wadena
Brainerd
105
82
Iron Mtn.
22
Escanaba
James
51
Fergus Falls
71
Mille Lacs L.
35
51
115
Breckenridge
75
Mississippi
St. Croix
53
8
Rhinelander
41
AKOTA
MINNESOTA
115
St. Cloud
Rice Lake
100
96
45°
Aberdeen
187
81
116
Ortonville
76
60
St. Croix Falls
123
8
WISCONSIN
Menominee
12
91
54
Green Bay
12
93
Willmar
St. Paul
Chippewa Falls
Wausau
31
36
Manistee
281
Watertown
29
Minneapolis
81
94
Eau Claire
Marshfield
Stevens Point
Appleton
46
10
Manitowoc
127
169
35
69
21
10
90
51
64
Oshkosh
Winnebago
43
Ludington
KOTA
Huron
14
75
Faribault
63
124
Winona
45
Tomah
60
62
Fond du Lac
102
Sheboygan
Brookings
51
PIPESTONE
Mankato
Rochester
14
90
31
Pipestone
60
99
La Crosse
Wisconsin Dells
94
MILWAUKEE
281
30
112
Albert Lea
20
Austin
61
Madison
18
72
Mitchell
65
26
Worthington
Fairmont
90
EFFIGY MOUNDS
122
18
15
Racine
James
29
Sioux Falls
92
Spirit Lake
Des Moines
18
Charles City
Prairie du Chien
Janesville
64
Kenosha
Case
86
Spencer
60
Mason City
88
218
150
Dubuque
Beloit
Waukegan
Missouri
75
Mississippi
Freeport
20
93
Rockford
77
Evanston
ncis
O'Neill
65
20
58
Ft. Dodge
70
Waterloo
90
90
Elgin
CHICAGO
brara
Sioux City
151
IOWA
89
Cedar Rapids
Aurora
INDIANA DUNES
281
Norfolk
77
Carroll
35
30
Marshalltown
218
Iowa
Clinton
39
CHICAGO PORTAGE
103
Joliet
Gary
48
12
Ames
Newton
63
Iowa City
HERBERT HOOVER
65
Davenport
63
5
51
57
65
ASKA
Columbus
30
Fremont
18
25
94
80
Des Moines
105
Rock Island
80
71
Ottawa
55
Kankakee
Loup
Platte
22
ILLINOIS
Rock
128
138
24
41
Kearney
Grand Island
Lincoln
61
Osceola
Ottumwa
95
Galesburg
86
Peoria
Illinois
116
Danville
IND.
96
80
47
34
Des Moines
34
Burlington
67
Bloomington
52
133
40°
Hastings
77
218
Keokuk
136
LINCOLN HOME
44
42
72
Champaign
Terre Haute
Republican
281
HOMESTEAD
73
135
134
Bethany
Kirksville
61
24
Decatur
36
55
Smith Center
53
Marysville
36
100
St. Joseph
36
Macon
67
Quincy
109
Jacksonville
Springfield
94
Mattoon
6A
41
ANSAS
81
69
Belleville
Solomon
Kansas
29
157
Moberly
54
Columbia
83
Hannibal
Mississippi
36
55
Alton
53
26
57
Flora
88
Wabash
25
70
Junction City
Topeka
Lawrence
114
Kansas City
35
49
54
Independence
129
70
St. LOUIS
60
50
Belleville
Vincennes
MISSOURI
KANSAS
Moberly

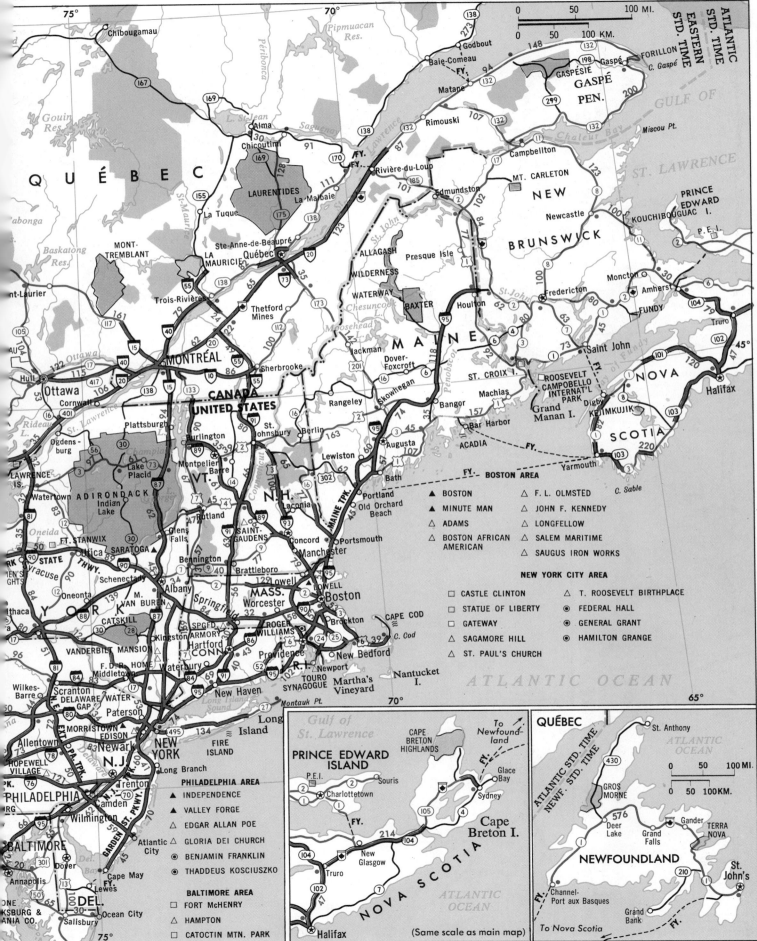

Legend:

- ◉ WASHINGTON MONUMENT
- ✕ MANASSAS
- ✕ MONOCACY
- ☐ FORT WASHINGTON PARK
- ☐ FREDERICK DOUGLASS HOME
- ☐ GREENBELT PARK
- ☐ J. F. KENNEDY CENTER
- ☐ L. B. JOHNSON MEM. GROVE
- ▲ CHESAPEAKE & OHIO CAN
- △ CLARA BARTON
- △ FORD'S THEATER
- △ PENNSYLVANIA AVENUE
- △ SEWALL-BELMONT HOUSE
- ◉ ARLINGTON HOUSE
- ◉ JEFFERSON MEMORIAL
- ◉ LINCOLN MEMORIAL
- ☐ NATIONAL CAPITAL PARKS
- ☐ NATIONAL MALL
- ☐ NATIONAL VISITOR CENTER
- ☐ PISCATAWAY PARK
- ☐ ROCK CREEK PARK
- ☐ T. ROOSEVELT ISLAND
- ☐ WHITE HOUSE
- ☐ WOLF TRAP FARM PARK

WASHINGTON, D.C. AREA

EASTERN STD. TIME
CENTRAL STD. TIME

0   50   100 MI.
0   50   100 KM.

(Same scale as main map)

INDEX OF THE WORLD

This index, arranged in strict alphabetical order, includes grand divisions, countries, states, colonial possessions, major geographical areas, cities, towns and other features (both physical and man-made). Page number and index keys are given for the map on which they are shown at the largest scale. Note that inset maps continue the sequence of the keys from the main map. Population figures, where available, are also included for countries, some internal political divisions, islands and island groups, and for cities and towns. An asterisk preceding the population denotes that it represents an area larger than the city proper (i.e., metropolitan area, municipality, etc.).

LIST OF ABBREVIATIONS

A.F.B.	Air Force Base
Afghan.	Afghanistan
Ala.	Alabama
Alg.	Algeria
Alta.	Alberta
Ant. & Barb.	Antigua & Barbuda
Antarc.	Antarctica
arch.	archipelago
Arg.	Argentina
Ariz.	Arizona
Ark.	Arkansas
A.S.S.R.	Autonomous Soviet Socialist Republic
Austr.	Australia
aut.	autonomous
Bah.	Bahamas
Bang.	Bangladesh
Belg.	Belgium
Bol.	Bolivia
Bots.	Botswana
Braz.	Brazil
Br., Brit.	British
Br. Col.	British Columbia
Bulg.	Bulgaria
Burk. Faso	Burkina Faso
Calif.	California
Camb.	Cambodia
Can.	Canada
cap.	capital
Cent. Afr. Rep.	Central African Republic
chan.	channel
Chan. Is.	Channel Islands
Col.	Colombia
Colo.	Colorado
Conn.	Connecticut
C. Rica	Costa Rica
Czech.	Czechoslovakia
D.C.	District of Columbia
Del.	Delaware
Dem.	Democratic
Den.	Denmark
depr.	depression
des.	desert
dist.	district
Dom. Rep.	Dominican Republic
E.	East, Eastern
Ecua.	Ecuador
E. Ger.	East Germany
El Sal.	El Salvador
Eng.	England
Equat. Guin.	Equatorial Guinea
est.	estuary
Eth.	Ethiopia
Fed.	Federal, Federated
Fin.	Finland
Fla.	Florida
for.	forest
Fr.	France, French
Fr. Poly.	French Polynesia
Ft.	Fort
Ga.	Georgia
Ger.	Germany
Greenl.	Greenland
Gt.	Great
Guad.	Guadeloupe
Guat.	Guatemala
Guy.	Guyana
har., harb.	harbor
Hond.	Honduras
Hung.	Hungary
isl., isls.	isle, island, islands
Ill.	Illinois
Ind.	Indiana
Indon.	Indonesia
Int'l	International
Ire.	Ireland
Isr.	Israel
isth.	isthmus
Iv. Coast	Ivory Coast
Jam.	Jamaica
Kans.	Kansas
Ky.	Kentucky
La.	Louisiana
Leb.	Lebanon
Lux.	Luxembourg
Madag.	Madagascar
Man.	Manitoba
Mass.	Massachusetts
Maur.	Mauritania
Md.	Maryland
Mex.	Mexico
Mich.	Michigan
Minn.	Minnesota
Miss.	Mississippi
Mo.	Missouri
Mong.	Mongolia
Mont.	Montana
Mor.	Morocco
Moz.	Mozambique
mt., mtn., mts.	mount, mountain, mountains
N., No.	North, Northern
N. Amer.	North America
Nat'l Pk.	National Park
N. Br.	New Brunswick
N.C.	North Carolina
N. Dak.	North Dakota
Nebr.	Nebraska
Neth.	Netherlands
Neth. Ant.	Netherlands Antilles
Nev.	Nevada
Newf.	Newfoundland
N.H.	New Hampshire
Nic.	Nicaragua
N. Ire.	Northern Ireland
N.J.	New Jersey
N. Korea	North Korea
N. Mex.	New Mexico
Nor.	Norway
N.S.	Nova Scotia
N.W.T.	Northwest Territories (Canada)
N.Y.	New York
N.Z.	New Zealand
Okla.	Oklahoma
Ont.	Ontario
Oreg.	Oregon
Pa.	Pennsylvania
Pak.	Pakistan
Pan.	Panama
Papua N.G.	Papua New Guinea
Par.	Paraguay
P.D.R. Yemen	People's Democratic Republic of Yemen
P.E.I.	Prince Edward Island
pen.	peninsula
Phil.	Philippines
Pk.	Park
plat.	plateau
Pol.	Poland
Port.	Portugal, Portuguese
P. Rico	Puerto Rico
prom.	promontory
prov.	province, provincial
pt., pte.	point, pointe
Que.	Québec
reg.	region
Rep.	Republic
res.	reservoir
R.I.	Rhode Island
riv.	river
Rom.	Romania
S.	South, Southern
sa.	serra, sierra
S. Africa	South Africa
S. Amer.	South America
São T. & Pr.	São Tomé & Príncipe
Sask.	Saskatchewan
S.C.	South Carolina
Scot.	Scotland
S. Dak.	South Dakota
Sen.	Senegal
Sing.	Singapore
S. Korea	South Korea
S. Leone	Sierra Leone
Sol. Is.	Solomon Islands
Sp.	Spain, Spanish
S.S.R.	Soviet Socialist Republic
St., Ste.	Saint, Sainte
St. Chris. & Nevis	St. Christopher & Nevis
str.	strait
St. Vinc. & Grens.	Saint Vincent & The Grenadines
Switz.	Switzerland
Tanz.	Tanzania
Tenn.	Tennessee
terr.	territory
Thai.	Thailand
Trin. & Tob.	Trinidad & Tobago
Tun.	Tunisia
U.A.E.	United Arab Emirates
U.K.	United Kingdom
Urug.	Uruguay
U.S.	United States
U.S.S.R.	Union of Soviet Socialist Republics
Va.	Virginia
Ven., Venez.	Venezuela
V.I. (Br.)	Virgin Islands (British)
V.I. (U.S.)	Virgin Islands (U.S.)
Viet.	Vietnam
vol.	volcano
Vt.	Vermont
W.	West, Western
Wash.	Washington
W. Ger.	West Germany
W. Indies	West Indies
Wis.	Wisconsin
W. Samoa	Western Samoa
W. Va.	West Virginia
Wyo.	Wyoming
Yugo.	Yugoslavia
Zim.	Zimbabwe

A

	Pop.	Key	Pg.
Aachen, W. Ger.	242,453	B 3	20
Aare (riv.), Switz.		E 3	37
Aba, Nigeria	177,000	H10	54
Abadan, Iran	296,081	F 5	68
Abakan, U.S.S.R.	128,000	K 4	46
Abeokuta, Nigeria	253,000	G10	54
Aberdeen, Md.	11,533	K 2	146
Aberdeen, Scot.	210,362	F 3	13
Aberdeen, S. Dak.	25,851	M 3	166
Aberdeen, Wash.	18,739	B 3	171
Abidjan, Iv. Coast	685,828	E 10	54
Abilene, Kans.	6,572	E 3	142
Abilene, Texas	98,315	E 5	168
Abington, Pa.	59,084	M 5	164
Abitibi (riv.), Ont.		J 5	108
Abraham Lincoln Birthplace Nat'l Hist. Site, Ky.		F 5	143
Abruzzi (reg.), Italy		D 3	32
Abu Dhabi (cap.), U.A.E.	347,000	F 5	60
Acadia Nat'l Pk., Maine		G 7	145
Acapulco, Mex.	309,254	K 8	119
Accra (cap.), Ghana	564,194	G11	54
Achinsk, U.S.S.R.	117,000	K 4	46
Aconcagua (mt.), Arg.		G10	93
Acre (riv.), Braz.		G 6	90
Acre, Isr.	34,400	C 2	67
Ada, Okla.	15,902	J 5	162
Adamawa (reg.), Africa		J 10	54
Adams Nat'l Hist Site, Mass.		D 7	147
Adamstown (cap.), Pitcairn	54	N 8	89
Adana, Turkey	475,384	F 4	64
Addis Ababa (cap.), Eth.	1,196,300	O10	54
Addison, Ill.	29,759	B 5	139
Adelaide, Austr.	882,520	D 8	86
Aden (cap.), P.D.R. Yemen	240,370	E 7	60
Adige (riv.), Italy		C 2	32
Adirondack (mts.), N.Y.		M 3	158
Admiralty (isls.), Papua N.G.		E 6	89
Adrar (reg.), Maur.		D 7	54
Adrian, Mich.	21,186	F 7	148
Adriatic (sea), Europe		F 4	6
Aegean (sea)		G 6	43
Afars & Issas, see Djibouti			
Afghanistan	15,540,000	A 2	70
Africa	469,000,000		52-57
Agadir, Morocco	61,192	D 5	54
Agaña (cap.), Guam	896	E 4	89
Agate Fossil Beds Natl Mon., Nebr.		A 2	153
Agawam, Mass.	26,271	D 4	147
Ageo, Japan	146,358	O 2	75
Agra, India	591,917	D 3	70
Aguascalientes, Mex.	181,277	H 6	119
Ahaggar (mts.), Alg.		H 7	54
Ahmadabad, India	1,591,832	C 4	70
Ahwaz (Ahvaz), Iran	329,006	F 5	68
Aiea, Hawaii	32,879	C 4	130
Aiken, S.C.	14,978	D 4	165
Air (mts.), Niger		H 8	54
Air Force Acad., Colo.	8,655	K 5	134
Aix-en-Provence, France	91,655	F 6	26
Ajaccio, France	47,056	B 7	26
Ajmer, India	262,851	C 3	70
Akashi, Japan	234,905	H 8	75
Akita, Japan	261,246	J 4	75
Akola, India	168,436	D 4	70
Akron, Ohio	237,177	G 3	161
Aktyubinsk, U.S.S.R.	191,000	F 4	46
Alabama (riv.), Ala.		C 8	129
Alabama (state), U.S.	3,893,888		129
Alameda, Calif.	63,852	J 2	133
Alamogordo, N. Mex.	24,024	C 6	157
Alamosa, Colo.	6,830	H 8	156
Aland (isls.), Fin.		L 6	16
Alaska (gulf) Alaska		K 3	130
Alaska (state), U.S.	401,851		130
Albacete, Spain	82,607	F 3	31
Albania	2,590,600	E 5	43
Albany, Ga.	74,550	D 7	137
Albany (cap.), N.Y.	101,727	N 5	158
Albany, Oreg.	26,678	D 3	163
Albert (Mobutu Sese Seko) (lake), Africa		M11	57
Alberta (prov.), Can.	2,237,724		114
Albert Lea, Minn.	19,200	E 7	149
Alborg, Den.	154,582	D 4	19
Albuquerque, N. Mex.	331,767	C 3	157
Alderney (isl.), Chan. Is.	1,686	E 8	11
Aleppo, Syria	639,428	C 4	64
Aleutian (isls.), Alaska		D 4	130
Alexandria, Egypt	2,318,655	M 5	54
Alexandria, La.	51,565	E 4	144
Alexandria, Va.	103,217	N 3	170
Algeria	17,422,000	F 6	54
Algiers (cap.), Alg.	1,365,400	G 4	54
Alhambra, Calif.	64,615	C10	133
Alicante, Spain	177,918	F 3	30
Aligarh, India	252,314	D 3	70
Al Kuwait (cap.), Kuwait	181,774	E 4	60
Allahabad, India	440,622	E 3	70
Allen Park, Mich.	34,196	B 7	148
Allentown, Pa.	103,758	L 4	164
Allepey-Cochin, India	160,166	D 7	70
Alliance, Ohio	24,315	H 4	161
Alma-Ata, U.S.S.R.	910,000	H 5	46
Almería, Spain	104,008	E 4	30
Alps (mts.), Europe		E 4	6
Altadena, Calif.	40,983	C 10	133
Altai (mts.), Asia		J 5	46
Alton, Ill.	34,171	A 2	139
Altoona, Pa.	57,078	F 4	164
Altun Shan (Altyn Tagh) (mts.), China		C 4	77
Altus, Okla.	23,101	D 5	162
Amagasaki, Japan	545,783	H 8	75
Amana, Iowa	300	K 5	141
Amarillo, Texas	149,230	C 2	168
Amazon (riv.), S. Amer.		J 4	90
American Fork, Utah	12,693	C 3	169
American Samoa	32,297	J 7	89
Americus, Ga.	16,120	D 6	137
Ames, Iowa	45,775	F 4	141
Amherst, N.S.	9,684	D 3	100
Amherst, Mass.	33,229	E 3	147
Amiens, France	129,453	D 3	26
Amistad Nat'l Rec. Area, Texas		D 8	168
Amman (cap.), Jordan	1,711,850	D 4	67
Amoy, see Xiamen, China			
Amravati, India	193,800	D 4	70
Amritsar, India	407,628	C 2	70
Amsterdam (cap.), Neth.	751,156	B 4	25
Amsterdam, N.Y.	21,872	M 5	158
Amudar'ya (riv.), Asia		G 5	46
Amur (riv.), Asia		D 4	46
Anaconda-Deer Lodge Co., Mont.	12,518	C 4	152
Anadyr', U.S.S.R.	7,703	S 3	46
Anaheim, Calif.	219,494	D11	133
Anchorage, Alaska	174,431	J 2	130
Ancona, Italy	88,427	D 3	32
Andalusia (reg.), Spain		C 4	31
Andaman (isls.), India		G 6	70
Anderson, Ind.	64,695	F 4	140
Anderson, S.C.	27,965	B 2	165
Andes (mts.), S. Amer.		F 10	93
Andizhan, U.S.S.R.	230,000	H 5	46
Andorra	31,000	G 1	31
Andorra la Vella (cap.), Andorra	12,000	G 1	31
Andover, Mass.	26,370	K 2	147
Andrew Johnson, Nat'l Hist. Site, Tenn.		Q 2	167
Andrews A.F.B., Md.	10,064	C 5	146
Andropov, U.S.S.R.	239,000	E 3	50
Andros (isl.), Bah.	8,397	B 1	124
Angara (riv.), U.S.S.R.		K 4	46
Angarsk, U.S.S.R.	239,000	L 4	46
Angel (falls), Ven.		H 2	90
Angers, France	136,603	C 4	26
Angkor Wat (ruins), Camb.		D 4	81
Angola	7,078,000	K 4	57
Anguilla (isl.)	6,519	F 3	124
Ankara (cap.), Turkey	1,701,064	E 3	64
Ankeny, Iowa	15,429	F 5	141
Ann (cape), Mass.		M 2	147
Annaba, Alg.	255,900	H 4	54
An Najaf, Iraq	128,096	D 5	68
Annandale, Va.	49,524	N 3	170
Annapolis (cap.), Md.	31,740	H 5	146
Annapolis Royal, N.S.	631	C 4	100
Annapurna (mt.), Nepal		E 3	70
Ann Arbor, Mich.	107,966	F 6	148
Anniston, Ala.	29,523	G 3	129
Anqing, China	160,000	J 5	77
Anshan, China	1,500,000	K 3	77
Ansonia, Conn.	19,039	C 3	135
Antakya, Turkey	77,518	G 4	64
Antananarivo (cap.), Madag.	451,808	R15	57
Antarctica			88
Antibes, France	44,236	G 6	26
Anticosti (isl.), Que.		E 3	106
Antietam Nat'l Battlfld., Md.		H 3	146
Antigua and Barbuda	72,000	G 3	124
Antilles (isls.), W. Indies		B-F 2-4	124
Antioch, Calif.	42,683	L 1	133
Antofagasta, Chile	125,100	F 8	90
Antsiranana (Diégo-Suarez), Madag.	40,443	R14	57
Antwerp, Belg.	224,543	E 6	25
Anyang, China	225,000	H 4	77
Aomori, Japan	264,202	K 3	75
Apalachee (bay), Fla.		B 2	136
Apennines (mts.), Italy		B-F 2-5	32
Apia (cap.), W. Samoa	33,100	J 7	89
Apostle Is. Nat'l Lakeshore, Wis.		C 1	173
Appalachian (mts.), U.S.		K 3	126
Appleton, Wis.	58,913	J 7	173
Appomattox Court House Nat'l Hist. Pk., Va.		F 6	170
Aqaba (gulf), Asia		C 4	60

	Pop.	Key	Pg.
Yangtze (Chang Jiang) (riv.), China		K 5	77
Yankton, S. Dak.	12,011	P 8	166
Yantai, China	180,000	K 4	77
Yaoundé (cap.), Cameroon	313,706	J 11	54
Yap (isl.), Fed. States of Micronesia	6,670	D 5	89
Yarmouth, Mass.	18,449	O 6	147
Yaroslavl', U.S.S.R.	597,000	E 3	50
Yazd, Iran	135,978	J 5	68
Yazoo City, Miss.	12,092	D 5	150
Yellow (sea), Asia		K 4	77
Yellow (Huang He) (riv.), China		J 4	77
Yellowknife (cap.), N.W.T.	9,483	E 3	96
Yellowstone (riv.), U.S.		E 1	126
Yellowstone Nat'l Pk., U.S.		E 2	126
Yemen Arab Republic	6,456,189	D 6	60
Yemen, People's Democratic Republic of	1,969,000	E 7	60
Yenisey (riv.), U.S.S.R.		J 3	46
Yogyakarta, Indon.	398,727	J 2	83
Yokohama, Japan	2,621,771	O 3	75

	Pop.	Key	Pg.
Yokosuka, Japan	389,557	O 3	75
Yonkers, N.Y.	195,351	H 1	158
Yorba Linda, Calif.	28,254	D11	133
York (cape), Austr.		G 2	86
York, Eng.	101,900	F 4	11
York, Pa.	44,619	J 6	164
York (riv.), Va.		L 6	170
Yorktown, Va.	550	M 6	170
Yosemite Nat'l Pk., Calif.		F 6	133
Yōsu, S. Korea	130,623	C 6	75
Youghiogheny (riv.), U.S.		D 6	164
Youngstown, Ohio	115,436	J 3	161
Ypres (Ieper), Belg.	20,825	B 7	25
Ypsilanti, Mich.	24,031	F 6	148
Yucatán (pen.), Mex.		P 7	119
Yucca Flat (basin), Nev.		E 6	154
Yucca House Nat'l Mon., Colo.		B 8	134
Yugoslavia	22,471,000	C 3	43
Yukon (terr.), Can.	23,153	C 3	96

	Pop.	Key	Pg.
Yukon (riv.), N. Amer.		C 3	94
Yukon, Okla.	17,112	G 3	162
Yuma, Ariz.	42,481	A 6	131
Yunnan (prov.), China		F 7	77

Z

	Pop.	Key	Pg.
Zaandam, Neth.	124,795	B 4	25
Zabrze, Pol.	197,214	A 4	45
Zagazig, Egypt	202,637	B 3	60
Zagreb, Yugo.	561,773	C 3	43
Zagros (mts.), Iran		E 4	68
Zaire	28,291,000	L 12	57
Zambezi (riv.), Africa		M15	57
Zambia	5,679,808	L 14	57
Zamboanga, Phil.	343,722	G 4	83
Zanesville, Ohio	28,655	G 6	161
Zanzibar, Tanz.	110,669	P13	57
Zaporozh'ye, U.S.S.R.	781,000	E 5	50

	Pop.	Key	Pg.
Zaragoza, see Saragossa, Spain			
Zaria, Nigeria	224,000	H 9	54
Zermatt, Switz.	3,101	E 4	37
Zhangjiakou (Kalgan), China	1,000,000	J 3	77
Zhdanov, U.S.S.R.	503,000	E 5	50
Zhengzhou (Chengchow), China	1,500,000	H 5	77
Zhitomir, U.S.S.R.	244,000	C 4	50
Zhuzhou, China	350,000	H 6	77
Zibo, China	1,750,000	J 4	77
Zigong, China	350,000	F 6	77
Zimbabwe	7,360,000	M15	57
Zion, Ill.	17,861	F 1	160
Zion Nat'l Pk., Utah		B 6	169
Zug, Switz.	51,300	G 2	37
Zugspitze (mt.), Europe		A 3	38
Zululand (reg.), S. Africa		N17	57
Zürich, Switz.	401,600	F 2	37
Zwickau, E. Ger.	123,069	E 3	20
Zwolle, Neth.	77,826	J 3	25

GLOSSARY OF GEOGRAPHICAL TERMS

A. = Arabic   Camb. = Cambodian   Ch. = Chinese   Dan. = Danish   Du. = Dutch   Finn. = Finnish   Fr. = French   Ger. = German   Ice. = Icelandic
It. = Italian   Jap. = Japanese   Nor. = Norwegian   Per. = Persian   Port. = Portuguese   Russ. = Russian   Sp. = Spanish   Sw. = Swedish   Turk. = Turkish

Term	Language	Meaning
Å	Nor., Sw.	Stream
Abajo	Sp.	Lower
Ada, Adasi	Turk.	Island
Altiplano	Sp.	Plateau
Älv, Alf, Elf	Sw.	River
Arrecife	Sp.	Reef
Baai	Du.	Bay
Bahía	Sp.	Bay
Bahr	Arabic	Marsh, Lake, Sea, River
Baia	Port.	Bay
Baie	Fr.	Bay, Gulf
Bañados	Sp.	Marshes
Barra	Sp.	Reef
Belt	Ger.	Strait
Ben	Gaelic	Mountain
Berg	Ger., Du.	Mountain
Bir	Aarbic	Well
Boca	Sp.	Gulf, Inlet
Bolshoi, Bolshaya	Russ.	Big
Bolsón	Sp.	Depression
Bong	Korean	Mountain
Bucht	Ger.	Bay
Bugt	Dan.	Bay
Bukhta	Russ.	Bay
Burnu, Burun	Turk.	Cape, Point
By	Dan., Nor., Sw.	Town
Cabo	Port., Sp.	Cape
Campos	Port.	Plains
Canal	Port., Sp.	Channel
Cap, Capo	Fr., It.	Cape
Catarátas	Sp.	Falls
Central, Centrale	Fr., It.	Middle
Cerrito, Cerro	Sp.	Hill
Ciénaga	Sp.	Swamp
Ciudad	Sp.	City
Col	Fr.	Pass
Cordillera	Sp.	Mt. Range
Côte	Fr.	Coast
Cuchilla	Sp.	Mt. Range
Dağ, Dagh	Turk.	Mountain
Dağlari	Turk.	Mt. Range
Dal	Nor., Sw.	Valley
Darya	Per.	Salt Lake
Dasht	Per.	Desert, Plain
Deniz, Denizi	Turk.	Sea, Lake
Desierto	Sp.	Desert
Eiland	Du.	Island
Elv	Dan., Nor.	River
Emi	Berber	Mountain
Erg	Arabic	Dune, Desert
Est, Este	Fr., Port., Sp.	East
Estrecho, Estreito	Sp., Port.	Strait
Étang	Fr.	Pond, Lagoon, Lake
Fjørd	Dan., Nor.	Fiord
Fleuve	Fr.	River
Gebel	Arabic	Mountain
Gebirge	Ger.	Mt. Range
Gobi	Mongol	Desert
Gol	Mongol, Turk.	Lake, Stream
Golf	Ger., Du.	Gulf
Golfe	Fr.	Gulf
Golfo	Sp., It., Port.	Gulf
Gölü	Turk.	Lake
Gora	Russ.	Mountain
Grand, Grande	Fr., Sp.	Big
Groot	Du.	Big
Gross	Ger.	Big
Grosso	It., Port.	Big
Guba	Russ.	Bay, Gulf
Gunto	Jap.	Archipelago
Gunung	Malay	Mountain
Higashi, Higasi	Jap.	East
Ho	Ch.	River
Hoek	Du.	Cape
Holm	Dan., Nor., Sw.	Island
Hu	Ch.	Lake
Hwang	Ch.	Yellow
Île	Fr.	Island
Insel	Ger.	Island
Irmak	Turk.	River
Isla	Sp.	Island
Isola	Sp.	Island
Jabal, Jebel	Arabic	Mountains
Järvi	Finn.	Lake
Jaure	Sw.	Lake
Jezira	Arabic	Island
Jima	Jap.	Island
Joki	Finn.	River
Kaap	Du.	Cape
Kabir, Kebir	Arabic	Big
Kanal	Russ., Ger.	Canal, Channel
Kap, Kapp	Nor., Sw., Ice.	Cape
Kawa	Jap.	River
Khrebet	Russ.	Mt. Range
Kiang	Ch.	River
Kita	Jap.	North
Klein	Du., Ger.	Small
Kô	Jap.	Lake
Ko	Thai.	Island
Koh	Camb., Khmer	Island
Köping	Sw.	Borough
Körfez, Körfezi	Turk.	Gulf
Kuh	Per.	Mountain
Kul	Sinkiang Turki	Lake
Kum	Turk.	Desert
Lac	Fr.	Lake
Lago	Port., Sp., It.	Lake
Lagôa	Port.	Lagoon
Laguna	Sp.	Lagoon
Lagune	Fr.	Lagoon
Llanos	Sp.	Plains
Mar	Sp., Port.	Sea
Mare	It.	Sea
Meer	Du.	Lake
Meer	Ger.	Sea
Mer	Fr.	Sea
Meseta	Sp.	Plateau
Minami	Jap.	Southern
Misaki	Jap.	Cape
Mittel	Ger.	Middle
Mont	Fr.	Mountain
Montagne	Fr.	Mountain
Montaña	Sp.	Mountains
Monte	Sp., It., Port.	Mountain
More	Russ.	Sea
Muong	Siamese	Town
Mys	Russ.	Cape
Nam	Burm., Lao.	River
Nevado	Sp.	Snow covered peak
Nieder	Ger.	Lower
Nishi, Nisi	Jap.	West
Nizhni, Nizhnyaya	Russ.	Lower
Nor	Mong.	Lake
Nord	Fr., Ger.	North
Norte	Sp., It., Port.	North
Nos	Russ.	Cape
Novi, Novaya	Russ.	New
Nusa	Malay	Island
O	Jap.	Big
Ö	Nor., Sw	Island
Ober	Ger.	Upper
Occidental, Occidentale	Sp., It.	Western
Oeste	Port.	West
Oriental	Sp., Fr.	Eastern
Orientale	It.	Eastern
Ost	Ger.	East
Ostrov	Russ.	Island
Ouest	Fr.	West
öy	Nor.	Island
Ozero	Russ.	Lake
Pampa	Sp.	Plain
Paso	Sp.	Pass
Passo	It., Port.	Pass
Pequeño	Sp.	Small
Peski	Russ.	Desert
Petit	Fr.	Small
Pic	Fr.	Mountain
Pico	Port., Sp.	Mountain, Peak
Pik	Russ.	Peak
Pointe	Fr.	Point
Poluostrov	Russ.	Peninsula
Ponta	Port.	Point
Presa	Sp.	Reservoir
Proliv	Russ.	Strait
Pulou, Pulo	Malay	Island
Punta	Sp., It., Port.	Point
Ras	Arabic	Cape
Ría	Sp.	Estuary
Río	Sp.	River
Rivier, Rivière	Du., Fr.	River
Rud	Per.	River
Saki	Jap.	Cape
Salto	Sp., Port.	Falls
San	Ch., Jap., Korean	Hill
See	Ger.	Sea, Lake
Selvas	Sp., Port.	Forest
Serra	Port.	Mts.
Serranía	Sp.	Mts.
Severni, Servernaya	Russ.	North
Shan	Ch., Jap.	Hill, Mts.
Shima	Jap.	Island
Shoto	Jap.	Islands
Sierra	Sp.	Mountains
Sjö	Nor., Sw.	Lake, Sea
Spitze	Ger.	Mt. Peak
Sredni, Srednyaya	Russ.	Middle
Stad	Dan., Nor., Sw.	City
Stari, Staraya	Russ.	Old
Su	Turk.	River
Sud, Süd	Sp., Fr., Ger.	South
Sul	Port.	South
Sungei	Malay	River
Sur	Sp.	South
Tagh	Turk.	Mt. Range
Tal	Ger.	Valley
Tandjong, Tanjung	Malay	Cape, Point
Tso	Tibetan	Lake
Val	Fr.	Valley
Velho	Port.	Old
Verkhni	Russ.	Upper
Vesi	Finn.	Lake
Vishni, Vishnyaya	Russ.	High
Vostochni, Vostochnaya	Russ.	East, Eastern
Wadi	Arabic	Dry River
Wald	Ger.	Forest
Wan	Jap.	Bay
Yama	Jap.	Mountain
Yug, Yuzhni, Yuzhnaya	Russ.	South, Southern
Zaliv	Russ.	Bay, Gulf
Zapadni, Zapadnaya	Russ.	Western
Zee	Du.	Sea
Zemlya	Russ.	Land
Zuid	Du.	South